P9-CET-937

EUROPE

NORTHERN
EUROPE
68

THE LOW
COUNTRIES
48

UNITED
KINGDOM AND
IRELAND
36

WESTERN
CENTRAL
EUROPE
52

EASTERN
EUROPE
64

FRANCE
44

SPAIN AND
PORTUGAL
40

ITALY
56

SOUTHEASTERN
EUROPE
60

RUSSIA
104

EUROPE
40
(see inset)

CENTRAL ASIA
110

WESTERN ASIA
108

EASTERN ASIA
126

JAPAN
130

THE PACIFIC OCEAN
26

THE MIDDLE EAST
114

SOUTHERN
ASIA
118

Ryukyu
Islands
130

NORTHERN
AFRICA
136

Mariana
Islands
150

Micronesia
150

Marshall
Islands
150

Maldives
118

SOUTHEAST ASIA
122

SOUTHERN
AFRICA
140

THE INDIAN OCEAN
30

THE PACIFIC ISLANDS
150

AUSTRALIA AND
PAPUA NEW GUINEA
146

NEW ZEALAND
150

ANTARCTICA
32

The Children's
World
Atlas

This first edition published by Barnes & Noble Publishing, Inc., by arrangement with Weldon Owen Inc.

Barnes & Noble Publishing, Inc.
122 Fifth Avenue
New York, NY 10011

ISBN 0-7607-5929-4

Printed and bound in Singapore

 04 05 06 07 08 MCH 10 9 8 7 6 5 4 3 2 1

Library of Congress Cataloging-in-Publication Data available upon request.

The Children's
World
Atlas

BARNES & NOBLE BOOKS
NEW YORK

Contents

How to use this atlas

Map Pages

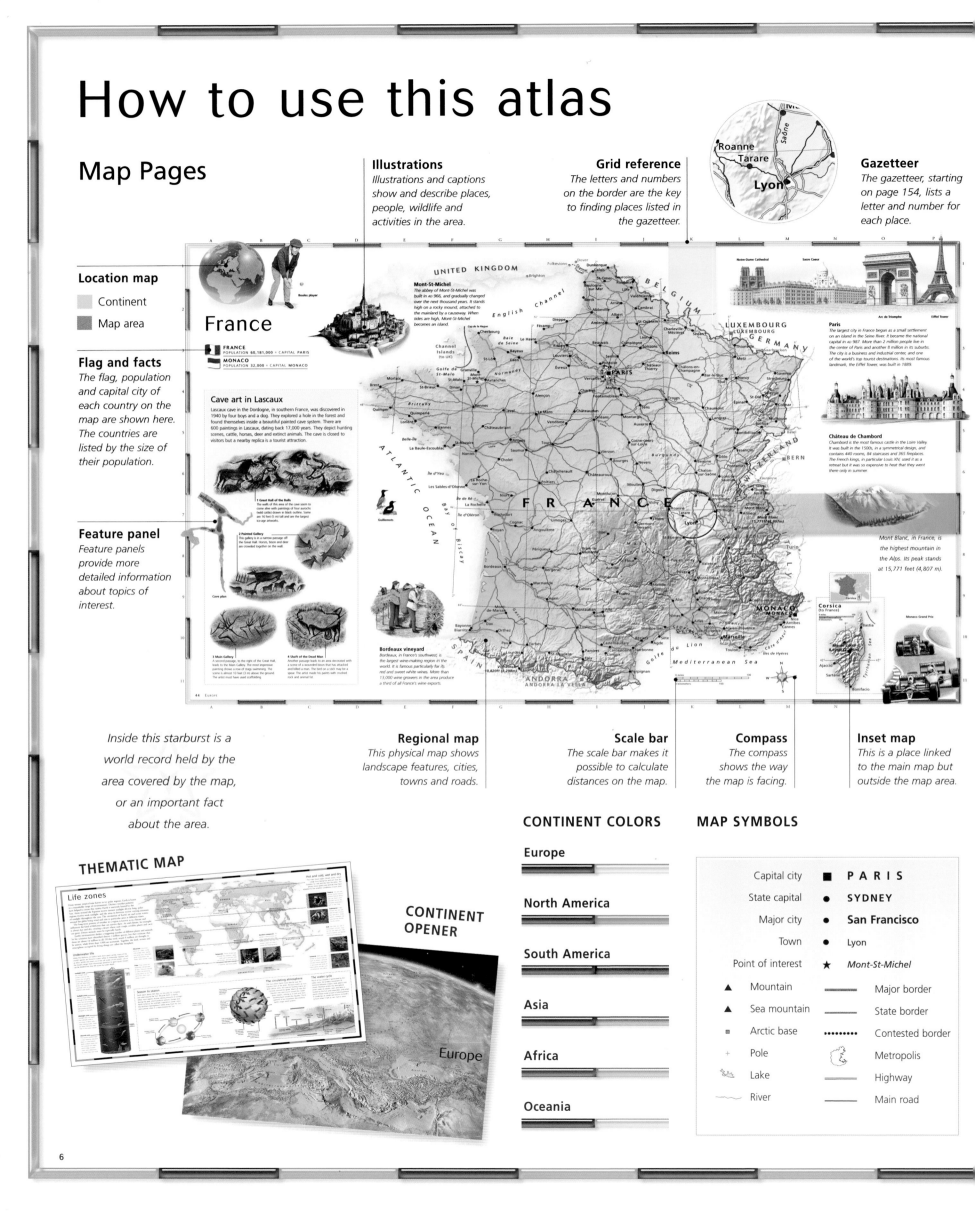

Illustrations
Illustrations and captions show and describe places, people, wildlife and activities in the area.

Grid reference
The letters and numbers on the border are the key to finding places listed in the gazetteer.

Gazetteer
The gazetteer, starting on page 154, lists a letter and number for each place.

Location map
Continent
Map area

France

FRANCE
POPULATION 60,181,000 • CAPITAL PARIS

MONACO
POPULATION 32,000 • CAPITAL MONACO

Flag and facts
The flag, population and capital city of each country on the map are shown here. The countries are listed by the size of their population.

Feature panel
Feature panels provide more detailed information about topics of interest.

Inside this starburst is a world record held by the area covered by the map, or an important fact about the area.

Regional map
This physical map shows landscape features, cities, towns and roads.

Scale bar
The scale bar makes it possible to calculate distances on the map.

Compass
The compass shows the way the map is facing.

Inset map
This is a place linked to the main map but outside the map area.

THEMATIC MAP

CONTINENT OPENER

Europe

CONTINENT COLORS

Europe

North America

South America

Asia

Africa

Oceania

MAP SYMBOLS

Capital city	■ PARIS
State capital	● SYDNEY
Major city	● San Francisco
Town	● Lyon
Point of interest	★ Mont-St-Michel
▲ Mountain	—— Major border
▲ Sea mountain	---- State border
▣ Arctic base	•••• Contested border
+ Pole	Metropolis
Lake	—— Highway
River	—— Main road

Fact File Pages

Quirky fact
This is a snippet of surprising or unusual information about the region.

Categories
The information in the fact file is divided into five categories, marked by blue banners.

Illustrations
Illustrations and photographs support the text entries.

Feature panel
Selected topics of interest are treated in more depth in colored feature panels.

History panel
This provides a timeline of events or a snapshot of a region's history.

Location finder
- Continent
- Map area

Land use image
This provides further information about how the land is used.

Inset map
This is an area linked to the region but outside the area of the main map.

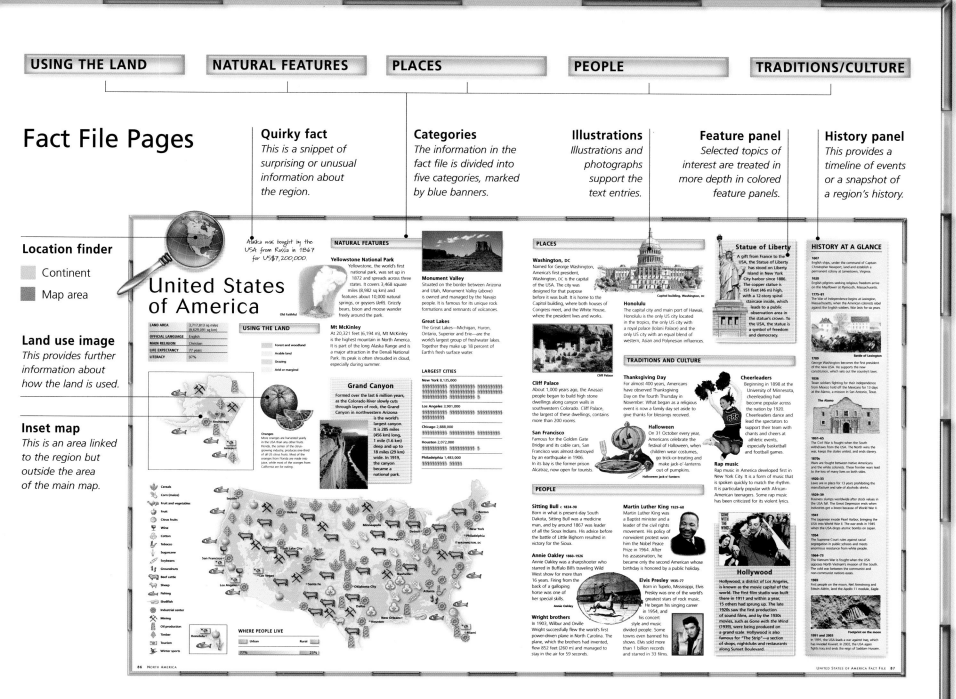

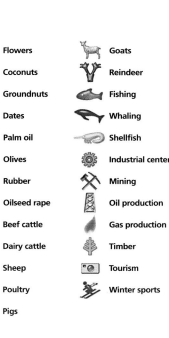

LAND USE

The colors of the map depict the different types of land in the region.

- Forest and woodland
- Arable land
- Grazing
- Arid or marginal

MAP ICONS

These symbols show how the land is used. They include farming, industry, mining and tourism.

Cereals	Vegetables	Flowers	Goats
Rice	Citrus fruits	Coconuts	Reindeer
Wheat	Bananas	Groundnuts	Fishing
Barley	Wine	Dates	Whaling
Corn (maize)	Cotton	Palm oil	Shellfish
Flax	Coffee	Olives	Industrial center
Jute	Tea	Rubber	Mining
Potatoes	Cocoa	Oilseed rape	Oil production
Fruit and vegetables	Tobacco	Beef cattle	Gas production
Fruit	Sugarcane	Dairy cattle	Timber
Vegetables	Sugar beet	Sheep	Tourism
		Poultry	Winter sports
		Pigs	

FACT FILE STATISTICS

LAND AREA	3,717,813 sq miles (9,629,091 sq km)
OFFICIAL LANGUAGE	English
MAIN RELIGION	Christian
LIFE EXPECTANCY	77 years
LITERACY	97%

This panel contains statistics about the country or region. If the fact file is about a region, the statistics of the countries in the region are combined.

POPULATION

LARGEST CITIES

New York 8,135,000

These diagrams show the population of the main cities in the region. Each figure represents 100,000 people.

URBAN AND RURAL

WHERE PEOPLE LIVE

- Urban
- Rural

75%   25%

This graph shows the percentage of people who live in urban and rural areas. If there are more than six countries in the region, the graphs show the countries with the highest and lowest percentages in the area and the regional average.

RIVERS AND MOUNTAINS

LONGEST RIVERS

Loire 634 miles (1,020 km)

HIGHEST MOUNTAINS

Mt Logan 19,551 feet (5,959 m)
Mt St Elias 18,009 feet (5,489 m)
Mt Lucania 17,146 feet (5,226 m)
King Peak 16,972 feet (5,173 m)

Where we live

Earth's 6 billion people are not spread evenly around the planet. Most live where resources are plentiful or can easily be obtained by trading. Therefore, few people live in deserts or polar regions, but many live in fertile areas close to energy sources, and near coasts and rivers. As the lights in the photograph below show, the continents of Europe and North America, and parts of Asia, are densely populated. Australia, Africa and South America are less densely populated, and most of their people live along the coast. The River Nile can be seen in Egypt. The image was made by combining information gathered by satellites over a period of nine months.

US–Mexico border
When seen from space, our planet looks very different. This satellite image, which has been artificially colored, clearly shows the contrast between developed and less-developed farmland. At the top, in red, are the gridded and irrigated fields of California's Imperial Valley in the USA, north of the border with Mexico. Below, in blue, are Mexico's less-developed farmlands. The border town of Mexicali-Caliexico is in the center of the photo.

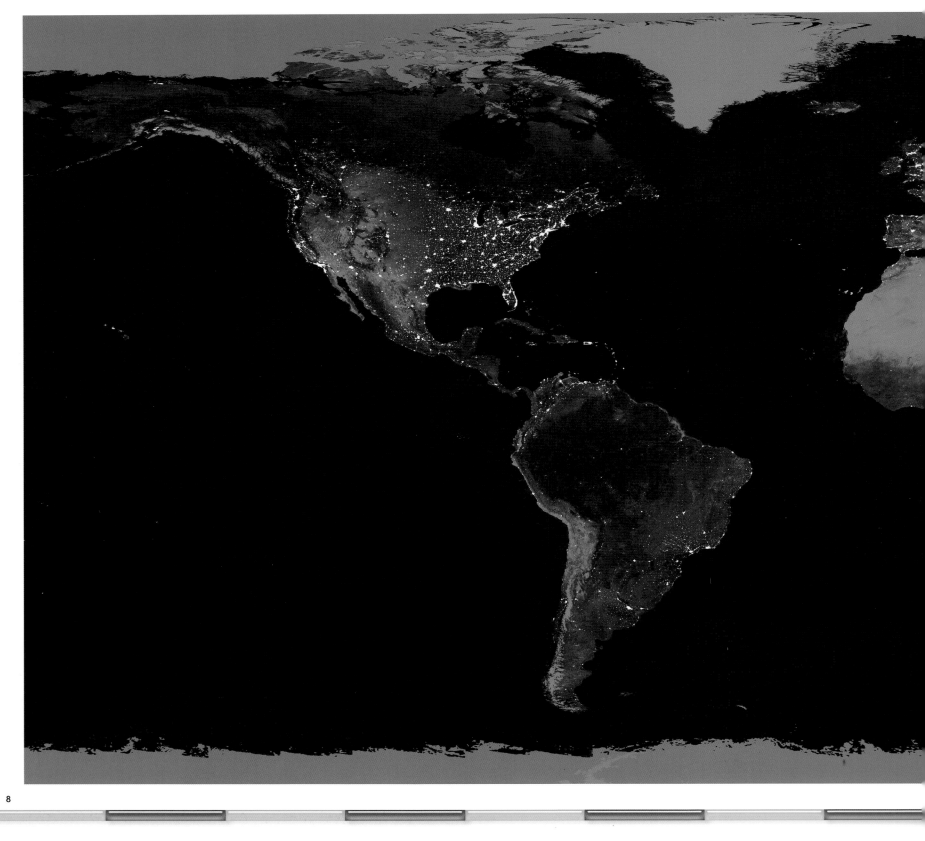

Istanbul, Turkey

In this view of Istanbul (*left*), city areas are blue-green and vegetation is red. Dividing the city is the busy shipping channel of the Bosporus, spanned by two bridges. The image also shows water depth—colder water is a deeper shade of blue.

Tokyo, Japan

Tokyo, with its surrounds, is the largest city in the world. In this view (*right*), the buildings (in blue) spread over a huge distance. The vegetation is colored red. Three rivers can be seen, as well as Tokyo's port area. The block-shaped islands are reclaimed land.

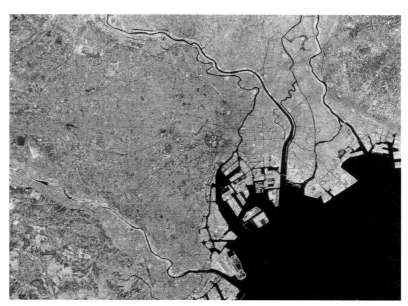

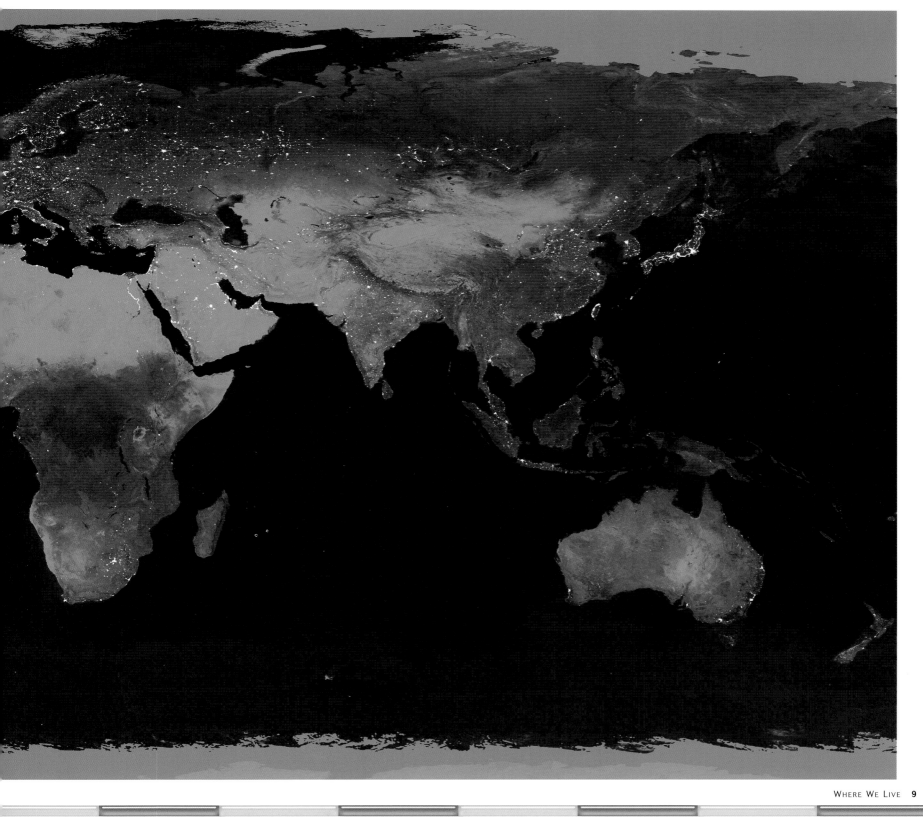

World weather

Since 1960, satellites orbiting high in the sky have sent back to Earth images of land and ocean, clouds and storms. Scientists now rely on these images to monitor the weather and predict how it will change. In the image below, taken from satellites 440 miles (700 km) above Earth, clouds swirl over the landmasses. The tropical region, around the Equator, is less cloudy than the areas to the north and south. The Sahara Desert in northern Africa and the dry lands of the Middle East can be seen, as well as the forests of South America. Greenland is the large white shape at the top. The light blue areas are seas and lakes.

Hurricanes

Hurricanes—also known as cyclones and typhoons—are powerful storms that produce winds of up to 150 miles an hour (250 km/h). These winds, and the heavy rain that follows, can cause enormous damage. Satellite images show hurricanes forming, and scientists can track their progress as they move toward land. This enables them to warn people of the coming danger. This image shows Hurricane Fran as it nears the east coast of the USA in 1996.

El Niño

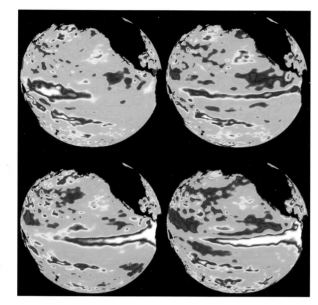

El Niño is an ocean current that develops off the coast of Peru every year. In some years, it flows much farther south than usual. This changes the temperature of the ocean, and produces extreme weather, such as droughts and flooding rains, over a wide area. These satellite images show El Niño developing in the Pacific Ocean over a six-month period. Landmasses are black and El Niño is the red and white tongue moving westward along the Equator.

1985

1990

Ozone hole

Antarctica

A "hole" in the sky

Ozone is a gas high in the atmosphere that absorbs most of the harmful rays from the Sun, and prevents heat from being lost from Earth. Since the 1980s, the amount of ozone over Antarctica has declined. The dark shades of blue show the growth of the ozone hole since 1985. The 2000 hole was the largest ever recorded—about three times the size of the USA.

2000

Earth's patterns

Photographs from space show things that cannot be seen on land. Many satellite images are artificially colored to make them clearer. They provide a large-scale view of natural events, such as volcanic eruptions, wildfires, dust storms, droughts and floods. They show how our cities are growing, and how our forests are disappearing. Using radar, satellites can "see" below the Sahara Desert to the rocks beneath. The view from space is now a vital tool in agricultural planning and weather forecasting. Satellite images help scientists understand how Earth's climate has changed over millions of years. And, as these pages show, they make interesting patterns.

Coastline, Guinea-Bissau
In this view of the coastline of Guinea-Bissau, in western Africa (*left*), the blue ribbons are rivers. The light blue areas are silt that has been deposited into the Atlantic Ocean at the bottom of the image.

Reservoir, Brazil
The Represa Três Marias winds across southeastern Brazil (*below*). This reservoir was built in 1960 to generate hydroelectric power for the state of Minas Gerais.

Grand Canyon, USA
Snow lies on the north and south rims of the Grand Canyon, Arizona (*above*). The canyon, the largest in the world, was carved out by the Colorado River. The image shows the lack of vegetation around this dramatic landform. The canyon's south rim, on the left of the photograph, is 1 mile (1.6 km) above its floor.

Comet scarring, Sahara
A comet slammed into the Sahara Desert millions of years ago and left the circular scars seen in this image (*left*).

Rain forest, Brazil
Brazil's remaining forest appears as bright red, while dark areas are cleared land, and black and gray patches are recently burned areas (*right*).

Mississippi River, USA
The Mississippi River (*left*) enters the Gulf of Mexico and dumps a load of silt that it has carried on its long journey through the Great Plains. The silt forms a delta at the river's mouth.

Fjords, Norway
Several of Norway's fjords—steep, narrow inlets from the sea—can be seen in this view of the southern part of the country (*right*).

Volcano, New Zealand
The snow-capped peak of volcanic Mt Taranaki (*below*) towers over the surrounding forest. It last erupted in 1755.

Malaspina Glacier, USA
The Malaspina Glacier, shown in light blue, fans out between Icy Bay and Yakutat Bay in Alaska (*right*). The red ridged area is a moraine, or deposit of rocks, that has built up as the glacier moved toward the sea. The moraine prevents the glacier from reaching the ocean, shown as a dark blue area at the bottom of the image.

Planet Earth

Earth is a giant ball of rock, just one of the many bodies that travel around the Sun. It was born about 4.6 billion years ago, when a swirling cloud of gas and dust gradually turned into the solar system. Inside the young Earth, radioactive materials began to decay and heat up. Rocks started to melt, with heavier metals sinking to the center, leaving lighter minerals on top. Eventually, Earth settled into four main layers—a thin rocky crust on the surface; a partly molten layer of rock called the mantle beneath the crust; an outer core of liquid iron and nickel; and an inner core of solid iron and nickel. Reaching temperatures of 5,400°F (3,000°C), the core is still extremely hot. This intense heat drives movements of the surface rocks and forms many of Earth's features.

Birth of a solar system

About 4.6 billion years ago, a cloud of gas and dust was drifting through space. Perhaps triggered by a nearby exploding star, the cloud began to collapse in on itself and rotate. The densest part of the cloud formed a core that grew hotter and larger as its gravity attracted more material. Eventually, this core became the young Sun. Around the Sun, some of the cloud formed a broad disk, called the solar nebula. Particles in the disk collided and stuck together, gradually growing bigger until they became the planets of the solar system.

1. Spinning disk
A cloud of dust and gas starts collapsing in on itself, forming a disk with a hot core. The core eventually becomes the Sun.

Our place in space

In the immensity of space, our planet is a mere speck. Earth orbits the Sun, one of the billions of stars in the Milky Way galaxy. The Milky Way and its companions in the Local Group are just a handful of the universe's 50 billion galaxies.

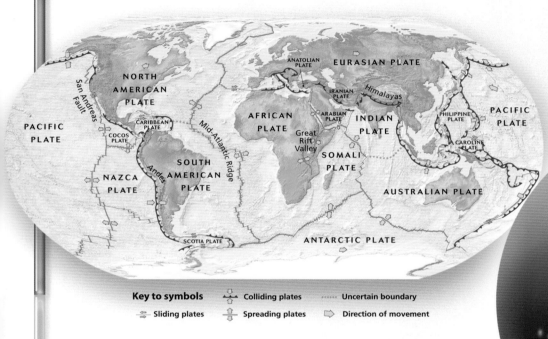

Key to symbols
- Colliding plates
- Sliding plates
- Spreading plates
- ···· Uncertain boundary
- ⇨ Direction of movement

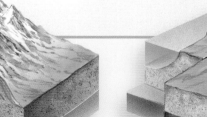

The Local Group
Our little corner of the universe is occupied by the Local Group, a cluster of about 30 galaxies.

Tectonic puzzle

Earth's rocky crust and the upper part of the mantle form a layer called the lithosphere. The lithosphere is broken up into several tectonic plates, like a giant jigsaw puzzle (above). These plates float on molten rock in the mantle, moving toward, away from, and past each other.

Crust: 3–43 miles (5–69 km) thick

Mantle: 1,800 miles (2,880 km) thick

Outer core: 1,400 miles (2,240 km) thick

Inner core: 750 miles (1,200 km) thick

Moving plates

As the hot rocks in Earth's mantle circulate, the tectonic plates above them gradually shift, moving about as fast as fingernails grow. On the surface, we see the results of these movements—valleys and mountains are formed, volcanoes erupt, and the ground rattles in earthquakes.

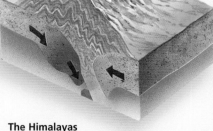

The Andes
South America's Andes Mountains formed when a plate carrying thin ocean crust slid under a plate of thicker continental crust. This movement pushed up the mountain range and formed volcanoes.

The Himalayas
The collision of two continental plates created the massive Himalayas mountain range in Asia. Because the plates were about as thick as each other, the crusts buckled and folded to form the peaks.

The San Andreas Fault
California's San Andreas Fault is the line where two plates—the Pacific and the North American—are sliding past each other. The friction between the two plates often jolts the ground in earthquakes.

2. Colliding particles
Particles in the disk smash into each other and stick together, gradually forming larger bodies.

3. The nine planets
The clumps in the disk keep colliding and building up until they form the nine planets. The solar system has been born.

Sun

Mercury

Venus

Earth

Mars

Jupiter

Uranus

Neptune

Saturn

Pluto

Sizing up the planets

Shown here to scale, all nine planets are dwarfed by the Sun. About 1,400 Earths would fit inside Jupiter, while 900 Jupiters could fit inside the Sun.

The Milky Way
Our galaxy, the Milky Way, is a giant spiral measuring about 100,000 light-years across.

The Great Rift Valley
In East Africa, two continental plates are slowly moving apart and have formed a wide valley known as the Great Rift Valley. Eventually, Africa will split, water will flood in, and a new ocean will form.

The Mid-Atlantic Ridge
The Mid-Atlantic Ridge marks where two ocean plates are separating. Molten rock from the mantle rises through the gap between the plates. When the rock cools, it adds to the underwater ridge.

The solar system
Earth is the third of the nine planets that orbit the Sun. The Sun itself is just one of the Milky Way's 200 billion stars.

Life zones

From steamy tropical rain forests to icy polar regions, Earth is home to a remarkable range of environments. Distinct weather patterns have helped to create this variety. Earth is unevenly heated by the Sun. Areas around the Equator receive intense sunlight all year long, polar regions receive weak sunlight, and the areas in between receive varying amounts of sunlight throughout the year. The circulation of Earth's air and ocean waters around the globe bring wind and rain to particular areas at different times.

The long-term pattern of weather in a region is known as its climate and influences the kind of lifeforms that can survive there. An arid climate, for example, is always hot and dry, creating a desert where only tough, scrubby plants and cacti can grow. Desert animals must be especially hardy.

Earth's environments shelter a staggering number of different plants and animals. So far, scientists have identified almost 2 million species, but they estimate that there are about 14 million in all. Of this total, nearly 8 million are thought to be insects, while fewer than 5,000 are mammals. Together, the land, oceans and atmosphere occupied by living things are called the biosphere.

Arctic Circle

Greatest temperature change in a day:
100°F (56°C), from 44°F (6.7°C)
to −56°F (−49°C),
at Browning, Montana,
USA, 1916

Strongest measured wind gust:
231 mph (372 km/h)
on Mt Washington,
New Hampshire, USA, 1934

Most snow in one year:
1,224 inches (31,102 mm)
on Mt Rainier, Washington,
USA, 1971–72

NORTH AMERICA

SOUTH AMERICA

Driest place:
0.02 inches (0.5 mm) per year
in Quillagua, Atacama Desert,
Chile, 1964–2001

Antarctic Circle

Underwater life

While the lifeforms on Earth's land show great variety, many of the world's species are found in water, either in freshwater habitats such as lakes, ponds and rivers, or in the salt water of the oceans. Life in the oceans ranges from microscopic plankton to giant squid. Oceans can be divided into four life zones by water depth.

Sunlight zone
The sunlight zone contains most of the ocean's life, including microscopic plankton; small and large fishes; sharks and rays; and mammals such as seals, dolphins and whales.

0

650 ft (198 m)

3,250 ft (990 m)

Twilight zone
Some sunlight filters through to the twilight zone, but not enough for plants to survive. Many of the fishes contain light-producing bacteria and glow in the dark.

Midnight zone
Sunlight does not reach the midnight zone, a vast mass of dark, cold, slow-moving water. There are fewer lifeforms here than in the waters above.

9,850 ft (3,000 m)

Abyssal zone
The ocean's bottom layer is near freezing and pitch black. In some places, black smokers spew out hot mineral-rich water, which helps mussels, clams and tubeworms to make their own food.

Mountain Mountain zones are colder, wetter and windier than nearby low-lying areas. Mountain goats move down the slopes when winter comes.

Polar Polar zones are extremely cold and dry all year. They are covered in either low-growing tundra plants or ice. The arctic fox's thick coat keeps it warm.

Season to season

Earth takes about 365 days, or one year, to complete one orbit around the Sun. Because Earth is slightly tilted, most regions receive varying amounts of sunlight during the year, which produce seasons. Europe and North America, for example, experience winter when the Northern Hemisphere is tilted away from the Sun, and summer when it is tilted toward the Sun.

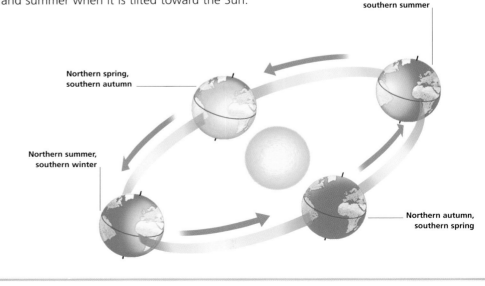

Northern winter, southern summer

Northern spring, southern autumn

Northern summer, southern winter

Northern autumn, southern spring

Hot and cold, wet and dry

This map shows eight climate zones, which range from being hot and wet near the Equator, to cold and dry near the poles. The photos show plants and animals that have adapted to the weather conditions in each zone.

EUROPE

ASIA

AFRICA

AUSTRALIA

ANTARCTICA

Hottest place:
136°F (57.3°C)
at El Azizia, Libya, 1922

Most rain in one year:
1,042 inches (26,461 mm)
at Cherrapunji, India, 1860–61

Tropic of Cancer

Equator

Tropic of Capricorn

Most rain in 24 hours:
73.5 inches (1,870 mm)
at Chilaos, La Réunion, 1952

Coldest place:
−129°F (−89.2°C)
at Vostok, Antarctica, 1983

Northern temperate The winters in these zones are long, snowy and very cold, while summers are cool. The moose's large size helps it survive the freezing winter.

Temperate These climates go through four seasons a year, with warm summers and cold winters. Animals such as honeybees cope with changes in weather and food supply.

Tropical Hot and wet all year round, tropical climates feature dense, lush rain forests with abundant animal life, including amphibians such as tree frogs.

Subtropical These climates are hot and wet through summer, but have drier, cooler winters. Anteaters eat juicy termites during the dry season.

Arid Very little rain falls in these desert climates. Days are hot and nights are cold. Desert scorpions can tolerate scorching temperatures.

Semiarid With too little rainfall for forest and too much for desert, semiarid climates feature expanses of grassland and herds of large grazing animals such as kangaroos and zebras.

The circulating atmosphere

The Sun strikes Earth more directly near the Equator than at the poles. Because warm air rises and cold air sinks, this uneven heating makes air circulate around the globe. Warm air near the Equator rises and moves toward the colder polar regions, sinking as it cools and then traveling back toward the Equator. These patterns of air movement also produce Earth's major wind systems.

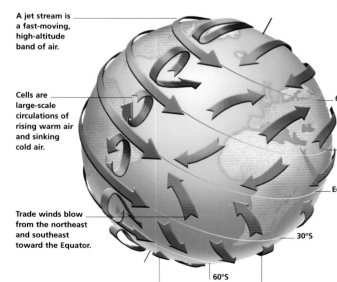

A jet stream is a fast-moving, high-altitude band of air.

Cells are large-scale circulations of rising warm air and sinking cold air.

Trade winds blow from the northeast and southeast toward the Equator.

Polar easterlies are cold winds blowing from the poles.

Westerlies are winds produced when air moving toward the poles is redirected by Earth's rotation.

60°N

30°N

Equator

30°S

60°S

The water cycle

Much of our weather is generated by the water cycle, the endless movement of moisture between oceans, land, plants and clouds. Moisture enters the atmosphere when water in oceans, rivers and lakes is heated by the Sun and evaporates, and when plants release water as part of photosynthesis. It condenses as clouds and returns to Earth's surface when it falls as rain, hail or snow.

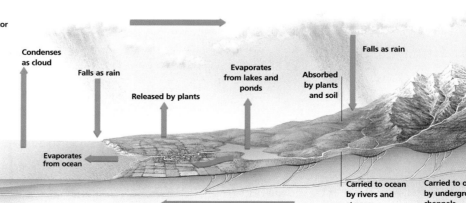

Condenses as cloud

Falls as rain

Released by plants

Evaporates from lakes and ponds

Absorbed by plants and soil

Falls as rain

Falls as snow

Evaporates from ocean

Carried to ocean by rivers and streams

Carried to ocean by underground channels

The world's people

More than 6 billion people live on our planet, and another 1 million are born every five days. There are now more than 10 times as many people as there were 400 years ago. This incredible population explosion happened because living standards and medical care have improved, allowing people to live longer than ever before. At the same time, birth rates—the number of babies born in each family—stayed high in many parts of the world. Until birth rates fall significantly, the world population will continue to grow, and may reach 10 billion by 2200.

Most of today's increase in population is in developing countries—ones with limited industry and technology. These include most of Asia and Africa, and parts of Central and South America. Many developing countries are finding it difficult to feed and care for their enormous populations. Countries with large industries and advanced technology are known as developed countries. They include Japan, Australia, and much of Europe and North America. Most of their populations have stopped growing, and some are shrinking.

Rich and poor

The gap between the world's rich and poor is growing. Developing countries are home to 75 percent of the world's people, but share just 20 percent of the world's wealth. On average, people in developing countries can expect to have less money, food, medical care, education and access to technology than people in developed countries. These graphs compare living standards in five countries, ranging from one of the world's wealthiest countries, Europe's Norway, to one of the poorest, Africa's Sierra Leone.

Many languages

About 6,000 different languages are spoken today, but more than half the people in the world have one of the 12 languages shown on this chart as their first language. English has fewer than half as many first-language speakers as Mandarin Chinese, but it is spoken by many more people as a second language and is becoming the main world language.

NUMBER OF NATIVE SPEAKERS

Language	Speakers	
Mandarin Chinese	874,000,000	
Hindi	366,000,000	
English	341,000,000	
Spanish	340,000,000	
Bengali	207,000,000	
Portuguese	176,000,000	
Russian	167,000,000	
Arabic	150,000,000	
Japanese	125,000,000	
German	100,000,000	
Korean	78,000,000	
French	77,000,000	

Many languages are now endangered. The language of Japan's indigenous people, the Ainu (left), is virtually extinct, with just a handful of elderly speakers remaining. On average, one language is lost every 10 days, and half of the world's 6,000 languages are likely to disappear by 2100.

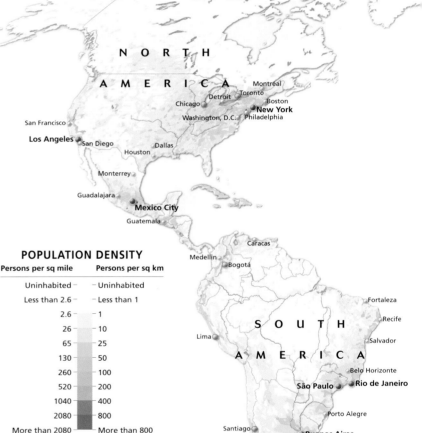

POPULATION DENSITY

Persons per sq mile	Persons per sq km
Uninhabited	Uninhabited
Less than 2.6	Less than 1
2.6	1
26	10
65	25
130	50
260	100
520	200
1040	400
2080	800
More than 2080	More than 800

World religions

The earliest signs of religious belief date back 60,000 years, and virtually every culture since has followed some kind of religion. There are now hundreds of different religious traditions in the world, but Hinduism, Buddhism, Judaism, Christianity and Islam have had the broadest influence. Hinduism and Buddhism both developed in Asia, while Judaism, Christianity and Islam started in the Middle East.

Islamic mosque

Stained glass window from Christian church

Ganesh, the Hindu god of wisdom

HOW THE WORLD WORSHIPS

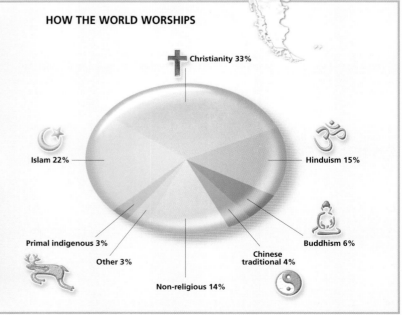

Christianity 33%
Islam 22%
Hinduism 15%
Buddhism 6%
Chinese traditional 4%
Non-religious 14%
Other 3%
Primal indigenous 3%

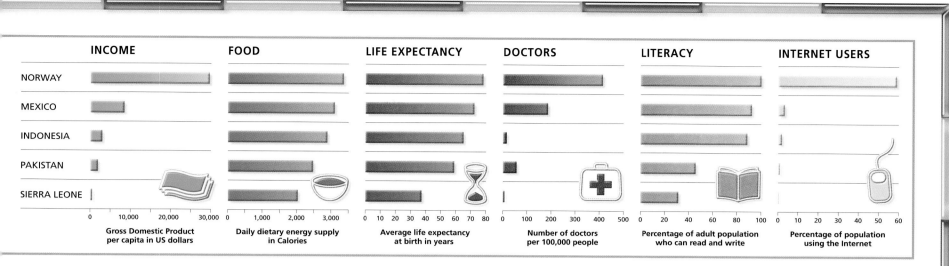

	INCOME	FOOD	LIFE EXPECTANCY	DOCTORS	LITERACY	INTERNET USERS
NORWAY						
MEXICO						
INDONESIA						
PAKISTAN						
SIERRA LEONE						

0 10,000 20,000 30,000	0 1,000 2,000 3,000	0 10 20 30 40 50 60 70 80	0 100 200 300 400 500	0 20 40 60 80 100	0 10 20 30 40 50 60
Gross Domestic Product per capita in US dollars	**Daily dietary energy supply in Calories**	**Average life expectancy at birth in years**	**Number of doctors per 100,000 people**	**Percentage of adult population who can read and write**	**Percentage of population using the Internet**

Where people live

The 6 billion people on Earth are spread very unevenly over its landmasses, with China, India and Europe the most crowded areas. People have tended to settle near rivers or the coast. About half of all people now live in cities.

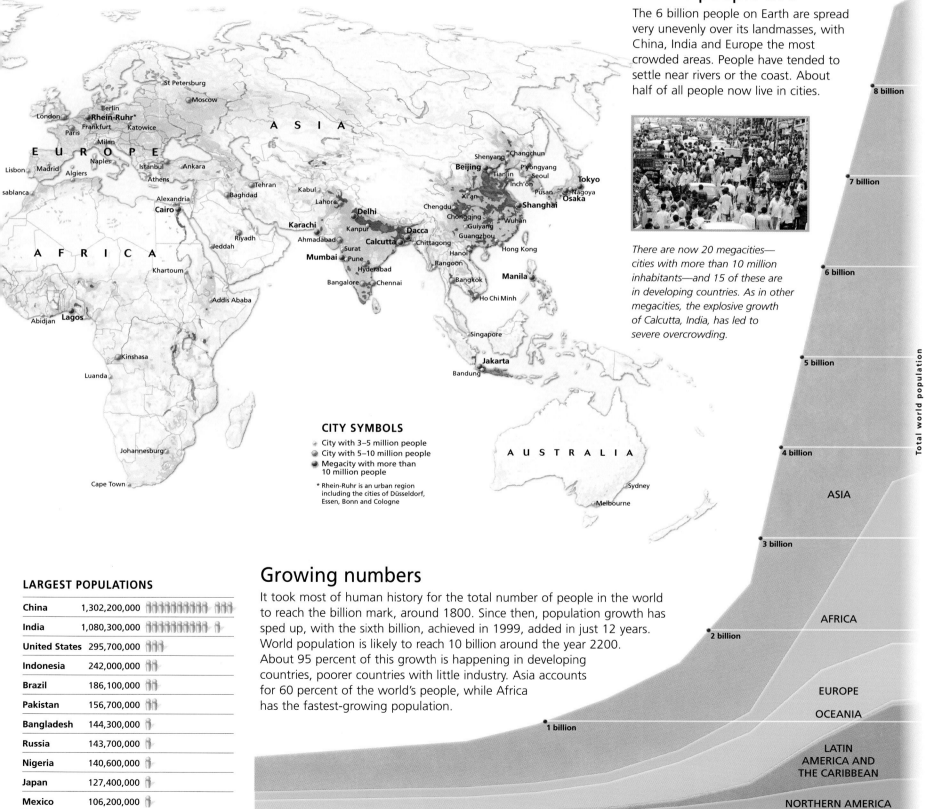

There are now 20 megacities— cities with more than 10 million inhabitants—and 15 of these are in developing countries. As in other megacities, the explosive growth of Calcutta, India, has led to severe overcrowding.

CITY SYMBOLS

- City with 3–5 million people
- City with 5–10 million people
- Megacity with more than 10 million people

* Rhein-Ruhr is an urban region including the cities of Düsseldorf, Essen, Bonn and Cologne

LARGEST POPULATIONS

China	1,302,200,000
India	1,080,300,000
United States	295,700,000
Indonesia	242,000,000
Brazil	186,100,000
Pakistan	156,700,000
Bangladesh	144,300,000
Russia	143,700,000
Nigeria	140,600,000
Japan	127,400,000
Mexico	106,200,000
Philippines	87,900,000

Growing numbers

It took most of human history for the total number of people in the world to reach the billion mark, around 1800. Since then, population growth has sped up, with the sixth billion, achieved in 1999, added in just 12 years. World population is likely to reach 10 billion around the year 2200. About 95 percent of this growth is happening in developing countries, poorer countries with little industry. Asia accounts for 60 percent of the world's people, while Africa has the fastest-growing population.

Geographic comparisons

Largest Islands

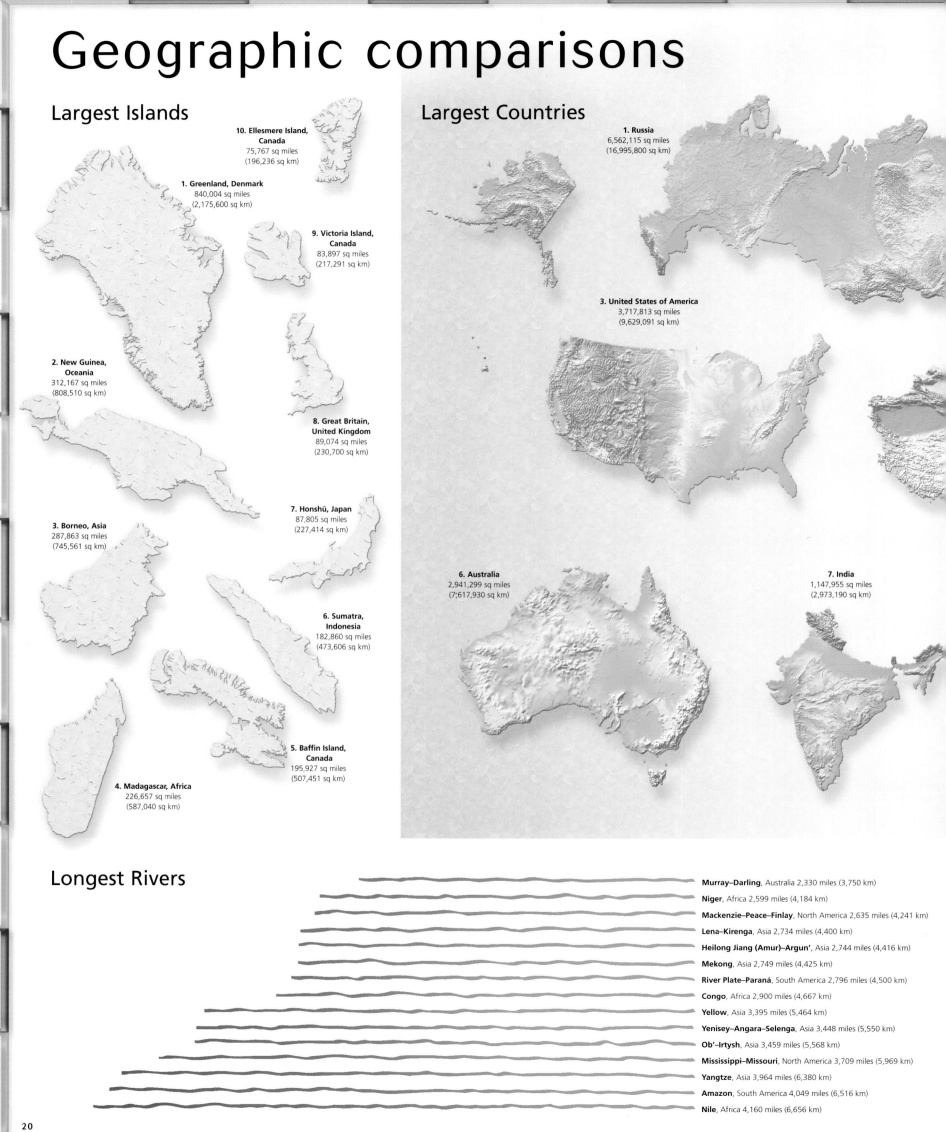

10. Ellesmere Island, Canada
75,767 sq miles
(196,236 sq km)

1. Greenland, Denmark
840,004 sq miles
(2,175,600 sq km)

9. Victoria Island, Canada
83,897 sq miles
(217,291 sq km)

2. New Guinea, Oceania
312,167 sq miles
(808,510 sq km)

8. Great Britain, United Kingdom
89,074 sq miles
(230,700 sq km)

7. Honshū, Japan
87,805 sq miles
(227,414 sq km)

3. Borneo, Asia
287,863 sq miles
(745,561 sq km)

6. Sumatra, Indonesia
182,860 sq miles
(473,606 sq km)

5. Baffin Island, Canada
195,927 sq miles
(507,451 sq km)

4. Madagascar, Africa
226,657 sq miles
(587,040 sq km)

Largest Countries

1. Russia
6,562,115 sq miles
(16,995,800 sq km)

3. United States of America
3,717,813 sq miles
(9,629,091 sq km)

6. Australia
2,941,299 sq miles
(7,617,930 sq km)

7. India
1,147,955 sq miles
(2,973,190 sq km)

Longest Rivers

Murray–Darling, Australia 2,330 miles (3,750 km)

Niger, Africa 2,599 miles (4,184 km)

Mackenzie–Peace–Finlay, North America 2,635 miles (4,241 km)

Lena–Kirenga, Asia 2,734 miles (4,400 km)

Heilong Jiang (Amur)–Argun', Asia 2,744 miles (4,416 km)

Mekong, Asia 2,749 miles (4,425 km)

River Plate–Paraná, South America 2,796 miles (4,500 km)

Congo, Africa 2,900 miles (4,667 km)

Yellow, Asia 3,395 miles (5,464 km)

Yenisey–Angara–Selenga, Asia 3,448 miles (5,550 km)

Ob'–Irtysh, Asia 3,459 miles (5,568 km)

Mississippi–Missouri, North America 3,709 miles (5,969 km)

Yangtze, Asia 3,964 miles (6,380 km)

Amazon, South America 4,049 miles (6,516 km)

Nile, Africa 4,160 miles (6,656 km)

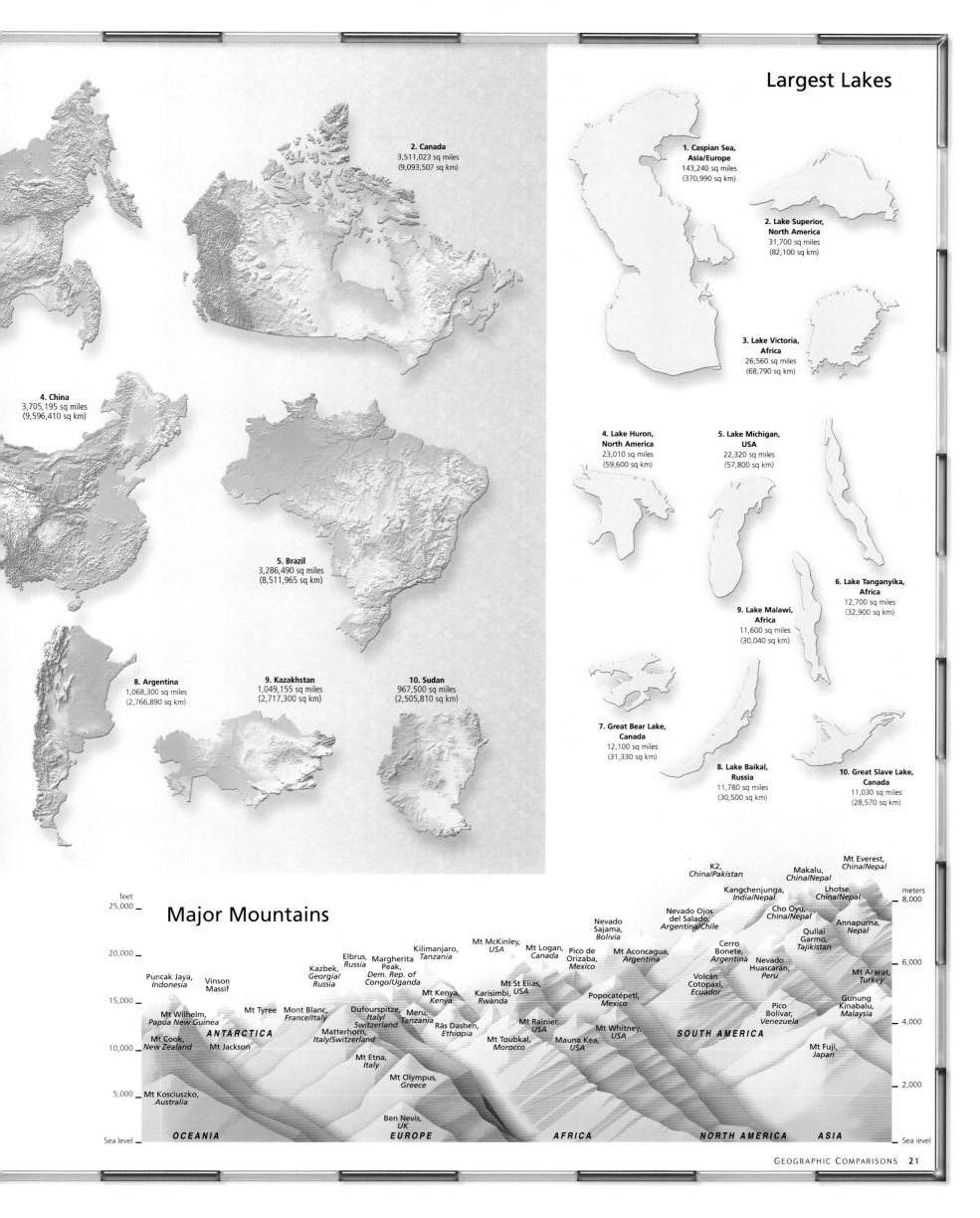

2. Canada
3,511,023 sq miles
(9,093,507 sq km)

4. China
3,705,195 sq miles
(9,596,410 sq km)

5. Brazil
3,286,490 sq miles
(8,511,965 sq km)

8. Argentina
1,068,300 sq miles
(2,766,890 sq km)

9. Kazakhstan
1,049,155 sq miles
(2,717,300 sq km)

10. Sudan
967,500 sq miles
(2,505,810 sq km)

Largest Lakes

1. Caspian Sea, Asia/Europe
143,240 sq miles
(370,990 sq km)

2. Lake Superior, North America
31,700 sq miles
(82,100 sq km)

3. Lake Victoria, Africa
26,560 sq miles
(68,790 sq km)

4. Lake Huron, North America
23,010 sq miles
(59,600 sq km)

5. Lake Michigan, USA
22,320 sq miles
(57,800 sq km)

6. Lake Tanganyika, Africa
12,700 sq miles
(32,900 sq km)

9. Lake Malawi, Africa
11,600 sq miles
(30,040 sq km)

7. Great Bear Lake, Canada
12,100 sq miles
(31,330 sq km)

8. Lake Baikal, Russia
11,780 sq miles
(30,500 sq km)

10. Great Slave Lake, Canada
11,030 sq miles
(28,570 sq km)

Major Mountains

feet
25,000
20,000
15,000
10,000
5,000
Sea level

meters
8,000
6,000
4,000
2,000
Sea level

Mt Everest, *China/Nepal*
K2, *China/Pakistan*
Makalu, *China/Nepal*
Kangchenjunga, *India/Nepal*
Lhotse, *China/Nepal*
Cho Oyu, *China/Nepal*
Nevado Ojos del Salado, *Argentina/Chile*
Annapurna, *Nepal*
Qullai Garmo, *Tajikistan*
Nevado Sajama, *Bolivia*
Cerro Bonete, *Argentina*
Mt McKinley, *USA*
Mt Logan, *Canada*
Pico de Orizaba, *Mexico*
Mt Aconcagua, *Argentina*
Nevado Huascarán, *Peru*
Mt Ararat, *Turkey*
Kilimanjaro, *Tanzania*
Elbrus, *Russia*
Margherita Peak, *Dem. Rep. of Congo/Uganda*
Kazbek, *Georgia/Russia*
Volcán Cotopaxi, *Ecuador*
Mt St Elias, *USA*
Popocatépetl, *Mexico*
Pico Bolívar, *Venezuela*
Gunung Kinabalu, *Malaysia*
Puncak Jaya, *Indonesia*
Vinson Massif
Mt Kenya, *Kenya*
Karisimbi, *Rwanda*
Meru, *Tanzania*
Mt Rainier, *USA*
Mt Whitney, *USA*
Mt Fuji, *Japan*
Mt Wilhelm, *Papua New Guinea*
Mt Tyree
Mont Blanc, *France/Italy*
Dufourspitze, *Italy/Switzerland*
Rās Dashen, *Ethiopia*
Mauna Kea, *USA*
SOUTH AMERICA
Matterhorn, *Italy/Switzerland*
Mt Toubkal, *Morocco*
Mt Cook, *New Zealand*
Mt Jackson
ANTARCTICA
Mt Etna, *Italy*
Mt Olympus, *Greece*
Mt Kosciuszko, *Australia*
Ben Nevis, *UK*
OCEANIA **EUROPE** **AFRICA** **NORTH AMERICA** **ASIA**

The physical world

CIRCUMFERENCE OF EARTH AROUND THE EQUATOR
24,902 miles (40,067 km)

AREA OF SEA
139,782,000 square miles (362,033,000 sq km)

AREA OF LAND ABOVE SEA LEVEL
57,151,000 square miles (148,021,000 sq km)

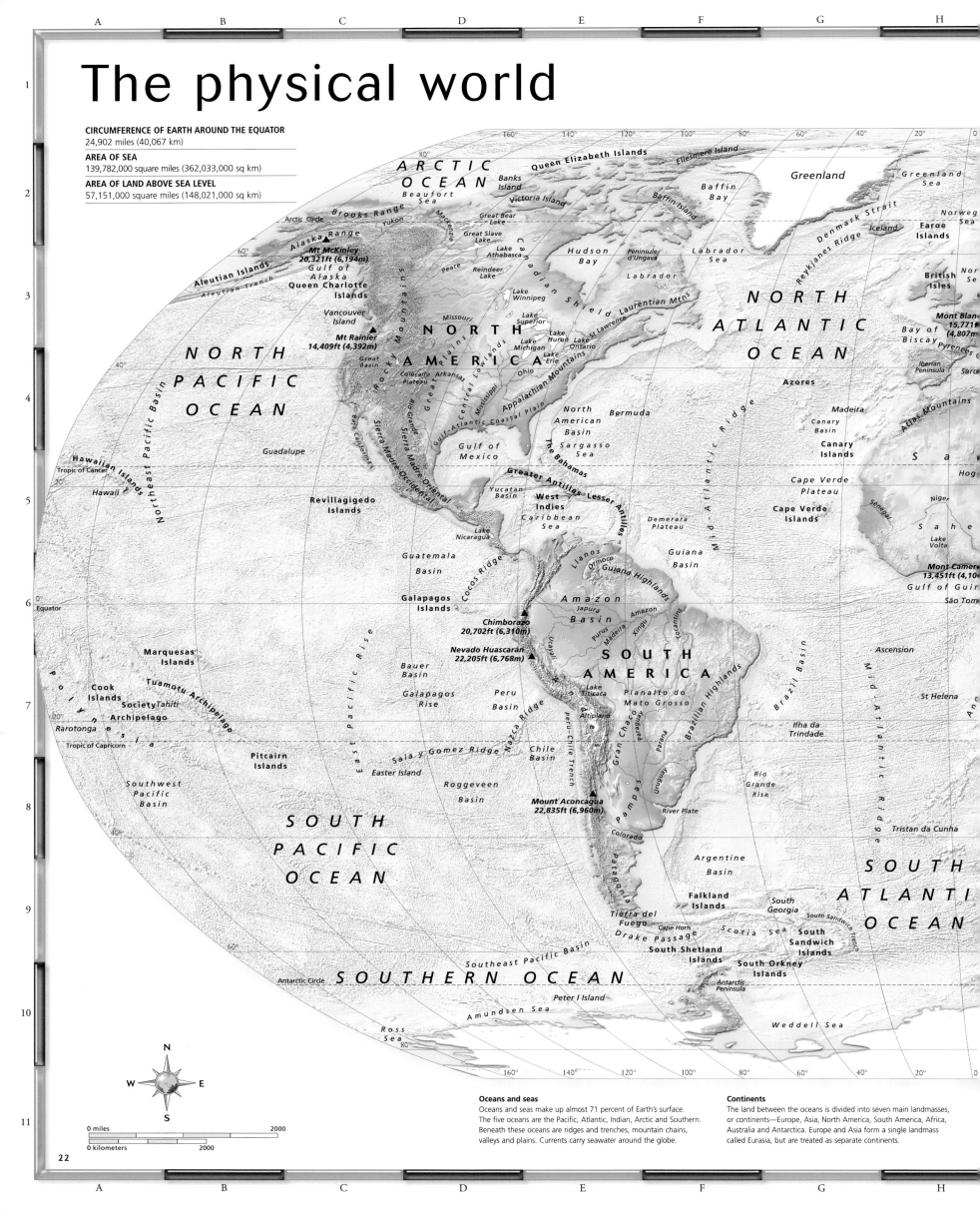

ARCTIC OCEAN
Queen Elizabeth Islands
Ellesmere Island
Greenland
Greenland Sea
Banks Island
Beaufort Sea
Baffin Bay
Baffin Island
Victoria Island
Norweg Sea
Denmark Strait
Iceland
Faroe Islands
Brooks Range
Arctic Circle
Yukon
Mackenzie
Great Bear Lake
Great Slave Lake
Reykjanes Ridge
Alaska Range
Mt McKinley 20,321ft (6,194m)
Gulf of Alaska
Lake Athabasca
Hudson Bay
Péninsule d'Ungava
Labrador Sea
British Isles
Nor Se
Aleutian Islands
Aleutian Trench
Queen Charlotte Islands
Peace
Reindeer Lake
Labrador
NORTH ATLANTIC OCEAN
Lake Winnipeg
Canadian Shield
St Lawrence
Laurentian Mtns
Mont Blanc 15,771 (4,807m)
Vancouver Island
Missouri
NORTH AMERICA
Lake Superior
Lake Michigan
Lake Huron
Lake Ontario
Lake Erie
Bay of Biscay
Iberian Peninsula
Pyrenees
NORTH PACIFIC OCEAN
Mt Rainier 14,409ft (4,392m)
Great Basin
Rocky Mountains
Great Plains
Colorado Plateau
Central Lowlands
Arkansas
Ohio
Mississippi
Appalachian Mountains
North American Basin
Bermuda
Azores
Madeira
Canary Basin
Atlas Mountains
Rio Grande
Sierra Madre Occidental
Sierra Madre Oriental
Baja California
Gulf of Mexico
Gulf-Central Coastal Plain
The Bahamas
Sargasso Sea
Canary Islands
Sa
Guadalupe
Tropic of Cancer
Hawaiian Islands
Yucatan Basin
Greater Antilles
Lesser Antilles
West Indies
Caribbean Sea
Cape Verde Plateau
Cape Verde Islands
Hog
Niger
Hawaii
Revillagigedo Islands
Lake Nicaragua
Demerara Plateau
Sahe
Lake Volta
Guatemala Basin
Cocos Ridge
Llanos
Orinoco
Guiana Highlands
Guiana Basin
Mont Camero 13,451ft (4,10
Gulf of Guin
São Tom
Galapagos Islands
Chimborazo 20,702ft (6,310m)
Amazon Basin
Japurá
Amazon
Equator
Nevado Huascarán 22,205ft (6,768m)
Purus
Madeira
Xingu
Tocantins
Marquesas Islands
East Pacific Rise
Bauer Basin
Ucayali
SOUTH AMERICA
Brazil Basin
Ascension
Cook Islands
Tuamotu Archipelago
Galapagos Rise
Peru Basin
Lake Titicaca
Planalto do Mato Grosso
Brazilian Highlands
Society Archipelago
Tahiti
Altiplano
Mid-Atlantic Ridge
St Helena
Rarotonga
Tropic of Capricorn
Nazca Ridge
Peru-Chile Trench
Gran Chaco
Paraguay
Paraná
Ilha da Trindade
Pitcairn Islands
Sala y Gomez Ridge
Chile Basin
Uruguay
Rio Grande Rise
Easter Island
Roggeveen Basin
Mount Aconcagua 22,835ft (6,960m)
Pampas
River Plate
Southwest Pacific Basin
Colorado
Argentine Basin
SOUTH PACIFIC OCEAN
Patagonia
SOUTH ATLANTI OCEAN
Tristan da Cunha
Falkland Islands
South Georgia
Tierra del Fuego
Cape Horn
Drake Passage
Scotia Sea
South Sandwich Trench
South Sandwich Islands
Southeast Pacific Basin
South Shetland Islands
South Orkney Islands
Antarctic Circle
SOUTHERN OCEAN
Peter I Island
Antarctic Peninsula
Ross Sea
Amundsen Sea
Weddell Sea

N W E S

0 miles 2000
0 kilometers 2000

Oceans and seas
Oceans and seas make up almost 71 percent of Earth's surface. The five oceans are the Pacific, Atlantic, Indian, Arctic and Southern. Beneath these oceans are ridges and trenches, mountain chains, valleys and plains. Currents carry seawater around the globe.

Continents
The land between the oceans is divided into seven main landmasses, or continents—Europe, Asia, North America, South America, Africa, Australia and Antarctica. Europe and Asia form a single landmass called Eurasia, but are treated as separate continents.

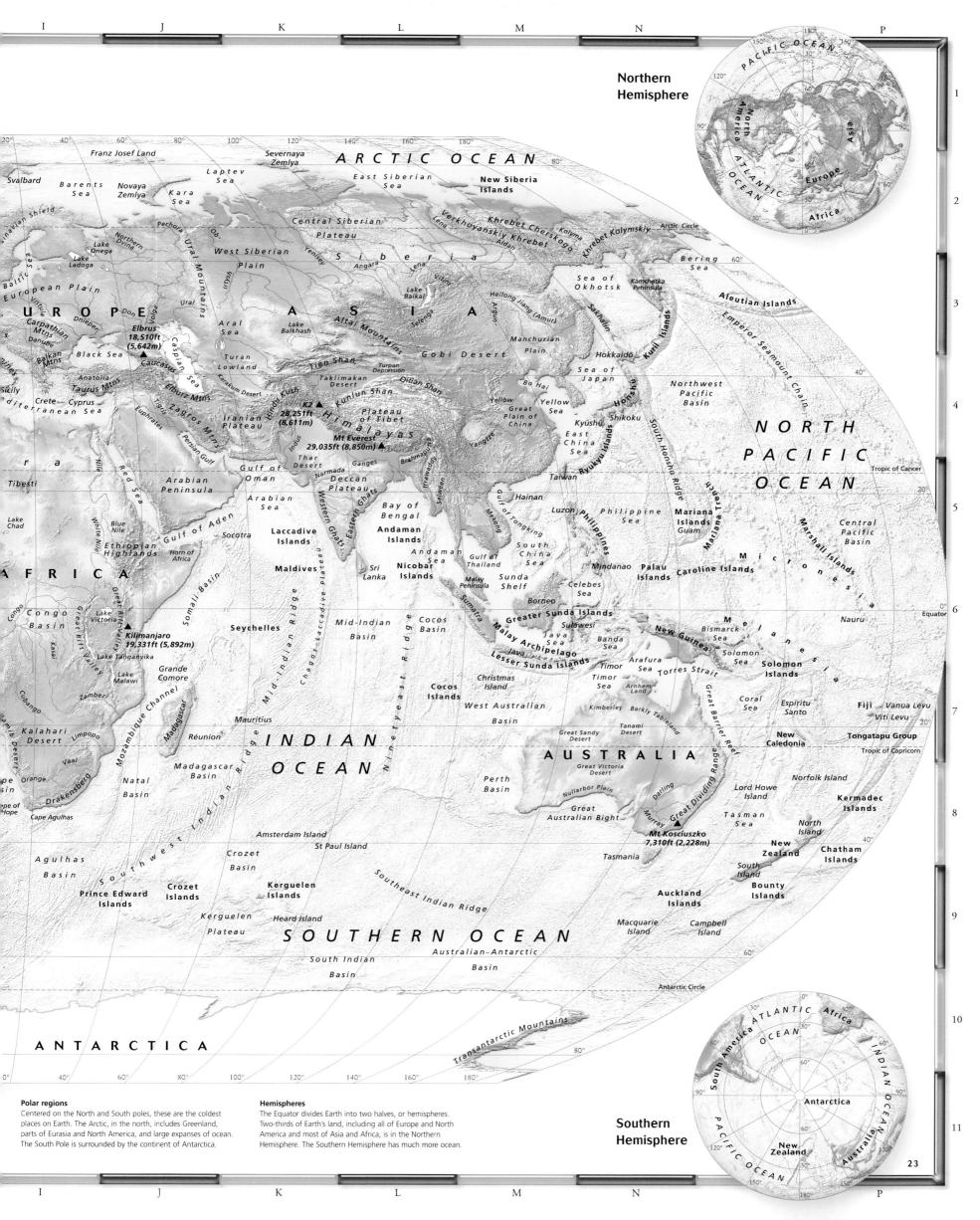

Northern Hemisphere

Southern Hemisphere

Polar regions
Centered on the North and South poles, these are the coldest places on Earth. The Arctic, in the north, includes Greenland, parts of Eurasia and North America, and large expanses of ocean. The South Pole is surrounded by the continent of Antarctica.

Hemispheres
The Equator divides Earth into two halves, or hemispheres. Two-thirds of Earth's land, including all of Europe and North America and most of Asia and Africa, is in the Northern Hemisphere. The Southern Hemisphere has much more ocean.

Countries of the world

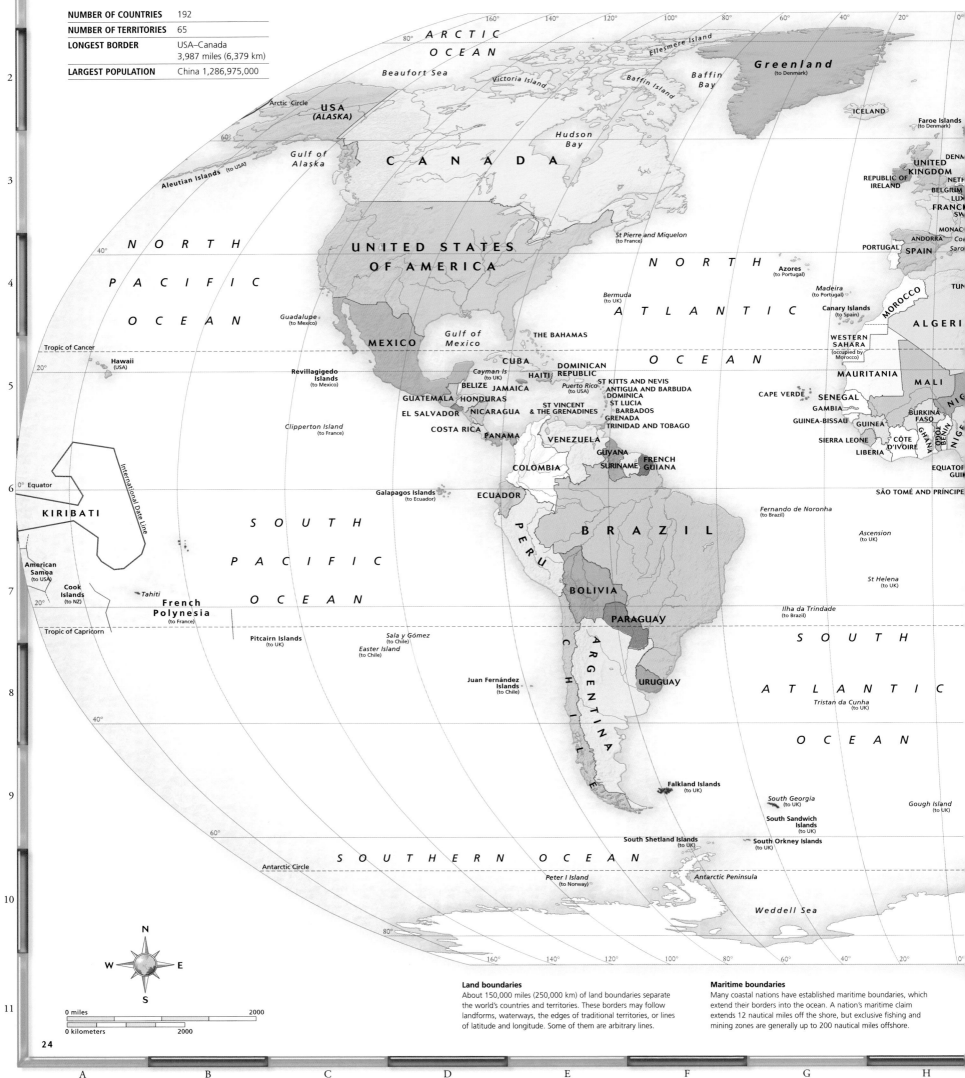

NUMBER OF COUNTRIES	192
NUMBER OF TERRITORIES	65
LONGEST BORDER	USA–Canada 3,987 miles (6,379 km)
LARGEST POPULATION	China 1,286,975,000

ARCTIC OCEAN

Beaufort Sea

Victoria Island

Baffin Island

Baffin Bay

Ellesmere Island

Greenland (to Denmark)

ICELAND

Faroe Islands (to Denmark)

Arctic Circle

USA (ALASKA)

Gulf of Alaska

Hudson Bay

C A N A D A

DENM

UNITED KINGDOM

REPUBLIC OF IRELAND

NETH

BELGIUM

LUX

FRANC

SW

Aleutian Islands (to USA)

N O R T H

P A C I F I C

O C E A N

St Pierre and Miquelon (to France)

UNITED STATES OF AMERICA

N O R T H

Azores (to Portugal)

A T L A N T I C

Bermuda (to UK)

Madeira (to Portugal)

PORTUGAL

SPAIN

MONAC

ANDORRA

Co

Sar

MOROCCO

Canary Islands (to Spain)

TUN

ALGERI

Tropic of Cancer

MEXICO

Gulf of Mexico

THE BAHAMAS

O C E A N

WESTERN SAHARA (occupied by Morocco)

MAURITANIA

MALI

Hawaii (USA)

20°

Guadalupe (to Mexico)

Revillagigedo Islands (to Mexico)

CUBA

DOMINICAN REPUBLIC

Cayman Is (to UK)

HAITI

BELIZE

JAMAICA

Puerto Rico (to USA)

ST KITTS AND NEVIS

ANTIGUA AND BARBUDA

DOMINICA

CAPE VERDE

SENEGAL

GAMBIA

GUINEA-BISSAU

GUINEA

SIERRA LEONE

CÔTE D'IVOIRE

LIBERIA

BURKINA FASO

GHANA

TOGO

NIGE

BENIN

NIG

GUATEMALA

HONDURAS

ST LUCIA

BARBADOS

EL SALVADOR

NICARAGUA

ST VINCENT & THE GRENADINES

GRENADA

TRINIDAD AND TOBAGO

Clipperton Island (to France)

COSTA RICA

PANAMA

VENEZUELA

EQUATOR

GUIN

SÃO TOMÉ AND PRÍNCIPE

COLOMBIA

GUYANA

SURINAME

FRENCH GUIANA

Galapagos Islands (to Ecuador)

ECUADOR

0° Equator

International Date Line

KIRIBATI

S O U T H

P A C I F I C

O C E A N

P E R U

B R A Z I L

Fernando de Noronha (to Brazil)

Ascension (to UK)

American Samoa (to USA)

Cook Islands (to NZ)

Tahiti

French Polynesia (to France)

BOLIVIA

St Helena (to UK)

20°

Tropic of Capricorn

Pitcairn Islands (to UK)

Sala y Gómez (to Chile)

Easter Island (to Chile)

PARAGUAY

Ilha da Trindade (to Brazil)

S O U T H

A T L A N T I C

Juan Fernández Islands (to Chile)

C H I L E

A R G E N T I N A

URUGUAY

O C E A N

Tristan da Cunha (to UK)

40°

Falkland Islands (to UK)

South Georgia (to UK)

Gough Island (to UK)

South Sandwich Islands (to UK)

60°

South Shetland Islands (to UK)

South Orkney Islands (to UK)

Antarctic Circle

S O U T H E R N   O C E A N

Peter I Island (to Norway)

Antarctic Peninsula

Weddell Sea

80°

N
W E
S

0 miles		2000
0 kilometers		2000

Land boundaries
About 150,000 miles (250,000 km) of land boundaries separate the world's countries and territories. These borders may follow landforms, waterways, the edges of traditional territories, or lines of latitude and longitude. Some of them are arbitrary lines.

Maritime boundaries
Many coastal nations have established maritime boundaries, which extend their borders into the ocean. A nation's maritime claim extends 12 nautical miles off the shore, but exclusive fishing and mining zones are generally up to 200 nautical miles offshore.

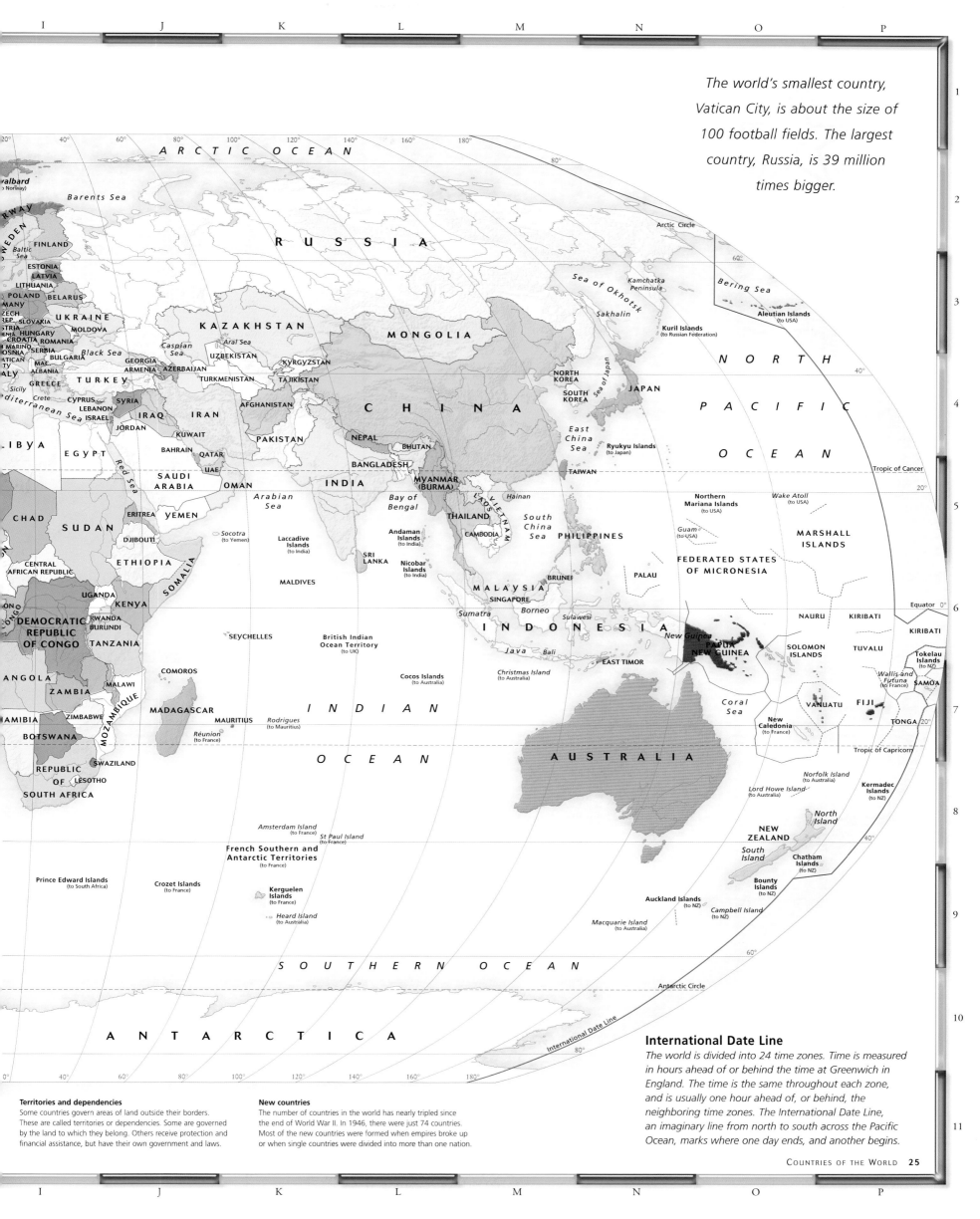

The world's smallest country, Vatican City, is about the size of 100 football fields. The largest country, Russia, is 39 million times bigger.

International Date Line

The world is divided into 24 time zones. Time is measured in hours ahead of or behind the time at Greenwich in England. The time is the same throughout each zone, and is usually one hour ahead of, or behind, the neighboring time zones. The International Date Line, an imaginary line from north to south across the Pacific Ocean, marks where one day ends, and another begins.

Territories and dependencies
Some countries govern areas of land outside their borders. These are called territories or dependencies. Some are governed by the land to which they belong. Others receive protection and financial assistance, but have their own government and laws.

New countries
The number of countries in the world has nearly tripled since the end of World War II. In 1946, there were just 74 countries. Most of the new countries were formed when empires broke up or when single countries were divided into more than one nation.

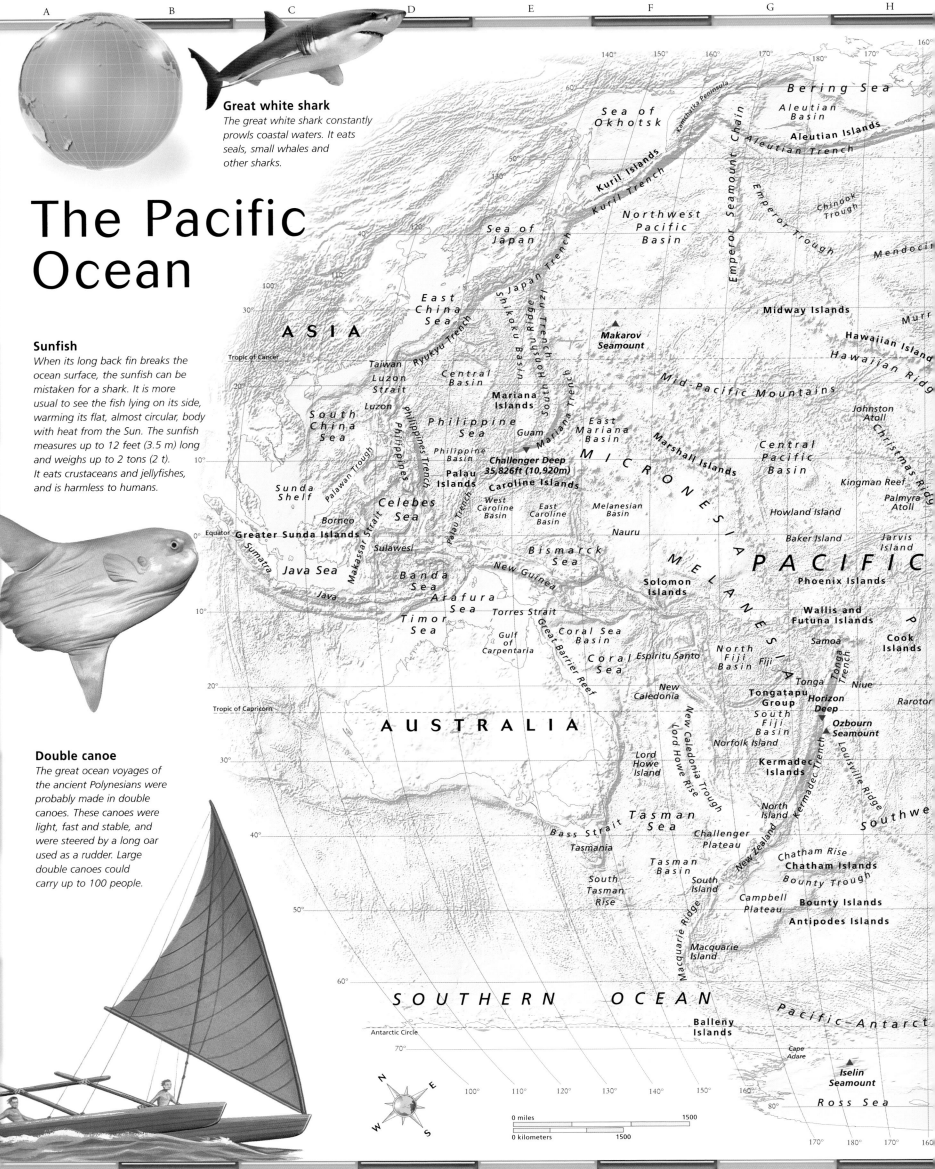

The Pacific Ocean

Great white shark

The great white shark constantly prowls coastal waters. It eats seals, small whales and other sharks.

Sunfish

When its long back fin breaks the ocean surface, the sunfish can be mistaken for a shark. It is more usual to see the fish lying on its side, warming its flat, almost circular, body with heat from the Sun. The sunfish measures up to 12 feet (3.5 m) long and weighs up to 2 tons (2 t). It eats crustaceans and jellyfishes, and is harmless to humans.

Double canoe

The great ocean voyages of the ancient Polynesians were probably made in double canoes. These canoes were light, fast and stable, and were steered by a long oar used as a rudder. Large double canoes could carry up to 100 people.

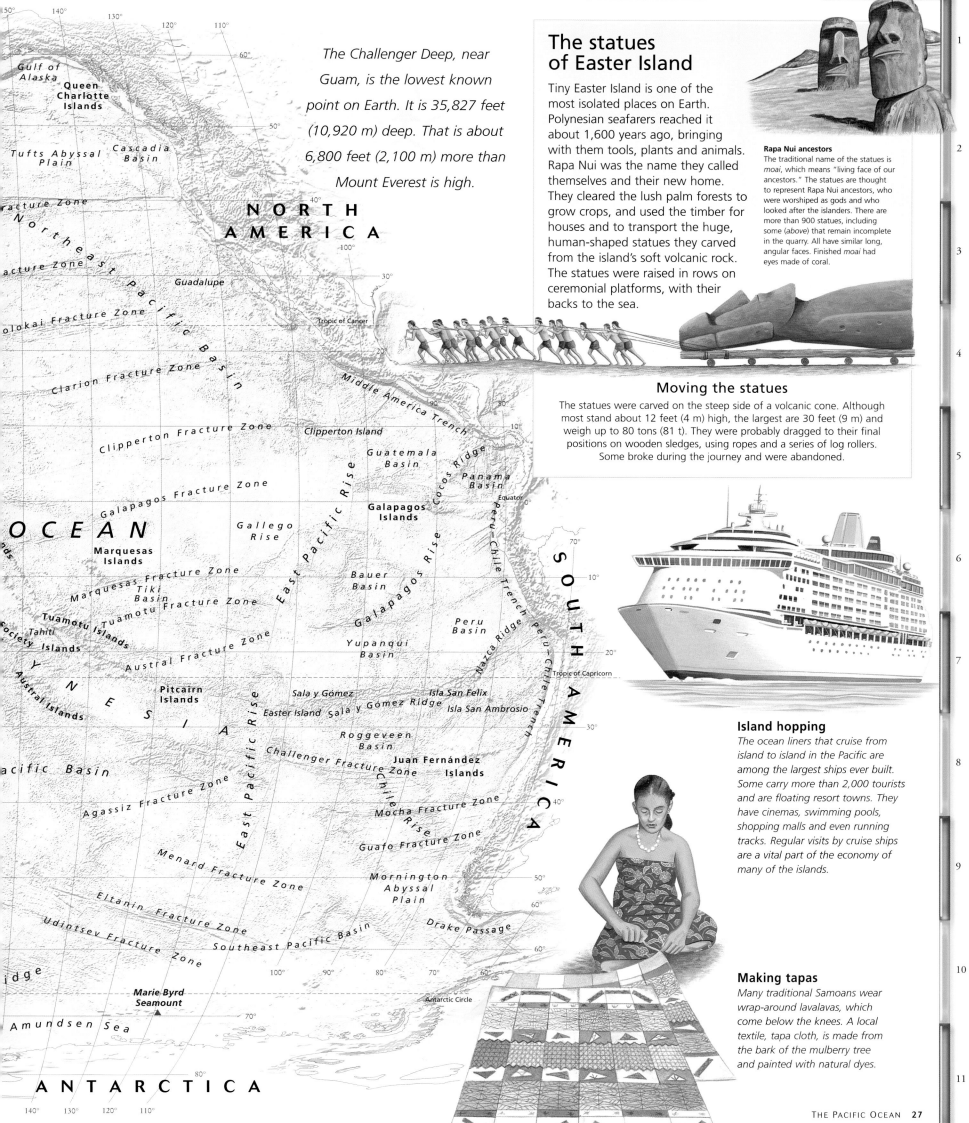

The Challenger Deep, near Guam, is the lowest known point on Earth. It is 35,827 feet (10,920 m) deep. That is about 6,800 feet (2,100 m) more than Mount Everest is high.

The statues of Easter Island

Tiny Easter Island is one of the most isolated places on Earth. Polynesian seafarers reached it about 1,600 years ago, bringing with them tools, plants and animals. Rapa Nui was the name they called themselves and their new home. They cleared the lush palm forests to grow crops, and used the timber for houses and to transport the huge, human-shaped statues they carved from the island's soft volcanic rock. The statues were raised in rows on ceremonial platforms, with their backs to the sea.

Rapa Nui ancestors
The traditional name of the statues is *moai*, which means "living face of our ancestors." The statues are thought to represent Rapa Nui ancestors, who were worshipped as gods and who looked after the islanders. There are more than 900 statues, including some (*above*) that remain incomplete in the quarry. All have similar long, angular faces. Finished *moai* had eyes made of coral.

Moving the statues

The statues were carved on the steep side of a volcanic cone. Although most stand about 12 feet (4 m) high, the largest are 30 feet (9 m) and weigh up to 80 tons (81 t). They were probably dragged to their final positions on wooden sledges, using ropes and a series of log rollers. Some broke during the journey and were abandoned.

Island hopping

The ocean liners that cruise from island to island in the Pacific are among the largest ships ever built. Some carry more than 2,000 tourists and are floating resort towns. They have cinemas, swimming pools, shopping malls and even running tracks. Regular visits by cruise ships are a vital part of the economy of many of the islands.

Making tapas

Many traditional Samoans wear wrap-around lavalavas, which come below the knees. A local textile, tapa cloth, is made from the bark of the mulberry tree and painted with natural dyes.

Map labels

Gulf of Alaska
Queen Charlotte Islands
Tufts Abyssal Plain
Cascadia Basin
Fracture Zone
Northeast Pacific Basin
Fracture Zone
Guadalupe
Molokai Fracture Zone
Clarion Fracture Zone
Clipperton Fracture Zone
Clipperton Island
Guatemala Basin
Cocos Ridge
Panama Basin
Galapagos Fracture Zone
Galapagos Islands
Gallego Rise
East Pacific Rise
Marquesas Islands
Marquesas Fracture Zone
Bauer Basin
Galapagos Rise
Peru-Chile Trench
Tiki Basin
Tuamotu Fracture Zone
Peru Basin
Tuamotu Islands
Tahiti
Society Islands
Yupanqui Basin
Nazca Ridge
Austral Fracture Zone
Peru-Chile Trench
Austral Islands
Pitcairn Islands
Sala y Gómez
Isla San Felix
Easter Island
Sala y Gómez Ridge
Isla San Ambrosio
Roggeveen Basin
East Pacific Rise
Challenger Fracture Zone
Juan Fernández Islands
Pacific Basin
Chile Trench
Agassiz Fracture Zone
Mocha Fracture Zone
Mocha Rise
Menard Fracture Zone
Guafo Fracture Zone
Mornington Abyssal Plain
Eltanin Fracture Zone
Drake Passage
Udintsev Fracture Zone
Southeast Pacific Basin
Ridge
Marie Byrd Seamount
Amundsen Sea

NORTH AMERICA
SOUTH AMERICA
OCEAN
POLYNESIA
ANTARCTICA

Tropic of Cancer
Equator
Tropic of Capricorn
Antarctic Circle

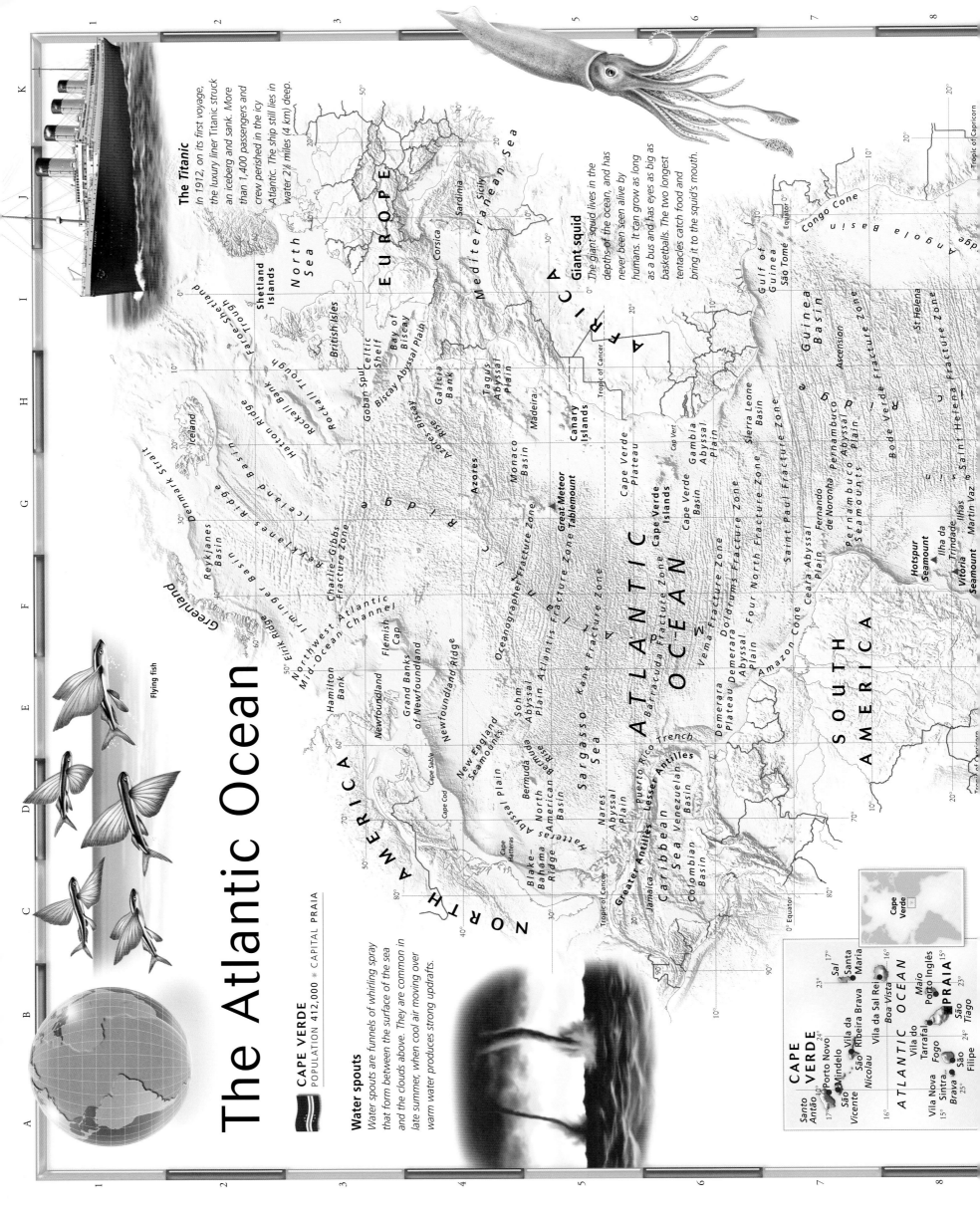

The Atlantic Ocean

CAPE VERDE
POPULATION 412,000 ✳ CAPITAL PRAIA

Water spouts
Water spouts are funnels of whirling spray that form between the surface of the sea and the clouds above. They are common in late summer, when cool air moving over warm water produces strong updrafts.

The *Titanic*
In 1912, on its first voyage, the luxury liner Titanic struck an iceberg and sank. More than 1,400 passengers and crew perished in the icy Atlantic. The ship still lies in water 2½ miles (4 km) deep.

Giant squid
The giant squid lives in the depths of the ocean, and has never been seen alive by humans. It can grow as long as a bus and has eyes as big as basketballs. The two longest tentacles catch food and bring it to the squid's mouth.

Flying fish

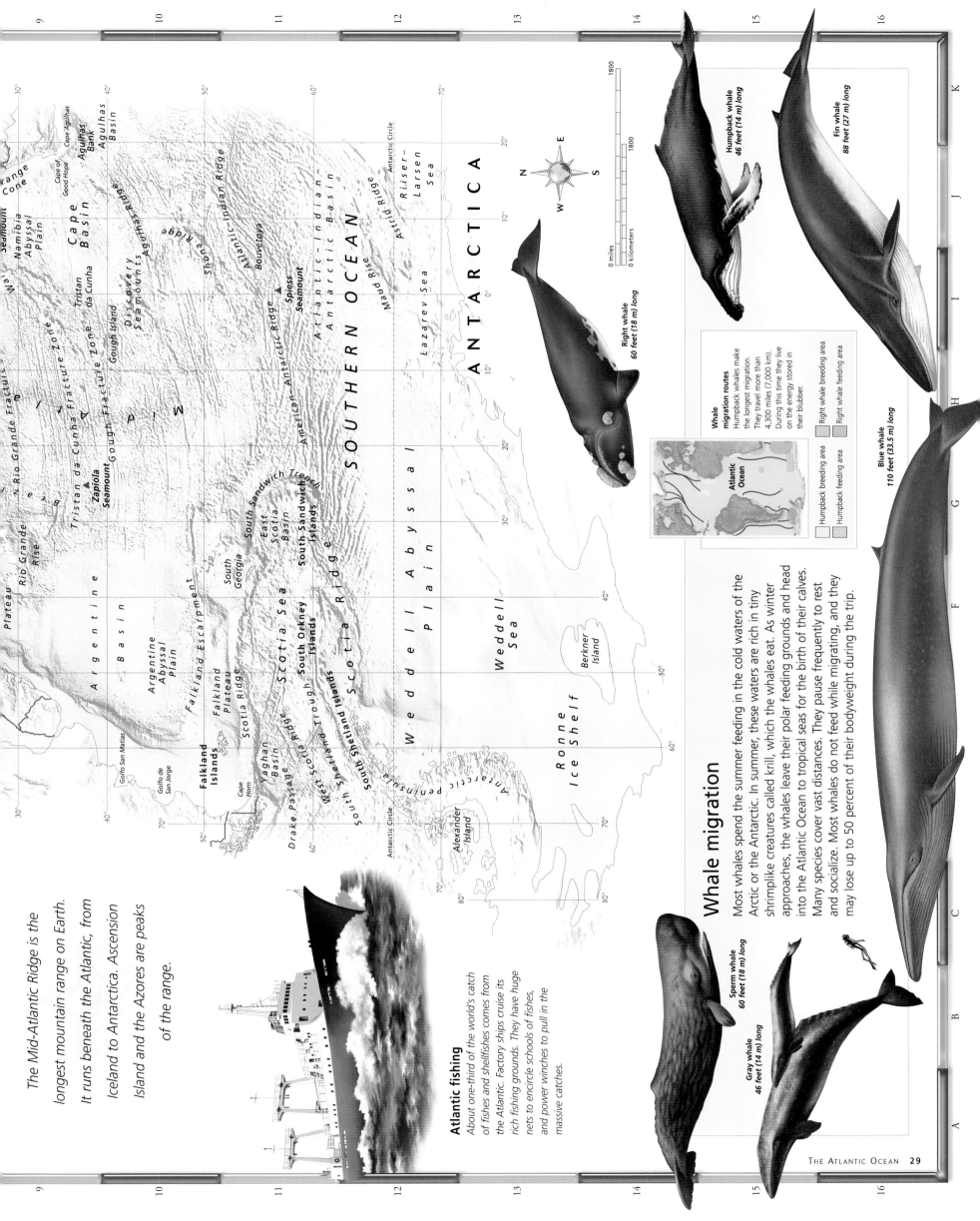

The Mid-Atlantic Ridge is the longest mountain range on Earth. It runs beneath the Atlantic, from Iceland to Antarctica. Ascension Island and the Azores are peaks of the range.

Atlantic fishing

About one-third of the world's catch of fishes and shellfishes comes from the Atlantic. Factory ships cruise its rich fishing grounds. They have huge nets to encircle schools of fishes, and power winches to pull in the massive catches.

Whale migration

Most whales spend the summer feeding in the cold waters of the Arctic or the Antarctic. In summer, these waters are rich in tiny shrimplike creatures called krill, which the whales eat. As winter approaches, the whales leave their polar feeding grounds and head into the Atlantic Ocean to tropical seas for the birth of their calves. Many species cover vast distances. They pause frequently to rest and socialize. Most whales do not feed while migrating, and they may lose up to 50 percent of their bodyweight during the trip.

Whale migration routes
Humpback whales make the longest migration. They travel more than 4,300 miles (7,000 km). During this time they live on the energy stored in their blubber.

Atlantic Ocean

☐ Humpback breeding area
☐ Right whale breeding area
☐ Humpback feeding area
☐ Right whale feeding area

Right whale
60 feet (18 m) long

Humpback whale
46 feet (14 m) long

Fin whale
88 feet (27 m) long

Blue whale
110 feet (33.5 m) long

Sperm whale
60 feet (18 m) long

Gray whale
46 feet (14 m) long

N

W — E

S

0 miles 1800
0 kilometers 1800

The Indian Ocean

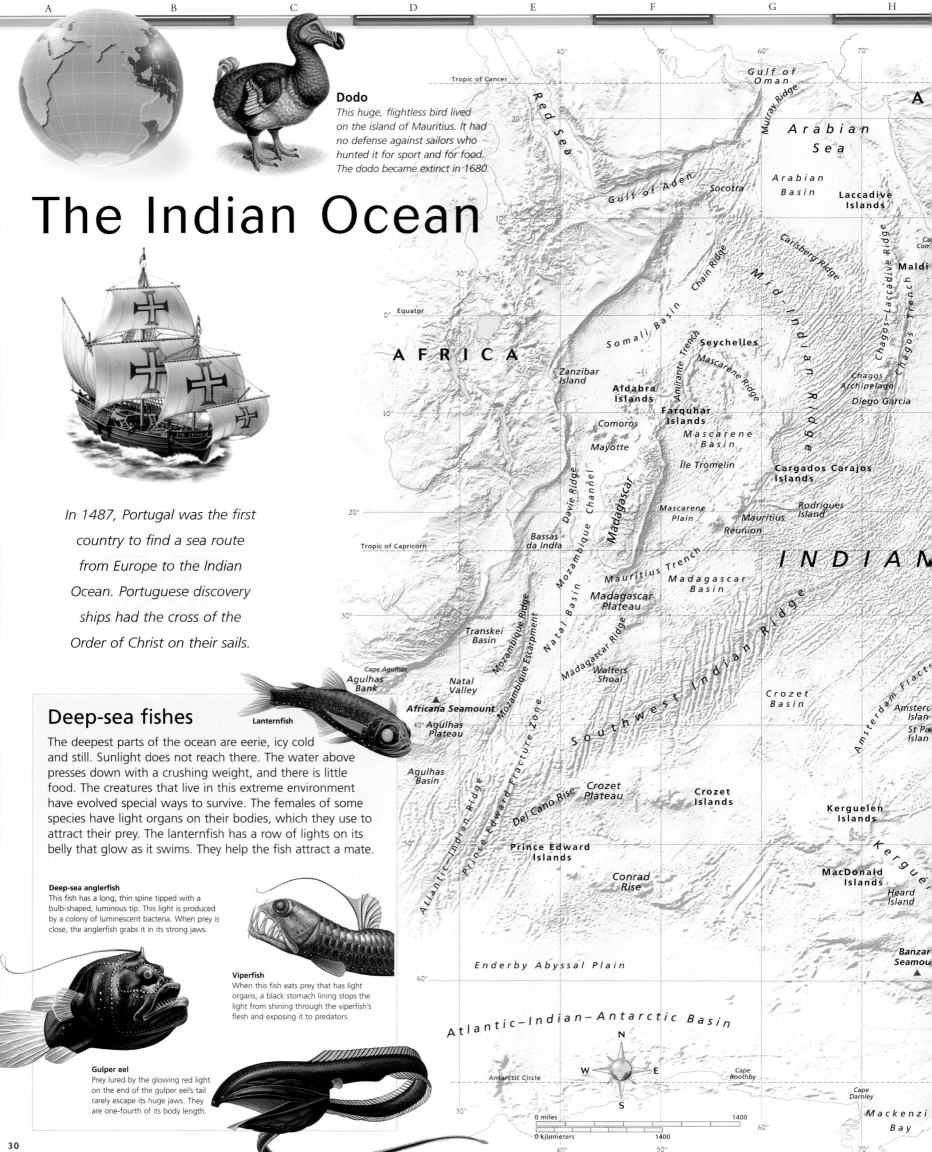

Dodo
This huge, flightless bird lived on the island of Mauritius. It had no defense against sailors who hunted it for sport and for food. The dodo became extinct in 1680.

In 1487, Portugal was the first country to find a sea route from Europe to the Indian Ocean. Portuguese discovery ships had the cross of the Order of Christ on their sails.

Deep-sea fishes

Lanternfish

The deepest parts of the ocean are eerie, icy cold and still. Sunlight does not reach there. The water above presses down with a crushing weight, and there is little food. The creatures that live in this extreme environment have evolved special ways to survive. The females of some species have light organs on their bodies, which they use to attract their prey. The lanternfish has a row of lights on its belly that glow as it swims. They help the fish attract a mate.

Deep-sea anglerfish
This fish has a long, thin spine tipped with a bulb-shaped, luminous tip. This light is produced by a colony of luminescent bacteria. When prey is close, the anglerfish grabs it in its strong jaws.

Viperfish
When this fish eats prey that has light organs, a black stomach lining stops the light from shining through the viperfish's flesh and exposing it to predators.

Gulper eel
Prey lured by the glowing red light on the end of the gulper eel's tail rarely escape its huge jaws. They are one-fourth of its body length.

Tropic of Cancer
Gulf of Oman
Red Sea
Gulf of Aden
Socotra
Arabian Sea
Arabian Basin
Laccadive Islands
Murray Ridge
Carlsberg Ridge
Chagos-Laccadive Ridge
Chagos Trench
Maldi
Chain Ridge
Mid-Indian Ridge
Equator
Somali Basin
Seychelles
Amirante Trench
Mascarene Ridge
Chagos Archipelago
Diego Garcia
AFRICA
Zanzibar Island
Aldabra Islands
Farquhar Islands
Mascarene Basin
Comoros
Mayotte
Île Tromelin
Cargados Carajos Islands
Davie Ridge
Madagascar
Mascarene Plain
Mauritius
Réunion
Rodrigues Island
Tropic of Capricorn
Bassas da India
Mozambique Channel
INDIAN
Mauritius Trench
Madagascar Basin
Natal Basin
Madagascar Plateau
Madagascar Ridge
Mozambique Ridge
Mozambique Escarpment
Transkei Basin
Walters Shoal
Cape Agulhas
Agulhas Bank
Natal Valley
Africana Seamount
Agulhas Plateau
Mozambique Fracture Zone
Southwest Indian Ridge
Crozet Basin
Amsterdam Fract
Amsterd Islan
St Pa Islan
Agulhas Basin
Atlantic-Indian Ridge
Prince Edward Fracture Zone
Del Cano Rise
Crozet Plateau
Crozet Islands
Kerguelen Islands
Prince Edward Islands
Conrad Rise
MacDonald Islands
Kergue
Heard Island
Banzar Seamou
Enderby Abyssal Plain
Atlantic-Indian-Antarctic Basin
Antarctic Circle
Cape Boothby
Cape Darnley
Mackenzi Bay

0 miles 1400
0 kilometers 1400

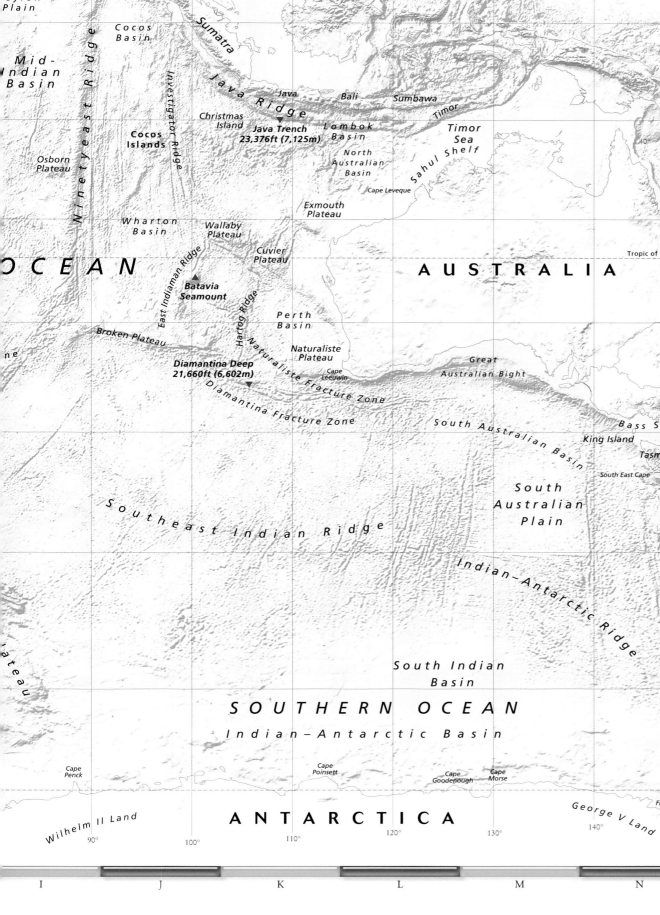

A

Ganges Cone
Bay of Bengal
Andaman Sea
Andaman Islands
Andaman Basin
Nicobar Islands
eylon Plain
Sri Lanka
Mid-Indian Basin
Cocos Basin
Ninetyeast Ridge
Investigator Ridge
Sumatra
Java Ridge
Java
Bali
Sumbawa
Timor
Christmas Island
Java Trench 23,376ft (7,125m)
Lombok Basin
North Australian Basin
Timor Sea
Sahul Shelf
Cape Leveque
Osborn Plateau
Cocos Islands
Wharton Basin
Wallaby Plateau
Exmouth Plateau
Cuvier Plateau
East Indiaman Ridge
Batavia Seamount
Hartog Ridge
Perth Basin
OCEAN
Broken Plateau
Naturaliste Fracture Zone
Naturaliste Plateau
Cape Leeuwin
Diamantina Deep 21,660ft (6,602m)
Diamantina Fracture Zone
AUSTRALIA
Tropic of Cancer
Tropic of Capricorn
Great Australian Bight
South Australian Basin
Bass Strait
King Island
Tasmania
South East Cape
South Australian Plain
Southeast Indian Ridge
Indian–Antarctic Ridge
South Indian Basin
SOUTHERN OCEAN
Indian–Antarctic Basin
Cape Penck
Cape Poinsett
Cape Goodenough
Cape Morse
Antarctic Circle
Fisher Bay
Wilhelm II Land
George V Land
ANTARCTICA
Equator

Manta ray

Rays are related to sharks. The manta ray grows to 23 feet (7 m) across and is the largest ray in the world. It feeds on plankton, small crustaceans and fishes. Manta rays are harmless to humans.

Pearl diver

Pearls form inside living mollusks in tropical waters. This process occurs naturally but, today, most pearls are specially farmed. A bead is inserted in the pearl oyster shell, and a pearl grows around it. Divers tend the oysters until the pearls are ready to be harvested.

Sea vent

Water heated by volcanic activity beneath the ocean floor bursts up through sea vents. Chimneys sometimes grow around these deep-sea hot springs. They are made of minerals that are contained in the very hot vent water. These minerals form particles on contact with the freezing ocean.

The polar regions

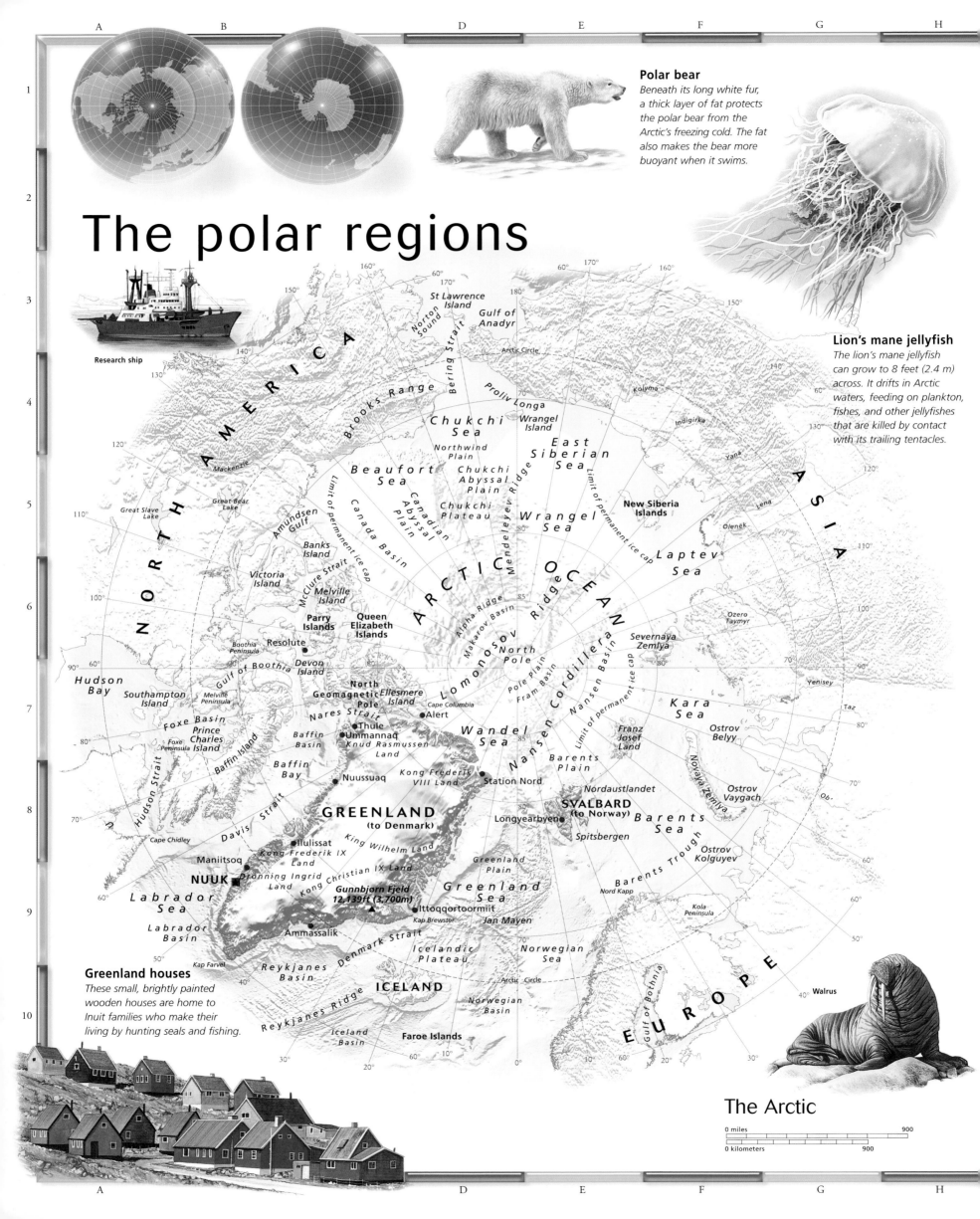

Polar bear
Beneath its long white fur, a thick layer of fat protects the polar bear from the Arctic's freezing cold. The fat also makes the bear more buoyant when it swims.

Lion's mane jellyfish
The lion's mane jellyfish can grow to 8 feet (2.4 m) across. It drifts in Arctic waters, feeding on plankton, fishes, and other jellyfishes that are killed by contact with its trailing tentacles.

Research ship

Greenland houses
These small, brightly painted wooden houses are home to Inuit families who make their living by hunting seals and fishing.

Walrus

The Arctic

0 miles   900
0 kilometers   900

Map labels

St Lawrence Island
Norton Sound
Bering Strait
Gulf of Anadyr
Arctic Circle
Proliv Longa
Kolyma
Indigirka
Wrangel Island
Brooks Range
Chukchi Sea
East Siberian Sea
Northwind Plain
Yana
NORTH AMERICA
Beaufort Sea
Chukchi Abyssal Plain
Canadian Abyssal Plain
Chukchi Plateau
Mendeleyev Ridge
Wrangel Sea
New Siberia Islands
ASIA
Lena
Mackenzie
Great Slave Lake
Great Bear Lake
Amundsen Gulf
Canada Basin
Laptev Sea
Olenëk
Banks Island
Victoria Island
McClure Strait
Melville Island
ARCTIC OCEAN
Alpha Ridge
Makarov Basin
Lomonosov Ridge
Nansen Cordillera
Severnaya Zemlya
Ozero Taymyr
NORTH
Parry Islands
Queen Elizabeth Islands
North Pole
Nansen Basin
Boothia Peninsula
Resolute
Devon Island
Gulf of Boothia
Pole Plain
Fram Basin
Limit of permanent ice cap
Yenisey
Hudson Bay
Southampton Island
Melville Peninsula
North Geomagnetic Pole
Ellesmere Island
Cape Columbia
Alert
Kara Sea
Taz
Foxe Basin
Prince Charles Island
Nares Strait
Thule
Ummannaq
Knud Rasmussen Land
Wandel Sea
Barents Plain
Franz Josef Land
Ostrov Belyy
Foxe Peninsula
Baffin Basin
Baffin Island
Baffin Bay
Nuussuaq
Kong Frederik VIII Land
Station Nord
Novaja Zemlya
Ostrov Vaygach
Nordaustlandet
Ob
Cape Chidley
Davis Strait
GREENLAND (to Denmark)
SVALBARD (to Norway)
Barents Sea
Longyearbyen
Spitsbergen
Ostrov Kolguyev
Ilulissat
King Wilhelm Land
Greenland Plain
Maniitsoq
Kong Frederik IX Land
NUUK
Dronning Ingrid Land
Kong Christian IX Land
Gunnbjorn Fjeld 12,139ft (3,700m)
Ittoqqortoormiit
Greenland Sea
Barents Trough
Nord Kapp
Labrador Sea
Kap Brewster
Jan Mayen
Kola Peninsula
Labrador Basin
Ammassalik
Kap Farvel
Reykjanes Basin
Denmark Strait
Icelandic Plateau
Norwegian Sea
Arctic Circle
Norwegian Basin
Gulf of Bothnia
EUROPE
Reykjanes Ridge
ICELAND
Norwegian Basin
Iceland Basin
Faroe Islands

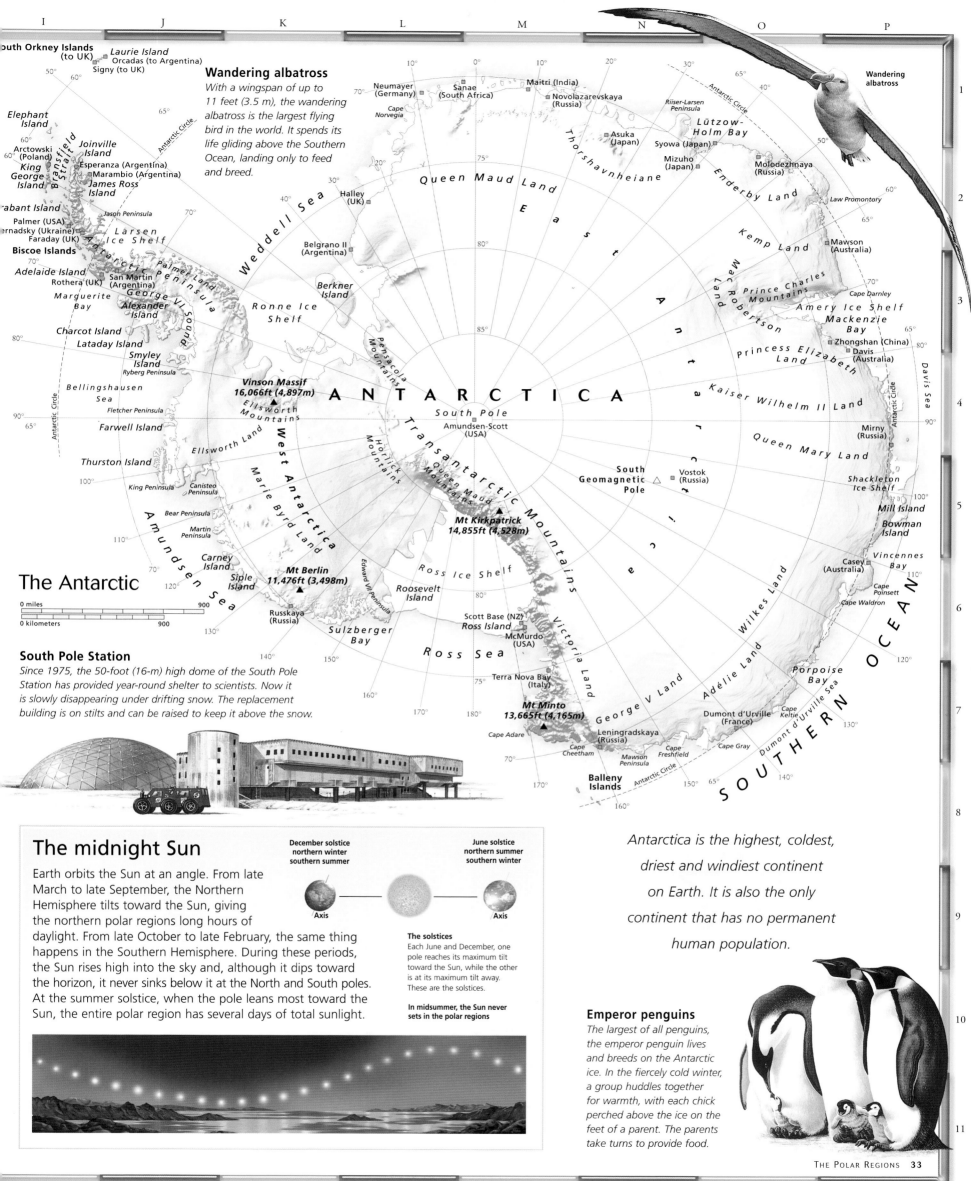

Wandering albatross

With a wingspan of up to 11 feet (3.5 m), the wandering albatross is the largest flying bird in the world. It spends its life gliding above the Southern Ocean, landing only to feed and breed.

Wandering albatross

The Antarctic

0 miles 900
0 kilometers 900

South Pole Station

Since 1975, the 50-foot (16-m) high dome of the South Pole Station has provided year-round shelter to scientists. Now it is slowly disappearing under drifting snow. The replacement building is on stilts and can be raised to keep it above the snow.

Map labels

South Orkney Islands (to UK)
Laurie Island
Orcadas (to Argentina)
Signy (to UK)
Elephant Island
Arctowski (Poland)
Joinville Island
King George Island
Esperanza (Argentina)
Marambio (Argentina)
James Ross Island
Brabant Island
Palmer (USA)
Vernadsky (Ukraine)
Faraday (UK)
Jason Peninsula
Biscoe Islands
Larsen Ice Shelf
Adelaide Island
Rothera (UK)
San Martin (Argentina)
Marguerite Bay
Palmer Land
George VI Sound
Charcot Island
Alexander Island
Lataday Island
Ronne Ice Shelf
Smyley Island
Ryberg Peninsula
Bellingshausen Sea
Fletcher Peninsula
Farwell Island
Ellsworth Land
Thurston Island
King Peninsula
Canisteo Peninsula
Ellsworth Mountains
Vinson Massif 16,066ft (4,897m)
West Antarctica
Bear Peninsula
Amundsen Sea
Martin Peninsula
Carney Island
Marie Byrd Land
Siple Island
Mt Berlin 11,476ft (3,498m)
Russkaya (Russia)
Sulzberger Bay
Edward VII Peninsula
Roosevelt Island
Ross Ice Shelf
Scott Base (NZ)
Ross Island
McMurdo (USA)
Terra Nova Bay (Italy)
Mt Minto 13,665ft (4,165m)
Cape Adare
Leningradskaya (Russia)
Cape Cheetham
Mawson Peninsula
Balleny Islands
Neumayer (Germany)
Cape Norvegia
Sanae (South Africa)
Maitri (India)
Novolazarevskaya (Russia)
Queen Maud Land
Halley (UK)
Asuka (Japan)
Belgrano II (Argentina)
Berkner Island
Pensacola Mountains
Horlick Mountains
Queen Maud Mountains
Transantarctic Mountains
ANTARCTICA
South Pole
Amundsen-Scott (USA)
Mt Kirkpatrick 14,855ft (4,528m)
South Geomagnetic Pole
Vostok (Russia)
Victoria Land
George V Land
Adélie Land
Cape Freshfield
Cape Gray
Dumont d'Urville (France)
Dumont d'Urville Sea
Weddell Sea
East Antarctica
Thorshavnheiane
Lützow-Holm Bay
Syowa (Japan)
Mizuho (Japan)
Molodezhnaya (Russia)
Riiser-Larsen Peninsula
Enderby Land
Kemp Land
Law Promontory
Mawson (Australia)
Prince Charles Mountains
Mac. Robertson Land
Cape Darnley
Amery Ice Shelf
Mackenzie Bay
Zhongshan (China)
Davis (Australia)
Princess Elizabeth Land
Kaiser Wilhelm II Land
Davis Sea
Queen Mary Land
Mirny (Russia)
Shackleton Ice Shelf
Mill Island
Bowman Island
Vincennes Bay
Casey (Australia)
Cape Poinsett
Cape Waldron
Wilkes Land
Porpoise Bay
Cape Keltie
SOUTHERN OCEAN
Antarctic Circle

The midnight Sun

Earth orbits the Sun at an angle. From late March to late September, the Northern Hemisphere tilts toward the Sun, giving the northern polar regions long hours of daylight. From late October to late February, the same thing happens in the Southern Hemisphere. During these periods, the Sun rises high into the sky and, although it dips toward the horizon, it never sinks below it at the North and South poles. At the summer solstice, when the pole leans most toward the Sun, the entire polar region has several days of total sunlight.

December solstice
northern winter
southern summer

June solstice
northern summer
southern winter

Axis

Axis

The solstices
Each June and December, one pole reaches its maximum tilt toward the Sun, while the other is at its maximum tilt away. These are the solstices.

In midsummer, the Sun never sets in the polar regions

Antarctica is the highest, coldest, driest and windiest continent on Earth. It is also the only continent that has no permanent human population.

Emperor penguins

The largest of all penguins, the emperor penguin lives and breeds on the Antarctic ice. In the fiercely cold winter, a group huddles together for warmth, with each chick perched above the ice on the feet of a parent. The parents take turns to provide food.

Norwegian
Sea

Iceland

Faroe
Islands

Shetland
Islands

ATLANTIC OCEAN

Köle

Outer Hebrides

Ben Nevis
4,406ft
(1,343m)

Orkney
Islands

Atlantic

North
Sea

Scand

Skagerrak

Vänern Vättern

Kattegat

Jutland

Öland

British Isles

Pennines

Fyn Sjaelland

Bornholm

Ireland

Irish Sea

Elbe

United Kingdom

Oder

Thames

Hartz
Mountains

Ore Mountains

English Channel

Rhine

Mosel

Bohemian
Forest

Seine

Black
Forest

Danube

Loire

Jura Vosges

Alps

Dolomites

Dinari

Lake
Geneva

Bay of
Biscay

Garonne

Massif
Central

Mont Blanc
15,771ft
(4,807m)

Po

Apennines

Adriatic Sea

Rhône

Pyrenees

Duero

Ebro

Aneto
11,168ft (3,404m)

Ligurian Sea

Corsica

Tyrrhenian Sea

Vesuvius
4,202ft (1,281m)

Iberian
Peninsula

Balearic Islands

Minorca

Sardinia

Sierra Morena

Ibiza

Majorca

Guadalquivir

Sistemas Béticos

Mediterranean Sea

Sicily

Mt Etna
10,902ft (3,323m)

Malta

Novaya
Zemlya

*Kara
Sea*

*Barents
Sea*

Inarijärvi

Ostrov
Kolguyev

Pechora

Lappland

Kola
Peninsula

White Sea

Ural Mountains

Gulf of Bothnia

avian Shield

Lake
Onega

Northern Dvina

Åland

Gulf of Finland

Lake Ladoga

Rybinsk
Reservoir

Kama

Baltic Sea

otland

Lake
Peipus

Volga

Gulf of
Riga

Valdai
Hills

Kuybyshev
Reservoir

Vistula

Dnieper

Volga Uplands

North European Plain

Kiev
Reservoir

Central Russian Uplands

Tsimlyansk
Reservoir

Carpathian Mountains

Dniester

Dnieper

Don

Europe

Great
Hungarian
Plain

Transylvanian Alps

Sea of
Azov

Crimea

Danube

Elbrus
18,510ft
(5,642m)
▲

Caspian Sea

Danube

Balkan Mountains

Black Sea

Caucasus

Rhodope Mountains

ALPS

Pindus Mountains

Sea of
Marmara

Aegean Sea

Dodecanese

onian

Peloponnese

Sea

Crete

Rhodes

United Kingdom and Ireland

UNITED KINGDOM
POPULATION 60,095,000 ✴ CAPITAL LONDON

IRELAND
POPULATION 3,924,000 ✴ CAPITAL DUBLIN

Loch Ness monster

Loch Ness, in the Scottish Highlands, is the largest freshwater lake in the United Kingdom. It is 788 feet (240 m) deep and about 23 miles (37 km) long. Although many people believe they have seen a monster rather like a dinosaur in the lake, there is still no proof that it exists.

Scottish Highland band

Bagpipers traditionally led regiments into battle. The tunes inspired the soldiers and frightened their enemies. The sound of bagpipes carries a long way. Today, military bands of pipers and drummers play on ceremonial occasions.

Hadrian's Wall

The emperor Hadrian ordered his army to build and patrol a wall at the northernmost boundary of Roman territory, to keep out invaders. Built between AD 122 and AD 129, near what is now the Scottish border, it extended 73 miles (118 km). Parts of it remain.

Stonehenge

The circle of standing stones on Salisbury Plain, in southwestern England, was built between 2900 BC and 1800 BC. While the function of this monument remains unknown, one theory is that the circle formed an astronomical observatory for predicting the best times to plant and harvest.

The first stage
The first builders of Stonehenge laid out a circular bank of earth and a ditch about 380 feet (116 m) in diameter. They raised a huge stone, the Heel Stone, at the entrance.

The second stage
Around 2800 BC, an inner stone circle, the Bluestone Circle, was built. The stone used may have come from another monument.

The third stage
Stonehenge as it looks today was built around 1800 BC. It consists of a ring of 30 stones topped by stone lintels. Within this ring are taller pairs of stones set in a horseshoe shape.

The summer solstice

At sunrise on the summer solstice, which is the longest day of the year, the Sun shines straight through the Heel Stone.

Positioning the stones
Many of the stones were probably brought great distances to the site. Each one was levered into a deep pit with sloping sides, called a posthole.

Pulling the stones upright
A system of ropes was attached to each stone. Because of the immense weight, hundreds of people were needed to pull the stones upright.

Raising the lintels
Each lintel, or cross beam, was shaped to the curve of the circle. A timber scaffold was built so that the lintels could be raised to the top of the stones.

Securing the lintels
A groove carved into the base of each lintel fitted into pegs carved on the top of each stone, ensuring that the two fitted securely together.

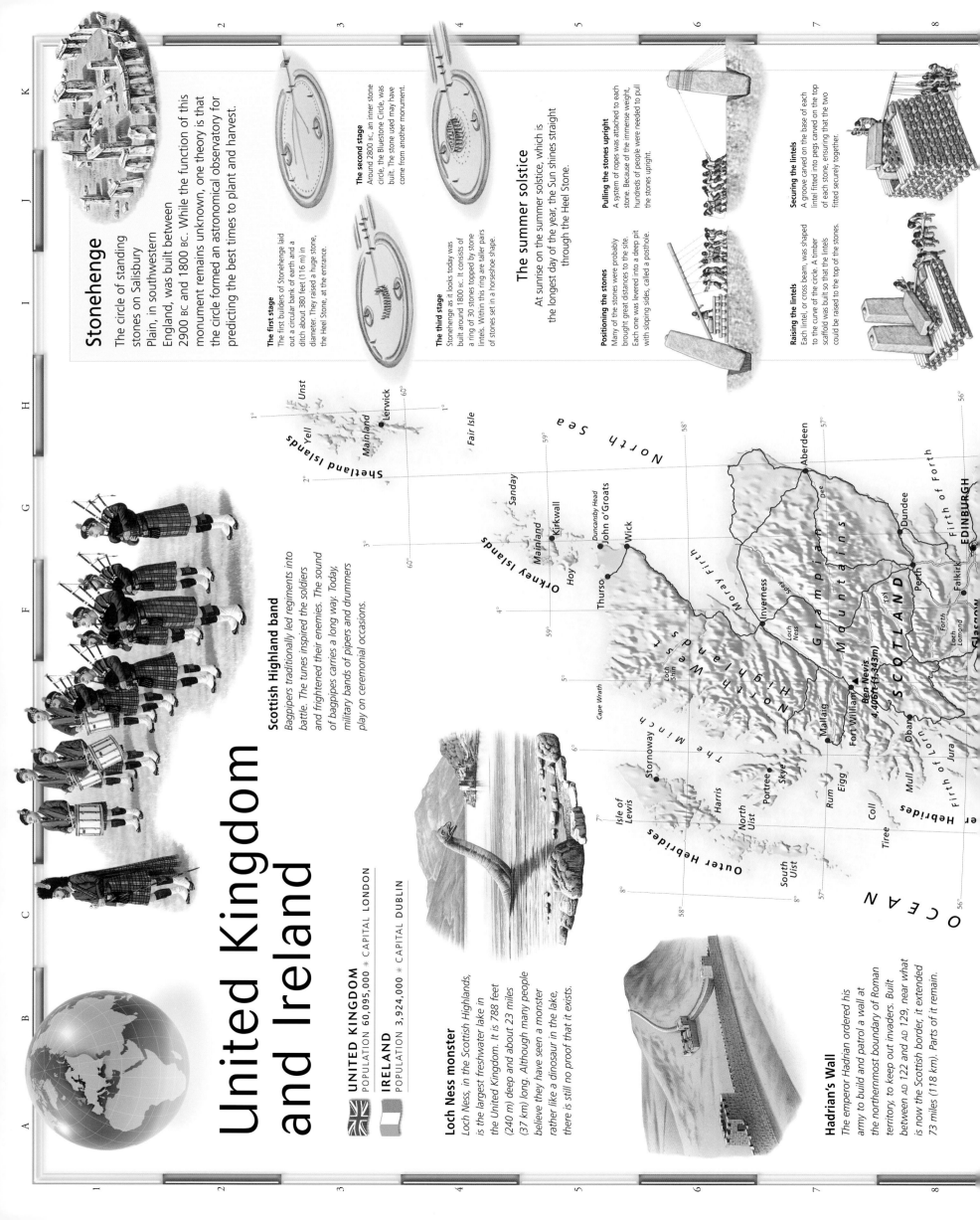

Shetland Islands
Unst
Yell
Mainland
Lerwick
Fair Isle

North Sea

Sanday
Orkney Islands
Mainland
Kirkwall
Hoy
Duncansby Head
John o'Groats
Wick
Thurso

Cape Wrath
North West Highlands
Inverness
Loch Ness
Moray Firth
Aberdeen
Dee

Loch Shin

Isle of Lewis
Stornoway
Harris
North Uist
South Uist
Tiree
Coll
Rum
Eigg
Skye
Portree
Mallaig
Fort William
Ben Nevis 4,406ft (1,343m)
The Minch

Grampian Mountains
SCOTLAND
Perth
Dundee
Firth of Forth
EDINBURGH
Falkirk
Forth
Firth of Lorn
Oban
Mull
Jura
Inner Hebrides
Outer Hebrides
Loch Lomond
Glasgow

OCEAN

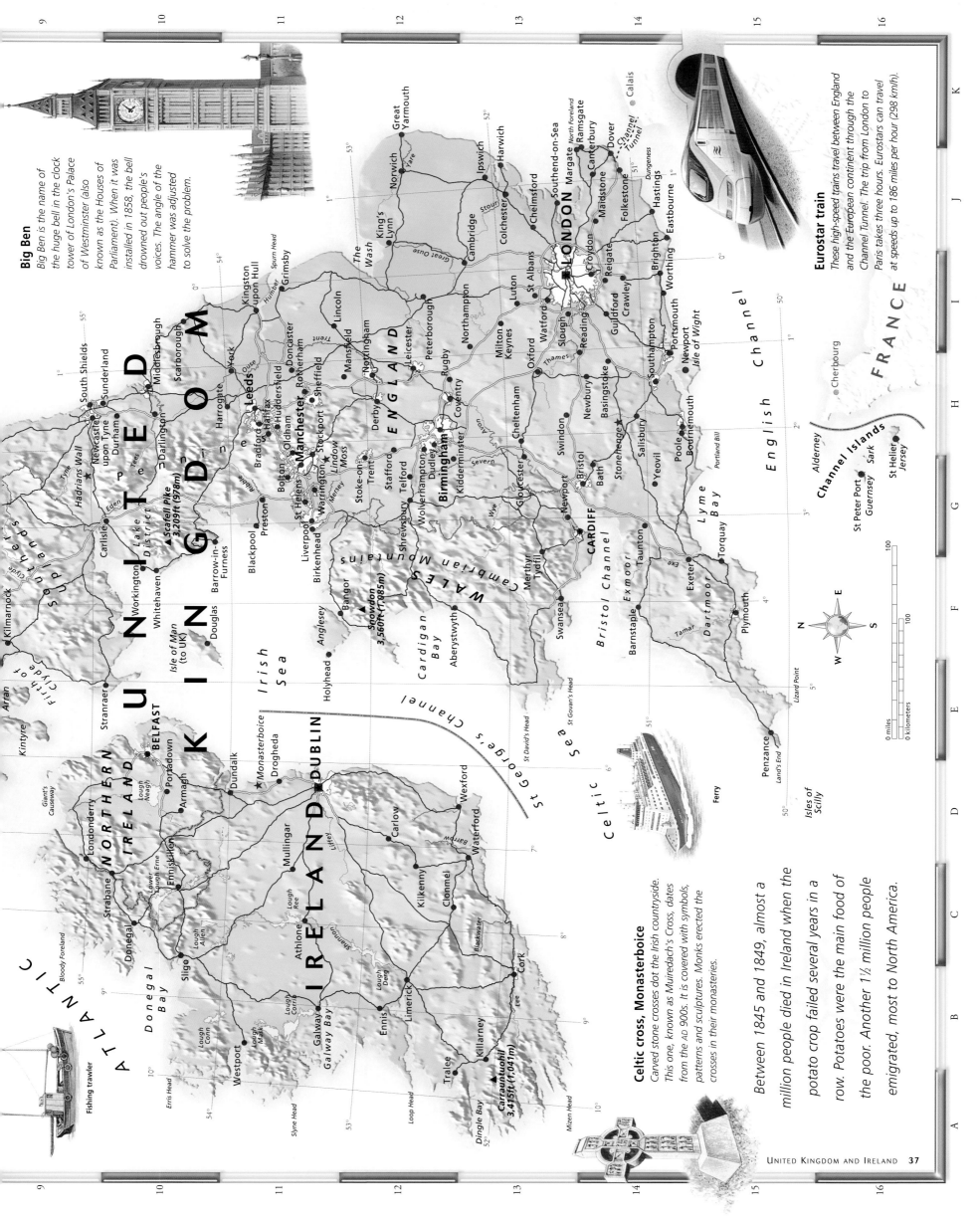

Big Ben

Big Ben is the name of the huge bell in the clock tower of London's Palace of Westminster (also known as the Houses of Parliament). When it was installed in 1858, the bell drowned out people's voices. The angle of the hammer was adjusted to solve the problem.

Eurostar train

These high-speed trains travel between England and the European continent through the Channel Tunnel. The trip from London to Paris takes three hours. Eurostars can travel at speeds up to 186 miles per hour (298 km/h).

Celtic cross, Monasterboice

Carved stone crosses dot the Irish countryside. This one, known as Muiredach's Cross, dates from the AD 900s. It is covered with symbols, patterns and sculptures. Monks erected the crosses in their monasteries.

Between 1845 and 1849, almost a million people died in Ireland when the potato crop failed several years in a row. Potatoes were the main food of the poor. Another 1½ million people emigrated, most to North America.

Fishing trawler

Ferry

Map labels

ATLANTIC OCEAN

NORTHERN IRELAND

Bloody Foreland
Erris Head
Donegal
Londonderry
Strabane
Giant's Causeway
Sligo
Lough Allen
Enniskillen
Lower Lough Erne
Lough Neagh
Portadown
Armagh
Dundalk
Drogheda
Monasterboice
BELFAST
Stranraer
Kintyre
Arran
Kilmarnock
Firth of Clyde
Southern Uplands

Donegal Bay
Westport
Lough Conn
Lough Mask
Lough Corrib
Galway
Galway Bay
Slyne Head
Loop Head
Lough Ree
Mullingar
Athlone
Lough Derg
Ennis
Limerick
Lee
Cork
Killarney
Tralee
Dingle Bay
Mizen Head
Carrauntuohil 3,415ft (1,041m)

IRELAND

DUBLIN
Liffey
Carlow
Kilkenny
Clonmel
Waterford
Wexford
Barrow
Blackwater
Shannon

St George's Channel

Irish Sea

Celtic Sea

St David's Head
St Govan's Head
Holyhead
Anglesey
Bangor
Snowdon 3,560ft (1,085m)
Aberystwyth
Cardigan Bay
WALES
Cambrian Mountains
Swansea
CARDIFF
Merthyr Tydfil
Newport
Bristol Channel

Isle of Man (to UK)
Douglas
Barrow-in-Furness
Blackpool
Preston
Liverpool
Birkenhead
St Helens
Warrington
Lindow Moss
Stockport
Manchester
Bolton
Oldham
Huddersfield
Halifax
Bradford
Leeds
Harrogate
UNITED KINGDOM
Workington
Whitehaven
Carlisle
Lake District
Scafell Pike 3,209ft (978m)
Eden
Ribble

ATLANTIC OCEAN
Kilmarnock
Hadrian's Wall
Newcastle upon Tyne
South Shields
Sunderland
Durham
Darlington
Middlesbrough
Scarborough
Tyne
Tees

York
Ouse
Kingston upon Hull
Spurn Head
Grimsby
The Wash
Humber
Doncaster
Rotherham
Sheffield
Lincoln
Mansfield
Nottingham
Derby
Stoke-on-Trent
Stafford
Telford
Shrewsbury
Birmingham
Wolverhampton
Dudley
Kidderminster
Trent
Severn
Wye

ENGLAND
Leicester
Peterborough
Northampton
Rugby
Coventry
Cheltenham
Gloucester
Avon
Merthyr Tydfil
Bristol
Bath
Stonehenge
Salisbury
Yeovil
Poole
Bournemouth

Great Yarmouth
Norwich
Yare
King's Lynn
Cambridge
Stour
Ipswich
Harwich
Colchester
Chelmsford
Great Ouse
LONDON
Luton
St Albans
Watford
Milton Keynes
Oxford
Slough
Croydon
Reigate
Reading
Newbury
Basingstoke
Guildford
Crawley
Thames
Southend-on-Sea
North Foreland
Ramsgate
Margate
Canterbury
Maidstone
Dover
Folkestone
Channel Tunnel
Calais
Hastings
Eastbourne
Brighton
Worthing
Southampton
Portsmouth
Newport
Isle of Wight
Swindon

English Channel
Lyme Bay
Exmoor
Barnstaple
Taunton
Exe
Exeter
Dartmoor
Tamar
Torquay
Plymouth
Penzance
Land's End
Lizard Point
Isles of Scilly

Alderney
Cherbourg
Channel Islands
St Peter Port
Guernsey
Sark
St Helier
Jersey
Portland Bill
F R A N C E

In 1690, the remains of a mammoth were discovered near the present-day Kings Cross Station in London.

United Kingdom and Ireland

UNITED KINGDOM LAND AREA	94,526 sq miles (244,820 sq km)
OFFICIAL LANGUAGE	English
MAIN RELIGION	Christian
LIFE EXPECTANCY	78 years
LITERACY	99%

IRELAND LAND AREA	27,135 sq miles (70,280 sq km)
OFFICIAL LANGUAGE	English
MAIN RELIGION	Christian
LIFE EXPECTANCY	77 years
LITERACY	98%

Sheep
Sheep are the United Kingdom's chief livestock. Farming sheep is particularly important in areas such as Wales where the soil is too poor for raising cattle and growing crops.

The population of Ireland is 95% ethnic Irish.

USING THE LAND

- Forest and woodland
- Arable land
- Grazing

Cereals | **Sheep**
Potatoes | **Fishing**
Fruit and vegetables | **Shellfish**
Sugar beet | **Industrial center**
Oilseed rape | **Mining**
Beef cattle | **Gas production**
Dairy cattle | **Timber**
| **Tourism**

Glasgow
Edinburgh
Belfast
Newcastle upon Tyne
DUBLIN
Leeds
Manchester
Birmingham
Cardiff
LONDON

Oil mining
Oil was discovered in the United Kingdom under the North Sea in the early 1970s. Extracting it proved difficult. Oil rigs were built to provide a stable surface for drilling into the seabed. By 2001, the United Kingdom had become the 12th-largest oil producer in the world.

WHERE PEOPLE LIVE

Urban   Rural

UNITED KINGDOM
89%   11%

IRELAND
59%   41%

LARGEST CITIES

London 7,465,000

Glasgow 1,101,000

Dublin 1,028,000

Birmingham 969,000

Edinburgh 461,000

Black Death

In the late 1340s, the Black Death, a type of bubonic plague, swept through Europe, killing more than a third of the people. By 1348 it had arrived in England. Over the next few centuries, the plague continued to strike, and Londoners fled the city (*above*) with each outbreak. It was finally wiped out by the Great Fire of London in 1666.

NATURAL FEATURES

Lake District ENGLAND
In this beautiful national park in the northern highland area of England (*below*), ice has worn away the land to create valleys and form what are England's largest lakes. The Lake District attracts millions of visitors each year.

Lake District

Norfolk Broads ENGLAND
These shallow, inland waterways, which were caused by peat diggings in the 14th century, crisscross Norfolk. The area is popular with visitors, who hire boats to sail from town to town.

Giant's Causeway NORTHERN IRELAND
This 3-mile (5-km) stretch of basalt columns was formed when molten lava erupted from beneath the sea and cooled very quickly. Some columns are nearly 20 feet (6 m) tall.

Giant's Causeway

Scottish Highlands SCOTLAND
The Scottish Highlands, which make up more than half of Scotland's landmass, have numerous rivers and lochs (lakes). Many native species have died out, but the shaggy-haired Highland cattle (*left*) still wander freely.

Highland cattle

TRADITIONS AND CULTURE

Wimbledon
Every year since 1877, one of the most famous tennis tournaments in the world has been held at Wimbledon, a suburb of London.

Scottish tartans
Originally hand-woven from woolen material, Scottish tartans are a symbol of Scotland. Items of clothing, especially kilts, are made from different patterns to represent different clans, or families.

Welsh choirs
Almost every town in Wales has a voice choir. There are male, female, mixed and children's choirs, many of which compete in the annual eisteddfod, a festival of music and arts.

St Patrick's Day
Celebrated on 17 March, this day began as a religious holiday to commemorate St Patrick, the patron saint of Ireland. Today, Irish people around the world gather together, wear green clothes and parade through the streets.

Arthurian legends
King Arthur, according to the legends, became king of Britain when he was 15 years old. He married Guinevere and created the knights of the round table. When he went to fight a war in Rome, he left his castle in the care of his nephew Mordred, who betrayed him.

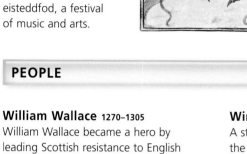

King Arthur fighting Mordred

It's said that if you kiss the Blarney Stone in Ireland, you'll become a clever talker.

PEOPLE

William Wallace 1270–1305
William Wallace became a hero by leading Scottish resistance to English rule. In 1297, he captured Stirling Castle, but was later defeated by Edward I and executed.

Shakespeare 1564–1616
Recognized as England's greatest dramatist and poet, Shakespeare wrote more than 150 poems and 36 plays. One of his most famous plays is *Romeo and Juliet*.

William Shakespeare

Isaac Newton 1642–1727
Isaac Newton, an influential scientist of the 17th century, invented the reflecting telescope in 1668. Although it was only 6 inches (15 cm) long, it could magnify objects more than 30 times.

Florence Nightingale 1820–1910
In 1854 Florence Nightingale led a group of nurses to work in military hospitals during the Crimean War. Her patients called her the "Lady with the Lamp." After the war, she established a school for nurses in England.

Winston Churchill 1874–1965
A statesman and orator, Churchill was the prime minister of Britain during World War II. His speeches inspired the people during the difficult war years.

The Beatles 1959–70
The Beatles, comprising John Lennon, Paul McCartney, George Harrison and Ringo Starr, were a world-famous rock-and-roll group. They also produced and starred in movies.

The Beatles

Henry VIII
The son of Henry VII and Elizabeth York, Henry VIII (1491–1547) had six wives. Of these, he divorced two and had two beheaded. When the pope refused Henry permission to divorce his first wife, he broke away from the Roman Catholic Church and created the Church of England. His actions aided the Protestant movement in Europe.

The monarchy
The British monarchy is the oldest institution of government in the United Kingdom. James VI of Scotland became the first king of the United Kingdom in 1603. Until the end of the 17th century, the monarch had the right to make and pass legislation, but this is no longer the case. The British monarchy is hereditary—the crown is inherited by the next eligible family member.

Royal carriage

PLACES

London ENGLAND
The Romans chose a small town on the Thames River as their capital in the 1st century AD, and named it Londinium. After being ruled by the Saxons and the Normans, today it is England's capital.

Canterbury Cathedral

Canterbury Cathedral ENGLAND
This cathedral is the seat of the Anglican Church. Archbishop Thomas Becket was murdered there in 1170 and the cathedral is now a site for pilgrims.

Dublin IRELAND
Starting as a permanent Viking settlement in AD 841, Dublin, built on the banks of the River Liffey, is the capital of Ireland and the center of its government.

Edinburgh SCOTLAND
The capital city of Scotland, Edinburgh is a financial, legal and cultural center. Edinburgh Castle stands in the medieval Old Town, once the center of the city.

Roman baths ENGLAND
Ancient Romans spent some leisure time in baths (hot and cold swimming pools), such as those in Bath (*right*). These baths are filled with the water from three natural hot springs.

HISTORY AT A GLANCE

3000–100 BC
The Celts spread over much of Europe, gradually moving into Britain between 500 and 100 BC.

54 BC
Julius Caesar, Roman general and statesman, travels from Gaul and invades England.

AD 43–410
England and Wales become part of the Roman empire. Boudicca, Queen of the Iceni, a tribe of Britons, leads a revolt against the Roman soldiers and sets fire to London.

c AD 450
Anglo-Saxons arrive in Britain, and settle in southern and eastern England.

AD 871–899
Alfred the Great rules as king of Wessex. He prevents the Danish conquest of Britain and draws up a legal code.

The Alfred Jewel

1066
William the Conqueror, Duke of Normandy, invades England, kills King Harold at the Battle of Hastings (*below*) and becomes king.

Bayeux tapestry

1215
The Magna Carta, a charter limiting the king's power and making him responsible to English law, is signed by King John.

1509–47
Henry VIII rules England and breaks away from the Catholic Church. He eventually unites Wales and England under one system of government.

1642
Civil war breaks out in England between those loyal to King Charles I (Royalists) and supporters of the parliament against Charles (Roundheads).

1837–1901
Queen Victoria rules the United Kingdom, and the British empire expands to cover one-fourth of the world and its people.

1914–18
The United Kingdom enters World War I when Germany invades Belgium. About 750,000 of the British armed forces die, and the war leaves the United Kingdom with severe economic problems.

1922
Ireland splits into Northern Ireland, which remains in the United Kingdom, and the Irish Free State, which is a self-governing member of the empire.

World War II Spitfire aircraft

1939–45
World War II is fought. The United Kingdom and France declare war on Germany after it invades Poland. With the Allies, the United Kingdom defeats Germany and Japan, and then helps to establish the United Nations.

1949
The Irish Free State becomes the Republic of Ireland and leaves the British Commonwealth.

1997
Referendums are held in Scotland and Wales and both vote in favor of greater control over their affairs. They set up their own parliamentary governing bodies.

Spain and Portugal

Basque folk dancer

The Alhambra

For almost 800 years, from AD 711 until 1492, Spain was ruled by the Islamic Moors. The Alhambra, in Granada, is one of the most beautiful and practical buildings from this period. It was built in the 1300s as a fortress against the Spanish, and was later used as a palace for the sultan and his family. It features cool, airy courtyards and pavilions, trickling fountains and wonderful gardens.

Tower of the Ladies
The oldest decorations in the Alhambra are here, with views into the valley.

Hall of the Two Sisters
This hall is in the center of a series of chambers where the sultan's family lived.

Court of the Lions
A fountain carved with lions stands in the middle of this shaded courtyard.

Mosaic
Decorative patterns of tiles and semi-precious stones are a common feature of Islamic art. The mosaics of the Alhambra are extremely complicated and beautiful.

Court of the Myrtles
This peaceful walkway leads to the throne room.

Azores (to Portugal)

Corvo
Flores
ATLANTIC OCEAN
Graciosa
Nova Lajes
São Jorge   Terceira
Horta   Angra do
Faial   Pico   Heroísmo
Ribeira
Grande
São Miguel
Ponta
Degada
Santa Maria

0 miles   125
0 kilometers   125

Madeira (to Portugal)

Ilha de
Porto Santo
Porto Santo
Ilha da
Madeira   ATLANTIC
OCEAN
Câmara
de Lobos   Machico
Funchal
Deserta
Grande
Ilhas
Desertas
Bugio

0 miles   40
0 kilometers   40

Canary Islands (to Spain)

ATLANTIC OCEAN
Alegranza
Graciosa
Lanzarote
Santa Cruz   Arrecife
de la Palma   San Cristóbal   Lobos
La Palma   de la Laguna   Puerto
Santa Cruz   del Rosario
Pico del Teide   de Tenerife   Fuerteventura
12,198ft (3,718m)
La Gomera   Las Palmas de
Tenerife   Gran Canaria
El Hierro   Gran   **Pico de las Nieves**
Canaria   **6,394ft (1,949m)**

Azores

Madeira

Canary Islands

0 miles   100
0 kilometers   100

Map labels

Cabo Ortegal
Ferrol   Avilés   Gijó
A Coruña   Luarca   Villaviciosa   Asturi
Betanzos   Vilalba   Oviedo   Miere
Santiago del   Lugo
Compostela   Cordiller
Cabo Fisterra
Ribeira   Lalín   Leó
Pontevedra   Ponferrada   Astorga
Ourense   Benavente
Vigo   Ponteareas
Cabo Silleiro   Toro
Viana do   Ponte   Zamora   Duero
Castelo   da Barca   Bragança
Póvoa de Varzim   Braga
Matosinhos   Porto   Vila Real   Salamanca
Vila Nova   Embalse de
de Gaia   Almendra
Ovar
Aveiro   Viseu   Ciudad
Guarda   Rodrigo   Béjar
Figueira da Foz   Coimbra   S i s t
Covilhã   Alman.
Plasencia   8,504ft (2,592
Leiria   Castelo   Tajo
Branco   Embalse
de Valdecañas
Caldas da Rainha   Cáceres   S
Cabo Carvoeiro   Torres   Trujillo
Novas   Portalegre   Embalse de
Torres Vedras   Santarém   Garcia Sola   Herre
del Dup
Sintra   Elvas   Badajoz   Embalse
LISBON   Estremoz   de Orellana   Embals
(LISBOA)   Barreiro   Mérida   del Zúja
Setúbal   Évora   Almendralejo
Cabo Espichel   Alcácer do Sal   Zafra
Sines   Beja
Cabo de Sines   Cortegana   S i e r r a
Écija
Algarve   Seville   Carmona
Huelva   Dos Hermanas   Osuna
Lagos   Ayamonte
Cabo de   Faro   Tavira   Golfo   Andalucía
São Vincente   Olhão   de Cádiz   Lebrija
Cabo de Santa Maria   Sanlúcar de
Barrameda   Ronda
El Puerto de
Santa María   Jerez de
Cádiz   la Frontera   Marb
San Fernando
Barbate
Cabo Trafalgar   Algeciras   Gibr
GIB
(to U
Tanger   Ceuta
Strait of Gibraltar   Punta
Almina
MOROCCO

PORTUGAL
ATLANTIC OCEAN

Cork trees

One-third of the world's cork oaks grow in Portugal. It takes nearly 60 years before they are mature enough for the cork bark to be harvested.

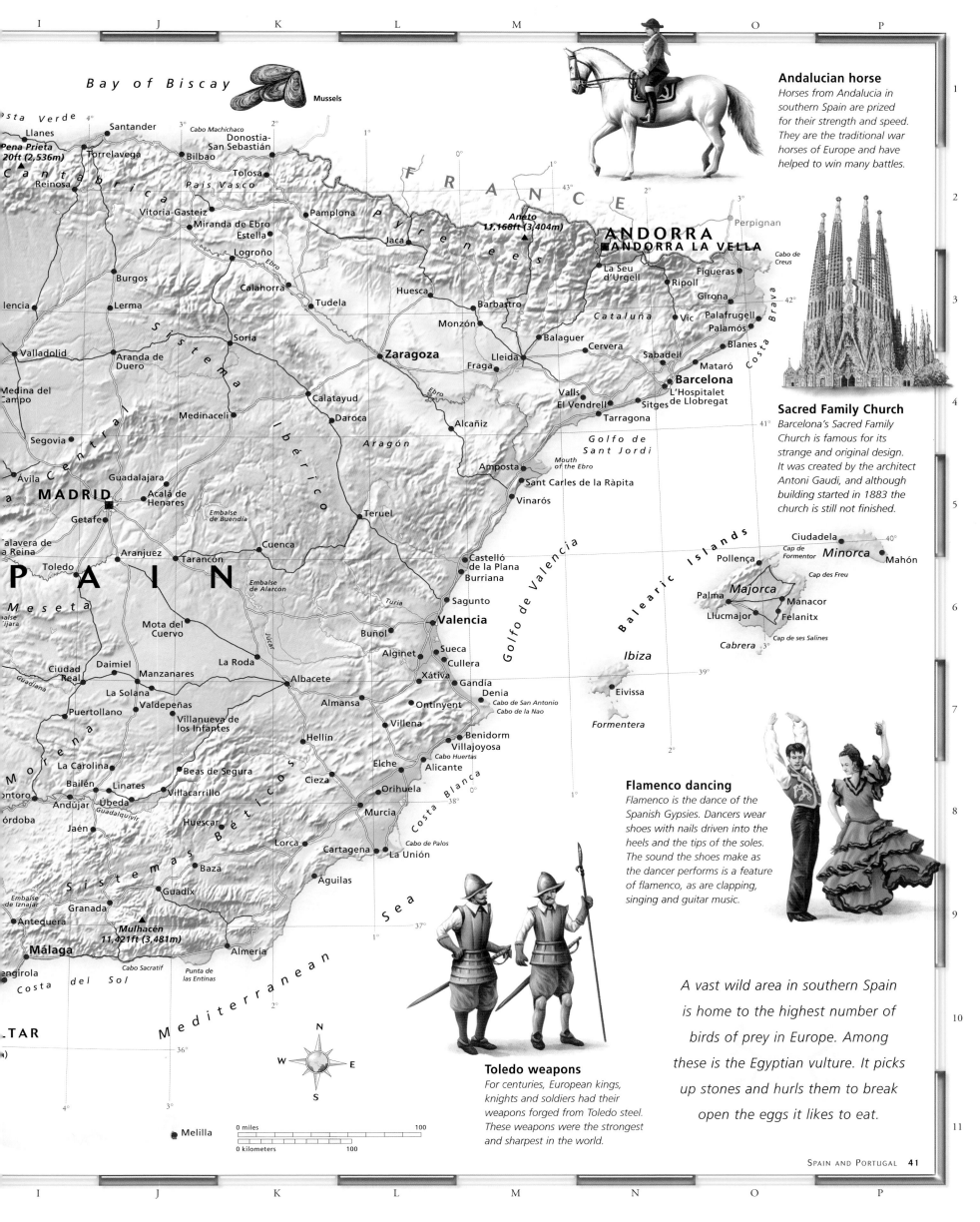

Bay of Biscay

Mussels

Costa Verde

Andalucian horse
Horses from Andalucia in southern Spain are prized for their strength and speed. They are the traditional war horses of Europe and have helped to win many battles.

Santander
Llanes
Peña Prieta
20ft (2,536m)
Torrelavega
Reinosa
Cantabrica
Pais Vasco
Cabo Machichaco
Donostia-
San Sebastián
Bilbao
Tolosa
FRANCE
Pyrenees
Pamplona
Vitoria-Gasteiz
Miranda de Ebro
Estella
Jaca
Aneto
11,168ft (3,404m)
ANDORRA
ANDORRA LA VELLA
Perpignan
Logroño
Huesca
La Seu
d'Urgell
Ripoll
Figueres
Cabo de
Creus
Burgos
Calahorra
Ebro
Barbastro
Vic
Girona
Palafrugell
Palamós
Lerma
Tudela
Monzón
Cataluña
Blanes
Costa
Brava
Valladolid
Aranda de
Duero
Soria
Zaragoza
Balaguer
Lleida
Fraga
Cervera
Sabadell
Mataró
Barcelona
L'Hospitalet
de Llobregat

Sacred Family Church
Barcelona's Sacred Family Church is famous for its strange and original design. It was created by the architect Antoni Gaudi, and although building started in 1883 the church is still not finished.

Medina del
Campo
Sistema
Iberico
Calatayud
Daroca
Alcañiz
Valls
El Vendrell
Sitges
Tarragona
Segovia
Medinaceli
Aragón
Golfo de
Sant Jordi
Ávila
Guadalajara
Sistema
Central
Amposta
Mouth
of the Ebro
MADRID
Acalá de
Henares
Sant Carles de la Ràpita
Ciudadela
Cap de
Formentor
Minorca
Getafe
Embalse
de Buendía
Teruel
Vinarós
Pollença
Mahón
Talavera de
la Reina
Aranjuez
Tarancón
Cuenca
Castelló
de la Plana
Burriana
Balearic
Islands
Majorca
Cap des Freu
Palma
Manacor
Toledo
SPAIN
Embalse
de Alarcón
Turia
Sagunto
Golfo de Valencia
Llucmajor
Felanitx
Cabrera
Cap de ses Salines
Meseta
Mota del
Cuervo
Jucar
Valencia
Buñol
Ibiza
Ciudad
Real
Daimiel
La Roda
Albacete
Alginet
Sueca
Cullera
Eivissa
Guadiana
Manzanares
Xátiva
Gandía
La Solana
Valdepeñas
Almansa
Ontinyent
Denia
Cabo de San Antonio
Cabo de la Nao
Formentera
Puertollano
Villanueva de
los Infantes
Villena
Benidorm
Villajoyosa

Flamenco dancing
Flamenco is the dance of the Spanish Gypsies. Dancers wear shoes with nails driven into the heels and the tips of the soles. The sound the shoes make as the dancer performs is a feature of flamenco, as are clapping, singing and guitar music.

Morena
La Carolina
Bailén
Linares
Villacarrillo
Hellín
Elche
Cabo Huertas
Alicante
Andújar
Úbeda
Guadalquivir
Cieza
Orihuela
Sistemas
Béticos
Jaén
Huéscar
Murcia
Costa Blanca
Cabo de Palos
Córdoba
Lorca
Cartagena
La Unión
Baza
Águilas
Embalse
de Iznajar
Guadix
Granada
Mulhacén
11,421ft (3,481m)
Almería
Mediterranean
Sea
Antequera
Málaga
Cabo Sacratif
Punta de
las Entinas
Fengirola
Costa
del
Sol
LTAR

Toledo weapons
For centuries, European kings, knights and soldiers had their weapons forged from Toledo steel. These weapons were the strongest and sharpest in the world.

N
W
E
S

0 miles 100
0 kilometers 100

Melilla

A vast wild area in southern Spain is home to the highest number of birds of prey in Europe. Among these is the Egyptian vulture. It picks up stones and hurls them to break open the eggs it likes to eat.

Spain and Portugal

USING THE LAND

- Cereals
- Citrus fruits
- Wine
- Fishing
- Olives
- Beef cattle
- Sheep
- Industrial center
- Mining
- Timber
- Tourism
- Forest and woodland
- Arable land
- Grazing

Olives
More olive oil is produced in Spain than in any other country. Over 1 million tons (1.02 million t) of olives are grown each year, most of which are crushed for olive oil. Olive groves are a common sight all over Spain.

SPAIN LAND AREA	194,897 sq miles (504,782 sq km)
OFFICIAL LANGUAGE	Spanish
MAIN RELIGION	Christian
LIFE EXPECTANCY	79 years
LITERACY	97%

PORTUGAL LAND AREA	35,672 sq miles (92,391 sq km)
OFFICIAL LANGUAGE	Portuguese
MAIN RELIGION	Christian
LIFE EXPECTANCY	76 years
LITERACY	87%

Portugal's most famous wine is called port—named after Porto, a major seaport.

Cod fishing
Cod is a favorite fish in Portugal. The Bay of Biscay has the most plentiful supplies of cod, tuna and sardines. Supplies have been severely reduced in recent years, causing problems in the local fishing industry. Although fishing is still a way of life for many coastal people, many fishermen have turned to other jobs.

Map labels: Bilbao, ANDORRA LA VELLA, Zaragoza, Barcelona, Porto, MADRID, Valencia, LISBON, Murcia, Seville, Málaga, Cádiz

Citrus fruits
The areas around Valencia, Spain, are part of La Huerta, which means "the orchard," because they are bursting with fresh produce. Orange and lemon groves stretch through the countryside.

Saffron farming
Saffron, the aromatic spice ingredient of Spain's famous rice dish, paella, is made from the stigmas of the saffron crocus flower. It takes 250,000 flowers to make just 1 pound (500 g) of saffron.

NATURAL FEATURES

Azores PORTUGAL
This archipelago of nine main islands in three separate groups lies about 1,000 miles (1,600 km) west of Portugal. The islands, formed by volcanic activity and earthquakes, have a subtropical, humid climate in which plants thrive. The island of Pico has the highest point in Portugal, at 7,713 feet (2,351 m).

The Pyrenees SPAIN
Stretching 270 miles (432 km) from the Bay of Biscay to the Mediterranean Sea, this rugged mountain range forms a barrier between Spain and France. During summer, warm air masses from Africa are trapped in the high regions, and cause rainfall to the south.

Mediterranean lynx

Doñana SPAIN
This wetland area south of Seville is Europe's largest nature reserve. Many rare animals roam the area, including the endangered Mediterranean lynx (above), fewer than 50 of which exist today. During winter, Doñana is home to thousands of migratory birds. A royal hunting ground for many centuries, it was made a national park in 1969.

Meseta SPAIN
Lying in the dry center of Spain, this high, arid plateau covers about two-thirds of the country and extends into Portugal. Warm air from the Pyrenees settles here, producing long, hot summers. In winter, conditions change and icy winds whip across the wide expanse. Parts of the meseta are mountainous.

La Tomatina

Every August, at the height of the tomato season, the town of Buñol, near Valencia, hosts the biggest food fight in the world. More than 20,000 entrants from Spain and beyond converge on the main street, ready to hurl tomatoes at anyone in sight. Part of a week-long festival, the battle is short-lived—about an hour—but in that time, many truckloads of tomatoes are reduced to pulp.

WHERE PEOPLE LIVE

	Urban	Rural
SPAIN	77%	23%
PORTUGAL	63%	37%

LARGEST CITIES

Madrid 3,291,000

Barcelona 1,541,000

Valencia 742,000

Seville 676,000

Zaragoza 646,000

PLACES

Madrid SPAIN
As Spain's capital, Madrid is the focus for industry, business and leisure. It is home to the Prado, a great art museum. King Juan Carlos lives in Madrid in the Royal Palace. Madrid is one of the highest capital cities in Europe.

Guggenheim Museum

Guggenheim Museum SPAIN
This distinctive modern building (*above*) in Bilbao, designed by the architect Frank O. Gehry, was opened in 1997. With its curving walls clad in thin sheets of titanium, the outside of the museum looks like a huge, free-form ship.

Santiago de Compostela SPAIN
Known as the Town of the Apostle, this university town's name comes from the apostle Saint James, who is buried there. It is the final destination on a popular pilgrimage trail, and has many religious monuments. Impressive processions pass through the streets during Easter week.

PEOPLE

Trajan AD 53–117
The first Roman emperor to be born outside Italy, in what is now Spain, Trajan tried to extend the empire to the east. He improved social welfare and commissioned many new buildings.

Queen Isabella 1451–1504

In 1469, Isabella of Castile married Ferdinand of Aragón, uniting their Catholic kingdoms to form the basis of modern Spain.

Christopher Columbus 1451–1506
This Italian-born sailor left Spain in 1492, in search of western trade routes to India. Three months later, he reached the Americas, not sure where he was. His accidental discovery made Spain a rich and powerful nation.

Vasco da Gama 1460–1524
This Portuguese navigator made three voyages to India (in 1497–99, 1502–03 and 1524), which opened up a new sea route from Europe to Asia and helped to make Portugal a world power.

Évora PORTUGAL
This city, east of Lisbon, was for many years an important military center for the Roman empire. It has also been under Moorish and Spanish control. Ruins of Roman buildings can still be seen throughout the city.

Lisbon PORTUGAL
Lisbon, Portugal's capital, is the country's main seaport. In the 8th century, it was invaded by Moors from Africa, and the city's buildings retain influences from this time. One of the greatest earthquakes ever recorded struck Lisbon in 1755, killing 30,000 people.

Alcazar, Segovia SPAIN
The Alcazar (*right*) takes its name from the Arabic word for castle. Isabella was crowned there in 1474. Built in the Middle Ages, it was rebuilt after being destroyed by fire in 1862.
The Alcazar at Segovia

Spanish Armada
The Armada was the name given to the Spanish navy under the rule of Phillip II in the 1500s. A flotilla of 130 ships, with 27,000 men on board, set sail to invade Britain in 1588. However, the English navy was better prepared. Using fire ships, it split the Spanish fleet apart and forced the Spaniards to return home in defeat. Spain's reputation as a maritime power was lost forever.

Pablo Picasso 1881–1973
This modern Spanish artist experimented with several different styles in his life. His Cubist period produced masterpieces such as *La Casserole Émailée* (*below*).

La Casa Mila

Gaudí's Barcelona
The city of Barcelona is adorned with the eye-catching architecture of Spain's most distinctive architect, Antoni Gaudí (1852–1926). Gaudí's buildings combined his love of the natural world with his knowledge of metalwork. The apartment block La Casa Mila (*above*) was built between 1906 and 1910 in the center of Barcelona. Its ornate roof and curved walls were inspired by the nearby ocean.

Portuguese water dogs were said to have sailed with the Spanish Armada in 1588 as messenger dogs between ships.

TRADITIONS AND CULTURE

Running of the bulls
This tradition is part of an annual festival held each July in Pamplona. As a climax to the 10 days of festivities, six bulls are released into the cobbled streets, behind crowds of young men who dodge the beasts' sharp horns.

Running of the bulls

Spanish food
Small plates of spicy food called tapas are eaten as snacks or appetizers. Rice is a favorite dish in many parts, often prepared with saffron, seafood and meat in paella. A specialty of the Andalucian region, in the south, is gazpacho—a chilled, tomato-based soup.

Jai alai
This game originated in the Basque region and is said to be the fastest ball game in the world. A player must fling the ball from a scooped basket called a *cesta* against a wall. The other player then catches it.

HISTORY AT A GLANCE

Cave painting, Altamira

15,000 BC
Prehistoric people create paintings depicting wild beasts in caves at Altamira, in northern Spain.

218 BC
Romans attack Hannibal's army and gradually move into the area. They remain until AD 409, when they are attacked by the Goths. The Goths rule until AD 711.

AD 711
Moorish Muslims invade southern Spain and Portugal from north Africa. In 1139 they lose control of Portugal and face problems in Spain.

1469
Monarchs Ferdinand and Isabella marry to form one reign, which is the start of modern Spain. By 1492, the Moors are driven out of Spain. The Jews are also expelled.

1492
Christopher Columbus discovers the Americas, and Spain begins to form its empire. The golden age of discovery and cultural activity starts 50 years later and lasts more than 100 years. In 1500, Portugal claims Brazil as a colony.

1561
The first permanent Spanish settlement in the Philippines is founded at Cebu. The Spaniards rule until independence in 1898.

1640
Portugal, a subject of Spain since 1580, gains independence. The country is ruled by kings until it becomes a republic in 1910.

1808–26
The Wars of Independence break out after Latin American countries rebel against the colonial rule imposed by Napoleonic Spain. The Spanish empire rapidly declines: Argentina becomes independent in 1816, Chile in 1817, Peru in 1824 and Bolivia in 1825. Brazil becomes independent from Portugal in 1822.

1926
The republic of Portugal is overthrown in a military coup. The dictator António Salazar is prime minister from 1932 until 1968.

1931
National elections result in overwhelming support for Spain as a republic.

Spanish Civil War

1936
The Spanish Civil War breaks out and military dictator General Franco takes power by 1939. He replaces the Spanish parliament with fascist rule: more than 100,000 are executed.

1974
After Salazar's death in 1970, the virtually bloodless Revolution of the Carnations in Portugal leads to democracy in 1974.

1975
Franco dies and King Juan Carlos I becomes ruler of Spain. He introduces democratic laws with more freedom than under Franco's rule.

France

FRANCE
POPULATION 60,181,000 ∗ CAPITAL PARIS

MONACO
POPULATION 32,000 ∗ CAPITAL MONACO

Boules player

Mont-St-Michel
The abbey of Mont-St-Michel was built in AD 966, and gradually changed over the next thousand years. It stands high on a rocky mound, attached to the mainland by a causeway. When tides are high, Mont-St-Michel becomes an island.

Cave art in Lascaux

Lascaux cave in the Dordogne, in southern France, was discovered in 1940 by four boys and a dog. They explored a hole in the forest and found themselves inside a beautiful painted cave system. There are 600 paintings in Lascaux, dating back 17,000 years. They depict hunting scenes, cattle, horses, deer and extinct animals. The cave is closed to visitors but a nearby replica is a tourist attraction.

Cave plan

1 Great Hall of the Bulls
The walls of this area of the cave seem to come alive with paintings of four aurochs (wild cattle) drawn in black outline. Some are 16 feet (5 m) tall and are the largest ice-age artworks.

2 Painted Gallery
This gallery is in a narrow passage off the Great Hall. Horses, bison and deer are crowded together on the wall.

3 Main Gallery
A second passage, to the right of the Great Hall, leads to the Main Gallery. The most impressive painting shows a row of stags swimming. The scene is almost 10 feet (3 m) above the ground. The artist must have used scaffolding.

4 Shaft of the Dead Man
Another passage leads to an area decorated with a scene of a wounded bison that has attacked and killed a man. The bird on a stick may be a spear. The artist made his paints with crushed rock and animal fat.

Guillemots

Bordeaux vineyard
Bordeaux, in France's southwest, is the largest wine-making region in the world. It is famous particularly for its red and sweet white wines. More than 13,000 wine growers in the area produce a third of all France's wine exports.

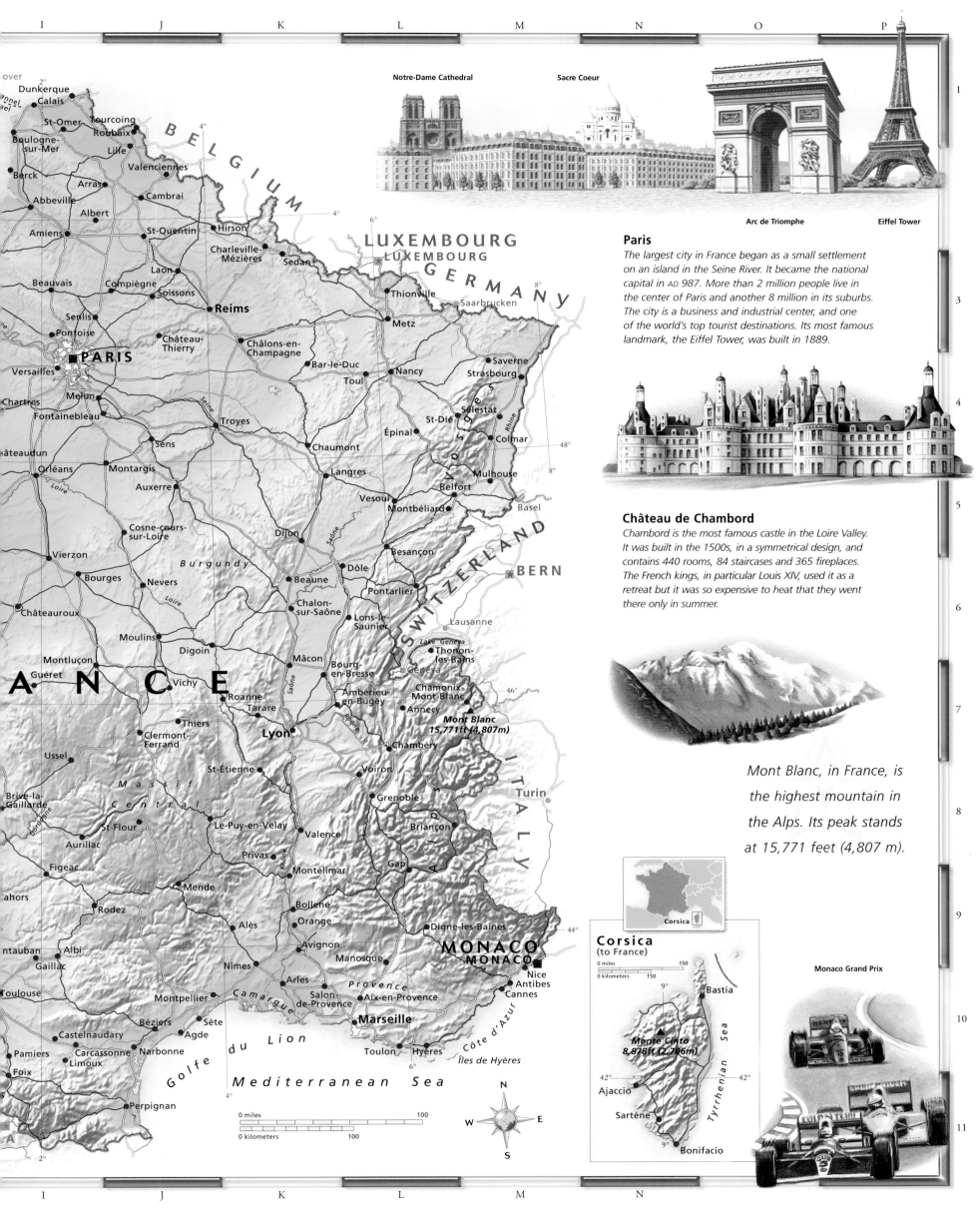

Map labels (grid references across top)

I   J   K   L   M   N   O   P

BELGIUM

LUXEMBOURG
LUXEMBOURG

GERMANY

SWITZERLAND

BERN

ITALY

Notre-Dame Cathedral

Sacre Coeur

Arc de Triomphe

Eiffel Tower

Map place names

Dunkerque, Calais, St-Omer, Tourcoing, Roubaix, Boulogne-sur-Mer, Lille, Berck, Valenciennes, Arras, Abbeville, Cambrai, Albert, Amiens, St-Quentin, Hirson, Beauvais, Charleville-Mézières, Sedan, Laon, Compiègne, Soissons, Senlis, Reims, Pontoise, Thionville, Saarbrucken, Château-Thierry, Châlons-en-Champagne, Metz, PARIS, Versailles, Bar-le-Duc, Nancy, Saverne, Strasbourg, Chartres, Melun, Toul, Sélestat, Fontainebleau, Troyes, Chaumont, Épinal, St-Dié, Colmar, Orléans, Sens, Langres, Mulhouse, Châteaudun, Montargis, Vesoul, Belfort, Auxerre, Dijon, Besançon, Montbéliard, Basel, Vierzon, Burgundy, Dôle, Bourges, Nevers, Beaune, Pontarlier, Châteauroux, Moulins, Chalon-sur-Saône, Lausanne, Digoin, Lons-le-Saunier, Montluçon, Mâcon, Bourg-en-Bresse, Lake Geneva, Thonon-les-Bains, Guéret, Vichy, Geneva, FRANCE, Roanne, Tarare, Ambérieu-en-Bugey, Chamonix Mont-Blanc, Annecy, Thiers, Lyon, **Mont Blanc 15,771ft (4,807m)**, Clermont-Ferrand, St-Étienne, Chambéry, Ussel, Voiron, Brive-la-Gaillarde, Massif Central, Grenoble, Turin, St-Flour, Le-Puy-en-Velay, Briançon, Aurillac, Valence, Figeac, Privas, Gap, Cahors, Mende, Rodez, Montélimar, Bollène, Orange, Digne-les-Baines, Montauban, Albi, Avignon, **MONACO MONACO**, Gaillac, Nîmes, Manosque, Nice, Antibes, Toulouse, Arles, Aix-en-Provence, Cannes, Montpellier, Salon-de-Provence, Provence, Béziers, Sète, Castelnaudary, Agde, **Marseille**, Pamiers, Carcassonne, Narbonne, Limoux, Toulon, Hyères, Côte d'Azur, Foix, Camargue, Îles de Hyères, Perpignan, Golfe du Lion, Mediterranean Sea

Seine, Loire, Rhône, Saône, Rhine, Dordogne

Paris

The largest city in France began as a small settlement on an island in the Seine River. It became the national capital in AD 987. More than 2 million people live in the center of Paris and another 8 million in its suburbs. The city is a business and industrial center, and one of the world's top tourist destinations. Its most famous landmark, the Eiffel Tower, was built in 1889.

Château de Chambord

Chambord is the most famous castle in the Loire Valley. It was built in the 1500s, in a symmetrical design, and contains 440 rooms, 84 staircases and 365 fireplaces. The French kings, in particular Louis XIV, used it as a retreat but it was so expensive to heat that they went there only in summer.

Mont Blanc, in France, is the highest mountain in the Alps. Its peak stands at 15,771 feet (4,807 m).

Corsica (to France)

0 miles 150
0 kilometers 150

Bastia, **Monte Cinto 8,878ft (2,706m)**, Ajaccio, Sartène, Bonifacio, Tyrrhenian Sea, Corsica

Monaco Grand Prix

0 miles 100
0 kilometers 100

N   E   S   W

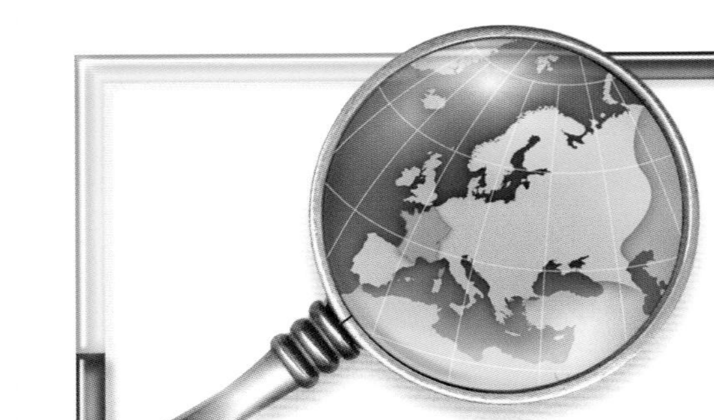

France

LAND AREA	210,669 sq miles (545,630 sq km)
OFFICIAL LANGUAGE	French
MAIN RELIGION	Christian
LIFE EXPECTANCY	79 years
LITERACY	99%

Monaco has been ruled by the Grimaldi dynasty for more than 700 years.

NATURAL FEATURES

Massif Central
This vast and rugged plateau in central and southern France covers almost one-sixth of the country. The higher slopes are forested, and cattle and sheep graze on the lower grasslands.

Corsica
About one-fifth of this mountainous, rocky Mediterranean island is forested with chestnuts, pines and oak trees. The scent of its shrubby underbrush carries for miles, and has given Corsica the name "the scented isle."

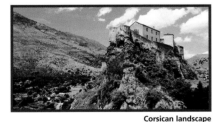

Corsican landscape

Normandy beaches
Normandy's shoreline features towering chalk cliffs, golden tourist beaches and elegant resorts. The cliffs of Jobourg are the highest in Europe. Parts of the coast have very swift tides, reaching speeds of 6 miles per hour (10 km/h) in spring.

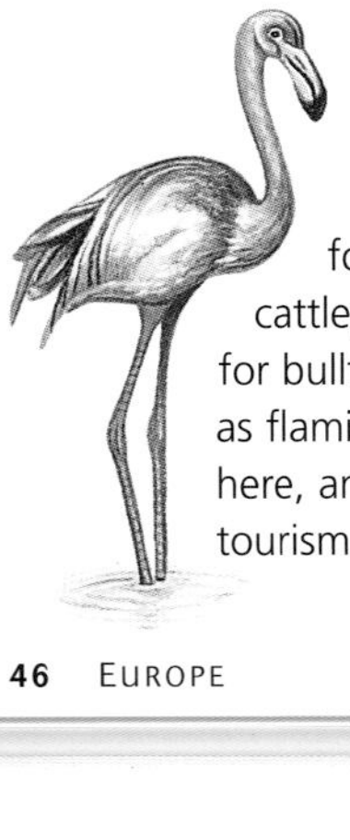

The Camargue
One of Europe's largest wetlands, this sparsely populated area is known for its free-ranging herds of cattle, horses and bulls (raised for bullfights) and for birds such as flamingoes (*left*). Rice is grown here, and salt is harvested. Nature tourism is a major industry.

USING THE LAND

Fishing
Fishing is still a major industry despite its decline over several years as a result of overfishing in the Atlantic Ocean. Recently there has been a move to develop fish farms to make up for the decrease in fish numbers.

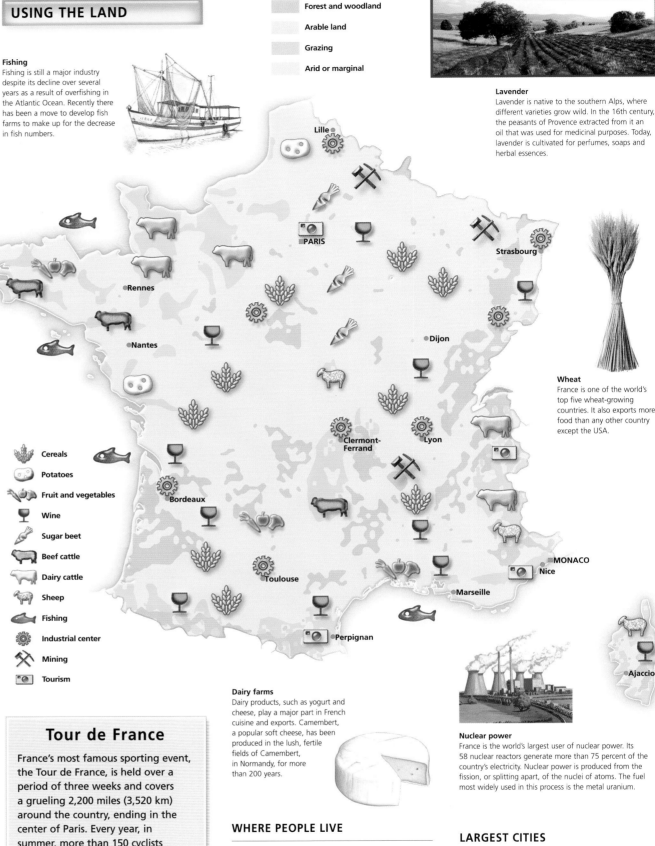

Lavender
Lavender is native to the southern Alps, where different varieties grow wild. In the 16th century, the peasants of Provence extracted from it an oil that was used for medicinal purposes. Today, lavender is cultivated for perfumes, soaps and herbal essences.

Forest and woodland
Arable land
Grazing
Arid or marginal
Lille
PARIS
Strasbourg
Rennes
Nantes
Dijon
Clermont-Ferrand
Lyon
Bordeaux
Toulouse
Marseille
MONACO
Nice
Perpignan
Ajaccio
Cereals
Potatoes
Fruit and vegetables
Wine
Sugar beet
Beef cattle
Dairy cattle
Sheep
Fishing
Industrial center
Mining
Tourism

Wheat
France is one of the world's top five wheat-growing countries. It also exports more food than any other country except the USA.

Dairy farms
Dairy products, such as yogurt and cheese, play a major part in French cuisine and exports. Camembert, a popular soft cheese, has been produced in the lush, fertile fields of Camembert, in Normandy, for more than 200 years.

Nuclear power
France is the world's largest user of nuclear power. Its 58 nuclear reactors generate more than 75 percent of the country's electricity. Nuclear power is produced from the fission, or splitting apart, of the nuclei of atoms. The fuel most widely used in this process is the metal uranium.

Tour de France

France's most famous sporting event, the Tour de France, is held over a period of three weeks and covers a grueling 2,200 miles (3,520 km) around the country, ending in the center of Paris. Every year, in summer, more than 150 cyclists compete in this world-famous race.

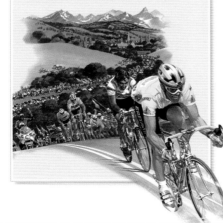

WHERE PEOPLE LIVE

Urban	Rural
75%	25%

LONGEST RIVERS

Loire 634 miles (1,020 km)

Rhône 505 miles (813 km)

Seine 485 miles (780 km)

Garonne 357 miles (575 km)

LARGEST CITIES

Paris 2,108,000

Marseille 826,000

Lyon 444,000

Toulouse 417,000

Nice 330,000

Eiffel Tower

Once the tallest structure in the world, the Eiffel Tower was erected as a temporary exhibit for the Centennial Exposition in Paris in 1889 by engineer Alexandre-Gustave Eiffel. When radio was invented, the tower began its long career as an antenna. It carried the first transatlantic radio–telephone call. Each year, about 6 million people visit the tower.

PEOPLE

Joan of Arc 1412–31

Joan of Arc, France's patron saint, led French troops to victory against the English at Orléans in 1429. Captured soon after and accused of witchcraft, she was burned at the stake in 1431.

Victor Hugo 1802–85

The most famous of the French Romantic writers, Victor Hugo is best known for his novels *The Hunchback of Notre Dame* and *Les Misérables*.

Louis Pasteur 1822–95

During his brilliant scientific career, Pasteur invented pasteurization, proved that germs cause many diseases and produced a rabies vaccine. His work provided the basis for a number of branches of science and medicine.

The Water-Lily Pond, by Claude Monet

Claude Monet 1841–1946

One of the great Impressionist artists, Monet is known for his atmospheric paintings of landscapes, water-lilies (*above*) and Rouen Cathedral.

Charles de Gaulle 1890–1970

An outstanding international figure, General de Gaulle became president of the Fifth Republic in 1959, achieving independence for Algeria in 1962. He resigned from office in 1969.

PLACES

Carcassonne

The walled city of Carcassonne lies on the top of a steep bank of the Aude River. It was often besieged in the Middle Ages, and was restored in the 19th century. It has the finest remains of medieval fortifications in Europe.

Carcassonne

Lyon

The Romans founded Lyon in 43 BC, and it later became the capital of Gaul. Today, the city is a center of banking, textiles and pharmaceuticals, but most people associate it with food. It is famed for its fine cuisine, which is sourced from the fertile agricultural land and many vineyards of the region.

The Louvre was formerly the royal family's main residence.

Chartres Cathedral

Chartres Cathedral

The people of Chartres, helped by lavish contributions from the king and nobles, built this cathedral (*above*) in just over 25 years (1195–1220). With its twin west towers, rose windows and figured stained glass, it is one of the finest examples of French Gothic architecture.

Château de Versailles

This palace (*below*) was built between 1668 and 1710 by Louis XIV to display his power and wealth. Set in an immense park, it is more than a quarter of a mile (400 m) long. World War I officially ended here when the Treaty of Versailles was signed in 1919.

Versailles

TRADITIONS AND CULTURE

Perfume and fashion

The French are known for their style and elegance. French perfumes, such as those produced by Chanel, and French fashion designers, such as Pierre Cardin, are famous worldwide.

French cuisine

Good food is essential to the French way of life. The kitchen is the center of the household, and meals are an important part of French leisure activity. Almost every part of France boasts its own ham and wine, and its cheeses are famous all over the world. Nearly every meal is accompanied by bread of some sort, and breakfast often includes a buttery pastry called a croissant.

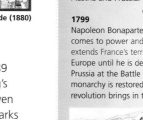

Croissants

Cafes

Cafes began in the 17th century as places to sample the popular new drinks chocolate and coffee. Le Procope, founded in 1686 in Paris, claims to be the world's oldest coffee house. Writers, artists, intellectuals and students met in cafes to talk and work.

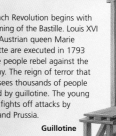

Bastille Day parade (1880)

Bastille Day

Each year on 14 July, parades and ceremonies commemorate the 1789 destruction of the Bastille, the king's prison. At the time, it held only seven prisoners. The fall of the Bastille marks the birth of the French Republic.

Napoleon

Born in Corsica in 1769, Napoleon Bonaparte was a general and reformer of law, education and the army. His goal was the military conquest of Europe. He declared himself emperor of France in 1804, but was forced to abdicate in 1814. He died in exile in 1821 on the island of St Helena.

HISTORY AT A GLANCE

700–500 BC
The Celtic Gauls gradually arrive in France from the north and east.

58–50 BC
Julius Caesar defeats the Gauls and France becomes part of the Roman empire until AD 476, when the Romans lose control of the region to the Franks and Visigoths.

Asterix the Gaul

AD 506
The Franks unite under Clovis, convert to Christianity and grow in power. Their leader, Charlemagne, is crowned the Holy Roman Emperor by the pope in AD 800. By this time, the Franks rule most of Germany, Italy and the Low Countries.

1066
Led by William the Conqueror, the Normans from northern France conquer England, making William the most powerful ruler in France.

1337–1453
England and France fight the Hundred Years' War, an on-and-off struggle over a series of disputes, including who was the rightful king of France. After a great deal of suffering on both sides, the English are eventually driven out of France. France loses nearly a third of its population when plague breaks out in 1348.

1643
Louis XIV—the Sun King—becomes king of France at the age of five and rules until 1715. French culture appears to be at its height.

1685
Religious persecution provokes the emigration of 400,000 Protestant Huguenots.

1789
The French Revolution begins with the storming of the Bastille. Louis XVI and his Austrian queen Marie Antoinette are executed in 1793 after the people rebel against the monarchy. The reign of terror that follows sees thousands of people executed by guillotine. The young republic fights off attacks by Austria and Prussia.

Guillotine

1799
Napoleon Bonaparte comes to power and extends France's territory through much of Europe until he is defeated by England and Prussia at the Battle of Waterloo in 1815. The monarchy is restored until 1848, when another revolution brings in the Second Republic.

Battle of Waterloo

1914–18
World War I devastates France and more than 1.3 million French soldiers die. France fights on the side of the British, Russians, Americans and Italians against Germany, Austria and Turkey.

1939–44
Germany occupies France during World War II. The French resistance works underground to help the Allied powers defeat the Germans. On D-Day—6 June 1944—the largest invasion fleet in history, comprising 156,000 troops and a vast armada of ships, planes and tanks, lands at five beaches on the Normandy coast. This campaign to liberate France is successful within months.

The Low Countries

NETHERLANDS
POPULATION 16,151,000 ✳ CAPITAL AMSTERDAM

BELGIUM
POPULATION 10,289,000 ✳ CAPITAL BRUSSELS

LUXEMBOURG
POPULATION 454,000 ✳ CAPITAL LUXEMBOURG

Clogs

Land below the sea

A third of the land in the Netherlands is below sea level, including the cities of Amsterdam and Rotterdam. Nearly two-thirds of the population lives below sea level. For centuries, reclaiming land from the sea for housing and farming, and keeping it drained, have been essential to the country's survival. Dikes and canals hold back the sea, and windmills drain the land.

The windmills at Kinderdijk
The Netherlands was once dotted with thousands of working windmills. Kinderdijk, near Rotterdam, has 19 windmills dating from 1740 lined up in long rows. They are still used to pump excess water from reclaimed land and keep it drained.

Afsluitdijk (the barrier dyke)
This 19-mile (30-km) barrier was built in 1932 as part of a project to reclaim 1,274 square miles (3,330 sq km) of land from the Zuider Zee (South Sea). IJsselmeer lake was created at the same time.

The Maaslandkering storm surge barrier
In 1997 the storm surge barrier outside Rotterdam was completed. During a severe storm, two massive gates can be closed to protect the land on either side from floods.

THE LOW COUNTRIES

Amsterdam
Rotterdam
The Hague

Dutch trade

For 200 years, starting in the early 1600s, the Dutch had a vast and powerful trading network in the Dutch East Indies (now named Indonesia). Merchant ships carried cargoes of gold to India and on to Asia, using it to buy jade, porcelain, spices, tea, coffee, sugar and tobacco to sell in Europe.

The canals of Amsterdam

The city of Amsterdam was founded in 1275. A network of canals was built to criss-cross the city because the land on which it is built is low and at risk of flooding. Today there are 165 canals and 1,281 bridges. The best way to get around the busy streets is by bicycle.

GERMANY

NETHERLANDS

West Frisian Islands
Schiermonnikoog
Ameland
Terschelling
Vlieland
Texel
Den Helder
Mackerel

Waddenzee
Afsluitdijk
IJsselmeer
North Sea

Delfzijl
Eemshaven
Zuidhorn
Groningen
Haren
Dokkum
Leeuwarden
Sneek
Joure
Heerenveen
Wolvega
Steenwijk
Meppel
Staphorst
Zwolle
IJssel
Kampen
Emmeloord
Lelystad
Nunspeet

Vlagtwedde
Stadskanaal
Borger
Emmen
Coevorden
Assen
Beilen
Hoogeveen

Almelo
Oldenzaal
Hengelo
Enschede
Rijssen
Goor
Haaksbergen
Eibergen
Winterswijk
Deventer
Dieren
Zutphen
Doetinchem

Epe
Apeldoorn
Barneveld
Ede
Arnhem
Veenendaal
Amersfoort
Zeist
Rhine

Schagen
Heerhugowaard
Hoorn
Alkmaar
Purmerend
Zaandam
AMSTERDAM
Almere
Hilversum
Utrecht
Nieuwegein
Gouda
Alphen
Zoetermeer
Haarlem
Amstelveen
Sassenheim
Leiden
Delft
THE HAGUE
('S-GRAVENHAGE)
Europoort
Rotterdam

Harlingen
Afsluitdijk

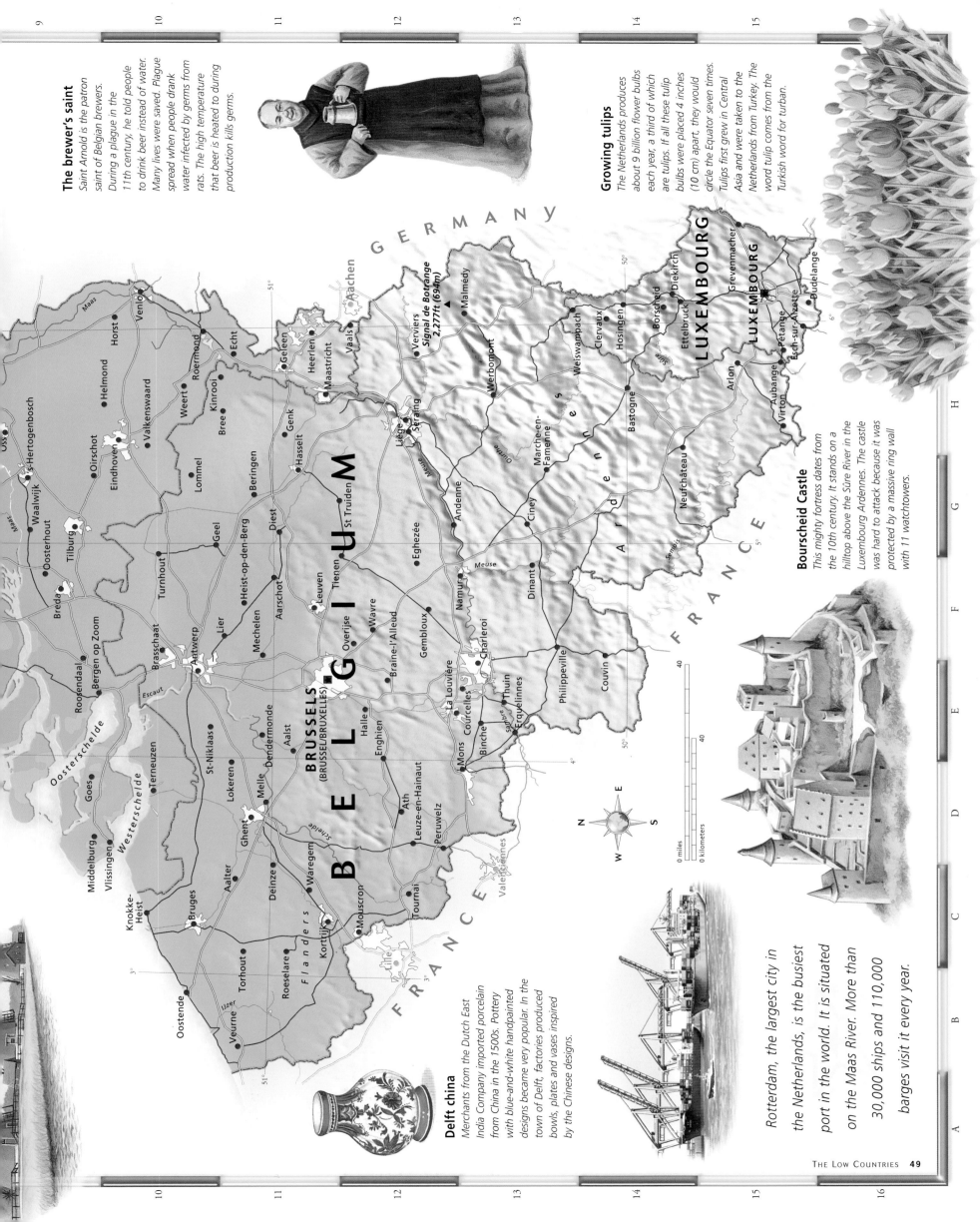

The brewer's saint

Saint Arnold is the patron saint of Belgian brewers. During a plague in the 11th century, he told people to drink beer instead of water. Many lives were saved. Plague spread when people drank water infected by germs from rats. The high temperature that beer is heated to during production kills germs.

Growing tulips

The Netherlands produces about 9 billion flower bulbs each year, a third of which are tulips. If all these tulip bulbs were placed 4 inches (10 cm) apart, they would circle the Equator seven times. Tulips first grew in Central Asia and were taken to the Netherlands from Turkey. The word tulip comes from the Turkish word for turban.

GERMANY

FRANCE

BELGIUM

BRUSSELS
(BRUSSEL/BRUXELLES)

LUXEMBOURG

LUXEMBOURG

Flanders

Ardennes

Signal de Botrange
2,277ft (694m)

N
W — E
S

0 miles   40
0 kilometers   40

Delft china

Merchants from the Dutch East India Company imported porcelain from China in the 1500s. Pottery with blue-and-white handpainted designs became very popular. In the town of Delft, factories produced bowls, plates and vases inspired by the Chinese designs.

Rotterdam, the largest city in the Netherlands, is the busiest port in the world. It is situated on the Maas River. More than 30,000 ships and 110,000 barges visit it every year.

Bourscheid Castle

This mighty fortress dates from the 10th century. It stands on a hilltop above the Sure River in the Luxembourg Ardennes. The castle was hard to attack because it was protected by a massive ring wall with 11 watchtowers.

The Low Countries

NETHERLANDS LAND AREA	16,033 sq miles (41,526 sq km)
OFFICIAL LANGUAGE	Dutch
MAIN RELIGION	Christian
LIFE EXPECTANCY	79 years
LITERACY	99%

BELGIUM LAND AREA	11,780 sq miles (30,510 sq km)
OFFICIAL LANGUAGE	Dutch/French/German
MAIN RELIGION	Christian
LIFE EXPECTANCY	78 years
LITERACY	98%

Luxembourgish is the national language of Luxembourg.

WHERE PEOPLE LIVE

Urban	Rural

BELGIUM
97% | 3%

NETHERLANDS
89% | 11%

NATURAL FEATURES

Ardennes BELGIUM–LUXEMBOURG
This chain of wooded hills covers 3,860 square miles (10,00 sq km) in northern Luxembourg, southern Belgium and northeast France. Under many of the hills are extensive cave systems, which are just one of the tourist attractions. The Ardennes is Belgium's most heavily forested region and also its least populated.

Beemster Polder
THE NETHERLANDS
Reclaimed in the 17th century from an area that used to be an inland sea, this oldest polder (reclaimed land) in the Netherlands is still divided into the rectangular plots of land that were drawn up in 1612.

Waddenzee
THE NETHERLANDS
This is the part of the North Sea between the Dutch mainland and the West Frisian Islands. Texel, the largest of these islands, is home to more than 300 species of birds, including the Eurasian spoonbill, and many migratory birds. It is one of the most important breeding grounds in Europe.

Eurasian spoonbill

Soignes Forest BELGIUM
Covering an area of about 10,000 acres (4,000 ha), this forest contains five nature reserves. Originally part of the ancient Charbonnière forest of Gaul, in which aurochs and elk roamed, it is known for its lofty beech trees.

Soignes Forest

USING THE LAND

	Forest and woodland
	Arable land
	Grazing

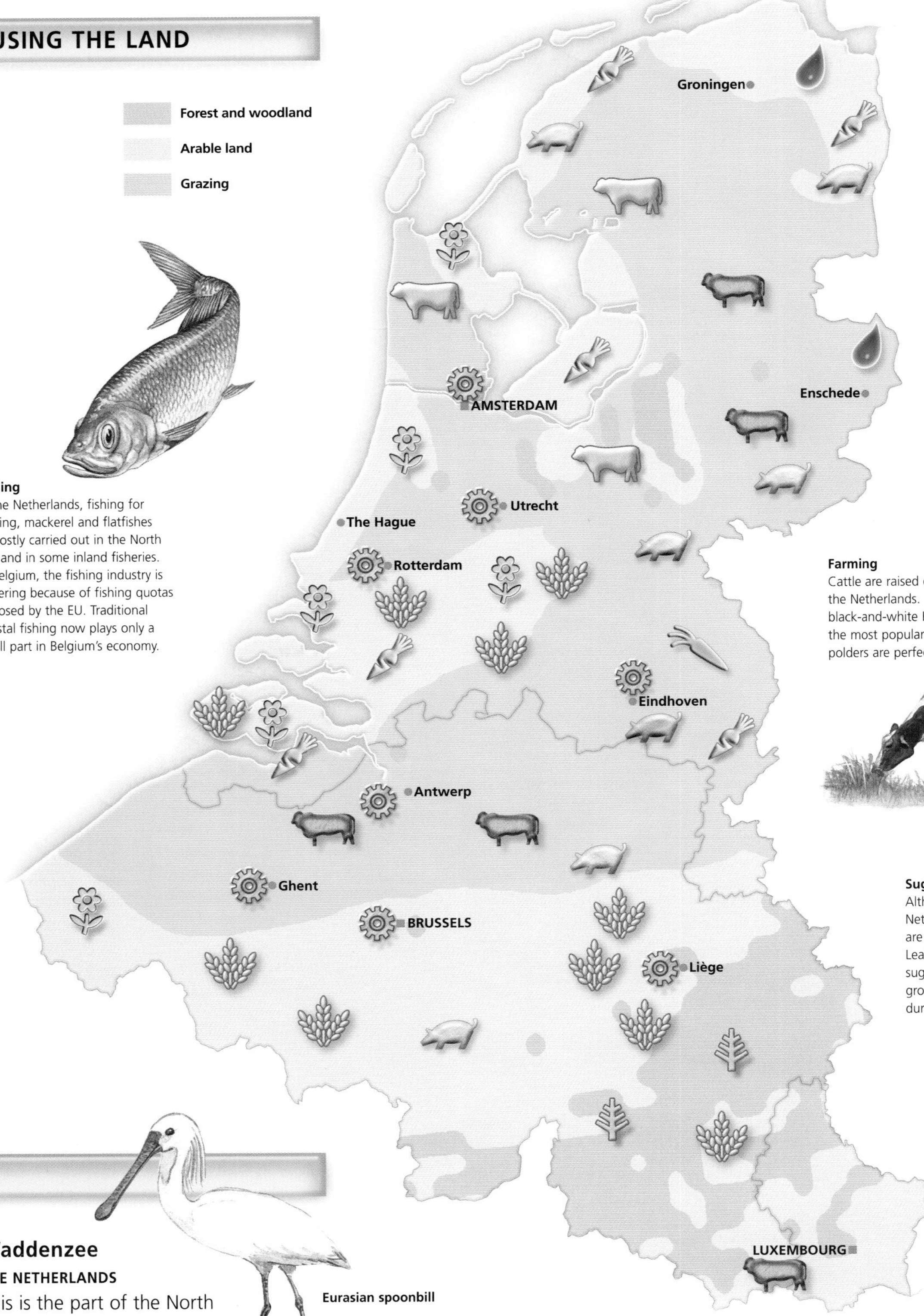

Fishing
In the Netherlands, fishing for herring, mackerel and flatfishes is mostly carried out in the North Sea and in some inland fisheries. In Belgium, the fishing industry is suffering because of fishing quotas imposed by the EU. Traditional coastal fishing now plays only a small part in Belgium's economy.

Map labels: Groningen, Enschede, AMSTERDAM, The Hague, Utrecht, Rotterdam, Eindhoven, Antwerp, Ghent, BRUSSELS, Liège, LUXEMBOURG

	Cereals
	Potatoes
	Vegetables
	Sugar beet
	Flowers
	Beef cattle
	Dairy cattle
	Pigs
	Gas production
	Timber

Farming
Cattle are raised on many farms throughout the Netherlands. Dairy cows, especially the black-and-white Holstein and Friesian, are the most popular varieties. The country's fertile polders are perfect for dairy farming.

Sugar beet
Although most farms in the Netherlands are small, their yields are among the world's highest. Leading crops include potatoes and sugar beet (*below*). Many farmers grow their crops in glasshouses during the winter.

Cheese markets

Many cheese-producing towns, such as Edam, Gouda and Alkmaar, retain their traditional cheese markets. Large, round balls of cheese are carried from the public weighing house to the cheese market, or *kaasmarkt*, on wooden sledges. The porters dress in white shirts and trousers, and wear leather slings to help them carry the heavy sledge. Gouda and Edam cheeses are world famous.

Edam cheese

LARGEST CITIES

Brussels 984,000

Amsterdam 742,000

Rotterdam 603,000

The Hague 470,000

Antwerp 451,000

Great painters

The 16th and 17th centuries were golden years for painting in Belgium and the Netherlands. The Flemish master Peter Paul Rubens painted for royal families, and is famous for his portraits, such as the *Portrait of a Boy* (*above*). Rembrandt, one of the most gifted Dutch painters, also specialized in portraits, using light and shade for dramatic effect.

TRADITIONS AND CULTURE

Belgian chocolate
Belgium is the world's third-largest producer of chocolates, which are exported all over the world. Some fine chocolate makers still fill and decorate their chocolates by hand.

Wooden shoes
Some Dutch people wear traditional wooden shoes that are shaped like ordinary shoes to help keep their feet warm and dry in the damp. Clogs, the pointy-toed, wooden shoes that are sold as tourist souvenirs, are not worn.

St Nicholas
Each year the people of the Netherlands celebrate the festival of Sinterklaas, or St Nicholas, the patron saint of sailors. On 6 December, the children exchange presents. Over the years, "Sinterklaas" became "Santa Claus."

Elfstedentocht
Also called the "Eleven Cities' Journey," this skating competition takes place on frozen canals that pass through 11 towns in Friesland, covering a distance of 125 miles (200 km).

Moules-frite—mussels with fries—is the national dish of Belgium.

PEOPLE

Desiderius Erasmus 1466–1536
Born in Rotterdam, Erasmus was a thinker and writer of the Renaissance period. He spent his life studying and writing about Christianity.

Abel Tasman c 1603–59
This navigator was chosen by the governor-general of the Dutch East Indies to explore the south Pacific. In 1642 he discovered what is now Tasmania, Australia, naming it Van Diemen's Land for his patron.

Vincent van Gogh 1853–90
Van Gogh's early paintings were mostly of farms and peasants. His later works were of orchards and sunflowers (*left*).

He had a unique brush style and loved to use bright, vivid colors. He is the greatest Dutch painter since Rembrandt.

Sunflowers

Mata Hari 1876–1917
Born in Friesland, Mata Hari's real name was Margarethe Geertruide Zelle. Well known as a dancer, she was accused of being a spy for Germany during World War I and was executed by the French.

Hergé 1907–83
Born in Brussels, Georges Rémi (known as Hergé) was a cartoonist. He created the children's cartoon series *The Adventures of Tintin* (*left*), which tells of the journeys of a boy reporter called Tintin and his white terrier, Snowy.

Anne Frank 1929–45
In 1942, during World War II, Anne Frank and her family hid for two years in an Amsterdam warehouse to avoid capture. Anne kept a diary of her life until taken to Auschwitz.

Anne Frank

PLACES

Amsterdam THE NETHERLANDS
Amsterdam is one of the Netherlands' two capitals (the other is The Hague). It began as a fishing village, and is now a busy port and commercial center.

Amsterdam

City of Luxembourg LUXEMBOURG
The capital of Luxembourg, which is one of Europe's oldest and smallest countries, this city is one of Europe's most important financial centers.

Brussels BELGIUM
Belgium's capital Brussels (*below*) is home to the headquarters of the European Union (EU) and the North Atlantic Treaty Organization (NATO).

Bruges BELGIUM
In the Middle Ages, Bruges was one of the largest and most influential of all European cities. An extensive network of canals runs through the city, which has beautiful gabled buildings and cobblestone streets.

The Hague THE NETHERLANDS
This city is the seat of government of the Netherlands. It is home to the Dutch parliament building and is the official residence of the Dutch royal family.

European Union

The European Union (EU) is an organization of democratic European countries that promotes cooperation among its members. Originally, this cooperation was mostly in the areas of politics, trade and economics, but now it involves such issues as human rights, international security and environmental protection.

HISTORY AT A GLANCE

c 50 BC
Julius Caesar invades the areas now known as the Low Countries. He conquers the land south of the Rhine, but the Frisians north of the Rhine are unconquered.

AD 406–511
Germanic tribes, called the Franks, end Roman rule in the Low Countries. Under Clovis I (king from c 481 to 511) the Franks rule most of Gaul.

AD 713–814
Charles Martel, a Frankish prince, conquers the Frisians and controls the Frankish empire, which reaches its peak between AD 768 and 814 under Charles's grandson, Charlemagne.

AD 925–1350
The Netherlands is ruled by the king of Germany, except for Flanders, which is ruled by France.

1350–1420
The dukes of French Burgundy, such as John the Fearless, become powerful, and the area is called the "Burgundian Netherlands."

John the Fearless

1504
The Low Countries again become part of the Holy Roman Empire.

1579
Seven provinces break away from Spanish rule and form the Union of Utrecht. This union is called the United Provinces of the Netherlands.

1602
The Dutch East India Company is formed and establishes profitable trade routes throughout Europe and East Asia.

1795–1813
The French, led by Napoleon Bonaparte, invade the Netherlands and control the United Provinces.

1814
The Congress of Vienna approves the United Kingdom of the Netherlands, including Belgium and Luxembourg. William I of Orange is king.

Congress of Vienna

1830
Belgians gain their independence after revolting against King William's control. Luxembourg becomes independent nine years later.

1847–48
Belgium and the Netherlands adopt important constitutional reforms.

1940–44
The Germans invade and occupy the Netherlands and Belgium until the end of World War II.

1957
Belgium, France, Italy, Luxembourg, West Germany and the Netherlands form the European Economic Community (EEC) to help free up trade among its members.

1967
The North Atlantic Treaty Organization (NATO) moves its headquarters from France to Belgium.

1992
The members of the European Community sign the Maastricht Treaty, which later establishes the European Union.

2002
Members of the European Union adopt euro notes and coins as their common currency.

Euro

Western Central Europe

Switzerland is one of the world's most rugged countries. Mountains make up more than 70 percent of its area.

Barge on Rhine River

GERMANY
POPULATION 82,398,000 ✳ CAPITAL BERLIN

AUSTRIA
POPULATION 8,188,000 ✳ CAPITAL VIENNA

SWITZERLAND
POPULATION 7,319,000 ✳ CAPITAL BERN

LIECHTENSTEIN
POPULATION 33,000 ✳ CAPITAL VADUZ

Brandenburg Gate
This monumental gateway in Berlin was built between 1788 and 1791. On its top is a statue of a chariot drawn by four horses, representing victory. The gate was damaged in World War II but has since been restored.

Farming
Wheat, barley, corn and sugar beets are grown in the region's richer soils. In the poorer soils of north Germany, rye, oats and potatoes are the main crops.

Car manufacture
The Ruhr valley in Germany is the world's largest car producer after the USA and Japan. German cars are noted for their style and reliability.

Hohensalzburg Castle
This massive fortress dominates the city of Salzburg in Austria. It was built by Archbishop Gebhard in the 11th century to protect the city from attacks by the neighboring Bavarians.

Tugboat
In the North Sea, tugboats bring ships and tankers safely through narrow or shallow waterways, and maneuver them into tight docking bays.

Bavarian

POLAND

DENMARK

NETHERLANDS

GERMANY

Baltic Sea

North Sea

Pommersche Bay

Kap Arkona

Oderhaff

Oder

Schwedt

Neubrandenburg

Eberswalde-Finow

BERLIN

Potsdam

Frankfurt an der Oder

Cottbus

Hoyerswerda

Görlitz

Bautzen

Dresden

Chemnitz

Zwickau

Gera

Jena

Weimar

Erfurt

Gotha

Eisenach

Leipzig

Halle

Dessau

Magdeburg

Brandenburg

Stendal

Wittenberge

Lutherstadt Wittenberg

Elbe

Saale

Werra

Fulda

Nordhausen

Göttingen

Kassel

Marburg

Siegen

Greifswald

Stralsund

Rostock

Lübecker Bay

Wismar

Schwerin

Schweriner See

Kummerower See

Peene

Müritz

Plauer See

Fehmarn

Fehmarn Belt

Mecklenburger Bay

Kieler Bay

Flensburg

Kiel

Neumünster

Lübeck

Heide

Elmshorn

Hamburg

Lüneburg

Uelzen

Elbe

Celle

Wolfsburg

Braunschweig

Salzgitter

Goslar

Hannover

Hildesheim

Leine

Weser

Hameln

Detmold

Paderborn

Minden

Bielefeld

Gütersloh

Lippstadt

Osnabrück

Münster

Hamm

Herne

Bochum

Dortmund

Hagen

Wuppertal

Remscheid

Solingen

Bergisch Gladbach

Leverkusen

Essen

Bottrop

Duisburg

Düsseldorf

Neuss

Krefeld

Moers

Wesel

Mönchengladbach

Aachen

Düren

Cologne

Bonn

Rhine

Siegen

Nordhorn

Rheine

Ems

Oldenburg

Delmenhorst

Bremen

Weser

Bremervörde

Bremerhaven

Cuxhaven

Wilhelmshaven

Helgoländer Bay

North Frisian Islands

East Frisian Islands

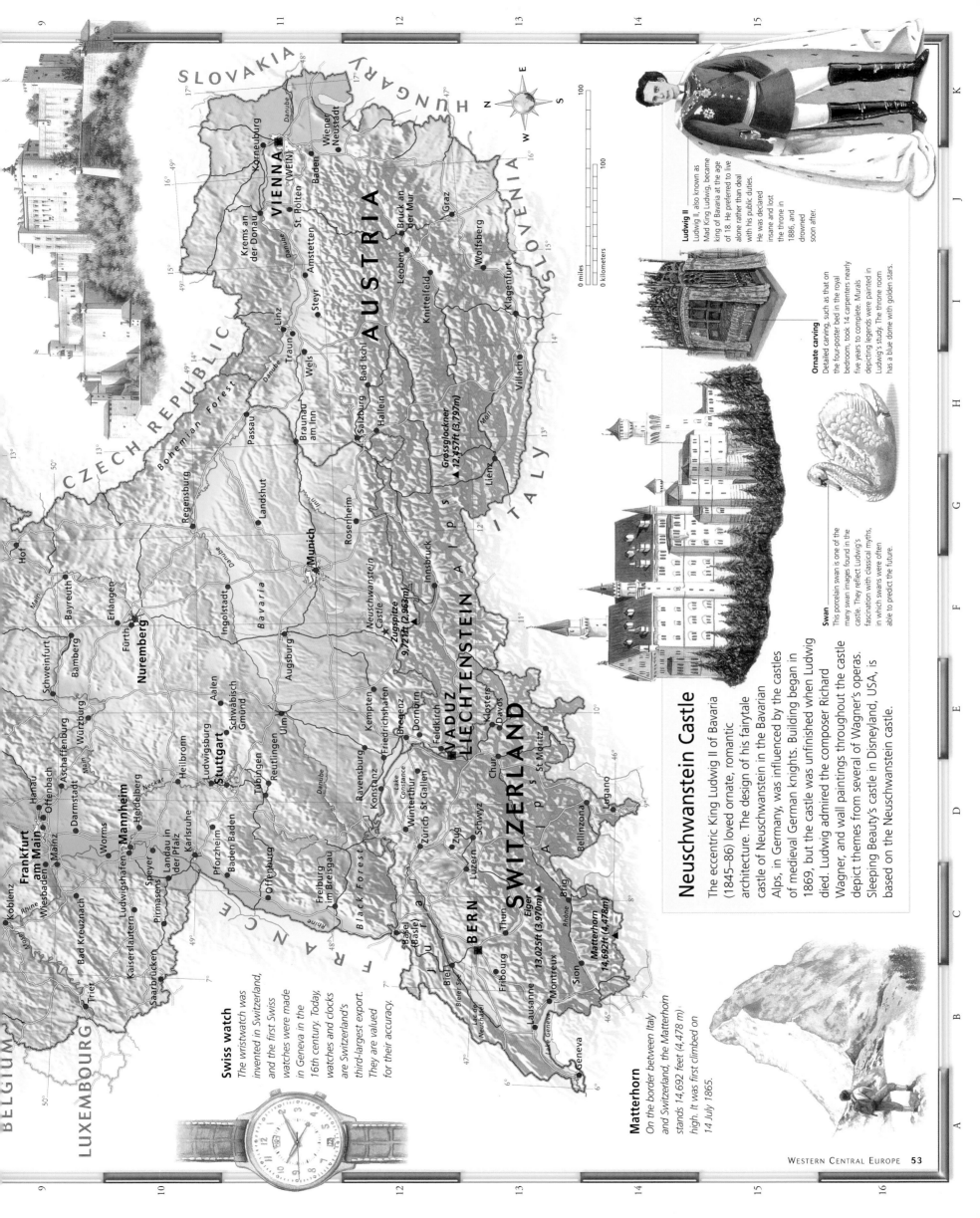

BELGIUM

LUXEMBOURG

SLOVAKIA

HUNGARY

SLOVENIA

CZECH REPUBLIC

FRANCE

AUSTRIA

A l p s

ITALY

Bavaria

Bohemian Forest

Black Forest

SWITZERLAND

LIECHTENSTEIN

VADUZ

BERN

Map labels

Hof
Bayreuth
Erlangen
Bamberg
Schweinfurt
Nuremberg
Fürth
Coburg
Würzburg
Aschaffenburg
Frankfurt am Main
Hanau
Offenbach
Wiesbaden
Mainz
Darmstadt
Worms
Mannheim
Heidelberg
Koblenz
Bad Kreuznach
Kaiserslautern
Saarbrücken
Trier
Speyer
Ludwigshafen
Pirmasens
Landau in der Pfalz
Karlsruhe
Pforzheim
Baden-Baden
Offenburg
Stuttgart
Heilbronn
Ludwigsburg
Aalen
Schwäbisch Gmünd
Tübingen
Reutlingen
Ulm
Augsburg
Ingolstadt
Regensburg
Landshut
Passau
Munich
Rosenheim
Kempten
Ravensburg
Konstanz
Friedrichshafen
Bregenz
Dornbirn
Feldkirch
Chur
Klosters
Davos
St. Moritz
Lugano
Bellinzona
Brig
Sion
Montreux
Lausanne
Geneva
Fribourg
Thun
Brienzer See
Freiburg im Breisgau
Winterthur
Zürich
St. Gallen
Zug
Luzern
Schwyz
Neckar
Main
Rhine
Mosel
Saar
Rhône
Lake Geneva
Lac de Neuchâtel
Bieler See
Lake Constance
Jura
Eiger 12,025ft (3,970m) ▲
Matterhorn 14,692ft (4,478m) ▲
Innsbruck
Neuschwanstein Castle
Zugspitze 9,721ft (2,963m) ▲
Grossglockner 12,457ft (3,797m) ▲
Inn
Danube
Krems an der Donau
Amstetten
St. Pölten
Linz
Traun
Wels
Steyr
Braunau am Inn
Salzburg
Hallein
Bad Ischl
Leoben
Knittelfeld
Bruck an der Mur
Graz
Wolfsberg
Klagenfurt
Villach
Lienz
Moll
Korneuburg
VIENNA (WIEN)
Baden
Wiener Neustadt
Frankfurt am Main
Mannheim
Stuttgart
Nuremberg
Munich
VIENNA

Scale

N
W E
S

0 miles   100
0 kilometers   100

Swiss watch

The wristwatch was invented in Switzerland, and the first Swiss watches were made in Geneva in the 16th century. Today, watches and clocks are Switzerland's third-largest export. They are valued for their accuracy.

Matterhorn

Matterhorn
On the border between Italy and Switzerland, the Matterhorn stands 14,692 feet (4,478 m) high. It was first climbed on 14 July 1865.

Neuschwanstein Castle

The eccentric King Ludwig II of Bavaria (1845–86) loved ornate, romantic architecture. The design of his fairytale castle of Neuschwanstein in the Bavarian Alps, in Germany, was influenced by the castles of medieval German knights. Building began in 1869, but the castle was unfinished when Ludwig died. Ludwig admired the composer Richard Wagner, and wall paintings throughout the castle depict themes from several of Wagner's operas. Sleeping Beauty's castle in Disneyland, USA, is based on the Neuschwanstein castle.

Swan
This porcelain swan is one of the many swan images found in the castle. They reflect Ludwig's fascination with classical myths, in which swans were often able to predict the future.

Ornate carving
Detailed carving, such as that on the four-poster bed in the royal bedroom, took 14 carpenters nearly five years to complete. Murals depicting legends were painted in Ludwig's study. The throne room has a blue dome with golden stars.

Ludwig II
Ludwig II, also known as Mad King Ludwig, became king of Bavaria at the age of 18. He preferred to live alone rather than deal with his public duties. He was declared insane and lost the throne in 1886, and drowned soon after.

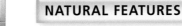

Tim Burners-Lee developed the world wide web in 1989 while working near Geneva.

Western Central Europe

GERMANY LAND AREA	134,836 sq miles (349,223 sq km)
OFFICIAL LANGUAGE	German
MAIN RELIGION	Christian
LIFE EXPECTANCY	78 years
LITERACY	99%

AUSTRIA LAND AREA	31,945 sq miles (82,738 sq km)
OFFICIAL LANGUAGE	German
MAIN RELIGION	Christian
LIFE EXPECTANCY	78 years
LITERACY	98%

SWITZERLAND LAND AREA	15,355 sq miles (39,770 sq km)
OFFICIAL LANGUAGE	German/French/Italian
MAIN RELIGION	Christian
LIFE EXPECTANCY	80 years
LITERACY	99%

WHERE PEOPLE LIVE

Urban | Rural

GERMANY
87% | 13%

SWITZERLAND
68% | 32%

AUSTRIA
65% | 35%

Neanderthals

Named for the Neander Valley near Düsseldorf in Germany, where their remains were discovered in 1856, the Neanderthals lived in Europe between 60,000 and 35,000 years ago. They had a thick brow line and sloping forehead, and were shorter and stockier than other early humans. Their disappearance is a mystery—perhaps it was because they did not develop technology.

USING THE LAND

- Cereals
- Potatoes
- Wine
- Sugar beet
- Beef cattle
- Dairy cattle
- Sheep
- Pigs
- Industrial center
- Mining
- Timber
- Winter sports

NATURAL FEATURES

Eisriesenwalt caves AUSTRIA
Discovered in 1879, these huge ice caves in Salzburg have more than 25 miles (40 km) of explored passageways and 39,000 cubic yards (30,000 m³) of ice.

Lake Geneva SWITZERLAND–FRANCE
Lake Geneva is one of the largest and most beautiful lakes in Europe. Sixty percent of its waters belong to Switzerland, the remainder to France. Château de Chillon (below) is a fortress built on the shores in the 11th century.

The Alps
Europe's most impressive mountain range extends along Germany's southern border with Austria, into the state of Bavaria. Although the peaks are snow-covered during winter, masses of edelweiss (left) blanket the alpine meadows in spring.

The Black Forest GERMANY
Named for its dense growth of spruce and fir trees that let little light into the area, this dramatic forest in southwest Germany has been the backdrop for many magical tales. Pollution, such as acid rain, has recently threatened the forest.

LARGEST CITIES

Berlin 3,387,000

Hamburg 1,731,000

Vienna 1,504,000

Munich 1,238,000

Cologne 970,000

Map labels: Kiel, Hamburg, Hannover, BERLIN, Essen, Leipzig, Dresden, Cologne, Frankfurt am Main, Nuremberg, Stuttgart, Linz, VIENNA, Munich, Salzburg, Basel, Zürich, VADUZ, Innsbruck, Graz, BERN, Klagenfurt, Geneva, Lugano

Forest and woodland
Arable land
Grazing
Arid or marginal

Chemicals
Germany is one of the world's leaders in chemicals production for both the local and export markets. Many corporations are developing measures to ensure that the environment is protected while chemicals are being manufactured.

Winter sports
The mountainous landscape of much of this region, as well as the extremely cold winters, make snow- and ice-related sports very popular. Many Germans, Swiss and Austrians love skiing, especially the cross-country style called *langlaufing*. In recent years, snowboarding (right) has also become popular.

HIGHEST MOUNTAINS

Monte Rosa massif 15,203 feet (4,634 m)

Dom 14,911 feet (4,545 m)

Weisshorn 14,780 feet (4,505 m)

Taschhorn 14,731 feet (4,490 m)

Classical music

Between 1750 and 1820, Vienna, Austria's capital, was the center of classical music. Two of the most gifted composers from this time were Ludwig van Beethoven (1770–1827), who at the age of 30 began to go deaf, and Wolfgang Amadeus Mozart (1756–91), who died at age 35 at the height of his musical powers. Both relied on the support of wealthy patrons, who provided the funds that enabled them to write music.

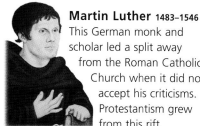
Ludwig van Beethoven

PEOPLE

Martin Luther 1483–1546
This German monk and scholar led a split away from the Roman Catholic Church when it did not accept his criticisms. Protestantism grew from this rift.

Gregor Mendel 1822–84
Known as the father of modern genetics, this Austrian monk, and later scientist, discovered why some plants and animals share the same characteristics.

Jean-Henri Dunant 1828–1910
In 1862, this Swiss journalist gathered together 36 people from 14 nations to form the International Red Cross. The Red Cross flag—a red cross on a white background—is the reverse of the Swiss flag.

Albert Einstein 1879–1955
Born in Germany, Einstein, a physicist, became a Swiss citizen in 1901. He published four research papers in 1905, the most influential being on his theory of relativity.

Albert Einstein

Maria von Trapp 1905–87
With her seven stepchildren and husband, this Austrian singer formed the Trapp Family Singers, who sang to audiences the world over. The film *The Sound of Music* is based on Maria's life.

Julie Andrews as Maria in The Sound of Music

TRADITIONS AND CULTURE

Oktoberfest
For 16 days during this beer festival in October, beer halls are filled with people drinking steins (*right*) of beer and enjoying oom-pah band music. The festival attracts more than 7 million visitors to Munich.

Fairy tales
Grimms' fairy tales were written by the brothers Grimm—two Germans who collected folktales about kings, magic and talking animals. The tales were often set in the forests and mountains of Germany.

Saint Bernard dog
This shaggy, densely coated dog breed was first reared in the 17th century by monks in the Saint Bernard Monastery, high in the Swiss Alps. Because of the dogs' ability to withstand very cold weather and their excellent sense of direction, they were able to help the guides who led people across the often dangerous Saint Bernard Pass.

Lipizzaner horses
This classic horse breed dates from 1580, and is a mix of Spanish, Arabian and Berber. It features in the dressage performances at the Spanish Riding School in Vienna.

Cuckoo clocks
Made in Germany since the 18th century, these decorative clocks (*right*) feature a mechanized cuckoo bird, which appears and sings as the clock strikes. The clock face can also be carved or painted.

Swiss cheese
Switzerland has a thriving dairy industry, and cheese-making is a family tradition that takes great skill. Emmentaler and Gruyère are the most popular varieties. A favorite Swiss dish is fondue, in which cheese is melted in a pot over a gentle flame, and pieces of bread are dipped into the pot.

Gruyère cheese

Liechtenstein is the world's largest exporter of false teeth.

PLACES

Berlin GERMANY
This capital city, divided into east and west after World War II but becoming one city again in 1989, began as a trading center in the 13th century. Its most famous landmark is the Brandenberg Gate.

Zurich SWITZERLAND
Situated either side of the Limmat River on Lake Zurich is Switzerland's capital city, a bustling business and cultural center, which earns one-fifth of the national income and has many visitors each year.

Vaduz LIECHTENSTEIN
This small capital city, although wealthy, has an atmosphere more like a village than a thriving center. Liechtenstein Castle, home of the prince, overlooks the city.

Vienna

Cologne Cathedral

Cologne Cathedral GERMANY
One of the world's largest Gothic structures, this cathedral is the most visited monument in Germany. Building started in 1248, but the cathedral was not completed until 1880. Its two large towers rise to 515 feet (157 m).

Vienna AUSTRIA
Vienna, on the Danube River, was once the capital of the Holy Roman Empire. It is now known for its architecture, much of which dates from the Habsburg period, and its music. Vienna is the birthplace of the noted composers Franz Schubert, Johann Strauss and Arnold Schoenberg.

HISTORY AT A GLANCE

AD 962
King Otto of Saxony rules the Holy Roman Empire as the first Holy Roman Emperor.

1200s
Three German cantons (districts) combine to form the Swiss Federation. More join over time. Zurich joins in 1351.

1278
Robert de Habsburg begins the Habsburg dynasty after taking control of Austria. By the 1500s this dynasty dominates most of Europe.

1455
Johann Gutenberg produces the Gutenberg Bible, the first European book printed with movable type.

Gutenberg Bible

1517
Martin Luther speaks out against the Roman Catholic Church. The Reformation follows. Luther establishes the Protestant Church.

1529
Ottoman Turks besiege Vienna but fail to take over the city.

1618–48
Protestants start the Thirty Years War as a protest against the Habsburg Holy Roman emperors. The Treaty of Westphalia ends the war.

1713
Liechtenstein becomes a principality under the Holy Roman Empire and gains independent sovereignty 150 years later.

1781
Joseph II of Austria abolishes serfdom in the Austrian empire.

1871
Prussian leader Otto von Bismarck forms the new German empire. The Victory column is built two years later in Berlin to commemorate unification and past victories.

Victory column

1914–18
Germany is defeated in World War I by the Allies and becomes a republic.

1933
Adolf Hitler leads the Nazi party into power. The following year Hitler gains total control and imposes his rule on the German people.

1938
Under Hitler's direction, tanks move into Vienna and occupy the city. Austria unites with Germany.

Adolf Hitler

1939–45
World War II occurs between Germany and the Allied forces. Millions of Jews are killed by Nazis during the Holocaust. Many German cities are bombed by the Allies. Germany is defeated and divided into East and West.

1961–89
The Berlin Wall separates the two halves of Berlin into East and West, and isolates West Berlin. The wall comes down in 1989, following the collapse of communism. Germany reunites.

Italy

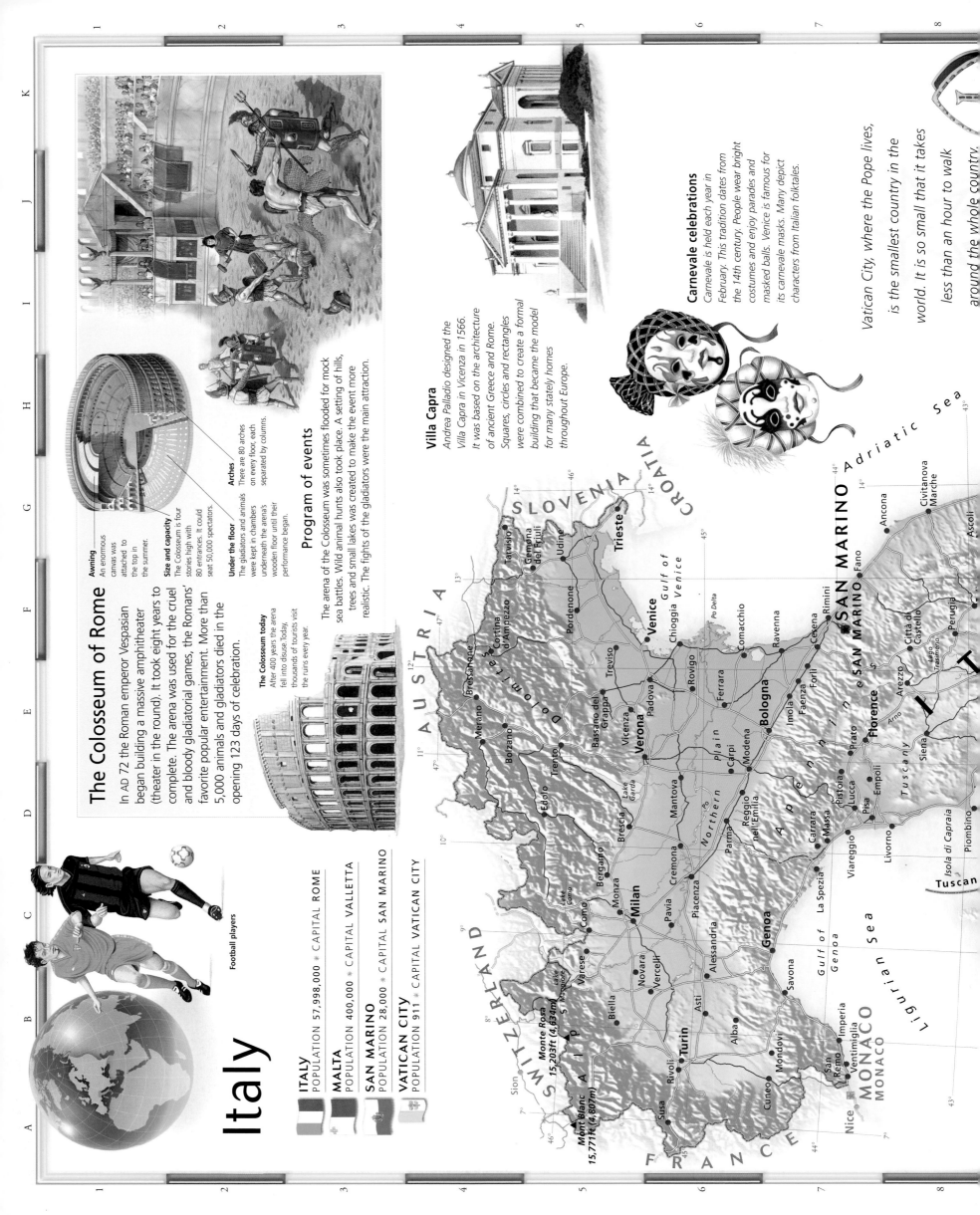

Football players

ITALY
POPULATION 57,998,000 * CAPITAL ROME

MALTA
POPULATION 400,000 * CAPITAL VALLETTA

SAN MARINO
POPULATION 28,000 * CAPITAL SAN MARINO

VATICAN CITY
POPULATION 911 * CAPITAL VATICAN CITY

The Colosseum of Rome

In AD 72 the Roman emperor Vespasian began building a massive amphitheater (theater in the round). It took eight years to complete. The arena was used for the cruel and bloody gladiatorial games, the Romans' favorite popular entertainment. More than 5,000 animals and gladiators died in the opening 123 days of celebration.

Awning
An enormous canvas was attached to the top in the summer.

Size and capacity
The Colosseum is four stories high with 80 entrances. It could seat 50,000 spectators.

Arches
There are 80 arches on every floor, each separated by columns.

Under the floor
The gladiators and animals were kept in chambers underneath the arena's wooden floor until their performance began.

The Colosseum today
After 400 years the arena fell into disuse. Today, thousands of tourists visit the ruins every year.

Program of events

The arena of the Colosseum was sometimes flooded for mock sea battles. Wild animal hunts also took place. A setting of hills, trees and small lakes was created to make the event more realistic. The fights of the gladiators were the main attraction.

Villa Capra

Andrea Palladio designed the Villa Capra in Vicenza in 1566. It was based on the architecture of ancient Greece and Rome. Squares, circles and rectangles were combined to create a formal building that became the model for many stately homes throughout Europe.

Carnevale celebrations

Carnevale is held each year in February. This tradition dates from the 14th century. People wear bright costumes and enjoy parades and masked balls. Venice is famous for its carnevale masks. Many depict characters from Italian folktales.

Vatican City, where the Pope lives, is the smallest country in the world. It is so small that it takes less than an hour to walk around the whole country.

Map labels

SLOVENIA
CROATIA
AUSTRIA
SWITZERLAND
FRANCE
MONACO

Adriatic Sea
Ligurian Sea
Gulf of Venice
Gulf of Genoa
Tyrrhenian Sea

Mont Blanc 15,771ft (4,807m)
Monte Rosa 15,203ft (4,634m)

Sion
Tarvisio
Gemona del Friuli
Udine
Trieste
Cortina d'Ampezzo
Bressanone
Merano
Bolzano
Trento
Edolo
Pordenone
Treviso
Venice
Chioggia
Po Delta
Comacchio
Ravenna
Cesena
Rimini
San Marino
Fano
Ancona
Civitanova Marche
Ascoli
Bassano del Grappa
Vicenza
Verona
Padova
Rovigo
Ferrara
Forlì
Faenza
Imola
Bologna
Modena
Carpi
Mantova
Reggio nell'Emilia
Parma
Piacenza
Cremona
Brescia
Bergamo
Monza
Milan
Pavia
Como
Lake Como
Lake Maggiore
Lake Garda
Varese
Novara
Vercelli
Alessandria
Asti
Biella
Turin
Rivoli
Susa
Cuneo
Mondovì
Alba
Savona
Ventimiglia
Imperia
San Remo
Nice
La Spezia
Carrara
Massa
Viareggio
Lucca
Pistoia
Prato
Florence
Arezzo
Siena
Empoli
Pisa
Livorno
Piombino
Isola di Capraia
Città di Castello
Perugia
Lago Trasimeno
Tuscany
Northern Plain
Dolomites
Apennines

ITALY

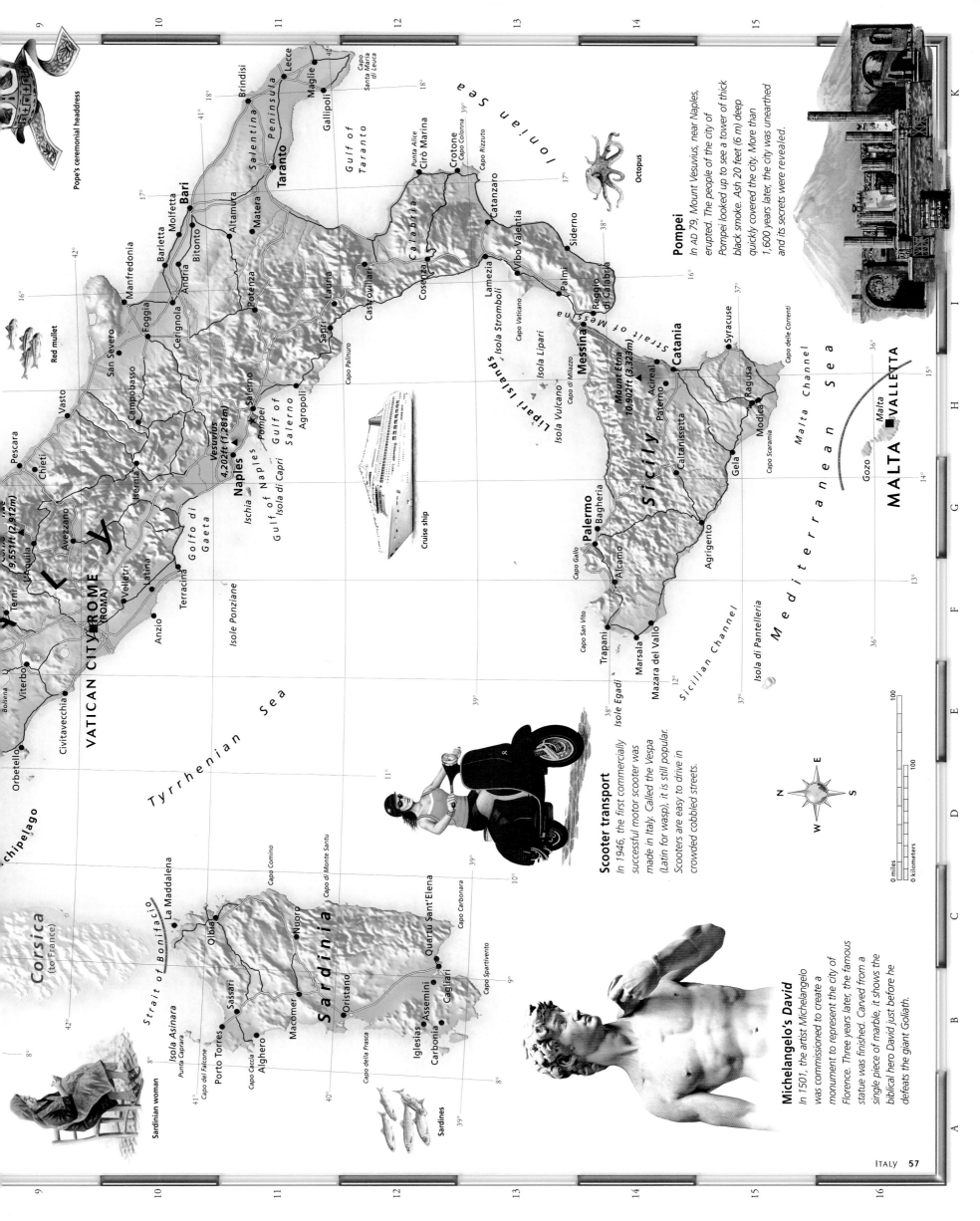

Pope's ceremonial headdress

Red mullet

Octopus

Sardinian woman

Sardines

Cruise ship

Pompei

In AD 79, Mount Vesuvius, near Naples, erupted. The people of the city of Pompei looked up to see a tower of thick black smoke. Ash 20 feet (6 m) deep quickly covered the city. More than 1,600 years later, the city was unearthed and its secrets were revealed.

Scooter transport

In 1946, the first commercially successful motor scooter was made in Italy. Called the Vespa (Latin for wasp), it is still popular. Scooters are easy to drive in crowded cobbled streets.

Michelangelo's David

In 1501, the artist Michelangelo was commissioned to create a monument to represent the city of Florence. Three years later, the famous statue was finished. Carved from a single piece of marble, it shows the biblical hero David just before he defeats the giant Goliath.

Italy

LAND AREA	113,522 sq miles (294,020 sq km)
OFFICIAL LANGUAGE	Italian
MAIN RELIGION	Christian
LIFE EXPECTANCY	79 years
LITERACY	98%

USING THE LAND

NATURAL FEATURES

Blue Grotto
On a clear day, the waters of this huge underground cave on the shore of the island of Capri reflect a beautiful deep blue. In Roman times, the grotto was a water monument for Emperor Tiberius, but it lay unused until the 1800s because local fishermen believed that it was haunted by evil spirits.

Sicily and Sardinia
These two Italian islands are off Italy's west coast. Sicily lies at the southern tip and Sardinia sits between Naples and Rome. Sicily has a mix of fine beaches and local historical treasures while Sardinia's windswept coastline is popular for fishing and water sports.

Dolomites
These majestic mountains, made of dolomite limestone, lie near the Austrian border on the edge of the Alps, in the northwest of Italy. Eighteen of the peaks rise to more than 10,000 feet (3,050 m).

Appennines
This steep mountain range extends for 860 miles (1,376 km) like a backbone down the center of Italy, between the east and west coasts. Most of Italy's rivers have their source in this range.

WHERE PEOPLE LIVE

Urban	Rural
67%	33%

LARGEST CITIES

Rome 2,453,000

Milan 1,180,000

Naples 991,000

Turin 855,000

Palermo 651,000

Mount Etna
Perched above the Sicilian town of Catania, Mount Etna is one of the world's most active volcanoes. Eruptions have occurred for more than 2.5 million years. Lava flows destroy villages and farmland every few years, and smaller eruptions happen even more often. Etna's name comes from the Greek for "I burn."

PEOPLE

Marco Polo 1254–1324
Born in Venice, Marco Polo set sail for China in 1271. He completed his journey by camel along the Silk Road and spent time in the emperor Kublai Khan's court. He did not return to Italy for 24 years.

Marco Polo's ship, *Santa Maria*

Leonardo da Vinci 1452–1519
A brilliant inventor, engineer, architect, scientist and artist, da Vinci was a leading figure of the Renaissance. He designed flying machines, such as the one below, based on his belief that humans could fly. His paintings, such as *Mona Lisa* and *The Last Supper*, are masterpieces.

Leonardo's flying machine

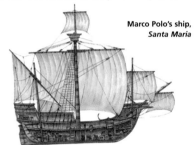

Galileo Galilei 1564–1642
Mathematician, astronomer, scientist: this genius made sense of the world by inventing the telescope, through which he viewed the planets.

Maria Montessori 1870–1952
Maria Montessori, Italy's first female medical student and later, a teacher, paved the way for a new way of teaching—the Montessori method.

Benito Mussolini 1883–1945
Prime minister from 1922 to 1943 and founder of fascism, this dictator carried out many social reforms and public works, but abolished democracy and banned trade unions and the free press.

Map legend

- Cereals
- Rice
- Vegetables
- Citrus fruits
- Wine
- Olives
- Beef cattle
- Dairy cattle
- Sheep
- Fishing
- Industrial center
- Tourism

- Forest and woodland
- Arable land
- Grazing
- Arid or marginal

Map cities: Turin, Milan, Venice, Genoa, Florence, SAN MARINO, ROME, Bari, Naples, Cagliari, Palermo, VALLETTA

Fruit and vegetables
Olive oil, garlic and tomatoes are a tasty basis for many of Italy's dishes. The country produces olives and vegetables of a very high quality. This is due to its Mediterranean climate of hot, dry summers and cool winters.

Winemaking
Different grape varieties are grown for wine throughout Italy. Tuscany's Chianti region is highly productive, while white frascati grapes are grown in the Lazio region around Rome.

Fishing
The waters of the Mediterranean Sea are home to sardines, tuna and anchovies. Fishing is an important industry for Italy.

PLACES

St Peter's Basilica VATICAN CITY
Each year, tourists flock to St Peter's Basilica (*above*). Built between 1506 and 1615, it is the church of the popes and a pilgrimage site for Roman Catholics. In front of it is a vast colonnaded square in which crowds gather to hear the pope speak.

Rome ITALY
Set on seven hills around the Tiber River, Rome is a thriving blend of ancient traditions and modern lifestyle. Italy's capital, it attracts millions of visitors who walk the city in search of its architectural treasures and appreciate its lively, buzzing atmosphere. Its attractions include ancient sites such as the Pantheon and the ruins of the Forum.

Milan ITALY
This northern city is a center of fashion, showcased each year at the Milan Fashion Show. Italian designers such as Miuccia Prada and Giorgio Armani are known all over the world.

Valletta MALTA
This seaport, Malta's capital, has been ruled by many different powers over the centuries. Once an important naval base, it was heavily bombed in World War II.

The Leaning Tower of Pisa
The most unusual feature of this bell tower in Pisa is its lean. Building stopped shortly after it began in 1173 as the subsiding ground below the tower caused it to tilt. Almost 200 years later, it was finally completed to a height of 180 feet (55 m), with 294 steps leading to the top. The bells in the tower are no longer rung, and concrete now supports the foundations under the ground.

Naples ITALY
Italy's most densely populated city, the seaport of Naples sits on the west coast's Bay of Naples, close to possible earthquake and volcano activity.

Florence ITALY
Florence is the cultural heart of Italy, showcasing such architectural marvels as the imposing Duomo (*below*). A center of the Renaissance, the city is home to the Uffizi gallery, which displays Italy's rich heritage of art. Notable Florentines include Michelangelo, Leonardo da Vinci, Galileo, Machiavelli, Dante and the city's most famous rulers, the Medici family.

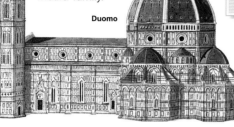

Duomo

TRADITIONS AND CULTURE

Pinocchio
This world-famous story of the wooden boy puppet who comes to life was written by Carlo Collodi and first published in 1890. Pinocchio learns about life through his adventures. His nose grows whenever he tells a lie.

Pinocchio

The Renaissance
In the 14th century there was a rebirth in art and classical knowledge, first in northern Italy and then throughout Europe. Ancient Greek thought was rediscovered and people began to view the world differently. There were great advances in art, science, literature and architecture. Michelangelo, one of the greatest Renaissance painters, brought a realism to art not seen before. His masterpiece, a series of frescoes painted on the ceiling of the Vatican's Sistine Chapel (*below*), took five years to complete.

Venice

This city consists of 118 small islands, linked by waterways and bridges, including the famous Rialto Bridge (*above*). In the 14th century, Venice was Europe's greatest seaport, and it is still a major Italian port today. Cars are banned from most of the city; water transport is provided by gondolas, vaporettos and power boats. Floods frequently bring the city to a halt. Industries include boatbuilding, textiles, furniture and glassworking. Tourism is an important source of income.

San Marino is the smallest republic in Europe and the oldest republic in the world.

Football (soccer)
Football is Italy's national sport. Most cities have their own first-grade teams, and some import highly paid players from other countries to play for them. Matches attract huge crowds.

Italian tastes
Italian people love their food. Their favorites are pizza (*right*) and pasta, which are both made from a dough of wheat grain mixed with water. There are hundreds of pasta varieties, from long spaghetti to small ravioli, served with many different sauces. Another favorite is Italian ice cream, or gelato.

Pizza

Italian design
Italian firms such as Alessi and Cappellini are known for their stylish and innovative designs, particularly in the areas of homewares, furniture and cars. Italy encourages good design through its design schools and exhibitions.

Alessi bottle opener

Opera
This combination of singing and drama originated in Italy in the 16th century. Italian operas include Verdi's *Rigoletto* and Puccini's *Tosca*. Famous modern opera singers include Luciano Pavarotti.

HISTORY AT A GLANCE
ANCIENT ROME

BEGINNINGS
According to legend, the city of Rome was founded in 753 BC by Romulus and Remus, twins who were raised by a wolf. The city-state was ruled by kings, until the final one, Tarquin the Cruel, was defeated in 509 BC by the Etruscans.

Romulus and Remus

THE REPUBLIC 509–27 BC
Two elected consuls ruled instead of the former kings. The consuls were advised by a council called the Senate, composed of wealthy citizens. During the 6th century BC, Rome became more powerful and by 275 BC controlled all of Italy. In the Punic Wars (264–146 BC), Rome fought Carthage for control of the Mediterranean and won. Further battles against Greece, Syria, Egypt and Macedonia were also successful.

JULIUS CAESAR
In 49 BC, as a popular general during the Roman Republic period, Julius Caesar led his army to victory over England and Germany. He made himself dictator of Rome and was murdered on 15 March 44 BC, known as the "ides of March."

THE EMPIRE 27 BC – AD 476
Rome's first emperor, Augustus, was Julius Caesar's nephew. He was crowned in 27 BC. The Roman empire continued to grow until it reached its largest point under Trajan (ruled AD 98–117). Rome ruled most of western Europe, including Britain, northern Africa and the Mediterranean Basin. However, the empire grew weaker and eventually split into two, with its eastern capital in Constantinople in 395. The fall of Rome was completed in 476 when Germanic tribes overran the city. The eastern empire continued until 1453, when the Ottomans captured Constantinople.

Roman soldiers

THE ARMY
The backbone of Rome's empire was its army—the most advanced and well-organized army of the ancient world. It was divided into 60 units, or legions, of foot soldiers, called legionaries. Each legion contained about 5,000 men. The army conquered many lands, expanding Rome's territory. Military life was harsh, but retired soldiers were given money or land to farm.

ROMAN ACHIEVEMENTS
The Romans invented concrete, which made it possible to build large, strong structures such as domed roofs and arched bridges. Roman roads were paved, and were known for their durability and straightness. Aqueducts supplied cities with water for public lavatories, fountains and bathhouses. The water flowed gently from a higher level to a lower one. Tiers of arches supported the pipes across steep valleys. Rome had an extensive and efficient sewerage system that was not bettered until the late 19th century.

Roman aqueduct

Southeastern Europe

ROMANIA
POPULATION 22,272,000 ✳ CAPITAL BUCHAREST

GREECE
POPULATION 10,666,000 ✳ CAPITAL ATHENS

SERBIA AND MONTENEGRO
POPULATION 10,665,000 ✳ CAPITAL BELGRADE

BULGARIA
POPULATION 7,538,000 ✳ CAPITAL SOFIA

CROATIA
POPULATION 4,422,000 ✳ CAPITAL ZAGREB

BOSNIA–HERZEGOVINA
POPULATION 3,990,000 ✳ CAPITAL SARAJEVO

ALBANIA
POPULATION 3,582,000 ✳ CAPITAL TIRANA

MACEDONIA
POPULATION 2,063,000 ✳ CAPITAL SKOPJE

SLOVENIA
POPULATION 1,936,000 ✳ CAPITAL LJUBLJANA

Diocletian's palace
This massive palace on the Adriatic coast in Split, Croatia, was built for the Roman emperor Diocletian in the late 3rd century AD. The palace is set out like a Roman fort, and now forms the city center.

Folk dancing
Ranging from simple, quick steps and gentle turns to lively jumping, traditional folk dances are enjoyed throughout Romania. Music and loud shouts accompany the dancers.

Rural life
Farming methods are changing as more country people move to the cities to find work. However, in some areas, the traditional way of life continues.

Greek evzones guards

The dalmatian is a breed of dog named for the Adriatic coastal region of Dalmatia, its first known home. These dogs once ran beside horsedrawn carriages to frighten highwaymen.

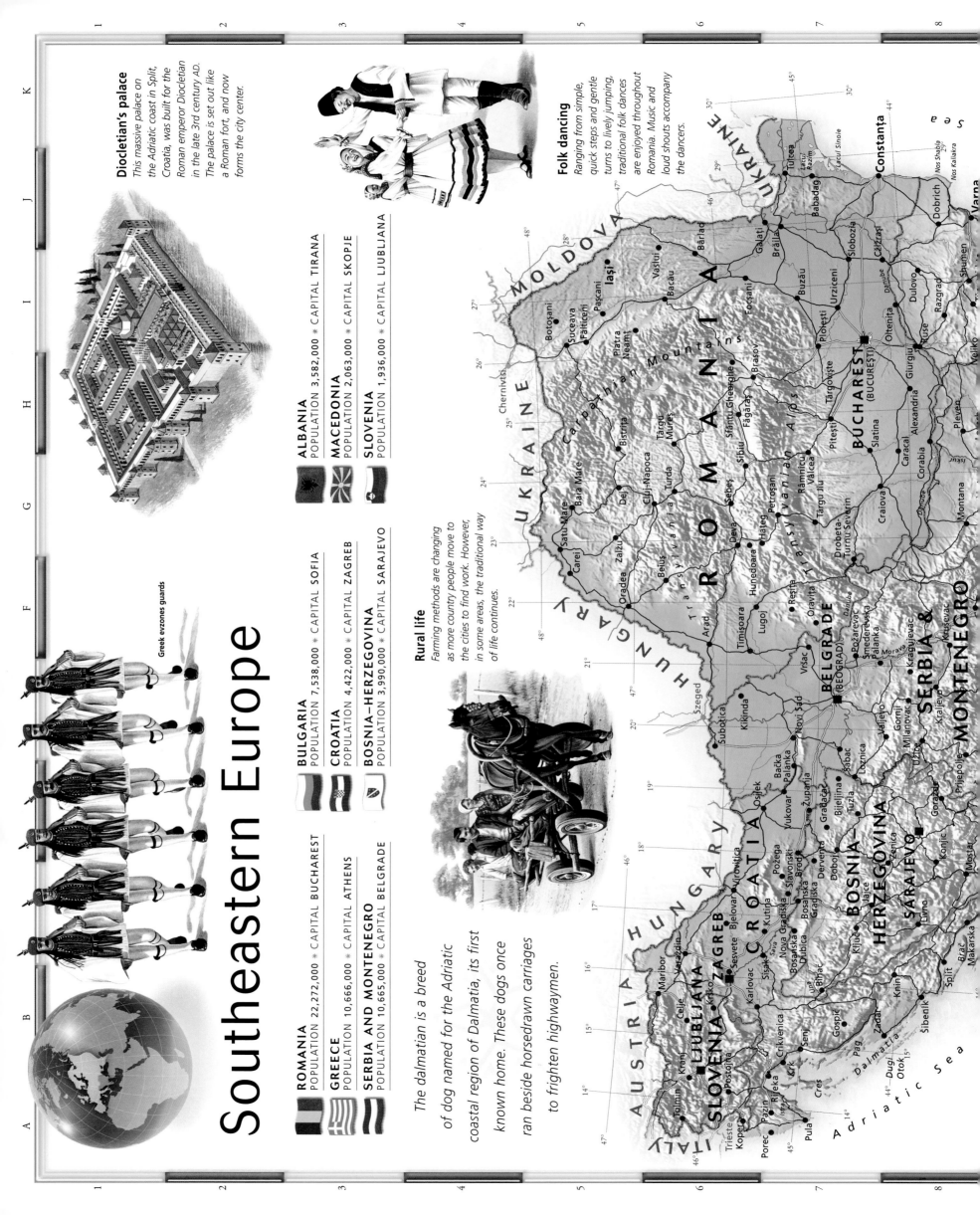

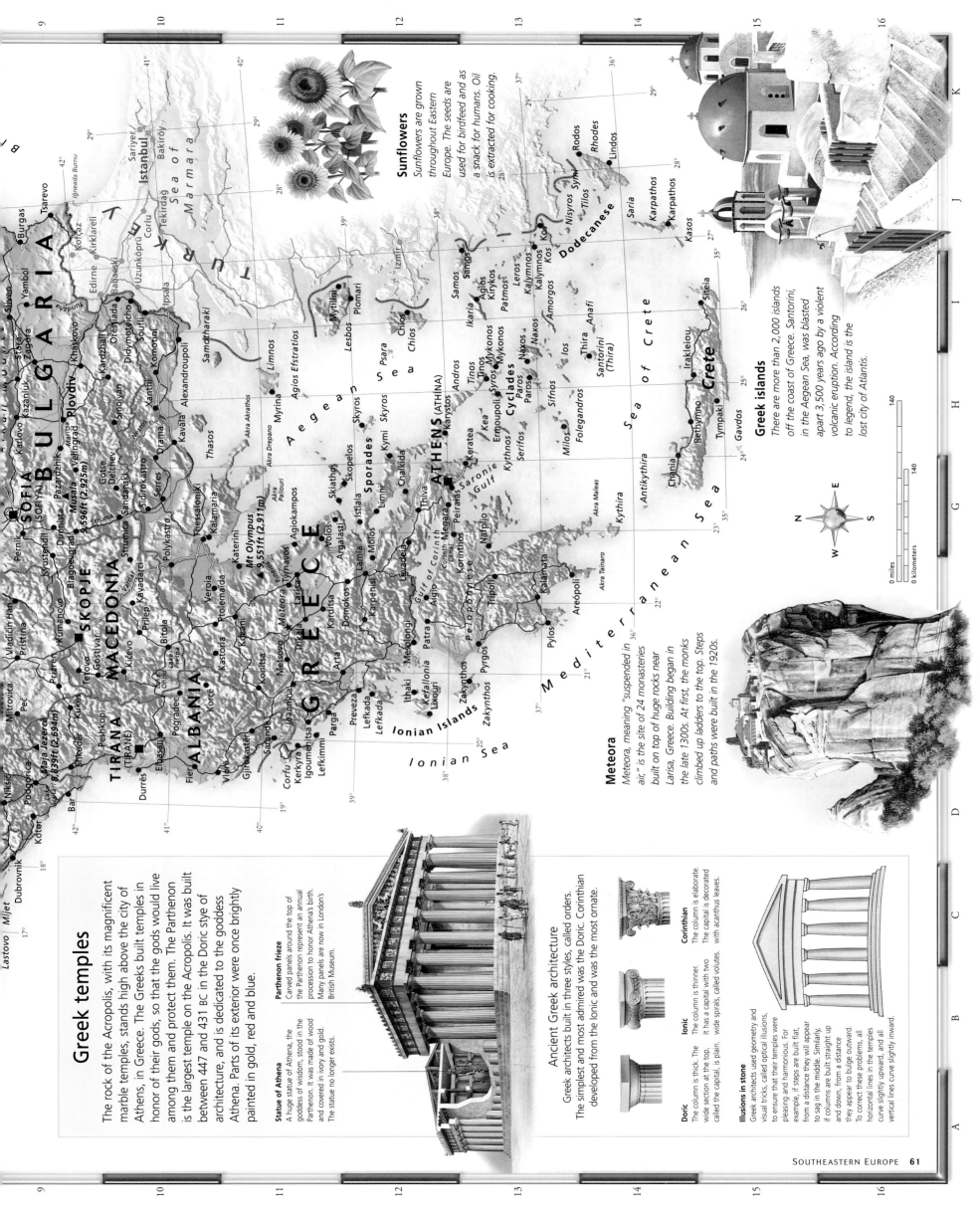

Greek temples

The rock of the Acropolis, with its magnificent marble temples, stands high above the city of Athens, in Greece. The Greeks built temples in honor of their gods, so that the gods would live among them and protect them. The Parthenon is the largest temple on the Acropolis. It was built between 447 and 431 BC in the Doric stye of architecture, and is dedicated to the goddess Athena. Parts of its exterior were once brightly painted in gold, red and blue.

Statue of Athena
A huge statue of Athena, the goddess of wisdom, stood in the Parthenon. It was made of wood and covered in ivory and gold. The statue no longer exists.

Parthenon frieze
Carved panels around the top of the Parthenon represent an annual procession to honor Athena's birth. Many panels are now in London's British Museum.

Ancient Greek architecture

Greek architects built in three styles, called orders. The simplest and most admired was the Doric. Corinthian developed from the Ionic and was the most ornate.

Doric
The column is thick. The wide section at the top, called the capital, is plain.

Ionic
The column is thinner. It has a capital with two wide spirals, called volutes.

Corinthian
The column is elaborate. The capital is decorated with acanthus leaves.

Illusions in stone
Greek architects used geometry and visual tricks, called optical illusions, to ensure that their temples were pleasing and harmonious. For example, if steps are built flat, from a distance they will appear to sag in the middle. Similarly, if columns are built straight up and down, from a distance they appear to bulge outward. To correct these problems, all horizontal lines in the temples curve slightly upward, and all vertical lines curve slightly inward.

Sunflowers

Sunflowers are grown throughout Eastern Europe. The seeds are used for birdfeed and as a snack for humans. Oil is extracted for cooking.

Meteora

Meteora, meaning "suspended in air," is the site of 24 monasteries built on top of huge rocks near Larisa, Greece. Building began in the late 1300s. At first, the monks climbed up ladders to the top. Steps and paths were built in the 1920s.

Greek islands

There are more than 2,000 islands off the coast of Greece. Santorini, in the Aegean Sea, was blasted apart 3,500 years ago by a violent volcanic eruption. According to legend, the island is the lost city of Atlantis.

Southeastern Europe

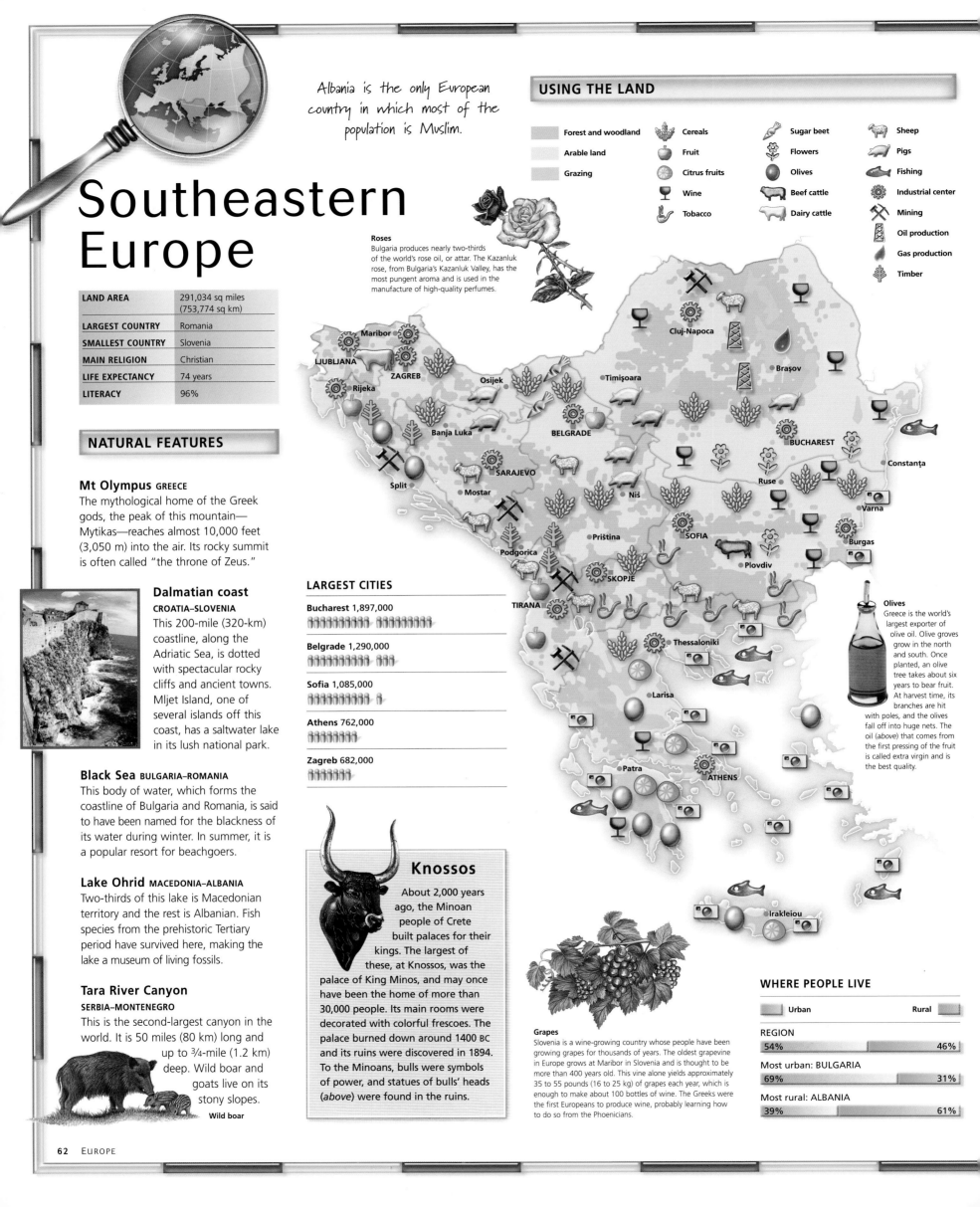

Albania is the only European country in which most of the population is Muslim.

LAND AREA	291,034 sq miles (753,774 sq km)
LARGEST COUNTRY	Romania
SMALLEST COUNTRY	Slovenia
MAIN RELIGION	Christian
LIFE EXPECTANCY	74 years
LITERACY	96%

NATURAL FEATURES

Mt Olympus GREECE
The mythological home of the Greek gods, the peak of this mountain—Mytikas—reaches almost 10,000 feet (3,050 m) into the air. Its rocky summit is often called "the throne of Zeus."

Dalmatian coast
CROATIA–SLOVENIA
This 200-mile (320-km) coastline, along the Adriatic Sea, is dotted with spectacular rocky cliffs and ancient towns. Mljet Island, one of several islands off this coast, has a saltwater lake in its lush national park.

Black Sea BULGARIA–ROMANIA
This body of water, which forms the coastline of Bulgaria and Romania, is said to have been named for the blackness of its water during winter. In summer, it is a popular resort for beachgoers.

Lake Ohrid MACEDONIA–ALBANIA
Two-thirds of this lake is Macedonian territory and the rest is Albanian. Fish species from the prehistoric Tertiary period have survived here, making the lake a museum of living fossils.

Tara River Canyon
SERBIA–MONTENEGRO
This is the second-largest canyon in the world. It is 50 miles (80 km) long and up to ¾-mile (1.2 km) deep. Wild boar and goats live on its stony slopes.

Wild boar

USING THE LAND

- Forest and woodland
- Arable land
- Grazing
- Cereals
- Fruit
- Citrus fruits
- Wine
- Tobacco
- Sugar beet
- Flowers
- Olives
- Beef cattle
- Dairy cattle
- Sheep
- Pigs
- Fishing
- Industrial center
- Mining
- Oil production
- Gas production
- Timber

Roses
Bulgaria produces nearly two-thirds of the world's rose oil, or attar. The Kazanluk rose, from Bulgaria's Kazanluk Valley, has the most pungent aroma and is used in the manufacture of high-quality perfumes.

Olives
Greece is the world's largest exporter of olive oil. Olive groves grow in the north and south. Once planted, an olive tree takes about six years to bear fruit. At harvest time, its branches are hit with poles, and the olives fall off into huge nets. The oil (above) that comes from the first pressing of the fruit is called extra virgin and is the best quality.

LARGEST CITIES

Bucharest 1,897,000

Belgrade 1,290,000

Sofia 1,085,000

Athens 762,000

Zagreb 682,000

Knossos
About 2,000 years ago, the Minoan people of Crete built palaces for their kings. The largest of these, at Knossos, was the palace of King Minos, and may once have been the home of more than 30,000 people. Its main rooms were decorated with colorful frescoes. The palace burned down around 1400 BC and its ruins were discovered in 1894. To the Minoans, bulls were symbols of power, and statues of bulls' heads (above) were found in the ruins.

Grapes
Slovenia is a wine-growing country whose people have been growing grapes for thousands of years. The oldest grapevine in Europe grows at Maribor in Slovenia and is thought to be more than 400 years old. This vine alone yields approximately 35 to 55 pounds (16 to 25 kg) of grapes each year, which is enough to make about 100 bottles of wine. The Greeks were the first Europeans to produce wine, probably learning how to do so from the Phoenicians.

Map labels: Maribor, LJUBLJANA, Rijeka, ZAGREB, Osijek, Cluj-Napoca, Brașov, Timișoara, Banja Luka, BELGRADE, BUCHAREST, Constanța, SARAJEVO, Split, Mostar, Niš, Ruse, Varna, Priština, SOFIA, Burgas, Podgorica, Plovdiv, SKOPJE, TIRANA, Thessaloniki, Larisa, Patra, ATHENS, Irakleiou

WHERE PEOPLE LIVE

	Urban	Rural
REGION	54%	46%
Most urban: BULGARIA	69%	31%
Most rural: ALBANIA	39%	61%

TRADITIONS AND CULTURE

Iliad and *Odyssey*

These two epic poems, written by the Greek poet Homer, tell the story of the Trojan War—a battle between Greece and Troy, in Asia Minor. The two poems are the earliest surviving examples of Greek literature.

Greek vase

Roma people

In the villages of Romania, these Gypsies perform their traditional folk music and dancing. Although little of their history is written down, their past is remembered through story-telling, usually in the Gypsy language called Romany.

Wagons at a Roma camp

Festivals

Many festivals are held throughout the year in southeastern Europe. In Bulgaria, at the *Martenitsa*, tiny red and white trims are tied to clothes to celebrate winter's end and the start of summer. For Greek Easter, red eggs are exchanged as gifts.

Macedonian folk music

The folk music of Macedonia has Turkish and Bulgarian influences. It is always linked to dancing. In the villages, the men play traditional instruments such as the *gaida*, or bagpipe, to accompany the folk dances.

Olympic Games

The Olympic Games have taken place since ancient Greek times, when they were held over five days every four years at Olympia, to honor the god Zeus. The best all-round athlete had to succeed in five events—discus and javelin throwing, running, jumping and wrestling. Chariot racing was the most popular event for the spectators.

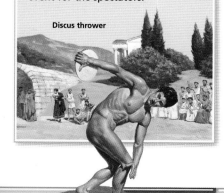

Discus thrower

PLACES

Dubrovnik CROATIA

This capital city, on the Dalmatian coast, was founded by Roman refugees in the 7th century. In the 1991–92 civil war, much of the city was destroyed by shell fire, but many of its historic buildings have now been restored.

Mostar BOSNIA–HERZOGOVINA

This medieval town is set in the Neretva River's valley. Its name means "bridge," for the 16th-century bridge that was destroyed in the shelling raids of the 1990s. Mostar is now divided into Muslim and Croat areas.

Bucharest ROMANIA

The tree-lined boulevards of this capital city have taken their inspiration from Paris. Monasteries and churches are clustered into the back streets of the city, and on a small island in Snagov Lake, to the city's north, is the supposed tomb of Dracula.

Predjama Castle

Predjama Castle SLOVENIA

Perched on a steep cliff, this stately castle sits at the entrance to a huge cave. Castle treasure, dating back to the 16th century when the legendary knight Erasmus of Predjama lived, has been found during recent restoration of the site.

Rhodes GREECE

The city of Rhodes, founded in 408 BC, is capital of the island of the same name. The city was home to the Colossus of Rhodes, a massive statue and one of the Seven Wonders of the World. The Old Town in the city is the oldest inhabited medieval town in Europe.

Shipka Memorial Church BULGARIA

The five golden domes of this huge church, built in 1902 after the Russo-Turkish war, tower over Shipka village. The church is dedicated to Russian leader Alexander Nevsky. Its crypt is the resting place for soldiers lost in battle.

Shipka Memorial Church

PEOPLE

Archimedes c 290–212 BC

This Greek inventor is famous for his discovery that the force weighing down on a submerged object is equal to the weight of the fluid the object displaces. He was also skilled in astronomy, mathematics and mechanics.

Constantin Brancusi 1876–1957

This Romanian sculptor is known for the dramatic, yet simple, lines and shapes in his work, made from bronze or wood. He designed a memorial (*left*) in Tirgu Jui Memorial Park in Romania, which gives the effect of an endless column.

Josip Tito 1892–1980

Born in Croatia, this revolutionary statesman led the former country of Yugoslavia (now Slovenia) from 1943 to 1980 under communist rule. He disagreed with many of Stalin's severe communist ideas.

Dracula

The legend of Dracula was inspired by the 15th-century Romanian prince Vlad Tepesset, also known as Vlad the Impaler. This brutal ruler led his people in raids against the Turks and punished his captured enemies harshly. He died in battle in 1476.

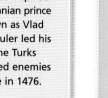

Dracula's castle

Mother Teresa 1910–97

Born in Macedonia, this nun dedicated her life to helping the sick and poor in Calcutta, India. She first went to India in 1928 and, in 1950, set up the Missionaries of Charity, which now has more than 450 centers around the world.

Mother Teresa

HISTORY AT A GLANCE
ANCIENT GREECE

GREEK MYTHOLOGY
The ancient stories about Greek gods and goddesses, and their adventures with magic and monsters, are among the best known in the world. Zeus was the king of gods and Hercules, the son of Zeus, was the most popular hero. In one of his feats, Hercules strangled the Nemean lion, then wore its skin as a cloak. Many of the gods were depicted in artworks (*above*).

GREEK THINKERS
Some of the greatest philosophers, or thinkers, of all time were from ancient Greece. They tried to work out how people should live and how the world worked. Socrates' ideas were about goodness, known as ethics. Plato, one of Socrates' students, developed a theory of ideals. Aristotle was taught by Plato. Pythagoras' theories have formed the basis for many of today's scientific understandings.

ATHENS
Spreading out from the Acropolis, a rocky hill that created natural protection from enemies, Athens had become the most powerful city-state by 500 BC. Athens is known as the birthplace of democracy, as its free male citizens were able to vote for the city's leaders .

SPARTA
The city-state of Sparta was established in the 10th century BC. Spartan warriors were known to be tough and strong in battle, and they fought to increase their territory. All Spartan men were soldiers, while girls were trained for outdoor life.

Temple of Apollo at Delphi

DELPHI
The ancient Greeks often received advice from oracles, or representatives of the gods. Apollo offered advice from his temple at Delphi by speaking through the most honored oracle, the Pythia. A road led up to Apollo's temple, lined with buildings that were filled with gifts for him.

PERSIAN WARS
The Persians, from the area in western Asia now known as Iran, tried to take over many of the Greek city-states to gain more power. They captured the state of Ionia but were fought off by soldiers of the Greek army, called hoplites, in the Battle of Marathon. The account of the Persian War, where the historian Herodotus interviewed survivors, was the first accurate written record of history.

Hoplite

ALEXANDER THE GREAT 356–323 BC
After King Philip II of Macedonia died in 337 BC, his son Alexander reigned. This young leader decided to conquer the Persian territories and beyond, creating the largest empire the world had ever seen. He was clever and courageous and his cavalry of 5,000 horsemen had great respect for him. He died at 32, which fragmented his empire and brought his era to an end.

Eastern Europe

Tobogganing
A toboggan is a long, flat-bottomed sled made of thin boards curved up at the front. The curved runners of the sled move easily over snow and ice. Tobogganing is a popular sport during the cold winters of Eastern Europe.

UKRAINE
POPULATION 48,055,000 ∗ CAPITAL KIEV

POLAND
POPULATION 38,623,000 ∗ CAPITAL WARSAW

BELARUS
POPULATION 10,322,000 ∗ CAPITAL MINSK

CZECH REPUBLIC
POPULATION 10,249,000 ∗ CAPITAL PRAGUE

HUNGARY
POPULATION 10,045,000 ∗ CAPITAL BUDAPEST

SLOVAKIA
POPULATION 5,430,000 ∗ CAPITAL BRATISLAVA

MOLDOVA
POPULATION 4,440,000 ∗ CAPITAL CHISINAU

LITHUANIA
POPULATION 3,593,000 ∗ CAPITAL VILNIUS

LATVIA
POPULATION 2,349,000 ∗ CAPITAL RIGA

ESTONIA
POPULATION 1,409,000 ∗ CAPITAL TALLINN

Gdańsk shipyards
Gdańsk, a port on the Baltic Sea, was once Poland's most prosperous city. In the 1980s, the shipyards were the base of the trade union group called Solidarity, which successfully opposed the communist government.

Astronomical clock
Prague's astronomical clock, on a wall of the city's town hall, was built in 1410. It includes an astrolabe (an early scientific instrument for measuring time), signs of the zodiac, sculptures and moving figures of the 12 apostles.

Budapest parliament
One of the largest parliament buildings in the world overlooks the Danube River in Budapest. It was built between 1884 and 1902, and has 691 rooms and more than 12 miles (19 km) of corridors.

The Estonian islands in the Gulf of Finland are a resting place for hundreds of species of birds migrating from the north to the Baltic Sea.

Gulf of Finland

Hiiumaa

Saarem

Ventspils

Liepāja

Maŭeikiai   Venta

Telšai

Klaipėda

LIT

Tauragė

Sovetsk

KALININGRAD
(to Russia)

Gusev

Marijam

Suwalki

Baltic Sea

Mierzeja
Helska   Zelenogradsk

Gulf of
Gdańsk   Kaliningrad
Chernyakhovsk

Gdynia   Gdańsk

Koszalin   Tczew   Elblag

Szczecin   Czluchow   Ostróda   Olsztyn   Augustow

Stargard
Szczeciński   Piła   Grudziądz

Gorzów
Wielkopolski   Bydgoszcz   Torun   Ciechanów   Łomža   Białyste

POLAND

Warta   Włocławek   Mazowiec

Poznań   Płock   Narew   Bug

Zielona   Konin   WARSAW
Góra   (WARSZAWA)

Leszno   Warta   Pruszków   Siedlce

Ostrów   Kalisz   Łódź   Bia
Wielkopolski   Podlas

GERMANY   Legnica   Piotrków   Radom   Vistula

Jelenia   Wrocław   Trybunalski   Lublin

Teplice   Góra   Snežka   Częstochowa   Kielce   Zamoś
Most   Liberec   5,266ft (1,602m)   Opole   Stalowa
Chomutov   Karlovy   Kladno   Wałbrzych   Zabrze Bytom   Wola
Vary   Gliwice   Dabrowa Górnicza   San
Plzeň   PRAGUE   Hradec Králové   Katowice   Sosnowiec   Kraków
(PRAHA)   Pardubice   Wodzisław Śląski   Rybnik   Tychy   Tarnów   Rzeszów

CZECH   Svitavy   Ostrava   Jastrzębie-Zdrój   Przmysl
REPUBLIC   Olomouc   Haríov   Bielsko-   Carpathian Mount
Bohemia   Frýdek-   Biala
Plechý   Jihlava   Mistek   Gerlachovský štit
4,521ft   Brno   Zlín   Žilina   8,711ft (2,655m)
(1,378m)   Pisek   Moravo   Ružomberok   Bardejov
České   Trenčín   Tatra Mountain   Prešov
Budějovice   Prievidza   Poprad
AUSTRIA   Trnava   SLOVAKIA   Michalovce
Košice   Uzhhor
VIENNA   Nitra   Zvolen
(WEIN)   BRATISLAVA   Miskolc   Mukache
Kékes
Györ   3,327ft (1,014m)   Eger   Nyíregyháza
Tatabánya   Sa
Szombathely   BUDAPEST   Debrecen   Ma
Székesfehérvár   Szolnok   Berettyóújfalu
Veszprém
HUNGARY
Zalaegerszeg   Balaton   Kecskemét   Békéscsaba
SLOVENIA   Nagykanizsa   Hódmezővásárhely
Kaposvár   Danube   Szeged
Szekszárd
Pécs   Arad
CROATIA   SERBIA   ROMANIA
& MON.

Wildcat

Tallinn

Tallinn, on the Gulf of Finland, is the capital of Estonia. The city started as a Danish fort in 1219. It became a thriving trade center in the mid-1300s, and merchants from around Europe sold their goods in its busy marketplace. Tallinn's medieval buildings, such as St Olaf's church and the town hall, are among the best preserved in Europe. The city is now a commercial fishing port.

Built to protect

Wealthy cities like Tallinn were often threatened by invaders. Dating from the 16th century, the imposing wall surrounding Tallinn's Old Town protected its citizens from enemies.

St Olaf's church
St Olaf's spire is a Tallinn landmark. The church, built in the 12th century, was the tallest in medieval Europe.

Watchtowers
There are 26 watchtowers. Soldiers armed with crossbows stood guard in them.

The town wall
Tallinn's massive wall was the strongest in Northern Europe.

Latvian folk dancers
Latvia proudly maintains its traditional folk songs and dances. One kind of folk song, called daina, tells stories that date back many hundreds of years.

Harvesting wheat
Wheat is grown throughout Eastern Europe. In some countries, such as Ukraine and Belarus, where there are many small farms, much of the work is done by hand.

Cossack dancer
The Cossacks are a group of people who live north of the Black Sea. They are known for their lively folk dances, which include athletic jumps, kicks and balancing acts.

Map labels

TALLINN, Narva laht, Kohtla-Järve, Narva, Haapsalu, Paide, Lake Peipus, ESTONIA, Pärnu, Viljandi, Võrtsjärv, Tartu, Võru, Lake Pskov, Valga, Valmiera, LATVIA, RĪGA, Ogre, Jelgava, Jēkabpils, Rēzekne, RUSSIA, Daugavpils, Panevėžys, Utena, Navapolatsk, Polatsk, Kėdainiai, Ukmergė, Vitsyebsk, Kaunas, VILNIUS, Maladzyechna, Orsha, Alytus, Barysaw, Lida, Hrodna, MINSK, Mahilyow, Slonim, Baranavichy, Slutsk, Babruysk, Zhlobin, Salihorsk, Svyetlahorsk, Homyel', Pinsk, Rechytsa, Mazyr, BELARUS, Pripet Marshes, Pripet, Kovel, Sarny, Chernihiv, Konotop, Sumy, Korosten', Chernobyl, Luts'k, Rivne, Romny, KIEV (KYYIV), Pryluky, Okhtyrka, Kharkiv, Zhytomyr, Fastiv, Poltava, UKRAINE, L'viv, Bila Tserkva, Cherkasy, Syeverodonets'k, Ternopil', Khmel'nyts'kyy, Kremenchuk, Slov''yans'k, Lysychans'k, Luhans'k, Vinnytsya, Kramators'k, Alchevs'k, Ivano-Frankivs'k, Uman', Oleksandriva, Kostyantynivka, Krasnyy Luch, Kam''yanets'-Podil's'kyy, Dniprodzerzhyns'k, Pavlohrad, Horlivka, Kirovohrad, Dnipropetrovs'k, Donets'k, Chernivtsi, Pervomays'k, Kryvyy Rih, Zaporizhzhya, Hora Hoverla 6,762ft (2,061m), Edinet, Yuzhnoukrayinsk, Nikopol', Bălţi, Ribnița, Mykolayiv, Mariupol', MOLDOVA, Melitopol', Berdyans'k, Iași, Dubăsari, CHIŞINĂU, Kherson, Sea of Azov, Tighina, Tiraspol, ROMANIA, Odesa, Ciadîr Lunga, Cahul, Kerch, Black Sea, Crimea, Galați, Brăila, Yevpatoriya, Simferopol', Sudak, Sevastopol', Yalta

0 miles 150
0 kilometers 150

Eastern Europe

LAND AREA	594,413 sq miles (1,539,522 sq km)
LARGEST COUNTRY	Ukraine
SMALLEST COUNTRY	Moldova
MAIN RELIGION	Christian
LIFE EXPECTANCY	71 years
LITERACY	88%

Sweet peppers
Peppers (*left*) are the main crop in some regions of Hungary, especially in the fertile district between Szeged and Kalocsa near the Danube River. Hungarians grow red peppers to make a seasoning called paprika, which is used in the dish Hungarian goulash.

WHERE PEOPLE LIVE

Urban	Rural

REGION

65%	35%

Most urban: CZECH REPUBLIC

75%	25%

Most rural: MOLDOVA

46%	54%

Chernobyl

In April 1986, an explosion and fire in the Chernobyl nuclear power plant, Ukraine, released huge amounts of radiation into the air. This poisoned food and water supplies, and caused health problems in Ukraine and surrounding areas. The pink in the image above shows how far the radioactivity had spread around the Northern Hemisphere by the tenth day after the explosion.

USING THE LAND

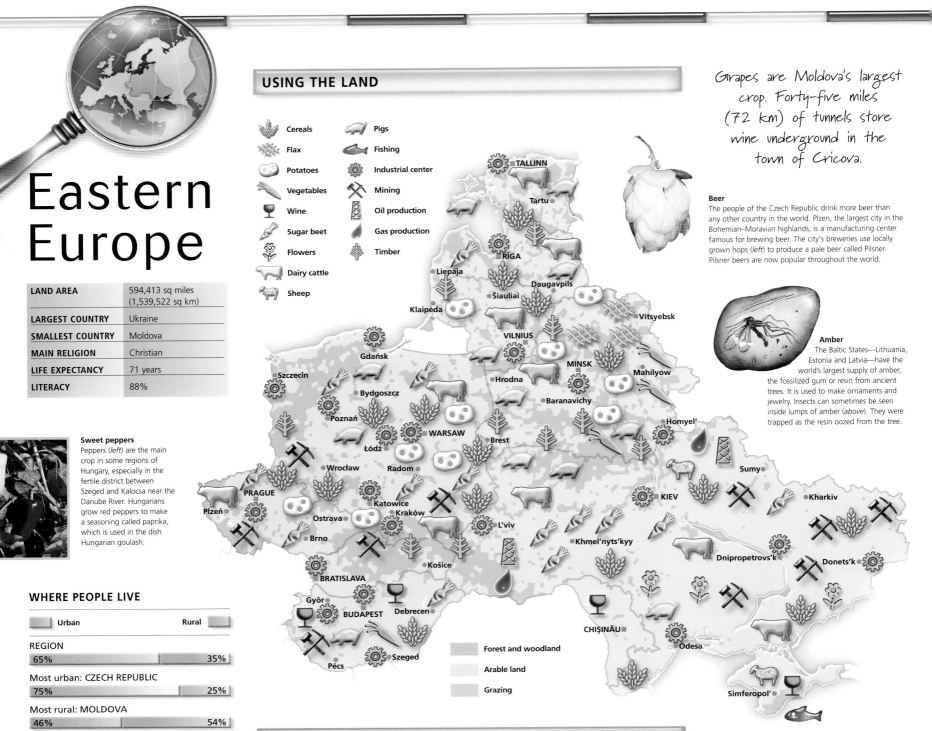

Cereals	Pigs
Flax	Fishing
Potatoes	Industrial center
Vegetables	Mining
Wine	Oil production
Sugar beet	Gas production
Flowers	Timber
Dairy cattle	
Sheep	

Forest and woodland

Arable land

Grazing

Grapes are Moldova's largest crop. Forty-five miles (72 km) of tunnels store wine underground in the town of Cricova.

Beer
The people of the Czech Republic drink more beer than any other country in the world. Plzen, the largest city in the Bohemian–Moravian highlands, is a manufacturing center famous for brewing beer. The city's breweries use locally grown hops (*left*) to produce a pale beer called Pilsner. Pilsner beers are now popular throughout the world.

Amber
The Baltic States—Lithuania, Estonia and Latvia—have the world's largest supply of amber, the fossilized gum or resin from ancient trees. It is used to make ornaments and jewelry. Insects can sometimes be seen inside lumps of amber (*above*). They were trapped as the resin oozed from the tree.

NATURAL FEATURES

Courland Lagoon LITHUANIA
Courland Lagoon, or Kursky Zaliv, is 56 miles (90 km) long and 28 miles (45 km) wide. It is separated from the Baltic Sea by the Courland Spit, a strip of sand dunes that is classified as a UNESCO World Heritage Site.

Bialowieza Forest POLAND–BELARUS
This nature reserve along the borders of Poland and Belarus is administered by both nations. The forest is home to many animals, such as lynx, boar, tarpan horses and a large herd of rare European bison called wisent (*below*).

Tatra mountains POLAND–SLOVAKIA
The Tatras, the highest of the central Carpathian Mountains, mark part of the border between Poland and Slovakia. Forests of spruce and firs thrive in the alpine climate. The chamois (*left*) lives in the high mountains, and is hunted for its skin, which is made into soft leather.

Chamois

Danube River
The second-longest river in Europe, the Danube flows through nine countries from southern Germany through eastern Europe to the Black Sea. It is a transport route for agricultural and industrial freight. Chemical pollution in the Danube has affected its wildlife and the water supply of farmlands on its banks.

LONGEST RIVERS

Danube 1,770 miles (2,850 km)

Dnieper 1,420 miles (2,285 km)

Vistula 651 miles (1,047 km)

Western Dvina 632 miles (1,020 km)

LARGEST CITIES

Kiev 2,581,000

Warsaw 2,200,000

Budapest 1,730,000

Brest 1,476,000

Kharkiv 1,418,000

PLACES

Warsaw POLAND
Located on the Vistula River in the center of Poland, Warsaw is Poland's capital and its largest city. The Old Town, built in the 13th century, is a mix of architectural styles and cobbled streets. Much of the city had to be rebuilt after World War II.

Bratislava SLOVAKIA
Bratislava, Slovakia's capital, is dominated by its huge castle that stands 300 feet (90 m) above the Danube. This was once the home of the Austrian royal family. Modern Bratislava is a center for learning, a transport hub and river port.

St Stephen's crown

When Stephen was crowned king of Hungary in AD 1000, he received a jeweled crown from Pope Sylvester II. That crown forms part of what is now called the Hungarian Holy Crown, held as a national treasure and relic. Stephen was made the patron saint of Hungary, and his crown is a symbol of Hungarian nationhood.

St Sophia's Cathedral UKRAINE
Completed in 1037, this is the oldest church in Kiev, the capital of Ukraine. It had fallen into ruin by the 13th century and was rebuilt between 1685 and 1707.

Budapest HUNGARY
The capital of Hungary, this city is divided by the Danube, with Buda on the east and Pest on the west. Buda is the city's historical heart and Pest is its economic, commercial and political center.

Riga LATVIA
Founded by German crusaders in 1201 and now the capital of Latvia, Riga is a shipping center. Its art nouveau buildings are among the finest in Europe.

Prague CZECH REPUBLIC
One of the oldest cities in Europe, Prague is situated on the Vltava River. It is the capital city, business hub and cultural center of the Czech Republic, and is known for its historic buildings.

Prague

TRADITIONS AND CULTURE

Midsummer's Eve LATVIA
This important festival in Latvia, also called St John's Eve, celebrates the middle of summer on 23–24 June. People light bonfires, sing and dance. They feast on special foods, such as caraway cheese and barley beer.

Puppetry CZECH REPUBLIC
A Czech tradition since medieval times, puppetry entertained and educated children. Czech puppeteers also used puppets to comment on the social and political concerns of the people. Puppetry remains very popular today.

Bohemian crystal CZECH REPUBLIC
Since the 15th century, the region of Bohemia in the western Czech Republic has manufactured Bohemian crystal. This is some of the world's finest and most expensive glassware.

Painted eggs UKRAINE
Exchanging hand-painted, decorated eggs as gifts has been an Easter tradition in Ukraine for centuries. Painting the eggs coincides with the arrival of spring. They are a symbol of rebirth, or the creation of new life.

Cowboys HUNGARY
Hungarian cowboys, or *csikósok*, manage herds of horses and cattle on the plains and grasslands of Hungary. They are admired for their skills on horseback.

Copernicus

Nicolaus Copernicus was born in Poland in 1473. An astronomer, physician and economist, he proposed the idea that Earth and other planets in the solar system revolved around the Sun. Until then, people believed that Earth was the center of the universe and everything revolved around it. He died in 1543, just after his theory was published.

Copernican solar system

PEOPLE

Attila the Hun c AD 406–53
In 434, Attila became king of the Huns. He united them and ruled their kingdom in present-day Hungary. He conquered lands from the Baltic to the Caspian Sea but failed to keep them under his control.

Frédéric Chopin 1810–49
Polish-born Frédéric Chopin gave his first public piano concert at the age of eight, and by 15 was composing music. He composed more than 200 pieces of music for the solo piano.

Rain by Marc Chagall

Marc Chagall 1887–1985
Born in present-day Belarus, Chagall moved to Paris in 1910. He is known for his unusual, dreamlike paintings, in which his figures sometimes float upside down. He was also a printmaker and stage designer.

Pope John Paul II born 1920
In 1978, Polish-born Karol Wojtyla became the first non-Italian pope since 1522 and took the name Pope John Paul II. He has visited more countries than any other pope in history.

Martina Navratilova born 1956
Born in Prague, Navratilova became a US citizen in 1981. She is one of the world's top women's tennis players, and has won a record 167 singles championships.

1918–20
Poland fights Russia, winning the Battle of Warsaw and gaining independence in 1920. Hungary, Estonia, Belarus, Latvia, Ukraine, Lithuania and Czechoslovakia also gain their independence in this period.

1938–39
Nazi Germany annexes first Sudetenland, the German-speaking part of Czechoslovakia, then the rest of Czechoslovakia. It then invades Poland, which leads the UK to declare war on Germany.

Polish cavalry (1939)

1939–45
The Soviet Union and Germany either invade or annex Estonia, Belarus, Latvia, Lithuania, Ukraine, Moldova (then part of Bessarabia) and Czechoslovakia. World War II breaks out.

1945–46
The victory of the Allies leads to the Soviet Union annexing western Ukraine, Estonia, part of Poland, western Belarus and part of Bessarabia (now Moldova). Poland regains some territory from Germany and Warsaw begins to rebuild.

1956
Hungary revolts against the Soviet Union. The revolt is put down by Soviet troops, who execute many of the revolution's leaders. The Soviets form a new government with János Kádár as prime minister.

Demonstration in Prague

1989
Protests, now known as the "velvet revolution," are held in Czechoslovakia to end communist rule. After nearly a decade of struggle, the Polish Solidarity campaign for independence is successful, and the first free elections are held. The border with Austria reopens.

1991
Moldova, Estonia, Lithuania, Latvia, Ukraine and Belarus gain their independence. Soviet forces withdraw from Czechoslovakia, and the country prepares to divide politically.

1993
Czechoslovakia forms two independent countries—the Czech Republic and Slovakia. Michal Kovac is elected president of Slovakia, and Vaclav Havel becomes president of the Czech Republic.

1999
Vaira Vike-Freiberga is elected president of Latvia, and becomes Eastern Europe's first female president. Hungary, the Czech Republic and Poland join as members of NATO.

Vaira Vike-Freiberga

2002
The European Union invites Hungary, Poland, Latvia, Lithuania, Estonia, Slovakia and the Czech Republic to join in 2004. Lithuania agrees to close Ignalina nuclear power station.

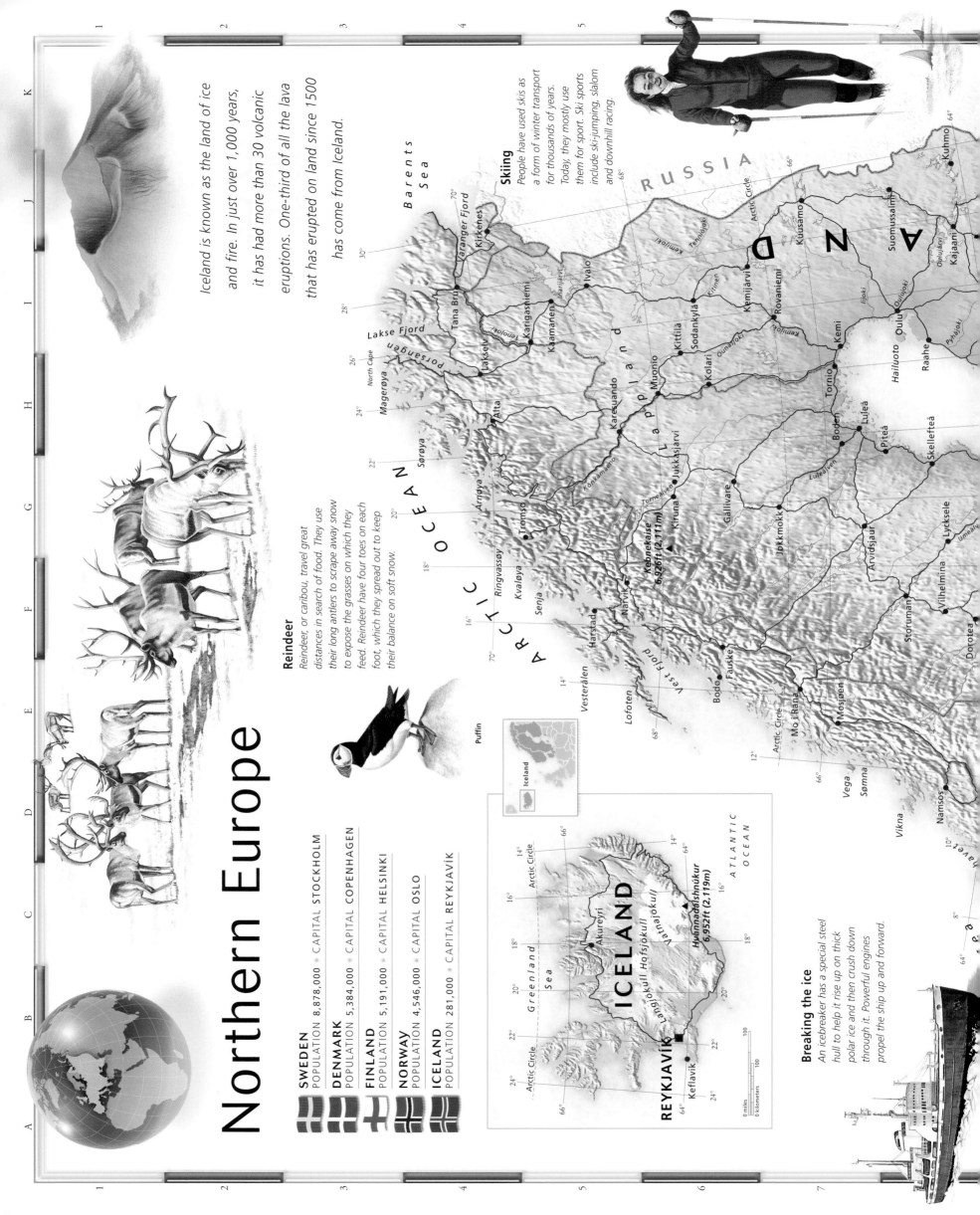

Northern Europe

Iceland is known as the land of ice and fire. In just over 1,000 years, it has had more than 30 volcanic eruptions. One-third of all the lava that has erupted on land since 1500 has come from Iceland.

SWEDEN
POPULATION 8,878,000 ★ CAPITAL STOCKHOLM

DENMARK
POPULATION 5,384,000 ★ CAPITAL COPENHAGEN

FINLAND
POPULATION 5,191,000 ★ CAPITAL HELSINKI

NORWAY
POPULATION 4,546,000 ★ CAPITAL OSLO

ICELAND
POPULATION 281,000 ★ CAPITAL REYKJAVIK

Skiing
People have used skis as a form of winter transport for thousands of years. Today, they mostly use them for sport. Ski sports include ski-jumping, slalom and downhill racing.

Reindeer
Reindeer, or caribou, travel great distances in search of food. They use their long antlers to scrape away snow to expose the grasses on which they feed. Reindeer have four toes on each foot, which they spread out to keep their balance on soft snow.

Puffin

Breaking the ice
An icebreaker has a special steel hull to help it rise up on thick polar ice and then crush down through it. Powerful engines propel the ship up and forward.

ICELAND

Iceland

Greenland Sea

Langjökull Hofsjökull Vatnajökull

Hvannadalshnúkur
6,952ft (2,119m)

ATLANTIC OCEAN

Akureyri

REYKJAVIK

Keflavik

Arctic Circle

0 miles   100
0 kilometers   100

Map labels

Barents Sea

ARCTIC OCEAN

RUSSIA

FINLAND

Lappland

Arctic Circle

Varanger Fjord
Kirkenes
Tana Bru
Kárášjohka
Karasjok
Kaamanen
Ivalo
Inari
Nellim
Kuusamo
Suomussalmi
Kuhmo
Kajaani

Lakse Fjord
North Cape
Magerøya
Porsangen
Lakselv
Alta
Kautokeino
Karesuando
Muonio
Kittilä
Sodankylä
Kolari
Rovaniemi
Kemijärvi
Kemi
Tornio
Oulu
Haukipudas
Raahe
Pyhäjoki

Søroya
Kvaløya
Senja
Ringvassøy
Arnøya
Tromsø
Jukkasjärvi
Kiruna
Gällivare
Jokkmokk
Boden
Luleå
Piteå
Skellefteå

Kebnekaise
6,926ft (2,111m)

Vesterålen
Lofoten
Harstad
Narvik
Vest Fjord
Fauske
Bodø
Mo i Rana
Mosjøen
Arvidsjaur
Storuman
Lycksele
Vilhelmina
Dorotea
Umeälven

Vega
Somna
Vikna
Namsos
Namdalen

Greenland Sea

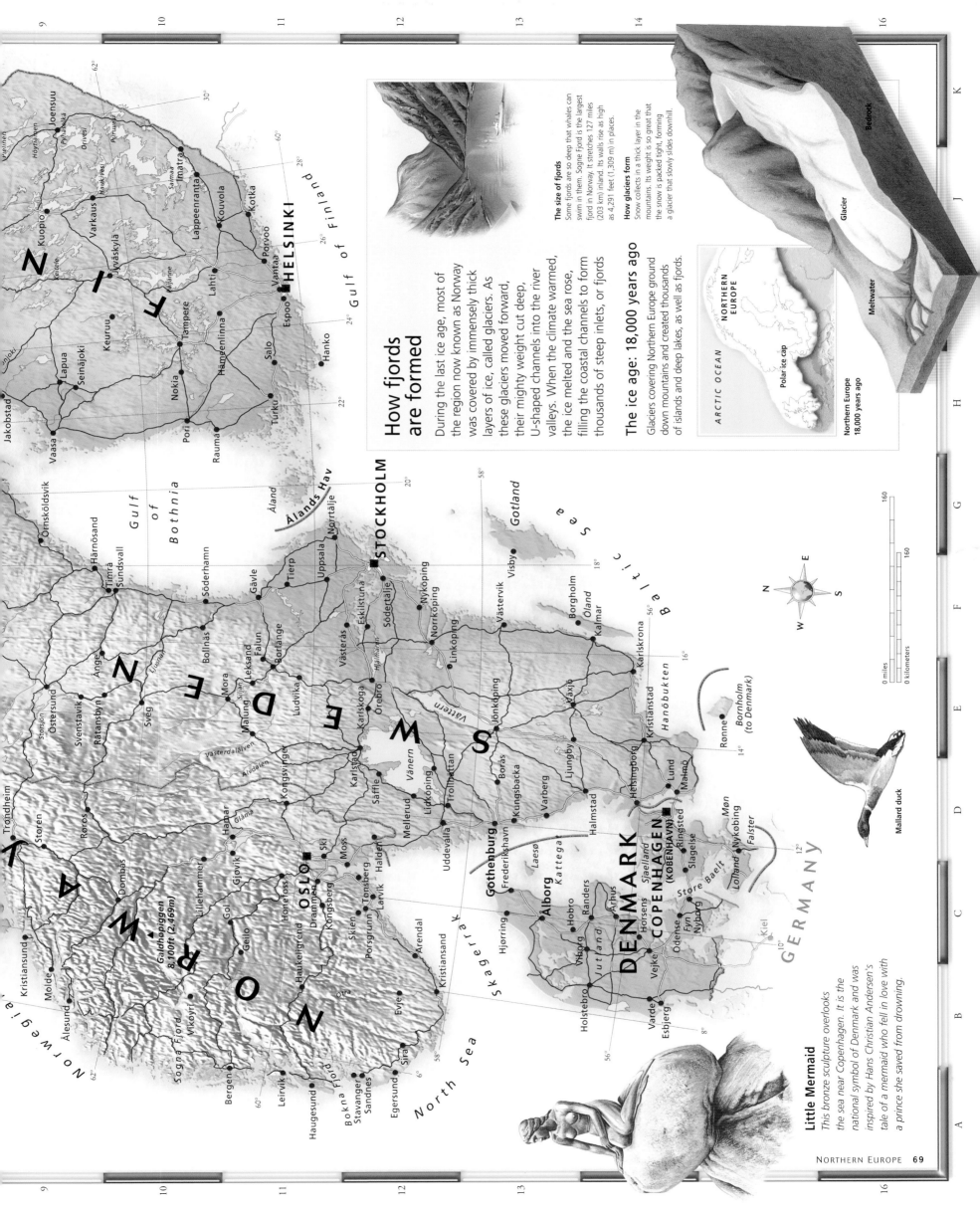

How fjords are formed

During the last ice age, most of the region now known as Norway was covered by immensely thick layers of ice, called glaciers. As these glaciers moved forward, their mighty weight cut deep, U-shaped channels into the river valleys. When the climate warmed, the ice melted and the sea rose, filling the coastal channels to form thousands of steep inlets, or fjords.

The ice age: 18,000 years ago

Glaciers covering Northern Europe ground down mountains and created thousands of islands and deep lakes, as well as fjords.

The size of fjords
Some fjords are so deep that whales can swim in them. Sogne Fjord is the largest fjord in Norway. It stretches 127 miles (203 km) inland. Its walls rise as high as 4,291 feet (1,309 m) in places.

How glaciers form
Snow collects in a thick layer in the mountains. Its weight is so great that the snow is packed tight, forming a glacier that slowly slides downhill.

Northern Europe 18,000 years ago

NORTHERN EUROPE

ARCTIC OCEAN

Polar ice cap

Bedrock
Glacier
Meltwater

Little Mermaid
This bronze sculpture overlooks the sea near Copenhagen. It is the national symbol of Denmark and was inspired by Hans Christian Andersen's tale of a mermaid who fell in love with a prince she saved from drowning.

Mallard duck

0 miles   160
0 kilometers   160

N
W E
S

FINLAND
HELSINKI
Kuopio, Joensuu, Hortlahen, Pyhäselkä, Orivesi, Viekinki, Imatra, Haukivesi, Salmaa, Kouvola, Kotka, Varkaus, Lappeenranta, Porvoo, Vantaa, Espoo, Lahti, Jyväskylä, Kajanne, Keuruu, Tampere, Nokia, Salo, Hanko, Hämeenlinna, Seinäjoki, Lapua, Pori, Rauma, Turku, Vaasa, Jakobstad

Gulf of Finland
Gulf of Bothnia
Åland
Ålands Hav

SWEDEN
STOCKHOLM
Örnsköldsvik, Härnösand, Timrå, Sundsvall, Söderhamn, Gävle, Tierp, Uppsala, Norrtälje, Östersund, Svenstavik, Rätansbyn, Sveg, Bollnäs, Mora, Malung, Leksand, Falun, Borlänge, Ludvika, Eskilstuna, Södertälje, Nyköping, Norrköping, Linköping, Örebro, Karlskoga, Karlstad, Säffle, Lidköping, Trollhättan, Borås, Jönköping, Växjö, Ljungby, Halmstad, Varberg, Kungsbacka, Uddevalla, Mellerud, Gothenburg, Frederikshavn

Vänern, Vättern, Hjälmaren, Siljan, Storsjön, Ljusnan, Västerås

Visby, Gotland, Västervik, Borgholm, Öland, Kalmar, Karlskrona, Kristianstad, Hanöbukten, Helsingborg, Lund, Malmö, Ronne, Bornholm (to Denmark)

Baltic Sea
Kattegat

NORWAY
OSLO
Trondheim, Støren, Røros, Kristiansund, Molde, Ålesund, Dombås, Lillehammer, Gjøvik, Hamar, Gol, Geilo, Kongsvinger, Ski, Drammen, Kongsberg, Honefoss, Tønsberg, Larvik, Halden, Moss, Skien, Porsgrunn, Haukeligrend, Arendal, Kristiansand, Evje, Sira, Egersund, Sandnes, Stavanger, Bergen, Leirvik, Haugesund

Galdhøpiggen 8,100ft (2,469m)
Sogna Fjord, Vikoyri, Bokna Fjord, Otra, Jotra, Glåma, Vesterdalälven, Älvdalen

Norwegian Sea
North Sea
Skagerrak

DENMARK
COPENHAGEN (KØBENHAVN)
Hjørring, Ålborg, Hobro, Randers, Århus, Horsens, Vejle, Holstebro, Viborg, Varde, Esbjerg, Odense, Nyborg, Slagelse, Ringsted, Roskilde, Nykøbing, Falster, Møn, Lolland, Laesø, Fyn, Sjælland, Jutland, Store Baelt, Kiel

GERMANY

NORTHERN EUROPE 69

Northern Europe

	Forest and woodland
	Arable land
	Grazing
	Arid or marginal

REYKJAVÍK

Reykjavík in Iceland is the world's northernmost capital. At midnight, you can see the Sun go down.

SWEDEN LAND AREA	173,732 sq miles (449,964 sq km)
OFFICIAL LANGUAGE	Swedish
MAIN RELIGION	Christian
LIFE EXPECTANCY	80 years
LITERACY	99%

DENMARK LAND AREA	16,639 sq miles (43,094 sq km)
OFFICIAL LANGUAGE	Danish
MAIN RELIGION	Christian
LIFE EXPECTANCY	77 years
LITERACY	99%

FINLAND LAND AREA	130,128 sq miles (337,030 sq km)
OFFICIAL LANGUAGE	Finnish
MAIN RELIGION	Christian
LIFE EXPECTANCY	78 years
LITERACY	99%

NORWAY LAND AREA	125,182 sq miles (324,220 sq km)
OFFICIAL LANGUAGE	Norwegian
MAIN RELIGION	Christian
LIFE EXPECTANCY	79 years
LITERACY	99%

Trondheim · Bergen · OSLO · Gothenburg · Århus · COPENHAGEN

Oulu · Umea · Turku · HELSINKI · STOCKHOLM

Fishing
The waters of Northern Europe are full of both freshwater and saltwater fishes. Salmon, trout and perch are found in the inland rivers and lakes, while mackerel, cod and herring live in coastal waters. Norway is one of the world's leading fishing countries, and has fish farms for salmon and trout in the fjord areas.

Timber
Much of Northern Europe is forested with coniferous, or cone-bearing, trees, including spruce and pine. Deciduous trees, such as birch, are grown in the southern regions. The timber from these forests is produced largely for export.

NATURAL FEATURES

Lake Vänern SWEDEN
This inland lake, the largest in Sweden and dating back to 6500 BC, is situated near the Göta Canal, an inland waterway connecting Stockholm and Gothenberg.

Aurora borealis
Auroras are streaks or curtains of colored light, caused when electrically charged particles from the Sun collide with Earth's atmosphere. The aurora borealis, or northern lights, is especially bright near the Arctic Circle. It can be seen many times a year in Northern Europe.

Arctic fox

Lappland
Pine and spruce trees cover most of this region, which takes in parts of Sweden, Norway, Russia and Finland. Lappland falls within the Arctic Circle and is home to animals such as the Arctic fox, whose coat changes color with the seasons.

Åland Islands FINLAND
Thousands of islands lie in Finland's Coastal Islands region—one of its four geographic areas. Although most of them are uninhabited, about 80 of the 6,500 islands in the Åland group, off the southwest coast, are home to Swedish-speaking Finns. In this group, the island of Åland is the largest.

Cereals		Fishing	
Sugar beet		Industrial center	
Beef cattle		Mining	
Sheep		Oil production	
Pigs		Gas production	
Reindeer		Timber	

WHERE PEOPLE LIVE

	Urban	Rural

DENMARK
85% | 15%

SWEDEN
83% | 17%

NORWAY
75% | 25%

FINLAND
67% | 33%

LARGEST CITIES

Stockholm 1,265,000

Copenhagen 1,101,000

Oslo 799,000

Helsinki 591,000

Gothenburg 510,000

Tollund Man

In 1950, two brothers from the small village of Tollund on Denmark's Jutland Peninsula, while digging up peat, discovered a well-preserved body from about 2,000 years ago. The peat covering Tollund Man was removed, revealing that he wore a pointed hat, tied under his chin.

Sami people

These traditional people live mainly in Lappland, which stretches across northern Norway, Sweden and Finland into the western part of Russia. They are the only people in Northern Europe allowed to herd reindeer, and many are now involved in fishing and handicrafts.

PEOPLE

Saint Bridget c 1303–73
The patron saint of Sweden, Saint Bridget is the most celebrated saint of Northern Europe. She founded the Brigittine order of nuns and monks, and helped sick and poor people.

Hans Christian Andersen 1805–75
The stories of this Danish fairy-tale writer often had characters who went through hard times in their search for happiness. One of Andersen's most famous tales is *The Ugly Duckling*.

Edvard Munch
1863–1944

This Norwegian artist created paintings, such as *The Scream* (*right*), which usually showed extremes of emotion. He moved to Paris in 1889 and learned from great French artists such as Paul Gauguin.

Roald Amundsen 1872–1928
In 1911, this Norwegian explorer, in an expedition with four others, was the first person to reach the South Pole. He was also the first to fly over the North Pole.

ABBA

ABBA 1973–83
In 1974, this Swedish pop music band won the Eurovision Song Contest. For the next six years, they topped music charts the world over with one hit after another.

TRADITIONS AND CULTURE

Nobel Prize

Annual prizes in literature, science and peace are awarded by the Nobel Foundation, which was established in 1900 using funds from Alfred Nobel, the Swedish inventor of dynamite.

Saunas
Many Swedish and Finnish people have saunas about once a week. They lie or sit on wooden slats in a hot, enclosed room, then plunge into cold water.

Runes

These are the characters, made up of sticks, in the Viking alphabet. Stones were carved with runic letters and stories in memory of events.

Trolls

These odd creatures are part of Norway's rich folklore. In early tales, trolls were very large creatures who turned to stone if they went out in the sun. The nokken is a water spirit troll and the hulder troll is female.

The *Kalevala*
Elias Lönnrot compiled this Finnish national epic from ancient spoken poetry he collected in Finland and Karelia. It was published in 1835.

Legoland, built with more than 45 million Lego bricks, is Denmark's most visited attraction.

PLACES

Reykjavík ICELAND
This lively capital city, founded in AD 874, was a small fishing village until the 20th century. It was a naval base in World War II. Today it is a fishing port and home to half of Iceland's industries.

Copenhagen DENMARK
Mostly situated on the east coast of Zealand, this thriving city is Denmark's center for industry, education and culture.

Helsinki FINLAND
Much of this city was rebuilt after fire destroyed it in the 19th century. The Helsinki Cathedral, a grand, domed building, was one of the main projects.

Bergen waterfront

Bergen NORWAY
As Norway's second-largest city and one of the country's chief ports, Bergen is a center for manufacture and trade. The waterfront is lined with wharves from the 13th century.

Stockholm SWEDEN
This picturesque city, Sweden's capital, is a blend of old and new. Its Old Town reflects the Middle Ages, sitting alongside modern life in the rest of the city.

Kronborg Castle DENMARK
This noble castle in Elsinore provided the setting for Hamlet's home in Shakespeare's play. It is one of Northern Europe's most renowned buildings.

Stavkirks

These wooden places of worship, known as stave churches, were built in Norway about 1,000 years ago after the Vikings converted to Christianity. They have high-pitched roofs and are decorated with a mix of Viking and Christian symbols. Dragons (a Viking symbol) often appear at the ends of the gables and crosses (a Christian symbol) are placed at the doors and windows.

Stavkirk in Vikøyri, built in 1130

HISTORY AT A GLANCE
THE VIKINGS

Viking pendants, worn in battle

NORSE MYTHS
Many myths and legends evolved during Viking times. The Vikings believed in gods and goddesses who lived in a place called Asgard. Each god had its own characteristics—Thor was the god of thunder and was very strong; Odin was the god of wisdom and war, and had magic powers; and Frey, a fertility god, had a boat in which all the gods could travel.

VIKING RAIDS
Between the 8th and 11th centuries, fierce Vikings from Norway, Sweden and Denmark, in search of more territory, metals and slaves, raided the far-flung lands of Europe and even North America. They were clever traders and craftsmen who told wonderful stories.

LONGSHIPS
The Vikings were skilled navigators who traveled in longships. The wooden hull was built from 16 overlapping planks. A carved figure, often a dragon, sat at the prow, or front, of the ship.

Viking longship

WEAPONS
A Viking warrior valued his weapons greatly. With his ax, shield and spear at his side, he was armed for any battle. Shields were usually wooden with an iron center to protect the warrior's hand, and the ax, made from iron, had engraved silver patterns on it.

HOUSES
Timber, straw or stone was used to make long, narrow houses, called longhouses. Early in the Viking age, houses did not have windows and were dark but, later, animal bladders were stretched across openings in the wall to let in some light. A hearth was always in the center.

BURIALS
Viking graves were often marked out in the shape of boats. Before Christianity, possessions were buried with the body for use in the next life. According to legend, dead warriors were taken by women to Valhalla—the Viking heaven.

Leif Eriksson sighting America

EXPLORERS
The Vikings were great adventurers, keen to explore lands near and far. In AD 982, Erik the Red discovered Greenland after he left Iceland in search of a new land. Leif Eriksson, one of Eric's sons, is thought to have been the first Viking to land in North America. Harald Haardraade, a member of the Byzantine fighting Vikings called the Varangian Guard, was the last Viking to land in England. The last of the warrior Viking kings, he was killed in battle in 1066.

ARCTIC OCEAN

Queen Elizabeth Islands   Axe
Heib
Islan
Parry Islands   Bathurst
Melville Island   Island
Banks   Prince of
Island   Wales Island
Victoria Island

Chukchi
Sea

Beaufort
Sea

Bering Strait

Brooks Range

Yukon

Great Bear
Lake

Mackenzie

Mt McKinley
20,321ft (6,194m)
Alaska ▲ Range

Bering
Sea

Great Slave
Lake

Aleutian Islands   Aleutian Range

Gulf of
Alaska

Coast Mountains

Mackenzie Mountains

Lake Athabasca

Pearce

Reindeer
Lake

Saskatchewan

Lake
Manitoba

Rocky Mountains

Grea

Mt Rainier
14,409ft (4,392m)
▲

Columbia

Coast Ranges

Cascade Range

Snake

Great Salt
Lake

PACIFIC OCEAN

Sierra Nevada

Mt Whitney
14,495ft (4,418m)
▲

▼ Death Valley
−282ft (−86m)

Great
Basin

Colorado
Plateau

▲ Mt Elbert
14,432ft (4,399m)

Colorado

Mojave
Desert

Grand
Canyon

Sonoran
Desert

Sierra Madre Oriental

Baja California

Gulf of California

Sierra Madre Occidental

Rio Grande

Volcan Popocatép
17,837ft (5,452

Sierra Madre

Ellesmere Island

Devon Island
merset
and

othia
insula

Greenland

Baffin Bay

Baffin Island

Davis Strait

Melville
Peninsula

Foxe
Basin

Hudson Strait

Labrador
Sea

Péninsule d'Ungava

Labrador

Hudson
Bay

Canadian Shield

ake
Vinnipeg

Lake
Nipigon

Laurentian Mountains

Reservoir
Manicouagan

Newfoundland

Lake Superior

Nova
Scotia

Great Lakes

Lake
Huron

Central Lowlands

Lake
Michigan

Lake Ontario

Central Plains

Lake Erie

Missouri

Ohio

Arkansas

Mississippi

ATLANTIC OCEAN

Appalachian Mountains

Gulf-Atlantic Coastal Plain

North America

Mississipi
Delta

The Bahamas

West Indies

Gulf of Mexico

Cuba

Greater Antilles

Leeward Islands

Yucatan
Peninsula

Pico de Orizaba
18,405ft (5,610m)

Caribbean Sea

Lesser Antilles

Sur

Lake
Nicaragua

of Panama

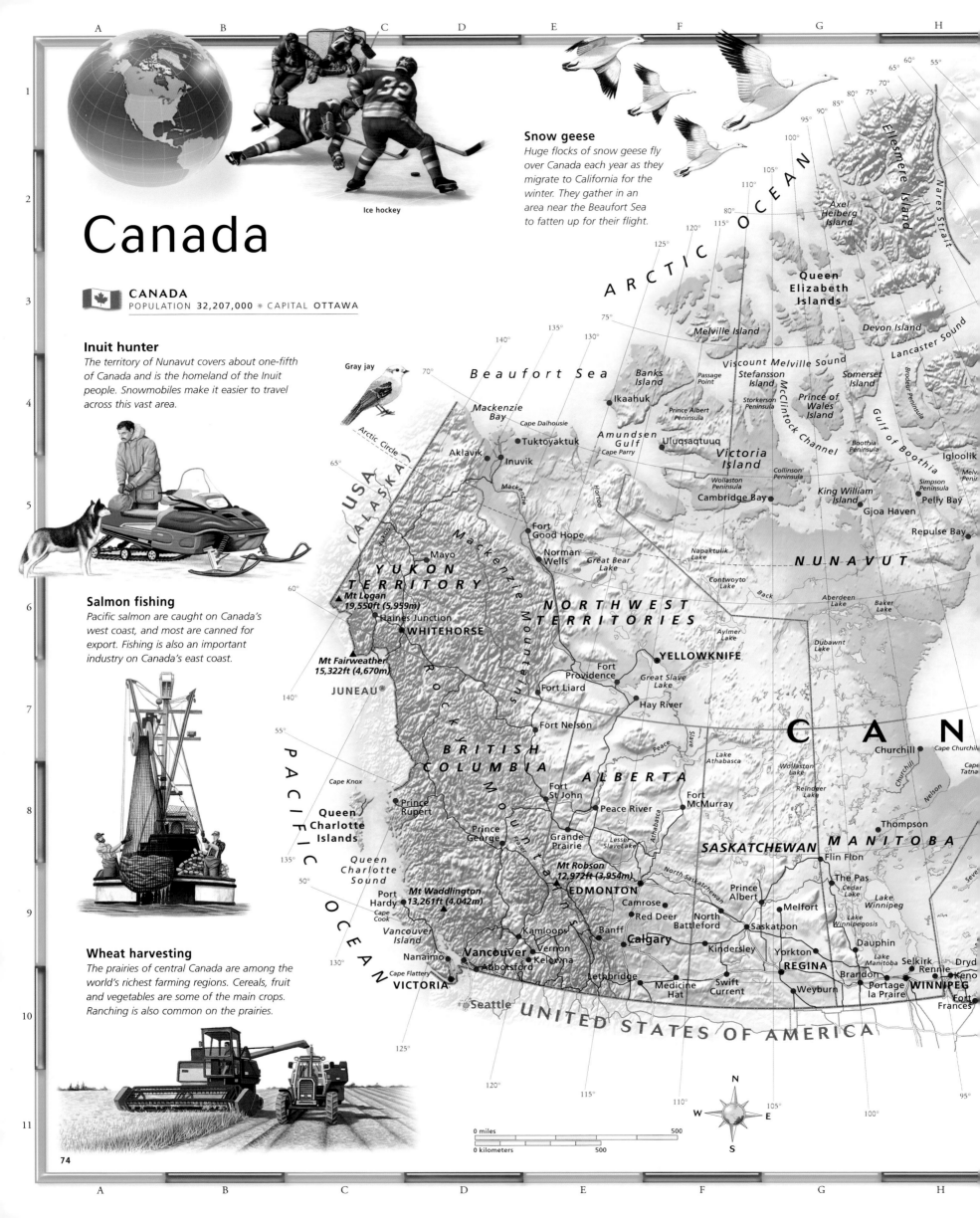

Canada

Ice hockey

Snow geese
Huge flocks of snow geese fly over Canada each year as they migrate to California for the winter. They gather in an area near the Beaufort Sea to fatten up for their flight.

CANADA POPULATION 32,207,000 ✳ CAPITAL OTTAWA

Inuit hunter
The territory of Nunavut covers about one-fifth of Canada and is the homeland of the Inuit people. Snowmobiles make it easier to travel across this vast area.

Salmon fishing
Pacific salmon are caught on Canada's west coast, and most are canned for export. Fishing is also an important industry on Canada's east coast.

Wheat harvesting
The prairies of central Canada are among the world's richest farming regions. Cereals, fruit and vegetables are some of the main crops. Ranching is also common on the prairies.

Gray jay

ARCTIC OCEAN

Queen Elizabeth Islands

Ellesmere Island

Nares Strait

Axel Heiberg Island

Melville Island

Devon Island

Lancaster Sound

Brodeur Peninsula

Beaufort Sea

Banks Island

Passage Point

Viscount Melville Sound

Stefansson Island

Prince of Wales Island

Somerset Island

Gulf of Boothia

Igloolik

Mackenzie Bay

Cape Dalhousie

Tuktoyaktuk

Amundsen Gulf

Cape Parry

Prince Albert Peninsula

Storkerson Peninsula

McClintock Channel

Boothia Peninsula

Aklavik

Inuvik

Uluqsaqtuuq

Victoria Island

Collinson Peninsula

King William Island

Simpson Peninsula

Pelly Bay

Ikaahuk

Wollaston Peninsula

Cambridge Bay

Gjoa Haven

Repulse Bay

Mackenzie

Fort Good Hope

Norman Wells

Great Bear Lake

Napaktulik Lake

NUNAVUT

Arctic Circle

YUKON TERRITORY

Mayo

▲ Mt Logan 19,550ft (5,959m)

Haines Junction

WHITEHORSE

Mt Fairweather 15,322ft (4,670m)

JUNEAU

Fort Providence

Fort Liard

YELLOWKNIFE

Great Slave Lake

Aylmer Lake

Contwoyto Lake

Back

Aberdeen Lake

Baker Lake

Dubawnt Lake

Mackenzie Mountains

NORTHWEST TERRITORIES

Hay River

Fort Nelson

Peace

Slave

Lake Athabasca

Churchill

Cape Churchill

C A N

Cape Tatna

BRITISH COLUMBIA

PACIFIC OCEAN

Cape Knox

Queen Charlotte Islands

Prince Rupert

Queen Charlotte Sound

Port Hardy

Cape Cook

Vancouver Island

Nanaimo

Cape Flattery

VICTORIA

Seattle

Fort St John

Prince George

Grande Prairie

Lesser Slave Lake

Mt Robson 12,972ft (3,954m)

EDMONTON

ALBERTA

Fort McMurray

Athabasca

Peace River

Wollaston Lake

Reindeer Lake

Churchill

Nelson

Thompson

M A N I T O B A

SASKATCHEWAN

Flin Flon

The Pas

Cedar Lake

Lake Winnipeg

Mt Waddlington 13,261ft (4,042m)

Kamloops

Vernon

Kelowna

Abbotsford

Vancouver

Red Deer

Camrose

Banff

Calgary

North Battleford

Kindersley

Saskatoon

Prince Albert

Melfort

Lake Winnipegosis

Yorkton

Dauphin

Lethbridge

Medicine Hat

Swift Current

REGINA

Weyburn

Lake Manitoba

Brandon

Selkirk

Rennie

Dryd

Keno

Portage la Prairie

WINNIPEG

Fort Frances

UNITED STATES OF AMERICA

0 miles 500

0 kilometers 500

N
W · E
S

74

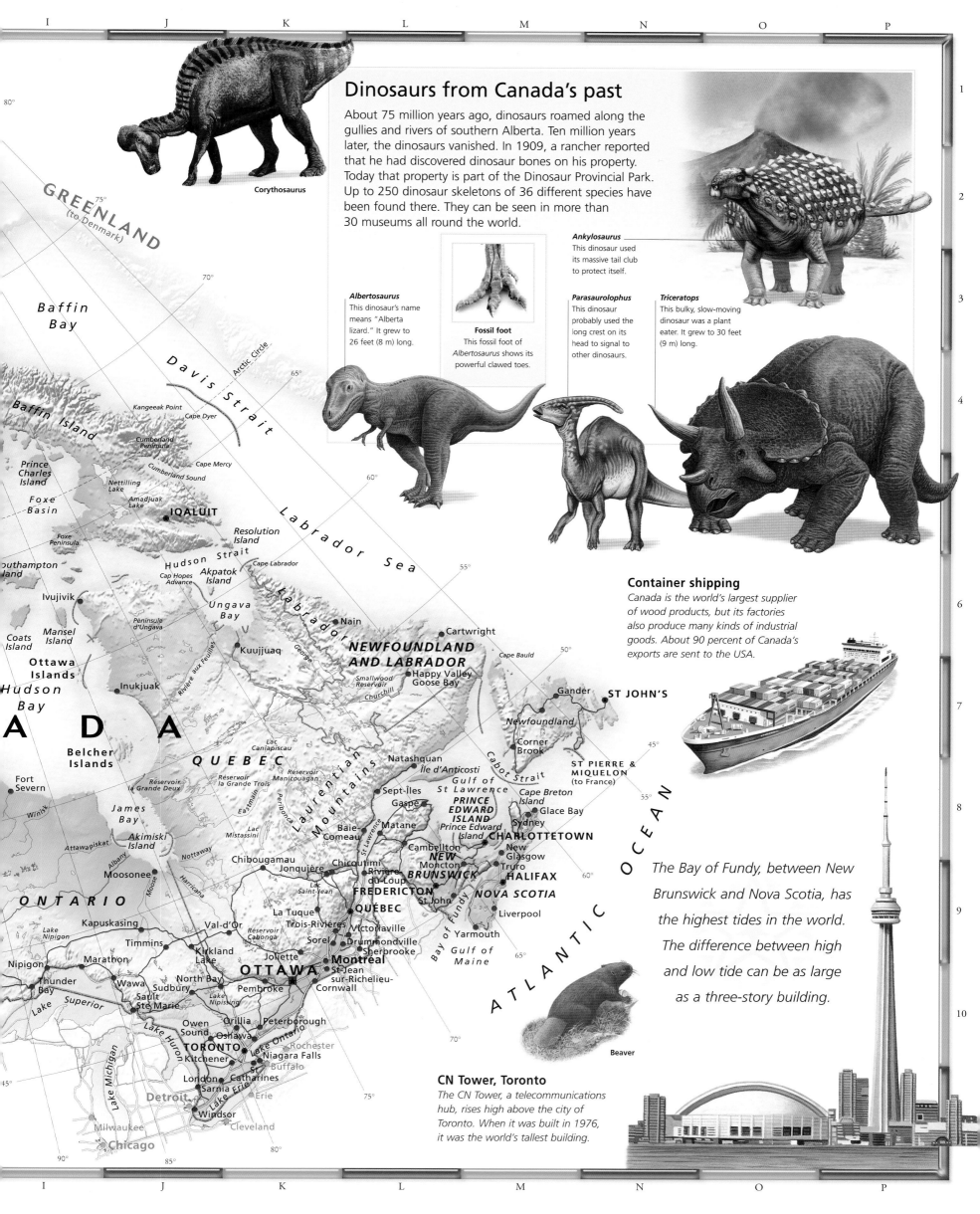

Corythosaurus

Dinosaurs from Canada's past

About 75 million years ago, dinosaurs roamed along the gullies and rivers of southern Alberta. Ten million years later, the dinosaurs vanished. In 1909, a rancher reported that he had discovered dinosaur bones on his property. Today that property is part of the Dinosaur Provincial Park. Up to 250 dinosaur skeletons of 36 different species have been found there. They can be seen in more than 30 museums all round the world.

Albertosaurus
This dinosaur's name means "Alberta lizard." It grew to 26 feet (8 m) long.

Fossil foot
This fossil foot of *Albertosaurus* shows its powerful clawed toes.

Ankylosaurus
This dinosaur used its massive tail club to protect itself.

Parasaurolophus
This dinosaur probably used the long crest on its head to signal to other dinosaurs.

Triceratops
This bulky, slow-moving dinosaur was a plant eater. It grew to 30 feet (9 m) long.

Container shipping
Canada is the world's largest supplier of wood products, but its factories also produce many kinds of industrial goods. About 90 percent of Canada's exports are sent to the USA.

The Bay of Fundy, between New Brunswick and Nova Scotia, has the highest tides in the world. The difference between high and low tide can be as large as a three-story building.

Beaver

CN Tower, Toronto
The CN Tower, a telecommunications hub, rises high above the city of Toronto. When it was built in 1976, it was the world's tallest building.

Map labels

GREENLAND (to Denmark)

Baffin Bay

Davis Strait

Arctic Circle

Kangeeak Point
Cape Dyer

Baffin Island

Cumberland Peninsula
Cape Mercy
Cumberland Sound

Prince Charles Island

Nettilling Lake
Amadjuak Lake
IQALUIT

Foxe Basin

Resolution Island

Foxe Peninsula

Labrador Sea

Hudson Strait
Cap Hopes Advance
Akpatok Island
Cape Labrador

...outhampton ...land

Ivujivik

Ungava Bay

Labrador

Nain

Cartwright

Coats Island

Mansel Island

Kuujjuaq

George

NEWFOUNDLAND AND LABRADOR

Cape Bauld

Ottawa Islands

Inukjuak

Rivière aux Feuilles

Smallwood Reservoir
Happy Valley Goose Bay

Churchill

Gander
ST JOHN'S

Hudson Bay

...ADA

Belcher Islands

QUEBEC

Lac Caniapiscau

Newfoundland

Corner Brook

Fort Severn

Réservoir la Grande Deux

Réservoir Manicouagan

Réservoir la Grande Trois

Laurentian Mountains

Natashquan
Île d'Anticosti

Gulf of St Lawrence

Cabot Strait

ST PIERRE & MIQUELON (to France)

James Bay

Eastmain

Peribonca

Sept-Îles
Gaspé

PRINCE EDWARD ISLAND

Cape Breton Island

Glace Bay

Akimiski Island

Attawapiskat

Lac Mistassini

Baie Comeau

Matane

Prince Edward Island

Sydney

Winisk

Chibougamau

Chicoutimi

CHARLOTTETOWN

ONTARIO

Nottaway

Jonquière

Rivière-du-Loup

Cambellton

New Glasgow

Truro

Albany

Harricana

Lac Saint-Jean

NEW BRUNSWICK

Moncton

HALIFAX

Moosonee

Moose

FREDERICTON

NOVA SCOTIA

Lake Nipigon

Kapuskasing

Val-d'Or

Réservoir Cabonga

Trois-Rivières

Victoriaville

QUÉBEC

St John

Liverpool

Timmins

Sorel

Drummondville

Bay of Fundy

Yarmouth

Nipigon

Kirkland Lake

Joliette

Montreal

Sherbrooke

Gulf of Maine

Thunder Bay

Marathon

North Bay

Pembroke

St-Jean-sur-Richelieu
Cornwall

OTTAWA

Wawa

Sudbury

Lake Nipissing

Lake Superior

Sault Ste Marie

Owen Sound

Orillia

Peterborough

ATLANTIC OCEAN

Lake Michigan

Kitchener

TORONTO

Oshawa

Rochester

Niagara Falls

St Catharines

Buffalo

Lake Ontario

London

Sarnia

Detroit

Lake Huron

Lake Erie

Erie

Cleveland

Windsor

Milwaukee

Chicago

Canada

LAND AREA	3,511,023 sq miles (9,093,507 sq km)
OFFICIAL LANGUAGE	English/French
MAIN RELIGION	Christian
LIFE EXPECTANCY	80 years
LITERACY	97%

Forest and woodland

Arable land

Grazing

Arid or marginal

USING THE LAND

- 🍁 Cereals
- 🥕 Fruit and vegetables
- 🍎 Fruit
- 🐑 Beef cattle
- 🐟 Fishing
- ⚙️ Industrial center
- ⛏️ Mining
- 🛢️ Oil production
- Gas production
- 🌲 Timber
- 📷 Tourism
- ⛷️ Winter sports

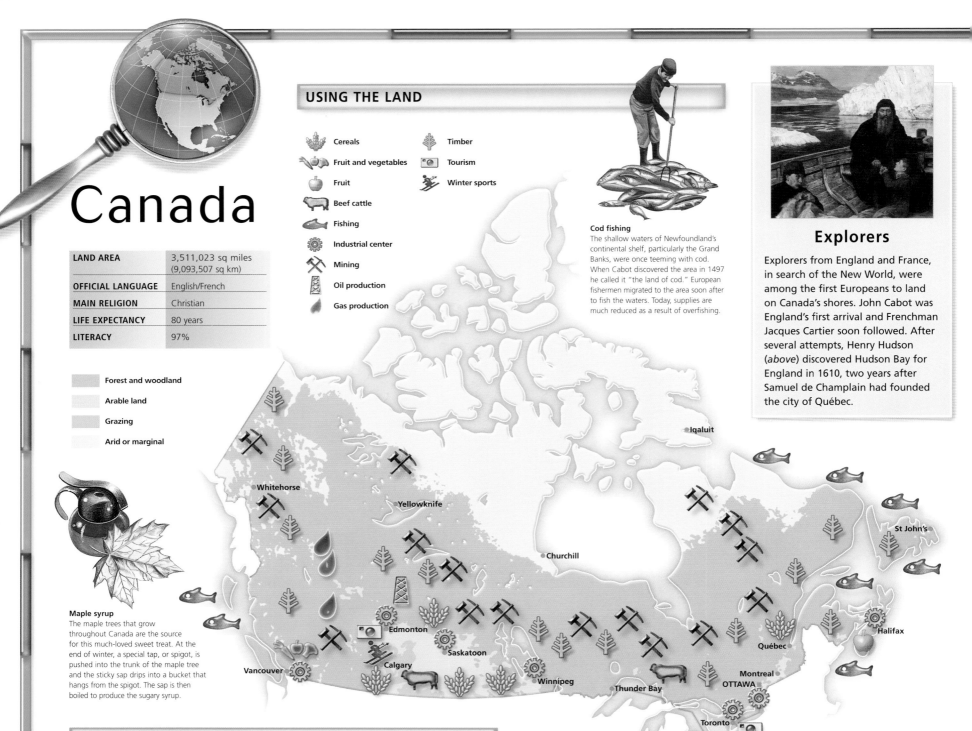

Cod fishing
The shallow waters of Newfoundland's continental shelf, particularly the Grand Banks, were once teeming with cod. When Cabot discovered the area in 1497 he called it "the land of cod." European fishermen migrated to the area soon after to fish the waters. Today, supplies are much reduced as a result of overfishing.

Explorers
Explorers from England and France, in search of the New World, were among the first Europeans to land on Canada's shores. John Cabot was England's first arrival and Frenchman Jacques Cartier soon followed. After several attempts, Henry Hudson (*above*) discovered Hudson Bay for England in 1610, two years after Samuel de Champlain had founded the city of Québec.

Maple syrup
The maple trees that grow throughout Canada are the source for this much-loved sweet treat. At the end of winter, a special tap, or spigot, is pushed into the trunk of the maple tree and the sticky sap drips into a bucket that hangs from the spigot. The sap is then boiled to produce the sugary syrup.

Iqaluit · Whitehorse · Yellowknife · St John's · Churchill · Edmonton · Halifax · Calgary · Saskatoon · Québec · Vancouver · Winnipeg · Montreal · Thunder Bay · OTTAWA · Toronto

NATURAL FEATURES

Hudson Bay
This inland sea on Canada's northern boundary is linked by channels and straits to both the Atlantic and Arctic oceans. Its coastal marshes provide a wetland habitat for an array of unique animals, notably bird species.

Nunavut
Established as Inuit territory in 1999, Nunavut (*below*), meaning "our people," is in the eastern Arctic region. The Inuit have claim to native land in this region, which includes Baffin and Ellesmere islands.

Rocky Mountains
This string of mountain ranges stretches for 3,000 miles (4,800 km) from the Yukon in Canada, down through the USA to Mexico. Banff National Park, home of the Moraine Lake, is in the Canadian Rockies.

Moraine Lake

The prairies
These flat, fertile, treeless grasslands east of the Rockies—which seem to stretch forever—now contain 75 percent of Canada's farmland, although they were once home to roaming buffalo herds.

St Lawrence River
The waters of Lake Ontario—one of the Great Lakes—flow into this river. The icy river supports a population of about 650 beluga whales.

Beluga whale

Forty percent of Toronto's population was born overseas— UNESCO voted it the world's most diverse city.

Wheat
This grain crop—Canada's largest agricultural export—is ideally suited to the natural grassland areas of the prairies. Two-thirds of Canadian wheat is grown in the Saskatchewan province. Once harvested, the grain is pooled, then stored in tall structures called silos (*above*), which dot the landscape.

WHERE PEOPLE LIVE

Urban — Rural

| 77% | 23% |

HIGHEST MOUNTAINS

| Mt Logan 19,551 feet (5,959 m) | Mt Lucania 17,146 feet (5,226 m) |
| Mt St Elias 18,009 feet (5,489 m) | King Peak 16,972 feet (5,173 m) |

LARGEST CITIES

Toronto 4,559,000

Montreal 3,264,000

Vancouver 1,883,000

Calgary 943,000

Ottawa 864,000

PLACES

Québec City
Situated above the mighty St Lawrence River, this capital city of Québec province has a predominantly French lifestyle, and over 90 percent of the population speaks French. Its Old Town is filled with classic 18th- and 19th-century houses.

Château Frontenac, Québec City

Vancouver
This busy port is Canada's contact point for trade with Japan and the East. Canada Place Pavilion overlooks the harbor, and the city's coastal setting, framed by hills and mountains, is ideal for outdoor sports.

St John's
Established in 1528 after John Cabot's discovery of its harbor, this city was the first British colony outside England, and is the oldest city in North America. It is where the Trans-Canada Highway starts.

Parliament building
Ottawa's parliament building (*above*), built in the mid-19th century and overlooking the Ottawa River, is the seat of Canada's government.

Dawson
During the gold rush of the late 1800s, this town (*below*) in the Klondike region was home to 40,000 people; now only about 2,000 people live there. Buildings from the gold rush have been preserved.

Basketball was invented in 1891 by James Naismith, a Canadian teacher, to occupy his students.

TRADITIONS AND CULTURE

Curling
Curling, one of Canada's most popular winter sports, is played on ice. Team members compete to slide a smooth, round stone toward a mark, called a tee.

Totem poles
These tall cedar poles depicting totems, or storytelling symbols, of different tribes were carved by native peoples, such as the Tlingits, of North America.

Tlingit totem pole

Buffalo jump
For almost 6,000 years, the native people of the North American Plains hunted buffalo by forcing them to run over a cliff, then collecting their carcasses. At Alberta, the Head-Smashed-In Buffalo Jump, named for a boy who was crushed by the falling beasts, has been declared a World Heritage Site by UNESCO.

Calgary Stampede
Every July, this huge 10-day rodeo in Calgary attracts cowboys who compete in a range of horse- and bull-racing events. In the chuckwagon-racing event (*above*), introduced in 1925, cowboys sit on a wagon behind teams of four horses and race around a track.

Inuit carvings
The Inuit have carved sculptures from stone and other materials for thousands of years. Today, the carvings are sold to collectors around the world.

Dog mushing
This activity, in which people travel across snow-covered land on sleds pulled by teams of dogs, is a competitive sport in Canada and Alaska. Huskies are used as they are intelligent and adapt well to cold conditions.

Huskies

Canadian Mounties
The Royal Canadian Mounted Police, called the Mounties, was established in 1873 to maintain order between new settlers and native people in Canada's northwest. The Mounties rode horses, wore distinctive red jackets and flat-brimmed hats, and, as legend goes, "always got their man." Today, they patrol in cars and ride horses only on special occasions.

PEOPLE

Laura Secord 1775–1868
In 1813, during the Battle of Beaver Dams, this courageous woman trekked through the wilds for 18 hours to inform the British that the USA intended to attack and take over Niagara Peninsula. Her news saved this territory.

Norman Bethune 1890–1939
Born in Ontario, this dedicated doctor pioneered many medical procedures, particularly in blood transfusions, that changed the lives of the sick. He worked with soldiers in China, and devised a public health system for Canada.

Joe Shuster 1914–92
This talented artist, who moved from Canada to Ohio, USA, in 1923, teamed up with writer Jerry Siegel to create *Superman*, one of the world's most successful comic strips.

Shuster's Superman

Pierre Trudeau 1919–2000
First elected as Canada's prime minister in 1968, and in power for 16 years, this progressive politician led the country through some of its most challenging times.

Jim Carrey born 1962
This internationally renowned actor is known for his comedy antics and impersonations, as well as character acting.

Jim Carrey in The Mask

HISTORY AT A GLANCE

c 20,000 BC
The first inhabitants, ancestors of the Inuit, come to Alaska from Asia via the Bering Strait.

AD 1000
Led by Leif Eriksson, the Vikings start to colonize the Newfoundland coast, but not permanently.

1497
John Cabot, an Italian–British explorer, reaches and names Newfoundland, claiming it for Britain.

1534
Jacques Cartier explores the Gulf of St Lawrence, then discovers the St Lawrence River and claims Canada for France.

Jacques Cartier

1605
The first European colony is established by France at Port Royal, Nova Scotia. Samuel de Champlain founds Québec three years later.

1663
Canada, known as New France, becomes a province of France.

1670
King Charles II of England allows the Hudson Bay Company to trap animals. Trade, especially in fur, is encouraged between England and Canada.

1754
Britain and France fight in the French and Indian War. France gives up Québec to Britain.

1759
Battle of the Plains of Abraham is fought outside Québec City and France is defeated by Britain. By 1763, the whole of Canada is in Britain's hands.

Québec soldier

1793
Alexander Mackenzie travels overland to reach the west coast of Canada—the Pacific Ocean. He is the first European to do so.

1846
The Oregon Treaty confirms Canada's northwest borders with the USA. The Dominion of Canada is established 21 years later.

1885
Canadian Pacific Railway is completed, creating a link across the country.

Canadian Pacific Railway

1949
Newfoundland becomes the newest province. Canada is a founding member of NATO.

1968
The Québec Party is formed, sparking independence for the province.

1989
Britain transfers all power relating to Canada in British law back to Canada.

Corvette

Like many Native American tribes, the Iroquois in the northeast made elaborate masks to wear at religious ceremonies. The wooden masks have deep wrinkles and distorted mouths and noses, and are topped with long strands of horsehair.

Northeastern United States

NEW YORK
POPULATION 19,011,000 * CAPITAL ALBANY

ILLINOIS
POPULATION 12,482,000 * CAPITAL SPRINGFIELD

PENNSYLVANIA
POPULATION 12,287,000 * CAPITAL HARRISBURG

OHIO
POPULATION 11,374,000 * CAPITAL COLUMBUS

MICHIGAN
POPULATION 9,991,000 * CAPITAL LANSING

NEW JERSEY
POPULATION 8,484,000 * CAPITAL TRENTON

VIRGINIA
POPULATION 7,188,000 * CAPITAL RICHMOND

MASSACHUSETTS
POPULATION 6,379,000 * CAPITAL BOSTON

INDIANA
POPULATION 6,115,000 * CAPITAL INDIANAPOLIS

WISCONSIN
POPULATION 5,402,000 * CAPITAL MADISON

MARYLAND
POPULATION 5,375,000 * CAPITAL ANNAPOLIS

KENTUCKY
POPULATION 4,066,000 * CAPITAL FRANKFORT

CONNECTICUT
POPULATION 3,425,000 * CAPITAL HARTFORD

WEST VIRGINIA
POPULATION 1,802,000 * CAPITAL CHARLESTON

MAINE
POPULATION 1,287,000 * CAPITAL AUGUSTA

NEW HAMPSHIRE
POPULATION 1,259,000 * CAPITAL CONCORD

RHODE ISLAND
POPULATION 1,059,000 * CAPITAL PROVIDENCE

DELAWARE
POPULATION 796,000 * CAPITAL DOVER

VERMONT
POPULATION 613,000 * CAPITAL MONTPELIER

WASHINGTON, DC
POPULATION 572,000 * NATIONAL CAPITAL

Baseball
Baseball is the national sport of the USA. It was probably adapted from an 18th-century English game called rounders. The first match played to an official set of rules was held in 1846. Two teams of nine players compete on a diamond-shaped field with four bases.

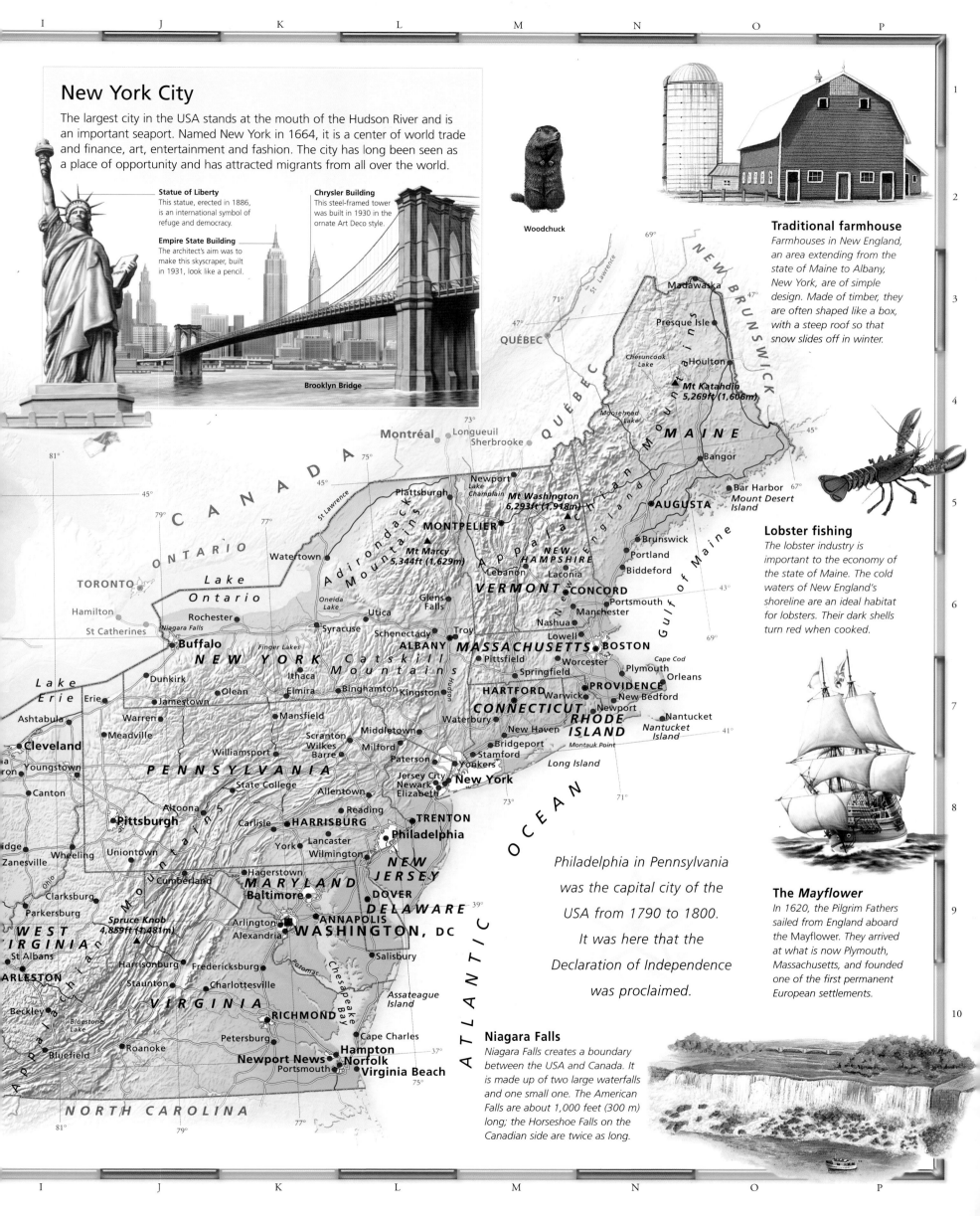

New York City

The largest city in the USA stands at the mouth of the Hudson River and is an important seaport. Named New York in 1664, it is a center of world trade and finance, art, entertainment and fashion. The city has long been seen as a place of opportunity and has attracted migrants from all over the world.

Statue of Liberty
This statue, erected in 1886, is an international symbol of refuge and democracy.

Empire State Building
The architect's aim was to make this skyscraper, built in 1931, look like a pencil.

Chrysler Building
This steel-framed tower was built in 1930 in the ornate Art Deco style.

Brooklyn Bridge

Woodchuck

Traditional farmhouse
Farmhouses in New England, an area extending from the state of Maine to Albany, New York, are of simple design. Made of timber, they are often shaped like a box, with a steep roof so that snow slides off in winter.

Lobster fishing
The lobster industry is important to the economy of the state of Maine. The cold waters of New England's shoreline are an ideal habitat for lobsters. Their dark shells turn red when cooked.

The *Mayflower*
In 1620, the Pilgrim Fathers sailed from England aboard the Mayflower. They arrived at what is now Plymouth, Massachusetts, and founded one of the first permanent European settlements.

Philadelphia in Pennsylvania was the capital city of the USA from 1790 to 1800. It was here that the Declaration of Independence was proclaimed.

Niagara Falls
Niagara Falls creates a boundary between the USA and Canada. It is made up of two large waterfalls and one small one. The American Falls are about 1,000 feet (300 m) long; the Horseshoe Falls on the Canadian side are twice as long.

CANADA
QUÉBEC
ONTARIO
Montréal
Longueuil
Sherbrooke
Toronto
Hamilton
St Catherines
Lake Ontario
Lake Erie
St Lawrence

NEW BRUNSWICK
Madawaska
Presque Isle
Houlton
Chésuncook Lake
Mt Katahdin 5,269ft (1,606m)
MAINE
Moosehead Lake
Bangor
Bar Harbor
Mount Desert Island
Gulf of Maine
AUGUSTA
Brunswick
Portland
Biddeford

Plattsburgh
Newport
Lake Champlain
Mt Washington 6,293ft (1,918m)
MONTPELIER
Mt Marcy 5,344ft (1,629m)
Adirondack Mountains
Watertown
VERMONT
NEW HAMPSHIRE
Lebanon
Laconia
CONCORD
Portsmouth
Manchester
Nashua
Lowell
Glens Falls
Oneida Lake
Rochester
Niagara Falls
Buffalo
Syracuse
Utica
Schenectady
Troy
ALBANY
MASSACHUSETTS
BOSTON
Pittsfield
Worcester
Cape Cod
Plymouth
Orleans
Springfield
Finger Lakes
NEW YORK
Catskill Mountains
Ithaca
Dunkirk
Olean
Elmira
Binghamton
Kingston
HARTFORD
PROVIDENCE
Warwick
New Bedford
Jamestown
Mansfield
CONNECTICUT
Newport
RHODE ISLAND
Nantucket
Nantucket Island
Waterbury
New Haven
Montauk Point
Cleveland
Ashtabula
Erie
Warren
Meadville
Scranton
Wilkes Barre
Middletown
Milford
Bridgeport
Stamford
Yonkers
Long Island
Youngstown
Canton
Williamsport
PENNSYLVANIA
Paterson
Jersey City
Newark
Elizabeth
New York
State College
Allentown
Altoona
Reading
Wheeling
Zanesville
Pittsburgh
Carlisle
HARRISBURG
TRENTON
Philadelphia
Uniontown
York
Lancaster
Wilmington
NEW JERSEY
Clarksburg
Parkersburg
Hagerstown
Cumberland
MARYLAND
Baltimore
DOVER
DELAWARE
WEST VIRGINIA
St Albans
Spruce Knob 4,859ft (1,481m)
Arlington
Alexandria
ANNAPOLIS
WASHINGTON, DC
Salisbury
CHARLESTON
Beckley
Harrisonburg
Fredericksburg
Staunton
Charlottesville
Potomac
Chesapeake Bay
Assateague Island
Bluestone Lake
VIRGINIA
RICHMOND
Petersburg
Cape Charles
Bluefield
Roanoke
Newport News
Hampton
Norfolk
Portsmouth
Virginia Beach
NORTH CAROLINA
Appalachian Mountains
Hudson
Ohio
ATLANTIC OCEAN

Southeastern United States

Country music
Nashville, Tennessee, is the home of country music. This music style, with songs about heartbreak and poverty, became popular in the 1930s.

FLORIDA
POPULATION 16,397,000 ✳ CAPITAL TALLAHASSEE

GEORGIA
POPULATION 8,384,000 ✳ CAPITAL ATLANTA

NORTH CAROLINA
POPULATION 8,186,000 ✳ CAPITAL RALEIGH

TENNESSEE
POPULATION 5,740,000 ✳ CAPITAL NASHVILLE

ALABAMA
POPULATION 4,464,000 ✳ CAPITAL MONTGOMERY

SOUTH CAROLINA
POPULATION 4,063,000 ✳ CAPITAL COLUMBIA

MISSISSIPPI
POPULATION 2,858,000 ✳ CAPITAL JACKSON

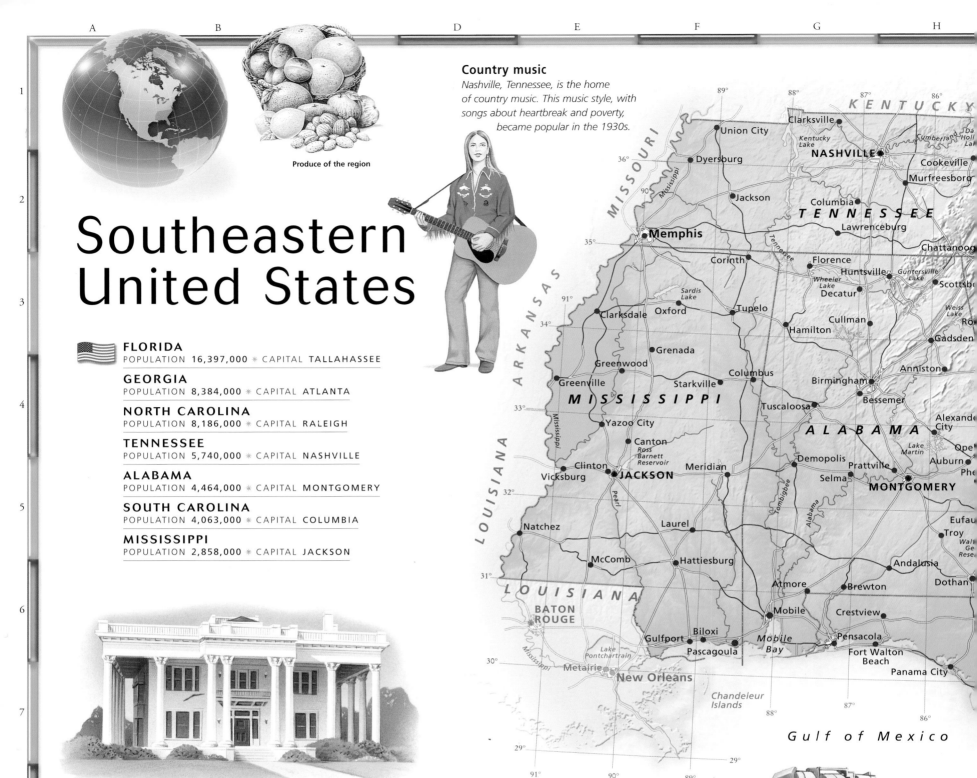

Plantation mansion
In the early 1800s, wealthy plantation owners in the southern states built large, elegant homes inspired by classical Greek architecture. These mansions featured imposing covered porches with pillars, sweeping staircases and huge ballrooms. They were often painted white.

In 1803, the USA paid France US$15 million for 828,000 square miles (2,144,500 sq km) of land west of the Mississippi River. This Louisiana Purchase, as it was called, doubled the nation's size.

Mississippi steamboat
The Mississippi is the largest river in North America and one of the world's busiest commercial waterways. Steam-powered boats carried building and farm goods, food and people along the river throughout the 1900s. Today, paddle-wheelers are tourist boats.

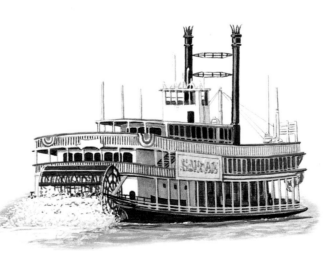

Cotton farming
The USA is one of the world's largest cotton producers. Cotton plantations were established in the southern states in the early 1800s. The invention of machinery for harvesting and cleaning the cotton revolutionized the industry in the mid-1800s and reduced the need for human labor.

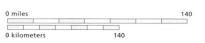

Gulf of Mexico

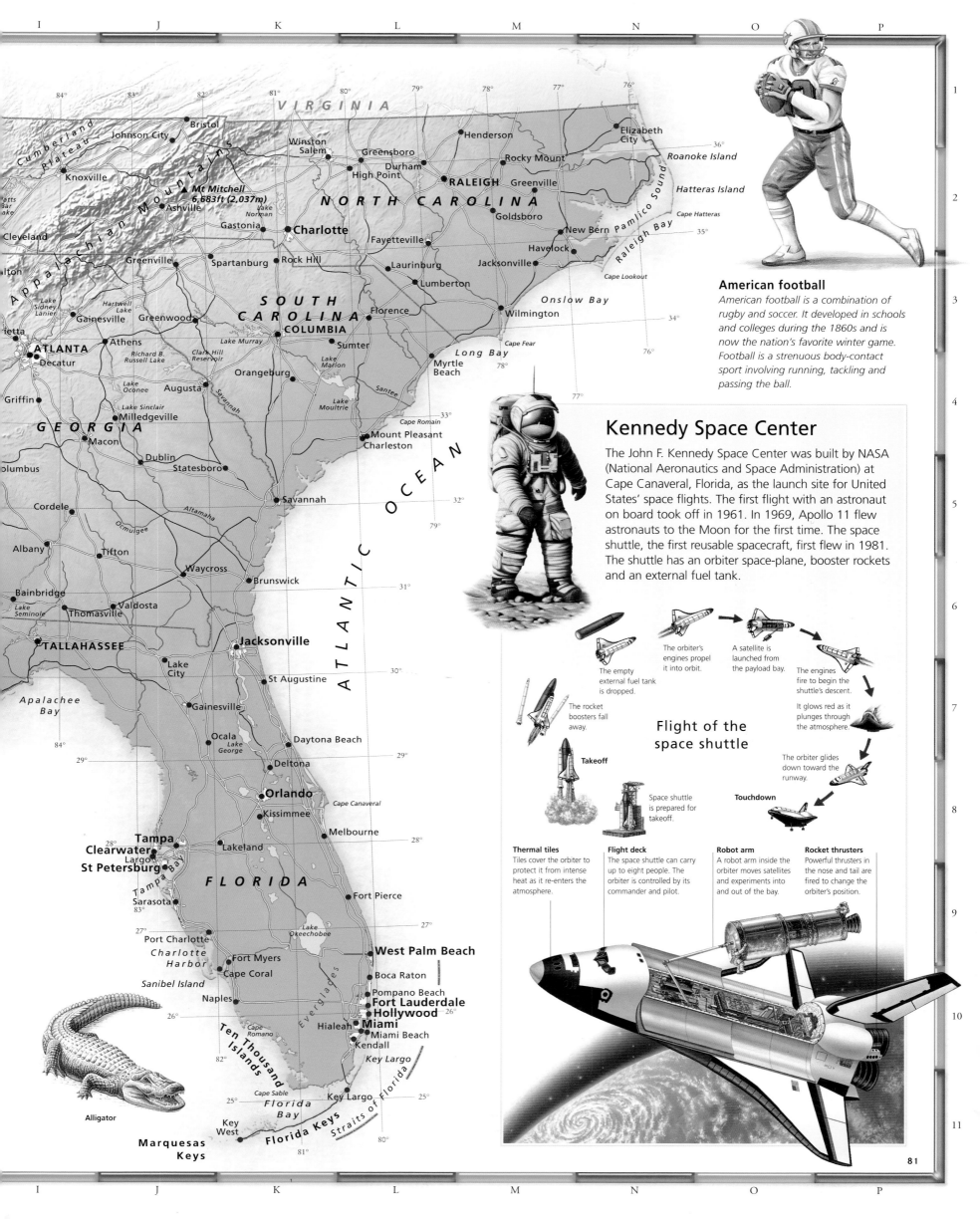

Map grid columns: I J K L M N O P
Map grid rows: 1 2 3 4 5 6 7 8 9 10 11

VIRGINIA

Johnson City
Bristol
Cumberland Plateau
Knoxville
Cleveland
Watts Bar Lake
Mt Mitchell 6,683ft (2,037m)
Ashville
Lake Norman
Winston Salem
Greensboro
Durham
High Point
Henderson
Elizabeth City
Roanoke Island
Hatteras Island
36°

NORTH CAROLINA
RALEIGH
Greenville
Goldsboro
Rocky Mount
New Bern
Pamlico Sound
Cape Hatteras
35°

Charlotte
Gastonia
Fayetteville
Havelock
Jacksonville
Raleigh Bay

Greenville
Spartanburg
Rock Hill
Laurinburg
Lumberton
Cape Lookout

SOUTH CAROLINA
Florence
Onslow Bay
34°

COLUMBIA
Sumter
Wilmington

Orangeburg
Lake Murray
Lake Marion
Long Bay
Myrtle Beach
Cape Fear
76°
78°

Augusta
Lake Moultrie
Santee
33°
Cape Romain

GEORGIA
Milledgeville
Lake Sinclair
Clark Hill Reservoir
Mount Pleasant
Charleston

Macon
Dublin
Statesboro

Cordele
Altamaha
Savannah
32°
ATLANTIC OCEAN
79°

Albany
Tifton
Ocmulgee

Waycross
Brunswick
31°

Bainbridge
Valdosta
Lake Seminole
Thomasville

TALLAHASSEE
Jacksonville
30°

Lake City
St Augustine

Apalachee Bay
Gainesville
29°

Ocala
Lake George
Daytona Beach
29°

Deltona

FLORIDA
Orlando
Cape Canaveral
77°

Kissimmee
Melbourne
28°

Tampa
Clearwater
Largo
St Petersburg
Lakeland
28°

Tampa Bay
Sarasota
83°
Fort Pierce

Port Charlotte
Lake Okeechobee
27°

Charlotte Harbor
Fort Myers
West Palm Beach
Boca Raton
Pompano Beach
Fort Lauderdale
Hollywood
Hialeah
Miami
Miami Beach
Kendall
26°

Cape Coral
Naples
Everglades

Ten Thousand Islands
Cape Romano
82°

Alligator

Cape Sable
Key Largo
25°
Florida Bay
Florida Keys
Straits of Florida

Marquesas Keys
Key West
81°
80°

American football

American football is a combination of rugby and soccer. It developed in schools and colleges during the 1860s and is now the nation's favorite winter game. Football is a strenuous body-contact sport involving running, tackling and passing the ball.

Kennedy Space Center

The John F. Kennedy Space Center was built by NASA (National Aeronautics and Space Administration) at Cape Canaveral, Florida, as the launch site for United States' space flights. The first flight with an astronaut on board took off in 1961. In 1969, Apollo 11 flew astronauts to the Moon for the first time. The space shuttle, the first reusable spacecraft, first flew in 1981. The shuttle has an orbiter space-plane, booster rockets and an external fuel tank.

Flight of the space shuttle

The empty external fuel tank is dropped.

The rocket boosters fall away.

The orbiter's engines propel it into orbit.

A satellite is launched from the payload bay.

The engines fire to begin the shuttle's descent.

It glows red as it plunges through the atmosphere.

The orbiter glides down toward the runway.

Takeoff
Space shuttle is prepared for takeoff.

Touchdown

Thermal tiles
Tiles cover the orbiter to protect it from intense heat as it re-enters the atmosphere.

Flight deck
The space shuttle can carry up to eight people. The orbiter is controlled by its commander and pilot.

Robot arm
A robot arm inside the orbiter moves satellites and experiments into and out of the bay.

Rocket thrusters
Powerful thrusters in the nose and tail are fired to change the orbiter's position.

Central United States

Bison herds
Herds of bison once roamed the Great Plains. When settlers arrived, they were hunted almost to extinction. Today, their numbers are gradually increasing.

Gateway Arch
The arch overlooking the Mississippi River in St Louis, Missouri, commemorates the westward expansion of the USA in the 1800s. Built in 1965, it is 630 feet (198 m) tall.

The Sioux
This nomadic tribe lived in tepees and hunted buffalo on the Great Plains. Sioux women embroidered ceremonial buckskins with beads and porcupine quills.

TEXAS
POPULATION 21,325,000 * CAPITAL AUSTIN

MISSOURI
POPULATION 5,630,000 * CAPITAL JEFFERSON CITY

MINNESOTA
POPULATION 4,972,000 * CAPITAL ST PAUL

LOUISIANA
POPULATION 4,465,000 * CAPITAL BATON ROUGE

COLORADO
POPULATION 4,418,000 * CAPITAL DENVER

OKLAHOMA
POPULATION 3,460,000 * CAPITAL OKLAHOMA CITY

IOWA
POPULATION 2,923,000 * CAPITAL DES MOINES

KANSAS
POPULATION 2,695,000 * CAPITAL TOPEKA

ARKANSAS
POPULATION 2,692,000 * CAPITAL LITTLE ROCK

NEW MEXICO
POPULATION 1,829,000 * CAPITAL SANTA FE

NEBRASKA
POPULATION 1,713,000 * CAPITAL LINCOLN

MONTANA
POPULATION 904,000 * CAPITAL HELENA

SOUTH DAKOTA
POPULATION 757,000 * CAPITAL PIERRE

NORTH DAKOTA
POPULATION 634,000 * CAPITAL BISMARCK

WYOMING
POPULATION 494,000 * CAPITAL CHEYENNE

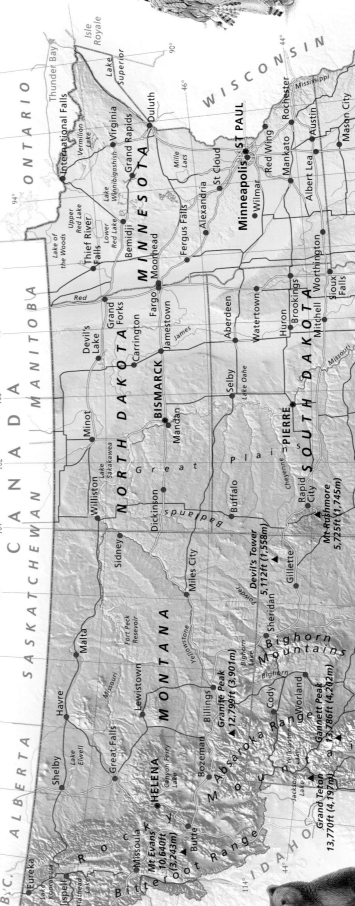

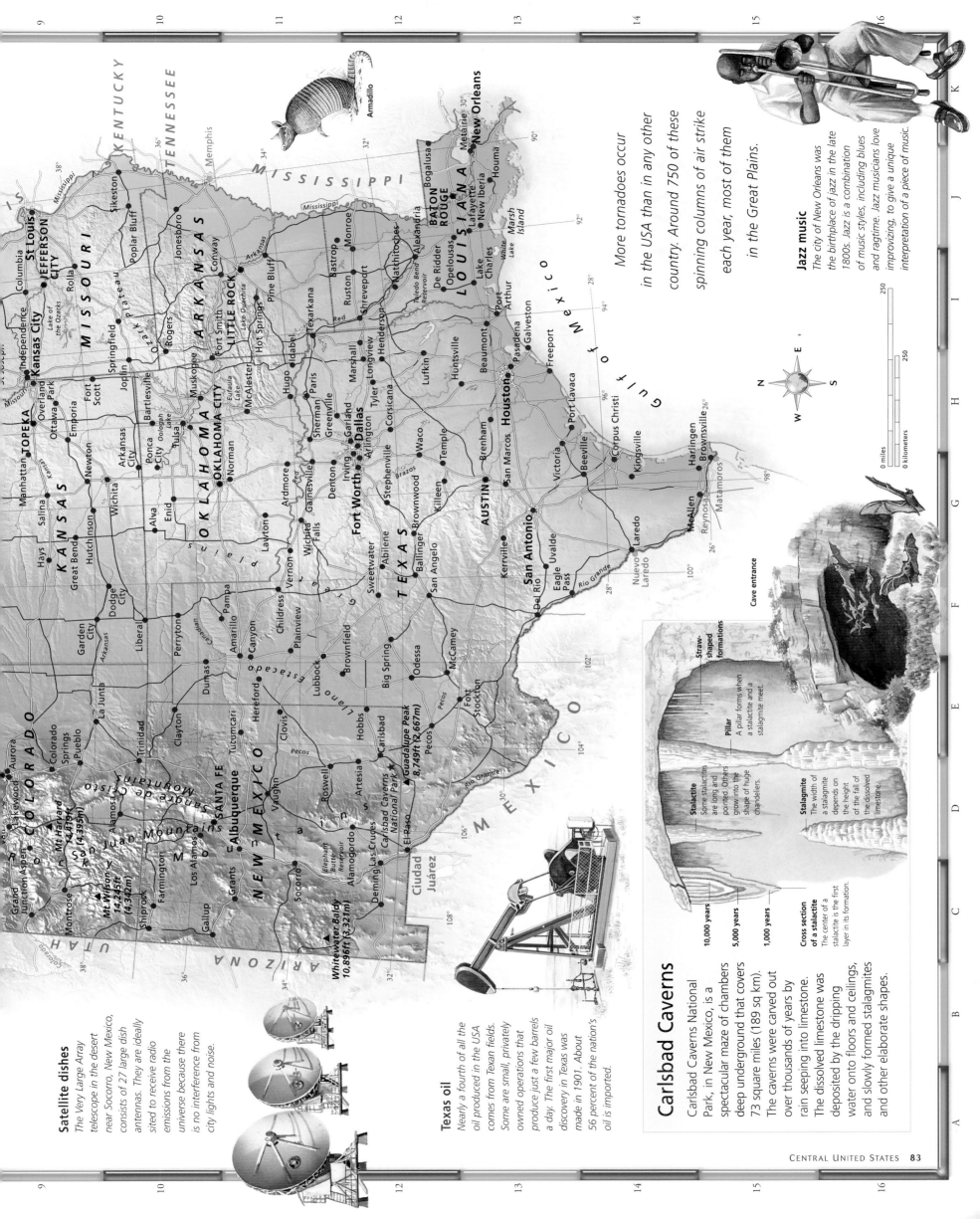

Armadillo

KENTUCKY
TENNESSEE
MISSISSIPPI
Memphis
Mississippi

Sikeston
Poplar Bluff
Jonesboro
Conway
Batesville
Rogers
Springfield
Rolla
Columbia
St Louis
JEFFERSON CITY
Independence
Kansas City
Overland Park
Ottawa Park
Emporia
Fort Scott
Joplin
MISSOURI

Lake of the Ozarks
Ozark Plateau

ARKANSAS
LITTLE ROCK
Pine Bluff
Hot Springs
Fort Smith
Muskogee
McAlester
Eufaula Lake
Lake Ouachita
Idabel
Hugo
Paris
Sherman
Greenville
Texarkana
Red

LOUISIANA
BATON ROUGE
New Orleans
Metairie
Bogalusa
Houma
New Iberia
Lafayette
Alexandria
Natchitoches
Monroe
Ruston
Shreveport
Bastrop
De Ridder
Opelousas
Lake Charles
Port Arthur
White Lake
Marsh Island
Toledo Bend Reservoir

Gulf of Mexico
Mexico

OKLAHOMA CITY
Norman
Ponca City
Tulsa
Bartlesville
Oologah Lake
Enid
Alva
Lawton
Ardmore
Gainesville
Denton
Sherman
Garland
Dallas
Fort Worth
Arlington
Irving
Corsicana
Tyler
Longview
Henderson
Marshall
Waco
Temple
Killeen
Brownwood
Stephenville
Abilene
Sweetwater
Ballinger
San Angelo
Vernon
Wichita Falls
Childress
Plainview
Lubbock
Brownfield
Big Spring
Odessa
McCamey
Fort Stockton
Pecos
Carlsbad
Artesia
Roswell
Hobbs

TEXAS
AUSTIN
San Marcos
Brenham
Houston
Pasadena
Galveston
Freeport
Port Lavaca
Victoria
Beeville
Corpus Christi
Kingsville
San Antonio
Uvalde
Eagle Pass
Del Rio
Nuevo Laredo
Laredo
McAllen
Harlingen
Brownsville
Matamoros
Reynosa
Beaumont
Huntsville
Lufkin

Kerrville

Rio Grande
Pecos
Brazos
Llano Estacado

NEW MEXICO
SANTA FE
Albuquerque
Los Alamos
Santa Fe
Grants
Gallup
Socorro
Vaughn
Tucumcari
Clovis
Clayton
Hereford
Canyon
Amarillo
Pampa
Perryton
Dumas
Dalhart

Las Cruces
Deming
Alamogordo
Elephant Butte Reservoir
El Paso
Ciudad Juárez
MEXICO

Carlsbad Caverns National Park
Guadalupe Peak 8,749ft (2,667m)
Whitewater Baldy 10,896ft (3,321m)
Mt Wilson 14,245ft (4,342m)
Sangre de Cristo Mountains
San Juan Mountains

COLORADO
Aurora
Lakewood
Grand Junction
Aspen
Montrose
Colorado Springs
Pueblo
Trinidad
La Junta
Garden City
Dodge City
Liberal

KANSAS
TOPEKA
Manhattan
Salina
Hays
Great Bend
Hutchinson
Wichita
Newton
Arkansas City

ARIZONA
UTAH

Mt Harvard 14,419ft (4,395m)

Satellite dishes

The Very Large Array telescope in the desert near Socorro, New Mexico, consists of 27 large dish antennas. They are ideally sited to receive radio emissions from the universe because there is no interference from city lights and noise.

Texas oil

Nearly a fourth of all the oil produced in the USA comes from Texan fields. Some are small, privately owned operations that produce just a few barrels a day. The first major oil discovery in Texas was made in 1901. About 56 percent of the nation's oil is imported.

Carlsbad Caverns

Carlsbad Caverns National Park, in New Mexico, is a spectacular maze of chambers deep underground that covers 73 square miles (189 sq km). The caverns were carved out over thousands of years by rain seeping into limestone. The dissolved limestone was deposited by the dripping water onto floors and ceilings, and slowly formed stalagmites and other elaborate shapes.

Cross section of a stalactite
The center of a stalactite is the first layer in its formation.

10,000 years
5,000 years
1,000 years

Strawshaped formations

Stalactite
Some stalactites are long and pointed. Others grow into the shape of huge chandeliers.

Pillar
A pillar forms when a stalactite and a stalagmite meet.

Stalagmite
The width of a stalagmite depends on the height of the fall of the dissolved limestone.

Cave entrance

More tornadoes occur in the USA than in any other country. Around 750 of these spinning columns of air strike each year, most of them in the Great Plains.

Jazz music

The city of New Orleans was the birthplace of jazz in the late 1800s. Jazz is a combination of music styles, including blues and ragtime. Jazz musicians love improvizing, to give a unique interpretation of a piece of music.

N W E S

0 miles 250
0 kilometers 250

Western United States

CALIFORNIA
POPULATION 34,501,000 * CAPITAL SACRAMENTO

WASHINGTON
POPULATION 5,988,000 * CAPITAL OLYMPIA

ARIZONA
POPULATION 5,307,000 * CAPITAL PHOENIX

OREGON
POPULATION 3,473,000 * CAPITAL SALEM

UTAH
POPULATION 2,270,000 * CAPITAL SALT LAKE CITY

NEVADA
POPULATION 2,106,000 * CAPITAL CARSON CITY

IDAHO
POPULATION 1,321,000 * CAPITAL BOISE

HAWAII
POPULATION 1,224,000 * CAPITAL HONOLULU

ALASKA
POPULATION 635,000 * CAPITAL JUNEAU

The tallest tree in the world is a coast redwood in California called the Stratosphere Giant.

It is more than 369 feet (112 m) tall.

Bald eagle

In 1782, a team of judges chose the bald eagle as the national bird of the United States of America. They liked its fierce expression, and preferred it to its rival in the competition, the wild turkey.

Silicon Valley

In the early 1980s, an area in the San Jose and Santa Clara valleys in California became a center for high-technology industries. Silicon is a material used in electronic equipment such as computers.

Wind turbines

Wind is an important source of energy. Turbines harness the power of wind for electricity. About 1 percent of electricity in California is generated by wind.

Frontier wagon trail

Moose

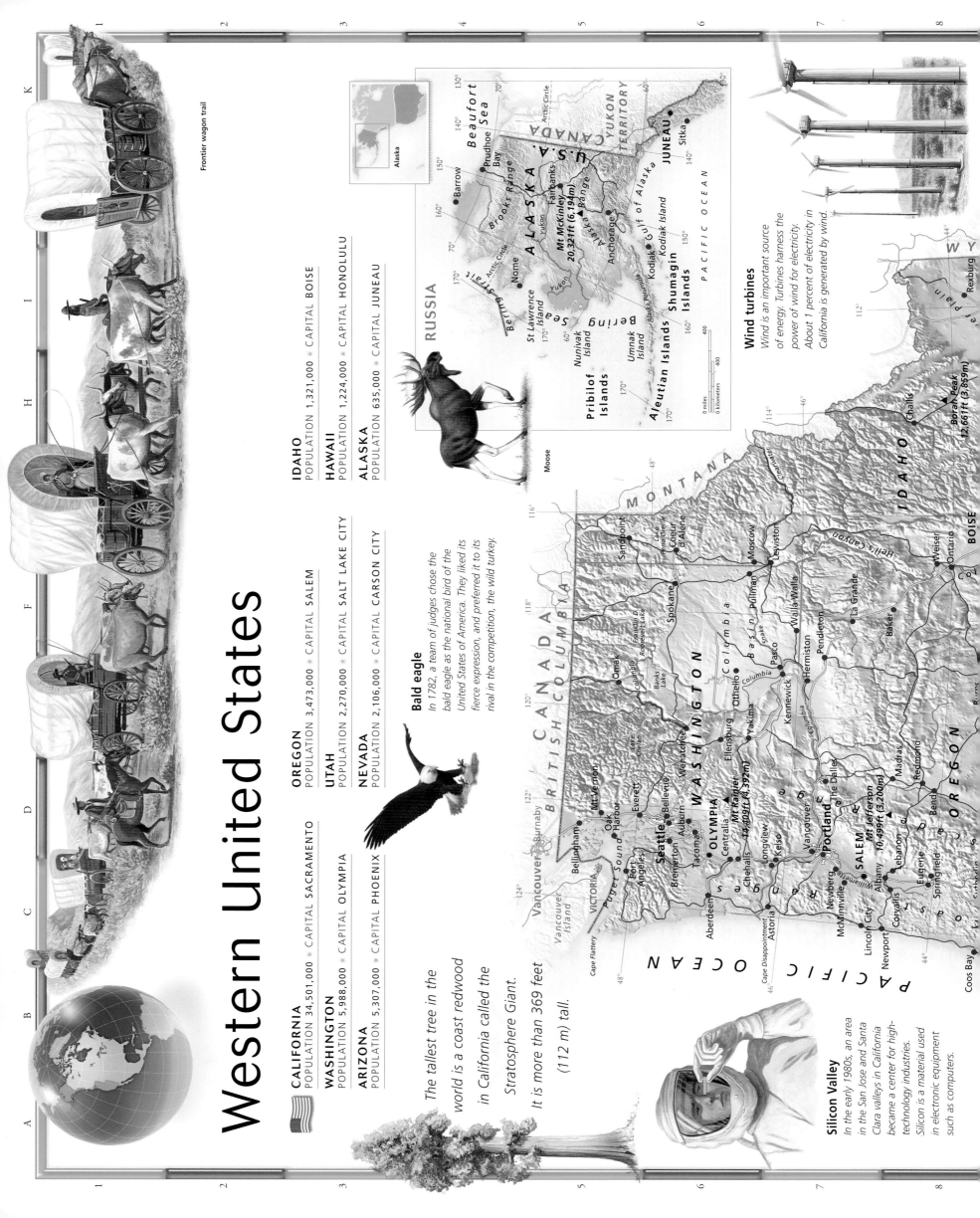

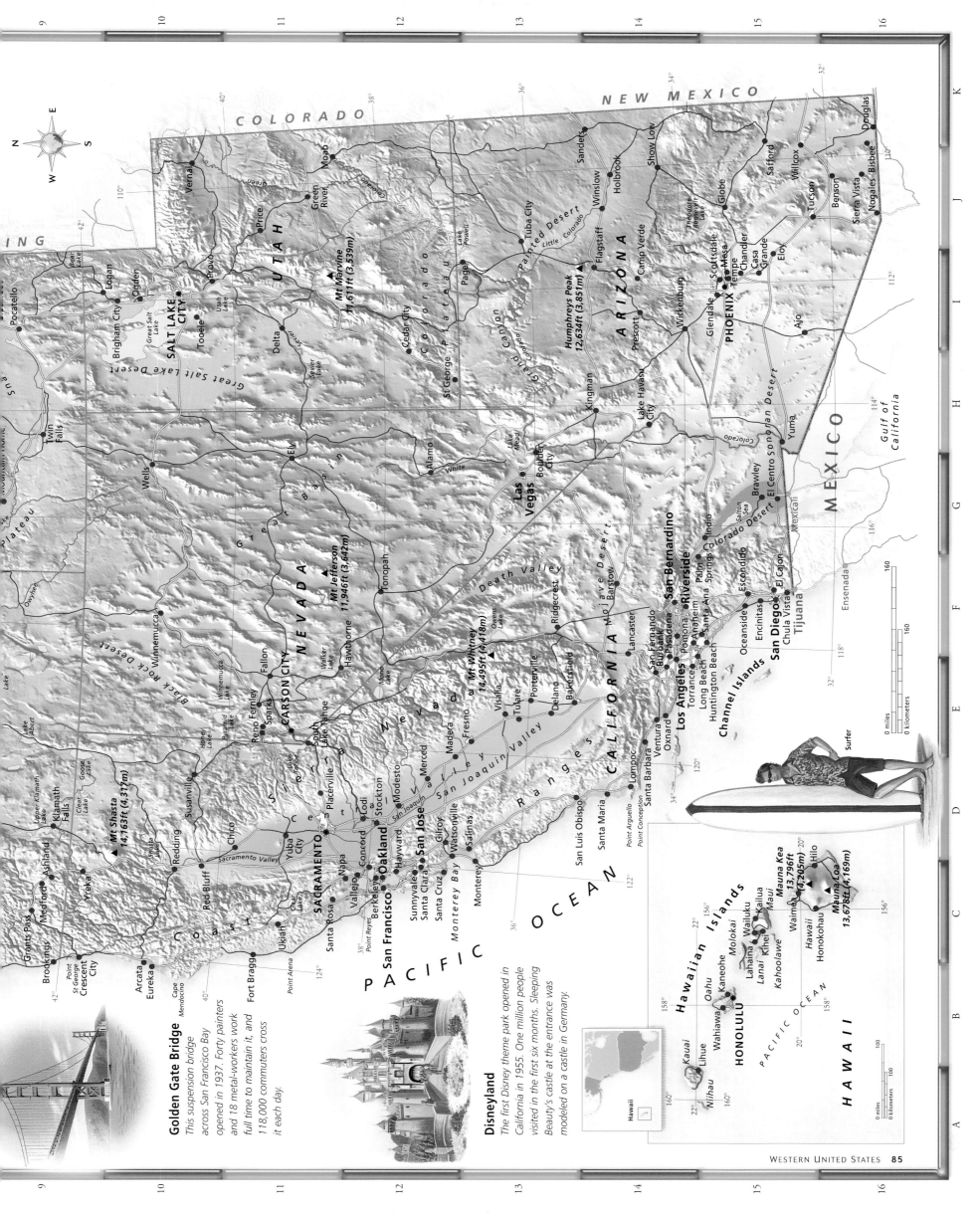

WYOMING

UTAH

NEVADA

CARSON CITY

CALIFORNIA

ARIZONA

MEXICO

PACIFIC OCEAN

Great Salt Lake Desert

Great Salt Lake

Black Rock Desert

Great Basin

Mojave Desert

Death Valley

Sonoran Desert

Colorado Desert

Gulf of California

Sierra Nevada

San Joaquin Valley

Sacramento Valley

Central Valley

Coast Ranges

Painted Desert

Colorado Plateau

Mt Marvine
11,611ft (3,539m)

Humphreys Peak
12,634ft (3,851m)

Mt Jefferson
11,946ft (3,642m)

Mt Whitney
14,495ft (4,418m)

Mt Shasta
14,163ft (4,317m)

Vernal
Price
Moab
Green River
Provo
Logan
Ogden
SALT LAKE CITY
Tooele
Brigham City
Pocatello
Twin Falls
Wells
Winnemucca
Delta
Cedar City
St George
Kingman
Lake Havasu City
Page
Tuba City
Winslow
Holbrook
Show Low
Sanders
Flagstaff
Camp Verde
Prescott
Wickenburg
Globe
Safford
Willcox
Sierra Vista
Nogales
Bisbee
Benson
Tucson
Eloy
Casa Grande
Chandler
Tempe
Mesa
Scottsdale
PHOENIX
Glendale
Ajo
Yuma
Mexicali
El Centro
Brawley
Indio
Palm Springs
Escondido
Oceanside
Encinitas
Chula Vista
Tijuana
Ensenada
San Diego
El Cajon
Riverside
San Bernardino
Santa Ana
Anaheim
Pomona
Pasadena
Burbank
San Fernando
Los Angeles
Long Beach
Huntington Beach
Torrance
Lancaster
Barstow
Ridgecrest
Bakersfield
Delano
Porterville
Tulare
Visalia
Fresno
Madera
Merced
Modesto
Stockton
Lodi
Placerville
Sacramento
Napa
Vallejo
Concord
Berkeley
Oakland
Hayward
San Francisco
San Jose
Sunnyvale
Santa Clara
Santa Cruz
Watsonville
Gilroy
Salinas
Monterey
Santa Maria
Santa Barbara
Ventura
Oxnard
San Luis Obispo
Lompoc
Redding
Red Bluff
Chico
Yuba City
Susanville
Reno
Sparks
Fernley
Fallon
Hawthorne
Tonopah
Alamo
Boulder City
Las Vegas
Elko
Eureka
Arcata
Ukiah
Santa Rosa
Fort Bragg
Crescent City
Brookings
Grants Pass
Medford
Ashland
Yreka
Klamath Falls
South Lake Tahoe

Pyramid Lake
Walker Lake
Honey Lake
Mono Lake
Owens Lake
Lake Mead
Lake Powell
Lake Tahoe
Utah Lake
Sevier Lake
Pyramid Lake
Goose Lake
Clear Lake
Upper Klamath Lake
Lake Abert
Bear Lake

Colorado
Green River
Little Colorado
Gila
San Joaquin
White
Owens

Channel Islands

Point Reyes
Point Arena
Cape Mendocino
Point Arguello
Point Conception
Point St George

Monterey Bay

Salton Sea

Theodore Roosevelt Lake

Grand Canyon

Golden Gate Bridge
This suspension bridge across San Francisco Bay opened in 1937. Forty painters and 18 metal-workers work full time to maintain it, and 118,000 commuters cross it each day.

Disneyland
The first Disney theme park opened in California in 1955. One million people visited in the first six months. Sleeping Beauty's castle at the entrance was modeled on a castle in Germany.

HAWAII

Hawaiian Islands

Kauai
Niihau
Oahu
Molokai
Lanai
Maui
Kahoolawe
Hawaii
Lihue
Wahiawa
Kaneohe
HONOLULU
Wailuku
Lahaina
Kihei
Kailua
Waimea
Honokohau
Hilo
Honolulu

Mauna Kea
13,796ft (4,205m)

Mauna Loa
13,678ft (4,169m)

PACIFIC OCEAN

Surfer

Hawaii

0 miles 160
0 kilometers 160

0 miles 100
0 kilometers 100

Alaska was bought by the USA from Russia in 1867 for US$7,200,000.

United States of America

LAND AREA	3,717,813 sq miles (9,629,091 sq km)
OFFICIAL LANGUAGE	English
MAIN RELIGION	Christian
LIFE EXPECTANCY	77 years
LITERACY	97%

USING THE LAND

- Forest and woodland
- Arable land
- Grazing
- Arid or marginal

Anchorage

Juneau

Oranges
More oranges are harvested yearly in the USA than any other fruits. Florida, the center of the citrus-growing industry, produces one-third of all US citrus fruits. Most of the oranges from Florida are made into juice, while most of the oranges from California are for eating.

NATURAL FEATURES

Yellowstone National Park
Yellowstone, the world's first national park, was set up in 1872 and spreads across three states. It covers 3,468 square miles (8,982 sq km) and features about 10,000 natural springs, or geysers (left). Grizzly bears, bison and moose wander freely around the park.

Old Faithful

Mt McKinley
At 20,321 feet (6,194 m), Mt McKinley is the highest mountain in North America. It is part of the long Alaska Range and is a major attraction in the Denali National Park. Its peak is often shrouded in cloud, especially during summer.

Monument Valley
Situated on the border between Arizona and Utah, Monument Valley (above) is owned and managed by the Navajo people. It is famous for its unique rock formations and remnants of volcanoes.

Great Lakes
The Great Lakes—Michigan, Huron, Ontario, Superior and Erie—are the world's largest group of freshwater lakes. Together they make up 18 percent of Earth's fresh surface water.

Grand Canyon
Formed over the last 6 million years, as the Colorado River slowly cuts through layers of rock, the Grand Canyon in northwestern Arizona is the world's largest canyon. It is 285 miles (456 km) long, 1 mile (1.6 km) deep and up to 18 miles (29 km) wide. In 1919, the canyon became a national park.

LARGEST CITIES

New York 8,135,000

Los Angeles 3,901,000

Chicago 2,888,000

Houston 2,072,000

Philadelphia 1,483,000

- Cereals
- Corn (maize)
- Fruit and vegetables
- Fruit
- Citrus fruits
- Wine
- Cotton
- Tobacco
- Sugarcane
- Soybeans
- Groundnuts
- Beef cattle
- Sheep
- Fishing
- Shellfish
- Industrial center
- Mining
- Oil production
- Timber
- Tourism
- Winter sports

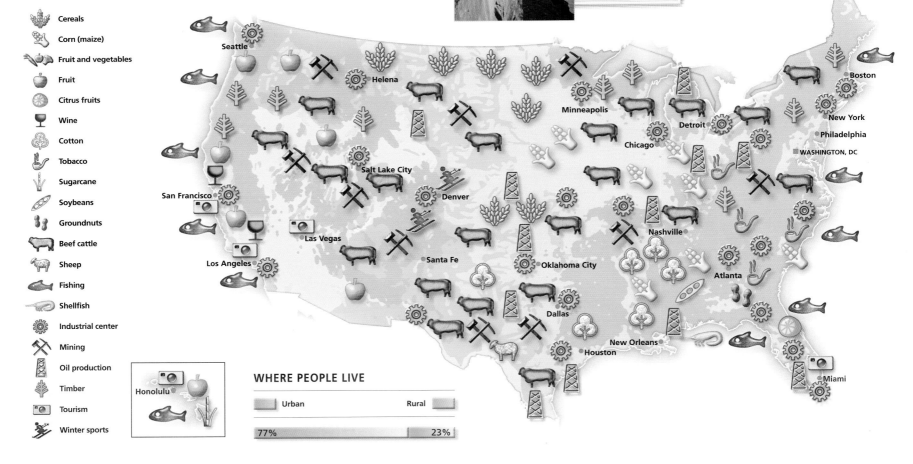

Seattle
Helena
Minneapolis
Detroit
Boston
New York
Philadelphia
WASHINGTON, DC
Chicago
Salt Lake City
San Francisco
Denver
Nashville
Las Vegas
Santa Fe
Oklahoma City
Atlanta
Los Angeles
Dallas
New Orleans
Houston
Miami

Honolulu

WHERE PEOPLE LIVE

Urban	Rural
77%	23%

PLACES

Washington, DC

Named for George Washington, America's first president, Washington, DC is the capital of the USA. The city was designed for that purpose before it was built. It is home to the Capitol building, where both houses of Congress meet, and the White House, where the president lives and works.

Capitol building, Washington, DC

Honolulu

The capital city and main port of Hawaii, Honolulu is the only US city located in the tropics, the only US city with a royal palace (Iolani Palace) and the only US city with an equal blend of western, Asian and Polynesian influences.

Cliff Palace

Cliff Palace

About 1,000 years ago, the Anasazi people began to build high stone dwellings along canyon walls in southwestern Colorado. Cliff Palace, the largest of these dwellings, contains more than 200 rooms.

San Francisco

Famous for the Golden Gate Bridge and its cable cars, San Francisco was almost destroyed by an earthquake in 1906. In its bay is the former prison Alcatraz, now open for tourists.

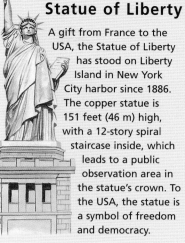

Statue of Liberty

A gift from France to the USA, the Statue of Liberty has stood on Liberty Island in New York City harbor since 1886. The copper statue is 151 feet (46 m) high, with a 12-story spiral staircase inside, which leads to a public observation area in the statue's crown. To the USA, the statue is a symbol of freedom and democracy.

TRADITIONS AND CULTURE

Thanksgiving Day

For almost 400 years, Americans have observed Thanksgiving Day on the fourth Thursday in November. What began as a religious event is now a family day set aside to give thanks for blessings received.

Halloween

On 31 October every year, Americans celebrate the festival of Halloween, when children wear costumes, go trick-or-treating and make jack-o'-lanterns out of pumpkins.

Halloween jack-o'-lantern

Cheerleaders

Beginning in 1898 at the University of Minnesota, cheerleading had become popular across the nation by 1920. Cheerleaders dance and lead the spectators to support their team with chants and cheers at athletic events, especially basketball and football games.

Rap music

Rap music in America developed first in New York City. It is a form of music that is spoken quickly to match the rhythm. It is particularly popular with African-American teenagers. Some rap music has been criticized for its violent lyrics.

Hollywood

Hollywood, a district of Los Angeles, is known as the movie capital of the world. The first film studio was built there in 1911 and within a year, 15 others had sprung up. The late 1920s saw the first production of sound films, and by the 1930s movies, such as *Gone with the Wind* (1939), were being produced on a grand scale. Hollywood is also famous for "The Strip"—a section of shops, nightclubs and restaurants along Sunset Boulevard.

PEOPLE

Sitting Bull c 1834–90

Born in what is present-day South Dakota, Sitting Bull was a medicine man, and by around 1867 was leader of all the Sioux Indians. His advice before the battle of Little Bighorn resulted in victory for the Sioux.

Annie Oakley 1860–1926

Annie Oakley was a sharpshooter who starred in Buffalo Bill's traveling Wild West show for more than 16 years. Firing from the back of a galloping horse was one of her special skills.

Annie Oakley

Wright brothers

In 1903, Wilbur and Orville Wright successfully flew the world's first power-driven plane in North Carolina. The plane, which the brothers had invented, flew 852 feet (260 m) and managed to stay in the air for 59 seconds.

Martin Luther King 1929–68

Martin Luther King was a Baptist minister and a leader of the civil rights movement. His policy of nonviolent protest won him the Nobel Peace Prize in 1964. After his assassination, he became only the second American whose birthday is honored by a public holiday.

Elvis Presley 1935–77

Born in Tupelo, Mississippi, Elvis Presley was one of the world's greatest stars of rock music. He began his singing career in 1954, and his concert style and music divided people. Some towns even banned his shows. Elvis sold more than 1 billion records and starred in 33 films.

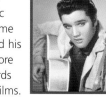

HISTORY AT A GLANCE

1607
English ships, under the command of Captain Christopher Newport, land and establish a permanent colony at Jamestown, Virginia.

1620
English pilgrims seeking religious freedom arrive on the *Mayflower* at Plymouth, Massachusetts.

1775–81
The War of Independence begins at Lexington, Massachusetts, when the American colonists rebel against the English soldiers. War lasts for six years.

Battle of Lexington

1789
George Washington becomes the first president of the new USA. He supports the new constitution, which sets out the country's laws.

1836
Texan soldiers fighting for their independence from Mexico hold off the Mexicans for 13 days at the Alamo, a mission in San Antonio, Texas.

The Alamo

1861–65
The Civil War is fought when the South withdraws from the USA. The North wins the war, keeps the states united, and ends slavery.

1870s
Wars are fought between Native Americans and the white colonists. These frontier wars lead to the loss of many lives on both sides.

1920–33
Laws are in place for 13 years prohibiting the manufacture and sale of alcoholic drinks.

1929–39
Business slumps worldwide after stock values in the USA fall. The Great Depression ends when industries get a boost because of World War II.

1941
The Japanese invade Pearl Harbor, bringing the USA into World War II. The war ends in 1945 when the USA drops atomic bombs on Japan.

1954
The Supreme Court rules against racial segregation in public schools and meets enormous resistance from white people.

1964–73
The Vietnam War is fought when the USA opposes North Vietnam's invasion of the South. The cold war between the communist and non-communist nations eases.

1969
First people on the moon, Neil Armstrong and Edwin Aldrin, land the Apollo 11 module, *Eagle*.

Footprint on the moon

1991 and 2003
In 1991, the USA leads a war against Iraq, which has invaded Kuwait. In 2003, the USA again fights Iraq and ends the reign of Saddam Hussein.

Mexico

MEXICO POPULATION **104,908,000** ✳ CAPITAL **MEXICO CITY**

Sombrero

Monarch butterflies

The monarch butterfly is a long-distance traveler. Each year, tens of millions of these colorful butterflies fly up to 2,500 miles (4,000 km) from Canada and the east coast of the USA to spend the winter in Mexico.

Cattle rancher

Only about one-fifth of Mexico is suitable for farming. The northern part is hot and dry, and cattle ranching is the main activity there. Mexico has large supplies of oil and is the world's biggest supplier of silver.

Piñata

A piñata is a papier-mâché container filled with toys and sweets. At Mexican celebrations, a piñata is hung from the ceiling or a tree branch, and children take turns trying to break it open with a stick to get the treats.

Traditional dancers

Folk dances and music are popular at fiesta time. Many of the dances performed today are based on Indian dances from before the Spanish conquest of Mexico.

The cardón cactus is the world's largest cactus. It grows in the deserts of the Baja California peninsula. Some are nearly 70 feet (21 m) high. These plants can live for more than 300 years.

San Diego
Tijuana
Mexicali
San Luis
Rio Colorado
Ensenada
UNITED STATES
El Paso
Ciudad Juárez
Cerro de La Encantada 10,157ft (3,096m)
Nogales
Agua Prieta
El Barreal
Cabo San Quintín
Caborca
Cananea
Magdalena
Nuevo Casas Grandes
Cumpas
El Sueco
Isla Ángel de la Guarda
Hermosillo
Chihuahua
Rosarito
Isla Cedros
Bahía Sebastián Vizcaíno
Isla Tiburón
Sonora
Cuauhtémoc
Punta Eugenia
Guerrero Negro
Empalme
Guaymas
Esperanza
Ciudad Obregón
Navojoa
Huatabampo
Punta Rosa
Loreto
San Blas
Los Mochis
Guasave
Guamúchil
Bahía La Paz
Culiacán
Isla Santa Margarita
La Paz
El Dorado
Tropic of Cancer
Santa Genoveva 7,894ft (2,406m)
Cabo San Lucas
Cabo San Lucas
Mazatlán
Escuina
Islas Marías
Punta de
Cabo Corrie

PACIFIC OCEAN

Gulf of California

Sierra San Pedro Mártir

Baja California

Sierra Madre

Colorado

Magdalena

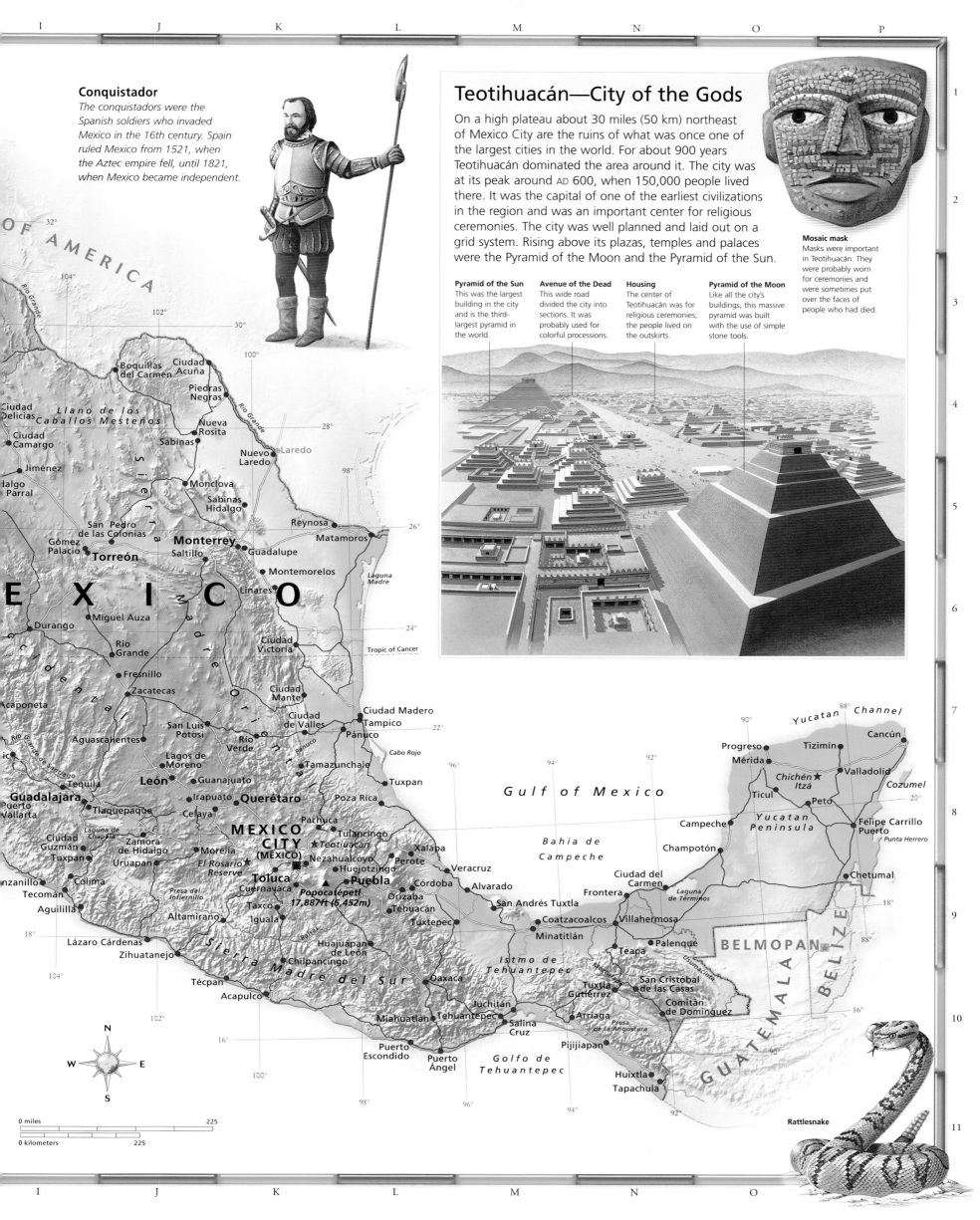

Conquistador

The conquistadors were the Spanish soldiers who invaded Mexico in the 16th century. Spain ruled Mexico from 1521, when the Aztec empire fell, until 1821, when Mexico became independent.

Teotihuacán—City of the Gods

On a high plateau about 30 miles (50 km) northeast of Mexico City are the ruins of what was once one of the largest cities in the world. For about 900 years Teotihuacán dominated the area around it. The city was at its peak around AD 600, when 150,000 people lived there. It was the capital of one of the earliest civilizations in the region and was an important center for religious ceremonies. The city was well planned and laid out on a grid system. Rising above its plazas, temples and palaces were the Pyramid of the Moon and the Pyramid of the Sun.

Mosaic mask
Masks were important in Teotihuacán. They were probably worn for ceremonies and were sometimes put over the faces of people who had died.

Pyramid of the Sun
This was the largest building in the city and is the third-largest pyramid in the world.

Avenue of the Dead
This wide road divided the city into sections. It was probably used for colorful processions.

Housing
The center of Teotihuacán was for religious ceremonies; the people lived on the outskirts.

Pyramid of the Moon
Like all the city's buildings, this massive pyramid was built with the use of simple stone tools.

Rattlesnake

Central America and the Caribbean

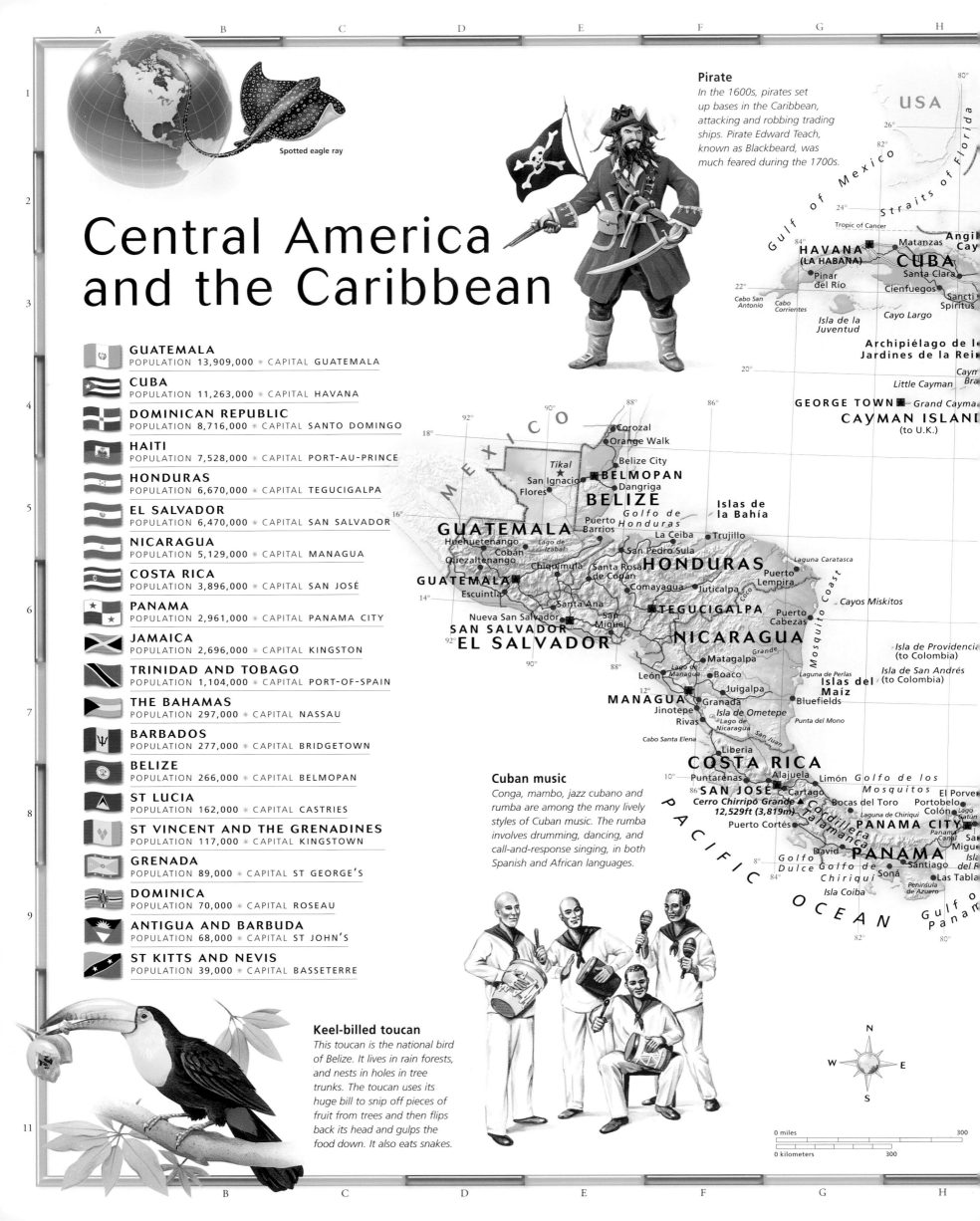

Spotted eagle ray

GUATEMALA
POPULATION 13,909,000 * CAPITAL GUATEMALA

CUBA
POPULATION 11,263,000 * CAPITAL HAVANA

DOMINICAN REPUBLIC
POPULATION 8,716,000 * CAPITAL SANTO DOMINGO

HAITI
POPULATION 7,528,000 * CAPITAL PORT-AU-PRINCE

HONDURAS
POPULATION 6,670,000 * CAPITAL TEGUCIGALPA

EL SALVADOR
POPULATION 6,470,000 * CAPITAL SAN SALVADOR

NICARAGUA
POPULATION 5,129,000 * CAPITAL MANAGUA

COSTA RICA
POPULATION 3,896,000 * CAPITAL SAN JOSÉ

PANAMA
POPULATION 2,961,000 * CAPITAL PANAMA CITY

JAMAICA
POPULATION 2,696,000 * CAPITAL KINGSTON

TRINIDAD AND TOBAGO
POPULATION 1,104,000 * CAPITAL PORT-OF-SPAIN

THE BAHAMAS
POPULATION 297,000 * CAPITAL NASSAU

BARBADOS
POPULATION 277,000 * CAPITAL BRIDGETOWN

BELIZE
POPULATION 266,000 * CAPITAL BELMOPAN

ST LUCIA
POPULATION 162,000 * CAPITAL CASTRIES

ST VINCENT AND THE GRENADINES
POPULATION 117,000 * CAPITAL KINGSTOWN

GRENADA
POPULATION 89,000 * CAPITAL ST GEORGE'S

DOMINICA
POPULATION 70,000 * CAPITAL ROSEAU

ANTIGUA AND BARBUDA
POPULATION 68,000 * CAPITAL ST JOHN'S

ST KITTS AND NEVIS
POPULATION 39,000 * CAPITAL BASSETERRE

Cuban music

Conga, mambo, jazz cubano and rumba are among the many lively styles of Cuban music. The rumba involves drumming, dancing, and call-and-response singing, in both Spanish and African languages.

Keel-billed toucan

This toucan is the national bird of Belize. It lives in rain forests, and nests in holes in tree trunks. The toucan uses its huge bill to snip off pieces of fruit from trees and then flips back its head and gulps the food down. It also eats snakes.

0 miles 300
0 kilometers 300

Voodoo

Voodoo is a form of religion practiced in Haiti and other countries. Based on a belief in spirits and in healing, it involves rituals and the use of objects such as bottles decorated with symbolic, colorful designs .

Queen angelfishes

These fishes live in tropical waters around coral reefs in the Caribbean. They feed on sponges and algae, and grow to 18 inches (45 cm). Friendly and inquisitive, angelfishes swim alongside divers.

Guatemala produces more coffee than any other Central American country. It is one of the world's leading exporters of coffee.

Palm trees

The Caribbean islands are often hit by violent hurricanes in the summer months. Palm trees are well suited to this extreme weather because they have strong, flexible trunks that sway in the wind and are not easily uprooted.

Map labels:

Cooper's Town, Great Abaco, Grand Bahama, eeport, THE BAHAMAS, Eleuthera, NASSAU, Rock Sound, Cat Island, Exuma Cays, San Salvador, Andros Island, Tropic of Cancer, Long Island, Clarence Town, Crooked Island, Acklins Island, Mayaguana Island, Great Inagua Island, Matthew Town, Caicos Islands, TURKS & CAICOS ISLANDS (to U.K.), Turks Islands, COCKBURN TOWN

ATLANTIC OCEAN

Camagüey, Las Tunas, Holguín, Bayamo, Santiago de Cuba, Guantánamo, Guantánamo Bay (to U.S.A.), Windward Passage, Hispaniola, Cap-Haïtien, Port-de-Paix, Puerto Plata, Gonaïves, Santiago, San Francisco de Macoris, Hinche, DOMINICAN REPUBLIC, San Pedro de Macoris, HAITI, Jérémie, Les Cayes, PORT-AU-PRINCE, Barahona, SANTO DOMINGO, La Romana, Mayagüez, Caguas, SAN JUAN, Ponce, PUERTO RICO (to U.S.A.)

Montego Bay, JAMAICA, Spanish Town, KINGSTON, ndeville, Jamaica Channel, Greater Antilles

VIRGIN ISLANDS (to U.S.A.), BRITISH VIRGIN ISLANDS (to U.K.), ROAD TOWN, St Croix, CHARLOTTE AMALIE, ST KITTS & NEVIS, BASSETERRE, PLYMOUTH, MONTSERRAT (to U.K.), BASSE-TERRE, Leeward Islands, ANGUILLA (to U.K.), THE VALLEY, Barbuda, ANTIGUA & BARBUDA, ST JOHN'S, Antigua, Pointe-à-Pitre, GUADELOUPE (to France), Marie-Galante, ROSEAU, DOMINICA, MARTINIQUE (to France), FORT-DE-FRANCE, ST LUCIA, CASTRIES, Lesser Antilles

Caribbean Sea

ARUBA (to Netherlands), ORANJESTAD, WILLEMSTAD, NETHERLANDS ANTILLES (to Netherlands), Curaçao, Bonaire, Islas Los Roques, Isla Orchila, Isla Blanquilla, Lesser Antilles, ST VINCENT & THE GRENADINES, KINGSTOWN, St Vincent, The Grenadines, BARBADOS, BRIDGETOWN, Windward Islands, GRENADA, ST GEORGE'S, Tobago, PORT OF SPAIN, TRINIDAD & TOBAGO, San Fernando, Trinidad

Cartagena, COLOMBIA, Gulf of Darién, La Palma, Maracaibo, Gulf of Venezuela, VENEZUELA, CARACAS, Isla La Tortuga, Isla de Margarita

Luxury yacht

Panama Canal

For hundreds of years, trading ships sailing between the east and west coasts of North America had to travel a long and dangerous route around Cape Horn in South America. In 1904, work began in Panama on carving a link between the Pacific and Atlantic oceans that would take many days off the trip. Thousands of laborers worked for 10 years, cutting through forests, hills and swamps to build the Panama Canal. It is about 51 miles (82 km) long from deep water to deep water, and a minimum of 300 feet (91 m) wide.

Raising a ship: stage one
Boat enters lock on lowest level. Gates close.

Stage two
Water flows in from higher level.

Stage three
Boat is raised to the higher level.

Stage four
Gates at higher end open. Boat moves forward.

A feat of engineering

The Panama Canal has a series of water-filled chambers, called locks, that separate two sections at different heights. This enables ships to be raised and lowered through the uneven, mountainous land on which the canal is built. Gatún Locks has a system of three locks that lifts ships 85 feet (26 m) to Gatún Lake.

Pacific Ocean, Miraflores Locks, Gaillard Cut, Gatún Lake, Gatún Locks, Atlantic Ocean

Miraflores Locks
This system of locks raises or lowers ships 31 feet (9 m) on the Pacific Ocean side of the canal. The final segment to the ocean is 7 miles (11 km) long.

Sapodilla, a Central American plant, produces chicle, the gum in most chewing gum.

Mexico, Central America and the Caribbean

LAND AREA	1,024,715 sq miles (2,654,000 sq km)
LARGEST COUNTRY	Mexico
SMALLEST COUNTRY	St Kitts-Nevis
MAIN RELIGION	Christian
LIFE EXPECTANCY	70 years
LITERACY	87%

NATURAL FEATURES

Soufrière Hills MONTSERRAT
In July 1995, this volcano began erupting and spitting out lava. The volcanic activity still continues, and has destroyed almost half of Montserrat.

Las Baulas COSTA RICA
This national park, which covers about 4 sq miles (10 sq km) of swamps and beaches, was founded in 1995 to protect endangered wildlife species, especially leatherback turtles, which nest there each year.

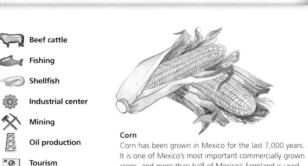
Leatherback turtle

Baja peninsula

Baja peninsula MEXICO
This is the world's longest peninsula. Its extremely arid land supports some hardy lizards, such as the gila monster and the Mexican beaded lizard. More than 120 species of cactus thrive there.

Lake Nicaragua NICARAGUA
This freshwater lake is the largest in Central America. It is home to the slow-moving bull shark, which is one of the most frequent attackers of humans.

Belize's reefs BELIZE
Parallel to the coastline, and fringed by tiny islands called cays, Belize's barrier reef is famous for its sponges, coral and fishes. Just beyond is Lighthouse Reef, with its underwater cave, the Blue Hole.

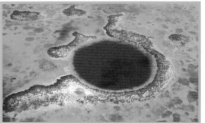
Blue Hole, Lighthouse Reef, Belize

USING THE LAND

- Corn (maize)
- Fruit
- Bananas
- Cotton
- Coffee
- Sugarcane
- Beef cattle
- Fishing
- Shellfish
- Industrial center
- Mining
- Oil production
- Tourism

Corn
Corn has been grown in Mexico for the last 7,000 years. It is one of Mexico's most important commercially grown crops, and more than half of Mexico's farmland is used for its cultivation. Tortillas, the flat bread that most Mexicans eat every day, are made from corn flour.

- Forest and woodland
- Arable land
- Grazing
- Arid or marginal

Tijuana · La Paz · Monterrey · Guadalajara · MEXICO CITY · Puebla · Acapulco · Mérida · BELMOPAN · GUATEMALA · SAN SALVADOR · TEGUCIGALPA · MANAGUA · SAN JOSÉ · PANAMA CITY · HAVANA · PORT-AU-PRINCE · KINGSTON · SANTO DOMINGO · SAN JUAN · PORT OF SPAIN

There are more Spanish speakers in Mexico than any other country.

Bananas
Bananas are especially important in Honduras, which is one of the poorest countries in the Western Hemisphere. Grown along the northern lowlands near the Caribbean Sea, they are a leading source of income.

Cigars
Cigars from Havana, Cuba, are famous as being among the finest in the world, and exporting them is one of Cuba's best sources of foreign revenue. The choicest tobacco comes from western Cuba. The highest-quality cigars are rolled by hand.

The quetzal

This beautiful jungle bird lives in the dense rain forests of Central America. The male is especially brightly colored, with a long, green, feathered tail that can add up to 3 feet (90 cm) to its length. The Aztecs believed the quetzal to be a symbol of freedom because it dies in captivity. Anyone caught killing a quetzal could be sentenced to death. Today, the quetzal is the national emblem of Guatemala, and appears on its flag and postage stamps.

Resplendent quetzal

LARGEST CITIES

Mexico City 8,750,000

Havana 2,359,000

Santo Domingo 2,241,000

Guadalajara 1,672,000

Puebla 1,371,000

WHERE PEOPLE LIVE

Urban	Rural

REGION
54% — 46%

Most urban: THE BAHAMAS
88% — 12%

Most rural: ST KITTS-NEVIS
34% — 66%

Blue agave
This plant is cultivated in Mexico. It produces a sweet sap, which is fermented to make a mild alcoholic drink called pulque. Pulque is then distilled and made into a stronger drink called tequila. Tequila, Mexico's national drink, is named for the town in which it was first made.

PLACES

Havana CUBA
The capital and largest city in Cuba, Havana is also its commercial and industrial center. The old colonial city includes the Spanish governor's palace and the 18th-century Havana Cathedral.

Colonial architecture, Havana

Mexico City MEXICO
Built on the ruins of Tenochtitlán in the 16th century, this city is one of the most populated urban areas in the world. It is home to Mexico's government and is its industrial and business center. Its cathedral (*below*) forms part of the main square.

Temple of the Magician MEXICO
In Uxmal lie the ruins of the Mayan Temple of the Magician (*below*), named

for the legend of a boy who built the temple in one night. The Mayans often built a new temple over an old one. This one has been built five separate times.

Antigua GUATEMALA
Built in the 16th century, Antigua, the capital of Guatemala in colonial days, was badly damaged by an earthquake in 1773. It is a city of old, historic buildings, although many of them are now preserved only as ruins.

San Juan PUERTO RICO
The second-oldest city in the Americas, San Juan is Puerto Rico's main seaport. In the early 16th century it was a walled city and the site of Spanish fortifications, many of which have been restored and are tourist attractions today.

The smallest bird in the world is the bee hummingbird, from Cuba.

PEOPLE

Montezuma 1466–1520
An Aztec emperor who extended Aztec land to include most of south-central Mexico, Montezuma was captured by Hernán Cortés in 1519. He was killed in 1520 when the Aztecs rebelled.

Hernán Cortés
Sent by the Spanish governor of Cuba in 1519 to explore the coast of Mexico, Cortés spent the next two years conquering central and southern Mexico. By 1521, Cuauhtémoc, the last Aztec emperor, had surrendered to Cortés, and the Aztec empire became a Spanish colony. When Cortés took over Tenochtitlán, the Aztec capital, he tore down all the buildings.

Frida Kahlo 1907–54
This Mexican painter is famous for her

brightly colored self-portraits, which reflected her tragic life. Kahlo taught herself to paint after she was severely injured in a traffic accident in 1925.

Fidel Castro born c 1926
Largely unchallenged as leader of Cuba since 1959, Castro has a poor relationship with the USA. However, he has improved Cuba's health and education standards.

Bob Marley 1945–81
Marley was a Jamaican musician and composer who popularized reggae music—a mix of native styles, rock and soul, with lyrics about social and political problems.

TRADITIONS AND CULTURE

Spirit dances GUATEMALA
A number of the Guatemalan folk dances re-enact old spiritual rituals and historical events. The Dance of the Conquistadores depicts the fierce battles between the Guatemalans and Hernán Cortés.

Calypso music TRINIDAD AND TOBAGO
The West Indies is the home of calypso music—a lively style of music, with lyrics

that express the mood and beliefs of the people. The Carnival in Trinidad is the most important musical event of the year. Bands and dancers fill the streets.

Day of the Dead MEXICO
In this festival, Mexicans remember their loved ones who have died. Families have feasts for the living next to the graves of the dead, and children exchange toy skeletons or dolls to honor them.

Chilies
Mexicans are very fond of chilies, and grow more than 100 varieties. Chilies range in color from green to red and black. The most common is the jalapeño chili, which is very hot.

Mayan sun calendar

Early calendars
Mayans were one of the first people to develop a reliable system of measuring the passing of time. They used two main systems for counting days which, when used together, produced a 52-year cycle called the Calendar Round. The first system was a 260-day year, and the second was a 365-day year, based on the orbit of Earth around the Sun.

HISTORY AT A GLANCE
GREAT CIVILIZATIONS

Aztec gold mask

OLMECS 1150–800 BC
The Olmecs were the first people to develop an advanced culture in Mexico. They lived near the rivers and swamps in southeast Mexico, in what are now the states of Veracruz and Tabasco. They devised their own way of writing and counting, and worked out a basic calendar. They carved huge stone heads with flat faces, wearing a type of helmet, to honor their gods, warriors and kings. An important Olmec settlement was found at La Venta, leading some historians to believe that Olmec culture began there.

Olmec head

MAYANS AD 250–900
The Mayans were the most advanced of all the Native American peoples. They settled in villages and developed agriculture in southern Mexico, Guatemala and northern Belize. They built stone cities, palaces and temple pyramids decorated with fine carvings. Religion played a large part in the life of the Mayans. Priests climbed the stairs of the pyramids and performed ceremonies in the temple at the top, offering sacrifices—animal and human—to their gods. The Mayans developed a system of picture writing, or hieroglyphics, and made paper from the bark of wild fig trees.

Mayan temple, Tikal, Guatemala

TOLTECS 900–1200
These were a warrior people who invaded central Mexico from the north, burning the city of Teotihuacán, one of the most important cultural centers in Mexico. The Toltecs were craftspeople, skilled in intricate sculptures, such as this huge carved statue of a soldier (*right*). They worshiped many gods, in particular, Quetzalcóatl, the Feathered Serpent, whose image (a snake crowned with quetzal feathers) adorns many of the buildings at Chichén Itzá and Tula.

Toltec carved stone column

AZTECS 1428–1521
The Aztecs came from the northwest and built their capital, Tenochtitlán (now Mexico City), in the Valley of Mexico. They had one of the most advanced cultures in the Americas, and created art, sculpture, poetry and music. They were deeply religious, and their religion affected every aspect of their lives. They worshiped more than 120 gods—nearly every event, day, month and city had its own special god. The Aztecs built many huge temples and elaborate sculptures to worship their gods. They especially honored Huitzilopochtli, a fierce god to whom they sacrificed thousands of people every year.

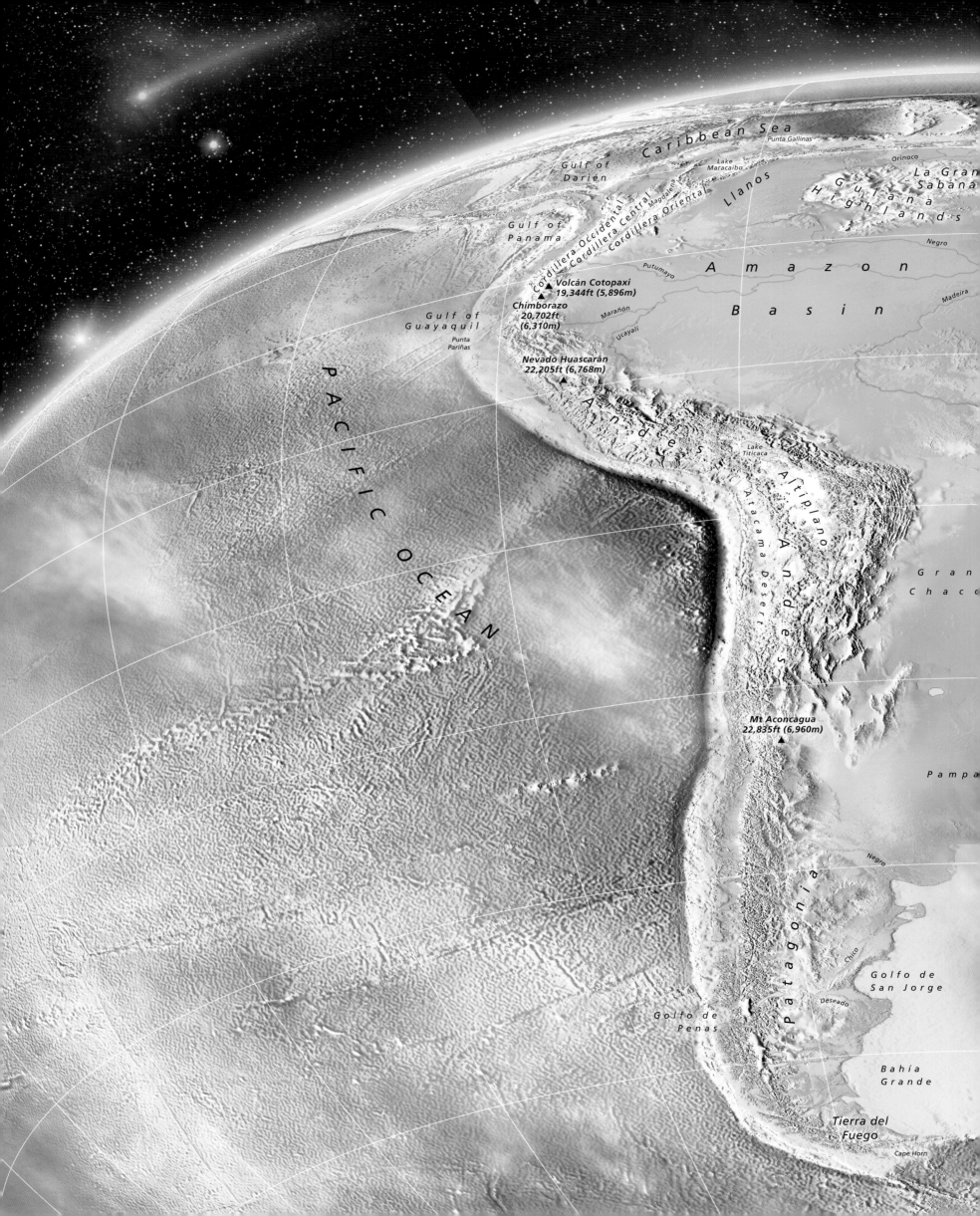

Caribbean Sea

Gulf of
Darién

Punta Gallinas

Lake
Maracaibo

Orinoco

La Gran
Sabana

Cordillera Occidental
Cordillera Central
Cordillera Oriental

Magdalena

Llanos

Guiana
Highlands

Gulf of
Panama

▲ Volcán Cotopaxi
19,344ft (5,896m)

▲ Chimborazo
20,702ft
(6,310m)

Putumayo

Marañón

Amazon

Negro

Madeira

Gulf of
Guayaquil

Punta
Pariñas

Ucayali

Nevado Huascarán
22,205ft (6,768m)
▲

Basin

A n d e s

Lake
Titicaca

Altiplano

A n d e s

Atacama Desert

Gran
Chaco

PACIFIC OCEAN

Mt Aconcagua
22,835ft (6,960m)
▲

Pampa

Negro

Chico

Golfo de
San Jorge

Golfo de
Penas

P a t a g o n i a

Deseado

Tierra del
Fuego

Bahía
Grande

Cape Horn

Tumuc-Humac
Mountains

Amazon

Xingu

Araguaia

Tocantins

Planalto da
Borborema

Cabo de
São Roque

A T L A N T I C

Planalto
do Mato
Grosso

São Francisco

O C E A N

Paraguay

B r a z i l i a n
H i g h l a n d s

Paraná

Serra
Geral

Serra do Mar

Mesopotamia

araná

Uruguay

Lagoa dos
Patos

River Plate

Lagoa Mirim

South America

Falkland
Islands

South
Georgia

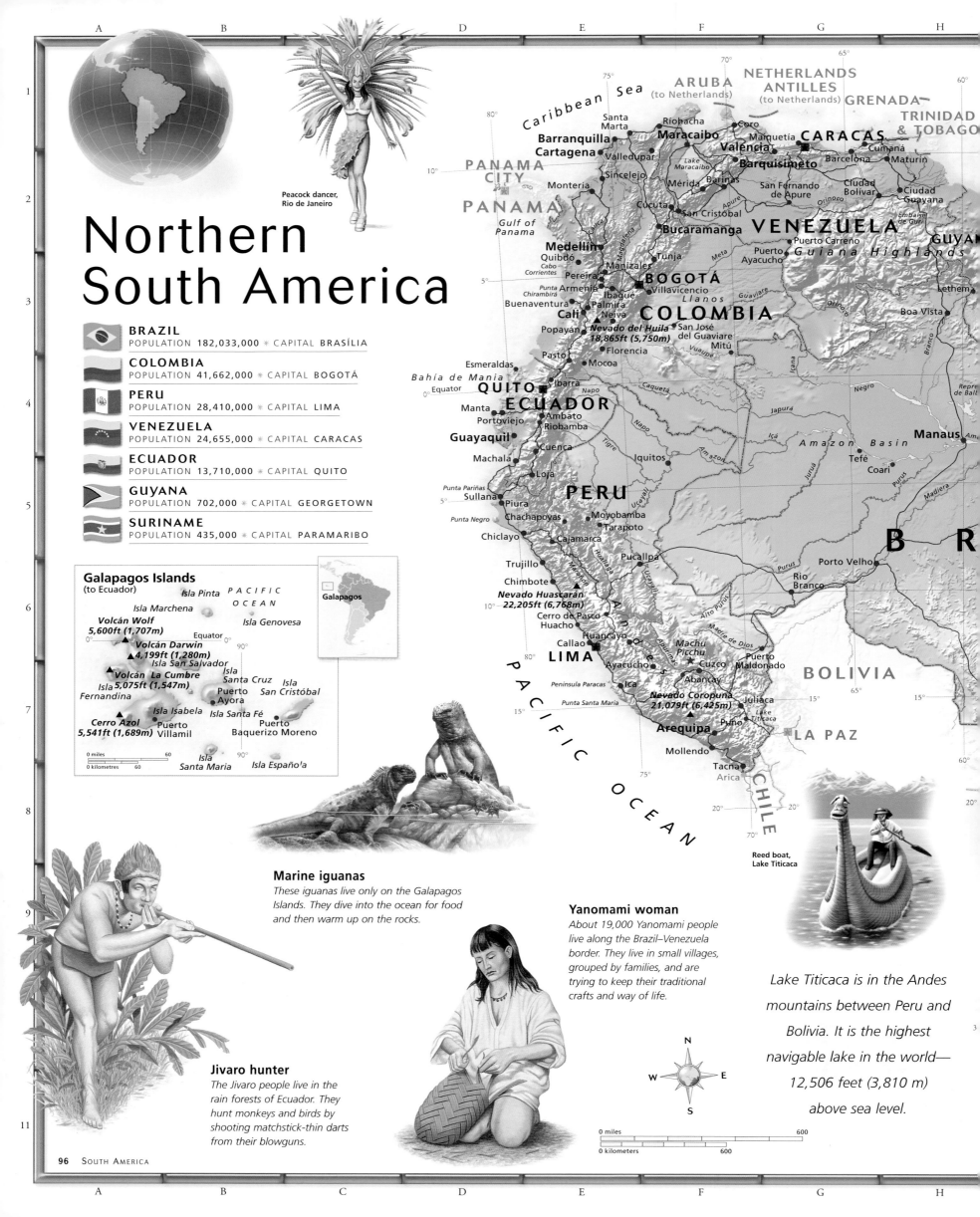

Northern South America

Peacock dancer, Rio de Janeiro

BRAZIL
POPULATION 182,033,000 ✳ CAPITAL BRASÍLIA

COLOMBIA
POPULATION 41,662,000 ✳ CAPITAL BOGOTÁ

PERU
POPULATION 28,410,000 ✳ CAPITAL LIMA

VENEZUELA
POPULATION 24,655,000 ✳ CAPITAL CARACAS

ECUADOR
POPULATION 13,710,000 ✳ CAPITAL QUITO

GUYANA
POPULATION 702,000 ✳ CAPITAL GEORGETOWN

SURINAME
POPULATION 435,000 ✳ CAPITAL PARAMARIBO

Galapagos Islands
(to Ecuador)

PACIFIC OCEAN

Isla Pinta
Isla Marchena
Isla Genovesa
Volcán Wolf
5,600ft (1,707m)
Equator
Volcán Darwin
4,199ft (1,280m)
Isla San Salvador
Volcán La Cumbre
Isla **5,075ft (1,547m)**
Isla Santa Cruz
Isla Fernandina
Puerto Ayora
Isla San Cristóbal
Cerro Azol
5,541ft (1,689m)
Isla Isabela
Puerto Villamil
Isla Santa Fé
Puerto Baquerizo Moreno
Isla Santa Maria
Isla Española

Galapagos

0 miles 60
0 kilometres 60

Map labels

Caribbean Sea
ARUBA (to Netherlands)
NETHERLANDS ANTILLES (to Netherlands)
GRENADA
TRINIDAD & TOBAGO
Santa Marta
Ríohacha
Coro
Maiquetía
CARACAS
Cumaná
Maturín
Barranquilla
Maracaibo
Valéncia
Barcelona
Cartagena
Valledupar
Lake Maracaibo
Barquisimeto
PANAMA CITY
Sincelejo
Mérida
Barinas
San Fernando de Apure
Ciudad Bolívar
Ciudad Guayana
PANAMA
Montería
Cúcuta
Apure
Orinoco
Embalse de Guri
Gulf of Panama
San Cristóbal
VENEZUELA
Bucaramanga
Meta
GUYA
Medellín
Puerto Carreño
Guiana Highlands
Quibdó
Tunja
Puerto Ayacucho
Cabo Corrientes
Manizales
Lethem
Punta Chirambirá
Pereira
BOGOTÁ
Guaviare
Buenaventura
Ibagué
Villavicencio
Llanos
Boa Vista
Palmira
Cali
Neiva
COLOMBIA
Orinoco
Popayán
Nevado del Huila
18,865ft (5,750m)
San José del Guaviare
Mitú
Vaupé
Branco
Esmeraldas
Pasto
Mocoa
Florencia
Bahía de Mania
Caquetá
Negro
Repre de Ball
Equator
QUITO
Ibarra
Napo
Japurá
Manta
ECUADOR
Ambato
Riobamba
Içá
Amazon Basin
Tefé
Manaus
Portoviejo
Napo
Coari
Guayaquil
Cuenca
Tigre
Iquitos
Amazon
Juruá
Purus
Machala
Loja
Madiera
Punta Pariñas
PERU
Sullana
Moyobamba
Piura
Chachapoyas
Tarapoto
Punta Negro
Chiclayo
Cajamarca
Pucallpa
Purus
Porto Velho
Trujillo
Rio Branco
Chimbote
Nevado Huascarán
22,205ft (6,768m)
B
Cerro de Pasco
Huacho
Huancayo
Machu Picchu
Madre de Dios
Callao
Ayacucho
Cuzco
Puerto Maldonado
LIMA
Ica
Abancay
BOLIVIA
Peninsula Paracas
Nevado Coropuna
21,079ft (6,425m)
Juliaca
Punta Santa Maria
Lake Titicaca
Puno
Arequipa
LA PAZ
Mollendo
Tacna
Arica
CHILE
PACIFIC OCEAN

Marine iguanas
These iguanas live only on the Galapagos Islands. They dive into the ocean for food and then warm up on the rocks.

Reed boat, Lake Titicaca

Yanomami woman
About 19,000 Yanomami people live along the Brazil–Venezuela border. They live in small villages, grouped by families, and are trying to keep their traditional crafts and way of life.

Lake Titicaca is in the Andes mountains between Peru and Bolivia. It is the highest navigable lake in the world— 12,506 feet (3,810 m) above sea level.

Jivaro hunter
The Jivaro people live in the rain forests of Ecuador. They hunt monkeys and birds by shooting matchstick-thin darts from their blowguns.

N W E S

0 miles 600
0 kilometers 600

Quechua Indian

About 45 percent of Peru's people are Indians, and most of these are Quechua. Their ancestors were the Incas who once ruled Peru.

Kinkajou

Toucan

The Amazon

The mighty Amazon River flows from the highlands of Peru through Brazil to the coast near Macapá. Dense tropical rain forest surrounds the river and its many tributaries. Here, trees can grow as tall as 20-story buildings to reach sunlight. More kinds of animals live in these jungles than anywhere else on Earth. At least 1,500 kinds of birds fly above the forest and up to 3,000 kinds of fishes swim in the rivers. Lizards and snakes slither along the ground. More than 800 types of mammals—including the world's largest group of bats—and countless insects are all at home in the Amazon.

Layers of life

High above the ground is the rain-forest canopy. Its tall trees and vines are home to birds and monkeys. The middle forest is more sheltered. Many birds also live here, along with reptiles and thousands of insects. The forest floor is cool, damp and dark. Ferns, fungi and saplings grow here, providing shelter and food for animals that live on the ground.

Tamandua
The tamandua is a skilled climber in its search for ants, termites and bees.

Jaguar
A jaguar is on the watch for prey. This powerful big cat is at risk because of rain-forest clearing.

Palla's long-tongued bat
Bats of many kinds are found in the Amazon rain forest. They feed on insects, fruits and nectar.

Bushmaster snake
Snakes thrive on the rain-forest floor. The bushmaster is the largest poisonous snake in the Americas. It grows to 10 feet (3 m).

Hoatzin
The hoatzin is an unusual bird—it eats only leaves. Fifteen percent of all known bird species live in the Amazon rain forest.

Bird-eating spider
The bird-eating spider is a giant: it can be as wide as 11 inches (28 cm).

Rio de Janeiro

Rio de Janeiro—home to 7 million people—is Brazil's most famous city. It was named in January 1502 by the Portuguese explorer Gaspar de Lemos, who mistook its huge bay for a river and called it Rio de Janeiro (River of January). The mountain Corcovado rises straight up from the city and is topped by a huge statue, Christ the Redeemer.

Christ the Redeemer

Sugarloaf Mountain

Copacabana Beach

Guanabara Bay

Southern South America

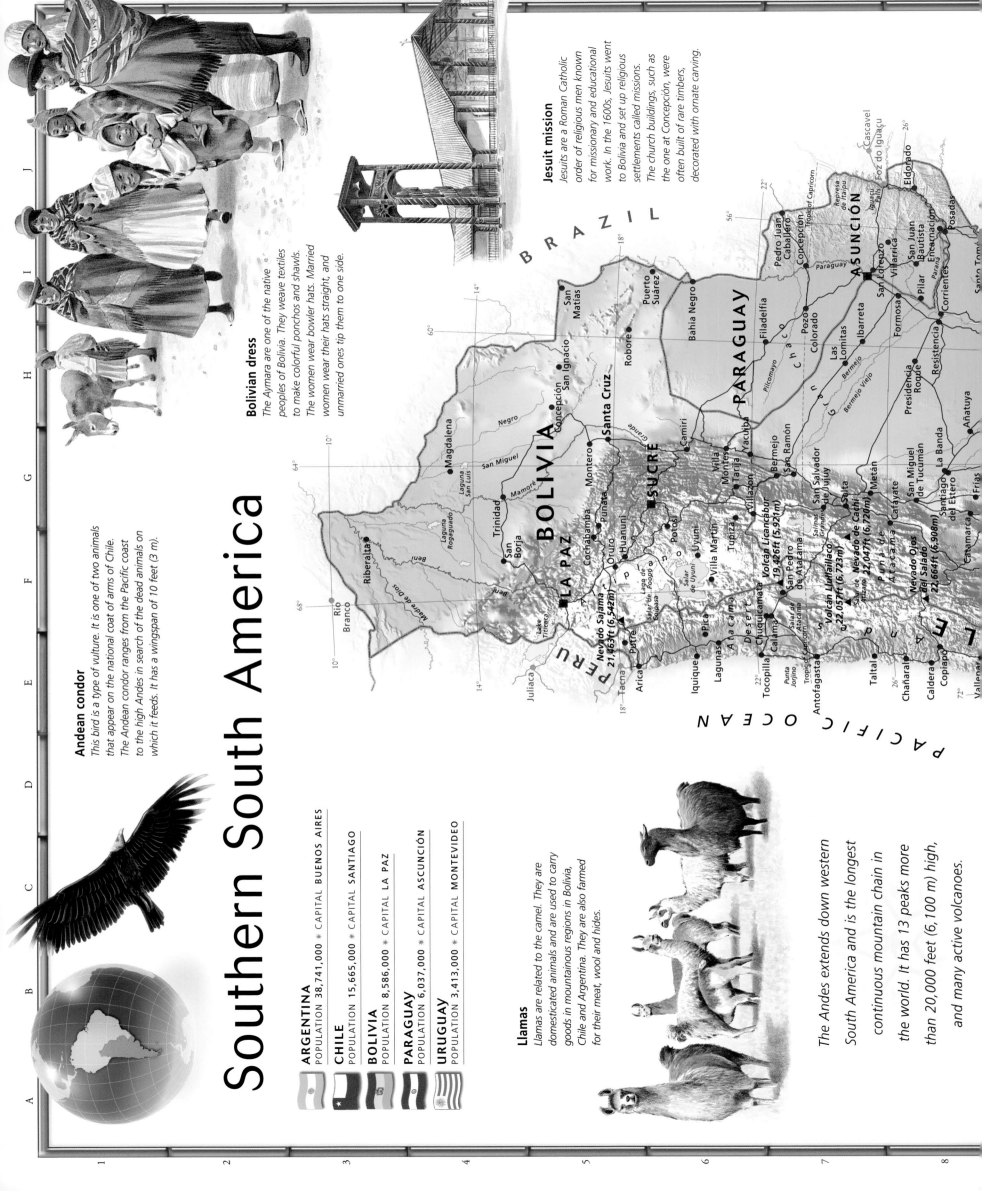

ARGENTINA
POPULATION 38,741,000 ∗ CAPITAL BUENOS AIRES

CHILE
POPULATION 15,665,000 ∗ CAPITAL SANTIAGO

BOLIVIA
POPULATION 8,586,000 ∗ CAPITAL LA PAZ

PARAGUAY
POPULATION 6,037,000 ∗ CAPITAL ASUNCIÓN

URUGUAY
POPULATION 3,413,000 ∗ CAPITAL MONTEVIDEO

Andean condor

This bird is a type of vulture. It is one of two animals that appear on the national coat of arms of Chile. The Andean condor ranges from the Pacific coast to the high Andes in search of the dead animals on which it feeds. It has a wingspan of 10 feet (3 m).

Bolivian dress

The Aymara are one of the native peoples of Bolivia. They weave textiles to make colorful ponchos and shawls. The women wear bowler hats. Married women wear their hats straight, and unmarried ones tip them to one side.

Jesuit mission

Jesuits are a Roman Catholic order of religious men known for missionary and educational work. In the 1600s, Jesuits went to Bolivia and set up religious settlements called missions. The church buildings, such as the one at Concepción, were often built of rare timbers, decorated with ornate carving.

Llamas

Llamas are related to the camel. They are domesticated animals and are used to carry goods in mountainous regions in Bolivia, Chile and Argentina. They are also farmed for their meat, wool and hides.

The Andes extends down western South America and is the longest continuous mountain chain in the world. It has 13 peaks more than 20,000 feet (6,100 m) high, and many active volcanoes.

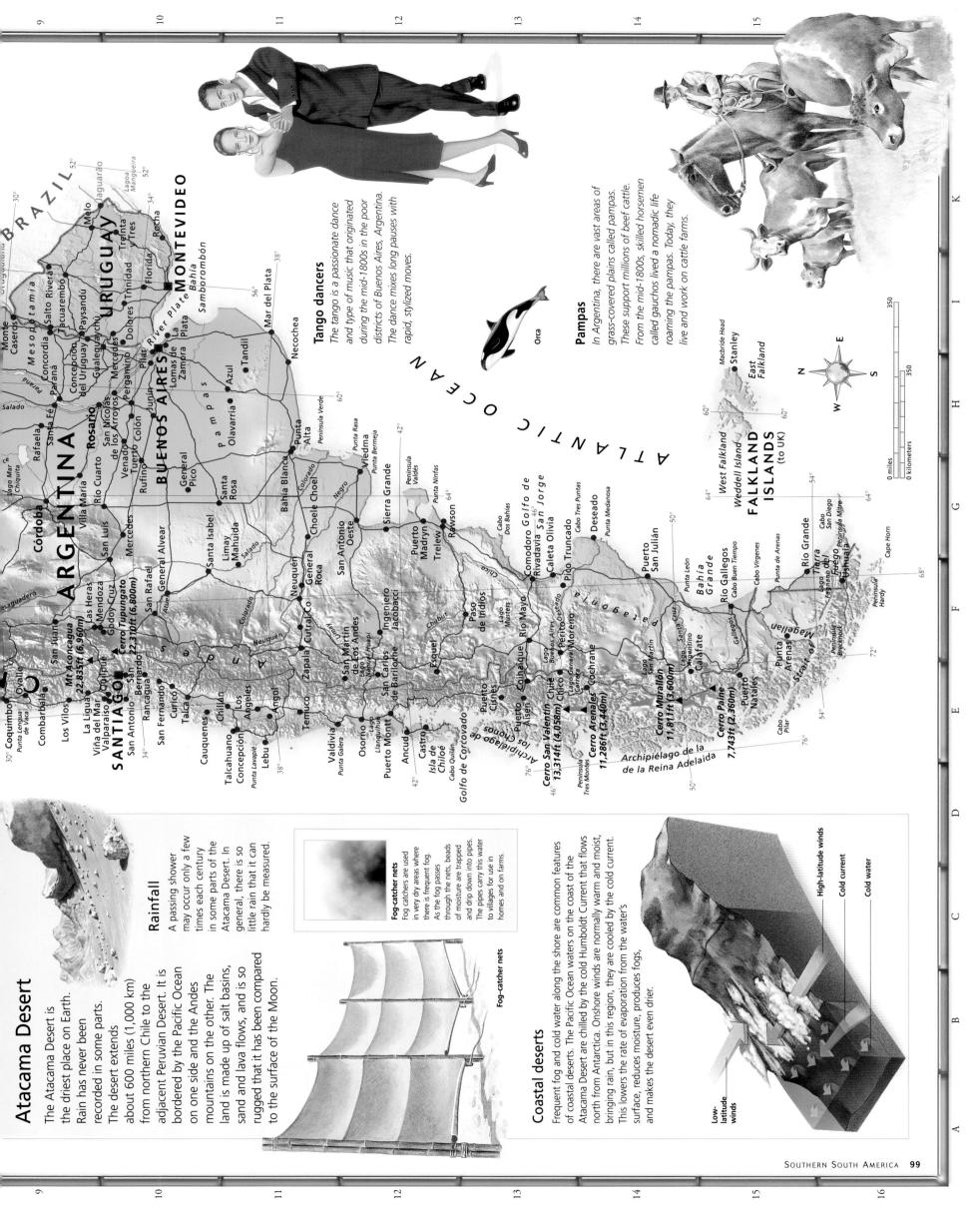

Atacama Desert

The Atacama Desert is the driest place on Earth. Rain has never been recorded in some parts. The desert extends about 600 miles (1,000 km) from northern Chile to the adjacent Peruvian Desert. It is bordered by the Pacific Ocean on one side and the Andes mountains on the other. The land is made up of salt basins, sand and lava flows, and is so rugged that it has been compared to the surface of the Moon.

Rainfall

A passing shower may occur only a few times each century in some parts of the Atacama Desert. In general, there is so little rain that it can hardly be measured.

Fog-catcher nets

Fog catchers are used in very dry areas where there is frequent fog. As the fog passes through the nets, beads of moisture are trapped and drip down into pipes. The pipes carry this water to villages for use in homes and on farms.

Fog-catcher nets

Coastal deserts

Frequent fog and cold water along the shore are common features of coastal deserts. The Pacific Ocean waters on the coast of the Atacama Desert are chilled by the cold Humboldt Current that flows north from Antarctica. Onshore winds are normally warm and moist, bringing rain, but in this region, they are cooled by the cold current. This lowers the rate of evaporation from the water's surface, reduces moisture, produces fogs, and makes the desert even drier.

Low-latitude winds

High-latitude winds

Cold current

Cold water

Tango dancers

The tango is a passionate dance and type of music that originated during the mid-1800s in the poor districts of Buenos Aires, Argentina. The dance mixes long pauses with rapid, stylized moves.

Orca

Pampas

In Argentina, there are vast areas of grass-covered plains called pampas. These support millions of beef cattle. From the mid-1800s, skilled horsemen called gauchos lived a nomadic life roaming the pampas. Today, they live and work on cattle farms.

South America

USING THE LAND

- Forest and woodland
- Arable land
- Grazing
- Arid or marginal

LAND AREA	6,731,004 sq miles (17,433,220 sq km)
LARGEST COUNTRY	Brazil
SMALLEST COUNTRY	Suriname
MAIN RELIGION	Christian
LIFE EXPECTANCY	72 years
LITERACY	93%

Cereals
Fruit
Citrus fruits
Bananas
Wine
Cotton
Coffee
Cocoa
Sugarcane
Soybeans
Rubber
Beef cattle
Sheep

Fishing
Shellfish
Industrial center
Mining
Oil production
Timber
Tourism

Anchovies
Peru is one of the top five fishing countries in the world, and anchovies are the main catch. Recent supplies have been affected by overfishing, and the seasonal changes to ocean currents called the El Niño effect. Most of the anchovies are dried to produce fish meal, which is sold for livestock feed.

Silver and tin
In 1545, huge silver deposits were found at Potosí, Bolivia, and it soon became the richest source of silver in the world. After four centuries of mining, the mine was largely exhausted. Tin has since become Bolivia's most important mineral.

Tomatoes and potatoes are originally from South America.

Potatoes
Potatoes grow wild in the Chilean highlands. Sliced, dried potato, called *chuño*, which was eaten centuries ago by the Incas, is still eaten today. It can be stored for months for later use.

NATURAL FEATURES

Moreno Glacier ARGENTINA
Moreno Glacier, at the southern tip of the Andes, is 30 miles (50 km) long and 2 miles (3 km) wide. Named for the naturalist Francisco Moreno, it is the largest glacier in Patagonia and the only one not decreasing in size.

Moreno Glacier

Salar de Uyuni BOLIVIA
The Salar (salt pan) de Uyuni was once a prehistoric lake. Today, it covers 4,680 square miles (12,120 sq km) of the Bolivian altiplano, or high plains. When it rains, the salt pan fills with a layer of water and shines like a mirror.

The Pantanal BRAZIL
Covering an area of 50,000 square miles (129,500 sq km), the Pantanal in western Brazil is the world's largest wetland. It sustains huge flocks of birds, as well as anacondas, crocodiles, deer and giant river otters.

Iguaçu Falls

Iguaçu Falls ARGENTINA–BRAZIL
These spectacular falls on the Argentine border with Brazil include 275 separate waterfalls, some of which drop 262 feet (80 m). The surrounding subtropical rain forest is home to howler monkeys, jaguars and tapirs.

Torres del Paine CHILE
The Torres (towers) del Paine are three jagged granite peaks that rise more than 6,560 feet (2,000 m) above the surrounding plain in Patagonia. The earliest was formed about 12 million years ago. Glaciers flow from the peaks.

Torres del Paine

Blue-footed booby

Galapagos Islands
About 600 miles (960 km) off the coast of Ecuador, the Galapagos Islands are home to many unique plants and animals. Some species of animals and birds, such as the blue-footed booby, are found only on these islands. The Galapagos tortoise, the world's largest living tortoise, can survive for up to 200 years—longer than any other animal.

WHERE PEOPLE LIVE

Urban — Rural

	Urban	Rural
REGION	73%	27%
Most urban: URUGUAY	91%	9%
Most rural: PARAGUAY	55%	45%

LARGEST CITIES

Buenos Aires 11,928,000

São Paulo 10,333,000

Lima 8,380,000

Bogotá 6,982,000

Map labels: CARACAS, GEORGETOWN, PARAMARIBO, CAYENNE, BOGOTÁ, Macapá, QUITO, Guayaquil, Manaus, Belém, Fortaleza, LIMA, Trujillo, Recife, Arequipa, LA PAZ, SUCRE, BRASÍLIA, Salvador, São Paulo, Rio de Janeiro, ASUNCIÓN, Porto Alegre, Córdoba, SANTIAGO, BUENOS AIRES, MONTEVIDEO, Bahía Blanca, Puerto Montt, Stanley, Punta Arenas

PLACES

La Paz BOLIVIA
At an altitude of 12,500 feet (3,812 m) at its center, La Paz, the administrative capital of Bolivia, is the highest capital city in the world. This hub of Bolivian commerce lies in a valley surrounded by Altiplano (high plains).

Cartagena COLOMBIA
Founded in 1533, Cartagena was once a slave port. Although the Spanish built forts to ward off British and French attacks, they were unsuccessful—in the 17th and 18th centuries Spain built the largest defense system in South America.

Machu Picchu
The Incas built this city on a ridge 50 miles (80 km) from Cuzco, in southern Peru, in the mid-1400s. They abandoned it 100 years later, and it was not rediscovered until 1911. The site is a 2-square-mile (5-sq-km) complex of granite buildings and plazas surrounded by farm terraces. It was probably a royal estate or religious center.

National Congress, Brasília

Brasília BRAZIL
The construction of Brasília, the capital of Brazil, began on an almost barren site in 1956. The city, complete with parks and artificial lakes, was laid out to a plan that, from the air, some say resembles a bow and arrow and others say a bird in flight.

Buenos Aires ARGENTINA
Buenos Aires was founded in the 16th century and became the capital of Argentina in the 18th century. More than a third of Argentina's people live in the city and its suburbs. Buenos Aires has a large number of theaters and museums.

Paramaribo SURINAME
This city, the capital of Suriname, was settled by the French around 1640. It became a British colony in 1651 and, in a deal in 1667, Britain swapped it for present-day New York, which was then owned by the Dutch.

Dutch colonial buildings

Amazon animals
The anaconda (*above*), which kills its prey by squeezing until it suffocates, is found in the Amazon River. It can reach 30 feet (9 m) in length. The goliath bird-eating spider, the largest in the world, lives in rain-forested regions. It eats young birds, frogs and even bats. When threatened, it makes a loud hissing noise by rubbing its legs together. The world's heaviest rodent, the capybara, is also a rain-forest dweller. It can weigh up to 145 pounds (65 kg).

PEOPLE

Atahuallpa c 1502–33
Atahuallpa was the last ruler of the Inca. In 1532, after a five-year struggle, he was captured by the Spaniards, who asked the Incas for a huge ransom for his release. Although the ransom was paid, Atahuallpa was executed in 1533.

Bernardo O'Higgins 1776–1842
A revolutionary leader who fought to achieve Chile's independence from Spain, O'Higgins became the director of Chile in 1817. However, he was unpopular and resigned in 1823.

Simón Bolívar 1783–1830
Bolívar (*right*), born in Venezuela, was called "the Liberator" for his role in helping several South American nations to gain independence. The country of Bolivia was named in his honor.

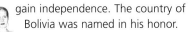

Eva Perón 1919–52
Known also as Evita, Eva was the popular wife of Juan Perón, the president of Argentina. She gained women the right to vote in 1947 and provided financial assistance to the poor.

Eva Perón

Pelé born 1940
Brazilian-born Pelé is a world-famous soccer player and the only player to have played in four World Cup championships. In 1999, Pelé was named the athlete of the century by the National Olympics Committee.

HISTORY AT A GLANCE
GREAT CIVILIZATIONS

Moche ear ornament

NAZCA
The Nazca people lived in southern Peru from about 200 BC to AD 600. They are best known for their distinctive pottery, which was decorated with bright, multicolored images of humans and animals, and for the huge depictions of animals and shapes they made on the desert floor. No one knows why these "Nazca lines" were created.

MOCHE
Moche was the main civilization on the north coast of Peru from the 1st to the 8th century. Two well-known remnants of this civilization are the Temple of the Sun and the Temple of the Moon. In 1987, tombs filled with treasures were found near Sipán. The most famous tomb is thought to contain the Lord of Sipán, a Moche warrior-priest.

Kalasasaya temple, Tiwanaku

TIWANAKU AND HUARI
These two civilizations held power in the south-central Andes from the 1st to the 9th century. The Tiwanaku built temples and pyramids south of Lake Titicaca. The Huari people established their city in the Ayacucho Basin. Huari buildings have not survived, but remnants of their pottery have been found.

CHIMÚ AND CHINCHA
The Chimú people appeared in the 10th century in the Moche Valley and built the city of Chan Chan as their capital. They dug irrigation canals to supply water to the city and their crops. Chincha, on the south coast of Peru, was a rich desert kingdom. It was a powerful commercial center that was brought under Inca control.

Inca statue

THE INCAS
The Incas were a group of tribes that lived around Cuzco in southern Peru. By the 13th century they began to expand, and in the 15th century were well established. At its height, the Inca empire was the largest in the Americas, extending 2,500 miles (4,000 km) from Colombia and Equador south to Chile and Argentina. In 1532, the empire fell to the Spanish conquistador Francisco Pizarro, who had with him only 167 men.

Francisco Pizarro

TRADITIONS AND CULTURE

Maté tea
Maté tea is made in a gourd (*below*) from a herb called yerba mate, and sipped through a metal straw called a *bombilla*. Groups of people often drink the tea together, passing the gourd and straw from person to person.

Gauchos
Gauchos are cowboys of the pampas of Argentina and Chile. Centuries ago, they led a tough, independent life. Now they work on ranches and are no longer self-reliant, but they still value their strength and independence.

Gauchos

Amazon peoples
People have lived in the Amazon rain forest for at least 10,000 years. They obtain a small amount of their food by hunting and gathering, but most of their food is harvested from small agricultural plots. Their traditional way of life is today threatened by the destruction of much of the rain forest.

Apus
People in parts of Peru have combined their traditional beliefs with Christianity. They worship apus, or spirits of the mountains, by marking the apu's home, such as a hill or a stream, with a type of Christian cross.

Hallaca
This traditional Christmas dish in Venezuela consists of a corn or maize dough filled with meat and seasonings, wrapped in a banana leaf and steamed. It is eaten after mass on Christmas Eve.

Kara Sea

North Siberi
Lowland

Ural Mountains

West Siberian Plain

Ob'

Yeni sey

Angar

Caspian
Depression

Kazakhskiy
Plain

Altai Mountain

Black Sea

Caucasus

Aral
Sea

Lake
Balkhash

Anatolia

Caspian Sea

Ustyurt
Plateau

Turan Lowland

Tien Shan

Cyprus

Karakum
Desert

Tarim Basin

Quilia

Syrian
Desert

Tigris

Iranian
Plateau

Taklimakan Desert

Euphrates

Zagros
Mountains

Hindu Kush

Kunlun Shan

An Nafūd

Indus

Plateau of
Tibet

Persian Gulf

Thar Desert

Himalaya

Mt Everest
29,035ft (8,850m)

Red Sea

Arabian
Peninsula

Gulf of
Oman

Gangetic Plain

Ganges

Brahmaputra

Rubʿ al Khālī

Indian

Subcontinent

Chin Hills

Irrawaddy

Gulf of Aden

Socotra

Arabian
Sea

Western Ghats

Deccan

Plateau

Eastern Ghats

Bay of
Bengal

Andaman
Islands

Laccadive
Islands

Laccadive Sea

Andaman
Sea

Maldives

Sri Lanka

Nicobar
Islands

I N D I A N   O C E A N

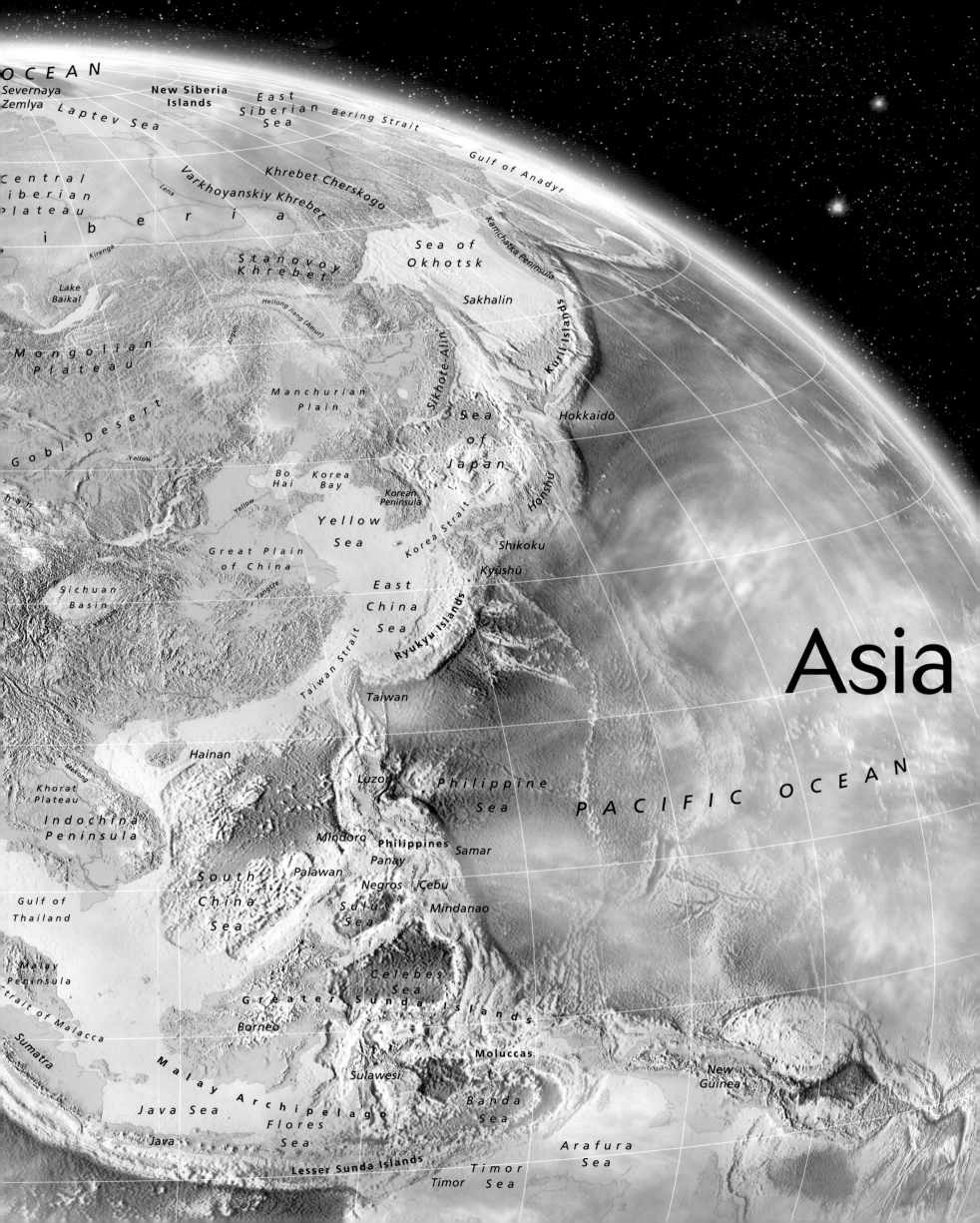

Sputnik

Russia

🏴 **RUSSIA**
POPULATION 144,526,000 ✳ CAPITAL MOSCOW

Nenets' camp
The Nenets live in the far northwest region of Russia. They are hunters and reindeer herders. Each season, when the reindeer migrate, the Nenets set up tents and cover them with animal skins for warmth.

St Basil's Cathedral
This ornate cathedral in Moscow was built by Czar Ivan the Terrible. Work began in 1554. When first built, the cathedral was painted white. The eight colorful domes are shaped rather like onions to shed heavy snow and rain.

Sturgeon
Up to 90 percent of the world's sturgeon comes from the Caspian Sea. The giant sturgeon grows to 19 feet (6 m) long and can live for 150 years. Sturgeon roe, or eggs, is called caviar. It is an expensive delicacy.

Siberian timber house
The homes of wealthy Siberians in the early 1800s were built of timber. Some of the finest are in Irkutsk, near Lake Baikal. They have shuttered windows and ornate decoration.

Russia is the largest country in the world. It covers two-thirds of Asia and one-third of Europe, and has 11 time zones. Russia was once part of a much larger country called the Soviet Union.

Wolf

Franz Josef Land

Novaya Zemlya

Kara Sea

Ostrov Belyy

Barents Sea

North Cape

Arctic Circle

Murmansk

Kandalaksha

Kola Peninsula

Ostrov Kolguyev

Ostrov Vaygach

Baydaratskaya Guba

Yamal Peninsula

Gydanskiy Peninsula

Obskaya Guba

Vorkuta

Noril'sk

Taz

FINLAND

White Sea

Pechorskoye More

Severodvinsk
Arkhangel'sk

Pechora

ESTONIA
LATVIA

St Petersburg

Gulf of Finland

Lake Ladoga

Lake Onega

Petrozavodsk

Pskov

Velikiye Novgorod

Velikiye Luki

Cherepovets

Vologda

Ukhta

Syktyvkar

Smolensk

Tver'

Rybinsk

BELARUS

Kaluga

Bryansk

Yaroslavl'

MOSCOW (MOSKVA)

Kolomna

Vladimir

Orel

Tula

Novomoskovsk

Kirov

Solikamsk

Berezniki

Ural Mountains

West Siberian Plain

Serov

UKRAINE

Kursk

Ryazan'

Lipetsk

Arzamas

Nizhniy Novgorod

Yoshkar-Ola

Glazov

Izhevsk

Perm

Belgorod

Michurinsk

Cheboksary

Kazan'

Sarapul

Neftekamsk

Nizhniy Tagil

Surgut

Staryy Oskol

Voronezh

Tambov

Saransk

Penza

Ul'yanovsk

Naberezhnyye Chelny

Pervoural'sk

Nizhnevartovsk

Donets'k

Kuznetsk

Syzran'

Tol'yatti

Oktyabr'skiy

Yekaterinburg

Ob'

Sea of Azov

Kerch

Shakhty

Saratov

Engel's

Samara

Ufa

Kamensk-Ural'skiy

Tobol'sk

Rostov-na-Donu

Balakovo

Volga

Zlatoust

Miass

Tyumen'

Novorossiysk

Krasnodar

Maykop

Sochi

Nevinnomyssk

Cherkessk

Armavir

Elista

Volgograd

Sterlitamak

Orenburg

Chelyabinsk

Kurgan

Ural'sk

Magnitogorsk

Orsk

Petropavlovsk

Omsk

R U S

Yeniseyskiy Kryazh

Yenisey

Pyatigorsk

Nal'chik

Caspian Depression

Astrakhan'

Atyrau

KAZAKHSTAN

Black Sea

Elbrus
18,510ft (5,642m)

Stavropol

GEORGIA

Caucasus

Caspian Sea

Makhachkala

T'BILISI

Groznyy

AZERBAIJAN

BAKU
(BAKI)

Semipalatinsk

Tomsk

Achinsk

Novosibirsk

Kemerovo

Krasnoyarsk

Kan

Kiselevsk

Barnaul

Novokuznetsk

Abakan

Rubtsovsk

Biysk

Zapadnyy Sayan

Gora Belukha
14,783ft (4,506m)

Kyzyl

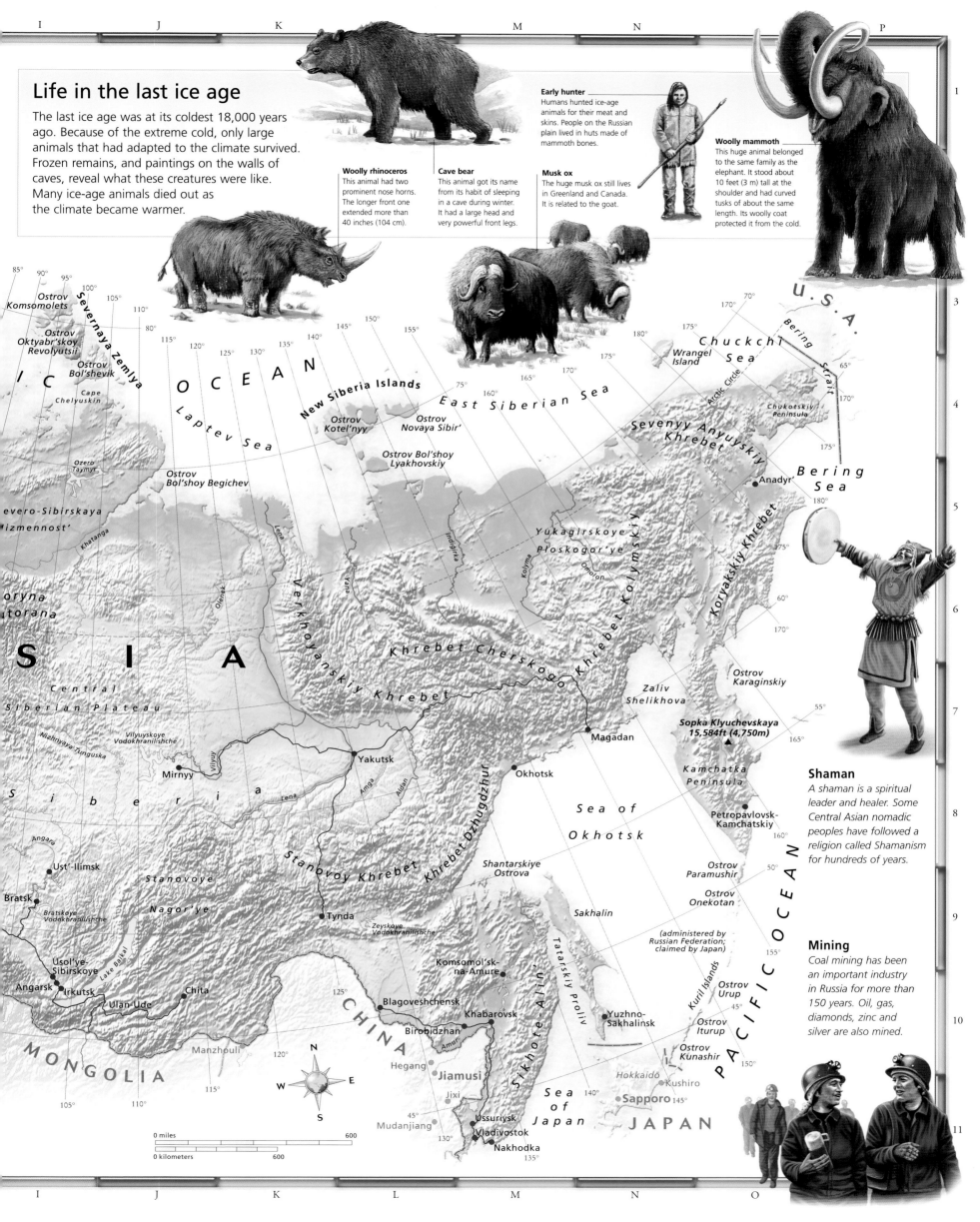

Life in the last ice age

The last ice age was at its coldest 18,000 years ago. Because of the extreme cold, only large animals that had adapted to the climate survived. Frozen remains, and paintings on the walls of caves, reveal what these creatures were like. Many ice-age animals died out as the climate became warmer.

Woolly rhinoceros
This animal had two prominent nose horns. The longer front one extended more than 40 inches (104 cm).

Cave bear
This animal got its name from its habit of sleeping in a cave during winter. It had a large head and very powerful front legs.

Musk ox
The huge musk ox still lives in Greenland and Canada. It is related to the goat.

Early hunter
Humans hunted ice-age animals for their meat and skins. People on the Russian plain lived in huts made of mammoth bones.

Woolly mammoth
This huge animal belonged to the same family as the elephant. It stood about 10 feet (3 m) tall at the shoulder and had curved tusks of about the same length. Its woolly coat protected it from the cold.

Shaman
A shaman is a spiritual leader and healer. Some Central Asian nomadic peoples have followed a religion called Shamanism for hundreds of years.

Mining
Coal mining has been an important industry in Russia for more than 150 years. Oil, gas, diamonds, zinc and silver are also mined.

Ostrov Komsomolets
Ostrov Oktyabr'skoy Revolyutsii
Ostrov Bol'shevik
Severnaya Zemlya
Cape Chelyuskin
Ozero Taymyr
IC
ARCTIC OCEAN
Laptev Sea
evero-Sibirskaya Nizmennost'
oryna torana
SIA
Central Siberian Plateau
New Siberia Islands
Ostrov Kotel'nyy
Ostrov Novaya Sibir'
Ostrov Bol'shoy Lyakhovskiy
Ostrov Bol'shoy Begichev
East Siberian Sea
Khatanga
Lena
Yana
Olenek
Indigirka
Kolyma
Omolon
Yukagirskoye Ploskogor'ye
Sevenyy Anyuyskiy Khrebet
Chuckchi Sea
Wrangel Island
Arctic Circle
Chukotskiy Peninsula
Bering Strait
U.S.A.
Bering Sea
Anadyr
Koryakskiy Khrebet
Ostrov Karaginskiy
Khrebet Cherskogo
Verkhoyanskiy Khrebet
Khrebet Kolymskiy
Zaliv Shelikhova
Sopka Klyuchevskaya 15,584ft (4,750m)
Magadan
Kamchatka Peninsula
Petropavlovsk-Kamchatskiy
Vilyuyskoye Vodokhranilishche
Nizhnyaya Tunguska
Mirnyy
Yakutsk
Vilyuy
Lena
Amga
Aldan
Okhotsk
Sea of Okhotsk
Ostrov Paramushir
Ostrov Onekotan
Khrebet Dzhugdzhur
Shantarskiye Ostrova
Siberia
Angara
Ust'-Ilimsk
Bratsk
Bratskoye Vodokhranilishche
Stanovoye Nagor'ye
Stanovoy Khrebet
Tynda
Zeyskoye Vodokhranilishche
Sakhalin
(administered by Russian Federation; claimed by Japan)
Ostrov Urup
Usol'ye-Sibirskoye
Angarsk
Irkutsk
Ulan-Ude
Lake Baikal
Chita
Komsomol'sk-na-Amure
Tatarskiy Proliv
Kuril Islands
Ostrov Iturup
Yuzhno-Sakhalinsk
Sikhote-Alin'
MONGOLIA
Manzhouli
CHINA
Blagoveshchensk
Khabarovsk
Birobidzhan
Amur
Hegang
Jiamusi
Jixi
Mudanjiang
Ussuriysk
Vladivostok
Nakhodka
Ostrov Kunashir
Hokkaidō
Kushiro
Sapporo
Sea of Japan
JAPAN
PACIFIC OCEAN

0 miles 600
0 kilometers 600
N W E S

Russia

LAND AREA	6,562,115 sq miles (16,995,800 sq km)
OFFICIAL LANGUAGE	Russian
MAIN RELIGION	Christian
LIFE EXPECTANCY	73 years
LITERACY	99%

NATURAL FEATURES

Russian steppe
The Russian steppe is a vast, low-lying plain in southern Russia. Much of the plain lies less than 650 feet (200 m) above sea level. The natural vegetation includes grasses, mosses, lichen and trees.

Ural Mountains
These mountains divide European Russia from Siberia, and form the traditional border between Europe and Asia. The Urals extend from the Arctic Circle south for 1,550 miles (2,500 km) to the arid region near the Kazakhstan border.

Russian taiga
An area of coniferous forest, lakes, bogs and rivers in northern Russia, the taiga is home to many small mammals as well as moose, wolves and the rare Siberian tiger.

Siberian tiger

Lake Baikal
Formed more than 25 million years ago, Lake Baikal, in Siberia, is the oldest and deepest lake in the world. More than 1 mile (1,620 m) deep, it holds one-fifth of Earth's freshwater supplies. Home to more than 1,200 native plant and animal species, it is threatened by industrial wastewater pollution.

Tunguska meteorite
On 30 June 1908, a huge area of the forest in Tunguska, in a remote part of Siberia, was destroyed by an enormous fireball. Many scientists believe it was the largest meteorite to fall to Earth in the last 2,000 years. No fragments of it were left behind.

USING THE LAND

Natural resources
Russia has enormous deposits of iron, coal, oil and natural gas (*left*). However, two-thirds of the country's oil and natural gas deposits are in Siberia, which is a long way from the major population centers. Siberia's harsh climate makes it difficult to extract them.

- Forest and woodland
- Arable land
- Grazing
- Arid or marginal

Lake Baikal

- Cereals
- Potatoes
- Beef cattle
- Reindeer
- Fishing
- Industrial center
- Mining
- Oil production
- Gas production
- Timber

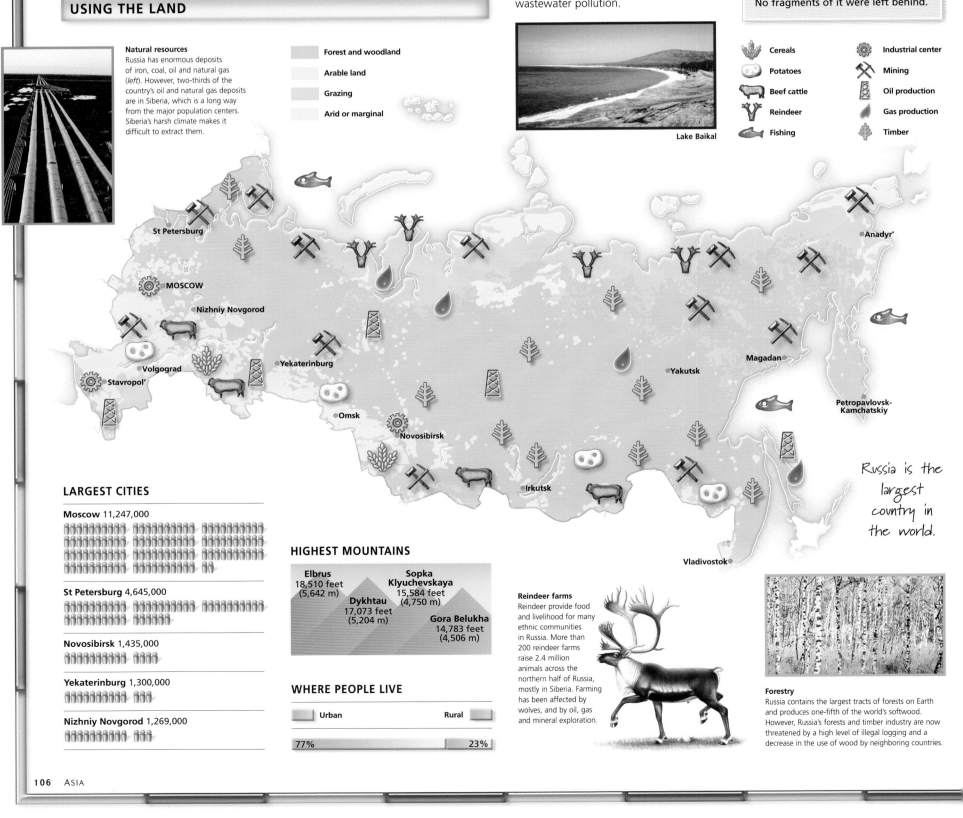

St Petersburg · MOSCOW · Nizhniy Novgorod · Volgograd · Stavropol' · Yekaterinburg · Omsk · Novosibirsk · Irkutsk · Yakutsk · Magadan · Anadyr' · Petropavlovsk-Kamchatskiy · Vladivostok

Russia is the largest country in the world.

LARGEST CITIES

Moscow 11,247,000

St Petersburg 4,645,000

Novosibirsk 1,435,000

Yekaterinburg 1,300,000

Nizhniy Novgorod 1,269,000

HIGHEST MOUNTAINS

- Elbrus 18,510 feet (5,642 m)
- Dykhtau 17,073 feet (5,204 m)
- Sopka Klyuchevskaya 15,584 feet (4,750 m)
- Gora Belukha 14,783 feet (4,506 m)

WHERE PEOPLE LIVE

Urban	Rural
77%	23%

Reindeer farms
Reindeer provide food and livelihood for many ethnic communities in Russia. More than 200 reindeer farms raise 2.4 million animals across the northern half of Russia, mostly in Siberia. Farming has been affected by wolves, and by oil, gas and mineral exploration.

Forestry
Russia contains the largest tracts of forests on Earth and produces one-fifth of the world's softwood. However, Russia's forests and timber industry are now threatened by a high level of illegal logging and a decrease in the use of wood by neighboring countries.

PEOPLE

Ivan the Terrible 1530–84
Ivan IV became the first czar (emperor) of Russia in 1547. Balanced against his political reform and territorial expansion was the fact that he instituted a reign of terror among the Russian nobility, killing thousands of people.

Catherine the Great 1729–96
Catherine II became czarina (empress) of Russia in 1796 as a result of a coup in which her husband (Peter the Great) was murdered. She successfully waged war against Turkey and Poland, increasing Russia's territory. During her reign, Russia enjoyed a period of stability.

Leo Tolstoy 1828–1910
One of the world's literary masters, Leo Tolstoy had a strong belief in the virtues of the simple peasant life—a belief that was reflected in his work. His most famous novel is *War and Peace*, an epic tale about Russia's struggle against France in the Napoleonic Wars.

Peter Tchaikovsky 1840–93
The compositions of the classical composer Peter Tchaikovsky are still played in concerts all over the world. His works include the ballets *Swan Lake* and *The Nutcracker*.

Grigory Rasputin 1871–1916

Born a Siberian peasant, this priest and mystic exerted a great deal of influence over the family of Czar Nicholas II and the court. Scandals surrounding Rasputin led to his murder by a group of nobles.

Trans-Siberian railroad
Stretching almost one-fourth of the way around the globe, the Trans-Siberian railroad is the longest rail system in the world. The journey from Moscow to Vladivostok makes 92 stops, takes eight days and covers 5,778 miles (9,244 km). The railroad was built between 1891 and 1904, in the reign of Alexander III.

TRADITIONS AND CULTURE

Icon painting

Icons are small religious images. Russia developed its own style of icon painting in the 15th century, using local saints and backgrounds. The icons illustrate legends, parables or rites of the Russian Orthodox Church. Painted icons are noted for their bright colors, including gold, and emphasis on strong outlines.

Matryoshka dolls
Also called "nesting dolls," these brightly painted, hollow wooden dolls are shaped so that they fit inside one another. They are an example of traditional Russian folk art. Sometimes matryoshka dolls represent a whole family, with some sets including more than 12 dolls.

Fabergé eggs
Created by Russian goldsmith and jeweler Peter Fabergé, these Easter eggs are his finest work. Fabergé made the first egg in 1884 as an Easter present for Czar Alexander III to give to his wife—thus beginning a tradition in the royal family. Each ornate jeweled egg contained an elaborate surprise gift for the czarina.

Russian ballet
Russia's ballet schools have produced many of the world's greatest ballet dancers, such as Rudolph Nureyev and Anna Pavlova. The Bolshoi Ballet, meaning "great ballet" in Russian, in Moscow is one of the world's leading ballet companies.

Troika rides
Far from being a thing of the past, horse-drawn sleighs in winter (and carriages in summer) are becoming more popular in Russia, not just as a novelty ride, but as transport for well-to-do business people and politicians.

Lenin
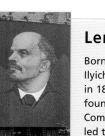
Born Vladimir Ilyich Ulyanov in 1870, Lenin founded the Communist Party, led the Russian Revolution and created the Soviet state, the world's first communist regime. His aim was to create a classless society ruled by workers, soldiers and peasants. He died in 1924 and people visit his tomb in the Kremlin, where his body is preserved.

PLACES

The Kremlin MOSCOW
This is a large walled area in the center of Moscow (*below*). Built in 1156 and much enlarged since, the Kremlin is the seat of the Russian government and the center of the Russian Orthodox Church. It also has magnificent palaces and churches that are open to the public.

The Kremlin

Velikiy Novgorod
This northwestern city is one of the oldest in Russia. It was a thriving cultural and trading center in medieval times. With its many fine historic buildings, it is a popular tourist destination.

Vladivostok
This major port and naval base is located on a peninsula in the Sea of Japan. Its name means "rule the East." Founded in 1860 as a military outpost, it was closed to foreigners during the Cold War.

St Petersburg
This city, built in 1703 by Peter the Great, is the second-largest city in Russia. For 200 years up to 1918, it was Russia's capital city. St Petersburg is a major industrial and commercial center and its port, although frozen for part of the year, is one of the largest in the world. Constructed in the 18th century for Catherine the Great as her winter palace, the Hermitage Museum (*below*) is the largest museum and art gallery in Russia.

Hermitage Museum, St Petersburg

HISTORY AT A GLANCE
RUSSIA SINCE 1917

Russian Revolution poster

RUSSIAN REVOLUTION
Czar Nicholas II was a poor leader in World War I, and his government collapsed in 1917. The Bolsheviks seized power in October of that year and brought Russia under communist control, with Lenin as leader. After a series of wars, the communists formed the Union of Soviet Socialist Republics (USSR), or Soviet Union, in 1922.

JOSEPH STALIN
By 1928, Stalin had assumed sole power over the USSR and remained as dictator until his death in 1953. He centralized industries and set up state farms. His rule was noted for its harshness.

WORLD WAR II
In 1941, Germany invaded the USSR and encircled the city of Leningrad. After much suffering, the Soviets broke the siege in 1944. At the end of the war, the USSR occupied much of eastern Europe.

The Battle of Leningrad memorial

COLD WAR
The so-called cold war between the USSR and the USA climaxed in October 1962, with the Cuban missile crisis—the USA's discovery of Soviet missiles in Cuba. Nuclear war was averted.

YURI GAGARIN
On 12 April 1961, this Soviet cosmonaut became the first man in space. Flying at a maximum altitude of 187 miles (299 km) in the Vostok I spacecraft, Gagarin orbited Earth once before landing. He never flew into space again.

Yuri Gagarin

POLITICAL REFORM
Mikhail Gorbachev, president of the USSR (1990–91), was a reformer within the Communist Party who worked to decentralize power in the USSR and improve ties with the USA.

BREAKUP OF THE USSR
Gorbachev's quest for openness (*glasnost*) and restructuring (*perestroika*) led to the breakup of the USSR and ended its control of eastern Europe. The USSR ceased to exist on 31 December 1991.

RUSSIAN FEDERATION
Russia faced many problems as it tried to become more democratic and develop a freer economy. In 1994, Russia invaded Chechnia to reassert its control over its former territory. In 2000, Vladimir Putin became president.

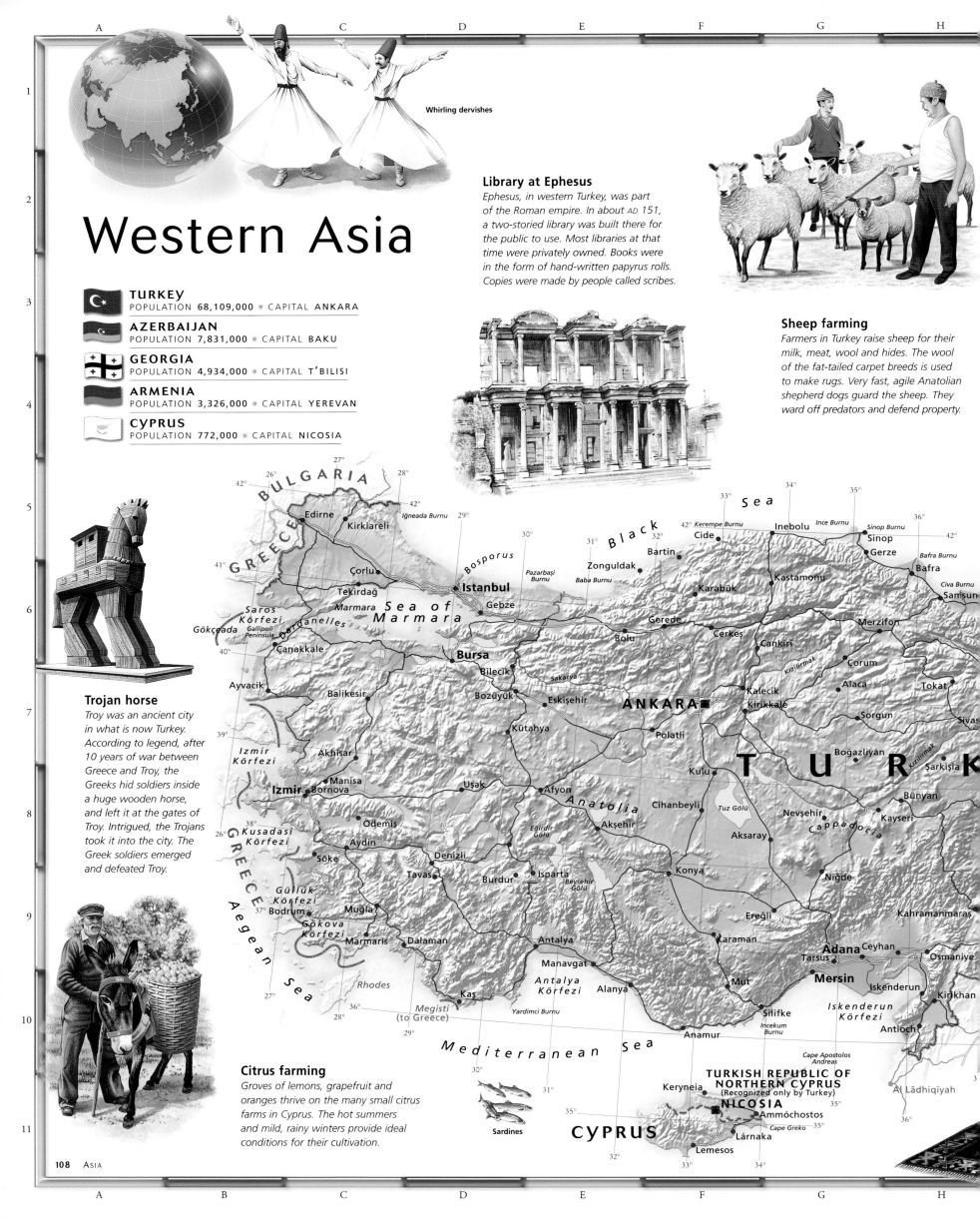

Western Asia

Whirling dervishes

TURKEY
POPULATION 68,109,000 ∗ CAPITAL ANKARA

AZERBAIJAN
POPULATION 7,831,000 ∗ CAPITAL BAKU

GEORGIA
POPULATION 4,934,000 ∗ CAPITAL T'BILISI

ARMENIA
POPULATION 3,326,000 ∗ CAPITAL YEREVAN

CYPRUS
POPULATION 772,000 ∗ CAPITAL NICOSIA

Library at Ephesus
Ephesus, in western Turkey, was part of the Roman empire. In about AD 151, a two-storied library was built there for the public to use. Most libraries at that time were privately owned. Books were in the form of hand-written papyrus rolls. Copies were made by people called scribes.

Sheep farming
Farmers in Turkey raise sheep for their milk, meat, wool and hides. The wool of the fat-tailed carpet breeds is used to make rugs. Very fast, agile Anatolian shepherd dogs guard the sheep. They ward off predators and defend property.

Trojan horse
Troy was an ancient city in what is now Turkey. According to legend, after 10 years of war between Greece and Troy, the Greeks hid soldiers inside a huge wooden horse, and left it at the gates of Troy. Intrigued, the Trojans took it into the city. The Greek soldiers emerged and defeated Troy.

Citrus farming
Groves of lemons, grapefruit and oranges thrive on the many small citrus farms in Cyprus. The hot summers and mild, rainy winters provide ideal conditions for their cultivation.

Sardines

Kurdish people

Kurds live in Turkey, Armenia, Iran, Iraq and Syria. They have no homeland of their own and their attempts to gain political independence have been crushed many times. Most Kurds are Muslims. They farm and herd sheep.

Rock formations of Cappadocia

An unusual landscape has formed at Cappadocia in central Turkey, as a result of lava eruptions from the now-extinct Mt Erciyes. Over centuries, wind and rain eroded the volcanic rock into strange, pointed formations. Early Christians made homes and churches in caves cut into the soft rock. Inside, they hid from their enemies.

Fresco
The walls of many of the cave churches are covered in paintings called frescoes. They are colorful, detailed representations of events from the Bible.

Sturgeon

Anchovies

Turquoise

Baku oil fields

Baku, on the Caspian Sea, is built on top of vast oil reserves. In the late 1900s, the city was supplying half the world's oil. Today, production is declining because the area has become severely polluted.

The Caspian Sea, a saltwater lake between Asia and Europe, is the largest inland expanse of water in the world. It is 750 miles (1,200 km) long and 270 miles (432 km) wide.

Turkish carpets

Turkey is famous for its beautiful handwoven carpets. Each carpet-producing region uses designs and colors that are unique to that area. The craftspeople often incorporate symbols into the design that relate to their own family history.

0 miles 140
0 kilometers 140

N
W E
S

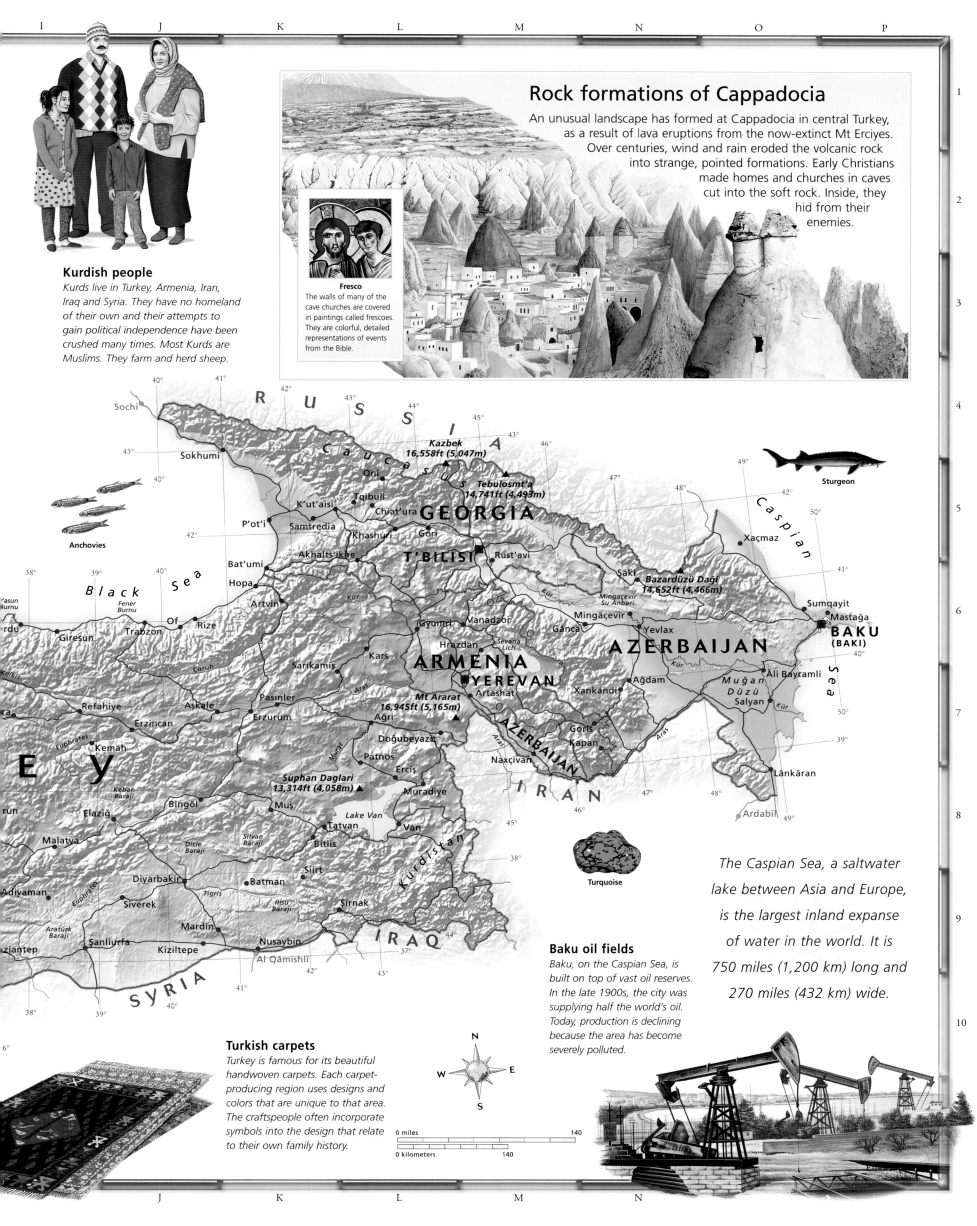

Map labels: RUSSIA, Sochi, Sokhumi, Caucasus, Kazbek 16,558ft (5,047m), Oni, Tebulosmt'a 14,741ft (4,493m), K'ut'aisi, Tqibuli, Chiat'ura, GEORGIA, P'ot'i, Samtredia, Khashuri, Gori, T'BILISI, Rust'avi, Xaçmaz, Caspian, Akhalts'ikhe, Bat'umi, Hopa, Artvin, Kür, Säki, Bazardüzü Daği 14,652ft (4,466m), Mingäçevir Su Anbari, Mingäçevir, Sumqayit, Mastağa, BAKU (BAKI), Giresun, Trabzon, Rize, Of, Gyumri, Vanadzor, Gäncä, Yevlax, AZERBAIJAN, Hrazdan, Sevana Lich, Ali Bayramli, Sarikamiş, Kars, ARMENIA, YEREVAN, Ağdam, Muğan Düzü, Salyan, Refahiye, Aşkale, Pasinler, Artashat, Xankändi, Erzincan, Erzurum, Aras, Mt Ararat 16,945ft (5,165m), Ağri, Gorls, Kapan, Kemah, Doğubeyazit, Naxçivan, Länkäran, Patnos, Erciş, AZERBAIJAN, IRAN, Elaziğ, Süphan Daglari 13,314ft (4,058m), Muradiye, Aras, Ardabil, Bingöl, Muş, Lake Van, Van, Malatya, Tatvan, Bitlis, Kurdistan, Adiyaman, Diyarbakir, Siirt, Siverek, Batman, Şirnak, Şanliurfa, Mardin, Kiziltepe, Nusaybin, Al Qämishli, IRAQ, SYRIA, ziantep, Black Sea, Yasun Burnu, Fener Burnu

Bactrian camel train
The two-humped bactrian camel can travel for four days without water. These camels have been used since ancient times to transport goods across the deserts of Central Asia.

Central Asia

PAKISTAN
POPULATION 150,695,000 ✳ CAPITAL ISLAMABAD

AFGHANISTAN
POPULATION 28,717,000 ✳ CAPITAL KABUL

UZBEKISTAN
POPULATION 25,982,000 ✳ CAPITAL TASHKENT

KAZAKHSTAN
POPULATION 16,764,000 ✳ CAPITAL ASTANA

TAJIKISTAN
POPULATION 6,864,000 ✳ CAPITAL DUSHANBE

KYRGYZSTAN
POPULATION 4,893,000 ✳ CAPITAL BISHKEK

TURKMENISTAN
POPULATION 4,776,000 ✳ CAPITAL ASHGABAT

The Aral Sea is an environmental disaster area. Harmful irrigation practices have turned two-thirds of the sea into desert over 30 years. The fishing industry is now in ruins.

Stranded fishing boats, Aral Sea

The Silk Road

The Silk Road is one of the most important trade routes in history. It was not a single road, but a network of shorter routes that linked scattered oasis settlements and market towns. From about 130 BC, goods from China were taken across the vast continent of Asia to the shores of the Mediterranean. Traders battled along the edges of deserts and braved dangerous mountain passes. Sometimes, camel trains were attacked by bandits. As well as goods, ideas, skills and religion also moved along the routes. Buddhism reached China from India in this way. The Silk Road declined in importance when a sea route from Europe to Asia was discovered in the late 15th century.

Turkey · China · India

—— Silk Road ■ Central Asia

Trading along the Silk Road

Few merchants ever traveled the full length of the route. Most covered just part of the journey, trading their wares for products from other countries, then returning home. Goods moved slowly and changed hands many times. Camel trains heading toward China carried gold, ivory, gems and glass.

Goods from Asia
Traders from Asia carried silk, furs, ceramics, jade and finely worked objects of bronze. Even in Roman times small quantities of Chinese goods were reaching Europe.

Uzbek clothing
The traditional layered clothing of the women of Uzbekistan is made from a multicolored silk fabric known as "the king of satins." Jewelry included a tiara with delicate pendants that followed the curve of the eyebrows.

Registan Square
This square in the ancient city of Samarkand, in Uzbekistan, was once a marketplace for traders traveling the Silk Road. Majestic Islamic buildings dating from the 14th century line the square.

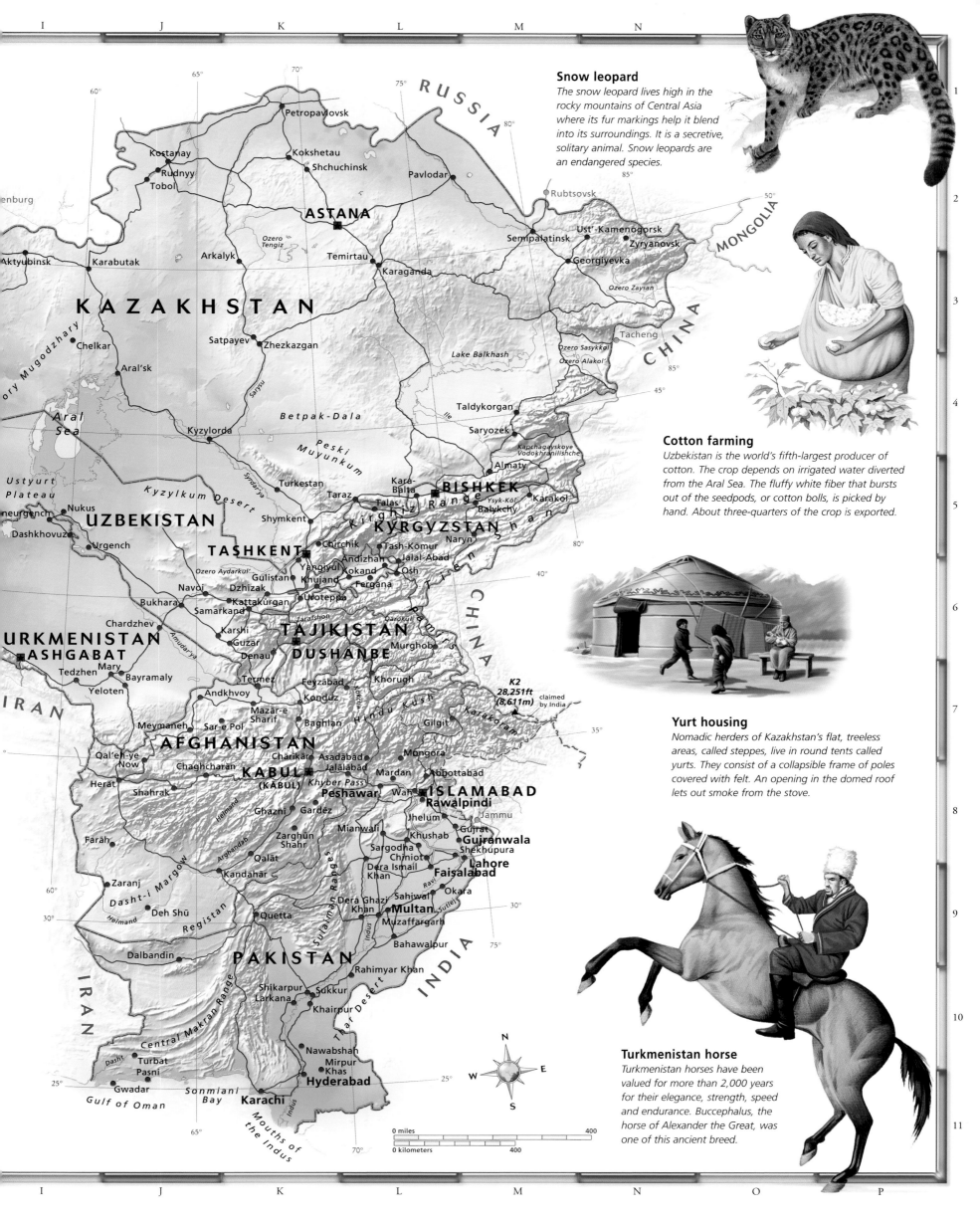

Snow leopard
The snow leopard lives high in the rocky mountains of Central Asia where its fur markings help it blend into its surroundings. It is a secretive, solitary animal. Snow leopards are an endangered species.

Cotton farming
Uzbekistan is the world's fifth-largest producer of cotton. The crop depends on irrigated water diverted from the Aral Sea. The fluffy white fiber that bursts out of the seedpods, or cotton bolls, is picked by hand. About three-quarters of the crop is exported.

Yurt housing
Nomadic herders of Kazakhstan's flat, treeless areas, called steppes, live in round tents called yurts. They consist of a collapsible frame of poles covered with felt. An opening in the domed roof lets out smoke from the stove.

Turkmenistan horse
Turkmenistan horses have been valued for more than 2,000 years for their elegance, strength, speed and endurance. Buccephalus, the horse of Alexander the Great, was one of this ancient breed.

RUSSIA
MONGOLIA
CHINA
IRAN
INDIA

KAZAKHSTAN
Petropavlovsk
Kostanay
Rudnyy
Tobol
Kokshetau
Shchuchinsk
Pavlodar
Rubtsovsk
Aktyubinsk
Karabutak
Arkalyk
Temirtau
ASTANA
Ust'-Kamenogorsk
Zyryanovsk
Semipalatinsk
Georgiyevka
Karaganda
Chelkar
Satpayev
Zhezkazgan
Ozero Tengiz
Ozero Zaysan
Tacheng
Aral'sk
Betpak-Dala
Lake Balkhash
Ozero Sasykköl
Ozero Alakol'
Aral Sea
Kyzylorda
Sarysu
Syrdar'ya
Ile
Taldykorgan
Saryozek
Kapchagayskoye Vodokhranilishche
Ustyurt Plateau
Peski Muyunkum
Turkestan
Taraz
Kara-Balta
BISHKEK
Almaty
neurgench
Nukus
Dashkhovuz
UZBEKISTAN
Shymkent
Talas
Karakol
Ysyk-Köl
Balykchy
Kyzylkum Desert
Urgench
KYRGYZSTAN
Kirghiz Range
Tien Shan
Chirchik
Tash-Kömur
Naryn
TASHKENT
Andizhan
Jalal-Abad
Yangiyul
Kokand
Osh
Ozero Aydarkul'
Khujand
Fergana
Navoi
Gulistan
Dzhizak
Uroteppa
Bukhara
Kattakurgan
URKMENISTAN
Chardzhev
Samarkand
Karshi
TAJIKISTAN
Murghob
Zarafshon
Qarokul
Amudar'ya
ASHGABAT
Guzar
Denau
DUSHANBE
Pamirs
Tedzhen
Mary
Bayramaly
Yeloten
Termez
Feyzabad
Khorugh
K2 28,251ft (8,611m)
claimed by India
Andkhvoy
Konduz
Vakhsh
Meymaneh
Sar-e Pol
Mazar-e Sharif
Baghlan
Gilgit
Hindu Kush
Karakoram
IRAN
Qal'eh-ye Now
Chaghcharan
AFGHANISTAN
Charikar
Asadabad
Jalalabad
Mardan
Abbottabad
Mongora
Herat
Shahrak
KABUL (KABUL)
Khyber Pass
Peshawar
Wah
ISLAMABAD
Ghazni
Gardez
Rawalpindi
Jhelum
Jammu
Farah
Zarghun Shahr
Mianwali
Khushab
Gujrat
Gujranwala
Arghandab
Qalat
Sargodha
Chiniot
Shekhupura
Zaranj
Kandahar
Dera Ismail Khan
Lahore
Faisalabad
Dasht-i Margow
Arghandab
Helmand
Ravi
Sutlej
Deh Shu
Quetta
Dera Ghazi Khan
Sahiwal
Okara
Multan
Registan
Muzaffargarh
Sulaiman Ranges
Indus
Dalbandin
Bahawalpur
PAKISTAN
Rahimyar Khan
INDIA
Shikarpur
Larkana
Sukkur
Thar Desert
Khairpur
Central Makran Range
Nawabshah
Mirpur Khas
Hyderabad
Dasht
Turbat
Pasni
Gwadar
Gulf of Oman
Sonmiani Bay
Karachi
Mouths of the Indus
Indus

N
W E
S

0 miles 400
0 kilometers 400

The city of Kandahar in Afghanistan was founded by Alexander the Great in the 4th century BC.

Western and Central Asia

LAND AREA	2,435,424 sq miles (6,307,720 sq km)
LARGEST COUNTRY	Kazakhstan
SMALLEST COUNTRY	Cyprus
MAIN RELIGION	Muslim
LIFE EXPECTANCY	64 years
LITERACY	88%

- Forest and woodland
- Arable land
- Grazing
- Arid or marginal

USING THE LAND

- Cereals
- Rice
- Wheat
- Fruit and vegetables
- Fruit
- Citrus fruits
- Wine
- Cotton
- Tobacco
- Sugar beet
- Dates
- Beef cattle
- Sheep
- Fishing
- Industrial center
- Mining
- Oil production
- Gas production

Opium poppies
Opium poppies, used to make drugs such as morphine and codine, are grown widely in Afghanistan. Sap from the seedpods is often traded illegally, and is used to produce the banned drug, heroin.

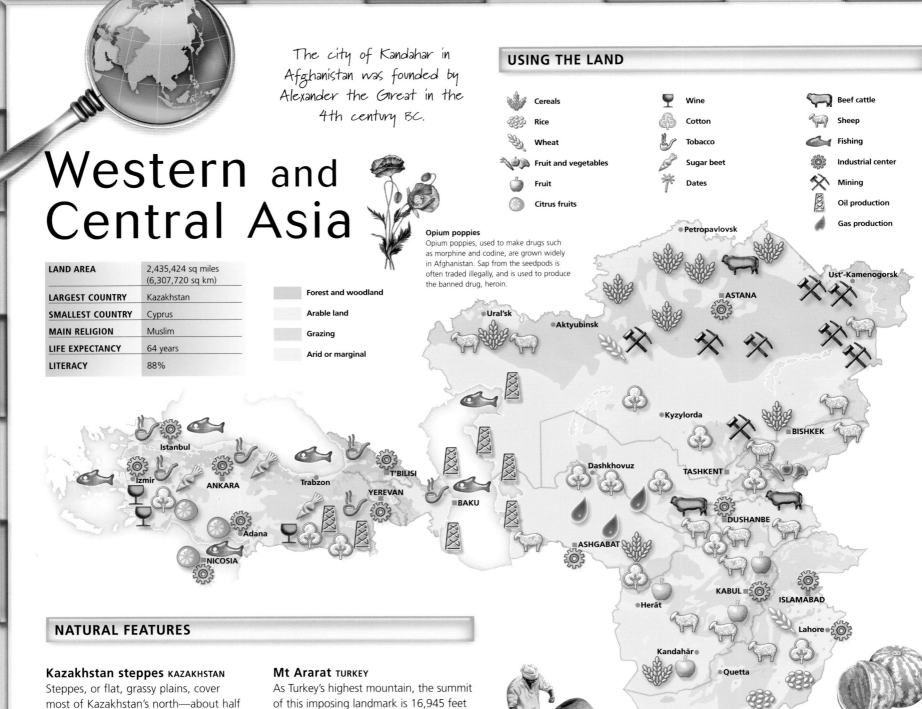

NATURAL FEATURES

Kazakhstan steppes KAZAKHSTAN
Steppes, or flat, grassy plains, cover most of Kazakhstan's north—about half of this country's total area. Farmers raise sheep and cattle in some parts.

Pammukale TURKEY
These chalk-coated cliffs look like a frozen waterfall. Calcium-rich spring waters flow over the cliffs to form pools, overhangs, stalactites and other formations.

Tien Shan
These largely unexplored, snow-capped mountains run for 1,500 miles (2,410 km) between Kazakhstan, Kyrgyzstan and China, along the steppe's southern edge.

North Anatolian Fault TURKEY
This fault, or deep crack in Earth's surface, runs from the Sea of Marmara to Lake Van. Shifting land either side of the fault can cause earthquakes, most recently in 1999, when more than 18,000 people died.

Mt Ararat TURKEY
As Turkey's highest mountain, the summit of this imposing landmark is 16,945 feet (5,165 m) above sea level. A glacier stretches down its northern face. The mountain is thought to be the resting place of Noah's Ark, referred to in the Old Testament of the Bible.

Khyber Pass

The Khyber Pass links Pakistan and Afghanistan through the Hindu Kush mountains. It is 33 miles (53 km) long. Invading armies have used it as a passage for centuries. The pass was well defended, and ancient fortresses and watchtowers still stand. It is walled by steep cliffs, and narrows to less than 10 feet (3 m) in parts.

Wheat
Wheat, which is grown extensively throughout this region, is used to make flat bread. The bread is sometimes cooked in a clay oven under the ground (*above*). Regional varieties include *nan*, *pide* and *chapatti*. *Jelabi* is an Afghan sweet bread that is deep-fried and coated in sugar syrup. Rice and other cereals are also grown in Western and Central Asia.

"Stan" at the end of a country's name means country.

Watermelons
In spring, snow from the Tien Shan mountains melts, providing water for irrigation. The fertile valleys of Kazakhstan are excellent for growing fruit crops, such as watermelons and citrus fruits.

WHERE PEOPLE LIVE

Urban	Rural

REGION
48% | 52%

Most urban: TURKEY
74% | 26%

Most rural: AFGHANISTAN
20% | 80%

LARGEST CITIES

Karachi 10,809,000

Istanbul 9,631,000

Lahore 5,904,000

Ankara 3,544,000

Hagia Sophia

Hagia Sophia, in Istanbul, Turkey, is one of the most spectacular examples of domed architecture in the world. It was built as a Christian church in the 6th century, in the Byzantine period. From 1453 until the 1930s, Hagia Sophia was used as a mosque. Many of its features—from the intricate mosaics and fountain, to the minarets (tall towers) built on each corner—are from this period. Today, it is used as a museum.

PEOPLE

Ismail al-Bukhari AD 810–870
This Arabic scholar wrote a book of sayings of the prophet Muhammad. Muslims believe it is second in value only to their holy book, the Koran.

Öz Beg ruled 1312–41
As khan, or ruler, of the Golden Horde—an area under Mongol rule—Öz Beg adopted Islam as his religion. The Uzbek people derive their name from his.

Timur the Great 1336–1405
Some say this Mongol ruler, known as

Tamerlane in Europe, was one of history's most bloodthirsty tyrants, while others believe he was wise and just. Today, pilgrims and tourists flock to his tomb in Samarkand.

Roxelana died 1558
Chosen from the sultan's harem as his favorite, Roxelana became the wife of the Ottoman ruler Süleyman, and advised him on political and social matters.

Mustafa Kemal Atatürk 1881–1938
This military hero became Turkey's first president and prime minister in 1923, after he led a nationalist movement to abolish Ottoman rule.

Mustafa Kemal Atatürk

Imran Khan born 1952
This world-class Pakistani cricketer first captained his country's cricket team in 1982. He is now a politician.

PLACES

Kabul AFGHANISTAN
Afghanistan's capital, Kabul, has been under constant attack over the centuries. Following Soviet occupation in the 1980s, civil war broke out, with warlords fighting for control of the city. From 1996 to 2002, Kabul was controlled by the repressive Taliban.

Istanbul TURKEY
Called Constantinople until its capture by the Ottomans in the 15th century, Istanbul is Turkey's grandest city. Much of its architecture is from Byzantine times.

Samarkand UZBEKISTAN
Samarkand, Uzbekistan's second-largest city, is also one of the world's oldest. Its culture is a blend of Iranian, Indian and Mongolian traditions.

Badshahi Mosque PAKISTAN
This 5,000-seat mosque (below) at Lahore is the largest in the Indian subcontinent. Its enclosed central space and beautiful pool are typical of Islamic architecture.

TRADITIONS AND CULTURE

Shari'a law
Often called Islamic law, this legal system has been inspired by religious traditions and writings, notably the Koran. Many of the laws relate to worship, politics, criminal acts and family life.

Buzkashi
In this regional sport, players compete on horseback to bring an animal carcass into a scoring circle. *Buzkashi* means "goat grabbing."

Hamam
These are traditional baths Turkish men and women still visit regularly. Bathers go through three stages—they lie on hot marble, making them sweat, then have a body massage, followed by a drink.

In Greek mythology, the goddess Aphrodite was born in the waves of Cyprus.

An imam, or Muslim leader

Tool artifacts

Mohenjo-daro PAKISTAN
The ruins of this ancient city lie on the banks of the Indus River. The well-planned city was built around 3000 BC, with buildings made from unbaked mud bricks. It was the largest city of the ancient Indus civilization.

Topkapi harem

In the 15th century, part of Turkey's Topkapi Palace (above) was home to a group of women chosen to look after the *padishah*, or ruler. Women in the Topkapi harem lived in the palace for life, and were forbidden to leave. At times, there were several thousand women in the harem.

Islamic art
Islamic art is brightly colored, with strong patterns and shapes. Calligraphy, or decorative handwriting, and geometric patterns (*above*)

are typical features of this style. Islamic designs decorate ceramics, glass, textiles, metalwork and woodwork.

Grand Bazaar
This shopping market in Istanbul's center, which started as just a few stalls in the 15th century, now contains 4,000 shops stretching through 60 streets. Everything from leather and carpets to sweets and spices (*below*) is for sale.

Constantinople

AD 330
The emperor Constantine I renames Byzantium as Constantinople and makes it the capital of the Eastern Roman and Byzantine empires. The city becomes the new financial and political center and remains powerful for the next 1,000 years, but slowly declines by the 12th century.

1401
The Safavid dynasty in Persia is founded by Shah Ismail I. In the years to come, wars are fought between the Safavids and Ottoman Turks.

1453
The Ottoman Turks, headed by Sultan Mehmet, capture Constantinople. During Mehmet's reign, the Grand Bazaar is redeveloped, which improves the city's economy. The architectural masterpiece, the Topkapi Palace, is built.

1457
The Ottomans rename the city of Constantinople as Istanbul, and declare it the capital of their growing empire. Five years later, the Ottoman Turks take over Bosnia.

1520
Süleyman I, known as Süleyman the Magnificent because of his successes in expanding the empire, is crowned ruler over the Ottoman empire. Art and architecture expand during his reign.

Süleyman the Magnificent

1522
The Turks capture the Greek Island of Rhodes in the Aegean Sea and by 1524 it becomes part of the Ottoman empire.

1526
The Turks invade Hungary in the Battle of Mohacs. The battle lasts only two hours and the Turks gain victory, claiming Hungary for the Ottomans.

1529
The Turks fail to capture the city of Vienna, capital of Austria. The Ottoman empire shows signs of losing power.

1571
The Turks are defeated at the Battle of Lepanto, a huge sea battle fought off the coast of Greece between a Turkish and a Christian fleet.

1590
The Turks and Persians make peace after years of fighting with each other. Shortly after this, the Ottoman empire starts to decline.

1909
The last of the 36 Ottoman sultans, Muhammed Vahiduddin starts his reign. His rule ends in 1922 after Mustafa Kemal Atatürk abolishes the Muslim rank of sultan and founds the Republic of Turkey in 1924.

Muhammed Vahiduddin

Desert oasis

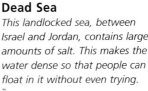

The Middle East

IRAN
POPULATION 68,279,000 * CAPITAL TEHRAN

IRAQ
POPULATION 24,683,000 * CAPITAL BAGHDAD

SAUDI ARABIA
POPULATION 24,294,000 * CAPITAL RIYADH

YEMEN
POPULATION 19,350,000 * CAPITAL ŞAN'Ā'

SYRIA
POPULATION 17,586,000 * CAPITAL DAMASCUS

ISRAEL
POPULATION 6,117,000 * CAPITAL JERUSALEM

JORDAN
POPULATION 5,460,000 * CAPITAL AMMĀN

LEBANON
POPULATION 3,728,000 * CAPITAL BEIRUT

OMAN
POPULATION 2,807,000 * CAPITAL MUSCAT

UNITED ARAB EMIRATES
POPULATION 2,485,000 * CAPITAL ABU DHABI

KUWAIT
POPULATION 2,183,000 * CAPITAL KUWAIT

QATAR
POPULATION 817,000 * CAPITAL DOHA

BAHRAIN
POPULATION 667,000 * CAPITAL AL MANĀMAH

Dead Sea
This landlocked sea, between Israel and Jordan, contains large amounts of salt. This makes the water dense so that people can float in it without even trying.

The world's largest known reserves of oil are in the Middle East. Saudi Arabia, Iraq, Iran, the United Arab Emirates and Kuwait are among the world's leading oil producers.

Jerusalem's holy sites

Jerusalem is one of the holiest cities in the world. Within its boundaries are sites central to the beliefs of the Jewish, Christian and Islamic faiths. Jews consider Jerusalem a holy city because it was the religious center and capital of the ancient Israelite nation. For Christians, it is the place where Jesus Christ taught and was crucified. Muslims believe that Muhammad, the founder of Islam, rose to heaven from Jerusalem. Over the centuries, followers of these faiths have often disagreed about who controls Jerusalem, and conflicts have occurred as a result.

Jewish rabbi

Western Wall
This wall is all that remains of the Jewish Temple destroyed by the Romans in AD 70. It is the Jews' holiest site. They pray here and leave prayers on pieces of paper between the stones.

Temple Mount
Muslims believe Muhammad was lifted to heaven from the rock that lies directly beneath the golden dome. It is one of the most sacred Islamic sites. Jews believe the rock is the place where Abraham prepared to sacrifice his son, Isaac.

Church of the Holy Sepulchre
This church is built over the site where many Christians believe Jesus Christ was crucified. It is said to contain the sepulchre (tomb) where he was buried. The building dates from 1149, the time of Crusades.

Muslim praying

Christian nun

Hunting with falcons
This is a traditional sport in Saudi Arabia. Young, preferably female, wild falcons are trained to kill prey and return it to their handler. A leather glove protects the handler's arm from sharp talons.

Map labels

Manbij, Aleppo, Antioch, Al Lādhiqīyah, Idlib, Ar Raqq, Tarṭūs, Hamāh, SYRIA, Tripoli, Ḥimṣ, Palmyr, LEBANON, Baʿalbek, BEIRUT (BAYRŪT), DAMASC (DIMASHQ), Soûr, Saida, As Suwaydā', Haifa, Nazareth, ISRAEL, Nablus, Syri, Tel Aviv-Jaffa, Jericho, Az Zarqā', Muq, JERUSALEM, Gaza, AMMĀN, Tura, EGYPT, Be'er Sheva, Dead Sea, Kāf, Suez Canal, Negev, JORDAN, Ma'ān, Ham, CAIRO (EL QĀHIRA), Suez, Sinai, Wadi Rum, At Tubay, Elat, Al 'Aqabah, Gulf of Aqaba, Gulf of Suez, Jabal al Lawz ▲ 8,461 ft (2,579 m), Al Ḥijaz, Tabūk, Hurghada, Ras Karkūmā, Nile, Rās Abū Madd, Medi, Rās Baridī, Tropic of Cancer, Yanbu' al Baḥr, Rābigh, Nubian Desert, Jeddah, M, SUDAN, Port Sudan, Suakin, ERITRE, Massawa, ASMARA, Mediterranean Sea

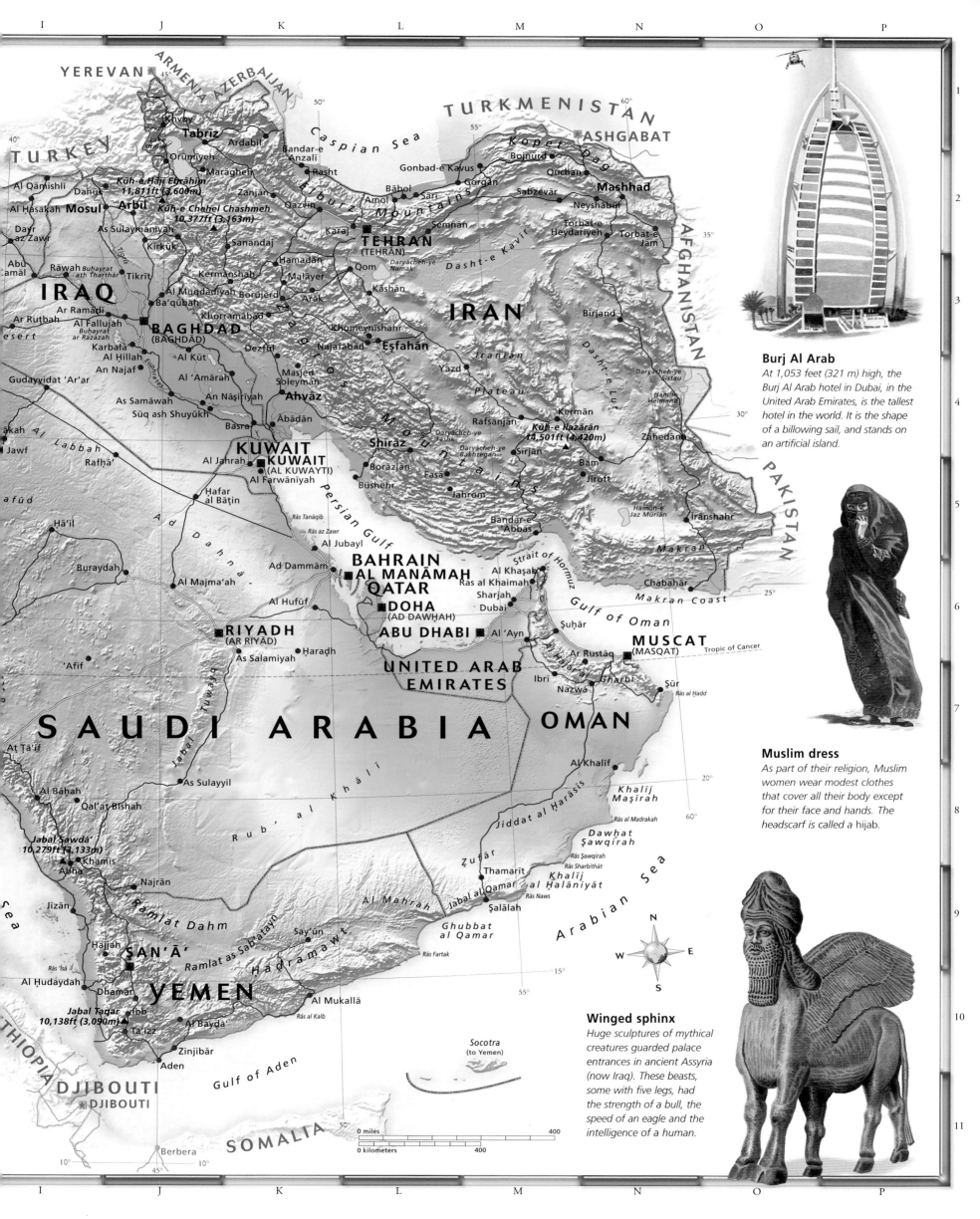

Burj Al Arab
At 1,053 feet (321 m) high, the Burj Al Arab hotel in Dubai, in the United Arab Emirates, is the tallest hotel in the world. It is the shape of a billowing sail, and stands on an artificial island.

Muslim dress
As part of their religion, Muslim women wear modest clothes that cover all their body except for their face and hands. The headscarf is called a hijab.

Winged sphinx
Huge sculptures of mythical creatures guarded palace entrances in ancient Assyria (now Iraq). These beasts, some with five legs, had the strength of a bull, the speed of an eagle and the intelligence of a human.

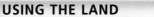

The Middle East

- Forest and woodland
- Arable land
- Grazing
- Arid or marginal

Frankincense
Thousands of years ago, frankincense was used for religious ceremonies and embalming. It comes from a small tree that is common in the southern part of Arabia. The bark is scraped off (*left*) and eventually a gum, frankincense, oozes out. Today, it is used in incense and perfumes.

LAND AREA	1,971,313 sq miles (5,105,677 sq km)
LARGEST COUNTRY	Iran
SMALLEST COUNTRY	Bahrain
MAIN RELIGION	Muslim
LIFE EXPECTANCY	73 years
LITERACY	78%

NATURAL FEATURES

Elburz and Zagros mountains IRAN
There are two mountain ranges in Iran, the Zagros and the Elburz. Mt Damavand, at more than 18,638 feet (5,681 m) above sea level, is Iran's highest peak. It is an almost extinct volcano, which still spouts occasional plumes of gas.

Mt Damavand

Mesopotamia IRAQ
Mesopotamia (from a Greek word that means "between the rivers") was the site of the world's earliest civilizations, from about 10,000 BC. It lay between the Tigris and Euphrates rivers. The northern region had a mild climate and fertile land, while the southern had lush, marshy areas.

Arz el Rab LEBANON
Arz el Rab, or Cedars of the Lord, is the oldest cedar grove in Lebanon. The mountains were once covered with cedar trees, since cut down over the centuries.

Wadi Rum JORDAN

This wadi, or river valley, is unusual for its deep, pinkish sands covered in small shrubs, and its occasional enormous rock formations, called *jebels,* that rise up into the sky, making the wadi look rather like the surface of the Moon.

Map legend:
- Rice
- Wheat
- Fruit
- Citrus fruits
- Cotton
- Coffee
- Dates
- Sheep
- Goats
- Fishing
- Industrial center
- Oil production
- Gas production

Map labels: Tabriz, Mashhad, Aleppo, Mosul, Al Lādhiqīyah, TEHRAN, BEIRUT, DAMASCUS, BAGHDAD, Eşfahān, Haifa, Ahvāz, Tel Aviv-Jaffa, AMMAN, JERUSALEM, Be'ér Sheva', Basra, Kermān, Zāhedān, KUWAIT, Shīrāz, Bandar-e 'Abbās, AL MANĀMAH, Dubai, DOHA, RIYADH, ABU DHABI, MUSCAT, Jeddah, ŞAN'Ā', Aden

Grain
Wheat, millet and barley are the main grain crops of the Middle East. The greatest problem is the lack of water but the area suitable for growing these crops has been extended by irrigation. Small crops are even planted in moist wadis (river valleys) in the desert.

WHERE PEOPLE LIVE

	Urban	Rural	

REGION

Urban 76%	Rural 24%

Most urban: KUWAIT

97%	3%

Most rural: YEMEN

24%	76%

The Crusades
In the 11th century, Palestine was under the control of the Muslims. In 1095, Pope Urban II joined with the Byzantine emperor to recapture the Holy Land (Palestine) from the Muslims for the Christians. For almost 200 years, until 1294, the armies of eight separate crusades raided Palestine. In periods of peace, the crusaders were accepted and entertained by the Muslims (*above*).

Oil
The Middle East has some of the world's largest and most productive oilfields. The most important are in Saudi Arabia, Iran, Iraq and Kuwait. Kuwait is the second-largest oil producer (Saudi Arabia is the largest) in the Middle East. During the 1991 Gulf War, the Iraqis set fire to many of the oil wells and oil refineries in Kuwait (*above*).

LARGEST CITIES

Tehran 8,068,000

Baghdad 5,949,000

Riyadh 3,823,000

Jeddah 2,818,000

Mashhad 2,082,000

TRADITIONS AND CULTURE

Damascus souks
Souks, or market stalls, are a common sight in the old section of Damascus, Syria. Famous for their crafts, the souks sell fine damask tapestries, glassware and carvings inlaid with mother-of-pearl.

Kibbutzim
These are groups of farms in Israel in which the owners share the work, the decision-making, the food and the earnings in return for the work they do for the community.

Camel racing
Camel races are popular in Saudi Arabia. Every year, more than 2,000 camels and riders compete in the grueling King's Cup Camel Race in Riyadh.

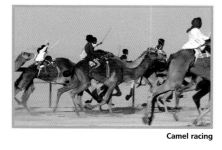
Camel racing

Over 95 percent of Saudi Arabia is desert. The Rub' al Khali desert is known as the Empty Quarter.

PLACES

Jericho ISRAEL
The ancient walled city of Jericho was first settled around 8350 BC. Now situated in the West Bank area, Jericho was handed over to Palestinian control in 1994 after years of unrest.

Petra JORDAN
Once a wealthy trading center, the city of Petra (*left*) was carved from red sandstone cliffs more than 2,000 years ago. It seems to have been abandoned at some time in the 6th century.

Baghdad IRAQ
The capital of Iraq and its largest city, Baghdad is situated near the Tigris River. The site has been settled since ancient times, and Baghdad was once one of the world's richest cities. Much of the city has been destroyed by recent wars.

Five pillars of Islam
Mecca, in Saudi Arabia, is the holiest city of Islam. One of the five duties (or pillars) of faith for Muslims is that they make a pilgrimage to Mecca (a hajj, *above*) at least once in their lifetime.

Birthplace of religions
The Middle East is the birthplace of three of the world's major religions: Christianity, Judaism and Islam. Judaism, which began in the area around 2000 BC, is the world's oldest major religion. Christianity, based on the teachings of Jesus Christ around 2,000 years ago, also reveres some of Judaism's scriptures as holy. Islam arose in the 7th century from the teachings of the prophet Muhammad.

Mecca SAUDI ARABIA
Every year, millions of Muslims make the pilgrimage to Mecca, the birthplace of Muhammad, to pray. Muslims think of Mecca as their homeland and even when they are elsewhere in the world, they face in the direction of Mecca to pray.

Esfahan IRAN
One of the largest cities in Iran, Esfahan is famous for its mosques, such as the 17th-century Royal Mosque, now called Masjid-e Iman, its medieval Islamic architecture and its public gardens.

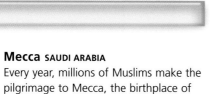
Royal Mosque

PEOPLE

Solomon c 1000 BC
Solomon, son of King David, was the third king of ancient Israel. He was known as a wise and clever king who established peace and unity in Israel.

King Solomon

Harun Al-Rashid AD 766–809
A ruler of the Abbasid dynasty, Harun Al-Rashid supported the arts, literature, mathematics and medicine. The capital, Baghdad, flourished under his rule.

Saladin 1138–93
Saladin, a Muslim sultan, captured Jerusalem from the Christians in 1187. The English king Richard the Lionheart fought against him in the Third Crusade, which ended in a truce in 1192.

Ibn Saud 1880–1953
From 1902, when he first attacked Riyadh, Ibn Saud's aim was to unify Arabia. He achieved this in 1932, when he brought tribal conflicts under control and became the king of Arabia.

Ayatollah Khomeini 1900–89
In 1979, this Muslim leader took control of Iran from the king and changed its government to an Islamic republic. Khomeini was its first leader.

Flying carpet

Arabian Nights
Also called *The Thousand and One Nights*, this collection of almost 200 folktales first appeared around the year AD 800. The stories tell of the heroic and romantic adventures of well-known characters, such as Sinbad the Sailor, Aladdin and Ali Baba. These tales have been collected from several countries, including Arabia, India, Egypt and Persia.

HISTORY AT A GLANCE
ANCIENT MESOPOTAMIA

c 5000 BC
Tribes, probably from Arabia, begin to settle into village life along the banks of the Tigris and Euphrates rivers—the area called Mesopotamia.

c 3000 BC
The Sumerians, an advanced culture whose inventions include writing, a calendar, systems of measurement and the wheel, live in this area.

c 2340 BC
Sargon of Agade, a military ruler from central Mesopotamia, conquers Syria and the Sumer, forming the kingdom of Akkad, the first nation-state in world history.

c 1760 BC
King Hammurabi, of the Amorite dynasty, establishes Babylon as an important trading center and the capital of Mesopotamia. He introduces laws, called the Code of Hammurabi, which are carved into a black stone called a stela (*right*).

Hammurabi

c 1600 BC
The Hittites, a people from an area that is now part of Turkey, sweep down into Babylon, conquer and plunder the city, and bring the dynasty of Hammurabi to an end.

c 1240 BC
The Assyrians, a people from the northern part of what is now Iraq, decide to expand into Babylon. After a series of battles, Hittite power collapses and the Assyrians control Babylon.

c 1200 BC
One of the oldest epics in world literature, *The Epic of Gilgamesh*, is written, telling the tale of Gilgamesh, a powerful king in ancient Sumeria.

c 1155 BC
The Assyrians create a unified empire by installing Assyrian rulers in each capital they conquer.

706–681 BC
Sennacherib succeeds his father, Sargon II, as king of Assyria. He makes Nineveh the capital city, and sets up a library of thousands of clay tablets of technical and scientific writings. In 689, he destroys the city of Babylon.

612 BC
The Medes, a people from Iran, join forces with the Babylonians to destroy the Assyrian empire.

Ishtar Gate

605–562 BC
King Nebuchadnezzar II captures Jerusalem and controls the southern area of Mesopotamia. He rebuilds Babylon and fortifies it with walls. One of its eight gates is the Ishtar Gate (*above*), named after Ishtar, goddess of love and war.

539 BC
The Persian king, Cyrus the Great, and his soldiers (*right*), incorporate Babylon into the rapidly growing Persian empire. Persia rules much of the Middle East until it is conquered by Alexander the Great.

331 BC
Macedonian general Alexander the Great conquers Babylon, ruling until his death in 323.

Persian soldier

Southern Asia

INDIA POPULATION 1,049,700,000 * CAPITAL NEW DELHI

BANGLADESH POPULATION 138,448,000 * CAPITAL DHAKA

NEPAL POPULATION 26,470,000 * CAPITAL KATHMANDU

SRI LANKA POPULATION 19,742,000 * CAPITAL COLOMBO

BHUTAN POPULATION 2,140,000 * CAPITAL THIMPHU

MALDIVES POPULATION 330,000 * CAPITAL MALE

The Himalayas

The Himalayas extend more than 1,600 miles (2,600 km) from northern Pakistan, through Kashmir and northern India, across Tibet and Nepal and into Bhutan. Although the mountains are known as the Himalayas, they are three separate ranges. The Great Himalaya range includes Mount Everest. Nearly a third of the world's mammal species live in the Himalayas. They include the snow leopard and the red panda. Rhododendrons bloom on the lower slopes and there are more than 250 species of orchids.

How the Himalayas were formed

The Himalayas were formed by the collision of two tectonic plates. The Indian Plate and the Eurasian Plate started on their collision course about 60 million years ago.

Continents in collision
One continent pushes over the top of the other and the rocks start to crumple and fold.

Rising mountains
Peaks are thrust upward as pressure continues. Fossils from the seabed move to the top of the mountains.

Growing sideways
Some land is pushed outward, so the mountain range then extends sideways.

On the move
The continents are carried along by Earth's tectonic plates. The plates are moving up to 8 inches (20 cm) per year in some places.

EURASIAN PLATE

INDIA today

Equator

INDIAN OCEAN

Sri Lanka

"INDIA" landmass

10 million years ago

38 million years ago

55 million years ago

71 million years ago

Indian elephants
The Indian, or Asian, elephant is smaller than the African elephant. It is a strong, calm animal that can carry people, logs and food.

Taj Mahal
The Taj Mahal near Agra, in northern India, was built in the mid-1600s by Mughal emperor Shah Jahan as a monument to his favorite wife. It is made of white marble and decorated with jewels and carvings.

The largest, most famous sapphire in the world was discovered in Sri Lanka more than 300 years ago. Surprisingly, it is called the Star of India.

Indian dancer
Dancing takes place at festivals throughout India. Some dances tell stories or are associated with a particular religion This dancer in Jaipur, in Rajasthan, is celebrating Holi, the festival that welcomes spring and honors elephants.

CHINA

Mishmi Hills

Dibrugarh

Tinsukia

Brahmaputra

CHINA

BHUTAN

THIMPHU

Kula Kangri 24,783ft (7,554m)

Mt Everest 29,035ft (8,850m)

KATHMANDU

NEPAL

Dharan

Annapurna 26,545ft (8,091m)

Dhangadhi

Bahraich

Faizabad

Gorakhpur

Ghaghara

Shahjahanpur

Pilibhit

Bareilly

Budaun

Sitapur

Fatehgarh

Lucknow

Rampur

Moradabad

Haldwani

Aligarh

Hathras

Firozabad

Agra

Mathura

Alwar

Faridabad

Ghaziabad

NEW DELHI

Delhi

Meerut

Muzaffarnagar

Karnal

Saharanpur

Dehra Dun

Chandigarh

Ludhiana

Patiala

Bathinda

Jalandhar

Hoshiarpur

Pathankot

Amritsar

Jammu

Srinagar

Line of Control

Jammu and Kashmir

Ladakh

K2 28,251ft (8,611m)

Karakoram Range

(Administered by China, claimed by India)

(Administered by China, claimed by India)

(Administered by China, claimed by India)

(Administered by China, claimed by India)

Hindu Kush

ISLAMABAD

PAKISTAN

Lahore

Gujranwala

Jhelum

Sikar

Bikaner

Jaipur

Rajasthan

Thar Desert

Hisar

Bhiwani

Rohtak

Sirsa

Ganganagar

Moga

Abohar

Punjab

Himalaya

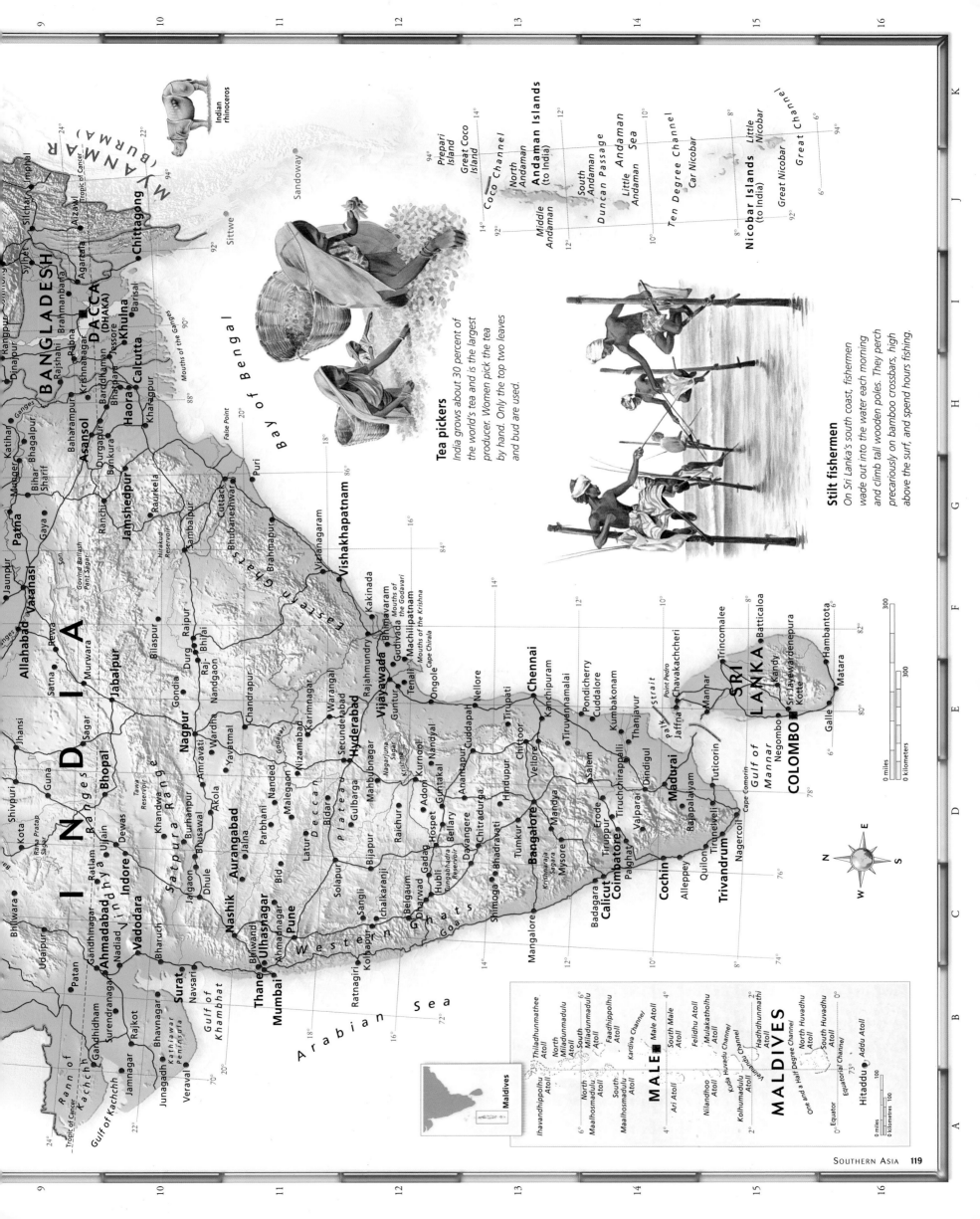

Tea pickers
India grows about 30 percent of the world's tea and is the largest producer. Women pick the tea by hand. Only the top two leaves and bud are used.

Stilt fishermen
On Sri Lanka's south coast, fishermen wade out into the water each morning and climb tall wooden poles. They perch precariously on bamboo crossbars, high above the surf, and spend hours fishing.

Southern Asia

The Maldives has over 1,200 islands, but only about 80 are open to foreigners.

Bhutan is the only country with a national park formed to protect the yeti.

INDIA TOTAL AREA	1,147,955 sq miles (2,973,190 sq km)
OFFICIAL LANGUAGE	English, Hindu and others
MAIN RELIGION	Hinduism
LIFE EXPECTANCY	63 years
LITERACY	59%

BANGLADESH TOTAL AREA	51,703 sq miles (133,910 sq km)
OFFICIAL LANGUAGE	Bangla (Bengali)
MAIN RELIGION	Muslim
LIFE EXPECTANCY	61 years
LITERACY	43%

NEPAL TOTAL AREA	52,819 sq miles (136,800 sq km)
OFFICIAL LANGUAGE	Nepali
MAIN RELIGION	Hinduism
LIFE EXPECTANCY	59 years
LITERACY	41%

SRI LANKA TOTAL AREA	24,996 sq miles (64,740 sq km)
OFFICIAL LANGUAGE	Sinhala
MAIN RELIGION	Buddhism
LIFE EXPECTANCY	72 years
LITERACY	92%

BHUTAN TOTAL AREA	18,147 sq miles (47,000 sq km)
OFFICIAL LANGUAGE	Dzongkha
MAIN RELIGION	Buddhism
LIFE EXPECTANCY	53 years
LITERACY	42%

One-fifth of the world's people live in Southern Asia.

WHERE PEOPLE LIVE

Urban	Rural

INDIA
28% | 72%

BANGLADESH
24% | 76%

SRI LANKA
23% | 77%

NEPAL
12% | 88%

BHUTAN
7% | 93%

Map legend

- Cereals
- Rice
- Jute
- Cotton
- Tea
- Groundnuts
- Rubber
- Beef cattle
- Goats
- Fishing
- Industrial center
- Mining
- Tourism

Map labels: Srinagar, Delhi, NEW DELHI, KATHMANDU, THIMPHU, Varanasi, DACCA, Ahmadabad, Calcutta, Chittagong, Mumbai, Hyderabad, Chennai, COLOMBO

LARGEST CITIES

Mumbai 12,623,000

Delhi 10,401,000

Dacca 9,363,000

Calcutta 4,853,000

HIGHEST MOUNTAINS

Kangchenjunga 28,169 feet (8,586 m)
Mt Everest 29,035 feet (8,850 m)
Lhotse 27,940 feet (8,516 m)
Makalu 27,765 feet (8,462 m)

USING THE LAND

- Forest and woodland
- Arable land
- Grazing
- Arid or marginal

Rice
Rice is grown throughout Southern Asia and is the largest single crop of Sri Lanka. Much rice cultivation is still performed by hand (below). A variety of long-grained rice called basmati, grown in northern India, is prized for its light, fluffy texture and delicate aroma. More than half the world's people depend on rice for survival.

Jute
Jute is a strong, fibrous plant used in rope, mats and sacking. Jute is one of Bangladesh's greatest income sources, and its largest export crop. However, the production of synthetic fibers is now threatening this industry's future.

Ladakh

NATURAL FEATURES

Thar Desert INDIA
Also known as the Great Indian Desert, the Thar covers 74,000 square miles (192,000 sq km) in northwest India. High winds erode the desert's sand dunes into constantly changing forms.

The Sundarbans INDIA–BANGLADESH
One of the largest mangrove swamps on Earth, the Sundarbans span the border between India and Bangladesh on the Bay of Bengal. They are home to rare species of animals, such as the Bengal tiger (below) and the Indian python.

Ladakh KASHMIR
The remote region of Ladakh, often called the Land of High Passes, lies across the disputed Kashmir Valley in the rainshadow of the Indian Himalayas. High plains and deep valleys dominate the landscape. It is one of the highest and driest regions in the world.

Mt Everest NEPAL
Located in the Himalayas on the border between Nepal and Tibet, Mt Everest is the highest point on Earth. The ultimate challenge for any mountain climber is to reach its summit, a steep and rugged area 29,035 feet (8,850 m) above sea level.

Bengal tiger

Shiva

Hindu gods

Hindus believe that their gods, even though they appear in separate forms, are part of one supreme god, Brahman. The three most important gods reflect the circle of life. First is Brahma, the creator of the world; then Vishnu, the preserver of the existing world; and finally, Shiva, the destroyer of the world.

PEOPLE

The Buddha c 566–486 BC

Siddhartha Gautama, founder of the Buddhist religion and known as the Buddha, began life as a Hindu. Dissatisfied with many Hindu teachings, he searched for spiritual answers and received "enlightenment," after which he taught about the true nature of the world.

Akbar 1542–1605

The grandson of the Mughal founder Babur, Akbar (*right*) was the greatest of India's Mughal emperors. He tolerated all religions and supported the arts.

Mahatma Gandhi 1869–1948

Called the Mahatma, or great soul, Gandhi helped to gain India's independence from Britain in 1947. Later, as head of the Indian National Congress, he led peaceful protests in an effort to unify the country. He was shot dead by a Hindu rebel.

Tenzing Norgay 1914–86

After six failed attempts, Tenzing Norgay, a Sherpa from Nepal, joined Edmund Hillary to become the first to conquer Mt Everest and return, in May 1953.

Indira Gandhi 1917–84

The first female prime minister of India, Indira Gandhi led her country twice, from 1966 to 1967, and from 1980 until she was assassinated by her guards in 1984. She supported social changes that improved the lives of many Indians.

PLACES

Mumbai INDIA

Located on an island connected by bridges to the mainland, Mumbai, India's largest city, provides much of the country's wealth through its port trade and film industry. In contrast, many of its citizens are poor and homeless.

Meenakshi Temple INDIA

Towering above the heart of Madurai is this temple complex (*below*), built

by the Nayaks in the 16th century. Towers carved with mythical figures enclose the main shrine, which honors the god Shiva and his wife Meenakshi.

Colombo SRI LANKA

The administrative capital of Sri Lanka, Colombo was founded in the mid-1300s at the mouth of the Kelani River. Many of Colombo's buildings date from its 450 years of European colonization.

Golden Temple

Golden Temple INDIA

This holiest of Sikh shrines (*above*) stands in the middle of a pool of water at Amritsar. It was built by Guru Arjun, one of the 10 Sikh gurus, and houses his original writings on the Sikh faith.

Thimpu BHUTAN

Located in the heart of the Himalayas, this small Buddhist city is the capital of the kingdom of Bhutan. Buildings constructed in the traditional Bhutanese style dominate the skyline.

Kathmandu NEPAL

The capital of Nepal, Kathmandu has a rich architectural heritage from several religions. This Buddhist temple, the Bodhnath Stupa (*left*), looks like a mandala from above, and is the largest of its kind.

TRADITIONS AND CULTURE

Tsechus BHUTAN

These annual festivals are held to celebrate Buddhism's arrival in Bhutan. Dancers wearing silk costumes and animal masks (*right*) act out traditional legends in the streets.

Sacred cows

For Hindus, many of whom live in southern Asia, cows are sacred beasts. No Hindu eats beef, and cows are free to roam.

Varanasi ghats INDIA

In Varanasi, India's most holy city, the ghats, or steps, of the Ganges River attract millions of pilgrims who bathe in the river's sacred waters. First light is the most blessed time to bathe.

Bollywood INDIA

Mumbai has the largest film industry in the world, producing about 800 films a year. Watching Bollywood films is one of the most popular pastimes for Southern Asians.

Kandy perahera SRI LANKA

Decorated elephants and hundreds of dancers take part in the 10-day perahera Buddhist festival, at Kandy. The sacred tooth, a relic of the Buddha, is displayed.

Sikhism INDIA

This religion, founded by Guru Nanak in the 15th century, combines Hindu and Islamic beliefs. Nine gurus succeeded Nanak and each added his mark to the Sikh faith, now followed by millions.

Indian cobra

Found in the rain forests, rice paddies and cultivated fields of India, the Indian cobra is highly venomous. When threatened, the snake rises up and spreads its neck vertebrae (*above*). To attack, the cobra "spits" by pressing on its venom glands, forcing venom out through its fangs. It can spit venom over 6½ feet (2 m).

THE MUGHALS 1526–1857
Babur (*above*), a Muslim leader from Afghanistan, founded the Mughal dynasty. Babur's grandson Akbar, a ruler at 15, brought more power and strength to the empire and formed his own religion. Shah Jahan, the grandson of Akbar, developed art and architecture, and created the Taj Mahal. The dynasty slowly declined after his rule, and was ended by Britain in 1857.

RIVAL STATES
As the Mughal empire became less powerful, other countries tried to take control of India. Portuguese seaman Vasco de Gama was the first European to land there, in Calicut in 1498, and Dutch, French and British ships arrived soon after. The Portuguese set up a factory in Goa and took control of Indian trade during the 16th century. Britain then gained trading control through the East India Company, set up in 1600.

SPICE TRADE
In the 17th century, trading companies were set up by other Europeans keen to trade with India for silk and spices. The British East India Company took spices, and later silks, back to England. France also competed for trade.

Indian spice market

THE BRITISH RAJ
In 1756, the prince of Bengal tried to regain power from the English. A year later, Britain, led by Robert Clive, won the Battle of Plassey, and took over the rule of Bengal and India. In 1858, Indian rule passed to the British crown. Many British people went to India and lived as they would in their homeland. In 1947, Britain agreed to release India from its control and it became independent.

Indians served the British during the Raj

SINCE INDEPENDENCE
Once India gained independence, Pakistan, a Muslim nation, wanted to split away. Riots broke out, and millions were killed as they tried to flee the unrest in the "partition" of India. Kashmir joined India, which has caused warring with Pakistan ever since. In 1971, with the support of India's army, East Pakistan gained independence from Pakistan and formed Bangladesh. In 1950, India became a democratic republic and is now governed by a coalition, or joint, government, headed by its own prime minister.

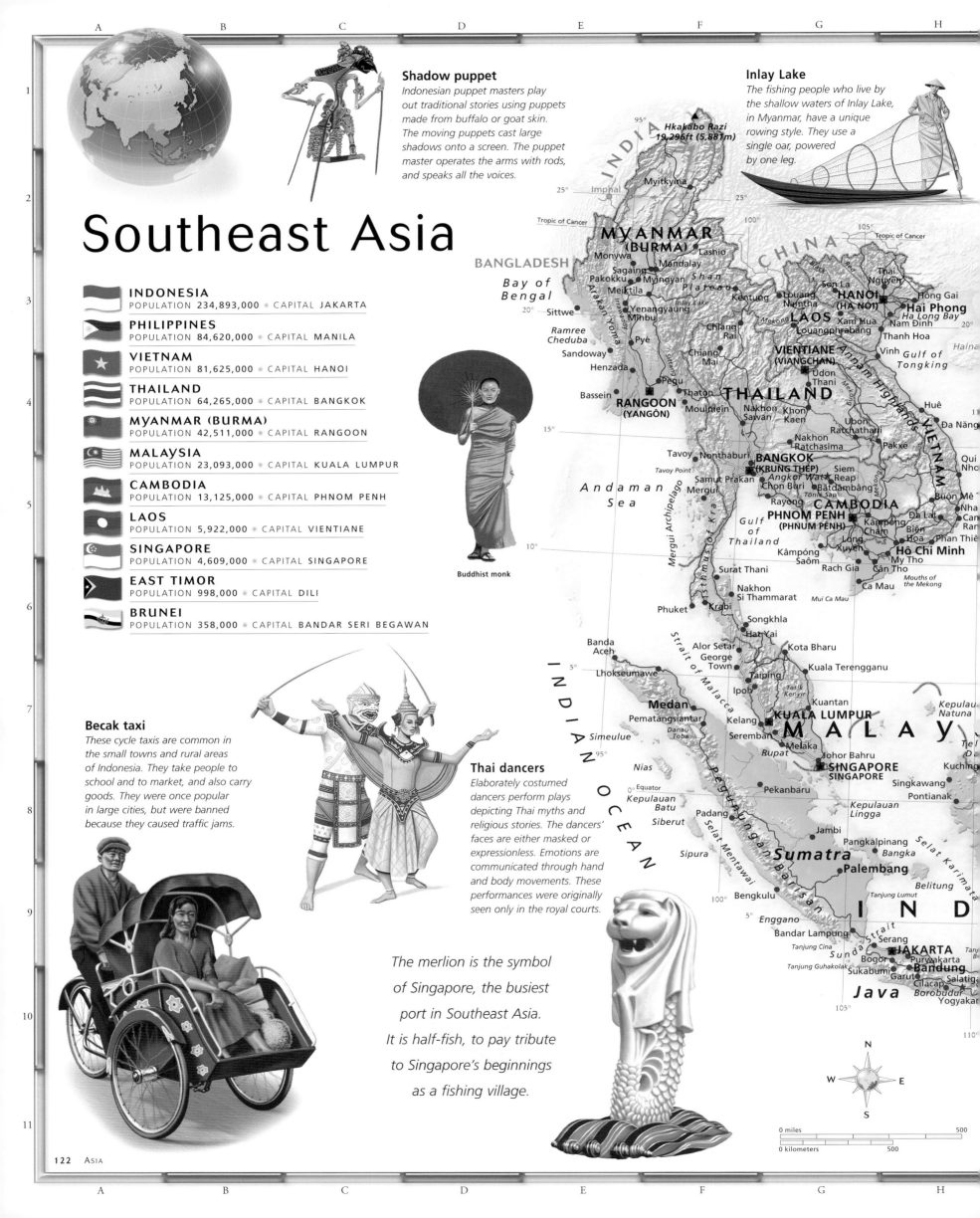

Southeast Asia

Shadow puppet
Indonesian puppet masters play out traditional stories using puppets made from buffalo or goat skin. The moving puppets cast large shadows onto a screen. The puppet master operates the arms with rods, and speaks all the voices.

Inlay Lake
The fishing people who live by the shallow waters of Inlay Lake, in Myanmar, have a unique rowing style. They use a single oar, powered by one leg.

INDONESIA
POPULATION 234,893,000 ✳ CAPITAL JAKARTA

PHILIPPINES
POPULATION 84,620,000 ✳ CAPITAL MANILA

VIETNAM
POPULATION 81,625,000 ✳ CAPITAL HANOI

THAILAND
POPULATION 64,265,000 ✳ CAPITAL BANGKOK

MYANMAR (BURMA)
POPULATION 42,511,000 ✳ CAPITAL RANGOON

MALAYSIA
POPULATION 23,093,000 ✳ CAPITAL KUALA LUMPUR

CAMBODIA
POPULATION 13,125,000 ✳ CAPITAL PHNOM PENH

LAOS
POPULATION 5,922,000 ✳ CAPITAL VIENTIANE

SINGAPORE
POPULATION 4,609,000 ✳ CAPITAL SINGAPORE

EAST TIMOR
POPULATION 998,000 ✳ CAPITAL DILI

BRUNEI
POPULATION 358,000 ✳ CAPITAL BANDAR SERI BEGAWAN

Buddhist monk

Becak taxi
These cycle taxis are common in the small towns and rural areas of Indonesia. They take people to school and to market, and also carry goods. They were once popular in large cities, but were banned because they caused traffic jams.

Thai dancers
Elaborately costumed dancers perform plays depicting Thai myths and religious stories. The dancers' faces are either masked or expressionless. Emotions are communicated through hand and body movements. These performances were originally seen only in the royal courts.

The merlion is the symbol of Singapore, the busiest port in Southeast Asia. It is half-fish, to pay tribute to Singapore's beginnings as a fishing village.

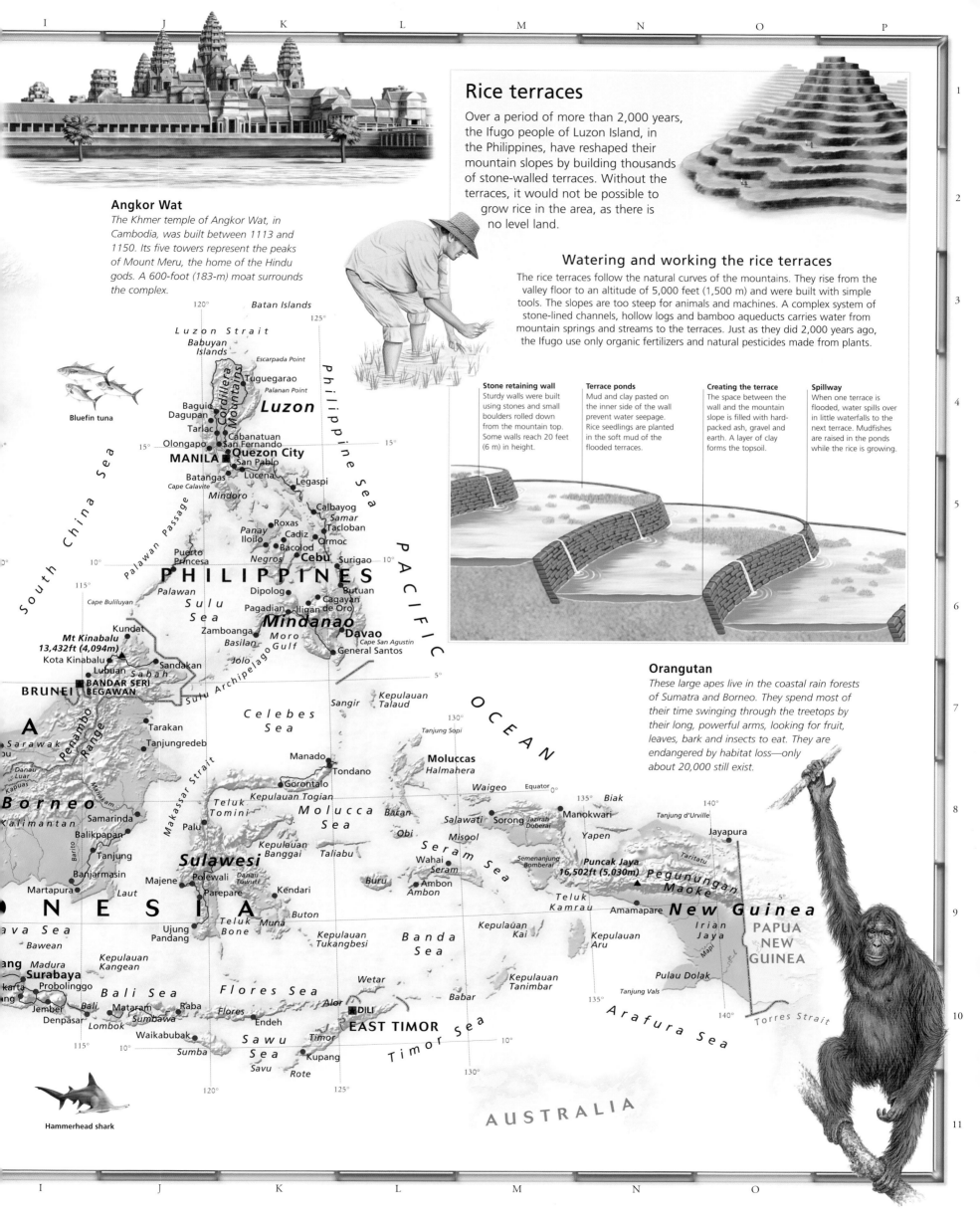

Angkor Wat

The Khmer temple of Angkor Wat, in Cambodia, was built between 1113 and 1150. Its five towers represent the peaks of Mount Meru, the home of the Hindu gods. A 600-foot (183-m) moat surrounds the complex.

Rice terraces

Over a period of more than 2,000 years, the Ifugo people of Luzon Island, in the Philippines, have reshaped their mountain slopes by building thousands of stone-walled terraces. Without the terraces, it would not be possible to grow rice in the area, as there is no level land.

Watering and working the rice terraces

The rice terraces follow the natural curves of the mountains. They rise from the valley floor to an altitude of 5,000 feet (1,500 m) and were built with simple tools. The slopes are too steep for animals and machines. A complex system of stone-lined channels, hollow logs and bamboo aqueducts carries water from mountain springs and streams to the terraces. Just as they did 2,000 years ago, the Ifugo use only organic fertilizers and natural pesticides made from plants.

Stone retaining wall
Sturdy walls were built using stones and small boulders rolled down from the mountain top. Some walls reach 20 feet (6 m) in height.

Terrace ponds
Mud and clay pasted on the inner side of the wall prevent water seepage. Rice seedlings are planted in the soft mud of the flooded terraces.

Creating the terrace
The space between the wall and the mountain slope is filled with hard-packed ash, gravel and earth. A layer of clay forms the topsoil.

Spillway
When one terrace is flooded, water spills over in little waterfalls to the next terrace. Mudfishes are raised in the ponds while the rice is growing.

Orangutan

These large apes live in the coastal rain forests of Sumatra and Borneo. They spend most of their time swinging through the treetops by their long, powerful arms, looking for fruit, leaves, bark and insects to eat. They are endangered by habitat loss—only about 20,000 still exist.

Bluefin tuna

Hammerhead shark

Southeast Asia

There are more than 13,000 islands in the Indonesian archipelago.

LAND AREA	1,689,703 sq miles (4,376,310 sq km)
LARGEST COUNTRY	Indonesia
SMALLEST COUNTRY	Singapore
MAIN RELIGION	Muslim
LIFE EXPECTANCY	70 years
LITERACY	76%

WHERE PEOPLE LIVE

Urban	Rural

REGION
43% — 57%

Most urban: SINGAPORE
100%

Most rural: CAMBODIA
16% — 84%

The small country of Brunei became rich when oil was discovered in 1929. The Sultan of Brunei owns the largest fleet of Rolls Royce cars in the world.

USING THE LAND

- Forest and woodland
- Arable land
- Grazing
- Arid or marginal

Krakatoa

In 1883, Krakatoa, a volcano on a small Indonesian island, erupted. The noise from the explosion was heard as far away as Australia and Japan. Several tsunamis (giant tidal waves) killed thousands of people—the largest killed 36,000. A steamship called the *Berouw* (above) was swept inland 1½ miles (2.4 km) by the force of one of the waves.

NATURAL FEATURES

Irian Jaya
Occupying the western half of New Guinea, Irian Jaya is an area of high mountains and dense rain forests. It is home to many animals, including the tree kangaroo, and the Arfak butterflies, which are found only in this region.

Tree kangaroo

Spice Islands
Lying between Sulawesi and New Guinea, the Spice Islands (Moluccas Islands) were the only source of spices, such as cloves, nutmeg and pepper, from the early 1500s to the late 1800s.

Lake Tonle Sap CAMBODIA
During the wet season, Lake Tonle Sap, the largest inland lake in Southeast Asia, floods. When the water subsides, the farmland is covered with rich, fertile soil.

Ha Long Bay VIETNAM

Ha Long Bay, or the Bay of the Descending Dragon, includes more than 1,600 rocky islands whose limestone cliffs are full of alcoves, caves and tunnels.

Timber
Timber is a prized resource in Southeast Asia, but its logging (*left*) has led to serious environmental problems in countries such as Thailand, Myanmar and Malaysia. Careless and often illegal logging has destroyed forests. Many species of animals have therefore lost their habitats and some may become extinct.

LARGEST CITIES

Manila 10,330,000

Jakarta 8,988,000

Bangkok 6,709,000

Rangoon 4,455,000

- Rice
- Tobacco
- Coconuts
- Palm oil
- Rubber
- Beef cattle
- Fishing
- Shellfish
- Industrial center
- Mining
- Oil production
- Gas production
- Timber
- Tourism

Fruits

An amazing variety of fruits are grown in the plantations of Southeast Asia. Tropical fruits, such as pineapples (*left*), bananas, melons and mangoes, are sold at local markets. Some countries, including Vietnam and Malaysia, export fruits to other countries, often in canned form.

PLACES

Jakarta INDONESIA
Jakarta, situated on the island of Java, was settled in the 5th century. It is the capital of Indonesia, its largest city and its industrial and commercial center.

Rangoon MYANMAR
Rangoon is the political center of Myanmar. Located on the Ayeyarwady delta, it is also a major trading port and industrial city.

Ho Chi Minh VIETNAM
Formerly called Saigon, this is the largest city in Vietnam. The busy streets are filled with people, market stalls and traffic. Its architecture is a mix of French colonial and Asian.

Getting around Ho Chi Minh

Grand Palace BANGKOK
Built in 1782, this palace on the east bank of the Choa Phraya River was the home of the Thai royal family until the late 1800s. It is now used for ceremonial purposes.

Borobodur INDONESIA
This is the largest Buddhist monument in the world. It was built on the island of Java in the 700s and 800s, and is shaped like a pyramid, with a square base and five tiers topped with three circular terraces.

Komodo dragon
The Komodo dragon is the biggest lizard in the world. It is an excellent swimmer and moves freely between several Indonesian islands. It can grow up to 10 feet (3 m) and weigh up to 200 pounds (90 kg). It has strong, thick legs with sharp claws, fanglike teeth and a lashing tail. Despite its size, it moves fast and can kill deer, goats and wild boar.

The Petronas Towers, 1,483 feet (452 m) high, in Kuala Lumpur, Malaysia, are the tallest buildings in the world.

Islamic traders

Arab merchants brought Islam to Southeast Asia in the 7th century. By the 13th century, sailing in ships called dhows (*above*), these Muslim sailors had set up a spice-trading network across Asia. Muhammad, the prophet and founder of Islam, had himself been a merchant, so Islamic merchants were well respected as honest traders.

PEOPLE

King Mongkut 1804–68
Also known as Rama IV, Thailand's King Mongkut was a Buddhist monk for 27 years before becoming king. In 1862, he hired a British governess to teach his children English. The musical *The King and I* was based on her journals.

Tunku Abdul Rahman 1903–90
Rahman, the prime minister of Malaya from 1957 to 1963, led the movement to set up the independent country of Malaysia. He then became Malaysia's prime minister from 1963 to 1970.

King Norodom Sihanouk born 1922
Born in Cambodia, Sihanouk became king in 1941 when he was 18. In 1955, he gave up his throne to form a political party and become prime minister. After many years of political unrest, Sihanouk became king again in 1993.

Aung San Suu Kyi born 1945
Aung San helped found the National League for Democracy and was awarded the Nobel Peace Prize in 1991 for her work toward democracy for Myanmar.

Aung San Suu Kyi

Xanana Gusmão born 1946
Gusmão, a former guerilla leader who fought against Indonesian rule, and was imprisoned for it, was elected president of East Timor in 2002.

TRADITIONS AND CULTURE

White elephants
In ancient times, the kings of Siam (now Thailand) and Burma (Myanmar) valued and protected these animals because they believed that they would bring them peace, power and riches.

Balinese festivals
Many Balinese festivals are based on religious traditions and feature elaborate costumes (*below*). Galungan, or Balinese New Year, begins on the first day of the Hindu calendar year and lasts for 10 days. Villages honor dead ancestors and celebrate good defeating evil.

Stilt villages
In many countries in Southeast Asia, houses are built up on stilts. In some regions, this is because the houses are built over water, but in others, it is to provide shelter and living quarters underneath for the farm animals, such as pigs, chicken and water buffalo.

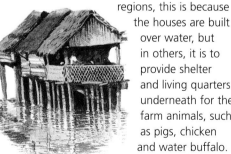

Stilt village

Ceremonial silks
For centuries, Thai people have been weaving silk that is famous worldwide. The colors and patterns have symbolic meanings and the silks are worn in ceremonies. Thai silk is printed by a process called silk-screen printing.

HISTORY AT A GLANCE

C 1,600,000 BC
Humanlike people live in Java. They are about 5 feet (150 cm) tall, with large eyebrow ridges, a heavy jaw, a small chin and a thick skull.

C 2100 BC
Humans live in Ban Chiang, a settlement in the Udon Thani province in Thailand. They cultivate rice and raise animals for food. They also make and use metal tools.

Pagan palace

AD 1044
King Anawratha comes to the throne of Burma and rules from its capital, Pagan. Over the next 13 years he defeats the Mon, who are an Austro-Asian people, and unifies Burma.

1350
King Ramathibodi I founds the new kingdom of Ayutthaya in Thailand. He sets up his capital on an island near the Chao Phraya River just north of present-day Bangkok. He unifies the people and establishes a legal system. The kingdom lasts until 1767.

Ayutthayan Buddha

1595–98
The first Dutch trading missions arrive in Indonesia and, several years later, the powerful Dutch East India Company is founded.

1782
King Rama I becomes king of Thailand. He is the first of the Chakri dynasty, which rules Thailand today. He moves the court to Bangkok, turning it from a small village to a royal city.

1959
The island of Singapore, previously a colony of Britain, gains self-government for its internal affairs. Britain remains responsible for its defense and foreign affairs.

Vietnam War

1965–73
The USA joins the South Vietnamese in their efforts to prevent the North Vietnamese and South Vietnamese rebels from taking over Vietnam. The USA is involved for eight years, the longest war in which it has taken part.

1967
Suharto takes over from Sukarno as president of Indonesia. He makes peace with Malaysia and helps form the Association of Southeast Asian States (ASEAN), which promotes trade and cooperation with western countries.

1975–79
Cambodia is ravaged by the dictator Pol Pot, the leader of the Khmer Rouge soldiers. Temples and mosques are destroyed, and thousands of Cambodians are tortured, executed and buried.

2002
East Timor, which has been ruled by force by Indonesia since 1975, becomes independent, elects Xanana Gusmão as president and joins the United Nations.

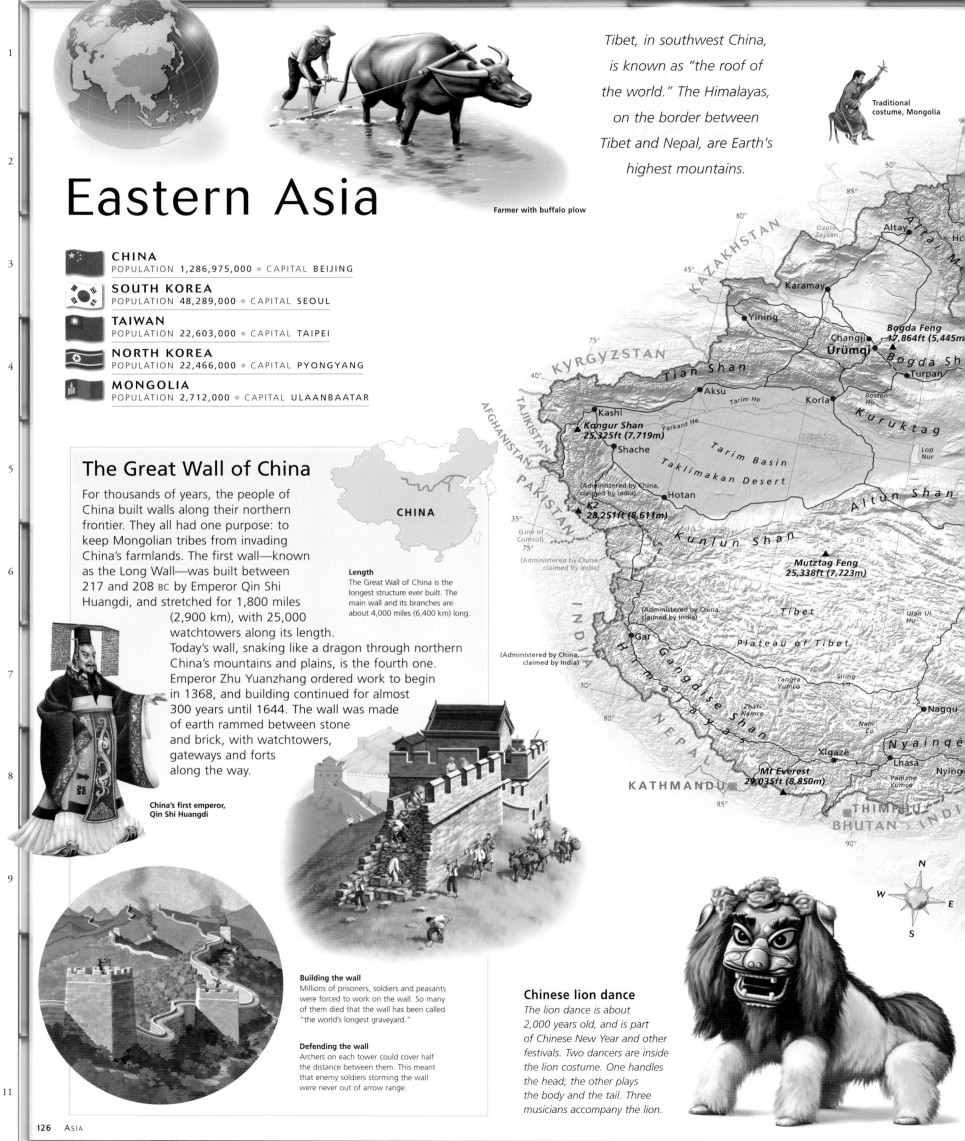

Eastern Asia

Tibet, in southwest China, is known as "the roof of the world." The Himalayas, on the border between Tibet and Nepal, are Earth's highest mountains.

Farmer with buffalo plow

Traditional costume, Mongolia

CHINA
POPULATION 1,286,975,000 * CAPITAL BEIJING

SOUTH KOREA
POPULATION 48,289,000 * CAPITAL SEOUL

TAIWAN
POPULATION 22,603,000 * CAPITAL TAIPEI

NORTH KOREA
POPULATION 22,466,000 * CAPITAL PYONGYANG

MONGOLIA
POPULATION 2,712,000 * CAPITAL ULAANBAATAR

The Great Wall of China

For thousands of years, the people of China built walls along their northern frontier. They all had one purpose: to keep Mongolian tribes from invading China's farmlands. The first wall—known as the Long Wall—was built between 217 and 208 BC by Emperor Qin Shi Huangdi, and stretched for 1,800 miles (2,900 km), with 25,000 watchtowers along its length.
Today's wall, snaking like a dragon through northern China's mountains and plains, is the fourth one. Emperor Zhu Yuanzhang ordered work to begin in 1368, and building continued for almost 300 years until 1644. The wall was made of earth rammed between stone and brick, with watchtowers, gateways and forts along the way.

CHINA

Length
The Great Wall of China is the longest structure ever built. The main wall and its branches are about 4,000 miles (6,400 km) long.

China's first emperor, Qin Shi Huangdi

Building the wall
Millions of prisoners, soldiers and peasants were forced to work on the wall. So many of them died that the wall has been called "the world's longest graveyard."

Defending the wall
Archers on each tower could cover half the distance between them. This meant that enemy soldiers storming the wall were never out of arrow range.

Chinese lion dance
The lion dance is about 2,000 years old, and is part of Chinese New Year and other festivals. Two dancers are inside the lion costume. One handles the head; the other plays the body and the tail. Three musicians accompany the lion.

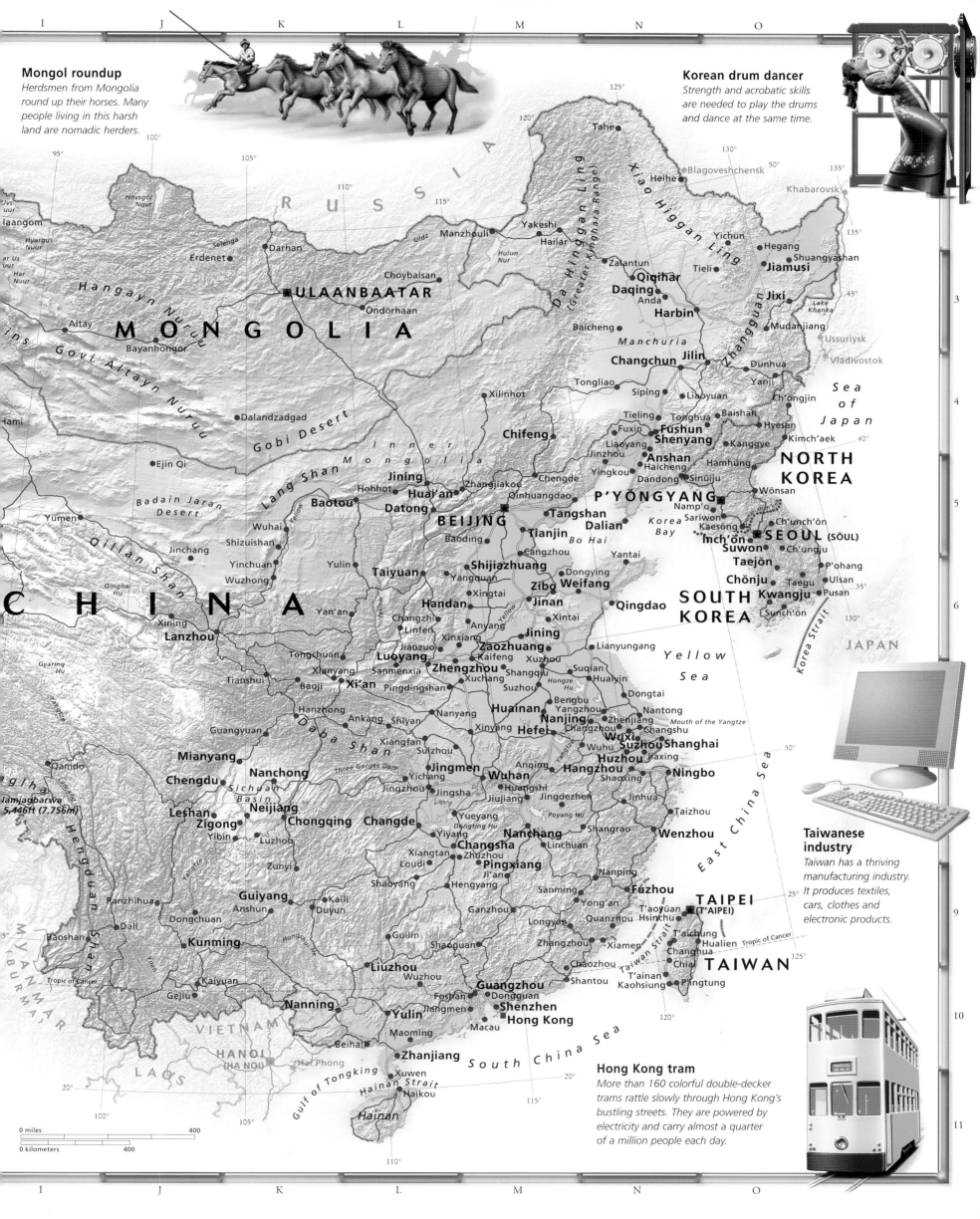

Mongol roundup
Herdsmen from Mongolia round up their horses. Many people living in this harsh land are nomadic herders.

Korean drum dancer
Strength and acrobatic skills are needed to play the drums and dance at the same time.

Taiwanese industry
Taiwan has a thriving manufacturing industry. It produces textiles, cars, clothes and electronic products.

Hong Kong tram
More than 160 colorful double-decker trams rattle slowly through Hong Kong's bustling streets. They are powered by electricity and carry almost a quarter of a million people each day.

Eastern Asia

CHINA LAND AREA	3,705,195 sq miles (9,596,410 sq km)
OFFICIAL LANGUAGE	Chinese/Mandarin
MAIN RELIGION	Buddhist/Taoist
LIFE EXPECTANCY	72 years
LITERACY	86%

SOUTH KOREA LAND AREA	37,911 sq miles (9,596,410 sq km)
OFFICIAL LANGUAGE	Korean
MAIN RELIGION	Christian
LIFE EXPECTANCY	75 years
LITERACY	98%

TAIWAN LAND AREA	12,456 sq miles (32,260 sq km)
OFFICIAL LANGUAGE	Mandarin
MAIN RELIGION	Buddhist/Taoist
LIFE EXPECTANCY	76 years
LITERACY	86%

NORTH KOREA LAND AREA	46,491 sq miles (120,410 sq km)
OFFICIAL LANGUAGE	Korean
MAIN RELIGION	Buddhist
LIFE EXPECTANCY	70 years
LITERACY	99%

MONGOLIA LAND AREA	600,543 sq miles (1,555,400 sq km)
OFFICIAL LANGUAGE	Khalkha Mongol
MAIN RELIGION	Buddhist
LIFE EXPECTANCY	63 years
LITERACY	99%

LARGEST CITIES

Seoul 9,552,000

Shanghai 9,111,000

Beijing 6,696,000

Tianjin 4,384,000

USING THE LAND

- Cereals
- Rice
- Tea
- Sugarcane
- Soybeans
- Beef cattle
- Sheep
- Pigs
- Fishing
- Industrial center
- Mining
- Oil production
- Timber
- Forest and woodland
- Arable land
- Grazing
- Arid or marginal

Tea plantations
During the 17th century, European traders came to China's coast to buy tea and other goods. Today, Chinese tea remains popular. Plantations in more than 20 provinces grow crops for local use and for export.

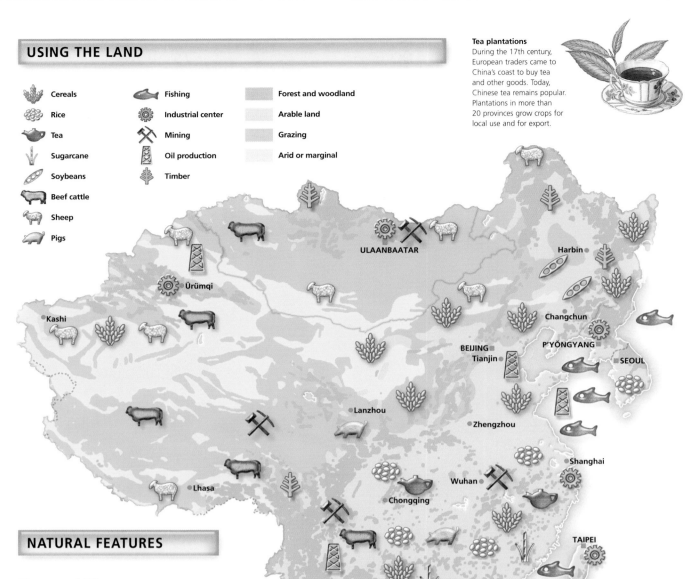

NATURAL FEATURES

Plateau of Tibet CHINA
This high, flat and dry region in southwest China, north of the Himalayas, is the largest plateau in the world. It is home to Tibetan farmers, who keep yaks (right) for meat and dairy products.

Yellow River CHINA
The name of this river comes from the yellow silt that gathers on its bed as it flows downstream. Because its floods cause so much damage, the Yellow River is also called "China's Sorrow."

Gobi Desert MONGOLIA–CHINA
Vast areas of the Gobi Desert are covered in rugged, bare rock, with little vegetation. The desert stretches across 500,000 square miles (1,300,000 sq km).

Guilin CHINA
Tourists flock to this scenic area in Guangxi province to see its unusual limestone mountain peaks, known as karst formations. These landscapes have inspired artists and poets for centuries.

Guilin mountains

Rice paddies
Rice, China's main crop, is grown in flooded fields called paddies. The seeds are sown elsewhere, and once the rice shoots appear, women plant them out into the paddies. When the rice stalks are ripe, they are harvested. The grains are shaken from the stalks and left to dry in the sun. Water buffalo are sometimes used to plow the rice fields.

WHERE PEOPLE LIVE

	Urban	Rural	

	Urban	Rural
SOUTH KOREA	81%	19%
TAIWAN	69%	31%
NORTH KOREA	60%	40%
MONGOLIA	58%	42%
CHINA	32%	68%

LONGEST RIVERS

Yangtze (Chang Jiang) 3,964 miles (6,380 km)

Yellow (Huang He) 3,395 miles (5,464 km)

Lancang Jiang (Mekong) 2,749 miles (4,425 km)

Heilong Jiang (Amur) 1,786 miles (2,874 km)

Three Gorges Dam

A massive dam is being built across the Yangtze River at Sandouping. Work began in 1993, and when complete, water from the dam will generate hydroelectricity to power China's industries. The water will flood an area the size of Singapore, washing away the homes of more than a million people, and destroying historic sites and magnificent scenery.

TRADITIONS AND CULTURE

Tai chi
Each morning, people all over China start their day outdoors with a series of gentle movements that they believe will help develop their mind, body and spirit. Tai chi started in the 3rd century AD.

Moon Festival
At this mid-autumn festival during the eighth full moon of the Chinese lunar year, people let off loud fireworks when the moon appears, and eat moon cakes (*left*).

Woodblock printing
People in Eastern Asia invented the first form of printing in the 8th century. They carved characters from printed blocks, covered them with ink, and pressed the inked block onto paper.

There are 300 million bicycles in China, and people need a licence to ride one.

Dragon boat racing
As part of the Dragon Boat Festival, celebrated in Taiwan as well as China, long, decorated boats race on waterways to commemorate the death of the poet Chu Yuan, who drowned in 299 BC. Rice dumplings are served on the day.

Dragon boat

Chinese art
For centuries, Chinese painters have created landscapes using ink and brush on silk or paper. Plants and animals, combined with calligraphy, are popular subjects for scrolls, fans or folded albums.

Terra-cotta warriors
In 1974, workers in Shaanxi province, China, discovered a pit of life-size pottery statues. Emperor Qin Shi Huangdi had ordered the terra-cotta warriors to be made so that they could protect him after his death. In one pit, 7,000 soldiers and 600 horses, originally painted in bright colors, were found. Although they were made from molds, no two faces are the same.

Koumiss, the national drink of Mongolia, is made from fermented mare's milk.

PLACES

Shanghai CHINA
Shanghai, on the Huangpu River, was first settled in AD 1000. This thriving port is China's chief industrial and commercial city, and has long been a center for foreign investment and trade.

The Forbidden City CHINA
The emperor once lived behind the walls of this elaborate complex, whose intricate features date from the Ming dynasty. Today, tourists are able to enter the area and walk around its grounds.

The Forbidden City

Seoul SOUTH KOREA
South Korea's capital, Seoul, is a modern city on the Han River. Many businesses have their headquarters in the center and the streets bustle with a quarter of the nation's population.

Potala Palace TIBET
This traditional home of the Dalai Lama, or priest-king, of Tibet sits on a rocky hill above the city of Lhasa. The 1,000-room palace was built in the 17th century.

Potala Palace

HISTORY AT A GLANCE
THE CHINESE DYNASTIES

XIA c 2205–c 1700 BC
People are living in communities and use tools by the time this first dynasty develops, but few records exist. Yu, a Xia emperor, builds the first of China's canals.

SHANG 1600–1050 BC
The Shang dynasty overthrows the Xia. People use bronze for the first time, for tools and pottery. The Shang develop a 12-month, 360-day calendar.

Bronze Shang pot

ZHOU 1050–221 BC
Local armies fight for land, with much bloodshed. Confucianism develops. Iron is used and ox-drawn plows, crossbows and irrigation are invented.

QIN 221–207 BC
The ruler of the Qin state overthrows the Zhou ruler. Local states are destroyed and unified into one nation. The word China comes from "Qin."

HAN 206 BC – AD 220
The country is run by a new national civil service, based on the teachings of Confucius. Factories produce silk, cloth, paper and farm tools.

JIN AD 265–420
Two Jin dynasties emerge—northern and southern—under the rule of the Emperor Sima Yan. China cannot maintain its unity.

SUI AD 581–618
China is reunified after three centuries of disunity. The Great Wall is rebuilt and planning for the Grand Canal begins. Defeat by the Turks causes this short dynasty to collapse.

Fashions from the Tang dynasty

TANG AD 618–907
A lively emperor brings a new age of prosperity and opportunity in art and culture. Paper money is introduced and Buddhism becomes popular.

LIAO AD 907–1125
China disintegrates during these years, following attacks from the north. Many areas fall into foreign hands. The south divides into small states.

SONG AD 960–1279
The country is once again united. Cities grow. This is a golden age for architecture, craft, science, painting and learning.

YUAN 1206–1368
Kublai Khan sets up the Mongol emperors in Beijing to rule the Silk Road. The Chinese resent their Mongol invaders.

MING 1368–1644
The ideals of the Tang and Song dynasties return under Zhou Yuanzhang. This is a time of stability and order.

The last emperor

QING 1644–1911
The Manchus seize China. The empire gradually weakens and the Manchus are overthrown. Still a child, Pu Yi is the last emperor of China.

MODERN CHINA 1949
After civil war, China becomes a communist regime and is renamed the People's Republic of China. Industry and agriculture are modernized.

PEOPLE

Confucius 551–479 BC
The values of this great thinker and teacher still form part of the Chinese way of life. Although he lived 2,500 years ago, his ideas on the family, school and nation are respected throughout China.

Zhang Heng AD 78–139
This Chinese mathematician and astronomer invented a seismoscope (*right*), for recording earthquakes. A ball fell out of a dragon's mouth into a frog's mouth when an earthquake occurred, making a loud noise, which woke the emperor.

Genghis Khan 1162–1227
One of the great Mongol leaders, Genghis Khan brought together the tribes of central Asia in 1209, and was crowned lord of all. His grandson was Kublai Khan.

Mao Zedong 1893–1976
The son of a peasant, Mao Zedong was a revolutionary leader. As head of the People's Republic of China, formed in 1949, Chairman Mao led China for almost 30 years under communist rule.

Dalai Lama born 1935
This spiritual leader of Tibet, now the 14th, has lived in exile in India since 1959. His title means "Ocean of Wisdom." In 1989, he received the Nobel Peace Prize.

Giant pandas
The number of giant pandas in China has dropped to 700 because the fountain bamboo forests that provide their food are being cleared for housing. These bears live in Sichuan province in central China.

Japan

JAPAN
POPULATION 127,214,000 ✳ CAPITAL
TOKYO

Earthquakes and volcanoes

Earth's crust is broken into pieces, called tectonic plates, that constantly move around. When a thick plate rides up over a thinner plate, the thinner one is forced down into the layer between Earth's crust and its core, a process called subduction. On the surface, volcanoes and earthquakes occur. There are three tectonic plates beneath Japan, and regular, sometimes devastating, earthquakes and volcanic eruptions take place on land.

The Ring of Fire

Japan sits on the Ring of Fire (in red). This chain includes more than half Earth's volcanoes and is the source of more than half its earthquakes.

Equator

JAPAN
PACIFIC OCEAN
— Ring of Fire

Double trouble
Japan lies on both the Pacific and the Philippine plates. The Pacific Plate moves 4 inches (10 cm) each year. The Philippine Plate moves at half that speed. These two plates cause many of Japan's earthquakes and volcanoes.

Pacific Plate
Eurasian Plate
JAPAN
Kobe • Tokyo •
Philippine Plate

How volcanoes form

Forces deep within Earth cause magma to burst through the crust and spit ash and fire.

Mid-ocean ridge
When plates under the ocean are pushed apart, magma rises through the gap. It cools and hardens to form a series of ridges on the ocean floor.

Island arc volcano
When two plates collide, ocean crust and island arc volcanoes form.

Magma upwelling

Ocean crust

Direction of plate movement

Trench

Magma upwelling

Hot-spot volcano
Sometimes, magma from a spot deep in the mantle forces its way through a weak spot in the middle of a plate to form a series of hot-spot volcanoes.

Continental volcano
When thin ocean crust meets thicker continental crust, the thin crust slides under the thicker one. This process forms a line of volcanoes.

Magma chamber
As magma rises from the mantle, it collects in the crust in large pockets called magma chambers.

Japanese cranes
These large wading birds are a symbol of loyalty and good luck. They make a loud sound like a bugle and are famous for their spectacular courtship dances and the great care they take of their young.

Japanese macaques
These animals, also called Japanese snow monkeys, live in the mountains of northern Honshū. The area is snow-covered for more than half the year. Japanese macaques keep warm by sitting in groups in hot volcanic springs.

Fishing

Map labels

RUSSIA

Kuril Islands

Ostrov Iturup
(Administered by
Russian Federation
claimed by Japan)

Ostrov Kunashir

Nemuro-kaikyō

Nosapu-misaki
Nemuro

Shari
Shiretoko-misaki
Kushiro
Kitami
Abashiri
Kussharo-ko
Teshikaga

Hokkaidō

Asahi-dake
7,513ft (2,290m) ▲

Horoshiri-dake
6,732ft (2,052m) ▲

Obihiro
Tokachi

Asahikawa
Tomakomai

Sea of Okhotsk

RUSSIA

Sakhalin

La Pérouse Strait

Sōya-wan
Wakkanai

Rebun-tō
Rishiri-tō

Teshio

Ishikari-wan
Otaru
Sapporo
Ebetsu
Shikotsu-ko
Tōya-ko
Uchiura-wan
Muroran
Hakodate
Tsugaru-kaikyō

Shakotan-misaki
Kamui-misaki
Benkei-misaki
Esan-misaki

Okushiri-tō

Henashi-zaki
Nyūdō-zaki

Erimo-misaki

PACIFIC OCEAN

J A P A N

Hachinohe
Aomori
Hirosaki
Towada-ko
Mutsu-wan
Shiriya-zaki

Iwate-san
6,696ft (2,041m) ▲
Morioka

Akita

Ishinomaki
Kinka-san
Sendai-wan
Sendai

Yamagata
Sakata
Nagano?
Tsuruoka

Fukushima

Niigata

Sadoga-shima

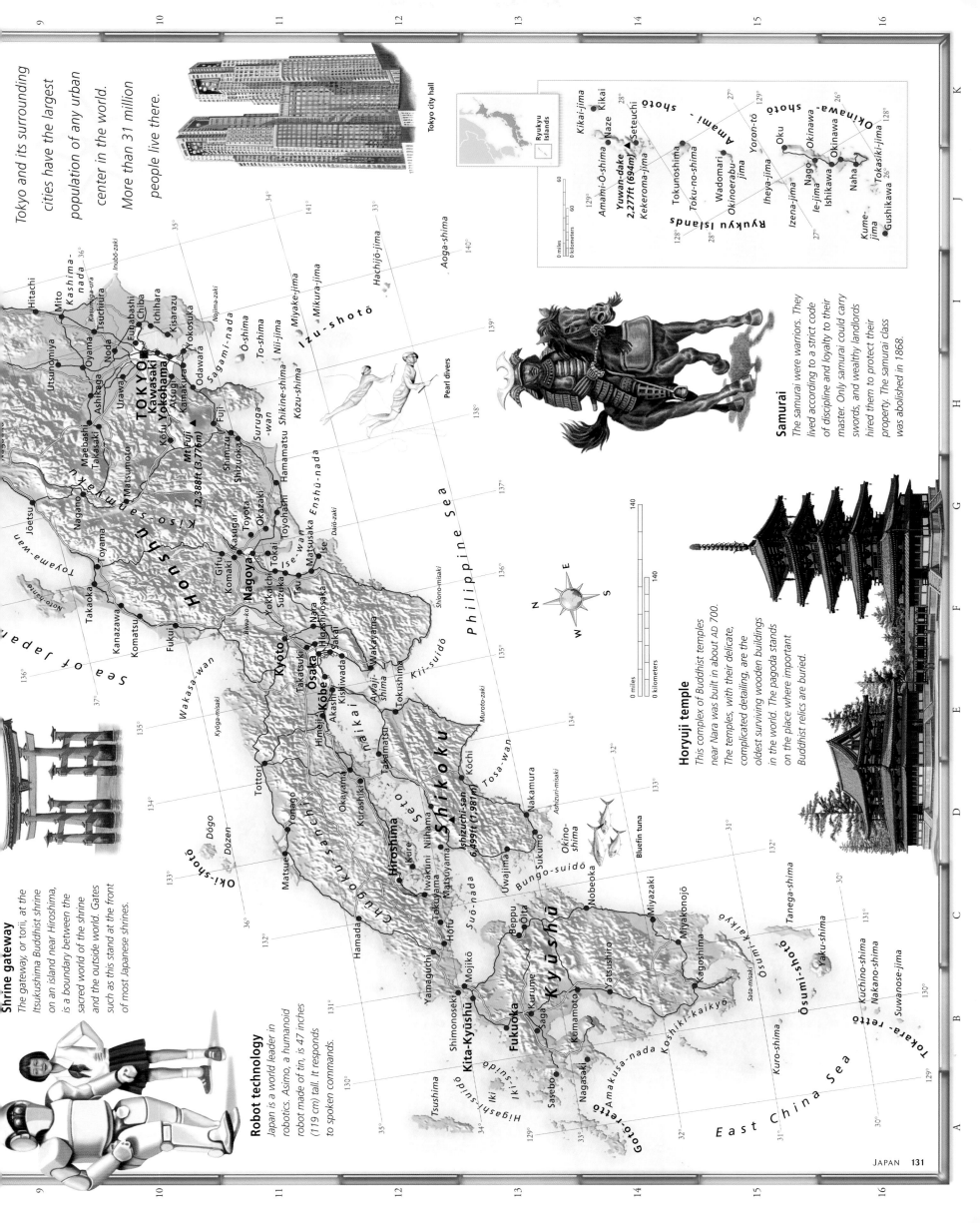

Tokyo and its surrounding cities have the largest population of any urban center in the world. More than 31 million people live there.

Tokyo city hall

Ryukyu Islands

Kikai-jima
Kikai
Amami-Ō-shima
Nase
Seteuchi
Yuwan-dake
2,277ft (694m) ▲
Kekeroma-jima
Amami - shotō
Tokunoshima
Tōku-no-shima
Wadomari
Okinoerabu-jima
Yoron-tō
Iheya-jima
Izena-jima
Oku
Nago
Ie-jima
Okinawa
Okinawa
Ishikawa
Naha
Tokasiki-jima
Kume-jima
Gushikawa
Okinawa-shotō
Ryukyu Islands

0 miles 60
0 kilometers 60

Samurai

The samurai were warriors. They lived according to a strict code of discipline and loyalty to their master. Only samurai could carry swords, and wealthy landlords hired them to protect their property. The samurai class was abolished in 1868.

Horyuji temple

This complex of Buddhist temples near Nara was built in about AD 700. The temples, with their delicate, complicated detailing, are the oldest surviving wooden buildings in the world. The pagoda stands on the place where important Buddhist relics are buried.

Shrine gateway

The gateway, or torii, at the Itsukushima Buddhist shrine on an island near Hiroshima, is a boundary between the sacred world of the shrine and the outside world. Gates such as this stand at the front of most Japanese shrines.

Robot technology

Japan is a world leader in robotics. Asimo, a humanoid robot made of tin, is 47 inches (119 cm) tall. It responds to spoken commands.

Hitachi
Mito
Tsuchiura
Funabashi
Chiba
Ichihara
Kisarazu
Utsunomiya
Ashikaga
Oyama
Noda
Urawa
TOKYO
Kawasaki
Yokohama
Kamakura
Yokosuka
Odawara
Maebashi
Takasaki
Matsumoto
Kōfu
Mt. Fuji
12,388ft (3,776m) ▲
Atsugi
Shimizu
Shizuoka
Nagano
Toyama
Takaoka
Kanazawa
Komatsu
Fukui
Gifu
Komaki
Nagoya
Kasugai
Toyota
Okazaki
Toyohashi
Ise
Tsu
Yokkaichi
Suzuka
Tōkai
Nara
Higashi-Ōsaka
Sakai
Kyōto
Osaka
Takatsuki
Himeji
Kobe
Akashi
Kishiwada
Wakayama
Awaji-shima
Tokushima
Takamatsu
Tottori
Matsue
Yonago
Okayama
Kurashiki
Niihama
Matsuyama
Imabari
Iwakuni
Kure
Hiroshima
Takamatsu
Kōchi
Nakamura
Sukumo
Uwajima
Hamada
Yamaguchi
Tokuyama
Hōfu
Ōita
Beppu
Shimonoseki
Mojikō
Kita-Kyūshū
Fukuoka
Kurume
Saga
Sasebo
Nagasaki
Kumamoto
Yatsushiro
Miyakonojō
Miyazaki
Nobeoka
Kagoshima

Honshū
Kyūshū
Shikoku
Ishizuchi-san
6,499ft (1,981m) ▲

Sea of Japan
East China Sea
Philippine Sea

Pearl divers
Bluefin tuna

Izu-shotō
Hachijō-jima
Aoga-shima
Miyake-jima
Mikura-jima
Ō-shima
To-shima
Nii-jima
Shikine-shima
Kōzu-shima

Oki-shotō
Dōgo
Dōzen

Tanega-shima
Yaku-shima
Ōsumi-shotō
Kuchino-shima
Nakano-shima
Suwanose-jima
Tokara-rettō

Tsushima
Iki
Gotō-rettō

N
E
S
W

0 miles 140
0 kilometers 140

JAPAN **131**

Japan

LAND AREA	144,689 sq miles (374,744 sq km)
OFFICIAL LANGUAGE	Japanese
MAIN RELIGION	Shinto/Buddhism
LIFE EXPECTANCY	81 years
LITERACY	99%

Japan has an average of 546 residents per square mile (337 per sq km)—one of the world's highest population densities.

WHERE PEOPLE LIVE

Urban	Rural
79%	21%

Rice plantations
About half the country's farmland is planted with rice, Japan's main food. Japan has abundant rainfall and many rivers that can be used for irrigation, allowing rice to be cultivated in paddies—fields that have been submerged under 2–4 inches (5–10 cm) of water. Farmers harvest their crops quickly with efficient machinery.

USING THE LAND

- Forest and woodland
- Arable land
- Rice
- Fruit
- Tobacco
- Beef cattle
- Fishing
- Industrial center
- Winter sports

Fruit and vegetables
Although four-fifths of the country is mountainous, and the soils are poor, Japan grows a wide variety of crops, including tomatoes, strawberries, cherries and carrots. Because of the limited amount of suitable farming land, Japanese farms are very small—seldom more than 2 acres (1 ha)—and every usable piece of land is planted.

Sapporo

Sendai

TOKYO
Yokohama

Nagoya

Kyōto

Ōsaka

Hiroshima

Fukuoka

Nakamura

Kagoshima

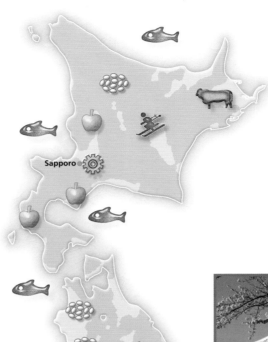

Fishing
Since earliest times, the Japanese have relied on the sea and waterways for food. Deep-sea fishes, such as mackerel and tuna, are plentiful. However, to keep up with the demand for freshwater species, such as trout and eel, fish farms have been developed. Seaweed is also part of many Japanese dishes—fishermen gather kelp along Hokkaido's coast, and laver seaweed, or *nori*, is grown in Kyushu.

LARGEST CITIES

Tokyo 8,274,000

Yokohama 3,517,000

Ōsaka 2,596,000

Nagoya 2,195,000

Sapporo 1,856,000

NATURAL FEATURES

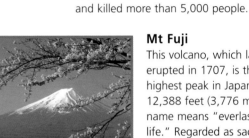

Earthquake damage

Earthquakes
Japan experiences about 1,000 mostly minor Earth tremors each year. In 1923, an earthquake in the Tokyo–Yokohama area killed 140,000 people. The 1995 Kobe quake lasted only 20 seconds, but caused US$200 billion worth of damage and killed more than 5,000 people.

Mt Fuji
This volcano, which last erupted in 1707, is the highest peak in Japan, at 12,388 feet (3,776 m). Its name means "everlasting life." Regarded as sacred, it is a place of pilgrimage and the subject of many paintings and poems.

Mt Fuji

Ryukyu islands
This archipelago of 55 islands—some flat and built from coral, others mountainous and volcanic—extends 400 miles (640 km). Agriculture is the main occupation. The main crops are rice, sweet potatoes, sugar and pineapples. The islanders have their own language.

Shirakami mountains
This uninhabited, mountainous area in northern Honshū contains Japan's last beech forest. Many plants and animals are found here, including the Asiatic bear.

Asiatic bear

Bullet train
The first section of the *Shinkansen*—a high-speed electric rail line between Tokyo and Fukuoka—opened in 1964. About 250 "bullet trains" operate along the line daily. On some sections they can reach speeds of 160 miles (260 km) per hour. The fastest trains can complete the 664-mile (1,062-km) trip in less than seven hours.

Great Buddha

Erected in 1252, this 37-foot (11-m) tall bronze statue is in the grounds of Kotokuin Temple in Kamakura. The wooden building that once housed it was destroyed by a tsunami in 1495. Today, more than 96 million people follow Buddhism, which came to Japan from China in the 6th century. This Buddha faces the ocean, thought to be an ideal place to meditate.

PEOPLE

Murasaki Shikibu AD 978–1014
This Japanese noblewoman created *The Tale of Genji*—one of the world's first novels. The story was painted on a scroll, with intricately detailed illustrations. She also kept a diary of her life at court.

Toyotomi Hideyoshi 1536–98
The son of a peasant, Hideyoshi rose to be a samurai, then a feudal lord. He conquered Japan and unified the country after more than a century of warfare.

The Great Wave Off Kanagawa

Katsushika Hokusai 1760–1849
This artist produced thousands of artworks by printing from carved wood blocks. His series "Thirty-six Views of Mount Fuji," which includes *The Great Wave Off Kanagawa*, is famous.

Emperor Hirohito 1901–89
Japan's longest-reigning monarch, Hirohito oversaw dramatic changes in Japan, through an era of military expansion that ended with defeat in World War II, to the country's emergence as an economic superpower.

TRADITIONS AND CULTURE

Cherry blossoms
The brief season of Japan's national flower, the cherry blossom, is eagerly awaited each spring. Many poems have been written about these flowers. During World War II, they symbolized the soldiers who died in the war. In peacetime, they represent the start of the school year.

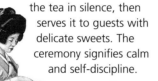

Shinto
Shinto is an ancient Japanese religion, based on the worship of spirits. There are more than 80,000 Shinto shrines in Japan. Before entering a shrine to pay their respects to the spirits, people wet their fingertips and rinse out their mouth.

Tea ceremony
This ancient ceremony takes great skill and concentration. The host prepares the tea in silence, then serves it to guests with delicate sweets. The ceremony signifies calm and self-discipline.

Hari-kiri, or seppuku, is a traditional form of ritual suicide.

PLACES

Tokyo
Tokyo, Japan's largest city, was founded in 1457 as the fortified town of Edo. In 1868, it became the capital and was renamed Tokyo. This bustling, crowded city is where much of the nation's political, economic and social activity takes place, and is home to one-fourth of the nation's people.

Kyoto
Founded in AD 794, Kyoto was the capital and home of the emperor's family for more than 1,000 years. A center of Buddhism and traditional culture, it is known for its historic temples and gardens, schools of tea ceremony and flower arranging, museums, geisha houses, artisans, theaters and festivals.

Golden Pavilion, Kyoto

Theater
Japan has three main types of traditional theater. Noh plays are short, with more symbolism than action. Lively Kabuki plays combine music, dance and mime with elaborate staging and costuming. Bunraku is a sophisticated form of puppet theater.

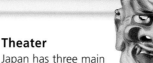
Noh mask

Rock gardens
The 2,000-year-old Japanese art of rock gardening follows strict rules to create serene spaces through harmony of the various elements. The patterns have spiritual and symbolic significance.

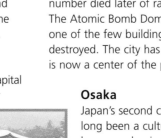

Sumo wrestling
Sumo wrestling, the national sport, is a popular spectacle in Japan. Following centuries-old rules and rituals, the two opponents, who eat special food to bulk up their size, use their strength and weight to try to knock each other out of a ring.

Hiroshima
On 6 August 1945, the USA dropped an atomic bomb on Hiroshima. Some 70,000 people died instantly or soon after the blast; a similar number died later of radiation sickness. The Atomic Bomb Dome (*above*) was one of the few buildings not completely destroyed. The city has been rebuilt, and is now a center of the peace movement.

Atomic Bomb Dome

Osaka
Japan's second city, Osaka has long been a cultural center, and has several universities. Its castle was built in the 16th century by the warlord Toyotomi Hideyoshi. Today, the city is a financial center with a busy port. Its industries include machinery, chemicals, metal production, textiles, paper and printing.

HISTORY AT A GLANCE

Jamon pottery

13,000 BC
Hunters and gatherers form the Jamon period. The first pottery is created.

300 BC
Settlers from Southeast Asia and Korea arrive, bringing their knowledge of rice-farming.

AD 500
The Yamato period starts. *Daimyo* (rulers) take control of large areas.

AD 710
The Nara period starts. Later this century, Japanese culture evolves, with a new writing system. Buddhism becomes the state religion.

AD 794
Kyoto is built as the new capital city. It remains Japan's principal city for more than 1,000 years.

1185
After defeating the Taira family, Minamoto Yoritomo establishes a rival government and becomes the first shogun.

1274
The Mongols invade Japan. A "divine wind" (kamikaze) sinks their ships and they retreat. A second Mongol invasion also fails.

1542
The first Europeans arrive in search of spices and silk to trade. Missionaries spread the Christian faith. Firearms are introduced.

Imperial Palace

1590
After a series of wars, Toyotomi Hideyoshi unifies Japan and takes control. Guns are banned and the samurai gain status.

1600
The Tokugama period starts. Edo (Tokyo) becomes the new capital. All foreigners are expelled from 1637—only the Dutch and Chinese are allowed to trade from Nagasaki. Christianity is banned in 1614.

1868
Emperor Meiji is made head of state and moves to Tokyo. A period of rapid modernization begins. Japan's national pride grows.

Zero plane

1941
Japan launches a surprise attack on Pearl Harbor and fights the USA and Allies in World War II.

1945
Japan surrenders after the USA drops atomic bombs over Hiroshima and Nagasaki.

1997
After a period of rapid growth, the Japanese economy enters a severe recession.

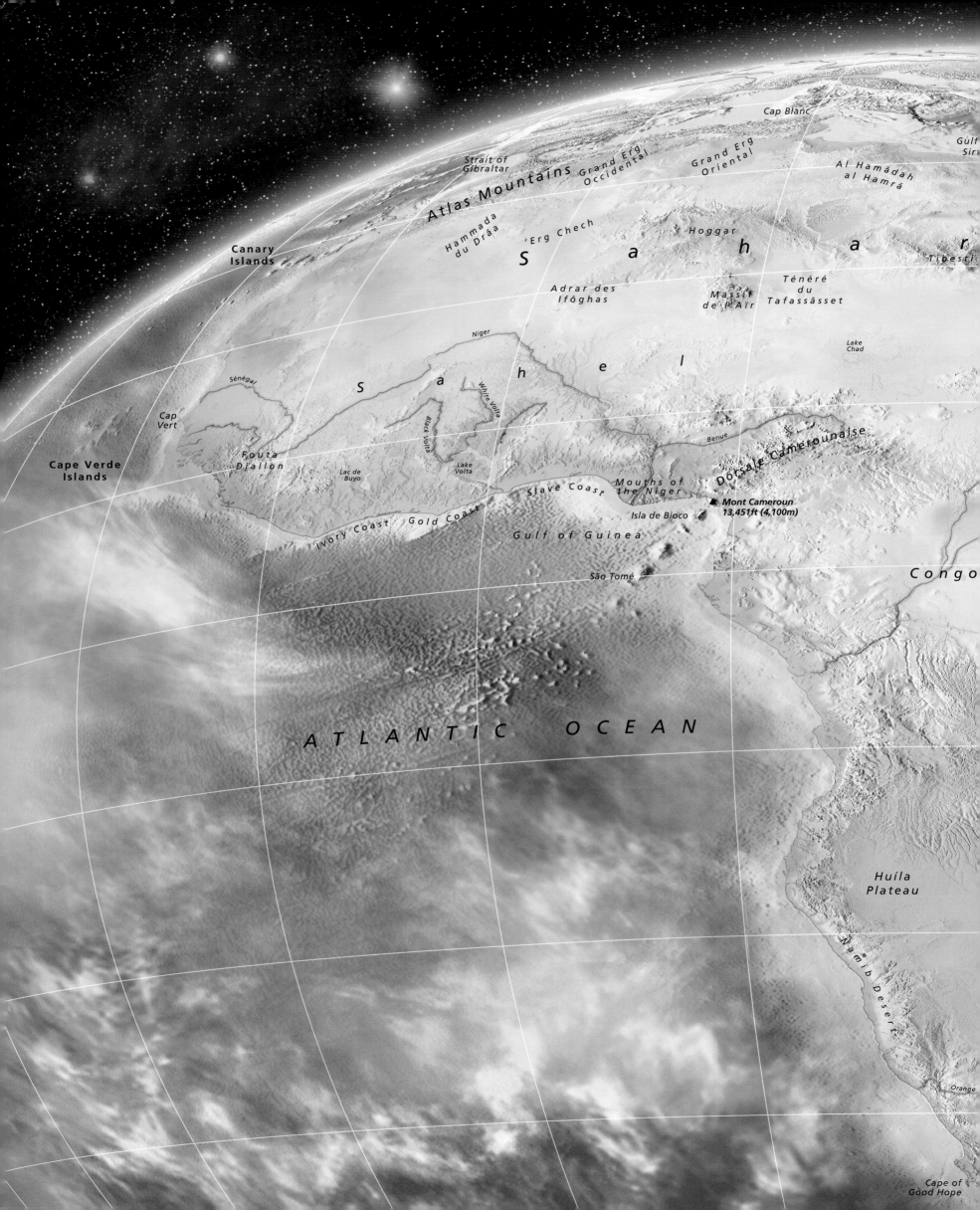

Cap Blanc

Gulf of
Sir

Strait of
Gibraltar

Atlas Mountains

Grand Erg
Occidental

Grand Erg
Oriental

Al Hamādah
al Hamrā

Canary
Islands

Hammada
du Drâa

'Erg Chech

S   a

Hoggar

h   a   r

Tibesti

Adrar des
Ifôghas

Massif
de l'Aïr

Ténéré
du
Tafassâsset

Niger

Cap
Vert

Sénégal

S   a   h   e   l

Lake
Chad

White Volta

Fouta
Djallon

Black Volta

Benue

Dorsale Camerounaise

Cape Verde
Islands

Lac de
Buyo

Lake
Volta

Slave Coast

Mouths of
the Niger

Mont Cameroun
13,451ft (4,100m)

Ivory Coast   Gold Coast

Gulf of Guinea

Isla de Bioco

São Tomé

Congo

ATLANTIC   OCEAN

Huíla
Plateau

Namib Desert

Orange

Cape of
Good Hope

Mediterranean Sea

Libyan
Desert

Qattâra
Depression

Nile
Delta

Sinai

Nile

Eastern Desert

Red Sea

Gulf of Aden

Rās Xaafuun

a

Massif
Ennedi

Marra
Plateau

Western Desert

Nubian
Desert

Blue Nile

White Nile

Lake
Tana

Ethiopian
Highlands

Ahmar
Mountains

Mendebo
Mountains

Horn of
Africa

Ubangi

Congo

Lake
Albert

Lake
Turkana

Great Rift Valley

Shebeli

Basin

Great Rift Valley

Lake
Victoria

Serengeti
Plain

Mt Kenya
17,057ft (5,199m)

Lake
Tanganyika

East African
Plateau

Kilimanjaro
19,331ft (5,892m)

Pemba Island

Zanzibar Island

Africa

Plateau
du Kasai

Lake
Malawi

Comoros
Islands

INDIAN   OCEAN

Zambezi

Lake
Kariba

Zambezi

Mozambique Channel

Madagascar

Okavango
Delta

Kalahari
Basin

Limpopo

Kalahari
Desert

Drakensberg

Great Karoo
Little Karoo

Cape
Agulhas

Northern Africa

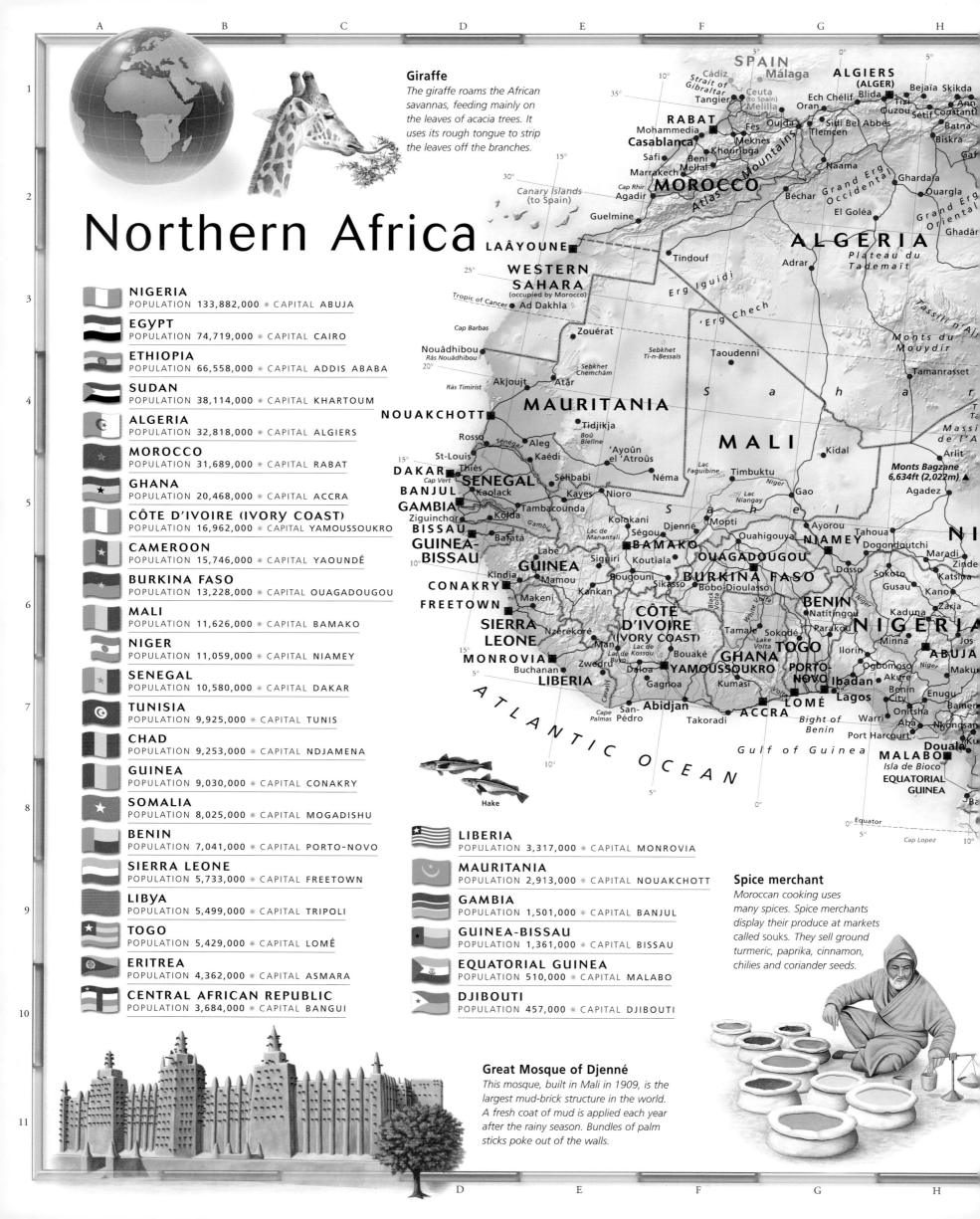

Giraffe
The giraffe roams the African savannas, feeding mainly on the leaves of acacia trees. It uses its rough tongue to strip the leaves off the branches.

NIGERIA
POPULATION 133,882,000 ✳ CAPITAL ABUJA

EGYPT
POPULATION 74,719,000 ✳ CAPITAL CAIRO

ETHIOPIA
POPULATION 66,558,000 ✳ CAPITAL ADDIS ABABA

SUDAN
POPULATION 38,114,000 ✳ CAPITAL KHARTOUM

ALGERIA
POPULATION 32,818,000 ✳ CAPITAL ALGIERS

MOROCCO
POPULATION 31,689,000 ✳ CAPITAL RABAT

GHANA
POPULATION 20,468,000 ✳ CAPITAL ACCRA

CÔTE D'IVOIRE (IVORY COAST)
POPULATION 16,962,000 ✳ CAPITAL YAMOUSSOUKRO

CAMEROON
POPULATION 15,746,000 ✳ CAPITAL YAOUNDÉ

BURKINA FASO
POPULATION 13,228,000 ✳ CAPITAL OUAGADOUGOU

MALI
POPULATION 11,626,000 ✳ CAPITAL BAMAKO

NIGER
POPULATION 11,059,000 ✳ CAPITAL NIAMEY

SENEGAL
POPULATION 10,580,000 ✳ CAPITAL DAKAR

TUNISIA
POPULATION 9,925,000 ✳ CAPITAL TUNIS

CHAD
POPULATION 9,253,000 ✳ CAPITAL NDJAMENA

GUINEA
POPULATION 9,030,000 ✳ CAPITAL CONAKRY

SOMALIA
POPULATION 8,025,000 ✳ CAPITAL MOGADISHU

BENIN
POPULATION 7,041,000 ✳ CAPITAL PORTO-NOVO

SIERRA LEONE
POPULATION 5,733,000 ✳ CAPITAL FREETOWN

LIBYA
POPULATION 5,499,000 ✳ CAPITAL TRIPOLI

TOGO
POPULATION 5,429,000 ✳ CAPITAL LOMÉ

ERITREA
POPULATION 4,362,000 ✳ CAPITAL ASMARA

CENTRAL AFRICAN REPUBLIC
POPULATION 3,684,000 ✳ CAPITAL BANGUI

LIBERIA
POPULATION 3,317,000 ✳ CAPITAL MONROVIA

MAURITANIA
POPULATION 2,913,000 ✳ CAPITAL NOUAKCHOTT

GAMBIA
POPULATION 1,501,000 ✳ CAPITAL BANJUL

GUINEA-BISSAU
POPULATION 1,361,000 ✳ CAPITAL BISSAU

EQUATORIAL GUINEA
POPULATION 510,000 ✳ CAPITAL MALABO

DJIBOUTI
POPULATION 457,000 ✳ CAPITAL DJIBOUTI

Hake

Spice merchant
Moroccan cooking uses many spices. Spice merchants display their produce at markets called souks. They sell ground turmeric, paprika, cinnamon, chilies and coriander seeds.

Great Mosque of Djenné
This mosque, built in Mali in 1909, is the largest mud-brick structure in the world. A fresh coat of mud is applied each year after the rainy season. Bundles of palm sticks poke out of the walls.

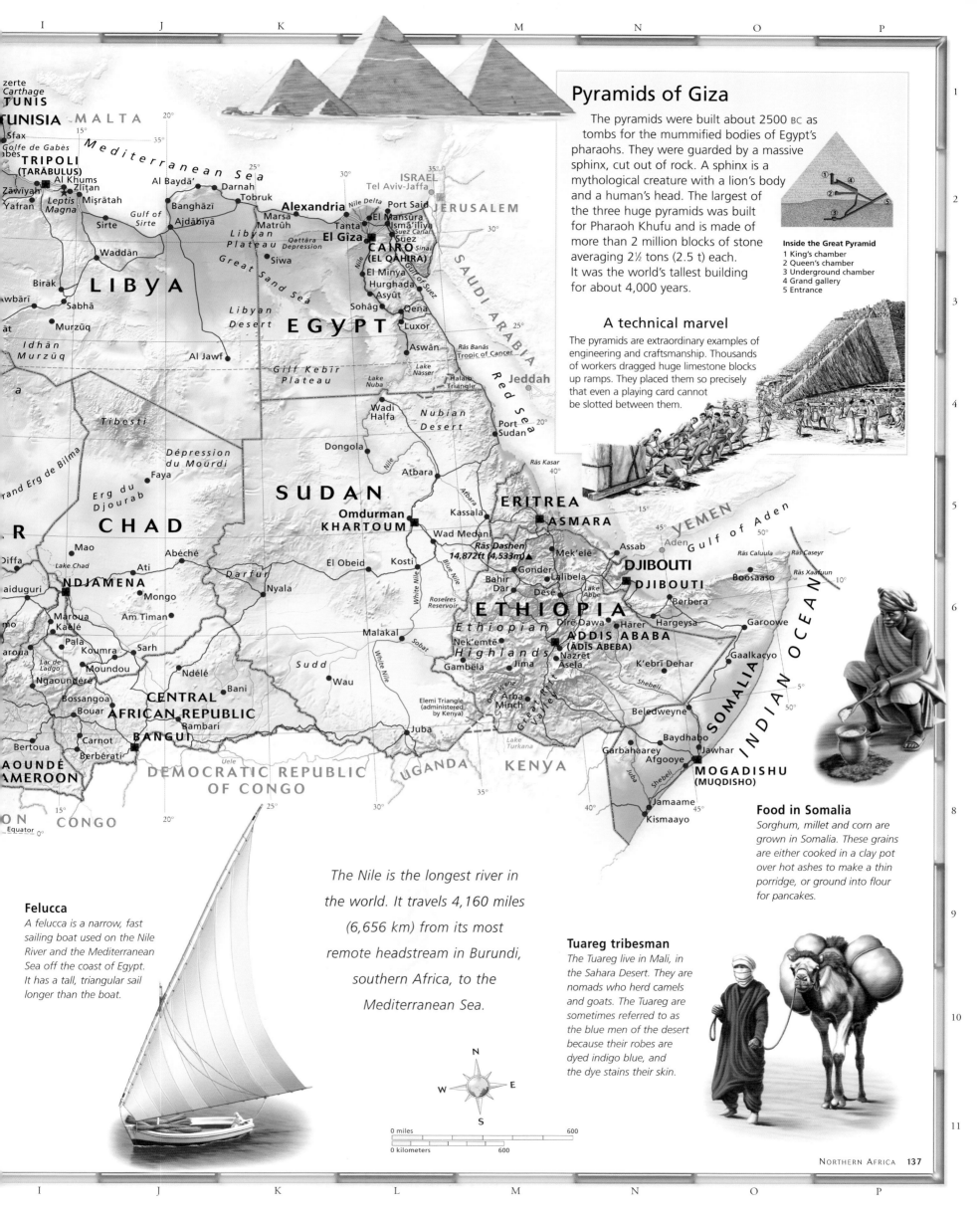

Map labels

zerte
Carthage
TUNIS
TUNISIA
MALTA
Sfax
Golfe de Gabès
abès
TRIPOLI
(ṬARĀBULUS)
Al Khums
Ẕlīṭan
Ẕāwiyah
Leptis
Magna
Miṣrātah
Yafran
Mediterranean Sea
Al Baydā'
Darnah
Tobruk
Sirte
Banghāzī
Ajdābiyā
Gulf of Sirte
Waddān
Marsa
Matrûh
Alexandria
Nile Delta
Port Said
ISRAEL
Tel Aviv-Jaffa
JERUSALEM
Birāk
Libyan
Plateau
Qattâra
Depression
El Mansûra
Ismâ'iliya
Tanta
El Gîza
CAIRO
(EL QAHIRA)
Suez
Suez Canal
Sinai
wbārī
LIBYA
Siwa
El Minya
Gulf of Suez
Sabhā
Great Sand Sea
EGYPT
Asyût
Sohâg
Hurghada
Murzûq
Libyan
Desert
Luxor
Qena
at
Idhān
Murzūq
Al Jawf
Gilf Kebīr
Plateau
Aswân
Rās Banās
Tropic of Cancer
Tibesti
Lake
Nuba
Lake
Nasser
Halaib
Triangle
Red Sea
SAUDI ARABIA
Jeddah
Dépression
du Mourdi
Wadi
Halfa
Nubian
Desert
Port
Sudan
Erg du
Djourab
Faya
rand Erg de Bilma
R
Dongola
Atbara
Nile
Rās Kasar
Omdurman
KHARTOUM
SUDAN
Kassala
ERITREA
ASMARA
Rās Dashen
14,872ft (4,533m)
YEMEN
Aden
Gulf of Aden
Rās Caluula
Rās Caseyr
Mao
CHAD
Abéché
Ati
Darfur
El Obeid
Kosti
Wad Medani
Blue Nile
Mek'elē
Gonder
Lālibela
Assab
Berbera
Boosaaso
Rās Xaafuun
Diffa
Lake Chad
NDJAMENA
Mongo
Nyala
White Nile
Bahir
Dar
Desē
Lake
Abbe
DJIBOUTI
DJIBOUTI
Garoowe
aiduguri
Am Timan
Roseires
Reservoir
ETHIOPIA
Dirē Dawa
Harēr
Hargeysa
Maroua
Kaélé
Pala
Koumra
Sarh
Malakal
Sobat
Ethiopian
Highlands
Nek'emtē
ADDIS ABABA
(ĀDĪS ABEBA)
Nazrēt
Asela
K'ebrī Dehar
Gaalkacyo
Mundou
Ndélé
Sudd
Wau
Gambēla
Jima
Shebeli
SOMALIA
INDIAN OCEAN
aroua
Lac de
Lagdo
Ngaoundéré
Bani
White Nile
Omo Wenz
Beledweyne
Bossangoa
Bouar
CENTRAL
AFRICAN REPUBLIC
Bambari
Arba
Minch
Elemi Triangle
(administered
by Kenya)
Great Rift Valley
Baydhabo
Bertoua
Carnot
Berbérati
BANGUI
Juba
Lake
Turkana
Garbahaarey
Afgooye
Jawhar
Shebeli
AOUNDÉ
MEROON
DEMOCRATIC REPUBLIC
OF CONGO
UGANDA
KENYA
Juba
MOGADISHU
(MUQDISHO)
ON
CONGO
Equator
Jamaame
Kismaayo

Pyramids of Giza

The pyramids were built about 2500 BC as tombs for the mummified bodies of Egypt's pharaohs. They were guarded by a massive sphinx, cut out of rock. A sphinx is a mythological creature with a lion's body and a human's head. The largest of the three huge pyramids was built for Pharaoh Khufu and is made of more than 2 million blocks of stone averaging 2½ tons (2.5 t) each. It was the world's tallest building for about 4,000 years.

Inside the Great Pyramid
1 King's chamber
2 Queen's chamber
3 Underground chamber
4 Grand gallery
5 Entrance

A technical marvel

The pyramids are extraordinary examples of engineering and craftsmanship. Thousands of workers dragged huge limestone blocks up ramps. They placed them so precisely that even a playing card cannot be slotted between them.

Food in Somalia

Sorghum, millet and corn are grown in Somalia. These grains are either cooked in a clay pot over hot ashes to make a thin porridge, or ground into flour for pancakes.

Felucca

A felucca is a narrow, fast sailing boat used on the Nile River and the Mediterranean Sea off the coast of Egypt. It has a tall, triangular sail longer than the boat.

The Nile is the longest river in the world. It travels 4,160 miles (6,656 km) from its most remote headstream in Burundi, southern Africa, to the Mediterranean Sea.

Tuareg tribesman

The Tuareg live in Mali, in the Sahara Desert. They are nomads who herd camels and goats. The Tuareg are sometimes referred to as the blue men of the desert because their robes are dyed indigo blue, and the dye stains their skin.

N
W   E
S

0 miles   600
0 kilometers   600

Northern Africa

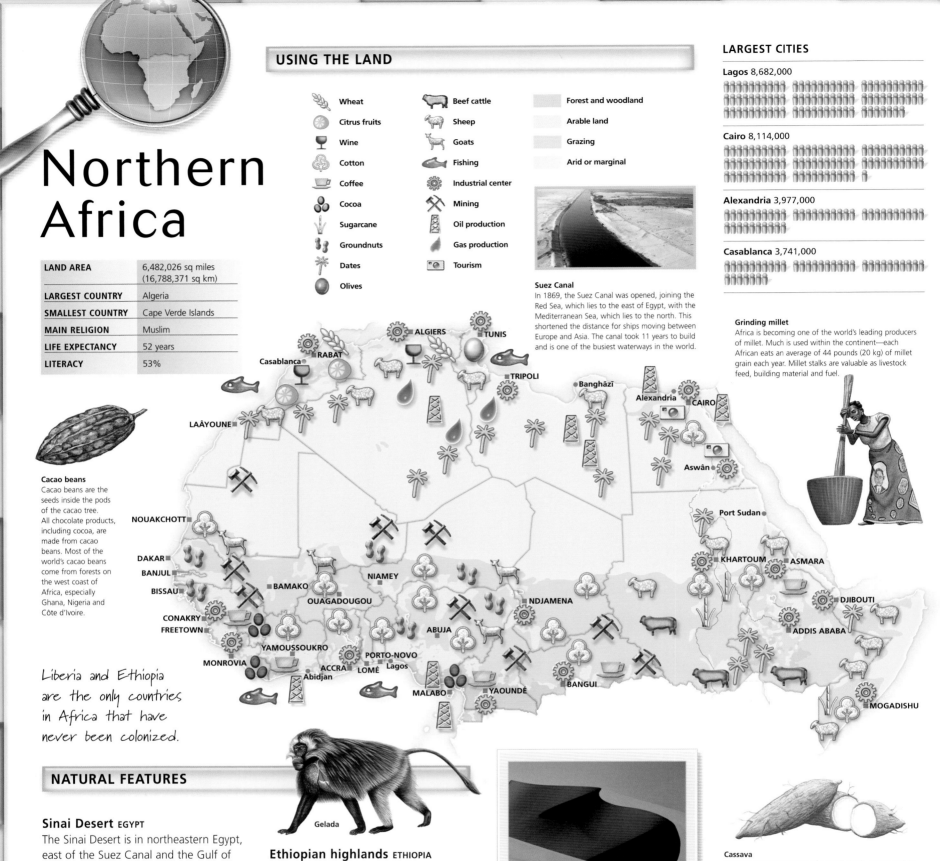

USING THE LAND

- 🌾 Wheat
- 🍊 Citrus fruits
- 🍷 Wine
- Cotton
- ☕ Coffee
- Cocoa
- Sugarcane
- Groundnuts
- 🌴 Dates
- Olives
- 🐄 Beef cattle
- 🐑 Sheep
- 🐐 Goats
- 🐟 Fishing
- ⚙ Industrial center
- ⛏ Mining
- Oil production
- Gas production
- Tourism
- Forest and woodland
- Arable land
- Grazing
- Arid or marginal

LAND AREA	6,482,026 sq miles (16,788,371 sq km)
LARGEST COUNTRY	Algeria
SMALLEST COUNTRY	Cape Verde Islands
MAIN RELIGION	Muslim
LIFE EXPECTANCY	52 years
LITERACY	53%

Suez Canal
In 1869, the Suez Canal was opened, joining the Red Sea, which lies to the east of Egypt, with the Mediterranean Sea, which lies to the north. This shortened the distance for ships moving between Europe and Asia. The canal took 11 years to build and is one of the busiest waterways in the world.

Cacao beans
Cacao beans are the seeds inside the pods of the cacao tree. All chocolate products, including cocoa, are made from cacao beans. Most of the world's cacao beans come from forests on the west coast of Africa, especially Ghana, Nigeria and Côte d'Ivoire.

Liberia and Ethiopia are the only countries in Africa that have never been colonized.

LARGEST CITIES

Lagos 8,682,000

Cairo 8,114,000

Alexandria 3,977,000

Casablanca 3,741,000

Grinding millet
Africa is becoming one of the world's leading producers of millet. Much is used within the continent—each African eats an average of 44 pounds (20 kg) of millet grain each year. Millet stalks are valuable as livestock feed, building material and fuel.

NATURAL FEATURES

Sinai Desert EGYPT
The Sinai Desert is in northeastern Egypt, east of the Suez Canal and the Gulf of Suez. It is a barren area, but it does have a number of oases, such as Wadi Ferain in the southwest, which has been used by the Bedouin for thousands of years.

Atlas Mountains MOROCCO–TUNISIA
These mountains are made up of three ranges that run from the northeast to the southwest and extend for 1,200 miles (2,000 km). The land between the mountains and the coast is fertile.

Ethiopian highlands ETHIOPIA
Covering two-thirds of the country and divided by the Great Rift Valley, the highlands have the country's richest farmland. A wide variety of animals live in the highlands—the gelada baboon is found only in this region.

Jungle CÔTE D'IVOIRE
Côte d'Ivoire is on the west coast of Africa along the Gulf of Guinea. Almost one-third of the country is a densely forested tropical jungle. The region's elephants are threatened because their habitat is being destroyed and animals are being killed to supply the ivory market.

Gelada

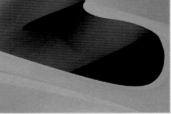

Sahara Desert

The Sahara is the largest desert in the world. It stretches across more than half of northern Africa, from the Atlantic Ocean to the Red Sea. Its rocky plains are barren and not suitable for farming. Most of the Saharan people are nomads who move their herds of camels, sheep and goats around to take advantage of available water and pasture land.

Cassava
Cassava, the starchy root of a small shrub, grows well in the hot climates of western Africa. The bark of the root is peeled off, the juice squeezed out and the remaining pulp is baked to make flat cakes. Cassava can also be dried and deep-fried, or fermented and made into an alcoholic drink. Cassava is also known as manioc or yuca.

WHERE PEOPLE LIVE

Urban		Rural

REGION
| 42% | 58% |

Most urban: LIBYA
| 87% | 13% |

Most rural: ETHIOPIA
| 17% | 83% |

Aswan High Dam

Before the Aswan High Dam was completed in 1970, Egyptian farmers depended on the River Nile to water their crops. The dam now provides Egypt with regular water supplies, but its construction was difficult. In the 1960s, Abu Simbel (*below*), the temple of Ramses II, had to be moved to save it from the rising waters.

TRADITIONS AND CULTURE

Musical storytelling ALGERIA

The Berbers of Algeria (*below*) use music and song to tell stories and record their history. They play their many instruments, including various kinds of drums, at traditional festivals and weddings.

Dinka people SUDAN

These are a group of closely related cattle-herding peoples living in central Africa. The women plant and raise most of the crops and the men are responsible for the goats, sheep and cattle.

Tribal religions

Followers of tribal religions worship spirits that they believe are in all living things. These spirits communicate through shamans (priests), who honor them in rituals.

Minarets

A minaret is a tall tower attached to a mosque. A *muezzin*, or crier, calls the followers of Islam to prayer five times each day from the balcony of the minaret.

Ethiopia uses the Julian calendar, and its dates are therefore seven years behind those used in most countries.

PLACES

Cairo EGYPT

Cairo, the capital of Egypt, is one of the oldest cities in Africa and among the world's most crowded. Its noisy and colorful streets have a mix of mosques, monuments, museums and bazaars.

Timbuktu MALI

Timbuktu began as a nomad camp in 1100, and later became a trading post for merchants crossing the Sahara. Today, the city is a center of Islamic learning.

Carthage TUNISIA

Carthage, founded in the 8th century BC, was one of the greatest cities and busiest seaports of ancient times. It was destroyed by the Romans in 146 BC.

Lalibela churches ETHIOPIA

These 11 churches, carved out of rock in the 13th century, were named for King Lalibela of the Zagwe dynasty. They are joined by a maze of tunnels and passages.

Nomadic Wodaabe people have male beauty contests.

Leptis Magna LIBYA

Originally a Phoenician port, Leptis Magna became part of the Roman empire in 111 BC. Its ruined buildings show that it was once a large and bustling city.

Leptis Magna

Marrakech MOROCCO

Marrakech, on the plains below the Atlas Mountains, was founded in 1062 by the Almoravid dynasty as the capital of its empire. It became one of Islam's great cities and today is a popular tourist resort, famous for its bazaars.

Liberia

Liberia, a small country on the west coast, is Africa's oldest republic. It was founded in 1822 by freed slaves from the USA, but today most of its people are native Africans. The name Liberia means "free land." Less than 4 percent of the land can be farmed, but there are rich reserves of iron ore.

Freed slave

PEOPLE

Queen of Sheba c 1000 BC

The Queen of Sheba features in the traditional stories of Muslims and Christians, but her homeland is not known. Ethiopians claim that their first emperor, Menelik I, was the son of the Queen of Sheba and King Solomon of Israel.

Hannibal c 287–c 183 BC

The Carthaginian general Hannibal led his army across the Alps by elephant in 218 BC to fight his enemies, the Romans. Many years later, he poisoned himself rather than surrender to Rome.

Ibn Batuta c AD 303–c 377

Born in Tangier, Morocco, Arab traveler and author Ibn Batuta visited western Africa, western Europe and Asia. He journeyed for 29 years recording his travels in his book *Rihla* (Journey).

Haile Selassie 1892–1975

Haile Selassie became emperor of Ethiopia in 1930 and set about modernizing his country. After a military rebellion, he was removed from power in 1974.

Kofi Annan born 1938

Kofi Annan was born in Kumasi, Ghana, and studied in the USA and Switzerland. He joined the United Nations in 1962 and was head of its peacekeeping department from 1993 to 1995. In 1997, he became the seventh Secretary General of the United Nations.

Kofi Annan

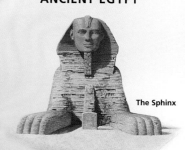

The Sphinx

RIVER NILE
Life in ancient Egypt revolved around the River Nile. Every year the river flooded its banks, watering the land and leaving behind rich, fertile soil in which the people grew crops.

PHARAOHS
Ancient Egyptians believed that their rulers, the pharaohs, were god-kings. They believed the pharaohs could control the weather, their crops and even Egypt's success in war and trade.

GODS AND GODDESSES
Ancient Egyptians worshiped hundreds of gods and goddesses. Some, such as the sun-god Re, were honored as great gods throughout the country, but others were recognized only in particular regions. Many gods appeared in animal form.

Gods and goddesses

HIEROGLYPHICS
The ancient Egyptians used hieroglyphics, a form of writing in which picture symbols represented objects, people, and even ideas and sounds.

PAPYRUS
Papyrus is a water plant. Egyptians sliced the stems to make paper. When one layer was placed on another, the plant's juices glued them together.

MUMMIES
A mummy is a dead body that has been dried out to stop it from decaying. The bodies were preserved by a special embalming process and stored inside a decorated coffin or case.

Mummy case

SPHINXES
The Egyptians built sphinxes to guard their temples or tombs. They usually had a human head (as a sign of intelligence) and a lion's body (as a sign of strength).

NEFERTITI
Nefertiti, an Egyptian queen of the 14th century BC, was the wife of the pharaoh Akhenaton. With her husband, she established a new religion based on Sun worship.

TUTANKHAMEN
Tutankhamen (*right*) was pharaoh of Egypt from about 1347 to 1339 BC. In 1922, his tomb containing thousands of golden treasures was discovered near Luxor.

CLEOPATRA
Cleopatra became queen of Egypt in 51 BC. She was the last pharaoh to rule Egypt. She was clever and ambitious, and was supported in battle by two Roman generals, Mark Antony and Julius Caesar.

Southern Africa

Wildlife safari

DEMOCRATIC REPUBLIC OF CONGO
POPULATION 56,625,000 * CAPITAL KINSHASA

SOUTH AFRICA
POPULATION 42,769,000 * CAPITAL PRETORIA

TANZANIA
POPULATION 35,922,000 * CAPITAL DODOMA

KENYA
POPULATION 31,639,000 * CAPITAL NAIROBI

UGANDA
POPULATION 25,633,000 * CAPITAL KAMPALA

MOZAMBIQUE
POPULATION 17,479,000 * CAPITAL MAPUTO

MADAGASCAR
POPULATION 16,980,000 * CAPITAL ANTANANARIVO

ZIMBABWE
POPULATION 12,577,000 * CAPITAL HARARE

MALAWI
POPULATION 11,651,000 * CAPITAL LILONGWE

ANGOLA
POPULATION 10,766,000 * CAPITAL LUANDA

ZAMBIA
POPULATION 10,307,000 * CAPITAL LUSAKA

RWANDA
POPULATION 7,810,000 * CAPITAL KIGALI

BURUNDI
POPULATION 6,096,000 * CAPITAL BUJUMBURA

CONGO
POPULATION 2,954,000 * CAPITAL BRAZZAVILLE

NAMIBIA
POPULATION 1,927,000 * CAPITAL WINDHOEK

LESOTHO
POPULATION 1,862,000 * CAPITAL MASERU

BOTSWANA
POPULATION 1,573,000 * CAPITAL GABORONE

GABON
POPULATION 1,322,000 * CAPITAL LIBREVILLE

MAURITIUS
POPULATION 1,210,000 * CAPITAL PORT LOUIS

SWAZILAND
POPULATION 1,161,000 * CAPITAL MBABANE

COMOROS
POPULATION 633,000 * CAPITAL MORONI

SÃO TOMÉ AND PRINCIPE
POPULATION 176,000 * CAPITAL SÃO TOMÉ

SEYCHELLES
POPULATION 80,000 * CAPITAL VICTORIA

Fang mask
The Fang tribespeople mainly live in the hot, humid rain forests of Gabon. The spiritual leader of each village wears ceremonial masks to bring good health and prosperity to the tribe.

Herero woman
Various tribes form the Herero group and speak a common language. They live in Namibia. In the late 19th century, Herero women were encouraged by German missionaries to dress in the style of clothing then worn in Europe. Their distinctive clothes remain much the same today.

Mountain gorilla
This gorilla inhabits forests in the mountains of Rwanda and Uganda. It lives in family groups led by one or two males, and eats bamboo shoots. It is now endangered.

0 miles / 500
0 kilometers / 500

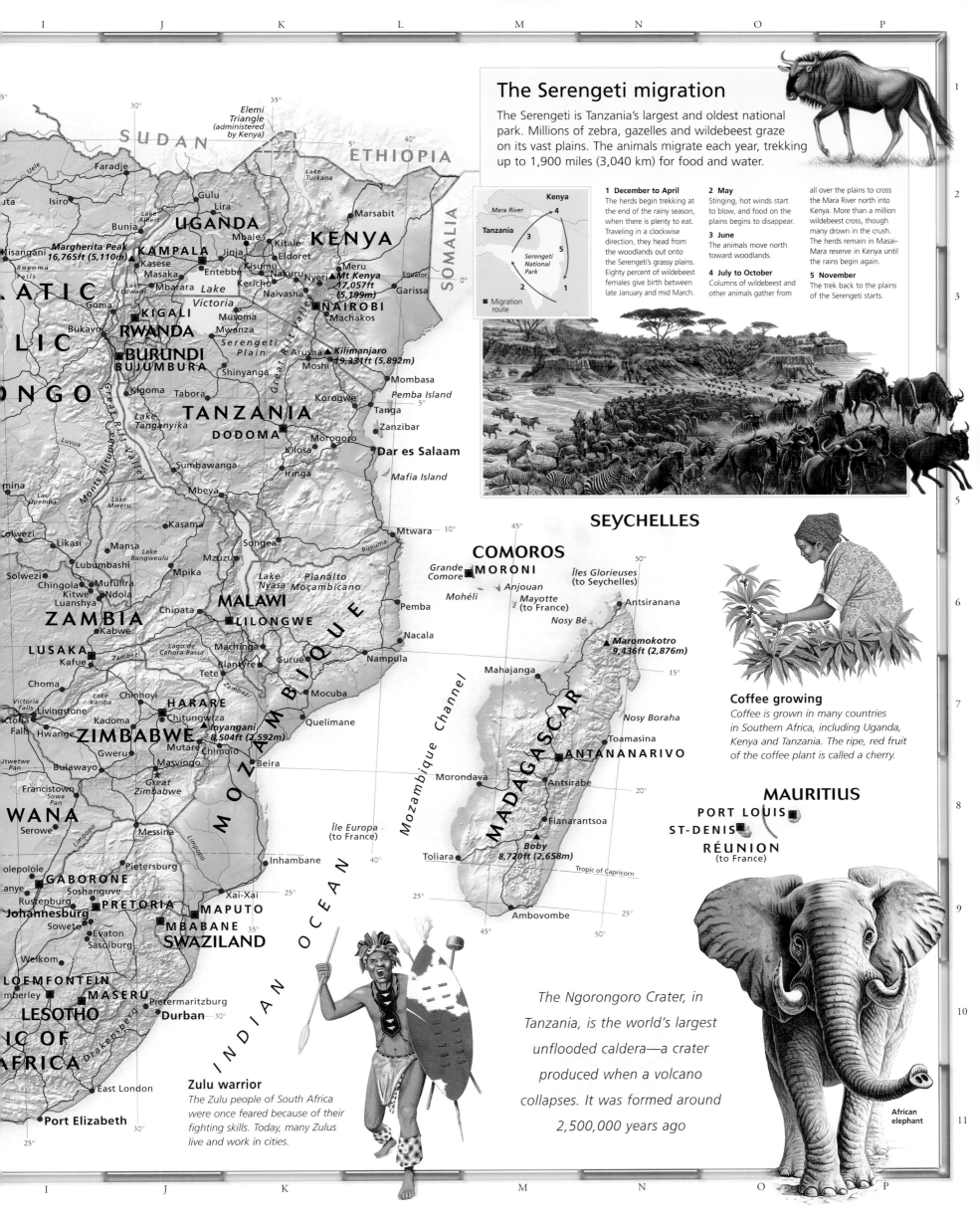

The Serengeti migration

The Serengeti is Tanzania's largest and oldest national park. Millions of zebra, gazelles and wildebeest graze on its vast plains. The animals migrate each year, trekking up to 1,900 miles (3,040 km) for food and water.

Kenya
Mara River
Tanzania
Serengeti National Park
■ Migration route

1 December to April
The herds begin trekking at the end of the rainy season, when there is plenty to eat. Traveling in a clockwise direction, they head from the woodlands out onto the Serengeti's grassy plains. Eighty percent of wildebeest females give birth between late January and mid March.

2 May
Stinging, hot winds start to blow, and food on the plains begins to disappear.

3 June
The animals move north toward woodlands.

4 July to October
Columns of wildebeest and other animals gather from all over the plains to cross the Mara River north into Kenya. More than a million wildebeest cross, though many drown in the crush. The herds remain in Masai-Mara reserve in Kenya until the rains begin again.

5 November
The trek back to the plains of the Serengeti starts.

Coffee growing
Coffee is grown in many countries in Southern Africa, including Uganda, Kenya and Tanzania. The ripe, red fruit of the coffee plant is called a cherry.

Zulu warrior
The Zulu people of South Africa were once feared because of their fighting skills. Today, many Zulus live and work in cities.

The Ngorongoro Crater, in Tanzania, is the world's largest unflooded caldera—a crater produced when a volcano collapses. It was formed around 2,500,000 years ago

African elephant

Southern Africa

USING THE LAND

- Forest and woodland
- Arable land
- Grazing
- Arid or marginal

Kenya has the world's youngest population. The average age is 18 years.

Rubber
The people of the Democratic Republic of Congo cut into the bark of the rubber tree to drain off the fluid that is made into rubber. This is called tapping. Some species of rubber trees grow only in the Democratic Republic of Congo. Rubber is one of the country's main exports. However, the use of synthetic rubber has led to a decline in demand.

Vanilla beans
Vanilla beans are harvested from the vanilla plant, which is a tropical orchid that takes about three years to flower. The world's leading producer of vanilla beans is the island of Madagascar.

LAND AREA	4,281,904 sq miles (11,090,080 sq km)
LARGEST COUNTRY	Democratic Republic of Congo
SMALLEST COUNTRY	Seychelles
MAIN RELIGION	Christian
LIFE EXPECTANCY	45 years
LITERACY	66%

NATURAL FEATURES

Congo River
The Congo, the fifth-longest river in the world, flows through western central Africa. People along its banks rely on the river for transport and trade.

Mt Kilimanjaro TANZANIA
Kilimanjaro is Africa's highest mountain. Although it is near the Equator in Tanzania, its summit is always covered in snow. It was once an active volcano.

Mt Kilimanjaro

Kalahari Desert
Most of the large Kalahari Desert is in Botswana, but it also extends to Namibia and South Africa. Although little rain falls, trees and grasses grow in the desert.

Victoria Falls
Victoria Falls forms part of the border between Zambia and Zimbabwe. The falls are fed by the Zambezi River. Their local name, *mosi-oa-tunya*, means "smoke that thunders" because the water can be heard 10 miles (16 km) away.

Ngorongoro Crater TANZANIA
The Ngorongoro Crater, at the eastern edge of the Serengeti Plain, is home to more than 30,000 animals. The crater has a constant supply of spring water.

Map legend:
- Corn (maize)
- Citrus fruits
- Wine
- Cotton
- Coffee
- Tea
- Cocoa
- Tobacco
- Beef cattle
- Sheep
- Fishing
- Industrial center
- Mining
- Oil production
- Timber

Map labels: SÃO TOMÉ, LIBREVILLE, BRAZZAVILLE, KINSHASA, LUANDA, Namibe, WINDHOEK, GABORONE, PRETORIA, Johannesburg, Bloemfontein, MASERU, MBABANE, MAPUTO, Durban, Cape Town, Port Elizabeth, KAMPALA, KIGALI, BUJUMBURA, NAIROBI, DODOMA, Zanzibar, Dar es Salaam, Lubumbashi, LUSAKA, LILONGWE, HARARE, Beira, MORONI, ANTANANARIVO

Diamond mining
South Africa's diamond mining industry began in 1867 with the discovery of a single diamond on the banks of the Orange River. Today, South Africa produces 9 percent of the world's diamonds, and exports 90 percent of what it mines. It is the world's fifth-largest rough diamond producer.

Great Rift Valley
The Great Rift Valley cuts across the entire length of Kenya, and extends north into Ethiopia and south into Tanzania. Millions of years ago, the land slowly moved apart, creating the valley. The area is rich in fossils, and is famous for the discovery of the bones of an early human, nicknamed Lucy, who lived 3 million years ago.

Reconstruction of Lucy

Boyoma Falls in the Democratic Republic of Congo has the world's greatest waterfall flow.

WHERE PEOPLE LIVE

Urban		Rural

REGION
| 36% | 64% |

Most urban: GABON
| 80% | 20% |

Most rural: RWANDA
| 6% | 94% |

LARGEST CITIES

Kinshasa 6,790,000

Cape Town 2,984,000

Dar es Salaam 2,538,000

Durban 2,531,000

Nairobi 2,504,000

PLACES

Cape Town SOUTH AFRICA
Cape Town is South Africa's oldest city and legislative capital. It was the first white settlement in South Africa, founded in 1652. Set between the coast and Table Mountain, Cape Town is a shipping and commercial center.

Stone Town TANZANIA
In historical Stone Town, on Zanzibar Island, African and Arabic cultures are brought together in a mix of cathedrals, mosques, temples and houses built in the 19th century on the island.

Stone Town

Nairobi KENYA
The capital of Kenya, Nairobi is a center of trade, industry, business and tourism, and one of the largest cities in Africa. It is home to several museums of African history, art and natural history.

Source of the Nile
For hundreds of years, explorers were puzzled about the starting point of the world's longest river, the Nile. In 1862, John Hanning Speke discovered that its primary source is Lake Victoria, whose waters rise from the Ruvironza River in the mountains of Burundi. The River Nile flows northward through a total of eight African countries from central Africa to the Mediterranean Sea.

Robben Island SOUTH AFRICA
Used for more than 400 years as a prison, Robben Island is best known for two ex-prisoners: anti-apartheid activists Nelson Mandela and Walter Sisulu.

Great Zimbabwe ZIMBABWE
This city, built by the Shona people in the 1100s, was once the center of a great empire. Its structures were made from stones put together without mortar.

PEOPLE

Shaka c 1787–1828
The son of a Zulu chieftain, Shaka was a fierce warrior. When his father died, Shaka took over the Zulu clan. Under his leadership, the Zulus established one of Africa's most powerful empires.

Louis Leakey 1893–1976
Archaeologist Louis Leakey and his wife Mary discovered fossils believed to be early human beings that lived in Africa about 2 million years ago. They found these fossils (called hominids) in Olduvai Gorge in Tanzania.

Nelson Mandela born 1918
After working as a lawyer, Mandela joined the African National Congress in 1944. He organized protests against the government and was sentenced to life in prison in 1964. Mandela was released in 1990, and in 1994 he became South Africa's first black president.

Christiaan Barnard 1922–2001
Born in South Africa, Christiaan Barnard was a heart surgeon in Cape Town. He pioneered open-heart surgery, and in 1967 became the first surgeon to transplant a human heart from one person to another.

HISTORY AT A GLANCE
SOUTH AFRICA

1488
Portuguese explorer Bartholomew Diaz rounds the Cape of Good Hope and calls it the "Cape of Storms" because of the terrible weather.

1652
The Dutch East India Company establishes a settlement at the Cape to supply its ships sailing between the East Indies and the Netherlands.

Dutch East India crest

1779
First war between the Xhosa tribe, who had been tending cattle and raising crops at the Cape since the 1500s, and the British and Dutch settlers.

1795
Britain annexes the Cape for the first time and many of the Afrikaner (Dutch-supporting) settlers go north to gain freedom from British rule.

1852
Afrikaners in the Transvaal gain independence from Britain. Shortly afterward, the Afrikaners establish the Orange Free State, one of the four provinces of the Union of South Africa.

1879
After many fierce battles, the Zulu kingdom finally loses its independence and is defeated by the British armies.

1880
The first Boer War between the British and the Afrikaners begins. The Afrikaners are victorious.

The second Boer War

1899–1902
The second Boer War, also called the South African War, takes place between the British and the Afrikaners. Although the Afrikaners fight fiercely, the British defeat them, and the Transvaal and the Orange Free State become British colonies.

1950
A policy of segregation, called apartheid, is implemented. People are officially classified into four distinct racial groups: black, white, colored and Asian.

Apartheid sign

1961
South Africa leaves the Commonwealth of Nations and becomes a republic. The African National Congress (ANC) begins to use weapons in its protests against the government.

1990
Nelson Mandela is released from prison; negotiations begin on voting rights for blacks.

1994
The ANC wins the first election after apartheid is abolished and Nelson Mandela becomes president. After an absence of 20 years, South Africa rejoins the United Nations.

1999
The ANC wins the general elections and Thabo Mbeki takes over as president.

TRADITIONS AND CULTURE

Chokwe masks
Masks once played an important role in the rituals of the Chokwe people of the Democratic Republic of Congo. Today, they are used mostly for entertainment.

Masai people
The Masai are a nomadic people who live in the grasslands of southern Kenya and northern Tanzania. Their daily life centers around the herding of cattle. Families and their herds live together in a compound known as a *kraal*.

San people of the Kalahari
The San live in the Kalahari region of Botswana and Namibia. In the past, the San survived by hunting animals with bows and snares, and gathering desert berries and insects. Today, few of them follow this traditional way of life.

San hunters

Zionist church
About 6 million people in southern Africa are followers of this faith, which combines the teachings of Christianity with traditional African beliefs and forms of worship such as dancing.

Animals of Madagascar
The forests of Madagascar, an island off the east coast of Africa, are home to an amazing variety of animals. Many species of birds, reptiles, insects and mammals exist only on this island. The best known are the lemurs, which have survived there for 58 million years. There are more than 20 species, ranging in size from the 11-inch (29-cm) mouse lemur to the 3-foot (90-cm) indri. Many are now endangered.

Ring-tailed lemur

Elephants can walk under water by sticking their trunks up in the air above the water like a snorkel.

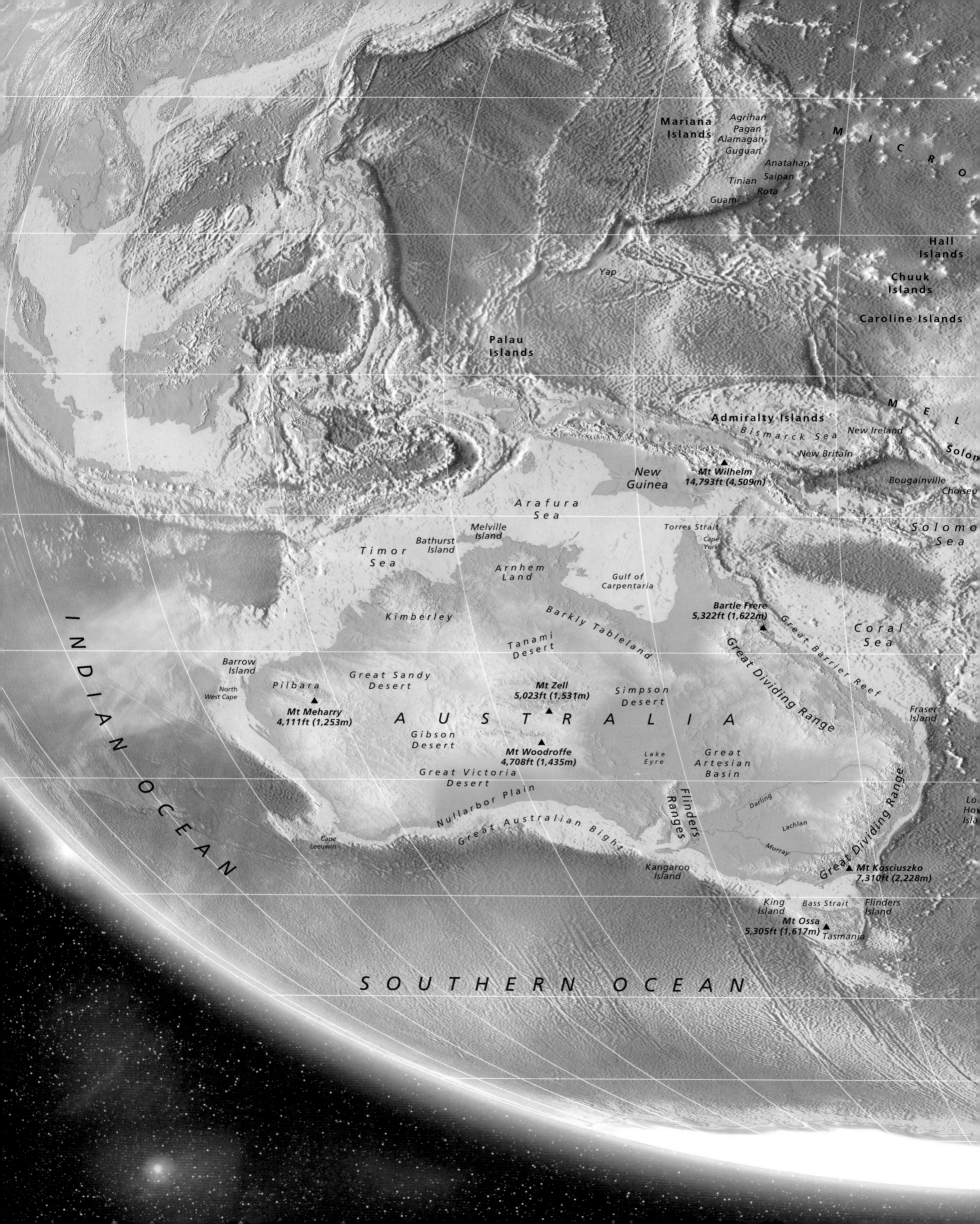

M I C R O

Mariana
Islands

Agrihan
Pagan
Alamagan
Guguan

Anatahan

Saipan
Tinian   *Rota*

Guam

Hall
Islands

Chuuk
Islands

Caroline Islands

Yap

Palau
Islands

M E L

Admiralty Islands

Bismarck Sea   *New Ireland*

New Britain

Solon

New
Guinea

▲ Mt Wilhelm
14,793ft (4,509m)

Bougainville

Choiseu

*Arafura
Sea*

Torres Strait

*Cape
York*

S o l o m o

Sea

*Melville
Island*

*Timor
Sea*

*Bathurst
Island*

*Arnhem
Land*

*Gulf of
Carpentaria*

C o r a l

S e a

Kimberley

Barkly Tableland

**Bartle Frere
5,322ft (1,622m)**
▲

Great Barrier Reef

*Tanami
Desert*

Great Dividing Range

*Barrow
Island*

Pilbara

**Great Sandy
Desert**

**Mt Zell
5,023ft (1,531m)**
▲

*Simpson
Desert*

*Fraser
Island*

*North
West Cape*

▲

**Mt Meharry
4,111ft (1,253m)**

A U S T R A L I A

*Gibson
Desert*

▲

**Mt Woodroffe
4,708ft (1,435m)**

*Lake
Eyre*

**Great
Artesian
Basin**

Great Dividing Range

**Great Victoria
Desert**

*Flinders
Ranges*

Darling

Lachlan

I N D I A N   O C E A N

Nullarbor Plain

Great Australian Bight

Murray

▲ **Mt Kosciuszko
7,310ft (2,228m)**

*Cape
Leeuwin*

*Kangaroo
Island*

*King
Island*   *Bass Strait*   *Flinders
Island*

*Lo
How
Isla*

▲ **Mt Ossa
5,305ft (1,617m)** *Tasmania*

S O U T H E R N   O C E A N

Pohnpei

Kosrae

Ralik Chain

Ratak Chain

Majuro

Tarawa
**Gilbert
Islands**

Nauru

Banaba

_S I A_

_E S I A_

lands

nta
bel

Malaita

uadalcanal

San
Cristobal

Ndeni

**Torres
Islands**

Espíritu
Santo

Malakula

Ouvéa

Lifou

Maré

**New
Caledonia**

Île des
Pins

**Santa Cruz
Islands**

**Banks
Islands**

Pentecost

Éfaté

Erromango

Tanna

Nanumea

**Ellice
Islands**

Nui

Funafuti
Nukulaelae

Niutao

Nuilakita

Rotuma

Vanua
Levu

Fiji

Vitu
Levu

Wallis

Futuna

Kingman Reef

Palmyra

Teraina

Tabuaeran

Christmas
Island

Howland Island
Baker Island

**Phoenix
Islands**

Nikumaroro

Kanton

Orona

Phoenix
Manra

Atafu
Nukunonu
Fakaofo

_P_

_O_

_L_

_Y_

_N_

_E_

_S_

_I_

_A_

Jarvis
Island

Malden
Island

**Northern
Cook Islands**

Starbuck
Island

Swains

Nassau

Tongareva

Rakahanga
Manihiki

Millennium

Vostok

Flint

Samoa

Savai'i

Upolu

Tutuila

**Niua
Group**

**Vava'u
Group**

**Ha'apai
Group**

**Tongatapu
Group**

Niue

Cook Islands

Suwarrow

Line Islands

Oceania

Raoul
Island

**Kermadec
Islands**

Norfolk
Island

asman

Sea

Mt Cook
12,316ft (3,754m)
▲

South
Island

Stewart
Island

**Snares
Islands**

**Antipodes
Islands**

Macquarie
Island

North
Island

**NEW
ZEALAND**

Chatham
Islands

**Bounty
Islands**

_P A C I F I C   O C E A N_

Australia and Papua New Guinea

Red kangaroo

Bird-of-paradise

Birds-of-paradise live in the forests of Papua New Guinea. To attract a mate, male birds gather in the treetops and call loudly, dance and display their long, brightly colored tail feathers. Female birds are drab and have short feathers.

AUSTRALIA
POPULATION 19,732,000 ✳ CAPITAL CANBERRA

PAPUA NEW GUINEA
POPULATION 5,296,000 ✳ CAPITAL PORT MORESBY

Iron ore mining

Australia is one of the world's largest producers of iron ore. Most comes from the Hamersley Range, in Western Australia. The massive trucks that cart iron ore are too big for public roads and never leave the mine.

Aboriginal dancers

Aboriginal Australians use dancing to express their beliefs and represent their lives. Some of the dances tell the stories of the Dreamtime—the time of the creation of all things. These dances and stories have been handed down by tribal elders over thousands of years.

Uluru rises 2,844 feet (867 m) above sea level and measures nearly 6 miles (9.5 km) around its base. It is the largest monolith (single piece of rock) in the world.

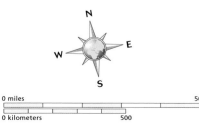

Dugongs

Arafura Sea

Timor Sea

Melville Island
Cobourg Peninsula
Goulbu Island

Bathurst Island
Van Diemen Gulf
DARWIN
Palmerston
★ Kakadu National Park
Arnher Land

Cape Ford
Joseph Bonaparte Gulf
Pine Creek
Katherine
Daly Waters

Bonaparte Archipelago
Wyndham
Kununurra
Top Springs

Cape Leveque
King Sound
Kimberley Plateau
King Leopold Ranges
Lake Argyle
Bungle Bungles

INDIAN OCEAN

Broome
Fitzroy Crossing
Fitzroy
Halls Creek

Eighty Mile Beach
Tanami Desert
Tennant Creek

Dampier
Port Hedland
Great Sandy Desert
Lake Gregory
Lake White
NORTHER TERRITOR

Barrow Island
Onslow
Percival Lakes
Lake Mackay

North West Cape
Hamersley Range
AUSTR

Exmouth
Newman
Lake Disappointment
MacDonnell Ranges
Alice Spring

Tropic of Capricorn
Gibson Desert
Lake Neale
Lake Amadeus
Uluru (Ayers Roc 2,844ft (867m)

Lake MacLeod
WESTERN AUSTRALIA
Great Victoria

Gascoyne
Carnarvon
Lake Carnegie
Desert

Shark Bay
Lake Wells
Cooba Pedy

Dirk Hartog Island
Denham
Murchison
Meekatharra

Lake Austin
SOUTH AUSTRALI

Geraldton
Mount Magnet
Lake Noondie
Lake Ballard
Lake Carey
Lake Minigwal
Nullarbor Plain
Tarcoola

Dongara
Lake Barlee
Lake Moore
Kalgoorlie
Eucla
Ced

Moora
Coolgardie
Lake Lefroy
Lake Cowan
Penong

PERTH
Northam
Norseman
Balladonia
Great Australian Bight

Fremantle
Mandurah
Brookton
Esperance

Bunbury
Wagin
Ravensthorpe
Ellisto

Busselton
SOUTHERN OCEAN

Augusta
Albany

N W E S

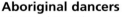

0 miles ———— 500
0 kilometers ———— 500

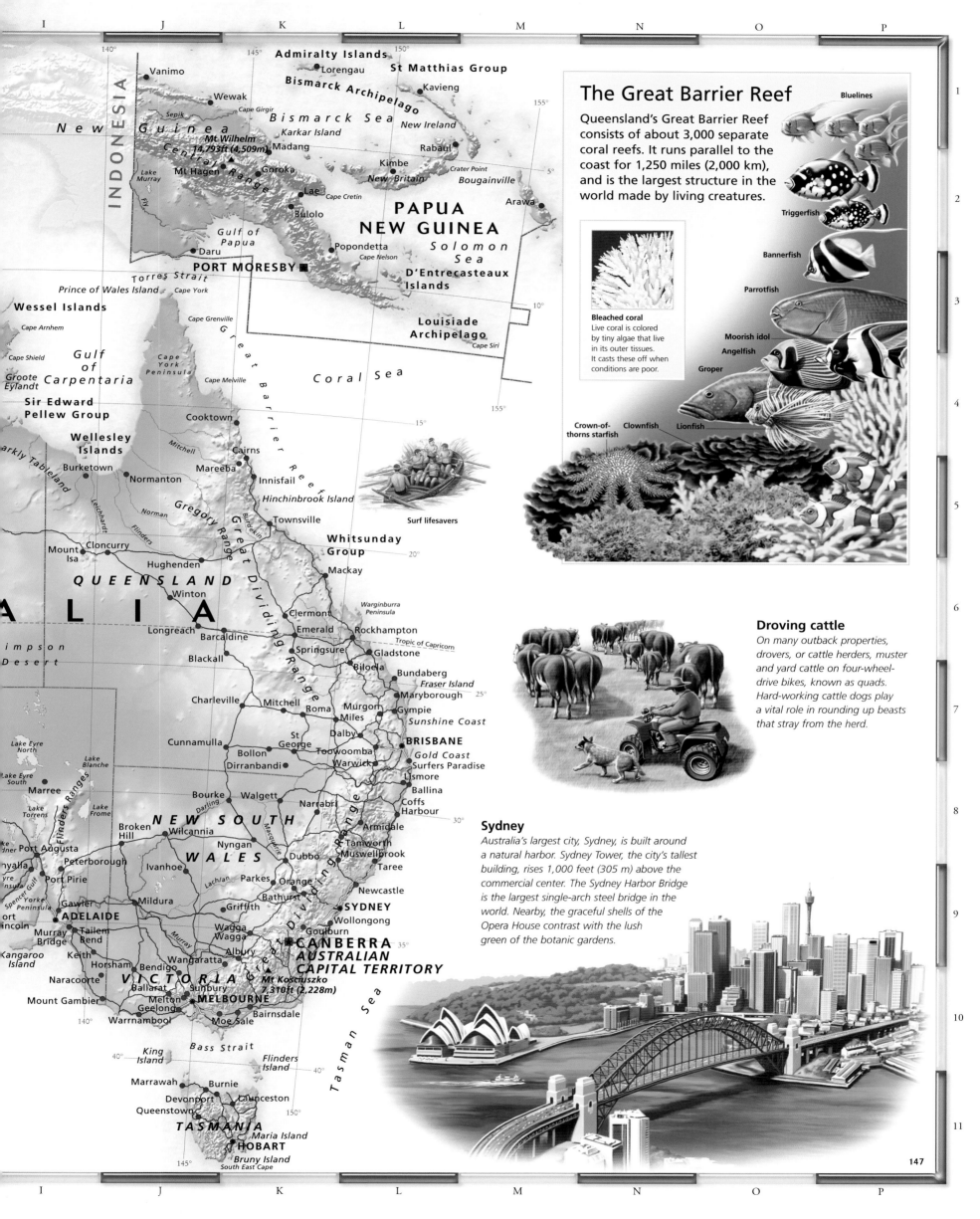

Map labels

I J K L M N O P

New Guinea

INDONESIA

Vanimo

Admiralty Islands

Lorengau

St Matthias Group

Wewak

Bismarck Archipelago

Kavieng

Cape Girgir

Sepik

Bismarck Sea

New Ireland

Karkar Island

Mt Wilhelm 14,793ft (4,509m)

Madang

Rabaul

Central Range

Mt Hagen

Goroka

Kimbe

Lake Murray

Lae

New Britain

Crater Point

Bougainville

Cape Cretin

Fly

Bulolo

Gulf of Papua

PAPUA NEW GUINEA

Solomon Sea

Arawa

Daru

Popondetta

Cape Nelson

D'Entrecasteaux Islands

PORT MORESBY

Torres Strait

Prince of Wales Island

Cape York

Louisiade Archipelago

Wessel Islands

Cape Grenville

Cape Siri

Cape Arnhem

Cape Shield

Gulf of Carpentaria

Groote Eylandt

Cape York Peninsula

Cape Melville

Coral Sea

Sir Edward Pellew Group

arkly Tableland

Wellesley Islands

Cooktown

Mitchell

Burketown

Cairns

Normanton

Mareeba

Norman

Innisfail

Great Barrier Reef

Hinchinbrook Island

Leichhardt

Flinders

Gregory Range

Townsville

Whitsunday Group

Surf lifesavers

Mount Isa

Cloncurry

Great Dividing Range

Mackay

Hughenden

Warginburra Peninsula

QUEENSLAND

Winton

Clermont

Emerald

Rockhampton

impson Desert

Longreach

Barcaldine

Springsure

Tropic of Capricorn

ALIA

Gladstone

Blackall

Biloela

Bundaberg

Fraser Island

Charleville

Mitchell

Roma

Murgon

Maryborough

Cunnamulla

St George

Miles

Gympie

Lake Eyre North

Dalby

Sunshine Coast

Lake Blanche

Bollon

Toowoomba

BRISBANE

Lake Eyre South

Dirranbandi

Warwick

Gold Coast

Marree

Surfers Paradise

Lismore

Flinders Ranges

Bourke

Walgett

Narrabri

Ballina

Darling

Coffs Harbour

Broken Hill

Wilcannia

Armidale

Lake Frome

NEW SOUTH WALES

Tamworth

Port Augusta

Nyngan

Macquarie

Muswellbrook

Peterborough

Ivanhoe

Dubbo

Taree

Parkes

Orange

Newcastle

Lachlan

Port Pirie

Mildura

Bathurst

SYDNEY

Gawler

Griffith

Wollongong

ADELAIDE

Wagga Wagga

Goulburn

Tailem Bend

Albury

CANBERRA

Murray Bridge

Wangaratta

AUSTRALIAN CAPITAL TERRITORY

Keith

Horsham

Bendigo

Kangaroo Island

Naracoorte

VICTORIA

Mt Kosciuszko 7,310ft (2,228m)

Ballarat

Sunbury

Mount Gambier

Melton

Geelong

MELBOURNE

Bairnsdale

Warrnambool

Moe Sale

Tasman Sea

King Island

Bass Strait

Flinders Island

Marrawah

Burnie

Devonport

Launceston

Queenstown

TASMANIA

Maria Island

HOBART

Bruny Island

South East Cape

The Great Barrier Reef

Queensland's Great Barrier Reef consists of about 3,000 separate coral reefs. It runs parallel to the coast for 1,250 miles (2,000 km), and is the largest structure in the world made by living creatures.

Bluelines

Triggerfish

Bannerfish

Parrotfish

Moorish idol

Angelfish

Groper

Bleached coral
Live coral is colored by tiny algae that live in its outer tissues. It casts these off when conditions are poor.

Crown-of-thorns starfish

Clownfish

Lionfish

Droving cattle

On many outback properties, drovers, or cattle herders, muster and yard cattle on four-wheel-drive bikes, known as quads. Hard-working cattle dogs play a vital role in rounding up beasts that stray from the herd.

Sydney

Australia's largest city, Sydney, is built around a natural harbor. Sydney Tower, the city's tallest building, rises 1,000 feet (305 m) above the commercial center. The Sydney Harbor Bridge is the largest single-arch steel bridge in the world. Nearby, the graceful shells of the Opera House contrast with the lush green of the botanic gardens.

147

Australia and Papua New Guinea

On the Aboriginal flag, the color black represents the people, red is the land, and yellow represents the Sun.

USING THE LAND

- Cereals
- Wine
- Coffee
- Sugarcane
- Coconuts
- Palm oil
- Rubber
- Beef cattle
- Sheep
- Fishing
- Industrial center
- Mining
- Oil production
- Gas production
- Timber
- Tourism

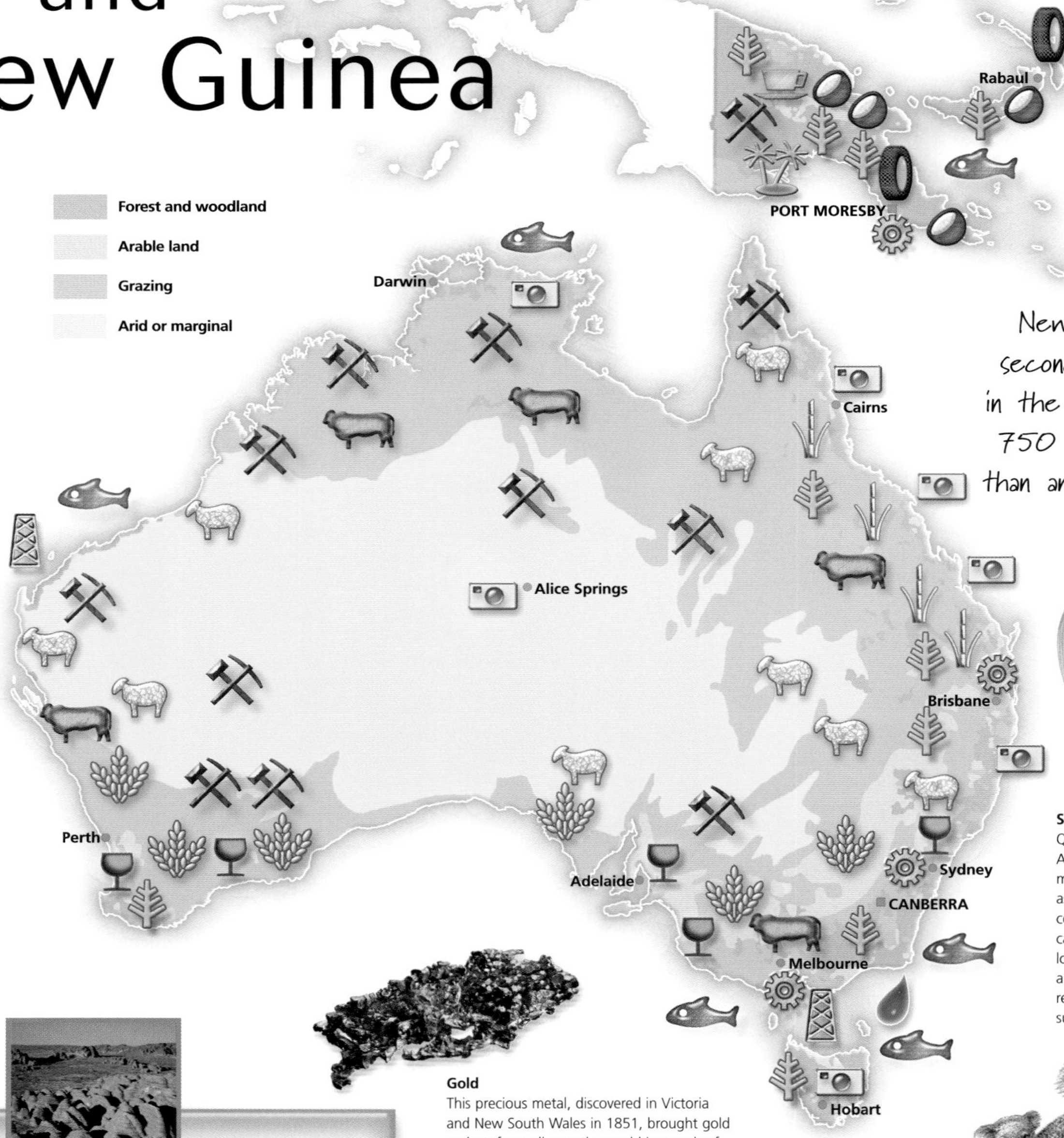

AUSTRALIA LAND AREA	2,941,299 sq miles (7,617,930 sq km)
OFFICIAL LANGUAGE	English
MAIN RELIGION	Christian
LIFE EXPECTANCY	80 years
LITERACY	99%

PAPUA NEW GUINEA LAND AREA	174,850 sq miles (452,860 sq km)
OFFICIAL LANGUAGE	English
MAIN RELIGION	Christian
LIFE EXPECTANCY	64 years
LITERACY	66%

- Forest and woodland
- Arable land
- Grazing
- Arid or marginal

New Guinea, the second largest island in the world, has over 750 languages—more than any other country.

LARGEST CITIES

Sydney 4,306,000

Melbourne 3,660,000

Brisbane 1,553,000

Perth 1,394,000

Adelaide 1,093,000

Sugarcane
Queensland produces most of Australia's sugarcane, grown on more than 6,000 farms for export as well as local use. Raw sugar comes from the juice inside the cane, which is extracted after the long stalks (above) are harvested and stripped of leaves. Ethanol, a renewable fuel, is produced from sugarcane waste.

Gold
This precious metal, discovered in Victoria and New South Wales in 1851, brought gold seekers from all over the world in search of their fortune. Today, Australia is the world's third-largest gold-mining country, with more than 300 tons (300 t) mined annually.

Map labels: Rabaul, PORT MORESBY, Darwin, Cairns, Alice Springs, Brisbane, Perth, Adelaide, Sydney, CANBERRA, Melbourne, Hobart

NATURAL FEATURES

Lake Eyre AUSTRALIA
This usually dry salt lake in the Simpson Desert fills with water only a few times each century, after heavy rains. Millions of birds gather around the lake to breed.

Tasmanian forests AUSTRALIA
The dense forests of the Tasmanian wilderness contain some of the world's oldest living plants. The Tasmanian tiger roamed the forests until last century.

Highlands PAPUA NEW GUINEA

The Southern Highlands have spectacular natural scenery. The Baiyer Wildlife Sanctuary is in the Western Highlands and Mt Wilhelm lies in the Eastern Highlands.

Bungle Bungles AUSTRALIA
These massive rock domes in Western Australia formed 350 million years ago. Their distinctive orange and black bands are best seen from the air. Pools and gorges lie among the domes.

Kakadu National Park AUSTRALIA
Lagoons and billabongs, or waterholes, are a common sight in the Kakadu National Park in Australia's Northern Territory. Much of the land in the park, which supports many animals and birds, floods every year for several months.

Waterlilies at Kakadu

WHERE PEOPLE LIVE

	Urban		Rural
AUSTRALIA	85%		15%
PAPUA NEW GUINEA	17%		83%

LONGEST RIVERS

Murray 1,566 miles (2,520 km)

Murrumbidgee 979 miles (1,575 km)

Darling 864 miles (1,390 km)

Lachlan 851 miles (1,370 km)

Koala and baby

Australian wildlife

Australia is home to two unusual groups of animals. Marsupials are mammals that carry their newborn in a pouch. Koalas, kangaroos and wombats are the most common marsupials. Kangaroos have strong hind legs and can bound along at great speed. Monotremes—platypus and echidnas—are unique animals that lay eggs. When the eggs hatch, they feed their young with milk.

PLACES

Parliament House AUSTRALIA
This modern concrete building, with its imposing flagpole, was opened in 1988 in Canberra, Australia's capital city. It is the seat of national government.

Parliament House

Melbourne AUSTRALIA
This cosmopolitan city, established in 1835, holds several world-renowned sporting events each year, including the Melbourne Cup horse race and the Australian Open tennis grand slam.

Adelaide AUSTRALIA
Named for Queen Adelaide in 1836, this small Australian city hosts the nation's most popular arts festival every two years. The city is surrounded by hills.

Darwin AUSTRALIA
This tropical city in the Northern Territory is Australia's closest point to Southeast Asia. In 1974, Cyclone Tracy devastated the city and it had to be rebuilt.

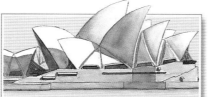

Sydney Opera House
Jutting into Sydney's harbor, this unique structure, with its curved sail-like roofs, has become one of Australia's most famous landmarks. In 1958, the designs of Danish architect Jørn Utzon were chosen from more than 200 competition entries, and work on the Opera House began. It took 15 years to complete. Musicians and actors from all over the world perform in its theaters and concert halls.

Port Moresby PAPUA NEW GUINEA
Local business people and foreigners populate this city, the largest in Papua New Guinea. The parliament building is in the style of a traditional spirit house.

Coober Pedy AUSTRALIA
Most buildings in this opal-mining town are underground, often in unused mines. Temperatures are so hot for much of the year that people prefer to live, and sometimes work, underground.

Underground house, Coober Pedy

PEOPLE

Captain Arthur Philip 1738–1814
As captain of the British fleet that landed on Australian soil in 1788, and first governor, Arthur Philip chose Sydney Cove as the site of a convict settlement.

Caroline Chisholm 1808–77
Called "the immigrants' friend," Caroline Chisholm set up quarters for 11,000 homeless convict women who came to Australia. She found work for many of these women on farms.

Ned Kelly 1854–80
This Victorian bushranger from an Irish convict family stole money from banks and animals from farms. He was found guilty of his crimes in 1880, and was hanged in Melbourne jail. He wore a metal face shield and suit of armor (*right*) to disguise himself, as well as for protection.

Ned Kelly

Sir Donald Bradman 1908–2001
Regarded as one of the best cricketers in the world, "the Don" (*right*) scored a batting average of 99.94. He played for Australia in 52 test matches over 20 years.

Edward Mabo 1936–92
This Aboriginal rights activist, in the Mabo decision of 1993, convinced the High Court of Australia to rule that ownership of land by Australian Aborigines before European settlement should be legally recognized.

Sir Michael Somare born 1936
This politician was the leader of Papua New Guinea's fight for independence. He became the country's first prime minister after independence in 1975. Over 10 years, the "big chief," as he was called, was twice voted into office, then out again.

TRADITIONS AND CULTURE

Sing-sings PAPUA NEW GUINEA
Dance, music and drama are combined at cultural festivals, called sing-sings. People wear elaborate costumes, and display carved masks outside spirit houses to protect the community. One tribe, the mudmen of Asaro (*right*), wear huge clay masks to imitate dead people in their dances.

Aboriginal art AUSTRALIA
The earliest Aboriginal paintings have been found in caves, drawn with yellow ocher and charcoal. Artists from different areas use a variety of styles, including dots (*below*), to create pictures that tell stories of their lives.

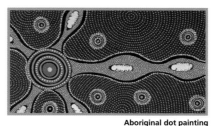
Aboriginal dot painting

Beaches
Most Australians live near the coast, so the beach is a popular destination for many families, especially at Christmas time. Ocean waves can be dangerous so surf lifesavers patrol the beach to keep swimmers safe.

Surf lifesavers

Four of the world's five deadliest snakes are found in Australia. The inland taipan is 50 times more venomous than the Indian cobra.

The Royal Flying Doctor Service

The outback
Australia is a vast country. People who live in the remote and sparsely populated outback areas rely on distance services to link them with the rest of the country. Doctors and nurses of the Royal Flying Doctor Service visit their outback patients by air. Many outback children are educated by lessons from the correspondence school or by two-way radio via the School of the Air.

HISTORY AT A GLANCE

C 50,000 BC
Aborigines arrive in Australia from New Guinea by crossing a land bridge. They occupy Fraser Cave, on the southern tip of Tasmania, about 30,000 years later.

Aboriginal tools

C 8000–6000 BC
New Guinea separates from Australia. Tribes develop in New Guinea's high mountain valleys.

AD 1688
William Dampier lands on the northwest coast of Australia in his ship *Cygnet*—the first European to land on Australian soil. Almost 100 years later, Captain James Cook lands on the east coast and claims it for Britain.

1788
The First Fleet, of 11 ships carrying 1,500 convicts and soldiers, arrives in Sydney Cove.

1851
Gold is discovered in Victoria and New South Wales, and the gold rush begins.

Convicts

1868
The last convicts are sent from Britain. They arrive in Western Australia. Free settlers migrate to Australia and the population grows.

1884
Britain annexes the southeast of New Guinea and Germany controls the northeast. Australia takes over the British area 20 years later.

1901
The six British colonies of Australia join to form a single federation of states, to be governed as one nation—the Commonwealth of Australia.

1914–18
Australia fights for Britain in World War I, along with New Zealand soldiers. They become known as ANZACs.

1921
German New Guinea comes under the control of Australia.

1939–45
Britain declares war on Germany, and Australia supports Britain in World War II. Japan occupies New Guinea from 1942 to 1945.

1975
Papua New Guinea gains its independence from Australia. Michael Somare is its first prime minister.

2000
Sydney hosts the Olympic Games. Sprinter Cathy Freeman wins a gold medal for Australia.

Cathy Freeman

New Zealand and the Pacific Islands

Brown kiwi
The kiwi cannot fly. Instead, it has strong legs for running, kicking and burrowing. Nostrils at the end of its long beak help it to sniff out insects to eat.

Parliament House
New Zealand's Parliament House is in Wellington. The circular building behind, known as the Beehive, contains the offices of government ministers.

NEW ZEALAND
POPULATION 3,951,000 ✳ CAPITAL WELLINGTON

FIJI
POPULATION 869,000 ✳ CAPITAL SUVA

SOLOMON ISLANDS
POPULATION 509,000 ✳ CAPITAL HONIARA

VANUATU
POPULATION 199,000 ✳ CAPITAL PORT VILA

SAMOA
POPULATION 178,000 ✳ CAPITAL APIA

FEDERATED STATES OF MICRONESIA
POPULATION 108,000 ✳ CAPITAL PALIKIR

TONGA
POPULATION 108,000 ✳ CAPITAL NUKU'ALOFA

KIRIBATI
POPULATION 99,000 ✳ CAPITAL TARAWA

MARSHALL ISLANDS
POPULATION 56,000 ✳ CAPITAL MAJURO

PALAU
POPULATION 20,000 ✳ CAPITAL KOROR

NAURU
POPULATION 13,000 ✳ CAPITAL YAREN

TUVALU
POPULATION 11,000 ✳ CAPITAL FUNAFUTI

Farming
Lush pastures grow in New Zealand's rich volcanic soil. They support large numbers of sheep, deer and cattle. Meat, wool and dairy products are the main exports.

Tiki
The tiki is a Maori fertility symbol. Tiki are carved from nephrite, a hard stone similar to jade that can be found on New Zealand's South Island.

Traditional house, Solomon Islands

Conch shell blower

FEDERATED STATES OF MICRONESIA

10° 135° Colonia ●Yap Uithi Gaferut
140° 145° West Fayu Hall Islands
Ngajangel Palau Ngulu Sorol Faraulep
KOROR Woleai Elato Ifalik Pulap Ulul Fayu Nomwin
Eauripik Ifalik Pulawat Pulusuk Weno **Chuuk Islands** Oroluk Kolonia
Losap **PALIKIR**
5° **Caroline Islands** Namoluk Pohnpei Mwokil Pingelap
PALAU Pulo Anna Merir Mortlock Islands Negetik Atoll Kosrae Tofol
Nukuoro

0 miles 300
0 kilometers 300

NORTHERN MARIANA ISLANDS (to USA)

Maug Islands
0 miles 150
0 km 150
146°
20° 20°
Asuncion
Agrihan
Mariana Islands
18° Pagan 18°
Alamagan
Guguan
16° 16°
Anatahan
SAIPAN Saipan
San Jose ● Tinian
14° Rota 14°
HAGÅTÑA GUAM (to USA)
Guam 146°

PACIFIC OCEAN

166° 168° 170° 172°
12° Bikini Rongelap Atoll Bikar 12°
Ailinginae Rongrik Utrik
10° Wotho Likiep Ailuk Mejit Island 10°
Ujae Kwajalein Wotje
Lae Namu Maloelap
8° Jabwat Aur 8°
Ralik Chain Ailinglaplap Majuro Arno
MARSHALL ISLANDS **MAJURO** Mili
6° Jaluit Knox 6°
Namorik Kili Island
Ebon 170° 172°
Ratak Chain
0 miles 150
0 km 150

Mariana Islands
Marshall Islands
Micronesia
Pacific Islands

Copra making

Copra is the meat of ripe coconuts that has been scraped out and dried in the sun. It is sold for processing into coconut oil. The oil is used in margarine, salad oils, soaps and cosmetics.

Frangipani flowers

New Zealand is in an active volcanic zone, with geysers, hot springs and pools of boiling mud. The greatest concentration of thermal activity is at Rotorua.

Spear fishing

Polynesians eat a lot of seafood. The men fish with nets, lines and spears. Women and children gather crabs and shellfish.

160° 155°
5° **Northern Line Islands** 5°
Christmas Island
Equator 0°
KIRIBATI
150°

awa Gilbert Islands
AIRIKI
175° 175° 170° 165°
International Date Line
P o l y n e s i a
KIRIBATI Kanton **SOUTH**
Orona
Phoenix Islands
TUVALU Central Line Islands
Funafuti **TOKELAU ISLANDS (to New Zealand)** **PACIFIC**
VAIAKU **OCEAN**
WALLIS AND FUTUNA ISLANDS (to France) **AMERICAN SAMOA (to USA)** Northern Cook Islands
Wallis **SAMOA** Savai'i
MATA'UTU Futuna Upolu **APIA** Tutuila
Niua Group **PAGO PAGO**
Vanua Levu **COOK ISLANDS (to New Zealand)**
Viti Levu **NIUE (to New Zealand)** Niue **ALOFI**
SUVA Southern Cook Islands
FIJI **NUKU'ALOFA** Tongatapu Eua Rarotonga **AVARUA** **FRENCH POLYNESIA (to France)**
TONGA
Austral Islands

145° 140° 135°
Nuku Hiva
Hiva Oa
Marquesas Islands
10°
Tuamotu Archipelago
15°
Îles Sous le Vent
Bora-Bora Raiatea
Moorea ● Tahiti **PAPEETE**
Society Archipelago
Groupe Actéon
20° 130°
PITCAIRN ISLANDS (to UK)
Gambier Islands
25° Pitcairn Island Henderson Island 25°
140° 135° 130°

0 miles 900
0 kilometers 900
N W E S

In 1893, New Zealand became the first country to grant women the right to vote.

New Zealand and the Pacific Islands

Forest and woodland

Arable land

Grazing

Arid or marginal

LAND AREA	128,126 sq miles (331,846 sq km)
LARGEST COUNTRY	New Zealand
SMALLEST COUNTRY	Nauru
MAIN RELIGION	Christian
LIFE EXPECTANCY	68 years
LITERACY	89%

The word "maori" means local, or original, people. White settlers were called "paheka."

Kiwifruit
First called a Chinese gooseberry after its place of origin, but now named after New Zealand's national bird, this delicious fruit is mainly grown near the Bay of Plenty in the north. The fruit, which grows on a vine, needs sunny conditions and rich soil to grow. New Zealand is the world's leading producer of kiwifruit.

NATURAL FEATURES

Yasawa Islands FIJI
This chain of coral islands, protected by reefs, lies off the northwest coast of Fiji's main island, Viti Levu. Beaches of white sand fringe the islands (below).

Tahitian mountains FRENCH POLYNESIA
The volcanic mountains of Tahiti run along the island's north and south coasts. The dense tropical rain forests that cover the mountains have provided inspiration for artists such as Paul Gauguin.

Milford Sound

Milford Sound NEW ZEALAND
These deep, fjordlike waterways (above), in South Island, are the final destination for trampers on the Milford Track, a famous walking trail through spectacular mountains and river valleys.

Wood and paper products
New Zealand is one of the largest paper and wood producers in the Pacific region. Kauri trees (above), which take more than 1,000 years to mature, were plentiful in New Zealand before European settlement, but are now protected because of years of logging. Many smaller islands in the Pacific region grow coconut trees for wood, copra (dried coconut meat) and palm oil production.

Wellington is the southernmost national capital in the world.

Auckland

Hamilton

Napier

WELLINGTON

Christchurch

Queenstown

Dunedin

Invercargill

Cereals	
Fruit	
Wine	
Beef cattle	
Dairy cattle	
Sheep	
Pigs	
Fishing	
Industrial center	
Timber	
Tourism	

Dairy food
New Zealand is the world's largest exporter of butter and cheese. Most dairy foods are exported, as more goods are produced than the small population needs. New Zealand's rich soils and grasslands provide fodder for the country's herds of cattle.

Tongariro National Park
NEW ZEALAND
In the center of New Zealand's North Island lies a Maori sacred area, situated on several active volcanoes, notably Mt Ruapehu (left), which erupted in 1995.

WHERE PEOPLE LIVE

Urban	Rural

REGION
49% — 51%

Most urban: NAURU
100%

Most rural: SOLOMON ISLANDS
19% — 81%

LARGEST CITIES

Auckland 374,000

Christchurch 340,000

Wellington 166,000

Hamilton 143,000

Dunedin 106,000

Tourism

Millions of tourists are attracted to the South Pacific islands each year, because of their beautiful beaches, coral reefs teeming with fishes and relaxed lifestyle. Most countries in the region rely on the income tourism brings. However, the high number of tourists can cause environmental problems, both on land and in the sea. Clean, fresh water is often in short supply, and an increased demand from visitors can reduce the amount available for local islanders.

Flightless birds

Several birds of New Zealand cannot fly. Before European settlement, the Maoris hunted the giant moa (*above*) to extinction. The kiwi, New Zealand's national bird, is like a hen but has stumps instead of wings. Flightless species of parrots include the kea, kaka and kakapo.

PEOPLE

Fletcher Christian 1764–93
Christian led the crew of the *Bounty* in a mutiny against Captain Bligh in 1789, and sailed for Pitcairn Island in the Pacific. His descendants still live there.

Te Rauparaha c 1768–1849
This fearless warrior and Maori chief signed the Treaty of Waitangi in 1840. New Zealand's rugby teams perform his haka (war song) before their matches.

Ernest Rutherford 1871–1937
Many call this New Zealand-born scientist the father of nuclear physics. He received world recognition for his discoveries relating to nuclear atoms.

Queen Salote Tupou III 1900–65
Queen Salote ruled the Kingdom of Tonga from 1918 until her death in 1965. She improved health and education, and helped to develop national pride.

Sir Edmund Hillary born 1919
This mountain climber from Auckland, New Zealand, made several attempts to climb the world's highest peak, Mt Everest. With the Sherpa Tenzing Norgay, he was first to reach the summit in May 1953.

Jonah Lomu born 1975
Jonah Lomu was a player in New Zealand's rugby team from 1994 to 2002. He played 63 international test matches in his 73 games.

TRADITIONS AND CULTURE

Family life SAMOA
In Samoa, the *aiga* (extended family) is all important. Each village is comprised of several *aiga*. The larger the extended family, the more important it is and the more influence it has in village affairs.

Maori culture NEW ZEALAND
As part of their traditional ceremonies, Maori men chant loudly in a haka, while women in traditional dress (*below*) perform a dance with twirling balls, called *poi*. The striking patterns painted on their faces are symbolic of the tattoos their ancestors wore.

PLACES

Sky Tower AUCKLAND
This striking structure in Auckland, New Zealand, is the tallest building in the Southern Hemisphere. It towers more than 1,075 feet (328 m) above the ground.

Queenstown NEW ZEALAND
Queenstown is a popular ski resort on Lake Wakatipu, South Island, nestled below the Remarkables mountain range. Breathtaking scenery surrounds the town.

Port Vila VANUATU
Vanuatu's capital, Port Vila, lies on the southwest coast of the island of Efate. The city's daily markets and bustling harbor attract many visitors.

Jean-Marie Tjibaou Cultural Center NOUMEA
This structure (*below*) was built on Tina Peninsula, Noumea, in 2000. It was designed by architect Renzo Piano and the unusual shapes reflect the traditional buildings of the local Kanak people.

War clubs MELANESIA
During the 18th and 19th centuries, warriors carried clubs to fight the enemy. A throwing club was strapped to the waist and thrown in battle. A bladed club was used to cut down the enemy. A chief's club, however, was ornamental.

Village chieftains SOUTH PACIFIC
As the village leader and part of a council of chiefs, the chieftain is responsible for the problems that arise in his community and has authority over the people.

Tramping NEW ZEALAND
Keen walkers from all over the world head for the many tracks in New Zealand to go tramping through the country's spectacular natural landscape. The summer months from November to April are the best times to tramp.

Royal Palace TONGA
This stately waterfront palace (*above*), built in 1867 in the capital Nuku'alofa, on the island of Tongatapu, is home to the royal family of Tonga.

Papeete FRENCH POLYNESIA
Papeete is the chief port of the island of Tahiti, and capital of French Polynesia. The lifestyle of this city is a lively mix of French, Polynesian and Chinese cultures.

Cook's voyages

Captain James Cook set sail from England three times between 1768 and 1779 on scientific expeditions to the South Pacific. On his first trip, he charted the coastlines of Tahiti, New Zealand and eastern Australia, claiming them as part of Britain. On his later trips he visited Tonga and many more Pacific islands. He was the first captain to give his crew fresh fruit to prevent the disease, scurvy.

Cook's ship *Endeavour*

HISTORY AT A GLANCE

40,000 BC
Early peoples begin to inhabit the island chains of the Pacific Ocean region.

4000 BC
Sea vessels are developed, which makes travel between island chains possible. Expert navigators follow the paths of birds to find new islands.

Double-hulled canoe used for exploration

AD 1000
Most Pacific islands are inhabited, and the first Maori settle in New Zealand.

1513
Spanish conquistador Vasco Nuñez de Balboa is the first European to sight the Pacific Ocean, on his voyage from Panama.

1560s
Alvaro de Mendana discovers the Marquesas Islands. He lands on the Solomon Islands, naming them for the biblical King Solomon.

1606
Pedro Fernandez de Quiros, from Portugal, discovers the Cook Islands and the New Hebrides.

1642
Dutch explorer Abel Tasman is the first European to sight New Zealand. He visits the mainland. More than 100 years later, James Cook maps the New Zealand coastline.

1818
The musket wars start in New Zealand, between British settlers and the Maori.

1840
The Treaty of Waitangi is signed between the Maori and British. The treaty protected Maori rights if they sold their land to the British. New Zealand becomes a British colony.

Treaty House, Waitangi

1843–72
The Maori wars, also known as the land wars, flare up in New Zealand over issues arising from the Treaty of Waitangi.

1893
Social reforms are introduced in New Zealand, including the suffrage (right to vote) for women.

1941–45
Parts of World War II are fought in the Pacific region. At the end of the war, the USA begins to test its nuclear weapons on Bikini atoll.

1962
Western Samoa (now Samoa) becomes the first independent Pacific nation. Eight years later, Fiji and Tonga gain independence from Britain.

1985
The Treaty of Rarotonga declares the South Pacific a nuclear-free zone. New Zealand bans all nuclear trade.

1995
The Waikato-Raupatu Claims Settlement Act for Maori land claims is passed.

Nuclear testing

Gazetteer

How to use the gazetteer

This gazetteer is a geographical index of places in this atlas. To find the city of Agra in India, for example, look up its name in the gazetteer.

The entry reads: **118   D8   Agra, India**

The number 118 indicates that Agra appears on the map on page 118. The reference D8 tells you that it can be found in square D8. Turn to page 118. Trace down from the letter D at the top of the page (or up from the letter D on the bottom of the page) and then across from the number 8 on the side of the page. You will find Agra within the square where the letter and number intersect.

The symbols below are used to indicate the geographic feature of each entry.

≈ **Bay**
Includes bays and gulfs

⊻ **Channel**
Includes channels, straits and passages

▢ **Country**

▣ **Dependent Territory**
Internal administrative region, province or state
eg Scotland, Falkland Islands, Manitoba, Queensland

▲ **Desert**
Includes sand dune features

⁙ **Geographic Area**
Includes regions eg Costa Blanca, Tuscany

◗ **Headland**
Includes headlands, points, capes, peninsulas and sand spits

🌴 **Island**
Includes atolls

🏝 **Island Group**

🝔 **Lake**
Includes reservoirs

▲ **Mountain**
Includes individual mountains and volcanoes

▰ **Mountain Range**

■ **National Capital**

🜨 **Ocean**

◆ **Physical Feature**
Includes plains, moors, wetlands, plateaus, peat bogs, mudflats, swamps and marshes

▬ **Polar Base**

🜄 **River**
Includes deltas, rivers, waterfalls, estuaries

🝐 **Sea**

★ **Special Feature**

⌂ **State Capital**

◼ **Underwater Feature**
Includes seamounts, reefs, abyssal plains

A name without a symbol indicates a town or city

Abbreviations

UNITED STATES OF AMERICA

Alabama	AL
Alaska	AK
Arizona	AZ
Arkansas	AR
California	CA
Colorado	CO
Connecticut	CT
Delaware	DE
District of Columbia	DC
Florida	FL
Georgia	GA
Guam	GU
Hawaii	HI
Idaho	ID
Illinois	IL
Indiana	IN
Iowa	IA
Kansas	KS
Kentucky	KY
Louisiana	LA
Maine	ME
Maryland	MD
Massachusetts	MA
Michigan	MI
Minnesota	MN
Mississippi	MS
Missouri	MO
Montana	MT
Nebraska	NE
Nevada	NV
New Hampshire	NH
New Jersey	NJ
New Mexico	NM
New York	NY
North Carolina	NC
North Dakota	ND
Ohio	OH
Oklahoma	OK
Oregon	OR
Pennsylvania	PA
Puerto Rico	PR
Rhode Island	RI
South Carolina	SC
South Dakota	SD
Tennessee	TN
Texas	TX
Utah	UT
Vermont	VT
Virginia	VA
Virgin Islands	VI
Washington	WA
West Virginia	WV
Wisconsin	WI
Wyoming	WY

CANADA

Alberta	AB
British Columbia	BC
Manitoba	MB
New Brunswick	NB
Newfoundland	NL
Northwest Territory	NT
Nova Scotia	NS
Nunavut	NU
Ontario	ON
Prince Edward Island	PE
Québec	QC
Saskatchewan	SK
Yukon Territory	YT

AUSTRALIA

Australian Capital Territory	ACT
New South Wales	NSW
Northern Territory	NT
Queensland	QLD
South Australia	SA
Tasmania	TAS
Victoria	VIC
Western Australia	WA

A

40	F 1	A Coruña, Spain
52	B 8	Aachen, Germany
53	E 10	Aalen, Germany
49	E 11	Aalst, Belgium
49	C 11	Aalter, Belgium
49	F 11	Aarschot, Belgium
136	H 7	Aba, Nigeria
115	K 4	Ābādān, Iran
104	H 9	Abakan, Russia
96	F 7	Abancay, Peru
130	I 2	Abashiri, Japan
45	I 2	Abbeville, France
74	D 10	Abbotsford, BC, Canada
111	L 8	Abbottabad, Pakistan
137	J 6	Abéché, Chad
36	G 7	Aberdeen, United Kingdom
82	G 6	Aberdeen, SD, United States
84	C 6	Aberdeen, WA, United States
74	G 6	Aberdeen Lake, NU, Canada 🝔
37	F 12	Aberystwyth, United Kingdom
115	I 9	Abhā, Saudi Arabia
136	F 7	Abidjan, Côte d'Ivoire
83	F 12	Abilene, TX, United States
118	C 7	Abohar, India
82	B 6	Absaroka Range, MT/WY, United States ▰
115	M 6	Abu Dhabi, United Arab Emirates ■
115	I 3	Abū Kamāl, Syria
136	H 6	Abuja, Nigeria ■
41	J 5	Acalá de Henares, Spain
89	I 7	Acaponeta, Mexico
89	K 10	Acapulco, Mexico
136	G 7	Accra, Ghana ■
104	H 9	Achinsk, Russia
57	H 14	Acireale, Italy
91	J 3	Acklins Island, The Bahamas 🌴
115	J 5	Ad Dahnā', Saudi Arabia ▲
136	E 3	Ad Dakhla, Western Sahara
115	K 6	Ad Dammām, Saudi Arabia
109	G 9	Adana, Turkey
137	M 6	Addis Ababa, Ethiopia ■
119	B 16	Addu Atoll, Maldives 🌴
147	I 9	Adelaide, SA, Australia ⌂
33	I 3	Adelaide Island, Antarctica 🌴
33	N 7	Adélie Land, Antarctica ⁙
115	J 10	Aden, Yemen
79	K 6	Adirondack Mountains, NY, United States ▰
109	I 9	Adiyaman, Turkey
147	K 1	Admiralty Islands, Papua New Guinea 🏝
119	D 12	Adoni, India
136	G 3	Adrar, Algeria
56	G 7	Adriatic Sea, Europe 🝐
61	H 11	Aegean Sea, Greece/Turkey 🝐
111	K 7	Afghanistan, Asia ▢
137	N 8	Afgooye, Somalia
115	I 7	'Afif, Saudi Arabia
30	D 7	Africana Seamount, Indian Ocean ◼
48	G 5	Afsluitdijk, Netherlands ◆
108	E 8	Afyon, Turkey
136	H 5	Agadez, Niger
136	F 2	Agadir, Morocco
119	I 9	Agartala, India
27	I 9	Agassiz Fracture Zone, Pacific Ocean ◼
109	N 7	Ağdam, Azerbaijan
45	J 10	Agde, France
44	H 9	Agen, France
61	G 11	Agiokampos, Greece
61	H 11	Agios Efstratios, Greece 🌴
61	I 13	Agios Kirykos, Greece
118	D 8	Agra, India
108	L 7	Ağri, Turkey
57	G 15	Agrigento, Italy
151	L 3	Agrihan, Northern Mariana Islands 🌴
57	H 11	Agropoli, Italy
88	G 3	Agua Prieta, Mexico
89	J 7	Aguascalientes, Mexico
41	K 9	Águilas, Spain
89	I 9	Aguililla, Mexico
30	C 7	Agulhas Bank, Indian Ocean ◼
30	D 8	Agulhas Basin, Indian Ocean ◼
30	D 7	Agulhas Plateau, Indian Ocean ◼
29	I 10	Agulhas Ridge, Atlantic Ocean ◼
150	E 1	Ahipara Bay, New Zealand ≈
119	B 10	Ahmadabad, India
119	C 11	Ahmadnagar, India
115	K 4	Ahvāz, Iran
61	F 12	Aigio, Greece
151	M 3	Ailinginae, Marshall Islands 🌴
151	N 4	Ailinglaplap, Marshall Islands 🌴
151	N 3	Ailuk, Marshall Islands 🌴
45	L 10	Aix-en-Provence, France
119	J 9	Aizawl, India
130	H 8	Aizu-Wakamatsu, Japan
45	N 11	Ajaccio, Corsica
137	J 2	Ajdābiyā, Libya
118	C 8	Ajmer, India
85	I 15	Ajo, AZ, United States
131	E 11	Akashi, Japan
109	L 5	Akhalts'ikhe, Georgia
108	C 7	Akhisar, Turkey
75	J 8	Akimiski Island, NU, Canada 🌴
130	H 7	Akita, Japan
136	E 4	Akjoujt, Mauritania
74	D 5	Aklavik, NT, Canada
119	D 10	Akola, India
75	J 6	Akpatok Island, NU, Canada 🌴
61	H 11	Akra Akrathos, Greece ◗
61	G 11	Akra Drepano, Greece ◗
61	G 14	Akra Maleas, Greece ◗
61	G 11	Akra Paliouri, Greece ◗
61	F 14	Akra Tainaro, Greece ◗
79	I 8	Akron, OH, United States
108	G 8	Aksaray, Turkey
108	E 8	Akşehir, Turkey
126	F 4	Aksu, China
110	H 5	Aktau, Kazakhstan
111	I 3	Aktyubinsk, Kazakhstan
136	H 7	Akure, Nigeria
68	C 5	Akureyri, Iceland
115	K 4	Al 'Amārah, Iraq
114	G 4	Al 'Aqabah, Jordan
115	M 6	Al 'Ayn, United Arab Emirates
115	I 8	Al Bāḥah, Saudi Arabia
115	J 10	Al Bayḍā', Yemen
137	J 2	Al Bayḍā', Libya
115	I 3	Al Fallujah, Iraq
115	K 5	Al Farwāniyah, Kuwait
115	M 6	Al Hajar'al Gharbī, Oman ▰
114	H 4	Al Ḥamād, Jordan/Saudi Arabia ▲
115	I 2	Al Ḥasakah, Syria
114	G 5	Al Hijāz, Saudi Arabia ⁙
115	J 4	Al Ḥillah, Iraq
115	I 10	Al Ḥudaydah, Yemen
115	K 6	Al Hufūf, Saudi Arabia
115	K 5	Al Jahrah, Kuwait
115	I 4	Al Jawf, Saudi Arabia
137	J 4	Al Jawf, Libya
115	K 5	Al Jubayl, Saudi Arabia
115	N 8	Al Khalif, Oman
115	M 6	Al Khaşab, Oman
137	I 2	Al Khums, Libya
115	J 4	Al Kūt, Iraq
115	I 4	Al Labbah, Saudi Arabi ⁙
114	H 2	Al Lādhiqīyah, Syria
115	L 9	Al Mahrah, Yemen ▰
115	J 6	Al Majma'ah, Saudi Arabia
115	L 6	Al Manāmah, Bahrain ■
115	K 10	Al Mukallā, Yemen
115	K 3	Al Muqdādīyah, Iraq
115	I 2	Al Qāmishlī, Syria
80	G 4	Alabama, United States ▣
80	G 5	Alabama, United States 🜄
108	G 7	Alaca, Turkey
90	G 8	Alajuela, Costa Rica
151	L 4	Alamagan, Northern Mariana Islands 🌴
85	G 12	Alamo, NV, United States
83	D 12	Alamogordo, NM, United States
83	D 10	Alamosa, CO, United States
69	G 11	Åland, Finland 🌴
69	G 11	Ålands Hav, Finland ⊻
109	E 10	Alanya, Turkey
84	J 5	Alaska, United States ▣
84	I 6	Alaska Peninsula, AL, United States ◗

22 B 3 Alaska Range, North America
41 K 7 Albacete, Spain
61 E 10 Albania, Europe
146 E 9 Albany, WA, Australia
81 I 5 Albany, GA, United States
79 L 6 Albany, NY, United States
84 C 7 Albany, OR, United States
75 J 9 Albany, Canada
150 F 4 Albatross Point, New Zealand
45 I 2 Albert, France
82 H 7 Albert Lea, MN, United States
74 E 8 Alberta, Canada
45 I 9 Albi, France
69 C 13 Ålborg, Denmark
83 D 11 Albuquerque, NM, United States
147 K 9 Albury, NSW, Australia
40 F 7 Alcácer do Sal, Portugal
57 F 14 Alcamo, Italy
41 L 4 Alcañiz, Spain
65 O 8 Alchevs'k, Ukraine
30 E 4 Aldabra Islands, Indian Ocean
105 L 8 Aldan, Russia
37 H 16 Alderney, United Kingdom
136 E 4 Aleg, Mauritania
40 D 10 Alegranza, Spain
44 H 4 Alençon, France
114 H 2 Aleppo, Syria
32 D 7 Alert, Canada
45 K 9 Alès, France
56 B 6 Alessandria, Italy
69 B 9 Ålesund, Norway
26 G 1 Aleutian Basin, Pacific Ocean
84 H 6 Aleutian Islands, AL, United States
26 G 2 Aleutian Trench, Pacific Ocean
80 H 4 Alexander City, AL, United States
33 J 3 Alexander Island, Antarctica
150 C 10 Alexandra, New Zealand
60 H 8 Alexandria, Romania
79 K 9 Alexandria, VI, United States
82 H 6 Alexandria, MN, United States
83 I 12 Alexandria, LA, United States
137 K 2 Alexandria, Egypt
61 I 10 Alexandroupoli, Greece
40 F 9 Algarve, Portugal
40 H 10 Algeciras, Spain
135 G 2 Algeria, Africa
57 B 11 Alghero, Italy
135 H 1 Algiers, Algeria
41 L 6 Alginet, Spain
109 O 7 Äli Bayramli, Azerbaijan
41 L 8 Alicante, Spain
146 H 6 Alice Springs, NT, Australia
118 E 8 Aligarh, India
48 F 6 Alkmaar, Netherlands
119 E 9 Allahabad, India
79 L 8 Allentown, PA, United States
119 D 14 Alleppey, India
82 E 8 Alliance, NE, United States
41 L 7 Almansa, Spain
40 H 5 Almanzor, Spain
111 M 5 Almaty, Kazakhstan
48 J 7 Almelo, Netherlands
40 G 7 Almendralejo, Spain
48 G 7 Almere, Netherlands
41 K 9 Almeria, Spain
45 K 10 Alofi, Niue
123 K 10 Alor, Indonesia
52 F 6 Alor Setar, Malaysia
78 H 5 Alpena, MI, United States
32 D 6 Alpha Ridge, Arctic Ocean
48 F 8 Alphen, Netherlands
23 I 3 Alps, Europe
68 H 4 Alta, Norway
23 K 3 Altai Mountains, Asia
81 J 5 Altamaha, United States
89 K 9 Altamirano, Mexico
57 J 11 Altamura, Italy
127 I 3 Altay, Mongolia
22 E 7 Altiplano, South America
96 F 6 Alto Purús, Peru
79 J 8 Altoona, PA, United States
126 G 5 Altun Shan, China
83 G 10 Alva, OK, United States
89 M 9 Alvarado, Mexico
69 D 11 Alvdalen, Sweden
118 D 8 Alwar, India
65 I 5 Alytus, Lithuania
137 J 6 Am Timan, Chad
75 J 5 Amadjuak Lake, NU, Canada
131 A 14 Amakusa-nada, Japan
123 N 9 Amamapare, Indonesia
131 J 14 Amami-Ō-shima, Japan
131 J 15 Amami-shotō, Japan
83 F 11 Amarillo, TX, United States
22 E 6 Amazon, South America
22 E 6 Amazon Basin, South America
28 E 6 Amazon Cone, Atlantic Ocean
96 E 4 Ambato, Ecuador
45 L 7 Ambérieu-en-Bugey, France
123 L 9 Ambon, Indonesia
123 L 9 Ambon, Indonesia
141 M 9 Ambovombe, Madagascar
48 H 4 Ameland, Netherlands
151 K 9 American Samoa, United States
29 G 11 American-Antarctic Ridge, Atlantic Ocean
48 G 8 Amersfoort, Netherlands
33 O 3 Amery Ice Shelf, Antarctica
105 L 8 Amga, Russia
45 I 2 Amiens, France
30 F 5 Amirante Trench, Indian Ocean
114 H 4 Ammān, Jordan
32 C 9 Ammassalik, Greenland
108 F 11 Ammóchostos, Cyprus
115 L 2 Amol, Iran
61 I 13 Amorgos, Greece
41 M 5 Amposta, Spain
119 D 10 Amravati, India
118 C 7 Amritsar, India
48 F 7 Amstelveen, Netherlands
48 G 7 Amsterdam, Netherlands
30 G 8 Amsterdam Fracture Zone, Indian Ocean
30 H 7 Amsterdam Island, France
53 I 11 Amstetten, Austria
111 J 6 Amudar'ya, Asia
74 E 4 Amundsen Gulf, NT, Canada
26 H 11 Amundsen Sea, Pacific Ocean
33 M 4 Amundsen-Scott, United States
105 L 10 Amur, China/Russia
114 H 5 An Nafūd, Saudi Arabia
115 J 4 An Najaf, Iraq
115 J 4 An Nāşiriyah, Iraq
105 O 5 Anadyr', Russia
61 I 14 Anafi, Greece
85 F 14 Anaheim, CA, United States
109 F 10 Anamur, Turkey
119 D 13 Anantapur, India
97 J 7 Anápolis, Brazil
151 L 4 Anatahan, Northern Mariana Islands
108 D 7 Anatolia, Turkey
98 G 8 Añatuya, Argentina
84 J 5 Anchorage, AL, United States
56 G 8 Ancona, Italy
99 E 12 Ancud, Chile
127 N 3 Anda, China
40 H 9 Andalucía, Spain
80 H 6 Andalusia, AL, United States
31 I 3 Andaman Basin, Indian Ocean
119 J 13 Andaman Islands, India
31 J 2 Andaman Sea, Indian Ocean
49 G 13 Andenne, Belgium
78 G 8 Anderson, IN, United States
22 E 7 Andes, South America
111 L 6 Andizhan, Uzbekistan
111 K 7 Andkhvoy, Afghanistan
41 N 3 Andorra, Europe
41 N 3 Andorra La Vella, Andorra
57 I 10 Andria, Italy
61 H 12 Andros, Greece
91 I 2 Andros Island, The Bahamas
41 I 8 Andújar, Spain
41 M 2 Aneto, Spain
23 L 3 Angara, Asia
105 I 10 Angarsk, Russia
69 E 9 Ånge, Sweden
44 G 5 Angers, France
90 H 2 Angillia Cays, Cuba
122 G 5 Angkor Wat, Cambodia
37 F 11 Anglesey, United Kingdom
99 E 11 Angol, Chile
140 G 6 Angola, Africa
28 I 8 Angola Basin, Atlantic Ocean
44 H 7 Angoulême, France
40 B 9 Angra do Heroísmo, Portugal
91 N 4 Anguilla, United Kingdom
141 M 6 Anjouan, Comoros
127 L 7 Ankang, China
108 F 7 Ankara, Turkey
78 H 7 Ann Arbor, MI, United States
136 H 1 Annaba, Algeria
122 G 3 Annam Highlands, Laos/Vietnam
79 K 9 Annapolis, MD, United States
118 G 8 Annapurna, Nepal
45 L 7 Annecy, France
80 H 4 Anniston, AL, United States
127 M 8 Anqing, China
127 N 5 Anshan, China
127 K 9 Anshun, China
109 E 9 Antalya, Turkey
109 E 10 Antalya Körfezi, Turkey
141 M 8 Antananarivo, Madagascar
33 I 2 Antarctic Peninsula, Antarctica
41 I 9 Antequera, Spain
45 M 10 Antibes, France
91 N 5 Antigua, Antigua and Barbuda
91 N 5 Antigua and Barbuda, North America
61 G 14 Antikythira, Greece
109 H 10 Antioch, Turkey
26 G 9 Antipodes Islands, New Zealand
98 E 7 Antofagasta, Chile
141 M 8 Antsirabe, Madagascar
141 N 6 Antsiranana, Madagascar
49 E 10 Antwerp, Belgium
127 M 6 Anyang, China
57 F 10 Anzio, Italy
131 I 12 Aoga-shima, Japan
130 H 6 Aomori, Japan
81 I 7 Apalachee Bay, FL, United States
48 I 7 Apeldoorn, Netherlands
22 H 3 Apennines, Europe
151 J 9 Apia, Samoa
97 I 3 Apoera, Suriname
78 E 3 Apostle Islands, WI, United States
22 D 4 Appalachian Mountains, North America
78 F 5 Appleton, WI, United States
96 F 2 Apure, Venezuela
96 F 6 Apurímac, Peru
115 I 3 Ar Ramādī, Iraq
114 H 2 Ar Raqqah, Syria
115 N 6 Ar Rustāq, Oman
115 I 3 Ar Rutbah, Iraq
30 G 2 Arabian Basin, Indian Ocean
23 J 5 Arabian Peninsula, Asia
30 G 2 Arabian Sea, Indian Ocean
97 L 6 Aracaju, Brazil
97 J 8 Araçatuba, Brazil
60 F 6 Arad, Romania
26 D 6 Arafura Sea, Pacific Ocean
41 L 4 Aragón, Spain
97 J 6 Araguaia, Brazil
97 J 5 Araguaína, Brazil
115 K 3 Arāk, Iran
122 E 3 Arakan Yoma, Myanmar
111 I 4 Aral Sea, Kazakhstan/Uzbekistan
111 J 4 Aral'sk, Kazakhstan
41 J 4 Aranda de Duero, Spain
41 J 5 Aranjuez, Spain
97 L 6 Arapiraca, Brazil
108 L 7 Aras, Azerbaijan/Turkey
109 I 9 Aratürk Baraji, Turkey
147 M 2 Arawa, Papua New Guinea
137 M 7 Ārba Minch, Ethiopia
115 J 2 Arbīl, Iraq
85 B 10 Arcata, CA, United States
99 D 14 Archipiélago de la Reina Adelaida, Chile
99 D 13 Archipiélago de los Chonos, Chile
90 H 3 Archipiélago de los Jardines de la Reina, Cuba
32 D 7 Arctic Ocean,
33 I 2 Arctowski, Poland
115 K 1 Ardabīl, Iran
49 F 14 Ardennes, Belgium
83 G 11 Ardmore, OK, United States
69 C 12 Arendal, Norway
61 F 14 Areópoli, Greece
96 F 7 Arequipa, Peru
56 E 8 Arezzo, Italy
61 G 12 Argalasti, Greece
99 F 9 Argentina, South America
29 E 10 Argentine Abyssal Plain, Atlantic Ocean
29 F 9 Argentine Basin, Atlantic Ocean
111 J 9 Arghandab, Afghanistan
23 M 3 Argun', Asia
69 C 14 Århus, Denmark
119 A 14 Ari Atoll, Maldives
98 E 5 Arica, Chile
85 I 14 Arizona, United States
111 J 3 Arkalyk, Kazakhstan
22 D 4 Arkansas, North America
83 I 10 Arkansas, United States
83 E 9 Arkansas, KS, United States
83 G 10 Arkansas City, KS, United States
104 E 5 Arkhangel'sk, Russia
45 K 10 Arles, France
79 K 9 Arlington, VI, United States
83 G 12 Arlington, TX, United States
136 H 5 Arlit, Niger
49 H 15 Arlon, Belgium
37 D 10 Armagh, United Kingdom
104 B 7 Armavir, Russia
96 E 3 Armenia, Colombia
109 M 7 Armenia, Asia
147 L 8 Armidale, NSW, Australia
48 H 8 Arnhem, Netherlands
146 H 4 Arnhem Land, NT, Australia
56 E 7 Arno, Italy
151 N 4 Arno, Marshall Islands
68 G 4 Arnøya, Norway
37 E 9 Arran, United Kingdom
45 I 2 Arras, France
40 D 10 Arrecife, Spain
89 N 10 Arriaga, Mexico
61 E 11 Arta, Greece
109 M 7 Artashat, Armenia
83 D 12 Artesia, NM, United States
108 K 6 Artvin, Turkey
91 L 7 Aruba, Netherlands
141 K 4 Arusha, Tanzania
68 G 7 Arvidsjaur, Sweden
104 D 6 Arzamas, Russia
115 K 7 As Salamiyah, Saudi Arabia
115 J 4 As Samāwah, Iraq
115 J 2 As Sulaymānīyah, Iraq
115 J 8 As Sulayyil, Saudi Arabia
114 H 3 As Suwaydā', Syria
111 L 7 Asadābād, Afghanistan
130 I 3 Asahi-dake, Japan
130 H 3 Asahikawa, Japan
119 H 9 Asansol, India
22 G 6 Ascension, Atlantic Ocean
53 D 9 Aschaffenburg, Germany
56 G 8 Ascoli Piceno, Italy
137 N 7 Āsela, Ethiopia
150 D 9 Ashburton, New Zealand
111 I 6 Ashgabat, Turkmenistan
131 H 9 Ashikaga, Japan
131 D 13 Ashizuri-misaki, Japan
85 C 9 Ashland, OR, United States
79 I 7 Ashtabula, OH, United States
81 J 2 Ashville, NC, United States
108 J 7 Aşkale, Turkey
137 M 5 Asmara, Eritrea
83 D 9 Aspen, CO, United States
137 N 5 Assab, Eritrea
79 L 10 Assateague Island, MD, United States
48 J 5 Assen, Netherlands
111 K 2 Astana, Kazakhstan
56 B 6 Asti, Italy
40 H 3 Astorga, Spain
84 C 7 Astoria, OR, United States
104 C 8 Astrakhan', Russia
29 I 12 Astrid Ridge, Atlantic Ocean
33 N 1 Asuka, Japan
98 I 7 Asunción, Paraguay
151 L 3 Asuncion, Northern Mariana Islands
137 L 3 Aswân, Egypt
137 L 3 Asyût, Egypt
115 I 7 Aţ Ţā'if, Saudi Arabia
114 H 5 Aţ Ţubayq, Jordan/Saudi Arabia
98 F 6 Atacama Desert, Chile
136 E 4 Atâr, Mauritania
137 L 5 Atbara, Sudan
137 M 5 Atbara, Sudan
49 D 12 Ath, Belgium
74 F 8 Athabasca, Canada
61 G 12 Athens, Greece
81 J 3 Athens, GA, United States
37 C 11 Athlone, Ireland
137 J 6 Ati, Chad
81 I 4 Atlanta, GA, United States
28 E 6 Atlantic Ocean
30 D 10 Atlantic-Indian Ridge, Indian Ocean
30 D 11 Atlantic-Indian-Antarctic Basin, Southern Ocean
28 E 5 Atlantis Fracture Zone, Atlantic Ocean
22 H 4 Atlas Mountains, Africa
80 G 6 Atmore, AL, United States
131 H 10 Atsugi, Japan
75 I 9 Attawapiskat, Canada
99 F 10 Atuel, Argentina
110 H 4 Atyrau, Kazakhstan
49 H 15 Aubange, Belgium
80 H 5 Auburn, AL, United States
84 D 6 Auburn, WA, United States
44 H 10 Auch, France
150 F 3 Auckland, New Zealand
23 O 9 Auckland Islands, Oceania
53 F 11 Augsburg, Germany
146 E 9 Augusta, WA, Australia
81 J 4 Augusta, GA, United States
79 N 5 Augusta, ME, United States
64 H 5 Augustów, Poland
151 N 3 Aur, Marshall Islands
119 C 11 Aurangabad, India
45 I 8 Aurillac, France
78 F 7 Auroa, IL, United States
83 D 9 Aurora, CO, United States
83 G 13 Austin, TX, United States
82 I 7 Austin, MN, United States
27 J 7 Austral Fracture Zone, Pacific Ocean
151 M 11 Austral Islands, French Polynesia
146 H 6 Australia, Oceania
147 K 9 Australian Capital Territory, Australia
53 I 12 Austria, Europe
45 J 5 Auxerre, France
151 L 10 Avarua, Cook Islands
40 F 5 Aveiro, Portugal
45 K 9 Avignon, France
41 I 5 Ávila, Spain
40 H 1 Avilés, Spain
37 H 13 Avon, United Kingdom
44 G 4 Avranches, France
131 E 12 Awaji-shima, Japan
150 E 1 Awanui, New Zealand
150 B 9 Awarua Point, New Zealand
137 I 3 Awbāri, Libya
74 G 2 Axel Heiberg Island, NU, Canada
96 F 7 Ayacucho, Peru
40 F 9 Ayamonte, Spain
108 C 8 Aydin, Turkey
74 F 6 Aylmer Lake, NT, Canada
136 G 5 Ayorou, Niger
136 E 4 'Ayoûn el 'Atroûs, Mauritania
108 B 7 Ayvacik, Turkey
114 H 4 Az Zarqā', Jordan
137 I 2 Az Zāwiyah, Libya
109 N 6 Azerbaijan, Asia
40 A 9 Azores, Portugal
28 G 4 Azores-Biscay Rise, Atlantic Ocean
99 H 11 Azul, Argentina

B

114 H 3 Ba'albek, Lebanon
108 E 6 Baba Burnu, Turkey
60 J 7 Babadag, Romania
123 L 10 Babar, Indonesia
115 L 2 Bābol, Iran
65 K 5 Babruysk, Belarus
123 K 3 Babuyan Islands, Philippines
97 K 5 Bacabal, Brazil
123 L 8 Bacan, Indonesia
60 I 6 Bacău, Romania
74 F 6 Back, Canada
61 D 7 Bačka Palanka, Serbia and Montenegro
123 K 5 Bacolod, Philippines
53 H 12 Bad Ischl, Austria
53 C 9 Bad Kreuznach, Germany
119 C 14 Badagara, India
127 J 5 Badain Jaran Desert, China
40 G 7 Badajoz, Spain
53 J 11 Baden, Austria
53 C 11 Baden Baden, Germany
82 E 6 Badlands, United States
136 D 5 Bafatá, Guinea-Bissau
32 C 7 Baffin Basin, Arctic Ocean
75 I 3 Baffin Bay, NU, Canada
75 I 4 Baffin Island, NU, Canada
108 H 6 Bafra, Turkey
108 H 5 Bafra Burnu, Turkey
97 I 10 Bagé, Brazil
115 J 3 Baghdad, Iraq
57 G 14 Bagheria, Italy
111 K 7 Baghlan, Afghanistan
123 J 4 Baguio, Philippines
91 I 1 Bahamas, The, North America
119 H 9 Baharampur, India
111 L 9 Bahawalpur, Pakistan

99 G 11 **Bahía Blanca**, Argentina
89 M 8 **Bahía de Campeche**, Mexico
96 D 4 **Bahía de Manta**, Ecuador
99 F 15 **Bahía Grande**, Argentina
88 G 6 **Bahía La Paz**, Mexico
98 I 6 **Bahia Negro**, Paraguay
88 E 4 **Bahía Sebastián Vizcaíno**, Mexico
137 M 6 **Bahir Dar**, Ethiopia
118 F 8 **Bahraich**, India
115 L 6 **Bahrain**, Asia
97 J 4 **Baía de Marajó**, Brazil
97 K 4 **Baía de São Marcos**, Brazil
60 G 5 **Baia Mare**, Romania
127 N 3 **Baicheng**, China
44 G 3 **Baie de Seine**, France
75 L 8 **Baie-Comeau**, QC, Canada
41 I 8 **Bailén**, Spain
81 I 6 **Bainbridge**, GA, United States
151 I 7 **Bairiki**, Kiribati
147 K 10 **Bairnsdale**, VIC, Australia
127 O 4 **Baishan**, China
88 E 3 **Baja California**, Mexico
84 F 8 **Baker**, OR, United States
26 G 6 **Baker Island**, Pacific Ocean
74 H 6 **Baker Lake**, NU, Canada
85 E 13 **Bakersfield**, CA, United States
109 P 6 **Baku**, Azerbaijan
41 M 3 **Balaguer**, Spain
104 C 7 **Balakovo**, Russia
64 F 10 **Balaton**, Hungary
150 C 10 **Balclutha**, New Zealand
41 N 7 **Balearic Islands**, Spain
123 I 10 **Bali**, Indonesia
123 J 10 **Bali Sea**, Indonesia
108 C 7 **Balikesir**, Turkey
123 J 8 **Balikpapan**, Indonesia
23 I 4 **Balkan Mountains**, Europe
146 F 9 **Balladonia**, WA, Australia
147 J 10 **Ballarat**, VIC, Australia
33 N 8 **Balleny Islands**, Antarctica
147 L 8 **Ballina**, NSW, Australia
83 F 12 **Ballinger**, TX, United States
89 K 9 **Balsas**, Mexico
65 J 9 **Bălți**, Moldova
23 I 3 **Baltic Sea**, Europe
79 K 9 **Baltimore**, MD, United States
111 M 5 **Balykchy**, Kyrgyzstan
115 M 5 **Bam**, Iran
136 E 5 **Bamako**, Mali
137 J 7 **Bambari**, Central African Republic
53 F 9 **Bamberg**, Germany
136 H 7 **Bamenda**, Cameroon
119 C 9 **Banas**, India
122 E 6 **Banda Aceh**, Indonesia
123 L 9 **Banda Sea**, Indonesia
122 G 9 **Bandar Lampung**, Indonesia
52 I 7 **Bandar Seri Begawan**, Brunei
115 M 5 **Bandar-e 'Abbās**, Iran
115 K 2 **Bandar-e Anzalī**, Iran
122 H 10 **Bandung**, Indonesia
74 E 9 **Banff**, AB, Canada
119 D 13 **Bangalore**, India
137 J 2 **Banghāzī**, Libya
122 H 8 **Bangka**, Indonesia
122 F 5 **Bangkok**, Thailand
119 H 9 **Bangladesh**, Asia
37 F 12 **Bangor**, United Kingdom
79 O 5 **Bangor**, ME, United States
137 J 7 **Bangui**, Central African Republic
137 K 7 **Bani**, Central African Republic
123 J 9 **Banjarmasin**, Indonesia
136 D 5 **Banjul**, Gambia
74 F 4 **Banks Island**, NT, Canada
84 E 6 **Banks Lake**, WA, United States
150 E 8 **Banks Peninsula**, New Zealand
119 H 10 **Bankura**, India
30 H 10 **Banzare Seamount**, Southern Ocean
127 M 5 **Baoding**, China
127 K 7 **Baoji**, China
127 I 9 **Baoshan**, China
127 L 5 **Baotou**, China
115 J 3 **Ba'qūbah**, Iraq
61 D 9 **Bar**, Serbia and Montenegro
79 O 5 **Bar Harbor**, ME, United States
91 K 4 **Barahona**, Dominican Republic
65 I 5 **Baranavichy**, Belarus
97 K 8 **Barbacena**, Brazil
91 O 6 **Barbados**, North America
41 M 3 **Barbastro**, Spain
40 H 10 **Barbate**, Spain
91 N 4 **Barbuda**, Antigua and Barbuda
147 K 6 **Barcaldine**, QLD, Australia
41 N 4 **Barcelona**, Spain
96 G 2 **Barcelona**, Venezuela
119 H 10 **Barddhaman**, India
118 E 8 **Bareilly**, India
32 E 8 **Barents Plain**, Arctic Ocean
32 F 8 **Barents Sea**, Arctic Ocean
32 E 9 **Barents Trough**, Arctic Ocean
57 J 10 **Bari**, Italy
96 F 2 **Barinas**, Venezuela
119 I 10 **Barisal**, Bangladesh
123 I 8 **Barito**, Indonesia
146 H 4 **Barkly Tableland**, NT, Australia
60 I 6 **Bârlad**, Romania
45 K 4 **Bar-le-Duc**, France
57 I 10 **Barletta**, Italy
104 G 9 **Barnaul**, Russia
48 H 8 **Barneveld**, Netherlands
37 F 14 **Barnstaple**, United Kingdom
96 F 2 **Barquisimeto**, Venezuela
28 E 6 **Barracuda Fracture Zone**, Atlantic Ocean
97 K 6 **Barragem de Sobradinho**, Brazil
96 E 1 **Barranquilla**, Colombia
40 E 7 **Barreiro**, Portugal
37 D 13 **Barrow**, Ireland
84 J 4 **Barrow**, AL, United States
146 D 6 **Barrow Island**, WA, Australia
37 G 10 **Barrow-in-Furness**, United Kingdom
85 F 14 **Barstow**, CA, United States
108 F 5 **Bartin**, Turkey
83 H 10 **Bartlesville**, OK, United States
65 J 5 **Barysaw**, Belarus
53 C 12 **Basel**, Switzerland
123 K 6 **Basilan**, Philippines
37 H 14 **Basingstoke**, United Kingdom
115 K 4 **Basra**, Iraq
147 J 10 **Bass Strait**, VIC, Australia
56 E 5 **Bassano del Grappa**, Italy
30 E 6 **Bassas da India**, France
122 E 4 **Bassein**, Myanmar
91 N 5 **Basseterre**, St Kitts and Nevis
91 N 5 **Basse-Terre**, Guadaloupe
45 N 10 **Bastia**, Corsica
49 H 14 **Bastogne**, Belgium
83 J 11 **Bastrop**, LA, United States
136 H 8 **Bata**, Equatorial Guinea
123 K 3 **Batan Islands**, Philippines
123 J 5 **Batangas**, Philippines
31 J 6 **Batavia Seamount**, Indian Ocean
122 G 5 **Bătdâmbâng**, Cambodia
37 G 14 **Bath**, United Kingdom
118 C 7 **Bathinda**, India
147 K 9 **Bathurst**, NSW, Australia
146 G 3 **Bathurst Island**, NT, Australia
109 K 9 **Batman**, Turkey
136 H 1 **Batna**, Algeria
83 J 12 **Baton Rouge**, LA, United States
119 F 15 **Batticaloa**, Sri Lanka
78 G 7 **Battle Creek**, MI, United States
109 K 6 **Bat'umi**, Georgia
27 L 6 **Bauer Basin**, Pacific Ocean
97 J 8 **Bauru**, Brazil
52 I 8 **Bautzen**, Germany
53 F 11 **Bavaria**, Germany
88 G 3 **Bavispe**, Mexico
123 I 9 **Bawean**, Indonesia
31 I 2 **Bay of Bengal**, Indian Ocean
41 J 1 **Bay of Biscay**, France/Spain
75 L 9 **Bay of Fundy**, NS, Canada
150 E 1 **Bay of Islands**, New Zealand
150 G 4 **Bay of Plenty**, New Zealand
91 I 4 **Bayamo**, Cuba
127 J 4 **Bayanhongor**, Mongolia
104 F 5 **Baydaratskaya Guba**, Russia
137 N 7 **Baydhabo**, Somalia
44 G 3 **Bayeux**, France
44 F 10 **Bayonne**, France
111 J 7 **Bayramaly**, Turkmenistan
53 F 9 **Bayreuth**, Germany
41 J 9 **Baza**, Spain
109 N 6 **Bazardüzü Dağl**, Azerbaijan
85 I 9 **Bear Lake**, ID/UT, United States
33 J 5 **Bear Peninsula**, Antarctica
41 J 8 **Beas de Segura**, Spain
32 C 5 **Beaufort Sea**, Arctic Ocean
83 I 13 **Beaumont**, TX, United States
45 K 6 **Beaune**, France
45 I 3 **Beauvais**, France
136 G 2 **Béchar**, Algeria
79 I 10 **Beckley**, WV, United States
114 G 4 **Be'ér Sheva'**, Israel
83 G 14 **Beeville**, TX, United States
127 L 10 **Beihai**, China
127 M 5 **Beijing**, China
48 J 5 **Beilen**, Netherlands
141 K 8 **Beira**, Mozambique
114 G 3 **Beirut**, Lebanon
60 F 6 **Beiuș**, Romania
40 F 8 **Beja**, Portugal
136 H 1 **Bejaïa**, Algeria
40 H 5 **Béjar**, Spain
64 G 10 **Békéscsaba**, Hungary
65 I 5 **Belarus**, Europe
75 J 8 **Belcher Islands**, NU, Canada
137 N 7 **Beledweyne**, Somalia
97 J 4 **Belém**, Brazil
37 E 10 **Belfast**, United Kingdom
45 L 5 **Belfort**, France
119 C 12 **Belgaum**, India
49 C 12 **Belgium**, Europe
104 B 6 **Belgorod**, Russia
61 E 7 **Belgrade**, Serbia and Montenegro
33 L 2 **Belgrano II**, Argentina
122 H 9 **Belitung**, Indonesia
90 E 5 **Belize**, North America
90 E 5 **Belize City**, Belize
119 D 12 **Bellary**, India
44 E 5 **Belle-Île**, France
84 D 6 **Bellevue**, WA, United States
84 D 5 **Bellingham**, WA, United States
33 J 4 **Bellingshausen Sea**, Southern Ocean
53 D 14 **Bellinzona**, Switzerland
90 E 5 **Belmopan**, Belize
97 K 8 **Belo Horizonte**, Brazil
82 H 5 **Bemidji**, MN, United States
36 E 7 **Ben Nevis**, United Kingdom
40 H 3 **Benavente**, Spain
84 D 8 **Bend**, OR, United States
147 J 10 **Bendigo**, VIC, Australia
127 M 7 **Bengbu**, China
122 G 9 **Bengkulu**, Indonesia
140 F 6 **Benguela**, Angola
98 F 4 **Beni**, Bolivia
136 F 2 **Beni Mellal**, Morocco
41 M 7 **Benidorm**, Spain
136 G 6 **Benin**, Africa
136 H 7 **Benin City**, Nigeria
130 G 4 **Benkei-misaki**, Japan
85 J 16 **Benson**, AZ, United States
131 C 13 **Beppu**, Japan
137 N 6 **Berbera**, Somalia
137 I 7 **Berbérati**, Central African Republic
45 I 2 **Berck**, France
65 N 9 **Berdyans'k**, Ukraine
65 N 10 **Berdyans'ka Kosa**, Ukraine
64 H 10 **Berettyóújfalu**, Hungary
104 E 7 **Berezniki**, Russia
56 C 5 **Bergamo**, Italy
69 A 11 **Bergen**, Norway
49 E 9 **Bergen op Zoom**, Netherlands
44 H 8 **Bergerac**, France
52 C 8 **Bergisch Gladbach**, Germany
26 H 1 **Bering Sea**, Pacific Ocean
32 D 4 **Bering Strait**, Arctic Ocean
49 G 11 **Beringen**, Belgium
85 C 12 **Berkeley**, CA, United States
33 K 3 **Berkner Island**, Antarctica
52 H 6 **Berlin**, Germany
98 G 7 **Bermejo**, Argentina
98 H 7 **Bermejo**, Argentina
98 H 7 **Bermejo Viejo**, Argentina
28 D 5 **Bermuda**, United Kingdom
28 D 5 **Bermuda Rise**, Atlantic Ocean
53 C 13 **Bern**, Switzerland
137 I 7 **Bertoua**, Cameroon
36 G 8 **Berwick-upon-Tweed**, United Kingdom
45 L 5 **Besançon**, France
80 G 4 **Bessemer**, AL, United States
40 F 2 **Betanzos**, Spain
111 K 4 **Betpak-Dala**, Kazakhstan
109 E 9 **Beysehir Gölü**, Turkey
45 J 10 **Béziers**, France
119 C 13 **Bhadravati**, India
119 G 9 **Bhagalpur**, India
119 C 10 **Bharuch**, India
119 H 10 **Bhatpara**, India
119 B 10 **Bhavnagar**, India
119 F 10 **Bhilai**, India
119 C 9 **Bhilwara**, India
119 F 12 **Bhimavaram**, India
118 E 8 **Bhind**, India
119 C 11 **Bhiwandi**, India
118 D 8 **Bhiwani**, India
119 D 10 **Bhopal**, India
119 G 11 **Bhubaneshwar**, India
119 D 10 **Bhusawal**, India
118 H 8 **Bhutan**, Asia,
123 N 8 **Biak**, Indonesia,
64 H 6 **Biała Podlaska**, Poland
64 H 5 **Białystok**, Poland
44 F 10 **Biarritz**, France
119 C 11 **Bid**, India
119 D 11 **Bidar**, India
79 N 6 **Biddeford**, ME, United States
53 B 12 **Biel**, Switzerland
52 C 7 **Bielefeld**, Germany
53 B 12 **Bieler See**, Switzerland
56 B 5 **Biella**, Italy
64 G 8 **Bielsko- Biała**, Poland
122 H 5 **Biên Hoa**, Vietnam
83 F 12 **Big Spring**, TX, United States
82 C 6 **Bighorn**, WY, United States
82 C 6 **Bighorn Lake**, MT, United States
82 D 6 **Bighorn Mountains**, MT/WY, United States
136 G 7 **Bight of Benin**, Africa
61 B 7 **Bihać**, Bosnia-Herzegovina
119 G 9 **Bihar Sharif**, India
119 C 12 **Bijapur**, India
61 D 7 **Bijeljina**, Bosnia-Herzegovina
118 C 8 **Bikaner**, India
151 N 2 **Bikar**, Marshall Islands
151 M 2 **Bikini**, Federated States of Micronesia
65 K 8 **Bila Tserkva**, Ukraine
119 F 10 **Bilaspur**, India
41 J 2 **Bilbao**, Spain
108 D 7 **Bilecik**, Turkey
82 C 6 **Billings**, MT, United States
147 L 7 **Biloela**, QLD, Australia
80 F 6 **Biloxi**, MS, United States
49 E 13 **Binche**, Belgium
79 L 7 **Binghamton**, NY, United States
108 J 8 **Bingöl**, Turkey
137 I 3 **Birāk**, Libya
118 G 8 **Biratnagar**, Nepal
115 N 3 **Birjand**, Iran
37 G 11 **Birkenhead**, United Kingdom
37 H 12 **Birmingham**, United Kingdom
80 G 4 **Birmingham**, AL, United States
105 M 10 **Birobidzhan**, Russia
85 K 16 **Bisbee**, AZ, United States
28 H 3 **Biscay Abyssal Plain**, Atlantic Ocean
33 I 3 **Biscoe Islands**, Antarctica
111 L 5 **Bishkek**, Kyrgyzstan
136 H 1 **Biskra**, Algeria
82 F 6 **Bismarck**, ND, United States
147 K 1 **Bismarck Archipelago**, Papua New Guinea
26 E 6 **Bismarck Sea**, Pacific Ocean
136 D 5 **Bissau**, Guinea Bissau
60 H 5 **Bistrița**, Romania
108 K 8 **Bitlis**, Turkey
61 F 10 **Bitola**, Macedonia
57 J 10 **Bitonto**, Italy
85 A 5 **Bitterroot Range**, MT, United States
131 F 11 **Biwa-ko**, Japan
104 G 9 **Biysk**, Russia
137 I 1 **Bizerte**, Tunisia
61 C 6 **Bjelovar**, Croatia
122 G 3 **Black**, Vietnam
53 C 12 **Black Forest**, Germany
85 E 10 **Black Rock Desert**, NV, United States
23 J 3 **Black Sea**, Europe
136 F 6 **Black Volta**, Burkina Faso
147 H 5 **Blackall**, QLD, Australia
85 I 9 **Blackfoot**, ID, United States
37 G 11 **Blackpool**, United Kingdom
37 C 13 **Blackwater**, Ireland
61 G 9 **Blagoevgrad**, Bulgaria
105 L 10 **Blagoveshchensk**, Russia
28 C 5 **Blake-Bahama Ridge**, Atlantic Ocean
41 O 3 **Blanes**, Spain
141 K 7 **Blantyre**, Malawi
150 E 7 **Blenheim**, New Zealand
136 H 1 **Blida**, Algeria
141 I 10 **Bloemfontein**, South Africa
37 C 9 **Bloody Foreland**, Ireland
78 E 8 **Bloomington**, IL, United States
78 F 9 **Bloomington**, IN, United States
23 J 5 **Blue Nile**, Africa
79 I 10 **Bluefield**, VI, United States
90 G 7 **Bluefields**, Nicaragua
79 I 10 **Bluestone Lake**, WV, United States
150 B 11 **Bluff**, New Zealand
127 M 5 **Bo Hai**, China
96 H 3 **Boa Vista**, Brazil
28 B 8 **Boa Vista**, Cape Verde
90 F 7 **Boaco**, Nicaragua
136 F 6 **Bobo-Dioulasso**, Burkina Faso
141 M 8 **Boby**, Madagascar
81 L 10 **Boca Raton**, LA, United States
90 G 8 **Bocas del Toro**, Panama
52 C 7 **Bochum**, Germany
28 G 8 **Bode Verde Fracture Zone**, Atlantic Ocean
68 H 7 **Boden**, Sweden
68 E 6 **Bodø**, Norway
109 C 9 **Bodrum**, Turkey
83 J 12 **Bogalusa**, LA, United States
108 G 7 **Boğazliyan**, Turkey
126 H 4 **Bogda Feng**, China
126 H 4 **Bogda Shan**, China
122 H 9 **Bogor**, Indonesia
96 F 3 **Bogotá**, Colombia
64 E 8 **Bohemia**, Czech Republic
64 D 8 **Bohemian Forest**, Czech Republic/Germany
84 G 8 **Boise**, ID, United States
115 M 2 **Bojnūrd**, Iran
69 A 12 **Bokna Fjord**, Norway
98 F 5 **Bolivia**, South America
45 K 9 **Bollene**, France
69 F 10 **Bollnäs**, Sweden
147 K 7 **Bollon**, QLD, Australia
56 E 7 **Bologna**, Italy
37 G 11 **Bolton**, United Kingdom
108 E 6 **Bolu**, Turkey
56 E 4 **Bolzano**, Italy
140 F 4 **Boma**, Democratic Republic of Congo
91 L 7 **Bonaire**, Netherlands Antilles
146 F 4 **Bonaparte Archipelago**, WA, Australia
118 I 8 **Bongaigaon**, India
45 N 11 **Bonifacio**, Corsica
52 C 8 **Bonn**, Germany
137 O 6 **Boosaaso**, Somalia
74 G 4 **Boothia Peninsula**, NU, Canada
89 J 4 **Boquillas del Carmen**, Mexico
151 M 10 **Bora-Bora**, French Polynesia
84 H 8 **Borah Peak**, ID, United States
69 D 13 **Borås**, Sweden
115 L 5 **Borāzjān**, Iran
44 G 8 **Bordeaux**, France
48 J 5 **Borger**, Netherlands
69 F 13 **Borgholm**, Sweden
69 E 11 **Borlänge**, Sweden
123 I 8 **Borneo**, Asia
69 E 15 **Bornholm**, Denmark
108 C 8 **Bornova**, Turkey
122 H 10 **Borobudur**, Indonesia
49 I 14 **Borscheid**, Luxembourg
115 K 3 **Borūjerd**, Iran
61 C 7 **Bosanska Dubica**, Bosnia-Herzegovina
61 C 7 **Bosanska Gradiška**, Bosnia-Herzegovina
61 C 7 **Bosnia-Herzegovina**, Europe
108 D 6 **Bosporus**, Turkey
137 J 7 **Bossangoa**, Central African Republic
126 G 4 **Bosten Hu**, China
79 N 6 **Boston**, MA, United States
61 G 9 **Botevgrad**, Bulgaria
60 I 5 **Botoșani**, Romania
140 H 8 **Botswana**, Africa
52 B 7 **Bottrop**, Germany
136 E 4 **Boû Bleïine**, Mauritania
136 F 6 **Bouaké**, Côte d'Ivoire
137 I 7 **Bouar**, Central African Republic
147 L 2 **Bougainville**, Papua New Guinea
136 E 6 **Bougouni**, Mali
85 G 13 **Boulder City**, NV, United States
45 I 1 **Boulogne-sur-Mer**, France
26 G 9 **Bounty Islands**, New Zealand
26 G 9 **Bounty Trough**, Pacific Ocean
45 K 7 **Bourg-en-Bresse**, France
45 I 6 **Bourges**, France
147 K 8 **Bourke**, NSW, Australia

Bay · Channel · Country · Dependent Territory · Desert · Geographic Area · Headland · Island · Island Group · Lake · Mountain

37 H 14 **Bournemouth**, United Kingdom
29 I 11 **Bouvetøya**, Atlantic Ocean
78 F 11 **Bowling Green**, KY, United States
33 P 5 **Bowman Island**, Antarctica
141 I 3 **Boyoma Falls**, Democratic Republic of Congo
82 B 6 **Bozeman**, MT, United States
108 D 7 **Bozüyük**, Turkey
33 I 2 **Brabant Island**, Antarctica
61 C 8 **Brač**, Croatia
37 H 11 **Bradford**, United Kingdom
40 F 4 **Braga**, Portugal
40 G 3 **Bragança**, Portugal
119 I 9 **Brahmanbaria**, Bangladesh
119 G 11 **Brahmapur**, India
23 L 5 **Brahmaputra**, Asia
60 J 7 **Brăila**, Romania
49 E 12 **Braine-l'Alleud**, Belgium
96 H 4 **Branco**, Brazil
140 G 8 **Brandberg**, Namibia
52 G 6 **Brandenburg**, Germany
74 G 10 **Brandon**, MB, Canada
33 I 2 **Bransfield Strait**, Antarctica
97 J 7 **Brasília**, Brazil
60 H 6 **Brașov**, Romania
49 E 10 **Brasschaat**, Belgium
64 F 9 **Bratislava**, Slovakia
105 I 9 **Bratsk**, Russia
105 I 9 **Bratskoye Vodokhranilishche**, Russia
53 H 11 **Braunau am Inn**, Austria
52 E 6 **Braunschweig**, Germany
28 A 8 **Brava**, Cape Verde
85 G 15 **Brawley**, CA, United States
96 H 5 **Brazil**, South America
29 G 9 **Brazil Basin**, Atlantic Ocean
22 F 7 **Brazilian Highlands**, South America
83 G 12 **Brazos**, TX, United States
140 F 4 **Brazzaville**, Congo
49 F 9 **Breda**, Netherlands
49 H 11 **Bree**, Belgium
53 E 12 **Bregenz**, Austria
52 D 6 **Bremen**, Germany
52 D 5 **Bremerhaven**, Germany
84 D 6 **Bremerton**, WA, United States
52 D 5 **Bremervörde**, Germany
83 H 13 **Brenham**, TX, United States
56 D 5 **Brescia**, Italy
56 E 4 **Bressanone**, Italy
65 I 6 **Brest**, Belarus
44 D 4 **Brest**, France
80 G 6 **Brewton**, AL, United States
45 L 8 **Briançon**, France
79 M 7 **Bridgeport**, RI, United States
91 O 6 **Bridgetown**, Barbados
53 C 13 **Brig**, Switzerland
85 I 10 **Brigham City**, UT, United States
37 I 14 **Brighton**, United Kingdom
57 K 11 **Brindisi**, Italy
147 L 7 **Brisbane**, QLD, Australia
37 G 14 **Bristol**, United Kingdom
81 J 1 **Bristol**, TN, United States
37 F 14 **Bristol Channel**, United Kingdom
74 D 7 **British Columbia**, Canada
91 N 4 **British Virgin Islands**, United Kingdom
44 E 4 **Brittany**, France
45 I 8 **Brive-la-Gaillarde**, France
64 F 8 **Brno**, Czech Republic
74 H 4 **Brodeur Peninsula**, NU, Canada
147 J 8 **Broken Hill**, NSW, Australia
31 I 6 **Broken Plateau**, Indian Ocean
82 G 7 **Brookings**, SD, United States
85 C 9 **Brookings**, OR, United States
22 C 2 **Brooks Range**, North America
146 E 9 **Brookton**, WA, Australia
146 F 5 **Broome**, WA, Australia
83 F 12 **Brownfield**, TX, United States
83 G 15 **Brownsville**, TX, United States
83 G 12 **Brownwood**, TX, United States
53 J 12 **Bruck an der Mur**, Austria
49 C 10 **Bruges**, Belgium
52 I 7 **Brunei**, Asia
81 K 6 **Brunswick**, GA, United States
79 N 5 **Brunswick**, ME, United States
147 K 11 **Bruny Island**, TAS, Australia
49 E 11 **Brussels**, Belgium
104 C 6 **Bryansk**, Russia
96 F 2 **Bucaramanga**, Colombia
136 E 7 **Buchanan**, Liberia
60 I 7 **Bucharest**, Romania
64 G 9 **Budapest**, Hungary
118 E 8 **Budaun**, India
96 E 3 **Buenaventura**, Colombia
99 G 10 **Buenos Aires**, Argentina
79 J 6 **Buffalo**, NY, United States
82 E 6 **Buffalo**, SD, United States
64 H 6 **Bug**, Poland/Ukraine
40 D 10 **Bugio**, Portugal
115 J 3 **Buḩayrat ar Razāzah**, Iraq
115 I 3 **Buḩayrat ath Tharthār**, Iraq
141 J 4 **Bujumbura**, Burundi
141 I 3 **Bukavu**, Democratic Republic of Congo
111 J 6 **Bukhara**, Uzbekistan
141 I 8 **Bulawayo**, Zimbabwe
61 J 9 **Bulgaria**, Europe
150 D 7 **Buller**, New Zealand
147 K 2 **Bulolo**, Papua New Guinea
146 E 9 **Bunbury**, WA, Australia
147 L 7 **Bundaberg**, QLD, Australia
146 G 5 **Bungle Bungles**, WA, Australia
131 C 13 **Bungo-suidō**, Japan
141 J 2 **Bunia**, Democratic Republic of Congo
41 L 6 **Buñol**, Spain
108 H 8 **Bünyan**, Turkey
122 H 5 **Buôn Mê Thuôt**, Vietnam
115 J 6 **Buraydah**, Saudi Arabia
85 E 14 **Burbank**, CA, United States
147 K 5 **Burdekin**, QLD, Australia
109 D 9 **Burdur**, Turkey
61 J 9 **Burgas**, Bulgaria
41 J 3 **Burgos**, Spain
45 J 6 **Burgundy**, France
119 D 10 **Burhanpur**, India
147 I 5 **Burketown**, QLD, Australia
136 F 6 **Burkina Faso**, Africa
147 K 11 **Burnie**, TAS, Australia
84 E 8 **Burns**, OR, United States
41 M 6 **Burriana**, Spain
108 D 6 **Bursa**, Turkey
123 L 9 **Buru**, Indonesia
141 J 4 **Burundi**, Africa
115 L 5 **Būshehr**, Iran
146 E 9 **Busselton**, WA, Australia
141 I 2 **Buta**, Democratic Republic of Congo
123 K 9 **Buton**, Indonesia
82 B 6 **Butte**, MT, United States
123 L 6 **Butuan**, Philippines
60 I 7 **Buzău**, Romania
65 K 6 **Byarezina**, Belarus
64 F 5 **Bydgoszcz**, Poland
64 G 7 **Bytom**, Poland

C

122 G 6 **Ca Mau**, Vietnam
123 K 4 **Cabanatuan**, Philippines
140 F 4 **Cabinda**, Angola
99 F 15 **Cabo Buen Tiempo**, Argentina
40 E 6 **Cabo Carvoeiro**, Portugal
96 E 3 **Cabo Corrientes**, Colombia
88 H 8 **Cabo Corrientes**, Mexico
90 G 3 **Cabo Corrientes**, Cuba
91 I 4 **Cabo Cruz**, Cuba
41 O 3 **Cabo de Creus**, Spain
41 M 7 **Cabo de la Nao**, Spain
41 L 8 **Cabo de Palos**, Spain
40 H 1 **Cabo de Penas**, Spain
41 M 7 **Cabo de San Antonio**, Spain
40 F 9 **Cabo de Santa Maria**, Portugal
40 E 9 **Cabo de São Vicente**, Portugal
40 E 8 **Cabo de Sines**, Portugal
99 G 13 **Cabo Dos Bahías**, Argentina
40 E 7 **Cabo Espichel**, Portugal
40 E 2 **Cabo Fisterra**, Spain
41 L 7 **Cabo Huertas**, Spain
41 J 1 **Cabo Machichaco**, Spain
97 J 3 **Cabo Norte**, Brazil
97 J 3 **Cabo Orange**, Brazil
40 F 1 **Cabo Ortegal**, Spain
99 E 15 **Cabo Pilar**, Chile
99 E 12 **Cabo Quilán**, Chile
89 L 7 **Cabo Rojo**, Mexico
41 J 10 **Cabo Sacratif**, Spain
90 G 3 **Cabo San Antonio**, Cuba
99 G 16 **Cabo San Diego**, Argentina
88 F 6 **Cabo San Lázaro**, Mexico
88 G 7 **Cabo San Lucas**, Mexico
88 G 7 **Cabo San Lucas**, Mexico
88 E 3 **Cabo San Quintín**, Mexico
90 F 7 **Cabo Santa Elena**, Costa Rica
40 E 3 **Cabo Silleiro**, Spain
40 G 10 **Cabo Trafalgar**, Spain
99 G 14 **Cabo Tres Puntas**, Argentina
99 F 15 **Cabo Vírgenes**, Argentina
88 F 3 **Caborca**, Mexico
75 M 7 **Cabot Strait**, Canada
41 O 6 **Cabrera**, Spain
40 G 6 **Cáceres**, Spain
97 L 8 **Cachoeiro do Itapemirim**, Brazil
78 G 5 **Cadillac**, MI, United States
40 G 10 **Cádiz**, Spain
123 K 5 **Cadiz**, Philippines
44 G 3 **Caen**, France
98 G 8 **Cafayate**, Argentina
123 K 6 **Cagayan de Oro**, Philippines
57 B 12 **Cagliari**, Italy
91 M 4 **Caguas**, Puerto Rico
45 I 9 **Cahors**, France
65 K 11 **Cahul**, Moldova
91 K 3 **Caicos Islands**, Turks and Caicos Islands
147 K 4 **Cairns**, QLD, Australia
137 L 5 **Cairo**, Egypt
96 E 5 **Cajamarca**, Peru
57 J 12 **Calabria**, Italy
99 E 15 **Calafate**, Argentina
41 K 3 **Calahorra**, Spain
45 I 1 **Calais**, France
98 F 7 **Calama**, Chile
41 K 4 **Calatayud**, Spain
123 K 5 **Calbayog**, Philippines
119 H 10 **Calcutta**, India
40 E 6 **Caldas da Rainha**, Portugal
98 E 8 **Caldera**, Chile
99 F 13 **Caleta Olivia**, Argentina
74 E 9 **Calgary**, AB, Canada
96 E 3 **Cali**, Colombia
119 C 14 **Calicut**, India
85 D 14 **California**, United States
96 E 6 **Callao**, Peru
57 G 14 **Caltanissetta**, Italy
122 H 5 **Cam Ranh**, Vietnam
97 L 7 **Camaçari**, Brazil
91 I 3 **Camagüey**, Cuba
40 C 9 **Câmara de Lobos**, Portugal
45 K 10 **Camargue**, France
75 L 8 **Cambellton**, NB, Canada
122 G 5 **Cambodia**, Asia
45 J 2 **Cambrai**, France
37 F 13 **Cambrian Mountains**, United Kingdom
37 I 13 **Cambridge**, United Kingdom
150 F 4 **Cambridge**, New Zealand
79 I 8 **Cambridge**, OH, United States
74 G 5 **Cambridge Bay**, NU, Canada
137 I 8 **Cameroon**, Africa
98 G 6 **Camiri**, Bolivia
85 I 14 **Camp Verde**, AZ, United States
23 O 9 **Campbell Island**, Oceania
26 G 9 **Campbell Plateau**, Pacific Ocean
89 O 8 **Campeche**, Mexico
97 M 5 **Campina Grande**, Brazil
97 J 9 **Campinas**, Brazil
97 I 8 **Campo Grande**, Brazil
57 H 10 **Campobasso**, Italy
97 L 8 **Campos dos Goytacazes**, Brazil
74 F 9 **Camrose**, AB, Canada
122 G 6 **Cân Tho**, Vietnam
74 G 7 **Canada**, North America
32 C 5 **Canada Abyssal Plain**, Arctic Ocean
83 F 10 **Canadian**, TX, United States
32 C 4 **Canadian Basin**, Arctic Ocean
22 D 2 **Canadian Shield**, North America
108 B 6 **Çanakkale**, Turkey
88 G 3 **Cananea**, Mexico
40 A 10 **Canary Islands**, Spain
22 G 4 **Canary Islands**, Africa
147 L 9 **Canberra**, ACT, Australia
89 P 7 **Cancún**, Mexico
127 M 5 **Cangzhou**, China
33 J 5 **Canisteo Peninsula**, Antarctica
108 F 6 **Cankiri**, Turkey
45 M 10 **Cannes**, France
97 J 10 **Canoas**, Brazil
37 J 14 **Canterbury**, United Kingdom
150 D 9 **Canterbury Bight**, New Zealand
150 D 9 **Canterbury Plains**, New Zealand
80 E 4 **Canton**, MS, United States
79 I 8 **Canton**, OH, United States
83 F 11 **Canyon**, TX, United States
82 B 6 **Canyon Ferry Lake**, MT, United States
136 D 3 **Cap Barbas**, Western Sahara
41 O 5 **Cap de Formentor**, Spain
44 F 2 **Cap de la Hague**, France
41 O 6 **Cap de ses Salines**, Spain
41 O 6 **Cap des Freu**, Spain
75 J 6 **Cap Hopes Advance**, QC, Canada
136 D 5 **Cap Vert**, Senegal
33 M 7 **Cape Adare**, Antarctica
23 I 8 **Cape Agulhas**, Africa
108 G 10 **Cape Apostolos Andreas**, Cyprus
147 I 3 **Cape Arnhem**, NT, Australia
29 J 9 **Cape Basin**, Atlantic Ocean
75 M 7 **Cape Bauld**, NL, Canada
85 B 9 **Cape Blanco**, OR, United States
30 F 11 **Cape Boothby**, Antarctica
75 M 8 **Cape Breton Island**, NS, Canada
150 E 1 **Cape Brett**, New Zealand
123 J 6 **Cape Buliluyan**, Philippines,
123 J 5 **Cape Calavite**, Philippines,
150 E 7 **Cape Campbell**, New Zealand
81 L 8 **Cape Canaveral**, FL, United States
79 L10 **Cape Charles**, VI, United States
33 M 7 **Cape Cheetham**, Antarctica
105 J 4 **Cape Chelyuskin**, Russia
32 B 8 **Cape Chidley**, Canada
119 E 12 **Cape Chirala**, India
74 H 7 **Cape Churchill**, MB, Canada
79 N 7 **Cape Cod**, MA, United States
32 D 7 **Cape Columbia**, Canada
119 D 15 **Cape Comorin**, India
74 C 9 **Cape Cook**, BC, Canada
81 K 10 **Cape Coral**, FL, United States
147 K 2 **Cape Cretin**, Papua New Guinea
74 E 4 **Cape Dalhousie**, NT, Canada
30 G 11 **Cape Darnley**, Antarctica
84 C 7 **Cape Disappointment**, WA, United States
75 J 4 **Cape Dyer**, NU, Canada
150 D 6 **Cape Farewell**, New Zealand
81 M 3 **Cape Fear**, NC, United States
84 C 5 **Cape Flattery**, WA, United States
146 G 4 **Cape Ford**, NT, Australia
150 D 7 **Cape Foulwind**, New Zealand
33 N 7 **Cape Freshfield**, Antarctica
147 K 1 **Cape Girgir**, Papua New Guinea
31 L 11 **Cape Goodenough**, Antarctica
33 O 7 **Cape Gray**, Antarctica
108 G 11 **Cape Greko**, Cyprus
147 J 3 **Cape Grenville**, QLD, Australia
81 O 2 **Cape Hatteras**, NC, United States
22 F 9 **Cape Horn**, South America
150 E 1 **Cape Karikari**, New Zealand
33 O 7 **Cape Keltie**, Antarctica
150 G 5 **Cape Kidnappers**, New Zealand
74 C 8 **Cape Knox**, BC, Canada
75 K 6 **Cape Labrador**, NL, Canada
31 K 7 **Cape Leeuwin**, Australia
146 F 5 **Cape Leveque**, WA, Australia
81 N 3 **Cape Lookout**, NC, United States
147 J 4 **Cape Melville**, QLD, Australia
85 B 10 **Cape Mendocino**, CA, United States
75 J 5 **Cape Mercy**, NU, Canada
31 L 11 **Cape Morse**, Antarctica
147 L 3 **Cape Nelson**, Papua New Guinea
33 L 1 **Cape Norvegia**, Antarctica
140 H 11 **Cape of Good Hope**, South Africa
150 F 7 **Cape Palliser**, New Zealand
136 E 7 **Cape Palmas**, Côte d'Ivoire/Liberia
74 E 4 **Cape Parry**, NT, Canada
31 I 11 **Cape Penck**, Antarctica
31 K 11 **Cape Poinsett**, Antarctica
150 A 10 **Cape Providence**, New Zealand
150 D 1 **Cape Reinga**, New Zealand
81 L 4 **Cape Romain**, SC, United States
81 K 10 **Cape Romano**, FL, United States
150 G 3 **Cape Runaway**, New Zealand,
28 E 4 **Cape Sable**, North America
81 K 11 **Cape Sable**, FL, United States
123 L 6 **Cape San Agustin**, Philippines
147 I 4 **Cape Shield**, NT, Australia
147 M 3 **Cape Siri**, Papua New Guinea
74 H 8 **Cape Tatnam**, MB, Canada
140 H 11 **Cape Town**, South Africa
150 G 6 **Cape Turnagain**, New Zealand
28 A 7 **Cape Verde**, Africa
28 G 6 **Cape Verde Basin**, Atlantic Ocean
28 G 6 **Cape Verde Islands**, Atlantic Ocean
28 G 5 **Cape Verde Plateau**, Atlantic Ocean,
33 P 6 **Cape Waldron**, Antarctica
36 E 5 **Cape Wrath**, United Kingdom
147 J 3 **Cape York**, QLD, Australia
147 J 4 **Cape York Peninsula**, QLD, Australia
91 K 4 **Cap-Haïtien**, Haiti
57 A 11 **Capo Caccia**, Italy
57 C 13 **Capo Carbonara**, Italy
57 J 13 **Capo Colonna**, Italy
57 C 11 **Capo Comino**, Italy
57 B 10 **Capo del Falcone**, Italy
57 B 12 **Capo della Frasca**, Italy
57 H 15 **Capo delle Correnti**, Italy
57 H 13 **Capo di Milazzo**, Italy
57 C 11 **Capo di Monte Santu**, Italy
57 G 14 **Capo Gallo**, Italy
57 I 12 **Capo Palinuro**, Italy
57 J 13 **Capo Rizzuto**, Italy
57 F 14 **Capo San Vito**, Italy
57 K 12 **Capo Santa Maria di Leuca**, Italy
57 H 15 **Capo Scaramia**, Italy
57 B 13 **Capo Spartivento**, Italy
57 I 13 **Capo Vaticano**, Italy
108 G 8 **Cappadocia**, Turkey
57 G 11 **Capri**, Italy
140 H 7 **Caprivi Strip**, Namibia
96 E 4 **Caquetá**, Colombia
119 K 14 **Car Nicobar**, India
60 G 8 **Caracal**, Romania
96 G 1 **Caracas**, Venezuela
78 E 10 **Carbondale**, IL, United States
45 I 10 **Carcassonne**, France
37 G 14 **Cardiff**, United Kingdom
37 F 12 **Cardigan Bay**, United Kingdom
60 F 5 **Carei**, Romania
30 G 5 **Cargados Carajos Islands**, Mauritius
37 G 10 **Carlisle**, United Kingdom
79 K 8 **Carlisle**, PA, United States
37 D 12 **Carlow**, Ireland
83 E 12 **Carlsbad**, NM, United States
30 F 2 **Carlsberg Ridge**, Indian Ocean
78 E 9 **Carlyle Lake**, IL, United States
40 H 8 **Carmona**, Spain
146 D 7 **Carnarvon**, WA, Australia
33 J 6 **Carney Island**, Antarctica
137 I 7 **Carnot**, Central African Republic
97 K 5 **Carolina**, Brazil
151 J 1 **Caroline Islands**, Federated States of Micronesia
23 I 3 **Carpathian Mountains**, Europe
56 D 6 **Carpi**, Italy
56 D 7 **Carrara**, Italy
37 A 13 **Carrauntuohil**, Ireland
82 F 5 **Carrington**, ND, United States
85 E 11 **Carson City**, NV, United States
41 L 8 **Cartagena**, Spain
96 E 2 **Cartagena**, Colombia
90 G 8 **Cartago**, Costa Rica
137 I 1 **Carthage**, Tunisia
75 L 6 **Cartwright**, NL, Canada
85 I 15 **Casa Grande**, AZ, United States
136 F 1 **Casablanca**, Morocco
150 B 9 **Cascade Point**, New Zealand
85 C 9 **Cascade Range**, OR/WA, United States
27 J 2 **Cascadia Basin**, Pacific Ocean
33 P 6 **Casey**, Australia
82 D 7 **Casper**, WY, United States
110 G 3 **Caspian Depression**, Kazakhstan/Russia
23 J 4 **Caspian Sea**, Asia
97 J 4 **Castanhal**, Brazil
41 M 6 **Castelló de la Plana**, Spain
45 I 10 **Castelnaudary**, France
40 G 6 **Castelo Branco**, Portugal
91 O 6 **Castries**, St Lucia
99 E 12 **Castro**, Chile
57 I 12 **Castrovillari**, Italy
91 J 2 **Cat Island**, The Bahamas
41 N 3 **Cataluña**, Spain
98 G 8 **Catamarca**, Argentina
57 H 14 **Catania**, Italy

Mountain Range · National Capital · Ocean · Physical Feature · Polar Base · River · Sea · Special Feature · State Capital · Underwater Feature

57	J 13	**Catanzaro**, Italy
79	L 7	**Catskill Mountains**, NY, United States ⛰
96	E 2	**Cauca**, Colombia ≀
23	J 4	**Caucasus**, Asia/Europe ⛰
99	E 10	**Cauquenes**, Chile
136	E 7	**Cavally**, Côte d'Ivoire/Libya ≀
97	J 10	**Caxias do Sul**, Brazil
97	J 3	**Cayenne**, French Guiana 🏛
90	H 4	**Cayman Brac**, Cayman Islands 🏝
90	H 4	**Cayman Islands**, United Kingdom ⊡
90	H 3	**Cayo Largo**, Cuba 🏝
90	G 6	**Cayos Miskitos**, Nicaragua 🏝
28	F 7	**Ceara Abyssal Plain**, Atlantic Ocean ▰
123	K 6	**Cebu**, Philippines
82	I 7	**Cedar**, IA, United States ≀
85	I 12	**Cedar City**, UT, United States
74	G 9	**Cedar Lake**, MB, Canada ∿
82	I 7	**Cedar Rapids**, IA, United States
146	H 8	**Ceduna**, SA, Australia
89	J 8	**Celaya**, Mexico
26	D 5	**Celebes Sea**, Pacific Ocean 🌊
60	B 6	**Celje**, Slovenia
52	E 6	**Celle**, Germany
37	D 14	**Celtic Sea**, Ireland/United Kingdom 🌊
28	H 3	**Celtic Shelf**, Atlantic Ocean ▰
137	J 7	**Central African Republic**, Africa □
26	D 4	**Central Basin**, Pacific Ocean ▰
151	M 8	**Central Line Islands**, Kiribati 🌴
22	D 4	**Central Lowlands**, North America ◇
111	J 10	**Central Makran Range**, Pakistan ⛰
26	G 5	**Central Pacific Basin**, Pacific Ocean ▰
147	J 1	**Central Range**, Papua New Guinea ⛰
23	K 2	**Central Siberian Plateau**, Asia ◇
85	D 10	**Central Valley**, CA, United States ◇
84	D 6	**Centralia**, WA, United States
57	I 10	**Cerignola**, Italy
108	F 6	**Cerkeş**, Turkey
99	E 14	**Cerro Arenales**, Chile ▲
96	A 7	**Cerro Azul**, Galapagos Islands ▲
90	G 8	**Cerro Chirripó Grande**, Costa Rica ▲
88	E 2	**Cerro de La Encantada**, Mexico ▲
96	E 6	**Cerro de Pasco**, Peru
99	E 14	**Cerro Murallón**, Argentina/Chile ▲
99	E 15	**Cerro Paine**, Chile ▲
99	E 13	**Cerro San Valentín**, Chile ▲
99	F 10	**Cerro Tupungato**, Argentina/Chile ▲
41	N 3	**Cervera**, Spain
56	F 7	**Cesena**, Italy
64	E 8	**České Budějovice**, Czech Republic
40	H 10	**Ceuta**, Spain
109	H 9	**Ceyhan**, Turkey
30	H 3	**Ceylon Plain**, Indian Ocean ▰
115	N 6	**Chābahār**, Iran
96	E 5	**Chachapoyas**, Peru
137	I 5	**Chad**, Africa □
111	J 8	**Chaghcharān**, Afghanistan
30	G 4	**Chagos Archipelago**, Indian Ocean ▰
30	H 4	**Chagos Trench**, Indian Ocean ▰
30	G 4	**Chagos-Laccadive Ridge**, Indian Ocean ▰
30	F 3	**Chain Ridge**, Indian Ocean ▰
61	G 12	**Chalkida**, Greece
26	E 5	**Challenger Deep**, Pacific Ocean ▰
27	K 8	**Challenger Fracture Zone**, Pacific Ocean ▰
26	G 8	**Challenger Plateau**, Pacific Ocean ▰
84	H 8	**Challis**, ID, United States
45	K 6	**Chalon- sur-Saône**, France
45	K 3	**Châlons-en-Champagne**, France
45	L 7	**Chambéry**, France
45	M 7	**Chamonix-Mont-Blanc**, France
89	O 8	**Champotón**, Mexico
98	E 8	**Chañaral**, Chile
80	F 7	**Chandeleur Islands**, LA, United States 🌴
118	D 7	**Chandigarh**, India
85	I 15	**Chandler**, AZ, United States
119	E 11	**Chandrapur**, India
127	N 4	**Changchun**, China
127	L 8	**Changde**, China
127	N 9	**Changhua**, Taiwan
126	G 4	**Changji**, China
127	L 8	**Changsha**, China
127	N 7	**Changshu**, China
127	L 6	**Changzhi**, China
127	M 7	**Changzhou**, China
61	G 14	**Chania**, Greece
37	G 16	**Channel Islands**, United Kingdom 🌴
85	E 15	**Channel Islands**, CA, United States 🌴
37	K 14	**Channel Tunnel**, United Kingdom/France ▰
127	M 10	**Chaozhou**, China
97	J 9	**Chapecó**, Brazil
33	J 3	**Charcot Island**, Antarctica 🏝
111	J 6	**Chardzhev**, Turkmenistan
111	K 7	**Chārīkār**, Afghanistan
49	F 13	**Charleroi**, Belgium
81	L 4	**Charleston**, SC, United States
79	I 10	**Charleston**, WV, United States ⌂
147	K 7	**Charleville**, QLD, Australia
45	K 3	**Charleville-Mézières**, France
28	F 3	**Charlie-Gibbs Fracture Zone**, Atlantic Ocean ▰
81	K 2	**Charlotte**, NC, United States
91	M 4	**Charlotte Amalie**, Virgin Islands 🏛
81	J 9	**Charlotte Harbor**, FL, United States ≈
79	J 10	**Charlottesville**, VI, United States
75	M 8	**Charlottetown**, PE, Canada ⌂
45	I 4	**Chartres**, France
44	G 5	**Châteaubriant**, France
45	I 5	**Châteaudun**, France
45	I 6	**Châteauroux**, France
45	J 3	**Château-Thierry**, France
44	H 6	**Châtellerault**, France
26	G 9	**Chatham Islands**, New Zealand 🌴
26	G 9	**Chatham Rise**, Pacific Ocean ▰
80	H 3	**Chattanooga**, TN, United States
45	K 4	**Chaumont**, France
119	E 14	**Chavakachcheri**, Sri Lanka
104	D 6	**Cheboksary**, Russia
78	H 4	**Cheboygan**, MI, United States
122	E 3	**Cheduba**, Myanmar 🏝
84	C 6	**Chehalis**, WA, United States
111	I 3	**Chelkar**, Kazakhstan
64	H 7	**Chelm**, Poland
37	J 13	**Chelmsford**, United Kingdom
37	H 13	**Cheltenham**, United Kingdom
104	E 8	**Chelyabinsk**, Russia
52	G 8	**Chemnitz**, Germany
127	M 5	**Chengde**, China
127	J 8	**Chengdu**, China
119	E 13	**Chennai**, India
44	G 3	**Cherbourg**, France
104	D 5	**Cherepovets**, Russia
65	L 8	**Cherkasy**, Ukraine
104	B 8	**Cherkessk**, Russia
65	L 6	**Chernihiv**, Ukraine
65	I 9	**Chernivtsi**, Ukraine
65	K 7	**Chernobyl**, Ukraine
64	H 4	**Chernyakhovsk**, Russia
79	K 9	**Chesapeake Bay**, United States ≈
79	N 4	**Chesuncook Lake**, ME, United States ∿
89	P 9	**Chetumal**, Mexico
82	D 8	**Cheyenne**, WY, United States ⌂
82	E 7	**Cheyenne**, SD, United States ≀
127	N 10	**Chiai**, Taiwan
122	F 4	**Chiang Mai**, Thailand
122	F 3	**Chiang Rai**, Thailand
109	L 5	**Chiat'ura**, Georgia
131	I 10	**Chiba**, Japan
75	K 9	**Chibougamau**, QC, Canada
78	F 7	**Chicago**, IL, United States
89	O 8	**Chichén Itzá**, Mexico, ✱
96	D 5	**Chiclayo**, Peru
99	F 13	**Chico**, Argentina ≀
85	D 11	**Chico**, CA, United States
75	K 9	**Chicoutimi**, QC, Canada
57	G 9	**Chieti**, Italy
127	M 4	**Chifeng**, China
88	H 4	**Chihuahua**, Mexico
83	F 11	**Childress**, TX, United States
99	E 11	**Chile**, South America □
99	E 13	**Chile Chico**, Chile
27	L 8	**Chile Rise**, Pacific Ocean ▰
99	E 11	**Chillán**, Chile
78	H 9	**Chillicothe**, OH, United States
89	K 9	**Chilpancingo**, Mexico
96	E 6	**Chimbote**, Peru
141	J 7	**Chimoio**, Mozambique
127	I 6	**China**, Asia □
141	I 6	**Chingola**, Zambia
141	J 7	**Chinhoyi**, Zimbabwe
111	L 8	**Chiniot**, Pakistan
26	G 2	**Chinook Trough**, Pacific Ocean ▰
56	F 6	**Chioggia**, Italy
61	I 12	**Chios**, Greece
61	H 12	**Chios**, Greece 🏝
141	J 6	**Chipata**, Zambia
90	E 6	**Chiquimula**, Guatemala
111	L 5	**Chirchik**, Uzbekistan
65	K 10	**Chişlnău**, Moldova 🏛
105	J 10	**Chita**, Russia
119	D 13	**Chitradurga**, India
119	I 10	**Chittagong**, Bangladesh
119	E 13	**Chittoor**, India
141	J 7	**Chitungwiza**, Zimbabwe
99	G 11	**Choele Choel**, Argentina
44	G 6	**Cholet**, France
141	I 7	**Choma**, Zambia
64	D 7	**Chomutov**, Moldova
122	G 5	**Chon Buri**, Thailand
127	O 4	**Ch'ŏngjin**, North Korea
127	K 8	**Chongqing**, China
127	O 6	**Chŏnju**, South Korea
127	L 3	**Choybalsan**, Mongolia
150	D 8	**Christchurch**, New Zealand
23	M 7	**Christmas Island**, Australia 🏝
150	L 7	**Christmas Island**, Kiribati 🏝
26	H 4	**Christmas Ridge**, Pacific Ocean ▰
99	F 12	**Chubut**, Argentina ≀
105	O 3	**Chuckchi Sea**, Russia 🌊
131	C 12	**Chūgoku-sanchi**, Japan ⛰
32	D 5	**Chukchi Abyssal Plain**, Arctic Ocean ▰
32	D 5	**Chukchi Plateau**, Arctic Ocean ▰
32	D 4	**Chukchi Sea**, Arctic Ocean 🌊
105	O 4	**Chukotskiy Peninsula**, Russia ▶
85	F 15	**Chula Vista**, CA, United States
127	O 5	**Ch'unch'ŏn**, South Korea
127	O 5	**Ch'ungju**, South Korea
98	E 6	**Chuquicamata**, Chile
53	D 13	**Chur**, Switzerland
74	H 7	**Churchill**, MB, Canada
74	H 8	**Churchill**, NL, Canada ≀
75	L 7	**Churchill**, MB, Canada ≀
151	L 1	**Chuuk Islands**, Federated States of Micronesia 🌴
65	K 10	**Ciadîr Lunga**, Moldova
108	F 5	**Cide**, Turkey
64	H 5	**Ciechanów**, Poland
91	I 3	**Ciego de Ávila**, Cuba
90	H 3	**Cienfuegos**, Cuba
41	K 8	**Cieza**, Spain
108	F 8	**Cihanbeyli**, Turkey
122	H 10	**Cilacap**, Indonesia
78	G 9	**Cincinnati**, OH, United States
49	G 13	**Ciney**, Belgium
57	J 12	**Cirà Marina**, Italy
56	F 8	**Città di Castello**, Italy
89	J 4	**Ciudad Acuña**, Mexico
96	G 2	**Ciudad Bolívar**, Venezuela
89	I 4	**Ciudad Camargo**, Mexico
89	K 7	**Ciudad de Valles**, Mexico
89	N 9	**Ciudad del Carmen**, Mexico
89	I 4	**Ciudad Delicias**, Mexico
96	H 2	**Ciudad Guayana**, Venezuela
89	I 8	**Ciudad Guzmán**, Mexico
88	H 2	**Ciudad Juárez**, Mexico
89	L 7	**Ciudad Madero**, Mexico
89	K 7	**Ciudad Mante**, Mexico
88	G 4	**Ciudad Obregón**, Mexico
41	I 7	**Ciudad Real**, Spain
40	G 5	**Ciudad Rodrigo**, Spain
89	K 6	**Ciudad Victoria**, Mexico
41	P 5	**Ciudadela**, Spain
108	H 6	**Civa Burnu**, Turkey ▶
56	G 8	**Civitanova Marche**, Italy
57	E 9	**Civitavecchia**, Italy
150	E 7	**Clarence**, New Zealand
150	E 7	**Clarence**, New Zealand ≀
91	J 3	**Clarence Town**, The Bahamas
27	I 4	**Clarion Fracture Zone**, Pacific Ocean ▰
81	J 4	**Clark Hill Reservoir**, GA, United States ∿
79	I 9	**Clarksburg**, WV, United States
80	E 3	**Clarksdale**, MS, United States
80	G 1	**Clarksville**, TN, United States
83	E 10	**Clayton**, NM, United States
85	C 11	**Clear Lake**, CA, United States ∿
85	D 9	**Clear Lake Reservoir**, CA, United States ∿
81	J 8	**Clearwater**, FL, United States
84	G 7	**Clearwater**, United States ≀
147	K 6	**Clermont**, QLD, Australia
45	J 7	**Clermont- Ferrand**, France
49	I 14	**Clervaux**, Luxembourg
81	I 2	**Cleveland**, TN, United States
79	I 7	**Cleveland**, OH, United States
80	E 5	**Clinton**, MS, United States
27	I 5	**Clipperton Fracture Zone**, Pacific Ocean ▰
27	K 5	**Clipperton Island**, Pacific Ocean 🏝
147	J 5	**Cloncurry**, QLD, Australia
37	C 12	**Clonmel**, Ireland
83	E 11	**Clovis**, NM, United States
60	G 6	**Cluj-Napoca**, Romania
150	C 10	**Clutha**, New Zealand ≀
37	F 9	**Clyde**, United Kingdom ≀
85	C 10	**Coast Ranges**, CA/OR/WA, United States ⛰
75	I 6	**Coats Island**, NU, Canada 🏝
89	M 9	**Coatzacoalcos**, Mexico
90	E 5	**Cobán**, Guatemala
146	H 3	**Cobourg Peninsula**, NT, Australia ▶
98	F 5	**Cochabamba**, Bolivia
119	D 14	**Cochin**, India
99	F 14	**Cochrane**, Chile
91	K 3	**Cockburn Town**, Turks Islands and Caicos 🏛
90	F 6	**Coco**, Honduras/Nicaragua ≀
119	J 13	**Coco Channel**, India ⧗
31	I 4	**Cocos Basin**, Indian Ocean ▰
31	I 5	**Cocos Islands**, Australia 🏝
27	L 5	**Cocos Ridge**, Pacific Ocean ▰
150	B 11	**Codfish Island**, New Zealand 🏝
82	C 7	**Cody**, WY, United States
84	G 6	**Coeur d'Alene**, ID, United States
48	J 6	**Coevorden**, Netherlands
147	L 8	**Coffs Harbour**, NSW, Australia
44	G 7	**Cognac**, France
99	E 13	**Coihaique**, Chile
119	D 14	**Coimbatore**, India
40	F 5	**Coimbra**, Portugal
97	L 8	**Colatina**, Brazil
37	J 13	**Colchester**, United Kingdom
89	I 9	**Colima**, Mexico
36	D 7	**Coll**, United Kingdom 🏝
74	G 5	**Collinson Peninsula**, NU, Canada ▶
45	M 4	**Colmar**, France
52	B 8	**Cologne**, Germany
96	E 3	**Colombia**, South America □
28	C 6	**Colombian Basin**, Atlantic Ocean ▰
119	E 15	**Colombo**, Sri Lanka 🏛
99	H 10	**Colón**, Argentina
90	H 8	**Colón**, Panama
151	J 1	**Colonia**, Federated States of Micronesia
22	E 8	**Colorado**, South America ≀
83	D 9	**Colorado**, United States ⊡
85	H 13	**Colorado**, United States ≀
88	E 2	**Colorado**, Mexico ≀
85	F 14	**Colorado Desert**, CA, United States ⌓
22	D 4	**Colorado Plateau**, North America ◇
83	D 9	**Colorado Springs**, CO, United States
80	G 2	**Columbia**, TN, United States
81	K 3	**Columbia**, SC, United States ⌂
83	I 9	**Columbia**, MO, United States
84	E 6	**Columbia**, United States ≀
84	F 6	**Columbia Basin**, WA, United States ◇
84	F 8	**Columbia Plateau**, ID/OR, United States ◇
80	F 4	**Columbus**, MS, United States
81	I 5	**Columbus**, GA, United States
78	G 9	**Columbus**, IN, United States
78	H 8	**Columbus**, OH, United States ⌂
82	G 8	**Columbus**, NE, United States
150	F 3	**Colville**, New Zealand
150	F 2	**Colville Channel**, New Zealand ⧗
56	F 6	**Comacchio**, Italy
90	E 6	**Comayagua**, Honduras
99	E 9	**Combarbalá**, Chile
89	N 10	**Comitán de Domínguez**, Mexico
56	C 5	**Como**, Italy
99	F 13	**Comodoro Rivadavia**, Argentina
141	M 6	**Comoros**, Africa □
45	J 3	**Compiègne**, France
136	D 6	**Conakry**, Guinea 🏛
99	E 11	**Concepción**, Chile
98	H 5	**Concepción**, Bolivia
98	I 7	**Concepción**, Paraguay
99	I 9	**Concepción del Uruguay**, Argentina
88	H 4	**Conchos**, Mexico ≀
79	M 6	**Concord**, NH, United States ⌂
85	C 12	**Concord**, CA, United States
99	I 9	**Concordia**, Argentina
23	I 6	**Congo**, Africa ≀
140	G 2	**Congo**, Congo/Democratic Republic of Congo ≀
23	I 6	**Congo Basin**, Africa ◇
28	J 7	**Congo Cone**, Atlantic Ocean ▰
79	M 7	**Connecticut**, United States ⊡
30	E 9	**Conrad Rise**, Southern Ocean ▰
60	J 8	**Constanța**, Romania
136	H 1	**Constantine**, Algeria
74	F 6	**Contwoyto Lake**, NU, Canada ∿
83	I 10	**Conway**, AR, United States
146	H 7	**Coober Pedy**, SA, Australia
151	L 9	**Cook Islands**, New Zealand ⊡
150	E 6	**Cook Strait**, New Zealand ⧗
80	H 2	**Cookeville**, TN, United States
147	K 4	**Cooktown**, QLD, Australia
146	F 8	**Coolgardie**, WA, Australia
91	I 1	**Cooper's Town**, The Bahamas
84	C 8	**Coos Bay**, OR, United States
69	C 14	**Copenhagen**, Denmark 🏛
98	E 8	**Copiapó**, Chile
99	E 9	**Coquimbo**, Chile
60	H 8	**Corabia**, Romania
26	F 7	**Coral Sea**, Pacific Ocean 🌊
26	E 6	**Coral Sea Basin**, Pacific Ocean ▰
81	I 5	**Cordele**, GA, United States
40	G 3	**Cordillera Cantabrica**, Spain ⛰
123	K 4	**Cordillera Mountains**, Philippines ⛰
90	G 8	**Cordillera Talamanca**, Costa Rica/Panama ⛰
41	I 8	**Córdoba**, Spain
99	G 9	**Córdoba**, Argentina
89	L 9	**Córdoba**, Mexico
61	D 11	**Corfu**, Greece 🏝
80	F 3	**Corinth**, MS, United States
61	G 12	**Corinth Canal**, Greece ≀
37	B 13	**Cork**, Ireland
108	C 6	**Çorlu**, Turkey
75	M 7	**Corner Brook**, NL, Canada
75	K 10	**Cornwall**, ON, Canada
96	F 1	**Coro**, Venezuela
150	F 3	**Coromandel Peninsula**, New Zealand ▶
90	E 4	**Corozal**, Belize
83	G 14	**Corpus Christi**, TX, United States
98	I 8	**Corrientes**, Argentina
45	N 9	**Corsica**, France ⊡
83	H 12	**Corsicana**, TX, United States
40	G 8	**Cortegana**, Spain
56	F 4	**Cortina d'Ampezzo**, Italy
108	J 7	**Çoruh**, Turkey ≀
108	G 7	**Çorum**, Turkey
97	I 8	**Corumbá**, Brazil
84	C 8	**Corvallis**, OR, United States
40	A 8	**Corvo**, Portugal 🏝
45	J 5	**Cosne-cours-sur-Loire**, France
41	L 8	**Costa Blanca**, Spain ⁙
41	O 4	**Costa Brava**, Spain ⁙
41	I 10	**Costa del Sol**, Spain ⁙
90	G 8	**Costa Rica**, North America □
40	H 1	**Costa Verde**, Spain ⁙
45	L 10	**Côte d'Azur**, France ⁙
136	F 6	**Côte d'Ivoire**, Africa □
52	I 7	**Cottbus**, Germany
82	H 8	**Council Bluffs**, IA, United States
49	E 13	**Courcelles**, Belgium
49	E 14	**Couvin**, Belgium
37	H 13	**Coventry**, United Kingdom
40	G 5	**Covilhã**, Portugal
89	P 8	**Cozumel**, Mexico 🏝
82	C 8	**Craig**, CO, United States
60	G 8	**Craiova**, Romania
85	D 9	**Crater Lake**, OR, United States ∿
147	L 2	**Crater Point**, Papua New Guinea ▶
37	I 14	**Crawley**, United Kingdom
56	D 6	**Cremona**, Italy
61	A 7	**Cres**, Croatia 🏝
85	C 9	**Crescent City**, CA, United States
82	H 8	**Creston**, IA, United States
80	H 6	**Crestview**, FL, United States
61	H 15	**Crete**, Greece 🏝
61	B 7	**Crikvenica**, Croatia
65	M 11	**Crimea**, Ukraine ▶
61	D 6	**Croatia**, Europe □
150	C 9	**Cromwell**, New Zealand
91	J 3	**Crooked Island**, The Bahamas 🏝
57	J 12	**Crotone**, Italy

≈ Bay ⧗ Channel □ Country ⊡ Dependent Territory ⌓ Desert ⁙ Geographic Area ▶ Headland 🏝 Island 🌴 Island Group ∿ Lake ▲ Mountain

▲▲ Mountain Range   ◼ National Capital   ⌕ Ocean   ◇ Physical Feature   ⬛ Polar Base   ↘ River   ◢ Sea   ✴ Special Feature   ⌂ State Capital   ◣ Underwater Feature

40 H 7 Embalse de Orellana, Spain
40 H 6 Embalse de Valdecañas, Spain
40 H 7 Embalse del Zújar, Spain
147 K 6 Emerald, QLD, Australia
48 H 6 Emmeloord, Netherlands
48 K 6 Emmen, Netherlands
88 G 4 Empalme, Mexico
26 G 3 Emperor Seamount Chain, Pacific Ocean
26 G 2 Emperor Trough, Pacific Ocean
56 D 7 Empoli, Italy
83 H 9 Emporia, KS, United States
52 C 6 Ems, Germany
98 I 8 Encarnación, Paraguay
85 F 15 Encinitas, CA, United States
123 K 10 Endeh, Indonesia
30 E 10 Enderby Abyssal Plain, Southern Ocean
33 O 2 Enderby Land, Antarctica
104 C 7 Engel's, Russia
122 F 9 Enggano, Indonesia
49 E 12 Enghien, Belgium
37 H 12 England, United Kingdom
37 G 15 English Channel, France/United Kingdom
83 G 10 Enid, OK, United States
37 B 12 Ennis, Ireland
37 C 10 Enniskillen, United Kingdom
48 J 7 Enschede, Netherlands
88 D 2 Ensenada, Mexico
131 G 11 Enshū-nada, Japan
141 J 3 Entebbe, Uganda
136 H 7 Enugu, Nigeria
48 I 7 Epe, Netherlands
45 L 4 Épinal, France
119 A 16 Equatorial Channel, Maldives
136 H 8 Equatorial Guinea, Africa
108 L 8 Erciş, Turkey
127 K 3 Erdenet, Mongolia
109 G 9 Ereğli, Turkey
52 F 8 Erfurt, Germany
136 F 3 'Erg Chech, Algeria/Mali
137 I 5 Erg du Djourab, Chad
136 F 3 Erg Iguidi, Algeria/Mauritania
79 J 7 Erie, PA, United States
130 I 4 Erimo-misaki, Japan
137 M 5 Eritrea, Africa
53 F 10 Erlangen, Germany
61 H 13 Ermoupoli, Greece
119 D 14 Erode, India
49 E 13 Erquelinnes, Belgium
37 A 10 Erris Head, Ireland
108 J 7 Erzincan, Turkey
108 K 7 Erzurum, Turkey
130 H 5 Esan-misaki, Japan
69 B 14 Esbjerg, Denmark
78 F 4 Escanaba, MI, United States
123 K 4 Escarpada Point, Philippines
49 E 10 Escaut, Belgium
49 I 15 Esch-sur-Alzette, Luxembourg
85 F 15 Escondido, CA, United States
88 H 7 Escuinapa, Mexico
90 D 6 Escuintla, Guatemala
115 L 3 Eşfahān, Iran
69 F 12 Eskilstuna, Sweden
108 E 7 Eskişehir, Turkey
96 D 4 Esmeraldas, Ecuador
146 F 9 Esperance, WA, Australia
33 I 2 Esperanza, Argentina
88 G 4 Esperanza, Mexico
150 H 9 Espiritu Santo, Vanuatu
69 I 11 Espoo, Finland
99 E 12 Esquel, Argentina
41 K 2 Estella, Spain
65 I 1 Estonia, Europe
40 F 7 Estremoz, Portugal
118 E 8 Etawah, India
137 M 6 Ethiopia, Africa
137 M 6 Ethiopian Highlands, Ethiopia
49 I 14 Ettelbruck, Luxembourg
151 J 10 Eua, Tonga
146 G 8 Eucla, WA, Australia
80 H 5 Eufaula, AL, United States
83 H 11 Eufaula Lake, OK, United States
84 D 8 Eugene, OR, United States
23 J 4 Euphrates, Asia
82 A 5 Eureka, MT, United States
85 B 10 Eureka, CA, United States
48 E 8 Europoort, Netherlands
52 B 8 Euskirchen, Germany
78 F 7 Evanston, IL, United States
82 B 8 Evanston, WY, United States
78 F 10 Evansville, IL, United States
141 I 9 Evaton, South Africa
84 D 5 Everett, WA, United States
81 K 10 Everglades, FL, United States
69 B 12 Evje, Norway
40 F 7 Évora, Portugal
44 H 3 Évreux, France
37 F 14 Exe, United Kingdom
37 F 14 Exeter, United Kingdom
37 F 14 Exmoor, United Kingdom
146 D 6 Exmouth, WA, Australia
31 K 5 Exmouth Plateau, Southern Ocean
91 I 2 Exuma Cays, The Bahamas
147 I 9 Eyre Peninsula, SA, Australia

F

119 B 14 Faadhippolhu Atoll, Maldives
56 E 7 Faenza, Italy
60 H 6 Făgăraş, Romania
40 B 9 Faial, Portugal
36 H 4 Fair Isle, United Kingdom
84 J 5 Fairbanks, AK, United States
150 C 9 Fairlie, New Zealand
111 L 9 Faisalabad, Pakistan
118 F 8 Faizabad, India
36 F 8 Falkirk, United Kingdom
29 E 10 Falkland Escarpment, Atlantic Ocean
99 H 15 Falkland Islands, United Kingdom
29 E 10 Falkland Plateau, Atlantic Ocean
85 E 11 Fallon, NV, United States
119 H 11 False Point, India
69 D 15 Falster, Denmark
60 I 5 Fălticeni, Romania
69 F 11 Falun, Sweden
56 F 7 Fano, Italy
33 I 2 Faraday, United Kingdom
141 J 2 Faradje, Democratic Republic of Congo
111 J 8 Farāh, Afghanistan
151 K 1 Faraulep, Federated States of Micronesia
150 E 6 Farewell Spit, New Zealand
82 G 6 Fargo, ND, United States
118 D 8 Faridabad, India
83 C 10 Farmington, NM, United States
40 F 9 Faro, Portugal
32 D 10 Faroe Islands, Denmark
28 H 2 Faroe-Shetland Trough, Atlantic Ocean
30 F 4 Farquhar Islands, Indian Ocean
33 J 4 Farwell Island, Antarctica
115 L 5 Fasā, Iran
65 K 8 Fastiv, Ukraine
118 E 8 Fatehgarh, India
68 F 6 Fauske, Norway
137 J 5 Faya, Chad
81 L 2 Fayetteville, NC, United States
151 L 1 Fayu, Federated States of Micronesia
44 H 2 Fécamp, France
151 M 1 Federated States of Micronesia, Pacific Ocean
52 F 4 Fehmarn, Germany
52 F 4 Fehmarn Belt, Denmark/Germany
97 L 6 Feira de Santana, Brazil
41 O 6 Felanitx, Spain
53 E 12 Feldkirch, Austria
119 B 14 Felidhu Atoll, Maldives
89 P 8 Felipe Carrillo Puerto, Mexico
108 J 6 Fener Burnu, Turkey
111 L 6 Fergana, Uzbekistan
82 G 6 Fergus Falls, MN, United States
28 G 7 Fernando de Noronha, Atlantic Ocean
85 E 11 Fernley, NV, United States
56 E 6 Ferrara, Italy
40 F 1 Ferrol, Spain
136 F 1 Fès, Morocco
111 L 7 Feyzābād, Afghanistan
141 M 8 Fianarantsoa, Madagascar
61 D 10 Fier, Albania
45 I 9 Figeac, France
40 E 5 Figueira da Foz, Portugal
41 O 3 Figueras, Spain
151 I 10 Fiji, Pacific Ocean
98 H 7 Filadelfia, Paraguay
78 H 8 Findlay, OH, United States
79 K 6 Finger Lakes, NY, United States
69 I 10 Finland, Europe
150 B 10 Fiordland, New Zealand
118 E 8 Firozabad, India
37 E 9 Firth of Clyde, United Kingdom
36 G 8 Firth of Forth, United Kingdom
36 D 8 Firth of Lorn, United Kingdom
31 N 11 Fisher Bay, Antarctica
146 F 5 Fitzroy, WA, Australia
146 F 5 Fitzroy Crossing, WA, Australia
85 I 14 Flagstaff, AZ, United States
82 C 8 Flaming Gorge Reservoir, WY, United States
49 C 11 Flanders, Belgium
82 A 5 Flathead Lake, MT, United States
28 F 3 Flemish Cap, Atlantic Ocean
52 E 4 Flensburg, Germany
33 J 4 Fletcher Peninsula, Antarctica
74 G 8 Flin Flon, MB, Canada
147 J 5 Flinders, QLD, Australia
147 K 10 Flinders Island, TAS, Australia
147 I 8 Flinders Ranges, SA, Australia
78 H 6 Flint, MI, United States
56 E 7 Florence, Italy
80 G 3 Florence, AL, United States
81 L 3 Florence, SC, United States
96 E 4 Florencia, Colombia
40 A 9 Flores, Portugal
90 E 5 Flores, Guatemala
123 J 10 Flores, Indonesia
123 K 10 Flores Sea, Indonesia
97 J 10 Florianópolis, Brazil
99 I 10 Florida, Uruguay
81 K 9 Florida, United States
81 K 11 Florida Bay, FL, United States
81 K 11 Florida Keys, FL, United States
147 J 2 Fly, Papua New Guinea
60 I 6 Focşani, Romania
57 I 10 Foggia, Italy
28 B 8 Fogo, Cape Verde
45 I 11 Foix, France
61 H 14 Folegandros, Greece
56 F 8 Foligno, Italy
37 J 14 Folkestone, United Kingdom
78 F 6 Fond du Luc, WI, United States
45 I 4 Fontainebleau, France
56 E 7 Forlì, Italy
41 N 7 Formentera, Spain
98 I 8 Formosa, Argentina
85 C 11 Fort Bragg, CA, United States
82 D 8 Fort Collins, CO, United States
82 H 7 Fort Dodge, IA, United States
74 H 10 Fort Frances, ON, Canada
74 E 5 Fort Good Hope, NT, Canada
81 L 10 Fort Lauderdale, FL, United States
74 E 7 Fort Liard, NT, Canada
74 F 8 Fort McMurray, AB, Canada
81 K 9 Fort Myers, FL, United States
74 E 7 Fort Nelson, BC, Canada
82 D 5 Fort Peck Reservoir, MT, United States
81 L 9 Fort Pierce, FL, United States
74 E 7 Fort Providence, NT, Canada
83 H 9 Fort Scott, KS, United States
75 I 8 Fort Severn, ON, Canada
83 H 11 Fort Smith, AR, United States
74 E 8 Fort St John, BC, Canada
83 E 13 Fort Stockton, TX, United States
80 G 6 Fort Walton Beach, FL, United States
78 G 8 Fort Wayne, IN, United States
36 E 7 Fort William, United Kingdom
83 G 12 Fort Worth, TX, United States
97 L 5 Fortaleza, Brazil
91 O 6 Fort-de-France, Martinique
36 F 8 Forth, United Kingdom
127 M 10 Foshan, China
28 F 6 Four North Fracture Zone, Atlantic Ocean
150 B 11 Foveaux Strait, New Zealand
150 C 8 Fox Glacier, New Zealand
75 I 5 Foxe Basin, NU, Canada
75 I 5 Foxe Peninsula, NU, Canada
97 J 9 Foz do Iguaçu, Brazil
41 M 4 Fraga, Spain
32 D 7 Fram Basin, Arctic Ocean
97 J 8 Franca, Brazil
44 G 7 France, Europe
140 F 3 Franceville, Gabon
141 I 8 Francistown, Botswana
78 G 10 Frankfort, KY, United States
53 D 9 Frankfurt am Main, Germany
52 I 6 Frankfurt an der Oder, Germany
84 F 5 Franklin D. Roosevelt Lake, WA, United States
150 C 8 Franz Josef Glacier, New Zealand
104 G 2 Franz Josef Land, Russia
74 D 8 Fraser, Canada
147 L 7 Fraser Island, QLD, Australia
79 K 10 Fredericksburg, VI, United States
75 L 9 Fredericton, NB, Canada
69 C 13 Frederikshavn, Denmark
83 H 13 Freeport, TX, United States
91 I 1 Freeport, The Bahamas
136 D 6 Freetown, Sierra Leone
53 C 11 Freiburg im Breisgau, Germany
146 E 9 Fremantle, WA, Australia
97 I 3 French Guiana, France
151 N 10 French Polynesia, France
89 J 7 Fresnillo, Mexico
85 E 13 Fresno, CA, United States
98 G 8 Frías, Argentina
53 B 13 Fribourg, Switzerland
53 E 12 Friedrichshafen, Germany
68 C 8 Frohavet, Norway
89 N 9 Frontera, Mexico
68 C 8 Frøya, Norway
64 F 8 Frýdek- Mistek, Czech Republic
41 I 10 Fuengirola, Spain
40 C 11 Fuerteventura, Spain
131 H 11 Fuji, Japan
131 F 10 Fukui, Japan
131 B 13 Fukuoka, Japan
130 H 8 Fukushima, Japan
52 E 8 Fulda, Germany
52 E 8 Fulda, Germany
131 I 10 Funabashi, Japan
151 I 8 Funafuti, Tuvalu
40 D 9 Funchal, Portugal
53 F 10 Fürth, Germany
127 N 4 Fushun, China
151 J 9 Futuna, Wallis and Futuna Islands
127 N 4 Fuxin, China
127 N 9 Fuzhou, China
69 C 14 Fyn, Denmark

G

137 O 6 Gaalkacyo, Somalia
137 I 2 Gabès, Tunisia
140 E 3 Gabon, Africa
141 I 9 Gaborone, Botswana
61 H 8 Gabrovo, Bulgaria
119 C 12 Gadag, India
80 H 3 Gadsden, AL, United States
151 K 1 Gaferut, Federated States of Micronesia
136 H 2 Gafsa, Tunisia
136 F 7 Gagnoa, Côte d'Ivoire
45 I 9 Gaillac, France
81 I 3 Gainesville, GA, United States
81 J 7 Gainesville, FL, United States
83 G 11 Gainesville, TX, United States
27 I 6 Galapagos Fracture Zone, Pacific Ocean
96 C 6 Galapagos Islands, Ecuador
27 L 7 Galapagos Rise, Pacific Ocean
60 J 7 Galaţi, Romania
69 C 10 Galdhøpiggen, Norway
78 E 8 Galesburg, IL, United States
28 H 4 Galicia Bank, Atlantic Ocean
119 E 16 Galle, Sri Lanka
27 K 6 Gallego Rise, Pacific Ocean,
99 F 15 Gallegos, Argentina
57 K 11 Gallipoli, Italy
108 B 6 Gallipoli Peninsula, Turkey
68 G 6 Gällivare, Sweden
83 C 10 Gallup, NM, United States
83 I 13 Galveston, TX, United States
37 B 11 Galway, Ireland
37 B 11 Galway Bay, Ireland
137 L 7 Gambēla, Ethiopia
136 D 5 Gambia, Africa
136 E 5 Gambia, Gambia/Senegal
28 H 6 Gambia Abyssal Plain, Atlantic Ocean
151 N 10 Gambier Islands, French Polynesia
140 G 3 Gamboma, Congo
109 N 6 Gäncä, Azerbaijan
75 M 7 Gander, NL, Canada
119 B 9 Gandhidham, India
119 C 9 Gandhinagar, India
41 M 7 Gandía, Spain
118 C 7 Ganganagar, India
126 F 7 Gangdise Shan, China
23 L 5 Ganges, Asia
31 I 2 Ganges Cone, Indian Ocean
31 I 1 Ganges Fan, Indian Ocean
82 C 7 Gannett Peak, WY, United States
127 M 9 Ganzhou, China
136 G 5 Gao, Mali
45 L 9 Gap, France
126 F 7 Gar, China
137 N 7 Garbahaarey, Somalia
83 F 9 Garden City, KS, United States
111 K 8 Gardēz, Afghanistan
141 L 3 Garissa, Kenya
83 H 12 Garland, TX, United States
44 G 8 Garonne, France
137 O 6 Garoowe, Somalia
137 I 6 Garoua, Cameroon
122 H 10 Garut, Indonesia
78 F 7 Gary, IN, United States
44 G 9 Gascony, France
146 D 7 Gascoyne, WA, Australia
75 L 8 Gaspé, QC, Canada
81 K 2 Gastonia, NC, United States
61 H 15 Gavdos, Greece
69 F 11 Gävle, Sweden
147 I 9 Gawler, SA, Australia
119 G 9 Gaya, India
114 G 4 Gaza, Israel
109 I 9 Gaziantep, Turkey
64 G 4 Gdańsk, Poland
64 G 4 Gdynia, Poland
108 D 6 Gebze, Turkey
49 G 10 Geel, Belgium
147 J 10 Geelong, VIC, Australia
69 C 11 Geilo, Norway
127 J 10 Gejiu, China
57 G 15 Gela, Italy
49 H 11 Geleen, Luxembourg
49 F 12 Gembloux, Belgium
140 G 2 Gemena, Democratic Republic of Congo
56 F 5 Gemona del Friuli, Italy
99 F 10 General Alvear, Argentina
99 G 10 General Pico, Argentina
99 F 11 General Roca, Argentina
123 K 6 General Santos, Philippines
53 B 14 Geneva, Switzerland
49 H 11 Genk, Belgium
56 C 7 Genoa, Italy
75 K 6 George, Canada
90 H 4 George Town, Cayman Islands
52 F 7 George Town, Malaysia
33 N 7 George V Land, Antarctica
33 J 3 George VI Sound, Antarctica
97 I 2 Georgetown, Guyana
81 I 4 Georgia, United States
109 M 5 Georgia, Asia
111 M 3 Georgiyevka, Kazakhstan
52 G 8 Gera, Germany
146 D 8 Geraldton, WA, Australia
108 F 6 Gerede, Turkey
64 G 8 Gerlachovský štít, Slovakia
52 F 7 Germany, Europe
108 G 5 Gerze, Turkey
41 J 5 Getafe, Spain
136 H 2 Ghadāmis, Algeria
118 F 8 Ghaghara, India
136 F 7 Ghana, Africa
136 H 2 Ghardaïa, Algeria
137 I 3 Ghāt, Libya
118 D 8 Ghaziabad, India
111 K 8 Ghaznī, Afghanistan
49 D 11 Ghent, Belgium
115 M 9 Ghubbat al Qamar, Oman/Yemen
37 D 9 Giant's Causeway, United Kingdom
40 H 10 Gibraltar, United Kingdom
146 F 7 Gibson Desert, WA, Australia
52 D 8 Giessen, Germany
131 F 11 Gifu, Japan
40 H 1 Gijón, Spain
151 I 7 Gilbert Islands, Kiribati
137 K 4 Gilf Kebir Plateau, Egypt
111 L 7 Gilgit, Pakistan

Bay · Channel · Country · Dependent Territory · Desert · Geographic Area · Headland · Island · Island Group · Lake · Mountain

▲▲ Mountain Range   **■** National Capital   🦢 Ocean   ◇ Physical Feature   ▬ Polar Base   🦢 River   ≈ Sea   ✷ Special Feature   🖰 State Capital   🔲 Underwater Feature

74 E 7 **Hay River**, NT, Canada
83 F 9 **Hays**, KS, United States
85 C 12 **Hayward**, CA, United States
30 H 9 **Heard Island**, Australia 🌴
48 I 5 **Heerenveen**, Netherlands
48 F 6 **Heerhugowaard**, Netherlands
49 I 11 **Heerlen**, Luxembourg
127 M 7 **Hefei**, China
127 O 2 **Hegang**, China
52 D 4 **Heide**, Germany
53 D 10 **Heidelberg**, Germany
127 N 2 **Heihe**, China
53 D 10 **Heilbronn**, Germany
23 M 3 **Heilong Jiang**, Asia 〰
49 F 11 **Heist-op-den-Berg**, Belgium
82 B 6 **Helena**, MT, United States ⌂
150 E 3 **Helensville**, New Zealand
52 C 4 **Helgoläner Bay**, Germany ≈
41 K 7 **Hellín**, Spain
84 G 8 **Hell's Canyon**, ID/OR, United States ◇
111 I 9 **Helmand**, Afghanistan/Iran 〰
49 H 10 **Helmond**, Netherlands
69 D 14 **Helsingborg**, Sweden
69 J 11 **Helsinki**, Finland 🏛
130 G 6 **Henashi-zaki**, Japan ◗
81 M 1 **Henderson**, NC, United States
78 F 10 **Henderson**, KY, United States
83 H 12 **Henderson**, TX, United States
151 P 11 **Henderson Island**, Pitcairn Islands 🌴
127 I 8 **Hengduan Shan**, China ⛰
48 J 7 **Hengelo**, Netherlands
127 L 9 **Hengyang**, China
122 E 4 **Henzada**, Myanmar
111 J 8 **Herāt**, Afghanistan
83 E 11 **Hereford**, TX, United States
84 E 7 **Hermiston**, OR, United States
88 G 4 **Hermosillo**, Mexico
52 C 7 **Herne**, Germany
40 H 6 **Herrera del Duque**, Spain
81 L 10 **Hialeah**, FL, United States
89 I 5 **Hidalgo del Parral**, Mexico
131 F 11 **Higashi-ōsaka**, Japan
131 A 13 **Higashi-suidō**, Japan ⧗
81 L 2 **High Point**, NC, United States
64 H 1 **Hiiumaa**, Estonia 🌴
52 E 7 **Hildesheim**, Germany
85 C 15 **Hilo**, HI, United States
48 G 7 **Hilversum**, Netherlands
23 K 4 **Himalayas**, Asia ⛰
131 E 11 **Himeji**, Japan
114 H 3 **Ḥimṣ**, Syria
91 K 4 **Hinche**, Haiti
147 K 5 **Hinchinbrook Island**, QLD, Australia 🌴
23 K 4 **Hindu Kush**, Asia ⛰
119 D 13 **Hindupur**, India
119 F 10 **Hirakud Reservoir**, India ∿
130 H 6 **Hirosaki**, Japan
131 C 12 **Hiroshima**, Japan
45 J 2 **Hirson**, France
118 D 7 **Hisar**, India
91 K 4 **Hispaniola**, Caribbean Sea 🌴
131 I 9 **Hitachi**, Japan
119 A 16 **Hitaddu**, Maldives
69 C 9 **Hitra**, Norway 🌴
151 O 9 **Hiva Oa**, French Polynesia 🌴
69 F 12 **Hjälmaren**, Sweden ∿
69 C 13 **Hjørring**, Denmark
122 F 1 **Hkakabo Razi**, Myanmar ▲
122 H 5 **Hô Chi Minh**, Vietnam
147 K 11 **Hobart**, TAS, Australia ⌂
83 E 12 **Hobbs**, NM, United States
69 C 13 **Hobro**, Denmark
64 G 10 **Hódmezővásarhely**, Hungary
53 G 9 **Hof**, Germany
68 C 6 **Hofsjökull**, Iceland ◇
131 C 12 **Hōfu**, Japan
22 H 5 **Hoggar**, Africa ◇
127 L 5 **Hohhot**, China
150 D 8 **Hokitika**, New Zealand
130 H 3 **Hokkaidō**, Japa 🌴
85 J 14 **Holbrook**, AZ, United States
91 I 3 **Holguín**, Cuba
81 L 10 **Hollywood**, FL, United States
69 B 14 **Holstebro**, Denmark
37 E 11 **Holyhead**, United Kingdom
65 K 6 **Homyel'**, Belarus
90 F 6 **Honduras**, North America ◻
69 C 11 **Hønefoss**, Norway
85 E 10 **Honey Lake**, CA, United States ∿
122 H 3 **Hông Gai**, Vietnam
127 M 10 **Hong Kong**, China
127 K 9 **Hongshui He**, China 〰
127 M 7 **Hongze Hu**, China ∿
150 G 9 **Honiara**, Solomon Islands 🏛
85 C 16 **Honokohau**, HI, United States
85 B 15 **Honolulu**, HI, United States ⌂
131 F 10 **Honshū**, Japan 🌴
48 J 6 **Hoogeveen**, Netherlands
48 F 6 **Hoorn**, Netherlands
108 K 6 **Hopa**, Turkey
78 F 10 **Hopkinsville**, KY, United States
65 I 9 **Hora Hoverla**, Ukraine ▲
26 G 7 **Horizon Deep**, Pacific Ocean ▰
33 L 4 **Horlick Mountains**, Antarctica ⛰
65 O 8 **Horlivka**, Ukraine
23 J 5 **Horn of Africa**, Africa ◗
130 I 4 **Horoshiri-dake**, Japan ▲
69 C 14 **Horsens**, Denmark
147 J 10 **Horsham**, VIC, Australia
49 I 10 **Horst**, Netherlands
40 B 9 **Horta**, Portugal
74 E 5 **Horton**, Canada 〰
118 D 7 **Hoshiarpur**, India
49 I 14 **Hosingen**, Luxembourg
119 D 12 **Hospet**, India
83 I 11 **Hot Springs**, AR, United States
126 F 5 **Hotan**, China
68 F 8 **Hoting**, Sweden
28 F 8 **Hotspur Seamount**, Atlantic Ocean ▰
78 F 3 **Houghton**, MI, United States
78 G 5 **Houghton Lake**, MI, United States ∿
79 O 4 **Houlton**, ME, United States
83 J 13 **Houma**, LA, United States
83 H 13 **Houston**, TX, United States
126 H 3 **Hovd**, Mongolia
127 J 2 **Hövsgöl Nuur**, Mongolia ∿
26 G 5 **Howland Island**, Pacific Ocean 🌴
36 F 5 **Hoy**, United Kingdom 🌴
52 H 7 **Hoyerswerda**, Germany
69 K 9 **Höytiäinen**, Finland ∿
64 E 7 **Hradec Králové**, Czech Republic
109 M 6 **Hrazdan**, Armenia
65 I 5 **Hrodna**, Belarus
127 N 9 **Hsinchu**, Taiwan
96 E 6 **Huacho**, Peru
127 L 5 **Huai'an**, China
127 M 7 **Huainan**, China
127 N 7 **Huaiyin**, China
89 L 9 **Huajuápan de León**, Mexico
127 O 9 **Hualien**, Taiwan
96 E 5 **Huallaga**, Peru 〰
140 G 6 **Huambo**, Angola
96 E 6 **Huancayo**, Peru
127 M 8 **Huangshi**, China
98 F 5 **Huanuni**, Bolivia
88 G 5 **Huatabampo**, Mexico
119 C 12 **Hubli**, India
37 H 11 **Huddersfield**, United Kingdom
79 L 7 **Hudson**, United States 〰
75 I 7 **Hudson Bay**, NU, Canada ≈
75 J 6 **Hudson Strait**, NU, Canada ⧗
122 H 4 **Huê**, Vietnam
90 D 5 **Huehuetenango**, Guatemala
89 L 9 **Huejotzingo**, Mexico
40 G 9 **Huelva**, Spain
41 L 3 **Huesca**, Spain
41 K 8 **Huéscar**, Spain
147 J 6 **Hughenden**, QLD, Australia
83 H 11 **Hugo**, OK, United States
140 G 7 **Huila Plateau**, Angola ◇
89 N 11 **Huixtla**, Mexico
127 M 3 **Hulun Nur**, China ∿
37 I 11 **Humber**, United Kingdom 〰
85 I 13 **Humphreys Peak**, AZ, United States ▲
60 G 6 **Hunedoara**, Romania
64 F 10 **Hungary**, Europe ◻
85 F 15 **Huntington Beach**, CA, United States
80 H 3 **Huntsville**, AL, United States
83 H 12 **Huntsville**, TX, United States
137 L 3 **Hurghada**, Egypt
82 G 7 **Huron**, SD, United States
83 G 9 **Hutchinson**, KS, United States
127 N 8 **Huzhou**, China
68 C 6 **Hvannadalshnúkur**, Iceland ▲
61 C 8 **Hvar**, Croatia 🌴
141 I 7 **Hwange**, Zimbabwe
127 I 2 **Hyargus Nuur**, Mongolia ∿
119 E 12 **Hyderabad**, India
111 K 11 **Hyderabad**, Pakistan
45 L 10 **Hyères**, France
127 O 4 **Hyesan**, North Korea

I

60 I 5 **Iași**, Romania
136 G 7 **Ibadan**, Nigeria
96 E 3 **Ibagué**, Colombia
96 E 4 **Ibarra**, Ecuador
98 H 7 **Ibarreta**, Argentina
115 J 10 **Ibb**, Yemen
22 H 4 **Iberian Peninsula**, Europe ◗
41 N 6 **Ibiza**, Spain 🌴
115 M 7 **Ibrī**, Oman
96 E 7 **Ica**, Peru
96 G 4 **Içá**, Brazil/Columbia 〰
96 G 4 **Içana**, Brazil 〰
68 C 5 **Iceland**, Europe ◻
28 G 3 **Iceland Basin**, Atlantic Ocean ▰
32 D 9 **Icelandic Plateau**, Arctic Ocean ⁙
119 C 12 **Ichalkaranji**, India
131 I 10 **Ichihara**, Japan
83 H 11 **Idabel**, OK, United States
84 G 8 **Idaho**, United States ▣
84 I 8 **Idaho Falls**, ID, United States
137 I 3 **Idhān Murzūq**, Libya ◓
114 H 2 **Idlib**, Syria
131 J 16 **Ie-jima**, Japan 🌴
151 K 1 **Ifalik**, Federated States of Micronesia 🌴
57 B 12 **Iglesias**, Italy
74 H 5 **Igloolik**, NU, Canada
108 C 5 **Iğneada Burnu**, Turkey ◗
61 E 11 **Igoumenitsa**, Greece
97 I 8 **Iguaçu Falls**, Argentina/Brazil 〰
89 K 9 **Iguala**, Mexico
97 L 5 **Iguatu**, Brazil
119 A 13 **Ihavandhippolhu Atoll**, Maldives 🌴
131 J 15 **Iheya-jima**, Japan 🌴
68 I 7 **Iijoki**, Finland 〰
69 J 9 **Iisalmi**, Finland
48 I 6 **IJssel**, Netherlands 〰
48 G 6 **IJsselmeer**, Netherlands ≈
49 B 10 **IJzer**, Belgium 〰
74 E 4 **Ikaahuk**, NT, Canada
61 I 13 **Ikaria**, Greece 🌴
140 H 3 **Ikela**, Democratic Republic of Congo
131 A 13 **Iki**, Japan 🌴
131 A 13 **Iki-suidō**, Japan ⧗
111 L 4 **Ile**, Kazakhstan 〰
44 F 7 **Île de Ré**, France 🌴
75 L 8 **Île d'Anticosti**, QC, Canada 🌴
44 G 7 **Île d'Oléron**, France 🌴
44 F 6 **Île d'Yeu**, France 🌴
141 L 8 **Île Europa**, France ▣
30 F 5 **Île Tromelin**, France 🌴
45 L 10 **Îles de Hyères**, France 🌴
141 M 6 **Îles Glorieuses**, Seychelles ▣
151 M 9 **Iles Sous le Vent**, French Polynesia 🏝
40 C 9 **Ilha da Madeira**, Portugal 🌴
28 G 8 **Ilha da Trindade**, Atlantic Ocean 🌴
97 J 4 **Ilha de Marajó**, Brazil 🌴
40 D 8 **Ilha de Porto Santo**, Portugal 🌴
40 D 9 **Ilhas Desertas**, Portugal 🏝
28 G 8 **Ilhas Martin Vaz**, Atlantic Ocean 🌴
97 L 7 **Ilhéus**, Brazil
123 K 6 **Iligan**, Philippines
109 K 9 **Ilisu Baraji**, Turkey ∿
78 E 8 **Illinois**, United States ▣
78 E 8 **Illinois**, IL, United States 〰
123 K 5 **Iloilo**, Philippines
136 G 6 **Ilorin**, Nigeria
32 C 8 **Ilulissat**, Greenland
69 J 10 **Imatra**, Finland
56 E 7 **Imola**, Italy
97 K 5 **Imperatriz**, Brazil
56 B 7 **Imperia**, Italy
119 J 9 **Imphal**, India
68 I 5 **Inarijärvi**, Finland ∿
130 H 8 **Inawashiro-ko**, Japan ∿
108 G 5 **Ince Burnu**, Turkey ◗
109 G 10 **Incekum Burnu**, Turkey ◗
127 O 5 **Inch'ŏn**, South Korea
83 H 9 **Independence**, MO, United States
119 C 9 **India**, Asia ◻
30 H 6 **Indian Ocean** 🌊
78 F 8 **Indiana**, United States ▣
31 K 10 **Indian-Antarctic Basin**, Southern Ocean ▰
31 L 9 **Indian-Antarctic Ridge**, Southern Ocean ▰
78 G 9 **Indianapolis**, IN, United States ⌂
105 L 5 **Indigirka**, Russia 〰
85 G 15 **Indio**, CA, United States
122 G 9 **Indonesia**, Asia ◻
119 D 10 **Indore**, India
23 K 4 **Indus**, Asia 〰
108 G 5 **Inebolu**, Turkey
99 F 12 **Ingeniero Jacobacci**, Argentina
53 F 11 **Ingolstadt**, Germany
141 K 9 **Inhambane**, Mozambique
122 F 3 **Inlay Lake**, Myanmar ∿
53 G 11 **Inn**, Germany 〰
37 D 9 **Inner Hebrides**, United Kingdom 🏝
127 L 4 **Inner Mongolia**, China ▣
147 K 5 **Innisfail**, QLD, Australia
53 F 12 **Innsbruck**, Austria
82 H 5 **International Falls**, MN, United States
131 I 10 **Inubō-zaki**, Japan ◗
75 J 7 **Inukjuak**, QC, Canada
74 D 5 **Inuvik**, NT, Canada
150 B 11 **Invercargill**, New Zealand
36 F 7 **Inverness**, United Kingdom
31 J 4 **Investigator Ridge**, Indian Ocean ▰
141 J 7 **Inyangani**, Zimbabwe ▲
61 E 11 **Ioannina**, Greece
61 E 12 **Ionian Islands**, Greece 🏝
61 D 12 **Ionian Sea**, Greece/Italy ◒
61 H 13 **Ios**, Greece 🌴
82 H 8 **Iowa**, United States ▣
82 I 8 **Iowa City**, IA, United States
97 K 8 **Ipatinga**, Brazil
52 F 7 **Ipoh**, Malaysia
37 J 13 **Ipswich**, United Kingdom
75 J 5 **Iqaluit**, NU, Canada ⌂
98 E 6 **Iquique**, Chile
96 F 5 **Iquitos**, Peru
61 H 14 **Irakleiou**, Greece
115 L 3 **Iran**, Asia ◻
115 M 4 **Iranian Plateau**, Iran ◇
115 N 5 **Īrānshahr**, Iran
89 J 8 **Irapuato**, Mexico
115 I 3 **Iraq**, Asia ◻
114 H 3 **Irbid**, Jordan
37 C 11 **Ireland**, Europe ◻
123 O 9 **Irian Jaya**, Indonesia ⁙
141 K 5 **Iringa**, Tanzania
97 I 5 **Iriri**, Brazil 〰
37 E 11 **Irish Sea**, Ireland/United Kingdom ◒
105 I 10 **Irkutsk**, Russia
28 F 3 **Irminger Basin**, Atlantic Ocean ▰
78 E 4 **Ironwood**, MI, United States
122 E 3 **Irrawaddy**, Myanmar 〰
23 K 3 **Irtysh**, Asia 〰
83 G 12 **Irving**, TX, United States
131 G 11 **Ise**, Japan
26 H 11 **Iselin Seamount**, Pacific Ocean ▰
57 G 10 **Isernia**, Italy
131 F 11 **Ise-wan**, Japan ≈
130 G 3 **Ishikari-wan**, Japan ≈
131 J 16 **Ishikawa**, Japan
130 I 7 **Ishinomaki**, Japan
131 D 13 **Ishizuchi-san**, Japan ▲
141 I 2 **Isiro**, Democratic Republic of Congo
109 H 10 **Iskenderun**, Turkey
109 G 10 **Iskenderun Körfezi**, Turkey ≈
61 G 8 **Iskur**, Bulgaria 〰
88 F 3 **Isla Ángel de la Guarda**, Mexico 🌴
88 E 4 **Isla Cedros**, Mexico 🌴
90 G 9 **Isla Coiba**, Panama 🌴
136 H 8 **Isla de Bioco**, Cameroon 🌴
99 E 12 **Isla de Chiloé**, Chile 🌴
90 G 3 **Isla de la Juventud**, Cuba 🌴
90 F 7 **Isla de Ometepe**, Nicaragua 🌴
90 H 8 **Isla del Rey**, Panama 🌴
96 B 8 **Isla Española**, Galapagos Islands 🌴
96 A 7 **Isla Fernandina**, Galapagos Islands 🌴
96 B 6 **Isla Genovesa**, Galapagos Islands 🌴
88 D 3 **Isla Guadalupe**, Mexico 🌴
96 B 7 **Isla Isabela**, Galapagos Islands 🌴
96 B 6 **Isla Marchena**, Galapagos Islands 🌴
96 B 6 **Isla Pinta**, Galapagos Islands 🌴
27 M 7 **Isla San Ambrosio**, Pacific Ocean 🌴
96 C 7 **Isla San Cristóbal**, Galapagos Islands 🌴
27 M 7 **Isla San Felix**, Pacific Ocean 🌴
96 A 6 **Isla San Salvador**, Galapagos Islands 🌴
96 B 7 **Isla Santa Cruz**, Galapagos Islands 🌴
96 B 7 **Isla Santa Fé**, Galapagos Islands 🌴
88 F 6 **Isla Santa Margarita**, Mexico 🌴
96 B 7 **Isla Santa Maria**, Galapagos Islands 🌴
88 F 4 **Isla Tiburón**, Mexico 🌴
111 L 8 **Islamabad**, Pakistan 🏛
90 F 5 **Islas de la Bahía**, Honduras 🏝
90 G 7 **Islas del Maíz**, Nicaragua 🏝
88 H 7 **Islas Marías**, Mexico 🏝
36 D 8 **Islay**, United Kingdom 🌴
36 D 5 **Isle of Lewis**, United Kingdom 🌴
37 F 10 **Isle of Man**, United Kingdom ▣
37 H 15 **Isle of Wight**, United Kingdom 🌴
78 F 3 **Isle Royale**, MI, United States 🌴
37 D 15 **Isles of Scilly**, United Kingdom 🏝
137 L 2 **Ismā'īlīya**, Egypt
57 B 10 **Isola Asinara**, Italy 🌴
57 E 15 **Isola di Pantelleria**, Italy 🌴
56 C 8 **Isola d'Capraia**, Italy 🌴
57 D 9 **Isola d'Elba**, Italy 🌴
57 G 11 **Isola d'Ischia**, Italy 🌴
57 H 13 **Isola Lipari**, Italy 🌴
57 H 13 **Isola Stromboli**, Italy 🌴
57 H 13 **Isola Vulcano**, Italy 🌴
57 E 14 **Isole Egadi**, Italy 🌴
57 F 11 **Isole Ponziane**, Italy 🌴
109 E 9 **Isparta**, Turkey
114 G 3 **Israel**, Asia ◻
108 D 6 **Istanbul**, Turkey ∿
122 F 6 **Isthmus of Kra**, Asia ◇
61 G 12 **Istiaia**, Greece
89 M 9 **Istmo de Tehuantepec**, Mexico ◇
61 A 7 **Istra**, Croatia ◗
97 L 7 **Itabuna**, Brazil
97 I 5 **Itaituba**, Brazil
56 E 8 **Italy**, Europe ◻
79 K 7 **Ithaca**, NY, United States
61 E 12 **Ithaki**, Greece
32 D 9 **Ittoqqortoormiit**, Greenland
68 I 5 **Ivalo**, Finland
147 J 9 **Ivanhoe**, NSW, Australia
65 I 8 **Ivano-Frankivs'k**, Ukraine
75 I 6 **Ivujivik**, QC, Canada
131 I 9 **Iwaki**, Japan
131 C 12 **Iwakuni**, Japan
130 H 6 **Iwate-san**, Japan ▲
131 J 15 **Izena-jima**, Japan 🌴
104 D 7 **Izhevsk**, Russia
108 C 8 **Izmir**, Turkey
108 B 7 **Izmir Körfezi**, Turkey ≈
26 E 3 **Izu Trench**, Pacific Ocean ▰
131 I 11 **Izu-shotō**, Japan 🏝

J

114 G 5 **Jabal al Lawz**, Saudi Arabia ▲
115 L 9 **Jabal al Qamar**, Oman ⛰
115 I 8 **Jabal Sawdā'**, Saudi Arabia ▲
115 J 10 **Jabal Taqar**, Yemen ▲
115 J 8 **Jabal Tuwayq**, Saudi Arabia ⛰
119 E 10 **Jabalpur**, India
151 N 4 **Jabwat**, Marshall Islands 🌴
41 L 2 **Jaca**, Spain
80 F 2 **Jackson**, TN, United States
80 E 5 **Jackson**, MS, United States ⌂
78 H 7 **Jackson**, MI, United States
82 B 7 **Jackson Lake**, WY, United States ∿
81 M 3 **Jacksonville**, NC, United States
81 K 6 **Jacksonville**, FL, United States
78 E 9 **Jacksonville**, IL, United States
41 I 8 **Jaén**, Spain
119 E 14 **Jaffna**, India
115 L 5 **Jahrom**, Iran
118 D 8 **Jaipur**, India
61 C 7 **Jajce**, Bosnia-Herzegovina
122 H 9 **Jakarta**, Indonesia 🏛
69 H 9 **Jakobstad**, Finland
111 L 6 **Jalal-Abad**, Kyrgyzstan
111 L 8 **Jalālābād**, Afghanistan
118 D 7 **Jalandhar**, India
119 C 10 **Jalgaon**, India
119 D 11 **Jalna**, India
151 N 4 **Jaluit**, Marshall Islands 🌴
137 N 8 **Jamaame**, Somalia
90 I 4 **Jamaica**, North America ◻

≈ Bay ⧗ Channel ◻ Country ▣ Dependent Territory ◓ Desert ⁙ Geographic Area ◗ Headland 🌴 Island 🏝 Island Group ∿ Lake ▲ Mountain

91	J 4	**Jamaica Channel**, Caribbean Sea ⧗
122	G 8	**Jambi**, Indonesia
82	G 6	**James**, ND, United States ∫
75	J 8	**James Bay**, ON, Canada ≈
33	I 2	**James Ross Island**, Antarctica 🏝
79	J 7	**Jamestown**, NY, United States
82	G 6	**Jamestown**, ND, United States
118	C 6	**Jammu**, India
118	D 6	**Jammu and Kashmir**, Asia ⁘
119	B 10	**Jamnagar**, India
119	G 10	**Jamshedpur**, India
32	D 9	**Jan Mayen**, Norway 🏝
78	E 6	**Janesville**, WI, United States
130	G 7	**Japan**, Asia ▣
26	E 3	**Japan Trench**, Pacific Ocean ◣
96	G 4	**Japurá**, Brazil/Columbia ∫
22	E 6	**Japurā**, South America ∫
97	J 4	**Jari**, Brazil ∫
26	H 5	**Jarvis Island**, Pacific Ocean 🏝
33	J 2	**Jason Peninsula**, Antarctica ▶
64	F 8	**Jastrzębie-Zdrój**, Poland
119	F 9	**Jaunpur**, India
122	G 10	**Java**, Indonesia 🏝
31	J 4	**Java Ridge**, Indian Ocean ◣
123	I 9	**Java Sea**, Indonesia ∿
31	K 5	**Java Trench**, Indian Ocean ◣
137	O 7	**Jawhar**, Somalia
123	O 8	**Jayapura**, Indonesia
123	M 8	**Jazirah Doberai**, Indonesia ▶
114	H 7	**Jeddah**, Saudi Arabia
83	I 9	**Jefferson City**, MO, United States ⌂
65	I 3	**Jēkabpils**, Latvia
64	E 7	**Jelenia Góra**, Poland
65	I 3	**Jelgava**, Latvia
123	I 10	**Jember**, Indonesia
52	F 8	**Jena**, Germany
91	J 4	**Jérémie**, Haiti
40	G 9	**Jerez de la Frontera**, Spain
114	G 4	**Jericho**, Israel
37	H 16	**Jersey**, United Kingdom 🏝
79	L 8	**Jersey City**, NJ, United States
114	G 4	**Jerusalem**, Israel ■
119	H 10	**Jessore**, Bangladesh
119	E 9	**Jhansi**, India
111	L 8	**Jhelum**, Pakistan
127	O 3	**Jiamusi**, China
127	M 9	**Ji'an**, China
127	M 10	**Jiangmen**, China
127	L 6	**Jiaozuo**, China
127	N 7	**Jiaxing**, China
115	M 8	**Jiddat al Ḩarāsīs**, Oman ▲
64	E 8	**Jihlava**, Czech Republic
127	O 4	**Jilin**, China
137	M 7	**Jīma**, Ethiopia
89	I 5	**Jiménez**, Mexico
127	M 6	**Jinan**, China
127	J 5	**Jinchang**, China
127	M 8	**Jingdezhen**, China
127	M 8	**Jingmen**, China
127	L 8	**Jingsha**, China
127	L 8	**Jingzhou**, China
127	N 8	**Jinhua**, China
127	L 5	**Jining**, China
127	M 6	**Jining**, China
141	K 3	**Jinja**, Uganda
90	F 7	**Jinotepe**, Nicaragua
127	N 5	**Jinzhou**, China
115	N 5	**Jīroft**, Iran
127	M 8	**Jiujiang**, China
127	O 3	**Jixi**, China
115	I 9	**Jīzān**, Saudi Arabia
97	M 5	**João Pessoa**, Brazil
118	C 8	**Jodhpur**, India
69	K 9	**Joensuu**, Finland
131	G 9	**Jōetsu**, Japan
141	I 9	**Johannesburg**, South Africa
36	G 5	**John o'Groats**, United Kingdom
81	J 1	**Johnson City**, TN, United States
26	H 4	**Johnston Atoll**, Pacific Ocean 🏝
52	G 7	**Johor Bahru**, Malaysia
97	J 9	**Joinville**, Brazil
33	I 2	**Joinville Island**, Antarctica 🏝
68	G 7	**Jokkmokk**, Sweden
78	F 7	**Joliet**, IL, United States
75	K 9	**Joliette**, QC, Canada
123	K 7	**Jolo**, Philippines 🏝
65	I 4	**Jonava**, Lithuania
83	J 10	**Jonesboro**, AR, United States
69	E 13	**Jönköping**, Sweden
75	K 9	**Jonquière**, QC, Canada
83	H 10	**Joplin**, MO, United States
114	H 4	**Jordan**, Asia ▣
136	H 6	**Jos**, Nigeria
146	G 4	**Joseph Bonaparte Gulf**, WA, Australia ≈
48	H 5	**Joure**, Netherlands
27	M 8	**Juan Fernandez Islands**, Pacific Ocean 🏝🏝
97	L 6	**Juàzeiro**, Brazil
97	L 5	**Juázeiro do Norte**, Brazil
137	L 7	**Juba**, Sudan
137	N 8	**Juba**, Somalia ∫
41	K 6	**Júcar**, Spain ∫
89	M 10	**Juchitán**, Mexico
90	F 7	**Juigalpa**, Nicaragua
97	K 8	**Juiz de Fora**, Brazil
68	G 6	**Jukkasjarvi**, Sweden
96	G 7	**Juliaca**, Peru
119	B 10	**Junagadh**, India
84	K 6	**Juneau**, AL, United States ⌂
99	H 10	**Junín**, Argentina
36	E 8	**Jura**, United Kingdom 🏝
53	B 12	**Jura**, France/Switzerland ⛰
65	I 3	**Jūrmala**, Latvia
96	G 5	**Juruá**, Brazil ∫
90	F 6	**Juticalpa**, Honduras
69	C 14	**Jutland**, Denmark ▶
69	I 10	**Jyväskylä**, Finland

K

126	E 5	**K2**, China/Pakistan ▲
68	I 5	**Kaamanen**, Finland
111	K 8	**Kabul**, Afghanistan ■
141	I 6	**Kabwe**, Zambia
141	J 7	**Kadoma**, Zimbabwe
136	H 6	**Kaduna**, Nigeria
136	E 5	**Kaédi**, Mauritania
137	I 6	**Kaélé**, Cameroon
127	O 5	**Kaesŏng**, North Korea
114	H 4	**Kāf**, Saudi Arabia
141	I 7	**Kafue**, Zambia
131	B 15	**Kagoshima**, Japan
85	C 15	**Kahoolawe**, HI, United States 🏝
109	H 9	**Kahramanmaraş**, Turkey
150	D 8	**Kaiapoi**, New Zealand
127	M 7	**Kaifeng**, China
150	E 7	**Kaikoura**, New Zealand
150	E 7	**Kaikoura Peninsula**, New Zealand ▶
127	K 9	**Kaili**, China
85	C 15	**Kailua**, HI, United States
33	N 4	**Kaiser Wilhelm II Land**, Antarctica ⁘
53	C 10	**Kaiserslautern**, Germany
150	C 11	**Kaitangata**, New Zealand
127	J 10	**Kaiyuan**, China
68	I 8	**Kajaani**, Finland
146	H 3	**Kakadu National Park**, NT, Australia ✱
65	M 9	**Kakhovs'ke Vodoskhovyshche**, Ukraine ∾
119	F 12	**Kakinada**, India
23	I 7	**Kalahari Desert**, Africa ▲
61	G 10	**Kalamaria**, Greece
61	F 13	**Kalamata**, Greece
78	G 7	**Kalamazoo**, MI, United States
108	F 7	**Kalecik**, Turkey
146	F 8	**Kalgoorlie**, WA, Australia
123	I 8	**Kalimantan**, Indonesia ⁘
64	G 4	**Kaliningrad**, Russia
64	H 4	**Kaliningrad**, Russia ▣
82	A 5	**Kalispell**, MT, United States
64	F 6	**Kalisz**, Poland
69	F 14	**Kalmar**, Sweden
104	C 6	**Kaluga**, Russia
61	I 13	**Kalymnos**, Greece
61	I 13	**Kalymnos**, Greece 🏝
131	H 10	**Kamakura**, Japan
105	O 8	**Kamchatka Peninsula**, Russia ▶
104	E 7	**Kamensk-Ural'skiy**, Russia
141	I 5	**Kamina**, Democratic Republic of Congo
74	D 9	**Kamloops**, BC, Canada
141	J 3	**Kampala**, Uganda ■
48	H 6	**Kampen**, Netherlands
122	G 5	**Kâmpóng Cham**, Cambodia
122	G 5	**Kâmpóng Saôm**, Cambodia
130	G 4	**Kamui-misaki**, Japan ▶
65	J 9	**Kam"yanets'- Podil's'kyy**, Ukraine
140	H 4	**Kananga**, Democratic Republic of Congo
131	F 10	**Kanazawa**, Japan
119	E 13	**Kanchipuram**, India
111	K 9	**Kandahār**, Afghanistan
104	D 4	**Kandalaksha**, Russia
119	E 15	**Kandy**, Sri Lanka
28	E 5	**Kane Fracture Zone**, Atlantic Ocean ◣
85	B 15	**Kaneohe**, HI, United States
147	I 9	**Kangaroo Island**, SA, Australia 🏝
75	J 4	**Kangeeak Point**, NU, Canada ▶
127	O 4	**Kanggye**, North Korea
78	F 8	**Kankakee**, IL, United States
136	E 6	**Kankan**, Guinea
136	H 6	**Kano**, Nigeria
118	E 8	**Kanpur**, India
83	F 9	**Kansas**, United States ▣
83	G 9	**Kansas**, KS, United States ∫
83	H 9	**Kansas City**, MO, United States
104	H 9	**Kansk**, Russia
151	K 8	**Kanton**, Kiribati 🏝
141	I 9	**Kanye**, Botswana
127	N 10	**Kaohsiung**, Taiwan
136	D 5	**Kaolack**, Senegal
52	H 4	**Kap Arkona**, Germany ▶
32	D 9	**Kap Brewster**, Greenland ▶
32	B 10	**Kap Farvel**, Greenland ▶
109	N 7	**Kapan**, Armenia
111	M 4	**Kapchagayskoye Vodokhranilishche**, Kazakhstan ∾
64	F 10	**Kaposvár**, Hungary
123	I 8	**Kapuas**, Indonesia ∫
75	J 9	**Kapuskasing**, ON, Canada
32	F 7	**Kara Sea**, Arctic Ocean ∿
111	L 5	**Kara-Balta**, Kyrgyzstan
108	F 6	**Karabük**, Turkey
111	I 3	**Karabutak**, Kazakhstan
111	K 11	**Karachi**, Pakistan
111	L 3	**Karaganda**, Kazakhstan
115	L 2	**Karaj**, Iran
111	M 5	**Karakol**, Kyrgyzstan
118	D 5	**Karakoram Range**, Asia ⛰
23	J 4	**Karakum Desert**, Asia ▲
109	F 9	**Karaman**, Turkey
126	G 3	**Karamay**, China
150	D 7	**Karamea Bight**, New Zealand ≈
115	J 3	**Karbalā'**, Iraq
61	F 11	**Karditsa**, Greece
119	B 14	**Kardiva Channel**, Maldives ⧗
61	H 10	**Kärdzhali**, Bulgaria
68	H 5	**Karesuando**, Finland
68	I 5	**Karigasniemi**, Finland
119	E 11	**Karimnagar**, India
147	K 1	**Karkar Island**, Papua New Guinea 🏝
61	B 6	**Karlovac**, Croatia
61	H 9	**Karlovo**, Bulgaria
64	D 7	**Karlovy Vary**, Czech Republic
69	E 12	**Karlskoga**, Sweden
69	E 14	**Karlskrona**, Sweden
53	D 10	**Karlsruhe**, Germany
69	E 12	**Karlstad**, Sweden
118	D 7	**Karnal**, India
61	J 14	**Karpathos**, Greece
61	J 14	**Karpathos**, Greece 🏝
61	F 12	**Karpenisi**, Greece
108	L 6	**Kars**, Turkey
111	J 6	**Karshi**, Uzbekistan
61	H 12	**Karystos**, Greece
109	D 10	**Kaş**, Turkey
23	I 6	**Kasai**, Africa ∫
141	J 5	**Kasama**, Zambia
141	J 3	**Kasese**, Uganda
115	L 3	**Kāshān**, Iran
126	E 4	**Kashi**, China
131	I 9	**Kashima-nada**, Japan ≈
61	J 14	**Kasos**, Greece 🏝
137	M 5	**Kassala**, Sudan
52	E 8	**Kassel**, Germany
108	G 6	**Kastamonu**, Turkey
61	F 11	**Kastoria**, Greece
131	G 11	**Kasugai**, Japan
131	I 9	**Kasumiga-ura**, Japan ∾
61	F 11	**Katerini**, Greece
146	H 4	**Katherine**, NT, Australia
119	B 10	**Kathiawar Peninsula**, India ▶
118	G 8	**Kathmandu**, Nepal ■
119	H 9	**Katihar**, India
64	F 7	**Katowice**, Poland
136	H 6	**Katsina**, Nigeria
111	K 6	**Kattakŭrgan**, Uzbekistan
69	D 13	**Kattegat**, Denmark ≈
85	B 14	**Kauai**, HI, United States 🏝
65	I 4	**Kaunas**, Lithuania
61	F 10	**Kavadarci**, Macedonia
61	H 10	**Kavala**, Greece
147	L 1	**Kavieng**, Papua New Guinea
131	H 10	**Kawasaki**, Japan
136	E 5	**Kayes**, Mali
108	G 8	**Kayseri**, Turkey
111	J 3	**Kazakhstan**, Asia ▣
104	D 7	**Kazan'**, Russia
61	H 9	**Kazanluk**, Bulgaria
109	L 4	**Kazbek**, Georgia ▲
61	H 13	**Kea**, Greece 🏝
82	F 8	**Kearney**, NE, United States
108	J 8	**Keban Baraji**, Turkey ∾
68	G 6	**Kebnekaise**, Sweden ▲
137	N 7	**K'ebrī Dehar**, Ethiopia
64	G 10	**Kecskemét**, Hungary
65	I 4	**Kėdainiai**, Lithuania
140	G 9	**Keetmanshoop**, Namibia
61	E 12	**Kefallonia**, Greece 🏝
68	B 6	**Keflavik**, Iceland
69	I 9	**Keitele**, Finland ∾
147	I 9	**Keith**, SA, Australia
131	J 14	**Kekeroma-jima**, Japan 🏝
64	G 9	**Kékes**, Hungary ▲
52	F 7	**Kelang**, Malaysia
108	I 7	**Kelkit**, Turkey ∫
74	E 9	**Kelowna**, BC, Canada
84	D 7	**Kelso**, WA, United States
108	I 7	**Kemah**, Turkey
104	H 9	**Kemerovo**, Russia
68	I 7	**Kemi**, Finland
68	I 6	**Kemijärvi**, Finland
68	I 6	**Kemijoki**, Finland ∫
33	O 2	**Kemp Land**, Antarctica ⁘
53	E 12	**Kempten**, Germany
81	L 10	**Kendall**, FL, United States
123	K 9	**Kendari**, Indonesia
111	I 5	**Keneurgench**, Turkmenistan
84	E 7	**Kennewick**, WA, United States
74	H 10	**Kenora**, ON, Canada
78	G 10	**Kentucky**, United States ▣
78	H 10	**Kentucky**, United States ∫
80	G 1	**Kentucky Lake**, TN, United States ∾
122	F 3	**Kentung**, Myanmar
141	K 2	**Kenya**, Africa ▣
123	N 9	**Kepulauan Aru**, Indonesia 🏝
123	K 8	**Kepulauan Banggai**, Indonesia 🏝
122	F 8	**Kepulauan Batu**, Indonesia 🏝
123	M 9	**Kepulauan Kai**, Indonesia 🏝
123	I 9	**Kepulauan Kangean**, Indonesia 🏝
122	G 8	**Kepulauan Lingga**, Indonesia 🏝
122	H 7	**Kepulauan Natuna**, Indonesia 🏝
123	L 7	**Kepulauan Talaud**, Indonesia 🏝
123	M 10	**Kepulauan Tanimbar**, Indonesia 🏝
123	K 8	**Kepulauan Togian**, Indonesia 🏝
123	L 9	**Kepulauan Tukangbesi**, Indonesia 🏝
61	G 13	**Keratea**, Greece
65	N 10	**Kerch**, Ukraine
108	F 5	**Kerempe Burnu**, Turkey ▶
30	G 8	**Kerguelen Islands**, France 🏝🏝
30	G 8	**Kerguelen Plateau**, Indian Ocean ◣
141	K 3	**Kericho**, Kenya
61	E 11	**Kerkyra**, Greece
26	G 8	**Kermadec Trench**, Pacific Ocean ◣
115	M 4	**Kermān**, Iran
115	K 3	**Kermanshah**, Iran
83	G 13	**Kerrville**, TX, United States
108	F 11	**Keryneia**, Cyprus
69	I 10	**Keuruu**, Finland
78	F 3	**Keweenaw Bay**, MI, United States ≈
81	K 11	**Key Largo**, FL, United States
81	L 10	**Key Largo**, FL, United States 🏝
81	K 11	**Key West**, FL, United States
105	M 10	**Khabarovsk**, Russia
111	K 10	**Khairpur**, Pakistan
115	M 9	**Khalīj al Ḩalāniyāt**, Oman ≈
115	N 8	**Khalīj Maşīrah**, Oman ≈
115	I 8	**Khamīs**, Saudi Arabia
119	D 10	**Khandwa**, India
119	H 10	**Kharagpur**, India
65	N 7	**Kharkiv**, Ukraine
137	L 5	**Khartoum**, Sudan ■
109	L 5	**Khashuri**, Georgia
61	H 9	**Khaskovo**, Bulgaria
105	I 6	**Khatanga**, Russia ∫
140	H 11	**Khayelitsha**, South Africa
65	L 10	**Kherson**, Ukraine
65	J 8	**Khmel'nyts'kyy**, Ukraine
115	L 3	**Khomeynīshahr**, Iran
122	G 4	**Khon Kaen**, Thailand
115	K 3	**Khorramābād**, Iran
111	L 7	**Khorugh**, Tajikistan
136	F 2	**Khouribga**, Morocco
105	L 7	**Khrebet Cherskogo**, Russia ⛰
105	L 9	**Khrebet Dzhugdzhur**, Russia ⛰
105	M 7	**Khrebet Kolymskiy**, Russia ⛰
111	K 6	**Khujand**, Tajikistan
119	I 10	**Khulna**, Bangladesh
111	L 8	**Khushab**, Pakistan
115	J 1	**Khvoy**, Iran
111	L 8	**Khyber Pass**, Afghanistan/Pakistan ◇
61	E 10	**Kičevo**, Macedonia
136	G 4	**Kidal**, Mali
37	G 13	**Kidderminster**, United Kingdom
52	E 4	**Kiel**, Germany
64	G 7	**Kielce**, Poland
52	E 4	**Kieler Bay**, Germany ≈
65	K 7	**Kiev**, Ukraine
141	J 3	**Kigali**, Rwanda ■
141	J 4	**Kigoma**, Tanzania
85	C 15	**Kihei**, HI, United States
131	E 12	**Kii-suidō**, Japan ⧗
131	K 14	**Kikai**, Japan
131	K 14	**Kikai-jima**, Japan 🏝
61	E 6	**Kikinda**, Serbia and Montenegro
140	G 4	**Kikwit**, Democratic Republic of Congo
151	N 4	**Kili Island**, Marshall Islands 🏝
141	K 4	**Kilimanjaro**, Tanzania ▲
37	C 12	**Kilkenny**, Ireland
37	B 13	**Killarney**, Ireland
83	G 12	**Killeen**, TX, United States
37	F 9	**Kilmarnock**, United Kingdom
141	K 5	**Kilosa**, Tanzania
147	L 2	**Kimbe**, Papua New Guinea
141	I 10	**Kimberley**, South Africa
146	F 4	**Kimberley Plateau**, WA, Australia ◇
127	O 4	**Kimch'aek**, North Korea
74	F 9	**Kindersley**, SK, Canada
136	D 6	**Kindia**, Guinea
33	I 2	**King George Island**, Antarctica 🏝
147	J 10	**King Island**, TAS, Australia 🏝
146	F 4	**King Leopold Ranges**, WA, Australia ⛰
33	J 5	**King Peninsula**, Antarctica ▶
146	F 4	**King Sound**, WA, Australia ≈
32	C 8	**King Wilhelm Land**, Greenland ⁘
74	G 5	**King William Island**, NU, Canada 🏝
37	J 12	**King's Lynn**, United Kingdom
85	H 14	**Kingman**, AZ, United States
26	H 5	**Kingman Reef**, Pacific Ocean ◣
79	L 7	**Kingston**, NY, United States
90	I 4	**Kingston**, Jamaica ■
37	I 11	**Kingston upon Hull**, United Kingdom
91	O 6	**Kingstown**, St Vincent and the Grenadines ■
83	G 14	**Kingsville**, TX, United States
130	I 8	**Kinka-san**, Japan ▶
49	H 10	**Kinrooi**, Belgium
140	G 4	**Kinshasa**, Democratic Republic of Congo ■
37	E 9	**Kintyre**, United Kingdom 🏝
111	L 5	**Kirghiz Range**, Kazakhstan/Kyrgyzstan ⛰
151	J 8	**Kiribati**, Pacific Ocean ▣
109	H 10	**Kirikhan**, Turkey
108	G 7	**Kirikkale**, Turkey
68	J 4	**Kirkenes**, Norway
75	J 9	**Kirkland Lake**, ON, Canada
108	C 5	**Kirklareli**, Turkey
82	I 8	**Kirksville**, MO, United States
115	J 2	**Kirkūk**, Iraq
36	G 5	**Kirkwall**, United Kingdom
104	D 6	**Kirov**, Russia
65	L 9	**Kirovohrad**, Ukraine
68	G 6	**Kiruna**, Sweden
141	I 3	**Kisangani**, Democratic Republic of Congo
131	I 10	**Kisarazu**, Japan
104	G 9	**Kiselevsk**, Russia
131	E 12	**Kishiwada**, Japan
137	N 8	**Kismaayo**, Somalia
131	G 10	**Kiso-sanmyaku**, Japan ⛰
81	K 8	**Kissimmee**, FL, United States

⛰ Mountain Range ■ National Capital ≋ Ocean ◇ Physical Feature ▬ Polar Base ∫ River ∿ Sea ✱ Special Feature ⌂ State Capital ◣ Underwater Feature

141 K 3 Kisumu, Kenya
131 B 13 Kita-Kyūshū, Japan
141 K 2 Kitale, Kenya
130 I 3 Kitami, Japan
75 J 10 Kitchener, ON, Canada
68 I 6 Kitinen, Finland
68 I 6 Kittilä, Finland
141 I 6 Kitwe, Zambia
108 G 7 Kizilirmak, Turkey
109 J 9 Kiziltepe, Turkey
64 E 7 Kladno, Czech Republic
53 I 13 Klagenfurt, Austria
64 H 4 Klaipėda, Lithuania
85 D 9 Klamath Falls, OR, United States
61 C 7 Ključ, Bosnia-Herzegovina
53 E 13 Klosters, Switzerland
61 B 8 Knin, Croatia
53 I 12 Knittelfeld, Austria
49 C 10 Knokke-Heist, Belgium
151 N 4 Knox, Marshall Islands
81 J 2 Knoxville, TN, United States
32 C 7 Knud Rasmussen Land, Greenland
131 E 11 Kōbe, Japan
53 C 9 Koblenz, Germany
131 D 13 Kōchi, Japan
84 I 6 Kodiak, AL, United States
84 J 6 Kodiak Island, AL, United States
131 H 10 Kōfu, Japan
65 J 1 Kohtla- Järve, Estonia
111 L 6 Kokand, Uzbekistan
111 L 7 Kokcha, Afghanistan
69 H 9 Kokkola, Finland
111 K 2 Kokshetau, Kazakhstan
104 E 4 Kola Peninsula, Russia
68 H 6 Kolari, Finland
136 D 5 Kolda, Senegal
119 C 12 Kolhapur, India
119 A 15 Kolhumadulu Atoll, Maldives
136 E 5 Kolokani, Mali
104 C 6 Kolomna, Russia
151 M 1 Kolonia, Federated States of Micronesia
141 I 5 Kolwezi, Democratic Republic of Congo
105 M 6 Kolyma, Russia
131 F 11 Komaki, Japan
131 F 10 Komatsu, Japan
61 H 10 Komotini, Greece
105 M 9 Komsomol'sk-na-Amure, Russia
111 K 7 Kondūz, Afghanistan
32 C 9 Kong Christian IX Land, Greenland
32 C 8 Kong Frederik IX Land, Greenland
32 D 8 Kong Frederik VIII Land, Greenland
69 C 11 Kongsberg, Norway
69 D 11 Kongsvinger, Norway
126 E 5 Kongur Shan, China
64 F 6 Konin, Poland
61 E 11 Konitsa, Greece
61 D 8 Konjic, Bosnia-Herzegovina
68 G 5 Könkämäeno, Sweden
65 L 7 Konotop, Ukraine
53 D 12 Konstanz, Germany
109 F 9 Konya, Turkey
60 A 6 Koper, Slovenia
115 M 1 Kopet Dag, Iran
61 E 10 Korçë, Albania
127 N 5 Korea Bay, North Korea
127 O 7 Korea Strait, South Korea,
61 G 13 Korinthos, Greece
130 I 8 Kōriyama, Japan
126 G 4 Korla, China
53 K 11 Korneuburg, Austria
141 L 4 Korogwe, Tanzania
151 I 1 Koror, Palau
65 K 7 Korosten', Ukraine
49 C 11 Kortrijk, Belgium
105 O 6 Koryakskiy Khrebet, Russia
131 B 14 Koshiki-kaikyō, Japan
61 E 9 Kosovska Mitrovica, Serbia and Montenegro
151 M 2 Kosrae, Federated States of Micronesia
111 J 2 Kostanay, Kazakhstan
137 L 6 Kosti, Sudan
65 N 8 Kostyantynivka, Ukraine
64 F 4 Koszalin, Poland
119 D 9 Kota, India
52 G 6 Kota Bharu, Malaysia
52 J 7 Kota Kinabalu, Malaysia
69 J 11 Kotka, Finland
61 D 9 Kotor, Serbia and Montenegro
137 I 6 Koumra, Chad
97 J 3 Kourou, French Guiana
136 F 6 Koutiala, Mali
69 J 11 Kouvola, Finland
65 I 7 Kovel, Ukraine
61 F 11 Kozani, Greece
131 H 11 Kōzu-shima, Japan
122 F 6 Krabi, Thailand
61 E 8 Kragujevac, Serbia and Montenegro
64 G 7 Kraków, Poland
61 E 8 Kraljevo, Serbia and Montenegro
65 N 8 Kramators'k, Ukraine
60 A 6 Kranj, Slovenia
104 B 7 Krasnodar, Russia
104 H 9 Krasnoyarsk, Russia
65 O 8 Krasnyy Luch, Ukraine
52 B 8 Krefeld, Germany
65 M 8 Kremenchuk, Ukraine
65 L 8 Kremenchuts'ka Vodoskhovyshche, Ukraine
53 J 11 Krems an der Donau, Austria
119 D 12 Krishna, India
119 H 9 Krishnanagar, India
119 D 13 Krishnaraja Sagara, India
69 B 12 Kristiansand, Norway
69 E 14 Kristianstad, Sweden
69 C 9 Kristiansund, Norway
61 A 7 Krk, Croatia
60 B 6 Krško, Greece
61 F 8 Kruševac, Serbia and Montenegro
65 M 9 Kryvyy Rih, Ukraine
52 G 7 Kuala Lumpur, Malaysia
52 G 7 Kuala Terengganu, Malaysia
52 G 7 Kuantan, Malaysia
52 H 8 Kuching, Malaysia
131 B 16 Kuchino-shima, Japan
119 A 15 Kuda Huvadu Channel, Maldives
115 J 2 Kūh-e Chehel Chashmeh, Iran
115 J 2 Kūh-e Ḥājī Ebrāhīm, Iraq
115 M 4 Kūh-e Ilazārān, Iran
68 J 8 Kuhmo, Finland
140 G 6 Kuito, Angola
61 E 9 Kukës, Albania
118 I 8 Kula Kangri, Bhutan
108 F 8 Kulu, Turkey
131 B 13 Kumamoto, Japan
61 F 9 Kumanovo, Macedonia
136 F 7 Kumasi, Ghana
136 H 7 Kumba, Cameroon
119 E 14 Kumbakonam, India
131 J 16 Kume-jima, Japan
52 G 5 Kummerower See, Germany
137 I 6 Kumo, Nigeria
52 J 6 Kundat, Malaysia
140 F 7 Kunene, Namibia
69 D 13 Kungsbacka, Sweden
23 K 4 Kunlun Shan, Asia
127 J 9 Kunming, China
146 G 4 Kununurra, WA, Australia
69 J 9 Kuopio, Finland
123 L 10 Kupang, Indonesia
109 M 6 Kür, Azerbaijan/Turkey
131 D 12 Kurashiki, Japan
109 L 9 Kurdistan, Turkey
131 D 12 Kure, Japan
104 E 8 Kurgan, Russia
105 N 10 Kuril Islands, Russia
26 E 2 Kuril Trench, Pacific Ocean
119 D 12 Kurnool, India
131 B 15 Kuro-shima, Japan
104 C 6 Kursk, Russia
126 G 4 Kuruktag, China
131 B 13 Kurume, Japan
110 H 5 Kuryk, Kazakhstan
108 B 8 Kusadasi Körfezi, Turkey
130 J 3 Kushiro, Japan
130 J 3 Kussharo-ko, Japan
108 D 7 Kütahya, Turkey
109 K 5 K'ut'aisi, Georgia
61 C 7 Kutina, Croatia
75 K 6 Kuujjuaq, QC, Canada
68 J 7 Kuusamo, Finland
115 K 4 Kuwait, Asia
115 K 5 Kuwait, Kuwait
104 C 7 Kuznetsk, Russia
68 F 4 Kvaløya, Norway
151 M 3 Kwajalein, Marshall Islands
127 O 6 Kwangju, South Korea
61 H 12 Kymi, Greece
131 E 10 Kyōga-misaki, Japan
131 F 11 Kyōto, Japan
111 L 5 Kyrgyzstan, Asia
61 G 14 Kythira, Greece
61 H 13 Kythnos, Greece
131 B 13 Kyūshū, Japan
61 F 9 Kyustendil, Bulgaria
65 K 7 Kyyivs'ke Vodoskhovyshche, Ukraine
104 H 10 Kyzyl, Russia
111 J 5 Kyzylkum Desert, Uzbekistan
111 J 4 Kyzylorda, Kazakhstan

L

98 G 8 La Banda, Argentina
44 F 5 La Baule-Escoublac, France
41 J 8 La Carolina, Spain
90 F 5 La Ceiba, Honduras
78 E 6 La Crosse, WI, United States
40 B 11 La Gomera, Spain
84 F 7 La Grande, OR, United States
83 E 10 La Junta, CO, United States
99 E 9 La Ligua, Chile
49 E 12 La Louvière, Belgium
57 C 10 La Maddalena, Italy
40 A 10 La Palma, Spain
91 I 8 La Palma, Panama
98 F 5 La Paz, Bolivia
88 G 6 La Paz, Mexico
130 G 1 La Pérouse Strait, Japan
99 I 10 La Plata, Argentina
98 F 8 La Rioja, Argentina
44 G 7 La Rochelle, France
44 G 6 La Roche-sur-Yon, France
41 K 7 La Roda, Spain
91 L 4 La Romana, Dominican Republic
99 E 9 La Serena, Chile
41 N 3 La Seu, Spain
41 J 7 La Solana, Spain
56 C 7 La Spezia, Italy
75 K 9 La Tuque, QC, Canada
41 L 8 La Unión, Spain
136 E 3 Laâyoune, Western Sahara
136 E 5 Labé, Guinea
75 K 6 Labrador, NL/QC, Canada
32 B 9 Labrador Basin, Arctic Ocean
32 B 9 Labrador Sea, Arctic Ocean
75 K 7 Lac Caniapiscau, QC, Canada
136 E 6 Lac de Buyo, Côte d'Ivoire
136 F 6 Lac de Kossou, Côte d'Ivoire
137 I 7 Lac de Ladgo, Cameroon
136 E 5 Lac de Manantali, Mali
53 B 13 Lac de Neuchâtel, Switzerland
136 F 5 Lac Faguibine, Mali
140 G 3 Lac Mai-Ndombe, Democratic Republic of Congo
75 K 8 Lac Mistassini, QC, Canada
136 F 5 Lac Niangay, Mali
140 G 3 Lac Ntomba, Democratic Republic of Congo
140 E 3 Lac Onangue, Gabon
75 K 9 Lac Saint-Jean, QC, Canada
74 H 9 Lac Seul, ON, Canada
141 I 5 Lac Upemba, Democratic Republic of Congo/Uganda
30 G 2 Laccadive Islands, India
147 J 9 Lachlan, NSW, Australia
79 M 6 Laconia, NH, United States
60 J 7 Lacul Razim, Romania
60 J 7 Lacul Sinoie, Romania
118 D 6 Ladakh, India/Pakistan
78 E 4 Ladysmith, WI, United States
147 K 2 Lae, Papua New Guinea
151 M 3 Lae, Marshall Islands
69 C 13 Laesø, Denmark
78 F 8 Lafayette, IN, United States
83 J 13 Lafayette, LA, United States
97 J 10 Lages, Brazil
99 E 14 Lago Argentino, Argentina
99 E 13 Lago Buenos Aires, Argentina
141 J 6 Lago de Cahora Bassa, Mozambique
90 E 5 Lago de Izabal, Guatemala
90 F 7 Lago de Managua, Nicaragua
90 F 7 Lago de Nicaragua, Nicaragua
98 F 5 Lago de Poopó, Bolivia
99 F 16 Lago Fagnano, Argentina
90 H 8 Lago Gatún, Panama
99 E 13 Lago General Carrera, Chile
99 E 12 Lago Llanquihué, Chile
99 G 9 Lago Mar Chiquita, Argentina
99 F 13 Lago Musters, Argentina
99 E 12 Lago Nahuel Huapi, Argentina
99 E 14 Lago San Martin, Argentina
97 J 10 Lagoa dos Patos, Brazil
97 I 11 Lagoa Mangueira, Brazil
97 I 11 Lagoa Mirim, Brazil/Uruguay
40 E 9 Lagos, Portugal
136 G 7 Lagos, Nigeria
89 J 7 Lagos de Moreno, Mexico
90 G 6 Laguna Caratasca, Honduras,
89 J 8 Laguna de Chapala, Mexico
90 G 8 Laguna de Chiriquí, Panama
90 G 7 Laguna de Perlas, Nicaragua
89 N 9 Laguna de Terminos, Mexico,
89 L 6 Laguna Madre, Mexico,
98 F 4 Laguna Rogaguado, Bolivia,
98 G 4 Laguna San Luis, Bolivia
98 E 6 Lagunas, Chile
85 C 15 Lahaina, HI, United States
111 M 9 Lahore, Pakistan
69 I 10 Lahti, Finland
137 N 6 Lake Abbe, Djibouti/Ethiopia
85 E 9 Lake Abert, OR, United States
141 J 2 Lake Albert, Democratic Republic of Congo/Uganda
146 G 7 Lake Amadeus, NT, Australia
146 G 4 Lake Argyle, WA, Australia
74 F 7 Lake Athabasca, AB/SK, Canada
146 E 8 Lake Austin, WA, Australia
105 I 10 Lake Baikal, Russia
111 M 4 Lake Balkhash, Kazakhstan
146 F 8 Lake Ballard, WA, Australia
141 J 5 Lake Bangweulu, Zambia
146 E 8 Lake Barlee, WA, Australia
147 I 8 Lake Blanche, SA, Australia
57 E 9 Lake Bolseno, Italy
146 F 8 Lake Carey, WA, Australia
146 F 7 Lake Carnegie, WA, Australia
22 t c Lake Chad, Africa
79 M 5 Lake Champlain, Canada/United States
83 I 13 Lake Charles, LA, United States
84 E 5 Lake Chelan, WA, United States
81 J 7 Lake City, FL, United States
56 C 5 Lake Como, Italy
53 D 12 Lake Constance, Europe
146 F 8 Lake Cowan, WA, Australia
146 F 6 Lake Disappointment, WA, Australia
37 G 10 Lake District, United Kingdom
141 J 3 Lake Edward, Democratic Republic of Congo/Uganda
82 B 5 Lake Elwell, MT, United States
79 I 7 Lake Erie, Canada/United States
147 I 7 Lake Eyre North, SA, Australia
147 I 8 Lake Eyre South, SA, Australia
147 I 8 Lake Frome, SA, Australia
147 I 8 Lake Gairdner, SA, Australia
56 D 5 Lake Garda, Italy
53 B 13 Lake Geneva, Italy/Switzerland
81 K 7 Lake George, FL, United States
146 G 5 Lake Gregory, WA, Australia
85 H 14 Lake Havasu City, AZ, United States
150 C 9 Lake Hawea, New Zealand
78 H 5 Lake Huron, Canada/United States
141 I 7 Lake Kariba, Zambia/Zimbabwe
127 P 3 Lake Khanka, China/Russia
82 A 5 Lake Koocanusa, MT, United States
104 C 4 Lake Ladoga, Russia
146 F 8 Lake Lefroy, WA, Australia
146 G 6 Lake Mackay, WA, Australia
146 D 7 Lake MacLeod, WA, Australia
56 B 5 Lake Maggiore, Italy/Switzerland
150 B 10 Lake Manapouri, New Zealand
74 H 9 Lake Manitoba, MB, Canada
96 F 2 Lake Maracaibo, Venezuela
81 K 4 Lake Marion, SC, United States
80 H 4 Lake Martin, AL, United States
85 H 13 Lake Mead, AZ/NV, United States
78 F 6 Lake Michigan, Canada/United States
146 F 8 Lake Minigwal, WA, Australia
146 E 8 Lake Moore, WA, Australia
81 L 4 Lake Moultrie, SC, United States
147 J 2 Lake Murray, Papua New Guinea
81 K 3 Lake Murray, SC, United States
141 J 5 Lake Mweru, Democratic Republic of Congo/Zambia
137 L 4 Lake Nasser, Egypt
146 G 6 Lake Neale, NT, Australia
75 I 9 Lake Nipigon, ON, Canada
75 J 10 Lake Nipissing, ON, Canada
146 E 8 Lake Noondie, WA, Australia
81 K 2 Lake Norman, NC, United States
137 L 4 Lake Nuba, Egypt/Sudan
141 K 6 Lake Nyasa, Africa
82 F 6 Lake Oahe, SD, United States
81 J 4 Lake Oconee, GA, United States
83 I 9 Lake of the Ozarks, MO, United States
82 H 5 Lake of the Woods, Canada/United States
150 C 9 Lake Ohau, New Zealand
61 E 10 Lake Ohrid, Albania/Macedonia
81 K 9 Lake Okeechobee, FL, United States
104 D 5 Lake Onega, Russia
79 K 6 Lake Ontario, Canada/United States
83 I 11 Lake Ouachita, AR, United States
84 F 8 Lake Owyhee, OR, United States
65 J 1 Lake Peipus, Estonia/Russia
84 G 6 Lake Pend Oreille, ID, United States
85 J 13 Lake Powell, AZ/UT, United States
61 E 10 Lake Prespa, Europe
150 C 9 Lake Pukaki, New Zealand
150 F 4 Lake Rotorua, New Zealand
82 E 5 Lake Sakakawea, ND, United States
61 D 9 Lake Scutari, Albania/Serbia and Montenegro
81 I 6 Lake Seminole, GA, United States
81 I 3 Lake Sidney Lanier, GA, United States
81 J 4 Lake Sinclair, GA, United States
78 H 7 Lake St Clair, Canada/United States
78 E 3 Lake Superior, Canada/United States
85 E 11 Lake Tahoe, CA/NV, United States
141 J 4 Lake Tanganyika, Africa
150 G 4 Lake Tarawera, New Zealand
150 F 4 Lake Taupo, New Zealand
150 B 10 Lake Te Anau, New Zealand
150 C 8 Lake Tekapo, New Zealand
96 G 7 Lake Titicaca, Bolivia/Peru
147 I 8 Lake Torrens, SA, Australia
56 F 8 Lake Trasimeno, Italy
141 K 2 Lake Turkana, Kenya
115 J 1 Lake Urmia, Iran
108 L 8 Lake Van, Turkey
141 J 3 Lake Victoria, Africa
136 G 6 Lake Volta, Ghana
150 F 6 Lake Wairarapa, New Zealand
150 B 10 Lake Wakatipu, New Zealand
150 C 9 Lake Wanaka, New Zealand
146 F 7 Lake Wells, WA, Australia
146 G 6 Lake White, WA, Australia
78 F 5 Lake Winnebago, WI, United States
82 H 5 Lake Winnibigoshish, MN, United States
74 H 9 Lake Winnipeg, MB, Canada
74 G 9 Lake Winnipegosis, MB, Canada
81 K 8 Lakeland, FL, United States
83 D 9 Lakewood, CO, United States
68 I 3 Lakse Fjord, Norway
68 H 4 Lakselv, Norway
137 M 6 Lalibela, Ethiopia
40 F 2 Lalín, Spain
57 I 13 Lamezia, Italy
61 F 12 Lamia, Greece
85 C 15 Lanai, HI, United States
127 I 8 Lancang, China
79 K 8 Lancaster, PA, United States
85 F 14 Lancaster, CA, United States
74 G 4 Lancaster Sound, NU, Canada
53 C 10 Landau in der Pfalz, Germany
37 E 15 Land's End, United Kingdom
53 G 11 Landshut, Germany
127 K 5 Lang Shan, China
68 B 6 Langjökull, Iceland
45 K 5 Langres, France
109 O 8 Länkäran, Azerbaijan

Bay · Channel · Country · Dependent Territory · Desert · Geographic Area · Headland · Island · Island Group · Lake · Mountain

78 G 7 **Lansing**, MI, United States ⌂
40 C 10 **Lanzarote**, Spain ⛱
127 J 6 **Lanzhou**, China
45 J 3 **Laon**, France
122 G 3 **Laos**, Asia □
69 J 10 **Lappeenranta**, Finland
68 G 6 **Lappland**, Finland ⁘
32 F 6 **Laptev Sea**, Arctic Ocean ∽
69 H 9 **Lapua**, Finland
57 G 9 **L'Aquila**, Italy
82 D 8 **Laramie**, WY, United States
82 D 7 **Laramie Mountains**, MT/WY, United States ⛰
83 G 14 **Laredo**, TX, United States
81 J 9 **Largo**, FL, United States
61 F 11 **Larisa**, Greece
111 K 10 **Larkana**, Pakistan
108 F 11 **Lárnaka**, Cyprus
33 J 2 **Larsen Ice Shelf**, Antarctica ◇
69 C 12 **Larvik**, Norway
83 D 12 **Las Cruces**, NM, United States
99 F 9 **Las Heras**, Argentina
98 H 7 **Las Lomitas**, Argentina
40 C 11 **Las Palmas de Gran Canaria**, Spain
90 H 9 **Las Tablas**, Panama
91 I 3 **Las Tunas**, Cuba
85 G 13 **Las Vegas**, NV, United States
122 F 3 **Lashio**, Myanmar
61 C 9 **Lastovo**, Croatia ⛱
33 J 3 **Lataday Island**, Antarctica ⛱
57 F 10 **Latina**, Italy
119 D 11 **Latur**, India
65 I 3 **Latvia**, Europe □
147 K 11 **Launceston**, TAS, Australia
80 F 5 **Laurel**, MS, United States
75 K 9 **Laurentian Mountains**, NL/QC, Canada ⛰
57 I 11 **Lauria**, Italy
33 J 1 **Laurie Island**, Argentina ⛱
81 L 3 **Laurinburg**, NC, United States
53 B 13 **Lausanne**, Switzerland
123 J 9 **Laut**, Indonesia ⛱
44 G 5 **Laval**, France
33 P 2 **Law Promontory**, Antarctica ▶
80 G 2 **Lawrenceburg**, TN, United States
83 G 11 **Lawton**, OK, United States
29 I 12 **Lazarev Sea**, Atlantic Ocean ∽
89 J 9 **Lázaro Cárdenas**, Mexico
44 H 3 **Le Havre**, France
44 H 5 **Le Mans**, France
79 M 6 **Lebanon**, NH, United States
84 C 8 **Lebanon**, OR, United States
114 H 3 **Lebanon**, Asia □
40 G 9 **Lebrija**, Spain
99 E 11 **Lebu**, Chile
57 K 11 **Lecce**, Italy
37 B 13 **Lee**, Ireland ≀
37 H 11 **Leeds**, United Kingdom
48 H 4 **Leeuwarden**, Netherlands
91 N 4 **Leeward Islands**, Caribbean Sea ⁂
61 E 12 **Lefkada**, Greece
61 E 12 **Lefkada**, Greece ⛱
61 E 11 **Lefkimmi**, Greece
123 K 5 **Legaspi**, Philippines
64 F 6 **Legnica**, Poland
37 H 12 **Leicester**, United Kingdom
147 I 5 **Leichhardt**, QLD, Australia ≀
48 F 8 **Leiden**, Netherlands
52 E 7 **Leine**, Germany ≀
52 G 8 **Leipzig**, Germany
40 E 6 **Leiria**, Portugal
69 A 11 **Leirvik**, Norway
69 E 11 **Leksand**, Sweden
48 H 7 **Lelystad**, Netherlands
108 F 11 **Lemesos**, Cyprus
105 K 5 **Lena**, Russia ≀
33 N 7 **Leningradskaya**, Russia ▬
53 I 12 **Leoben**, Austria
40 H 2 **León**, Spain
89 J 8 **León**, Mexico
90 F 7 **León**, Nicaragua
137 I 2 **Leptis Magna**, Libya ✱
45 J 8 **Le-Puy-en-Velay**, France
41 J 3 **Lerma**, Spain
61 I 13 **Leros**, Greece ⛱
36 H 3 **Lerwick**, United Kingdom
91 J 4 **Les Cayes**, Haiti
44 F 6 **Les Sables-d'Olonne**, France
61 I 12 **Lesbos**, Greece ⛱
127 J 8 **Leshan**, China
61 F 9 **Leskovac**, Serbia and Montenegro
141 I 10 **Lesotho**, Africa □
91 M 5 **Lesser Antilles**, Caribbean Sea ⁂
74 E 8 **Lesser Slave Lake**, AB, Canada ◢
64 F 6 **Leszno**, Poland
74 E 10 **Lethbridge**, AB, Canada
96 H 3 **Lethem**, Guyuna
49 F 11 **Leuven**, Belgium
49 D 12 **Leuze-en-Hainaut**, Belgium
61 G 12 **Levadeia**, Greece
52 B 8 **Leverkusen**, Germany
84 F 7 **Lewiston**, ID, United States
82 C 5 **Lewistown**, MT, United States
78 G 10 **Lexington**, KY, United States
82 F 8 **Lexington**, NE, United States
126 H 8 **Lhasa**, China
122 F 7 **Lhokseumawe**, Indonesia
41 N 4 **L'Hospitalet de Llobregat**, Spain
127 N 6 **Lianyungang**, China
127 N 4 **Liaoyang**, China
127 N 4 **Liaoyuan**, China
83 F 10 **Liberal**, KS, United States
64 E 7 **Liberec**, Czech Republic
90 F 7 **Liberia**, Costa Rica
136 E 7 **Liberia**, Africa □
140 E 3 **Libreville**, Gabon ◼
137 I 3 **Libya**, Africa □
137 K 3 **Libyan Desert**, Egypt/Libya ▲
137 K 2 **Libyan Plateau**, Egypt/Libya ◇
65 I 5 **Lida**, Belarus
69 D 12 **Lidköping**, Sweden
53 E 13 **Liechtenstein**, Europe □
49 H 12 **Liège**, Belgium
53 G 13 **Lienz**, Austria
64 H 3 **Liepāja**, Latvia
49 F 11 **Lier**, Belgium
37 D 11 **Liffey**, Ireland ≀
56 B 8 **Ligurian Sea**, France/Italy ∽
85 B 15 **Lihue**, HI, United States
141 I 5 **Likasi**, Democratic Republic of Congo
151 M 3 **Likiep**, Marshall Islands ⛱
45 J 2 **Lille**, France
69 D 10 **Lillehammer**, Norway
141 K 6 **Lilongwe**, Malawi ◼
96 E 7 **Lima**, Peru ◼
99 F 12 **Limay**, Argentina ≀
99 F 11 **Limay Mahuida**, Argentina
97 J 8 **Limeira**, Brazil
37 B 12 **Limerick**, Ireland
61 G 12 **Limni**, Greece
61 H 11 **Limnos**, Greece ⛱
44 H 7 **Limoges**, France
90 G 8 **Limón**, Costa Rica
45 I 10 **Limoux**, France
141 I 8 **Limpopo**, Botswana/Mozambique ≀
41 J 8 **Linares**, Spain
89 K 6 **Linares**, Mexico
127 M 8 **Linchuan**, China
37 I 12 **Lincoln**, United Kingdom
82 G 8 **Lincoln**, NE, United States ⌂
84 C 7 **Lincoln City**, OR, United States
97 I 2 **Linden**, Guyuna
61 J 14 **Lindos**, Greece
37 G 11 **Lindow Moss**, United Kingdom ◇
127 L 6 **Linfen**, China
97 L 8 **Linhares**, Brazil
69 E 12 **Linköping**, Sweden
53 I 11 **Linz**, Austria
57 H 14 **Lipari Islands**, Italy ⁂
104 C 6 **Lipetsk**, Russia
52 C 7 **Lippstadt**, Germany
141 J 2 **Lira**, Uganda
40 E 7 **Lisbon**, Portugal
147 L 8 **Lismore**, NSW, Australia
64 H 4 **Lithuania**, Europe □
119 J 14 **Little Andaman**, India ⛱
90 H 4 **Little Cayman**, Cayman Islands ⛱
85 J 13 **Little Colorado**, United States, United States ≀
119 K 15 **Little Nicobar**, India ⛱
83 I 11 **Little Rock**, AR, United States ⌂
127 L 10 **Liuzhou**, China
37 G 11 **Liverpool**, United Kingdom
75 M 9 **Liverpool**, NS, Canada
141 I 7 **Livingstone**, Zambia
61 C 8 **Livno**, Bosnia-Herzegovina
56 D 8 **Livorno**, Italy
61 E 12 **Lixouri**, Greece
37 E 15 **Lizard Point**, United Kingdom ▶
60 B 6 **Ljubljana**, Slovenia
69 E 13 **Ljungby**, Sweden
69 E 10 **Ljusnan**, Sweden ≀
41 I 1 **Llanes**, Spain
89 I 4 **Llano de los Caballos Mesteños**, Mexico ◇
83 E 12 **Llano Estacado**, United States, United States ◇
96 F 3 **Llanos**, Colombia ⁘
41 M 4 **Lleida**, Spain
41 O 6 **Llucmajor**, Spain
140 F 6 **Lobito**, Angola
40 C 10 **Lobos**, Spain ⛱
36 F 8 **Loch Lomond**, United Kingdom ◢
36 F 7 **Loch Ness**, United Kingdom ◢
36 E 6 **Loch Shin**, United Kingdom ◢
85 D 12 **Lodi**, CA, United States
64 G 6 **Łódź**, Poland
68 E 5 **Lofoten**, Norway ⛱
85 I 10 **Logan**, UT, United States
41 K 3 **Logroño**, Spain
45 I 5 **Loire**, France ≀
96 E 5 **Loja**, Ecuador
49 D 11 **Lokeren**, Belgium
69 D 15 **Lolland**, Denmark ⛱
99 I 10 **Lomas de Zamora**, Argentina
123 I 10 **Lombok**, Indonesia ⛱
31 K 5 **Lombok Basin**, Southern Ocean ▰
136 G 7 **Lomé**, Togo ◼
49 G 10 **Lommel**, Belgium
32 D 7 **Lomonosov Ridge**, Arctic Ocean ⛰
85 E 14 **Lompoc**, CA, United States
64 H 5 **Łomża**, Poland
37 I 13 **London**, United Kingdom ◼
75 J 11 **London**, ON, Canada
37 D 9 **Londonderry**, United Kingdom
97 J 9 **Londrina**, Brazil
81 L 4 **Long Bay**, NC/SC, United States ≈
85 E 15 **Long Beach**, CA, United States
79 M 8 **Long Island**, NY, United States ⛱
91 J 2 **Long Island**, The Bahamas ⛱
122 G 5 **Long Xuyên**, Vietnam
147 J 6 **Longreach**, QLD, Australia
83 I 12 **Longview**, TX, United States
84 C 7 **Longview**, WA, United States
127 M 9 **Longyan**, China
32 E 8 **Longyearbyen**, Savlbard
45 L 6 **Lons-le-Saunier**, France
37 A 12 **Loop Head**, Ireland ▶
126 H 5 **Lop Nur**, China ◢
41 K 8 **Lorca**, Spain
26 F 7 **Lord Howe Rise**, Pacific Ocean ▰
147 K 1 **Lorengau**, Papua New Guinea
88 F 5 **Loreto**, Mexico
44 E 5 **Lorient**, France
83 D 10 **Los Alamos**, NM, United States
99 E 11 **Los Angeles**, Chile
85 E 14 **Los Angeles**, CA, United States
88 G 5 **Los Mochis**, Mexico
99 E 9 **Los Vilos**, Chile
151 L 1 **Losap**, Federated States of Micronesia ⛱
122 G 3 **Louang Namtha**, Laos
122 G 3 **Louangphrabang**, Laos
140 F 4 **Loubomo**, Congo
127 L 9 **Loudi**, China
37 C 10 **Lough Allen**, Ireland ◢
37 B 10 **Lough Conn**, Ireland ◢
37 B 11 **Lough Corrib**, Ireland ◢
37 B 12 **Lough Derg**, Ireland ◢
37 B 11 **Lough Mask**, Ireland ◢
37 D 10 **Lough Neagh**, United Kingdom ◢
37 C 11 **Lough Ree**, Ireland ◢
147 L 3 **Louisiade Archipelago**, Papua New Guinea ⁂
83 I 13 **Louisiana**, United States ▣
78 G 10 **Louisville**, IN, United States
26 G 7 **Louisville Ridge**, Pacific Ocean ▰
44 G 10 **Lourdes**, France
44 H 3 **Louviers**, France
61 H 8 **Lovech**, Bulgaria
82 D 8 **Loveland**, CO, United States
79 N 6 **Lowell**, MA, United States
150 F 6 **Lower Hutt**, New Zealand
37 C 10 **Lower Lough Erne**, United Kingdom ◢
82 H 5 **Lower Red Lake**, MN, United States ◢
150 H 10 **Loyalty Islands**, New Caledonia ⁂
61 D 7 **Loznica**, Serbia and Montenegro
140 F 5 **Luanda**, Angola ◼
141 I 6 **Luanshya**, Zambia
40 G 1 **Luarca**, Spain
140 F 7 **Lubango**, Angola
83 E 11 **Lubbock**, TX, United States
52 E 5 **Lübeck**, Germany
52 F 4 **Lübecker Bay**, Germany ≈
64 H 7 **Lublin**, Poland
52 I 7 **Lubuan**, Malaysia
141 I 6 **Lubumbashi**, Democratic Republic of Congo
56 D 7 **Lucca**, Italy
123 K 5 **Lucena**, Philippines
118 E 8 **Lucknow**, India
140 G 9 **Lüderitz**, Namibia
118 D 7 **Ludhiana**, India
78 G 6 **Ludington**, MI, United States
69 E 11 **Ludvika**, Sweden
53 D 10 **Ludwigsburg**, Germany
53 D 10 **Ludwigshafen**, Germany
83 H 12 **Lufkin**, TX, United States
53 D 14 **Lugano**, Switzerland
40 G 2 **Lugo**, Spain
60 F 7 **Lugoj**, Romania
65 O 8 **Luhans'k**, Ukraine
68 H 7 **Luleå**, Sweden
68 G 7 **Luleälven**, Sweden ≀
81 L 3 **Lumberton**, NC, United States
150 B 10 **Lumsden**, New Zealand
69 D 14 **Lund**, Sweden
52 E 5 **Lüneburg**, Germany
127 L 7 **Luoyang**, China
141 I 6 **Lusaka**, Zambia ◼
52 G 7 **Lutherstadt Wittenberg**, Germany
37 I 13 **Luton**, United Kingdom
65 I 7 **Luts'k**, Ukraine
33 O 1 **Lützow-Holm Bay**, Antarctica ≈
141 I 4 **Luvua**, Democratic Republic of Congo ≀
49 I 15 **Luxembourg**, Luxembourg
49 H 15 **Luxembourg**, Europe □
137 L 3 **Luxor**, Egypt
53 C 13 **Luzern**, Switzerland
127 K 8 **Luzhou**, China
123 K 4 **Luzon**, Philippines ⛱
26 D 4 **Luzon Strait**, Pacific Ocean ⧗
65 I 8 **L'viv**, Ukraine
68 G 8 **Lycksele**, Sweden
37 G 15 **Lyme Bay**, United Kingdom ≈
45 K 7 **Lyon**, France
65 O 8 **Lysychans'k**, Ukraine

M

114 G 4 **Ma'ān**, Jordan
49 G 9 **Maas**, Netherlands ≀
49 H 11 **Maastricht**, Luxembourg
33 O 3 **Mac Robertson Land**, Antarctica ⁘
97 K 8 **Macaé**, Brazil
97 J 4 **Macapá**, Brazil
127 M 10 **Macau**, China
99 H 15 **Macbride Head**, Falkland Islands ▶
30 G 9 **MacDonald Islands**, Australia ⁂
146 G 6 **MacDonnell Ranges**, NT, Australia ⛰
61 F 10 **Macedonia**, Europe □
97 M 6 **Maceió**, Brazil
141 K 3 **Machakos**, Kenya
96 D 5 **Machala**, Ecuador
40 D 9 **Machico**, Portugal
119 F 12 **Machilipatnam**, India
141 J 6 **Machinga**, Malawi
96 F 6 **Machu Picchu**, Peru ✱
147 K 6 **Mackay**, QLD, Australia
22 D 2 **Mackenzie**, North America ≀
74 D 4 **Mackenzie Bay**, NT/YT, Canada ≈
74 D 5 **Mackenzie Mountains**, Canada ⛰
78 E 8 **Macomb**, IL, United States
57 B 11 **Macomer**, Italy
45 K 7 **Mâcon**, France
81 I 4 **Macon**, GA, United States
147 K 8 **Macquarie**, NSW, Australia ≀
26 F 9 **Macquarie Island**, Australia ⛱
26 F 10 **Macquarie Ridge**, Pacific Ocean ▰
141 M 9 **Madagascar**, Africa □
30 F 6 **Madagascar Basin**, Indian Ocean ▰
30 E 6 **Madagascar Plateau**, Indian Ocean ▰
30 E 7 **Madagascar Ridge**, Indian Ocean ▰
147 K 2 **Madang**, Papua New Guinea
79 N 3 **Madawaska**, NB, United States
40 C 8 **Madeira**, Portugal ⛱
22 E 6 **Madeira**, South America ≀
85 E 12 **Madera**, CA, United States
96 H 5 **Madiera**, Bolivia/Brazil ≀
78 E 6 **Madison**, WI, United States ⌂
84 D 8 **Madras**, OR, United States
96 F 6 **Madre de Dios**, Bolivia/Peru ≀
41 J 5 **Madrid**, Spain
123 I 10 **Madura**, Indonesia ⛱
119 D 14 **Madurai**, India
131 H 9 **Maebashi**, Japan
141 L 5 **Mafia Island**, Tanzania ⛱
105 N 7 **Magadan**, Russia
98 G 4 **Magdalena**, Bolivia
96 E 3 **Magdalena**, Colombia ≀
88 G 3 **Magdalena**, Mexico
88 F 3 **Magdalena**, Mexico ≀
52 F 7 **Magdeburg**, Germany
68 H 3 **Magerøya**, Norway ⛱
57 K 11 **Maglie**, Italy
104 E 8 **Magnitogorsk**, Russia
141 M 7 **Mahajanga**, Madagascar
123 I 8 **Mahakam**, Indonesia ≀
119 D 12 **Mahbubnagar**, India
150 G 5 **Mahia Peninsula**, New Zealand ▶
65 K 5 **Mahilyow**, Belarus
41 P 6 **Mahón**, Spain
37 J 14 **Maidstone**, United Kingdom
137 I 6 **Maiduguri**, Nigeria
53 D 9 **Main**, Germany ≀
79 N 4 **Maine**, United States ▣
36 F 5 **Mainland**, United Kingdom ⛱
36 G 3 **Mainland**, United Kingdom ⛱
53 D 9 **Mainz**, Germany
28 B 8 **Maio**, Cape Verde ⛱
96 G 1 **Maiquetía**, Venezuela
33 M 1 **Maitri**, India ▬
61 E 9 **Maja Jezercë**, Albania ▲
123 J 9 **Majene**, Indonesia
41 O 6 **Majorca**, Spain ⛱
151 N 4 **Majuro**, Marshall Islands ◼
151 N 4 **Majuro**, Marshall Islands ⛱
32 D 7 **Makarov Basin**, Arctic Ocean ▰
26 F 4 **Makarov Seamount**, Pacific Ocean ▰
61 C 8 **Makarska**, Croatia
123 J 8 **Makassar Strait**, Indonesia ⧗
110 H 3 **Makat**, Kazakhstan
136 D 6 **Makeni**, Sierra Leone
104 B 9 **Makhachkala**, Russia
115 N 5 **Makran**, Iran ⁘
115 N 6 **Makran Coast**, Iran ⁘
136 H 7 **Makurdi**, Nigeria
136 H 7 **Malabo**, Equatorial Guinea ◼
65 J 4 **Maladzyechna**, Belarus
41 I 9 **Málaga**, Spain
137 L 6 **Malakal**, Sudan
150 H 10 **Malakula**, Vanuatu ⛱
123 I 10 **Malang**, Indonesia
140 G 5 **Malanje**, Angola
108 I 8 **Malatya**, Turkey
141 J 6 **Malawi**, Africa □
23 M 6 **Malay Peninsula**, Asia ▶
115 K 3 **Malāyer**, Iran
52 G 7 **Malaysia**, Asia □
119 A 15 **Maldives**, Asia □
119 B 14 **Male**, Maldives ◼
119 B 14 **Male Atoll**, Maldives ⛱
119 D 11 **Malegaon**, India
84 E 8 **Malheur Lake**, OR, United States ◢
136 F 4 **Mali**, Africa □
36 E 7 **Mallaig**, United Kingdom
49 I 13 **Malmédy**, Belgium
69 D 14 **Malmö**, Sweden
151 N 3 **Maloelap**, Marshall Islands ⛱
57 H 16 **Malta**, Europe □
82 D 5 **Malta**, MT, United States
57 H 15 **Malta Channel**, Italy/Malta ⧗
69 E 11 **Malung**, Sweden
98 G 4 **Mamoré**, Bolivia ≀
136 E 6 **Mamou**, Guinea
136 E 6 **Man**, Côte d'Ivoire
41 O 6 **Manacor**, Spain
123 K 8 **Manado**, Indonesia
90 F 7 **Managua**, Nicaragua ◼
109 E 9 **Manavgat**, Turkey
114 H 2 **Manbij**, Syria
37 G 11 **Manchester**, United Kingdom
79 M 6 **Manchester**, NH, United States
127 N 3 **Manchuria**, China ⁘
23 M 3 **Manchurian Plain**, Asia ◇
122 F 3 **Mandalay**, Myanmar
82 F 6 **Mandan**, ND, United States
91 I 4 **Mandeville**, Jamaica
146 E 9 **Mandurah**, WA, Australia

⛰ Mountain Range ◼ National Capital ≋ Ocean ◇ Physical Feature ▬ Polar Base ≀ River ∽ Sea ✱ Special Feature ⌂ State Capital ▰ Underwater Feature

119 D 13 **Mandya**, India
57 I 10 **Manfredonia**, Italy
119 C 13 **Mangalore**, India
83 G 9 **Manhattan**, KS, United States
32 B 9 **Maniitsoq**, Greenland
123 J 5 **Manila**, Philippines
108 C 8 **Manisa**, Turkey
78 G 5 **Manistee**, United States
74 G 8 **Manitoba**, Canada
96 E 3 **Manizales**, Colombia
82 H 7 **Mankato**, MN, United States
119 E 15 **Mannar**, Sri Lanka
53 D 10 **Mannheim**, Germany
123 M 8 **Manokwari**, Indonesia
45 L 9 **Manosque**, France
141 J 5 **Mansa**, Zambia
75 I 6 **Mansel Island**, NU, Canada
37 H 12 **Mansfield**, United Kingdom
78 H 8 **Mansfield**, OH, United States
79 K 7 **Mansfield**, PA, United States
96 D 4 **Manta**, Ecuador
56 D 6 **Mantova**, Italy
150 F 3 **Manukau**, New Zealand
150 F 3 **Manukau Harbour**, New Zealand
41 J 7 **Manzanares**, Spain
89 I 9 **Manzanillo**, Mexico
127 M 2 **Manzhouli**, China
137 I 5 **Mao**, Chad
127 L 10 **Maoming**, China
123 O 9 **Mapi**, Indonesia
141 J 9 **Maputo**, Mozambique
99 I 11 **Mar del Plata**, Argentina
97 J 5 **Marabá**, Brazil
96 F 1 **Maracaibo**, Venezuela
136 H 5 **Maradi**, Niger
115 J 2 **Marāgheh**, Iran
33 I 2 **Marambio**, Argentina
96 E 6 **Marañón**, Peru
75 I 10 **Marathon**, ON, Canada
40 H 10 **Marbella**, Spain
52 D 8 **Marburg**, Germany
49 G 13 **Marche-en-Famenne**, Belgium
111 L 8 **Mardan**, Pakistan
109 J 9 **Mardin**, Turkey
147 K 5 **Mareeba**, QLD, Australia
37 J 13 **Margate**, United Kingdom
141 J 3 **Margherita Peak**, Democratic Republic of Congo/Uganda
33 I 3 **Marguerite Bay**, Antarctica
147 K 11 **Maria Island**, TAS, Australia
151 L 4 **Mariana Islands**, Northern Mariana Islands
26 E 5 **Mariana Trench**, Pacific Ocean
60 B 6 **Maribor**, Greece
33 K 5 **Marie Byrd Land**, Antarctica
27 J 10 **Marie Byrd Seamount**, Pacific Ocean
91 O 5 **Marie-Galante**, Guadaloupe
81 I 3 **Marietta**, GA, United States
64 H 4 **Marijampolė**, Lithuania
97 J 8 **Marília**, Brazil
97 J 9 **Maringá**, Brazil
78 H 8 **Marion**, OH, United States
40 G 9 **Marismas del Guadalquivir**, Spain
61 H 9 **Maritsa**, Bulgaria
65 O 9 **Mariupol'**, Ukraine
44 H 9 **Marmande**, France
108 C 6 **Marmara**, Turkey
109 C 9 **Marmaris**, Turkey
141 N 6 **Maromokotro**, Madagascar
137 I 6 **Maroua**, Cameroon
27 I 6 **Marquesas Fracture Zone**, Pacific Ocean
151 N 8 **Marquesas Islands**, French Polynesia
81 J 11 **Marquesas Keys**, FL, United States
78 F 4 **Marquette**, MI, United States
136 E 2 **Marrakech**, Morocco
147 J 11 **Marrawah**, TAS, Australia
147 I 8 **Marree**, SA, Australia
137 K 2 **Marsa Matrûh**, Egypt
141 L 2 **Marsabit**, Kenya
57 F 14 **Marsala**, Italy
45 L 10 **Marseille**, France
83 J 13 **Marsh Island**, LA, United States
83 I 12 **Marshall**, TX, United States
151 M 4 **Marshall Islands**, Pacific Ocean
123 I 9 **Martapura**, Indonesia
33 J 5 **Martin Peninsula**, Antarctica
91 O 6 **Martinique**, United States
111 J 7 **Mary**, Turkmenistan
147 L 7 **Maryborough**, QLD, Australia
79 K 9 **Maryland**, United States
141 J 3 **Masaka**, Uganda
30 F 5 **Mascarene Basin**, Indian Ocean
30 F 5 **Mascarene Plain**, Indian Ocean
30 F 4 **Mascarene Ridge**, Indian Ocean
141 I 10 **Maseru**, Lesotho
115 N 2 **Mashhad**, Iran
115 K 4 **Masjed Soleymān**, Iran
150 B 11 **Mason Bay**, New Zealand
82 I 7 **Mason City**, IA, United States
56 D 7 **Massa**, Italy
79 M 6 **Massachusetts**, United States
45 J 8 **Massif Central**, France
136 H 4 **Massif de l'Aïr**, Niger
109 P 6 **Mastağa**, Azerbaijan
150 F 6 **Masterton**, New Zealand
141 J 8 **Masvingo**, Zimbabwe
140 F 4 **Matadi**, Democratic Republic of Congo
90 F 7 **Matagalpa**, Nicaragua
150 H 3 **Matakaoa Point**, New Zealand
89 L 5 **Matamoros**, Mexico
75 L 8 **Matane**, QC, Canada
90 H 2 **Matanzas**, Cuba
119 E 16 **Matara**, Sri Lanka
123 J 10 **Mataram**, Indonesia
41 O 4 **Mataró**, Spain
150 B 10 **Mataura**, New Zealand
151 J 9 **Matā'utu**, Wallis and Futuna Islands
57 J 11 **Matera**, Italy
118 D 8 **Mathura**, India
97 I 7 **Mato Grosso**, Brazil
40 F 4 **Matosinhos**, Portugal
131 D 11 **Matsue**, Japan
131 G 10 **Matsumoto**, Japan
131 F 11 **Matsusaka**, Japan
131 C 12 **Matsuyama**, Japan
53 C 14 **Matterhorn**, Italy/Switzerland
91 J 3 **Matthew Town**, The Bahamas
96 H 2 **Maturín**, Venezuela
119 F 9 **Mau**, India
29 H 12 **Maud Rise**, Atlantic Ocean
64 H 3 **Maûeikiai**, Lithuania
151 K 2 **Maug Islands**, Northern Mariana Islands
85 C 15 **Maui**, HI, United States
140 H 8 **Maun**, Botswana
85 C 15 **Mauna Kea**, HI, United States
85 C 16 **Mauna Loa**, HI, United States
136 E 4 **Mauritania**, Africa
30 F 5 **Mauritius**, Mauritius
141 O 8 **Mauritius**, Africa
30 E 6 **Mauritius Trench**, Indian Ocean
33 P 2 **Mawson**, Australia
33 N 7 **Mawson Peninsula**, Antarctica
91 J 3 **Mayaguana Island**, The Bahamas
91 L 4 **Mayagüez**, Puerto Rico
104 B 7 **Maykop**, Russia
74 D 6 **Mayo**, YT, Canada
150 G 3 **Mayor Island**, New Zealand
141 M 6 **Mayotte**, France
57 F 14 **Mazara del Vallo**, Italy
111 K 7 **Mazār-e Sharif**, Afghanistan
88 H 7 **Mazatlán**, Mexico
64 H 6 **Mazowiecki**, Poland
65 K 6 **Mazyr**, Belarus
141 J 9 **Mbabane**, Swaziland
141 K 2 **Mbale**, Uganda
140 G 3 **Mbandaka**, Democratic Republic of Congo
140 F 5 **M'banza Congo**, Angola
141 J 3 **Mbarara**, Uganda
141 J 5 **Mbeya**, Tanzania
140 H 4 **Mbuji-Mayi**, Democratic Republic of Congo
83 H 11 **McAlester**, OK, United States
83 G 14 **McAllen**, TX, United States
83 E 12 **McCamey**, TX, United States
74 G 4 **McClintock Channel**, NU, Canada
32 C 6 **McClure Strait**, Canada
80 E 6 **McComb**, MS, United States
83 F 9 **McCook**, NE, United States
84 C 7 **McMinnville**, OR, United States
33 M 6 **McMurdo**, United States
79 J 7 **Meadville**, PA, United States
114 H 7 **Mecca**, Saudi Arabia
49 F 11 **Mechelen**, Belgium
52 F 4 **Mecklenburger Bay**, Germany
122 F 7 **Medan**, Indonesia
96 E 2 **Medellín**, Colombia
85 C 9 **Medford**, PR, United States
74 F 10 **Medicine Hat**, AB, Canada
114 H 6 **Medina**, Saudi Arabia
41 I 4 **Medina del Campo**, Spain
41 K 4 **Medinaceli**, Spain
23 I 4 **Mediterranean Sea**, Europe
146 E 7 **Meekatharra**, WA, Australia
118 D 7 **Meerut**, India
61 G 12 **Megara**, Greece
122 F 3 **Meiktila**, Myanmar
151 N 3 **Mejit Island**, Marshall Islands
137 M 5 **Mek'elē**, Ethiopia
136 F 1 **Meknès**, Morocco
23 M 5 **Mekong**, Asia
52 G 7 **Melaka**, Malaysia
26 F 5 **Melanesian Basin**, Pacific Ocean
147 J 10 **Melbourne**, VIC, Australia
81 K 8 **Melbourne**, FL, United States
74 G 9 **Melfort**, SK, Canada
41 J 11 **Melilla**, Spain
65 N 10 **Melitopol'**, Ukraine
49 D 11 **Melle**, Belgium
69 D 12 **Mellerud**, Sweden
99 J 9 **Melo**, Uruguay
147 J 10 **Melton**, VIC, Australia
45 I 4 **Melun**, France
146 G 3 **Melville Island**, NT, Australia
74 F 3 **Melville Island**, NT/NU, Canada
74 H 5 **Melville Peninsula**, NU, Canada
80 F 2 **Memphis**, TN, United States
27 J 9 **Menard Fracture Zone**, Pacific Ocean
45 J 9 **Mende**, France
32 D 6 **Mendeleyev Ridge**, Arctic Ocean
26 H 3 **Mendocino Fracture Zone**, Pacific Ocean
99 F 10 **Mendoza**, Argentina
48 I 6 **Meppel**, Netherlands
56 E 4 **Merano**, Italy
85 D 12 **Merced**, CA, United States
99 G 10 **Mercedes**, Argentina
99 I 10 **Mercedes**, Uruguay
98 I 8 **Mercedes**, Argentina
122 F 5 **Mergui**, Myanmar
122 F 6 **Mergui Archipelago**, Myanmar
40 G 7 **Mérida**, Spain
96 F 2 **Mérida**, Venezuela
89 O 8 **Mérida**, Mexico
80 F 5 **Meridian**, MS, United States
151 I 2 **Merir**, Palau
37 G 11 **Mersey**, United Kingdom
109 G 10 **Mersin**, Turkey
37 G 13 **Merthyr Tydfil**, United Kingdom
141 L 3 **Meru**, Kenya
108 G 6 **Merzifon**, Turkey
85 I 15 **Mesa**, AZ, United States
41 I 6 **Meseta**, Spain
99 H 9 **Mesopotamia**, Argentina/Uruguay
57 I 14 **Messina**, Italy
141 J 8 **Messina**, South Africa
96 F 3 **Meta**, Colombia/Venezuela
83 J 13 **Metairie**, LA, United States
98 G 7 **Metán**, Argentina
61 F 11 **Meteora**, Greece
61 C 8 **Metković**, Croatia
61 E 11 **Metsovo**, Greece
45 L 3 **Metz**, France
49 G 12 **Meuse**, Belgium
88 E 2 **Mexicali**, Mexico
89 J 6 **Mexico**, North America
89 K 8 **Mexico City**, Mexico
111 J 7 **Meymaneh**, Afghanistan
89 N 9 **Mezcalapa**, Mexico
89 L 10 **Miahuatlán**, Mexico
81 L 10 **Miami**, FL, United States
81 L 10 **Miami Beach**, FL, United States
111 L 8 **Mianwali**, Pakistan
127 K 8 **Mianyang**, China
104 E 8 **Miass**, Russia
78 G 6 **Michigan**, United States
104 C 6 **Michurinsk**, Russia
29 H 10 **Mid-Atlantic Ridge**, Atlantic Ocean
49 D 9 **Middelburg**, Netherlands
27 K 4 **Middle America Trench**, Pacific Ocean
119 J 13 **Middle Andaman**, India
78 H 11 **Middlesboro**, VI, United States
37 H 10 **Middlesbrough**, United Kingdom
79 L 7 **Middletown**, NY, United States
30 H 4 **Mid-Indian Basin**, Indian Ocean
30 F 3 **Mid-Indian Ridge**, Indian Ocean
26 F 4 **Mid-Pacific Mountains**, Pacific Ocean
26 G 3 **Midway Islands**, United States
40 H 2 **Mieres**, Spain
64 G 4 **Mierzeja Helska**, Poland
89 I 6 **Miguel Auza**, Mexico
131 I 11 **Mikura-jima**, Japan
56 C 5 **Milan**, Italy
147 J 9 **Mildura**, VIC, Australia
147 K 7 **Miles**, QLD, Australia
82 D 6 **Miles City**, MT, United States
79 L 7 **Milford**, PA, United States
150 B 9 **Milford Sound**, New Zealand
151 N 4 **Mili**, Marshall Islands
33 P 5 **Mill Island**, Antarctica
82 H 6 **Mille Lacs**, MN, United States
81 J 4 **Milledgeville**, GA, United States
61 G 13 **Milos**, Greece
37 I 13 **Milton Keynes**, United Kingdom
78 F 6 **Milwaukee**, WI, United States
89 M 9 **Minatitlán**, Mexico
122 E 3 **Minbu**, Myanmar
36 E 6 **Minch, The**, United Kingdom
123 K 6 **Mindanao**, Philippines
28 A 7 **Mindelo**, Cape Verde
52 D 6 **Minden**, Germany
123 J 5 **Mindoro**, Philippines
109 N 6 **Mingäşşevir**, Azerbaijan
109 N 6 **Mingaçevir Su Anbari**, Azerbaijan
136 H 6 **Minna**, Nigeria
82 H 6 **Minneapolis**, MN, United States
82 G 6 **Minnesota**, United States
41 P 5 **Minorca**, Spain
82 F 5 **Minot**, ND, United States
65 J 5 **Minsk**, Belarus
41 J 2 **Miranda de Ebro**, Spain
33 P 4 **Mirny**, Russia
105 J 8 **Mirnyy**, Russia
111 K 10 **Mirpur Khas**, Pakistan
118 J 7 **Mishmi Hills**, India
64 G 9 **Miskolc**, Hungary
123 L 8 **Misool**, Indonesia
137 I 2 **Mişrātah**, Libya
22 D 4 **Mississippi**, North America
80 E 4 **Mississippi**, United States
82 B 5 **Missoula**, MT, United States
22 D 3 **Missouri**, North America
83 I 9 **Missouri**, United States
147 K 7 **Mitchell**, QLD, Australia
147 J 4 **Mitchell**, QLD, Australia
82 G 7 **Mitchell**, SD, United States
131 I 9 **Mito**, Japan
96 F 3 **Mitú**, Colombia
131 I 11 **Miyake-jima**, Japan
131 C 14 **Miyakonojō**, Japan
131 C 14 **Miyazaki**, Japan
37 A 13 **Mizen Head**, Ireland
33 N 2 **Mizuho**, Japan
61 C 9 **Mljet**, Croatia
68 E 7 **Mo i Rana**, Norway
85 J 11 **Moab**, UT, United States
80 G 6 **Mobile**, AL, United States
80 G 6 **Mobile Bay**, AL, United States
27 L 9 **Mocha Fracture Zone**, Pacific Ocean
96 E 4 **Mocoa**, Colombia
141 K 7 **Mocuba**, Mozambique
56 D 6 **Modena**, Italy
85 D 12 **Modesto**, CA, United States
57 H 15 **Modica**, Italy
147 K 10 **Moe**, VIC, Australia
97 I 3 **Moengo**, Suriname
52 B 7 **Moers**, Germany
118 C 7 **Moga**, India
137 N 8 **Mogadishu**, Somalia
130 H 7 **Mogami**, Japan
136 F 1 **Mohammedia**, Morocco
141 M 6 **Mohéli**, Comoros
85 F 14 **Mojave Desert**, CA, United States
131 B 13 **Mojikō**, Japan
69 B 9 **Molde**, Norway
65 J 9 **Moldova**, Europe
141 I 9 **Molepolole**, Botswana
57 J 10 **Molfetta**, Italy
53 H 13 **Möll**, Austria
96 F 7 **Mollendo**, Peru
65 N 10 **Molochnyy Lyman**, Ukraine
33 O 2 **Molodezhnaya**, Russia
85 C 15 **Molokai**, HI, United States
26 H 4 **Molokai Fracture Zone**, Pacific Ocean
61 G 12 **Molos**, Greece
123 K 8 **Molucca Sea**, Indonesia
123 L 8 **Moluccas**, Indonesia
141 L 4 **Mombasa**, Kenya
69 D 15 **Møn**, Denmark
45 M 9 **Monaco**, Monaco
45 M 9 **Monaco**, Europe
28 G 4 **Monaco Basin**, Atlantic Ocean
37 D 11 **Monasterboice**, Ireland
52 B 8 **Mönchengladbach**, Germany
89 J 5 **Monclova**, Mexico
75 L 9 **Moncton**, NB, Canada
56 B 7 **Mondovi**, Italy
137 J 6 **Mongo**, Chad
127 J 3 **Mongolia**, Asia
111 L 7 **Mongora**, Pakistan
141 I 6 **Mongu**, Zambia
85 E 12 **Mono Lake**, CA, United States
83 J 12 **Monroe**, LA, United States
136 E 7 **Monrovia**, Liberia
49 D 13 **Mons**, Belgium
45 M 7 **Mont Blanc**, France/Italy
61 G 8 **Montana**, Bulgaria
82 C 6 **Montana**, United States
45 J 5 **Montargis**, France
45 I 9 **Montauban**, France
79 M 7 **Montauk Point**, NY, United States
45 L 5 **Montbéliard**, France
44 G 9 **Mont-de-Marsan**, France
57 G 9 **Monte Carno**, Italy
99 I 9 **Monte Caseros**, Argentina
45 N 10 **Monte Cinto**, Corsica
56 B 5 **Monte Rosa**, Italy
91 I 3 **Montego Bay**, Jamaica
45 K 9 **Montélimar**, France
89 K 6 **Montemorelos**, Mexico
85 C 13 **Monterey**, CA, United States
85 C 12 **Monterey Bay**, CA, United States
96 E 2 **Montería**, Colombia
98 G 5 **Montero**, Bolivia
89 K 5 **Monterrey**, Mexico
97 K 7 **Montes Claros**, Brazil
99 I 10 **Montevideo**, Uruguay
80 G 5 **Montgomery**, AL, United States
45 I 7 **Montluçon**, France
41 I 8 **Montoro**, Spain
79 M 5 **Montpelier**, VT, United States
45 J 10 **Montpellier**, France
75 K 10 **Montréal**, QC, Canada
53 B 13 **Montreux**, Switzerland
83 C 9 **Montrose**, CO, United States
136 H 5 **Monts Bagzane**, Niger
136 H 3 **Monts du Mouydir**, Algeria
141 I 5 **Monts Mitumba**, Democratic Republic of Congo
91 N 5 **Montserrat**, United Kingdom
44 F 4 **Mont-St-Michel**, France
122 E 3 **Monywa**, Myanmar
56 C 5 **Monza**, Italy
41 M 3 **Monzón**, Spain
146 E 8 **Moora**, WA, Australia
151 M 10 **Moorea**, French Polynesia
82 G 6 **Moorhead**, MN, United States
75 J 9 **Moose**, Canada
79 N 4 **Moosehead Lake**, ME, United States
75 J 9 **Moosonee**, ON, Canada
136 F 5 **Mopti**, Mali
69 E 11 **Mora**, Sweden
118 E 8 **Moradabad**, India
64 F 8 **Moraua**, Czech Republic
61 F 8 **Morava**, Serbia and Montenegro
36 F 6 **Moray Firth**, United Kingdom
89 J 8 **Morelia**, Mexico
118 D 8 **Morena**, India
130 I 6 **Morioka**, Japan
44 E 4 **Morlaix**, France
27 L 9 **Mornington Abyssal Plain**, Pacific Ocean
123 K 6 **Moro Gulf**, Philippines
136 F 2 **Morocco**, Africa
141 K 4 **Morogoro**, Tanzania
141 M 8 **Morondava**, Madagascar
141 M 6 **Moroni**, Comoros
150 F 3 **Morrinsville**, New Zealand
151 L 2 **Mortlock Islands**, Federated States of Micronesia
84 F 6 **Moscow**, WA, United States

Bay · Channel · Country · Dependent Territory · Desert · Geographic Area · Headland · Island · Island Group · Lake · Mountain

104 C 6 Moscow, Russia
53 C 9 Mosel, Europe
141 K 4 Moshi, Tanzania
68 E 7 Mosjøen, Norway
90 G 7 Mosquito Coast, Nicaragua
69 D 12 Moss, Norway
97 L 5 Mossoró, Brazil
64 D 7 Most, Czech Republic
61 C 8 Mostar, Bosnia-Herzegovina
115 I 2 Mosul, Iraq
41 J 6 Mota del Cuervo, Spain
150 G 3 Motiti Island, New Zealand
150 G 4 Motu, New Zealand
45 J 6 Moulins, France
122 F 4 Moulmein, Myanmar
137 I 7 Moundou, Chad
99 F 9 Mt Aconcagua, Argentina/Chile
108 M 7 Mt Ararat, Turkey
33 K 6 Mt Berlin, Antarctica
150 C 8 Mt Cook, New Zealand
79 O 5 Mount Desert Island, ME, United States
57 H 14 Mt Etna, Italy
82 B 6 Mt Evans, MT, United States
118 H 8 Mt Everest, China/Nepal
74 C 7 Mt Fairweather, BC, Canada
131 H 10 Mt Fuji, Japan
147 I 10 Mount Gambier, SA, Australia
147 J 2 Mt Hagen, Papua New Guinea
83 D 9 Mt Harvard, CO, United States
147 I 5 Mount Isa, QLD, Australia
84 D 7 Mt Jefferson, OR, United States
85 F 11 Mt Jefferson, NV, United States
79 N 4 Mt Katahdin, ME, United States
141 K 3 Mt Kenya, Kenya
52 J 6 Mt Kinabalu, Malaysia
33 M 5 Mt Kirkpatrick, Antarctica
147 K 10 Mt Kosciuszko, NSW, Australia
74 C 6 Mt Logan, YT, Canada
146 E 8 Mount Magnet, WA, Australia
79 L 6 Mt Marcy, NY, United States
85 I 11 Mt Marvine, UT, United States
84 J 5 Mt McKinley, AL, United States
33 M 7 Mt Minto, Antarctica,
81 J 2 Mt Mitchell, NC, United States
61 F 11 Mt Olympus, Greece
81 L 4 Mount Pleasant, SC, United States
84 D 6 Mt Rainier, WA, United States
74 E 9 Mt Robson, BC, Canada
150 F 5 Mt Ruapehu, New Zealand
82 E 7 Mt Rushmore, SD, United States
85 D 10 Mt Shasta, CA, United States
78 E 9 Mount Vernon, IL, United States
84 D 5 Mt Vernon, WA, United States
74 D 9 Mt Waddlington, BC, Canada
79 M 5 Mt Washington, NH, United States
85 F 13 Mt Whitney, CA, United States
147 K 1 Mt Wilhelm, Papua New Guinea
83 C 10 Mt Wilson, CO, United States
82 D 8 Mt Zirkel, CO, United States
85 G 9 Mountain Home, ID, United States
49 C 12 Mouscron, Belgium
41 M 5 Mouth of the Ebro, Spain
127 N 7 Mouth of the Yangtze, China
97 J 4 Mouths of the Amazon, Brazil
119 H 10 Mouths of the Ganges, Bangladesh
119 F 12 Mouths of the Godavari, India
111 K 11 Mouths of the Indus, Pakistan
119 E 12 Mouths of the Krishna, India
122 H 6 Mouths of the Mekong, Vietnam
96 E 5 Moyobamba, Peru
141 J 8 Mozambique, Africa
141 L 9 Mozambique Channel, Madagascar/Mozambique
30 D 7 Mozambique Escarpment, Indian Ocean
30 D 7 Mozambique Ridge, Indian Ocean
141 J 6 Mpika, Zambia
141 L 5 Mtwara, Tanzania
127 O 3 Mudanjiang, China
141 I 6 Mufulira, Zambia
109 O 7 Muğan Düzü, Azerbaijan
109 C 9 Muğla, Turkey
122 G 6 Mui Ca Mau, Vietnam
64 H 9 Mukacheve, Ukraine
119 B 15 Mulakatholhu Atoll, Maldives
41 J 9 Mulhacén, Spain
45 M 5 Mulhouse, France
36 D 8 Mull, United Kingdom
37 C 11 Mullingar, Ireland
111 L 9 Multan, Pakistan
119 B 11 Mumbai, India
123 K 9 Muna, Indonesia
78 G 8 Muncie, IN, United States
119 G 9 Munger, India
53 F 11 Munich, Germany
52 C 7 Münster, Germany
68 H 6 Muonio, Finland
114 H 4 Muqāţ, Jordan
108 L 8 Muradiye, Turkey
108 K 7 Murat, Turkey
146 E 7 Murchison, WA, Australia
41 L 8 Murcia, Spain
80 H 2 Murfreesboro, TN, United States
111 L 6 Murghob, Tajikistan
147 L 7 Murgon, QLD, Australia
52 G 5 Müritz, Germany
104 E 4 Murmansk, Russia
130 H 4 Muroran, Japan
131 E 13 Muroto-zaki, Japan
147 J 9 Murray, NSW/VIC, Australia
147 I 9 Murray Bridge, SA, Australia
26 H 3 Murray Fracture Zone, Pacific Ocean
30 G 2 Murray Ridge, Indian Ocean
150 G 4 Murupara, New Zealand
119 E 9 Murwara, India
137 I 3 Murzūq, Libya
108 K 8 Muş, Turkey
61 G 9 Musala, Bulgaria
115 N 6 Muscat, Oman
78 G 6 Muskegon, MI, United States
83 H 10 Muskogee, OK, United States
141 K 3 Musoma, Tanzania
147 L 8 Muswellbrook, NSW, Australia
109 F 10 Mut, Turkey
141 J 7 Mutare, Zimbabwe
130 H 5 Mutsu-wan, Japan
126 G 6 Mutztag Feng, China
111 L 9 Muzaffargarh, Pakistan
118 D 7 Muzaffarnagar, India
119 G 9 Muzaffarpur, India
141 J 3 Mwanza, Tanzania
140 H 5 Mwene-Ditu, Democratic Republic of Congo
151 M 2 Mwokil, Federated States of Micronesia
122 H 6 My Tho, Vietnam
122 F 2 Myanmar, Asia
122 F 3 Myingyan, Myanmar
122 F 2 Myitkyina, Myanmar
65 L 10 Mykolayiv, Ukraine
61 H 13 Mykonos, Greece
61 H 13 Mykonos, Greece
61 H 11 Myrina, Greece
81 L 4 Myrtle Beach, SC, United States
65 M 11 Mys Ayya, Ukraine
65 M 11 Mys Khersones, Ukraine
119 D 13 Mysore, India
61 I 11 Mytilini, Greece
141 K 6 Mzuzu, Malawi

N

136 G 2 Naama, Algeria
104 D 7 Naberezhnyye Chelny, Russia
114 G 3 Nāblus, Israel
141 L 6 Nacala, Mozambique
119 C 10 Nadiad, India
61 G 13 Nafplio, Greece
131 G 9 Nagano, Japan
131 G 9 Nagaoka, Japan
119 E 12 Nagarjuna Sagar, India
131 B 14 Nagasaki, Japan
119 D 15 Nagercoil, India
131 J 15 Nago, Japan
131 F 11 Nagoya, Japan
119 E 10 Nagpur, India
126 H 7 Nagqu, China
64 F 10 Nagykanizsa, Hungary
131 J 16 Naha, Japan
75 K 6 Nain, NL, Canada
141 K 3 Nairobi, Kenya
141 K 3 Naivasha, Kenya
115 L 3 Najafābād, Iran
115 J 9 Najrān, Saudi Arabia
131 D 13 Nakamura, Japan
131 B 16 Nakano-shima, Japan
105 M 11 Nakhodka, Russia
122 G 4 Nakhon Ratchasima, Thailand
122 F 4 Nakhon Sawan, Thailand
122 F 6 Nakhon Si Thammarat, Thailand
141 K 3 Nakuru, Kenya
104 B 8 Nal'chik, Russia
126 H 7 Nam Co, China
122 H 3 Nam Đinh, Vietnam
140 G 9 Namaqualand, Namibia
140 F 7 Namib Desert, Namibia
140 F 7 Namibe, Angola
140 G 8 Namibia, Africa
29 J 9 Namibia Abyssal Plain, Atlantic Ocean
127 I 8 Namjagbarwa, China
151 L 2 Namoluk, Federated States of Micronesia
151 M 4 Namorik, Marshall Islands
84 F 8 Nampa, ID, United States
127 O 5 Namp'o, North Korea
141 L 7 Nampula, Mozambique
68 D 8 Namsos, Norway
151 M 3 Namu, Marshall Islands
49 F 13 Namur, Belgium
74 D 9 Nanaimo, BC, Canada
127 M 8 Nanchang, China
127 K 8 Nanchong, China
45 L 4 Nancy, France
119 D 11 Nanded, India
119 E 12 Nandyal, India
127 N 7 Nanjing, China
127 K 10 Nanning, China
127 N 9 Nanping, China
32 E 7 Nansen Basin, Arctic Ocean
32 D 8 Nansen Cordillera, Arctic Ocean
44 F 6 Nantes, France
127 N 7 Nantong, China
79 N 7 Nantucket, MA, United States
79 N 7 Nantucket Island, MA, United States
127 L 7 Nanyang, China
85 C 12 Napa, CA, United States
74 F 5 Napaktulik Lake, NU, Canada
150 G 5 Napier, New Zealand
57 G 11 Naples, Italy
81 K 10 Naples, FL, United States
96 E 4 Napo, Ecuador/Peru
131 F 11 Nara, Japan
147 I 10 Naracoorte, SA, Australia
45 J 10 Narbonne, France
28 D 5 Nares Abyssal Plain, Atlantic Ocean
74 H 2 Nares Strait, NU, Canada/Greenland
64 H 6 Narew, Poland
23 K 5 Narmada, Asia
147 K 8 Narrabri, NSW, Australia
65 J 1 Narva, Estonia
65 J 1 Narva laht, Estonia
68 F 5 Narvik, Norway
111 M 5 Naryn, Kyrgyzstan
119 C 11 Nashik, India
79 M 6 Nashua, NH, United States
80 G 2 Nashville, TN, United States
91 I 2 Nassau, The Bahamas
97 M 5 Natal, Brazil
30 E 7 Natal Basin, Indian Ocean
30 D 7 Natal Valley, Indian Ocean
75 L 8 Natashquan, QC, Canada
80 E 5 Natchez, MS, United States
83 I 12 Natchitoches, LA, United States
136 G 6 Natitingou, Benin
31 J 7 Naturaliste Fracture Zone, Indian Ocean
31 K 7 Naturaliste Plateau, Southern Ocean
150 H 8 Nauru, Pacific Ocean
65 J 4 Navapolatsk, Belarus
111 J 6 Navoi, Uzbekistan
88 G 5 Navojoa, Mexico
119 B 10 Navsari, India
111 K 10 Nawabshah, Pakistan
109 M 7 Naxşivan, Azerbaijan
61 H 13 Naxos, Greece
61 I 13 Naxos, Greece
114 G 3 Nazareth, Israel
27 M 7 Nazca Ridge, Pacific Ocean
131 K 14 Naze, Japan
137 N 6 Nazrēt, Ethiopia
115 N 7 Nazwá, Oman
137 J 7 Ndélé, Central African Republic
137 I 6 Ndjamena, Chad
141 J 6 Ndola, Zambia
110 H 6 Nebitdag, Turkmenistan
82 F 8 Nebraska, United States
82 H 8 Nebraska City, NE, United States
53 D 10 Neckar, Germany
99 H 11 Necochea, Argentina
104 E 7 Neftekamsk, Russia
151 M 2 Negetik Atoll, Federated States of Micronesia
114 G 4 Negev, Israel
119 E 15 Negombo, Sri Lanka
99 G 11 Negro, Argentina
96 G 4 Negro, Bolivia/Brazil
123 K 6 Negros, Philippines
127 K 8 Neijiang, China
96 E 3 Neiva, Colombia
137 L 6 Nek'emtē, Ethiopia
119 E 13 Nellore, India
150 E 6 Nelson, New Zealand
74 H 8 Nelson, Canada
136 F 5 Néma, Mauritania
64 H 4 Nemunas, Lithuania
130 J 3 Nemuro, Japan
130 J 2 Nemuro-kaikyō, Japan
118 F 8 Nepal, Asia
61 C 9 Neretva, Bosnia-Herzegovina
61 H 10 Nestos, Greece
48 F 6 Netherlands, Europe
91 L 6 Netherlands Antilles, Netherlands
75 J 5 Nettilling Lake, NU, Canada
52 H 5 Neubrandenburg, Germany
49 H 14 Neufchâteau, Belgium
33 L 1 Neumayer, Germany
52 E 4 Neumünster, Germany
99 F 11 Neuquén, Argentina
99 F 11 Neuquén, Argentina
53 F 12 Neuschwanstein Castle, Germany
52 B 8 Neuss, Germany
53 C 9 Neuwied, Germany
85 F 11 Nevada, United States
96 F 7 Nevado Coropuna, Peru
98 F 7 Nevado de Cachi, Argentina
96 E 3 Nevado del Huila, Colombia
96 E 6 Nevado Huascarán, Peru
98 F 8 Nevado Ojos del Salado, Argentina/Chile
98 F 5 Nevado Sajama, Bolivia
45 J 6 Nevers, France
104 B 8 Nevinnomyssk, Russia
108 G 8 Nevşehir, Turkey
78 G 9 New Albany, IN, United States
97 I 2 New Amsterdam, Guyuna
79 N 7 New Bedford, MA, United States
81 M 2 New Bern, NC, United States
147 L 2 New Britain, Papua New Guinea
75 L 9 New Brunswick, Canada
150 G 10 New Caledonia, France
26 F 7 New Caledonia Trough, Pacific Ocean
118 D 8 New Delhi, India,
79 M 7 New England, United States
28 D 4 New England Seamounts, Atlantic Ocean
75 M 8 New Glasgow, NS, Canada
123 N 9 New Guinea, Asia/Oceania
79 M 5 New Hampshire, United States
79 M 7 New Haven, CT, United States
83 J 13 New Iberia, LA, United States
147 L 1 New Ireland, Papua New Guinea
79 L 9 New Jersey, United States
83 C 11 New Mexico, United States
83 K 13 New Orleans, LA, United States
150 E 5 New Plymouth, New Zealand
105 K 4 New Siberia Islands, Russia
147 K 8 New South Wales, Australia
79 J 7 New York, United States
79 L 8 New York, NY, United States
150 E 5 New Zealand, Pacific Ocean
79 L 8 Newark, NJ, United States
84 C 7 Newberg, OR, United States
37 H 14 Newbury, United Kingdom
147 L 9 Newcastle, NSW, Australia
37 H 9 Newcastle upon Tyne, United Kingdom
75 M 7 Newfoundland, NL, Canada
75 L 6 Newfoundland and Labrador, Canada
28 E 4 Newfoundland Ridge, Atlantic Ocean
146 E 6 Newman, WA, Australia
37 H 14 Newport, United Kingdom
79 M 5 Newport, VT, United States
79 N 7 Newport, RI, United States
84 C 8 Newport, OR, United States
79 K 10 Newport News, VI, United States
83 G 9 Newton, KS, United States
115 N 2 Neyshābūr, Iran
89 K 8 Nezahualcóyo, Mexico
151 I 1 Ngajangel, Palau
137 I 7 Ngaoundéré, Cameroon
151 J 1 Ngulu, Federated States of Micronesia
122 H 5 Nha Trang, Vietnam
79 J 6 Niagara Falls, Canada/United States
75 K 10 Niagara Falls, ON, Canada
136 G 5 Niamey, Niger
122 F 8 Nias, Indonesia
90 F 6 Nicaragua, North America
45 M 10 Nice, France
119 J 15 Nicobar Islands, India
108 F 11 Nicosia, Cyprus
48 G 8 Nieuwegein, Netherlands
109 G 9 Niğde, Turkey
22 H 5 Niger, Africa
136 H 5 Niger, Africa
136 G 6 Nigeria, Africa
130 G 8 Niigata, Japan
131 D 12 Niihama, Japan
85 A 15 Niihau, HI, United States
131 H 11 Nii-jima, Japan
48 H 8 Nijmegen, Netherlands
65 M 9 Nikopol', Ukraine
61 D 9 Nikšić, Serbia and Montenegro
119 A 15 Nilandhoo Atoll, Maldives
23 I 4 Nile, Africa
45 K 9 Nimes, France
31 I 6 Ninetyeast Ridge, Indian Ocean
127 N 8 Ningbo, China
136 E 5 Nioro, Mali
44 G 7 Niort, France
75 I 10 Nipigon, ON, Canada
61 F 8 Niš, Serbia and Montenegro
151 J 9 Niua Group, Tonga
26 H 7 Niue, Niue
151 K 10 Niue, New Zealand
119 E 11 Nizamabad, India
104 G 7 Nizhnevartovsk, Russia
104 D 6 Nizhniy Novgorod, Russia
104 E 7 Nizhniy Tagil, Russia
105 I 7 Nizhnyaya Tunguska, Russia
136 H 7 Nkongsamba, Cameroon
131 C 14 Nobeoka, Japan
131 I 10 Noda, Japan
85 J 16 Nogales, AZ, United States
88 G 3 Nogales, Mexico
131 I 10 Nojima-zaki, Japan
69 H 10 Nokia, Finland
84 I 4 Nome, AL, United States
151 L 1 Nomwin, Federated States of Micronesia
122 F 5 Nonthaburi, Thailand
32 E 9 Nord Kapp, Norway
32 E 8 Nordaustlandet, Svalbard
52 F 7 Nordhausen, Germany
52 C 6 Nordhorn, Germany
79 L 10 Norfolk, VI, United States
82 G 8 Norfolk, NE, United States
104 H 6 Noril'sk, Russia
147 J 5 Norman, QLD, Australia
83 G 11 Norman, OK, United States
74 E 5 Norman Wells, NT, Canada
44 G 4 Normandy, France
147 J 5 Normanton, QLD, Australia
69 F 12 Norrköping, Sweden
69 G 11 Norrtälje, Sweden
146 F 9 Norseman, WA, Australia
28 D 5 North American Basin, Atlantic Ocean
119 J 13 North Andaman, India
31 K 5 North Australian Basin, Southern Ocean
74 F 9 North Battleford, SK, Canada
75 J 10 North Bay, ON, Canada
68 I 3 North Cape, Norway
150 E 1 North Cape, New Zealand
81 L 2 North Carolina, United States
82 E 5 North Dakota, United States
22 H 3 North European Plain, Europe
26 G 7 North Fiji Basin, Pacific Ocean
37 K 13 North Foreland, United Kingdom

Mountain Range · National Capital · Ocean · Physical Feature · Polar Base · River · Sea · Special Feature · State Capital · Underwater Feature

52	D 3	**North Frisian Islands**, Germany 🌴
32	C 7	**North Geomagnetic Pole**, Arctic Ocean ◇
150	E 2	**North Head**, New Zealand ▶
119	B 15	**North Huvadhu Atoll**, Maldives 🏝
150	F 4	**North Island**, New Zealand 🏝
127	O 5	**North Korea**, Asia □
119	A 14	**North Maalhosmadulu Atoll**, Maldives 🏝
119	B 13	**North Miladunmadulu Atoll**, Maldives 🏝
82	F 8	**North Platte**, NE, United States
78	H 5	**North Point**, MI, United States ▶
32	D 6	**North Pole**, Arctic Ocean ◇
74	F 9	**North Saskatchewan**, Canada ∿
28	I 3	**North Sea**, Atlantic Ocean 🌊
36	D 6	**North Uist**, United Kingdom 🏝
146	D 6	**North West Cape**, WA, Australia ▶
36	E 7	**North West Highlands**, United Kingdom ⛰
146	E 9	**Northam**, WA, Australia
37	I 13	**Northampton**, United Kingdom
27	I 3	**Northeast Pacific Basin**, Pacific Ocean ▃
151	L 9	**Northern Cook Islands**, Cook Islands 🌴
23	J 2	**Northern Dvina**, Europe ∿
37	D 10	**Northern Ireland**, United Kingdom ▣
151	L 7	**Northern Line Islands**, Kiribati 🌴
151	K 3	**Northern Mariana Islands**, United States ▣
56	D 6	**Northern Plain**, Italy, ◇
146	H 6	**Northern Territory**, Australia, ▣
28	D 2	**Northwest Atlantic Mid-Ocean Channel**, Atlantic Ocean ⧗
26	F 2	**Northwest Pacific Basin**, Pacific Ocean ▃
74	E 6	**Northwest Territories**, Canada ▣
32	D 4	**Northwind Plain**, Arctic Ocean ▃
32	C 3	**Norton Sound**, United States ≈
69	B 11	**Norway**, Europe □
32	D 10	**Norwegian Basin**, Arctic Ocean ▃
32	E 9	**Norwegian Sea**, Arctic Ocean 🌊
37	J 12	**Norwich**, United Kingdom
61	J 9	**Nos Emine**, Bulgaria ▶
61	J 8	**Nos Kaliakra**, Bulgaria ▶
61	J 8	**Nos Shabla**, Bulgaria ▶
130	K 3	**Nosapu-misaki**, Japan ▶
141	N 6	**Nosy Bé**, Madagascar 🏝
141	N 7	**Nosy Boraha**, Madagascar 🏝
131	F 9	**Noto-hantō**, Japan ▶
75	J 9	**Nottaway**, Canada ∿
37	H 12	**Nottingham**, United Kingdom
136	D 4	**Nouâdhibou**, Mauritania
136	D 4	**Nouakchott**, Mauritania ▟
150	H 11	**Noumea**, New Caledonia ▟
61	C 7	**Nova Gradiška**, Croatia
97	K 8	**Nova Iguaçu**, Brazil
40	B 9	**Nova Lajes**, Portugal
75	M 9	**Nova Scotia**, Canada ▣
56	B 6	**Novara**, Italy
104	F 4	**Novaya Zemlya**, Russia 🏝
61	E 8	**Novi Pazar**, Serbia and Montenegro
61	E 7	**Novi Sad**, Serbia and Montenegro
97	J 10	**Novo Hamburgo**, Brazil
104	G 9	**Novokuznetsk**, Russia
33	M 1	**Novolazarevskaya**, Russia ≡
104	C 6	**Novomoskovsk**, Russia
104	B 7	**Novorossiysk**, Russia
104	G 9	**Novosibirsk**, Russia
141	I 8	**Ntwetwe Pan**, Botswana ≋
137	L 4	**Nubian Desert**, Sudan ◓
89	J 4	**Nueva Rosita**, Mexico
90	E 6	**Nueva San Salvador**, Netherlands Antilles
88	H 3	**Nuevo Casas Grandes**, Mexico
89	K 5	**Nuevo Laredo**, Mexico
151	O 8	**Nuku Hiva**, French Polynesia 🏝
151	K 10	**Nuku'alofa**, Tonga ▟
151	L 2	**Nukuoro**, Federated States of Micronesia 🏝
111	I 5	**Nukus**, Uzbekistan
146	G 8	**Nullarbor Plain**, WA, Australia ◓
74	G 6	**Nunavut**, Canada ▣
84	I 5	**Nunivak Island**, AK, United States 🏝
48	H 7	**Nunspeet**, Netherlands
57	C 11	**Nuoro**, Italy
53	F 10	**Nuremberg**, Germany
68	J 8	**Nurmes**, Finland
109	K 9	**Nusaybin**, Turkey
32	B 9	**Nuuk**, Greenland, ▟
32	C 8	**Nuussuaq**, Greenland
126	H 8	**Nyainqêntanglha Shan**, China ⛰
137	K 6	**Nyala**, Sudan
69	C 15	**Nyborg**, Denmark
141	K 3	**Nyeri**, Kenya
64	H 9	**Nyíegyháza**, Hungary
126	H 8	**Nyingchi**, China
69	D 15	**Nykøbing**, Denmark
69	F 12	**Nyköping**, Sweden
147	K 8	**Nyngan**, NSW, Australia
65	I 5	**Nyoman**, Belarus ∿
130	G 6	**Nyūdō-zaki**, Japan, ▶
136	E 6	**Nzérékoré**, Guinea

O

85	B 15	**Oahu**, HI, United States 🏝
84	D 5	**Oak Harbor**, WA, United States
85	C 12	**Oakland**, CA, United States
150	D 10	**Oamaru**, New Zealand
89	L 10	**Oaxaca**, Mexico
23	J 2	**Ob'**, Europe ∿
36	E 8	**Oban**, United Kingdom
123	L 8	**Obi**, Indonesia 🏝
130	I 3	**Obihiro**, Japan
104	G 6	**Obsakaya Guba**, Russia ≈
65	N 10	**Obytichna Kosa**, Ukraine ▶
81	J 7	**Ocala**, FL, United States
28	E 4	**Oceanographer Fracture Zone**, Atlantic Ocean ▃
85	F 15	**Oceanside**, CA, United States
81	J 5	**Ocmulgee**, United States ∿
131	H 10	**Odawara**, Japan
108	C 8	**Ödemiş**, Turkey
69	C 14	**Odense**, Denmark
64	F 7	**Oder**, Europe ∿
52	H 5	**Oderhaff**, Germany/Poland ≈
65	L 10	**Odesa**, Ukraine
83	E 12	**Odessa**, TX, United States
108	J 6	**Of**, Turkey
53	D 9	**Offenbach**, Germany
53	C 11	**Offenburg**, Germany
136	H 7	**Ogbomoso**, Nigeria
85	I 10	**Ogden**, UT, United States
65	I 3	**Ogre**, Latvia
22	D 4	**Ohio**, North America ∿
78	H 8	**Ohio**, United States ▣
150	F 5	**Ohura**, New Zealand
49	G 9	**Oirschot**, Netherlands
131	C 13	**Ōita**, Japan
111	L 9	**Okara**, Pakistan
140	H 7	**Okavango Delta**, Botswana ◇
131	D 12	**Okayama**, Japan
131	G 11	**Okazaki**, Japan
105	M 8	**Okhotsk**, Russia
65	M 7	**Okhtyrka**, Ukraine
131	J 16	**Okinawa**, Japan
131	K 15	**Okinawa**, Japan 🏝
131	K 16	**Okinawa-shotō**, Japan 🌴
131	J 15	**Okinoerabu-jima**, Japan 🏝
131	D 13	**Okino-shima**, Japan 🏝
131	C 11	**Oki-shotō**, Japan 🌴
83	G 10	**Oklahoma**, United States ▣
83	G 10	**Oklahoma City**, OK, United States ⌂
104	D 7	**Oktyabr'skiy**, Russia
131	K 15	**Oku**, Japan
130	G 5	**Okushiri-tō**, Japan 🏝
69	F 14	**Öland**, Sweden 🏝
99	H 11	**Olavarría**, Argentina
57	C 10	**Olbia**, Italy
52	D 5	**Oldenburg**, Germany
48	K 7	**Oldenzaal**, Netherlands
37	H 11	**Oldham**, United Kingdom
79	K 7	**Olean**, NY, United States
65	L 8	**Oleksandriva**, Ukraine
105	J 6	**Olenek**, Russia ∿
40	F 9	**Olhão**, Portugal
64	F 8	**Olomouc**, Czech Republic
123	J 4	**Olongapo**, Philippines
64	G 5	**Olsztyn**, Poland
60	I 8	**Oltenița**, Romania
84	D 6	**Olympia**, WA, United States ⌂
82	H 8	**Omaha**, NE, United States
84	E 5	**Omak**, WA, United States
115	M 7	**Oman**, Asia □
137	L 5	**Omdurman**, Sudan
137	M 7	**Omo Wenz**, Ethiopia ∿
105	N 6	**Omolon**, Russia ∿
104	F 8	**Omsk**, Russia
127	L 3	**Öndörhaan**, Mongolia
119	A 15	**One and a Half Degree Channel**, Maldives ⧗
79	K 6	**Oneida Lake**, NY, United States ≋
119	E 12	**Ongole**, India
109	L 5	**Oni**, Georgia
136	H 7	**Onitsha**, Nigeria
146	D 6	**Onslow**, WA, Australia
81	M 3	**Onslow Bay**, NC, United States ≈
84	F 8	**Ontario**, OR, United States
75	I 9	**Ontario**, Canada ▣
41	L 7	**Ontinyent**, Spain
83	H 10	**Oologah Lake**, OK, United States ≋
49	B 10	**Oostende**, Belgium
49	F 9	**Oosterhout**, Netherlands
49	D 9	**Oosterschelde**, Netherlands ≈
80	H 4	**Opelika**, AL, United States
83	J 12	**Opelousas**, LA, United States
64	F 7	**Opole**, Poland
150	G 4	**Opotiki**, New Zealand
60	F 5	**Oradea**, Romania
136	G 1	**Oran**, Algeria
45	K 9	**Orange**, France
147	K 9	**Orange**, NSW, Australia
140	G 10	**Orange**, Namibia/South Africa ∿
28	J 8	**Orange Cone**, Atlantic Ocean ▃
90	E 4	**Orange Walk**, Belize
81	K 4	**Orangeburg**, SC, United States
91	L 7	**Oranjestad**, Aruba ▟
60	F 7	**Oravița**, Romania
57	E 9	**Orbetello**, Italy
33	J 1	**Orcadas**, Argentina ≡
146	G 5	**Ord**, WA, Australia ∿
108	I 6	**Ordu**, Turkey
69	E 12	**Örebro**, Sweden
84	D 8	**Oregon**, United States ▣
65	M 8	**Orel**, Ukraine ∿
104	C 6	**Orel**, Russia
104	D 8	**Orenburg**, Russia
61	I 10	**Orestiada**, Greece
41	L 8	**Orihuela**, Spain
75	K 10	**Orillia**, ON, Canada
22	E 6	**Orinoco**, South America ∿
57	B 12	**Oristano**, Italy
69	K 9	**Orivesi**, Finland ≋
89	L 9	**Orizaba**, Mexico
36	F 5	**Orkney Islands**, United Kingdom 🌴
81	K 8	**Orlando**, FL, United States
45	I 5	**Orléans**, France
79	N 7	**Orleans**, MA, United States
123	K 5	**Ormoc**, Philippines
69	G 9	**Örnsköldsvik**, Sweden
151	M 1	**Oroluk**, Federated States of Micronesia 🏝
151	K 8	**Orona**, Kiribati 🏝
65	K 4	**Orsha**, Belarus
104	D 8	**Orsk**, Russia
44	G 10	**Orthez**, France
115	J 2	**Orūmīyeh**, Iran
98	F 5	**Oruro**, Bolivia
131	F 11	**Ōsaka**, Japan
31	I 5	**Osborn Plateau**, Indian Ocean ▃
111	L 6	**Osh**, Kyrgyzstan
140	G 7	**Oshakati**, Namibia
75	K 10	**Oshawa**, ON, Canada
131	H 11	**Ō-shima**, Japan 🏝
78	F 6	**Oshkosh**, WI, United States
61	D 6	**Osijek**, Croatia
65	N 7	**Oskol**, Ukraine ∿
69	C 11	**Oslo**, Norway ▟
109	H 9	**Osmaniye**, Turkey
52	C 6	**Osnabrück**, Germany
99	E 12	**Osorno**, Chile
49	H 9	**Oss**, Netherlands
69	E 9	**Östersund**, Sweden
64	F 8	**Ostrava**, Czech Republic
64	G 5	**Ostróda**, Poland
104	G 4	**Ostrov Belyy**, Russia 🏝
105	I 4	**Ostrov Bol'shevik**, Russia 🏝
105	J 5	**Ostrov Bol'shoy Begichev**, Russia 🏝
105	L 5	**Ostrov Bol'shoy Lyakhovskiy**, Russia 🏝
105	O 10	**Ostrov Iturup**, Russia 🏝
105	O 7	**Ostrov Karaginskiy**, Russia 🏝
104	F 4	**Ostrov Kolguyev**, Russia 🏝
105	I 3	**Ostrov Komsomolets**, Russia 🏝
105	L 4	**Ostrov Kotel'nyy**, Russia 🏝
105	N 10	**Ostrov Kunashir**, Russia 🏝
105	L 4	**Ostrov Novaya Sibir'**, Russia 🏝
105	I 3	**Ostrov Oktyabr'skoy Revolyutsii**, Russia 🏝
105	O 9	**Ostrov Onekotan**, Russia 🏝
105	O 9	**Ostrov Paramushir**, Russia 🏝
105	O 10	**Ostrov Urup**, Russia 🏝
104	F 5	**Ostrov Vaygach**, Russia 🏝
64	F 6	**Ostrów Wielkopolski**, Poland
131	B 15	**Ōsumi-kaikyō**, Japan ⧗
131	B 15	**Ōsumi-shotō**, Japan 🌴
40	H 9	**Osuna**, Spain
150	C 10	**Otago Peninsula**, New Zealand ▶
150	F 6	**Otaki**, New Zealand
130	G 4	**Otaru**, Japan
84	E 6	**Othello**, WA, United States
150	D 8	**Otira**, New Zealand
140	G 8	**Otjiwarongo**, Namibia
150	F 4	**Otorohanga**, New Zealand
69	B 11	**Otra**, Norway ∿
83	H 9	**Ottawa**, KS, United States
75	K 10	**Ottawa**, ON, Canada ▟
75	I 7	**Ottawa Islands**, NU, Canada 🌴
82	I 8	**Ottumwa**, IA, United States
136	F 6	**Ouagadougou**, Burkina Faso ▟
136	F 5	**Ouahigouya**, Burkina Faso
136	H 2	**Ouargla**, Algeria
140	G 2	**Ouésso**, Congo
136	G 1	**Oujda**, Morocco
68	I 8	**Oulu**, Finland
68	J 8	**Oulujärvi**, Finland ≋
68	I 8	**Oulujoki**, Finland ∿
68	H 6	**Ounasjoki**, Finland ∿
40	F 3	**Ourense**, Spain
49	G 13	**Ourthe**, Belgium ∿
37	H 11	**Ouse**, United Kingdom ∿
36	C 7	**Outer Hebrides**, United Kingdom 🌴
99	E 9	**Ovalle**, Chile
140	G 7	**Ovamboland**, Namibia ∷
40	F 4	**Ovar**, Portugal
49	F 12	**Overijse**, Belgium
83	H 9	**Overland Park**, KS, United States
40	H 2	**Oviedo**, Spain
75	J 10	**Owen Sound**, ON, Canada
85	F 13	**Owens Lake**, CA, United States ≋
78	F 10	**Owensboro**, KY, United States
85	F 9	**Owyhee**, United States ≋
37	H 13	**Oxford**, United Kingdom
150	D 8	**Oxford**, New Zealand
80	F 3	**Oxford**, MS, United States
85	E 14	**Oxnard**, CA, United States
131	H 9	**Oyama**, Japan
83	H 10	**Ozark Plateau**, United States, United States ◇
26	G 7	**Ozbourn Seamount**, Pacific Ocean ▃
111	M 4	**Ozero Alakol'**, Kazakhstan ≋
111	J 6	**Ozero Aydarkul'**, Uzbekistan ≋
111	M 3	**Ozero Sasykkol**, Kazakhstan ≋
105	I 5	**Ozero Taymyr**, Russia ≋
111	K 2	**Ozero Tengiz**, Kazakhstan ≋
65	K 11	**Ozero Yalpuh**, Ukraine ≋
111	N 3	**Ozero Zaysan**, Kazakhstan ≋

P

119	H 9	**Pabna**, Bangladesh
89	L 8	**Pachuca**, Mexico
26	H 6	**Pacific Ocean** ◎
26	G 10	**Pacific-Antarctic Ridge**, Pacific Ocean ▃
122	F 8	**Padang**, Indonesia
52	D 7	**Paderborn**, Germany
56	E 6	**Padova**, Italy
78	E 10	**Paducah**, KY, United States
150	F 3	**Paeroa**, New Zealand
61	B 7	**Pag**, Croatia 🏝
123	K 6	**Pagadian**, Philippines
151	L 3	**Pagan**, Northern Mariana Islands 🏝
85	I 13	**Page**, AZ, United States
151	K 9	**Pago Pago**, American Samoa ▟
65	I 1	**Paide**, Estonia
69	I 10	**Päijänne**, Finland ≋
85	I 13	**Painted Desert**, AZ, United States ◓
41	K 2	**Pais Vasco**, Spain ∷
111	K 9	**Pakistan**, Asia □
122	E 3	**Pakokku**, Myanmar
122	H 4	**Pakxé**, Laos
137	I 6	**Pala**, Chad
41	O 3	**Palafrugell**, Spain
41	O 3	**Palamós**, Spain
123	K 4	**Palanan Point**, Philippines ▶
151	J 2	**Palau**, Pacific Ocean □
26	D 6	**Palau Trench**, Pacific Ocean ≈
123	J 6	**Palawan**, Philippines 🏝
123	J 6	**Palawan Passage**, Philippines ⧗
26	C 5	**Palawan Trough**, Pacific Ocean ▃
122	G 9	**Palembang**, Indonesia
41	I 3	**Palencia**, Spain
89	N 9	**Palenque**, Mexico
57	G 14	**Palermo**, Italy
119	D 14	**Palghat**, India
119	C 9	**Pali**, India
151	M 1	**Palikir**, Federated States of Micronesia ▟
119	E 14	**Palk Strait**, India/Sri Lanka ⧗
85	F 15	**Palm Springs**, CA, United States
41	O 6	**Palma**, Spain
97	J 6	**Palmas**, Brazil
33	I 2	**Palmer**, United States ≡
33	J 3	**Palmer Land**, Antarctica ∷
146	G 3	**Palmerston**, NT, Australia
150	F 6	**Palmerston North**, New Zealand
57	I 13	**Palmi**, Italy
96	E 3	**Palmira**, Colombia
114	H 3	**Palmyra**, Syria
26	H 5	**Palmyra Atoll**, Pacific Ocean 🏝
123	J 8	**Palu**, Indonesia
45	I 10	**Pamiers**, France
111	L 6	**Pamirs**, Asia ⛰
81	N 2	**Pamlico Sound**, NC, United States ≈
83	F 11	**Pampa**, TX, United States
99	G 11	**Pampas**, Argentina ◇
41	K 2	**Pamplona**, Spain
90	H 8	**Panama**, North America □
27	M 5	**Panama Basin**, Pacific Ocean ▃
90	H 8	**Panama Canal**, Panama ⧗
80	H 7	**Panama City**, FL, United States
90	H 8	**Panama City**, Panama ▟
123	K 5	**Panay**, Philippines 🏝
65	I 4	**Panevėžys**, Lithuania
122	G 8	**Pangkalpinang**, Indonesia
97	I 8	**Pantanal**, Brazil ◇
89	L 7	**Pánuco**, Mexico
89	K 7	**Pánuco**, Mexico ∿
127	J 9	**Panzhihua**, China
151	M 10	**Papeete**, French Polynesia ▟
147	L 2	**Papua New Guinea**, Oceania □
98	H 6	**Paraguay**, South America □
98	I 7	**Paraguay**, Paraguay ∿
136	G 6	**Parakou**, Benin
97	I 2	**Paramaribo**, Suriname ▟
99	H 9	**Paraná**, Argentina
99	H 9	**Paraná**, South America ∿
119	D 11	**Parbhani**, India
64	E 7	**Pardubice**, Czech Republic
123	J 9	**Parepare**, Indonesia
61	E 11	**Parga**, Greece
97	I 4	**Parintins**, Brazil
45	I 4	**Paris**, France
83	H 11	**Paris**, TX, United States
79	I 9	**Parkersburg**, WV, United States
147	K 9	**Parkes**, NSW, Australia
56	D 6	**Parma**, Italy
97	L 4	**Parnaíba**, Brazil
97	K 6	**Parnaíba**, Brazil ∿
65	I 2	**Pärnu**, Estonia
61	H 13	**Paros**, Greece
61	H 13	**Paros**, Greece 🏝
32	C 6	**Parry Islands**, Canada 🏝
97	I 4	**Paru**, Brazil ∿
74	G 9	**Pas, The**, MB, Canada
83	H 13	**Pasadena**, TX, United States
85	F 14	**Pasadena**, CA, United States
80	F 6	**Pascagoula**, MS, United States
60	I 5	**Pașcani**, Romania
84	E 7	**Pasco**, WA, United States
108	K 7	**Pasinler**, Turkey
111	J 11	**Pasni**, Pakistan
99	F 13	**Paso de Indios**, Argentina
74	F 4	**Passage Point**, NT, Canada ▶

≈ Bay ⧗ Channel □ Country ▣ Dependent Territory ◓ Desert ∷ Geographic Area ▶ Headland 🏝 Island 🌴 Island Group ≋ Lake ▲ Mountain

53	H 11	**Passau**, Germany
97	J 10	**Passo Fundo**, Brazil
96	E 4	**Pasto**, Colombia
99	F 14	**Patagonia**, Argentina/Chile ⠿
119	B 9	**Patan**, India
57	H 14	**Paterno**, Italy
79	L 8	**Paterson**, NJ, United States
118	D 6	**Pathankot**, India
82	D 8	**Pathfinder Reservoir**, WY, United States 〰
118	D 7	**Patiala**, India
61	I 13	**Patmos**, Greece 🌴
119	G 9	**Patna**, India
108	L 7	**Patnos**, Turkey
78	F 9	**Patoka Lake**, IN, United States 〰
97	K 8	**Patos de Minas**, Brazil
61	F 12	**Patra**, Greece
44	G 10	**Pau**, France
56	C 6	**Pavia**, Italy
111	L 2	**Pavlodar**, Kazakhstan
65	N 8	**Pavlohrad**, Ukraine
99	I 9	**Paysandú**, Uruguay
108	E 6	**Pazarbaşi Burnu**, Turkey ▶
61	G 9	**Pazardzhik**, Bulgaria
61	A 7	**Pazin**, Croatia
22	D 3	**Peace**, North America ∿
74	E 8	**Peace River**, AB, Canada
80	E 5	**Pearl**, United States ∿
61	E 9	**Peć**, Serbia and Montenegro
104	E 5	**Pechora**, Russia ∿
104	E 5	**Pechorskoye More**, Russia, 🌊
83	E 12	**Pecos**, TX, United States
83	E 12	**Pecos**, NM, United States ∿
64	F 10	**Pécs**, Hungary
98	I 7	**Pedro Juan Caballero**, Paraguay
52	H 5	**Peene**, Germany ∿
150	E 8	**Pegasus Bay**, New Zealand ≈
122	F 4	**Pegu**, Myanmar
122	F 7	**Pegunungan Barisan**, Indonesia ⛰
123	N 9	**Pegunungan Maoke**, Indonesia ⛰
61	G 13	**Peiraias**, Greece
122	G 8	**Pekanbaru**, Indonesia
74	H 5	**Pelly Bay**, NU, Canada
97	J 10	**Pelotas**, Brazil
122	F 7	**Pematangsiantar**, Indonesia
141	L 6	**Pemba**, Mozambique
141	L 4	**Pemba Island**, Tanzania 🌴
75	K 10	**Pembroke**, ON, Canada
41	I 2	**Pena Prieta**, Spain ▲
123	I 8	**Penambo Range**, Indonesia/Malaysia ⛰
84	F 7	**Pendleton**, OR, United States
99	F 16	**Península Brecknock**, Chile ▶
90	H 9	**Península de Azuero**, Panama ▶
99	G 16	**Península Mitre**, Argentina ▶
96	E 7	**Peninsula Paracas**, Peru ▶
99	E 14	**Peninsula Tres Montes**, Chile ▶
99	G 12	**Peninsula Valdés**, Argentina ▶
99	H 11	**Peninsula Verde**, Argentina ▶
75	J 6	**Péninsule d'Ungava**, QC, Canada ▶
37	G 10	**Pennines**, United Kingdom ⛰
79	J 8	**Pennsylvania**, United States ▣
146	H 8	**Penong**, SA, Australia
80	G 6	**Pensacola**, FL, United States
33	L 3	**Pensacola Mountains**, Antarctica ⛰
104	C 7	**Penza**, Russia
37	E 15	**Penzance**, United Kingdom
78	E 8	**Peoria**, IL, United States
146	F 6	**Percival Lakes**, WA, Australia 〰
96	E 3	**Pereira**, Colombia
99	H 10	**Pergamino**, Argentina
69	H 9	**Perhonjoki**, Finland ∿
75	K 8	**Peribonca**, Canada ∿
44	H 8	**Périgueux**, France
99	F 13	**Perito Moreno**, Argentina
104	E 7	**Perm'**, Russia
28	H 7	**Pernambuco Abyssal Plain**, Atlantic Ocean ▰
28	G 7	**Pernambuco Seamounts**, Atlantic Ocean ▰
61	G 9	**Pernik**, Bulgaria
89	L 8	**Perote**, Mexico
45	J 11	**Perpignan**, France
83	F 10	**Perryton**, TX, United States
115	K 5	**Persian Gulf**, Asia ≈
36	F 8	**Perth**, United Kingdom
146	E 9	**Perth**, WA, Australia ⌂
31	K 6	**Perth Basin**, Southern Ocean ▰
96	E 5	**Peru**, South America ▣
27	M 7	**Peru Basin**, Pacific Ocean ▰
27	M 5	**Peru-Chile Trench**, Pacific Ocean ▰
56	F 8	**Perugia**, Italy
49	D 12	**Peruwelz**, Belgium
65	L 9	**Pervomays'k**, Ukraine
104	E 7	**Pervoural'sk**, Russia
57	G 9	**Pescara**, Italy
111	L 8	**Peshāwar**, Pakistan
61	E 10	**Peshkopi**, Albania
111	K 4	**Peski Muyunkum**, Kazakhstan ▲
49	I 15	**Pètange**, Luxembourg
78	E 5	**Petenwell Lake**, WI, United States 〰
22	E 10	**Peter I Island**, Antarctica 🌴
37	I 12	**Peterborough**, United Kingdom
147	I 9	**Peterborough**, SA, Australia
75	K 10	**Peterborough**, ON, Canada
79	K 10	**Petersburg**, VI, United States
89	P 8	**Peto**, Mexico
78	G 5	**Petoskey**, MI, United States
111	K 1	**Petropavlovsk**, Kazakhstan
105	O 8	**Petropavlovsk-Kamchatskiy**, Russia
60	G 7	**Petroşani**, Romania
104	D 5	**Petrozavodsk**, Russia
53	D 10	**Pforzheim**, Germany
122	H 5	**Phan Thiêt**, Vietnam
80	H 5	**Phenix City**, AL, United States
79	L 8	**Philadelphia**, PA, United States
49	F 13	**Philippeville**, Belgium
26	D 5	**Philippine Basin**, Pacific Ocean ▰
26	D 4	**Philippine Sea**, Pacific Ocean 🌊
123	K 3	**Philippine Sea**, Asia 🌊
26	D 4	**Philippines Trench**, Pacific Ocean ▰
122	G 5	**Phnom Penh**, Cambodia 🏛
85	I 15	**Phoenix**, AZ, United States ⌂
151	J 8	**Phoenix Islands**, Kiribati 🏝
122	F 6	**Phuket**, Thailand
56	C 6	**Piacenza**, Italy
60	I 5	**Piatra Neamț**, Romania
98	E 6	**Pica**, Chile
40	B 9	**Pico**, Portugal 🌴
40	C 11	**Pico de las Nieves**, Spain ▲
40	B 10	**Pico del Teide**, Spain ▲
99	F 13	**Pico Truncado**, Argentina
97	L 5	**Picos**, Brazil
150	E 6	**Picton**, New Zealand
89	K 4	**Piedras Negras**, Mexico
69	K 9	**Pielinen**, Finland 〰
82	F 7	**Pierre**, SD, United States ⌂
141	J 10	**Pietermaritzburg**, South Africa
141	J 9	**Pietersburg**, South Africa
89	N 10	**Pijijiapan**, Mexico
78	H 10	**Pikeville**, KY, United States
64	F 5	**Piła**, Poland
99	H 10	**Pilar**, Argentina
98	I 8	**Pilar**, Paraguay
98	H 7	**Pilcomayo**, Paraguay ∿
118	E 8	**Pilibhit**, India
90	G 3	**Pinar del Río**, Cuba
83	I 11	**Pine Bluff**, AR, United States
146	H 4	**Pine Creek**, NT, Australia
61	F 11	**Pineios**, Greece ∿
127	L 7	**Pingdingshan**, China
151	M 1	**Pingelap**, Federated States of Micronesia 🌴
127	N 10	**P'ingtung**, Taiwan
127	M 9	**Pingxiang**, China
65	J 6	**Pinsk**, Belarus
56	D 8	**Piombino**, Italy
64	G 7	**Piotrków Trybunalski**, Poland
97	J 9	**Piracicaba**, Brazil
53	C 10	**Pirmasens**, Germany
61	F 8	**Pirot**, Serbia and Montenegro
56	D 7	**Pisa**, Italy
64	E 8	**Pisek**, Czech Republic
56	D 7	**Pistoia**, Italy
151	P 11	**Pitcairn Island**, Pitcairn Islands 🌴
151	P 10	**Pitcairn Islands**, United Kingdom ▣
68	H 8	**Piteå**, Sweden
60	H 7	**Pitești**, Romania
79	J 8	**Pittsburgh**, PA, United States
79	M 7	**Pittsfield**, MA, United States
96	D 5	**Piura**, Peru
65	L 9	**Pivdennyy Buh**, Ukraine ∿
85	D 11	**Placerville**, CA, United States
83	F 11	**Plainview**, TX, United States
140	G 6	**Planalto do Bié**, Angola ◇
141	K 6	**Planalto Moçambicano**, Mozambique ◇
40	H 5	**Plasencia**, Spain
140	H 5	**Plateau du Kasai**, Democratic Republic of Congo ◇
136	G 3	**Plateau du Tademaït**, Algeria ◇
23	L 4	**Plateau of Tibet**, Asia ⛰
82	F 8	**Platte**, NE, United States ∿
79	L 5	**Plattsburgh**, NY, United States
53	G 9	**Plauen**, Germany
52	G 5	**Plauer See**, Germany 〰
64	D 8	**Plechý**, Czech Republic ▲
61	H 8	**Pleven**, Bulgaria
64	G 6	**Płock**, Poland
60	I 7	**Ploiești**, Romania
61	I 12	**Plomari**, Greece
61	H 9	**Plovdiv**, Bulgaria
37	F 15	**Plymouth**, United Kingdom
79	N 7	**Plymouth**, MA, United States
91	N 5	**Plymouth**, Montserrat 🏛
64	D 7	**Plzeň**, Czech Republic
56	D 6	**Po**, Italy ∿
56	F 6	**Po Delta**, Italy ∿
85	I 9	**Pocatello**, ID, United States
97	K 8	**Poços de Caldas**, Brazil
61	D 9	**Podgorica**, Serbia and Montenegro
61	E 10	**Pogradec**, Albania
127	P 6	**P'ohang**, South Korea
151	M 1	**Pohnpei**, Federated States of Micronesia 🌴
85	C 11	**Point Arena**, CA, United States ▶
85	D 14	**Point Arguello**, CA, United States ▶
85	D 14	**Point Conception**, CA, United States ▶
119	E 14	**Point Pedro**, Sri Lanka ▶
85	C 12	**Point Reyes**, CA, United States ▶
85	B 9	**Point St George**, CA, United States ▶
78	G 5	**Point Sturgeon**, WI, United States ▶
78	H 6	**Pointe Aux Barques**, MI, United States ▶
91	N 5	**Pointe-à-Pitre**, Guadaloupe
140	F 4	**Pointe-Noire**, Congo
44	H 6	**Poitiers**, France
64	G 5	**Poland**, Europe ▣
108	F 7	**Polatli**, Turkey
65	J 4	**Polatsk**, Belarus
32	D 7	**Pole Plain**, Arctic Ocean ▰
123	J 9	**Polewali**, Indonesia
41	O 6	**Pollença**, Spain
65	M 8	**Poltava**, Ukraine
61	F 10	**Polykastro**, Greece
52	H 4	**Pommersche Bay**, Germany ≈
85	F 14	**Pomona**, CA, United States
81	L 10	**Pompano Beach**, FL, United States
57	H 11	**Pompei**, Italy ✸
83	G 10	**Ponca City**, OK, United States
91	M 5	**Ponce**, Puerto Rico
119	E 14	**Pondicherry**, India
40	G 2	**Ponferrada**, Spain
97	L 8	**Ponta da Baleia**, Brazil ▶
40	C 9	**Ponta Degada**, Portugal
97	J 9	**Ponta Grossa**, Brazil
45	L 6	**Pontarlier**, France
40	F 3	**Ponte da Barca**, Portugal
40	F 3	**Ponteareas**, Spain
40	F 2	**Pontevedra**, Spain
122	H 8	**Pontianak**, Indonesia
45	I 3	**Pontoise**, France
65	J 4	**Ponya**, Belarus, ∿
37	H 14	**Poole**, United Kingdom
150	F 2	**Poor Knights Islands**, New Zealand 🌴
96	E 3	**Popayán**, Colombia
83	J 10	**Poplar Bluff**, MO, United States
89	K 9	**Popocatépetl**, Mexico ▲
147	K 3	**Popondetta**, Papua New Guinea
56	F 5	**Pordenone**, Italy
61	A 7	**Porec**, Croatia
69	H 10	**Pori**, Finland
150	F 6	**Porirua**, New Zealand
33	O 7	**Porpoise Bay**, Antarctica ≈
68	H 4	**Porsangen**, Norway ≈
69	C 12	**Porsgrunn**, Norway
84	C 5	**Port Angeles**, WA, United States
83	I 13	**Port Arthur**, TX, United States
147	I 8	**Port Augusta**, SA, Australia
150	C 10	**Port Chalmers**, New Zealand
81	J 9	**Port Charlotte**, FL, United States
141	I 11	**Port Elizabeth**, South Africa
136	H 7	**Port Harcourt**, Nigeria
74	C 9	**Port Hardy**, BC, Canada
146	E 6	**Port Hedland**, WA, Australia
78	H 6	**Port Huron**, MI, United States
83	H 13	**Port Lavaca**, TX, United States
147	I 9	**Port Lincoln**, SA, Australia
141	O 8	**Port Louis**, Mauritius 🏛
147	K 3	**Port Moresby**, Papua New Guinea 🏛
91	O 7	**Port of Spain**, Trinidad and Tobago 🏛
147	I 9	**Port Pirie**, SA, Australia
137	L 2	**Port Said**, Egypt
137	M 4	**Port Sudan**, Sudan
150	H 10	**Port Vila**, Vanuatu 🏛
37	D 10	**Portadown**, United Kingdom
74	H 10	**Portage la Praire**, MB, Canada
40	F 6	**Portalegre**, Portugal
91	K 4	**Port-au-Prince**, Haiti 🏛
91	K 4	**Port-de-Paix**, Haiti
85	E 13	**Porterville**, CA, United States
140	E 3	**Port-Gentil**, Gabon
79	N 6	**Portland**, ME, United States
84	D 7	**Portland**, OR, United States
37	G 15	**Portland Bill**, United Kingdom ▶
40	F 4	**Porto**, Portugal
97	J 10	**Porto Alegre**, Brazil
28	B 8	**Porto Inglês**, Cape Verde
28	A 7	**Porto Novo**, Cape Verde
40	D 9	**Porto Santo**, Portugal
57	B 11	**Porto Torres**, Italy
96	G 6	**Porto Velho**, Brazil
90	H 8	**Portobelo**, Panama
56	D 8	**Portoferraio**, Italy
136	G 7	**Porto-Novo**, Benin 🏛
96	D 4	**Portoviejo**, Ecuador
36	D 7	**Portree**, United Kingdom
37	I 14	**Portsmouth**, United Kingdom
78	H 9	**Portsmouth**, OH, United States
79	N 6	**Portsmouth**, NH, United States
79	K 11	**Portsmouth**, VI, United States
40	E 9	**Portugal**, Europe ▣
69	I 11	**Porvoo**, Finland
98	I 8	**Posadas**, Argentina
60	A 6	**Postojna**, Slovenia
57	I 11	**Potenza**, Italy
109	K 5	**P'ot'i**, Georgia
79	K 9	**Potomac**, United States ∿
98	G 6	**Potosí**, Bolivia
52	G 6	**Potsdam**, Germany
150	H 4	**Poverty Bay**, New Zealand ≈
40	F 4	**Póvoa de Varzim**, Portugal
82	D 7	**Powder**, MT, United States ∿
127	M 8	**Poyang Hu**, China 〰
89	L 8	**Poza Rica**, Mexico
61	F 7	**Požarevac**, Serbia and Montenegro
61	C 7	**Požega**, Croatia
64	F 6	**Poznań**, Poland
98	I 7	**Pozo Colorado**, Paraguay
64	E 7	**Prague**, Czech Republic
28	B 8	**Praia**, Cape Verde 🏛
56	E 7	**Prato**, Italy
80	H 5	**Prattville**, AL, United States
119	J 12	**Prepari Island**, India 🌴
89	N 10	**Presa de la Angostura**, Mexico 〰
89	J 9	**Presa del Infiernillo**, Mexico 〰
85	I 14	**Prescott**, AZ, United States
98	H 8	**Presidencia Roque**, Argentina
79	O 3	**Presque Isle**, ME, United States
37	G 11	**Preston**, United Kingdom
141	I 9	**Pretoria**, South Africa 🏛
61	E 12	**Preveza**, Greece
84	H 5	**Pribilof Islands**, AL, United States 🏝
85	J 11	**Price**, UT, United States
61	E 8	**Prijepolje**, Serbia and Montenegro
61	F 10	**Prilep**, Macedonia
74	F 9	**Prince Albert**, SK, Canada
74	F 4	**Prince Albert Peninsula**, NT, Canada ▶
75	I 5	**Prince Charles Island**, NU, Canada 🌴
33	O 3	**Prince Charles Mountains**, Antarctica ⛰
30	D 9	**Prince Edward Fracture Zone**, Indian Ocean ▰
30	E 9	**Prince Edward Islands**, Southern Ocean 🏝
75	M 8	**Prince Edward Island**, Canada ▣
74	D 8	**Prince George**, BC, Canada
147	J 3	**Prince of Wales Island**, QLD, Australia 🌴
74	G 4	**Prince of Wales Island**, NU, Canada 🌴
74	C 8	**Prince Rupert**, BC, Canada
33	O 4	**Princess Elizabeth Land**, Antarctica ⠿
140	E 3	**Príncipe**, São Tomé and Príncipe 🌴
65	J 6	**Pripet**, Belarus ∿
65	J 6	**Pripet Marshes**, Belarus/Ukraine ◇
61	F 9	**Priština**, Serbia and Montenegro
45	K 8	**Privas**, France
61	E 9	**Prizren**, Serbia and Montenegro
123	I 10	**Probolinggo**, Indonesia
97	I 3	**Professor Van Blommestein Meer**, Suriname 〰
89	O 7	**Progreso**, Mexico
32	D 4	**Proliv Longa**, Arctic Ocean ⧗
45	L 10	**Provence**, France ⠿
79	N 7	**Providence**, RI, United States ⌂
85	I 10	**Provo**, UT, United States
84	J 4	**Prudhoe Bay**, AL, United States
64	G 6	**Pruszków**, Poland
65	L 7	**Pryluky**, Ukraine
64	H 8	**Przemsyl**, Poland
61	H 12	**Psara**, Greece 🌴
104	C 5	**Pskov**, Russia
61	F 11	**Ptolemaïda**, Greece
65	J 5	**Ptsich**, Belarus ∿
96	E 6	**Pucallpa**, Peru
89	L 9	**Puebla**, Mexico
83	D 9	**Pueblo**, CO, United States
99	E 13	**Puerto Aisen**, Chile
89	L 10	**Puerto Ángel**, Mexico
96	G 3	**Puerto Ayacucho**, Venezuela
96	B 7	**Puerto Ayora**, Ecuador
96	B 7	**Puerto Baquerizo Moreno**, Ecuador
90	E 5	**Puerto Barrios**, Guatemala
90	G 6	**Puerto Cabezas**, Nicaragua
96	G 2	**Puerto Carreño**, Colombia
99	E 13	**Puerto Cisnes**, Chile
90	G 8	**Puerto Cortés**, Costa Rica
40	C 10	**Puerto del Rosario**, Spain
89	L 10	**Puerto Escondido**, Mexico
90	G 6	**Puerto Lempira**, Honduras
99	G 12	**Puerto Madryn**, Argentina
96	F 6	**Puerto Maldonado**, Peru
99	E 12	**Puerto Montt**, Chile
99	E 15	**Puerto Natales**, Chile
91	K 4	**Puerto Plata**, Dominican Republic
123	J 6	**Puerto Princesa**, Philippines
91	M 5	**Puerto Rico**, United States ▣
28	D 6	**Puerto Rico Trench**, Atlantic Ocean ▰
99	F 14	**Puerto San Julián**, Argentina
98	I 6	**Puerto Suárez**, Bolivia
89	I 8	**Puerto Vallarta**, Mexico
96	A 7	**Puerto Villamil**, Ecuador
41	I 7	**Puertollano**, Spain
84	C 5	**Puget Sound**, WA, United States ≈
150	F 3	**Pukekohe**, New Zealand
61	A 7	**Pula**, Croatia
151	K 1	**Pulap**, Federated States of Micronesia 🌴
123	N 10	**Pulau Dolak**, Indonesia 🌴
151	K 1	**Pulawat**, Federated States of Micronesia 🌴
84	F 6	**Pullman**, WA, United States
151	I 2	**Pulo Anna**, Palau 🌴
151	K 1	**Pulusuk**, Federated States of Micronesia 🌴
98	F 7	**Puna de Atacama**, Argentina ⛰
98	G 5	**Punata**, Bolivia
123	N 9	**Puncak Jaya**, Indonesia ▲
119	C 11	**Pune**, India
118	D 7	**Punjab**, India/Pakistan ⠿
96	F 7	**Puno**, Peru
57	J 12	**Punta Alice**, Italy ▶
40	H 10	**Punta Almina**, Spain ▶
99	H 11	**Punta Alta**, Argentina
99	F 15	**Punta Arenas**, Chile
99	G 12	**Punta Bermeja**, Argentina ▶
57	B 10	**Punta Caprara**, Italy ▶
96	E 3	**Punta Chirambirá**, Colombia ▶
99	F 15	**Punta de Arenas**, Argentina ▶
41	J 10	**Punta de las Entinas**, Spain ▶
88	H 8	**Punta de Mita**, Mexico ▶
90	G 7	**Punta del Mono**, Nicaragua ▶
88	E 4	**Punta Eugenia**, Mexico ▶
99	E 12	**Punta Galera**, Chile ▶
89	P 8	**Punta Herrero**, Mexico ▶
98	E 7	**Punta Jorjino**, Chile ▶

⛰ Mountain Range 🏛 National Capital ≈ Ocean ◇ Physical Feature ▬ Polar Base ∿ River 🌊 Sea ✸ Special Feature ⌂ State Capital ▰ Underwater Feature

99 E 11 **Punta Lavapié**, Chile ◗
99 E 9 **Punta Lengua de Vaca**, Chile ◗
99 F 14 **Punta León**, Argentina ◗
99 G 14 **Punta Medanosa**, Argentina ◗
96 D 5 **Punta Negro**, Peru ◗
99 G 12 **Punta Ninfas**, Argentina ◗
96 D 5 **Punta Pariñas**, Peru ◗
99 H 12 **Punta Rasa**, Argentina ◗
88 G 5 **Punta Rosa**, Mexico ◗
96 E 7 **Punta Santa Maria**, Peru ◗
90 F 8 **Puntarenas**, Costa Rica
119 G 11 **Puri**, India
48 F 7 **Purmerend**, Netherlands
96 H 5 **Purus**, Brazil/Peru ∿
69 K 10 **Puruvesi**, Finland 💧
122 H 9 **Purwakarta**, Indonesia
127 P 6 **Pusan**, South Korea
98 E 5 **Putre**, Chile
150 A 11 **Puysegur Point**, New Zealand ◗
104 B 8 **Pyatigorsk**, Russia
122 E 3 **Pyè**, Myanmar
68 I 8 **Pyhäjoki**, Finland ∿
69 K 9 **Pyhäselkä**, Finland 💧
61 F 13 **Pylos**, Greece
127 O 5 **P'yŏngyang**, North Korea 🏛
85 E 11 **Pyramid Lake**, NV, United States 💧
22 H 3 **Pyrenees**, Europe ▲
61 F 13 **Pyrgos**, Greece

Q

111 K 8 **Qalāt**, Afghanistan
115 I 8 **Qal'at Bishah**, Saudi Arabia
111 J 7 **Qal'eh-ye**, Afghanistan
127 I 8 **Qamdo**, China
111 L 6 **Qarokŭl**, Tajikistan 💧
115 L 6 **Qatar**, Asia □
137 K 2 **Qattâra Depression**, Egypt ◇
115 K 2 **Qazvīn**, Iran
137 L 3 **Qena**, Egypt
127 I 5 **Qilian Shan**, China ▲
127 N 6 **Qingdao**, China
127 J 6 **Qinghai Hu**, China 💧
127 M 5 **Qinhuangdao**, China
127 N 3 **Qiqihar**, China
115 L 3 **Qom**, Iran
127 N 9 **Quanzhou**, China
57 C 12 **Quartu Sant'Elena**, Italy
115 M 2 **Quchan**, Iran
75 J 8 **Québec**, Canada ▣
75 L 9 **Québec**, QC, Canada ⌂
74 C 8 **Queen Charlotte Islands**, BC, Canada 🏝
74 C 9 **Queen Charlotte Sound**, BC, Canada ≈
74 G 3 **Queen Elizabeth Islands**, NU, Canada 🏝
33 O 4 **Queen Mary Land**, Antarctica ⠿
33 L 2 **Queen Maud Land**, Antarctica ⠿
33 L 5 **Queen Maud Mountains**, Antarctica ▲
147 J 6 **Queensland**, Australia ▣
150 B 9 **Queenstown**, New Zealand
147 J 11 **Queenstown**, TAS, Australia
141 K 7 **Quelimane**, Mozambique
89 K 8 **Querétaro**, Mexico
111 K 9 **Quetta**, Pakistan
90 D 6 **Quezaltenango**, Guatemala
123 K 5 **Quezon City**, Philippines
122 H 5 **Qui Nhon**, Vietnam
96 E 3 **Quibdó**, Colombia
119 D 15 **Quilon**, India
99 E 10 **Quilpue**, Chile
44 E 4 **Quimper**, France
44 E 5 **Quimperlé**, France
78 D 8 **Quincy**, IL, United States
96 E 4 **Quito**, Ecuador 🏛

R

68 I 8 **Raahe**, Finland
123 J 10 **Raba**, Indonesia
136 F 1 **Rabat**, Morocco 🏛
147 L 2 **Rabaul**, Papua New Guinea
114 H 7 **Rābigh**, Saudi Arabia
122 G 6 **Rach Gia**, Vietnam
78 F 7 **Racine**, WI, United States
64 H 7 **Radom**, Poland
99 H 9 **Rafaela**, Argentina
115 J 5 **Rafḩā'**, Saudi Arabia
115 M 4 **Rafsanjān**, Iran
57 H 15 **Ragusa**, Italy
111 L 10 **Rahimyar Khan**, Pakistan
151 M 10 **Raiatea**, French Polynesia 🌴
119 D 12 **Raichur**, India
119 F 10 **Raipur**, India
119 F 10 **Raj- Nandgaon**, India
119 F 12 **Rajahmundry**, India
119 D 14 **Rajapalaiyam**, India
118 C 8 **Rajasthan**, India ⠿
119 B 10 **Rajkot**, India
119 H 9 **Rajshahi**, Bangladesh
150 D 8 **Rakaia**, New Zealand ∿
81 L 2 **Raleigh**, NC, United States ⌂
81 N 3 **Raleigh Bay**, NC, United States ≈
151 M 3 **Ralik Chain**, Marshall Islands 🏝
115 J 10 **Ramlat as Sab'atayn**, Yemen ◓
115 J 9 **Ramlat Dahm**, Yemen ◓
60 G 7 **Râmnicu Vâlcea**, Romania
118 E 8 **Rampur**, India
122 E 3 **Ramree**, Myanmar 🌴
37 K 14 **Ramsgate**, United Kingdom
119 D 9 **Rana Pratap Sagar**, India 💧
99 E 10 **Rancagua**, Chile
119 G 10 **Ranchi**, India
69 C 14 **Randers**, Denmark
150 D 8 **Rangiora**, New Zealand
122 F 4 **Rangoon**, Myanmar 🏛
119 H 9 **Rangpur**, Bangladesh
119 A 9 **Rann of Kachchh**, India ◇
82 E 7 **Rapid City**, SD, United States
151 L 10 **Rarotonga**, Cook Islands 🌴
114 H 6 **Rās Abū Madd**, Saudi Arabia ◗
115 N 7 **Rās al Ḩadd**, Oman ◗
115 K 10 **Rās al Kalb**, Yemen ◗
115 M 6 **Ras al Khaimah**, United Arab Emirates
115 N 8 **Rās al Madrakah**, Oman ◗
115 K 5 **Rās az Zawr**, Saudi Arabia ◗
114 H 6 **Rās Barīdī**, Saudi Arabia ◗
137 O 5 **Rās Caluula**, Somalia ◗
137 O 5 **Rās Caseyr**, Somalia ◗
137 M 5 **Rās Dashen**, Ethiopia ▲
115 L 9 **Rās Fartak**, Yemen ◗
115 I 10 **Rās 'Īsá**, Yemen ◗
114 H 6 **Rās Karkūmā**, Saudi Arabia ◗
137 M 5 **Rās Kasar**, Sudan ◗
115 M 9 **Rās Naws**, Oman ◗
136 D 4 **Rās Nouâdhibou**, Mauritania ◗
115 M 8 **Rās Şawqirah**, Oman ◗
115 M 9 **Rās Sharbithāt**, Oman ◗
115 K 5 **Rās Tanāqib**, Saudi Arabia ◗
136 D 4 **Rās Timirist**, Mauritania ◗
137 O 6 **Rās Xaafuun**, Somalia ◗
115 K 2 **Rasht**, Iran
151 M 3 **Ratak Chain**, Marshall Islands 🏝
69 E 9 **Rätansbyn**, Sweden
119 D 9 **Ratlam**, India
119 B 12 **Ratnagiri**, India
69 H 10 **Rauma**, Finland
119 G 10 **Raurkela**, India
56 F 7 **Ravenna**, Italy
53 E 12 **Ravensburg**, Germany
146 F 9 **Ravensthorpe**, WA, Australia
111 L 9 **Ravi**, India/Pakistan ∿
115 I 3 **Rāwah**, Iraq
111 L 8 **Rawalpindi**, Pakistan
99 G 12 **Rawson**, Argentina
122 G 5 **Rayong**, Thailand
61 I 8 **Razgrad**, Bulgaria
37 I 14 **Reading**, United Kingdom
79 L 8 **Reading**, PA, United States
130 G 2 **Rebun-tō**, Japan 🌴
65 K 6 **Rechytsa**, Belarus
97 M 6 **Recife**, Brazil
98 H 8 **Reconquista**, Argentina
83 G 11 **Red**, OK, United States ∿
122 G 3 **Red**, Vietnam ∿
85 C 10 **Red Bluff**, CA, United States
74 E 9 **Red Deer**, AB, Canada
23 J 4 **Red Sea**, Africa/Asia 🌊
82 I 7 **Red Wing**, MN, United States
85 C 10 **Redding**, CA, United States
97 J 6 **Redençao**, Brazil
84 D 8 **Redmond**, OR, United States
150 D 7 **Reefton**, New Zealand
108 I 7 **Refahiye**, Turkey
53 G 10 **Regensburg**, Germany
56 D 6 **Reggio**, Italy
57 I 14 **Reggio di Calabria**, Italy
74 G 10 **Regina**, SK, Canada ⌂
111 J 9 **Registan**, Afghanistan ◓
140 G 8 **Rehoboth**, Namibia
37 I 14 **Reigate**, United Kingdom
45 J 3 **Reims**, France
74 G 8 **Reindeer Lake**, MB/SK, Canada 💧
41 I 2 **Reinosa**, Spain
52 C 8 **Remscheid**, Germany
78 E 10 **Rend Lake**, IL, United States 💧
44 F 4 **Rennes**, France
74 H 10 **Rennie**, MB, Canada
85 E 11 **Reno**, NV, United States
96 H 4 **Represa de Balbina**, Brazil 💧
97 I 9 **Represa de Itaipu**, Brazil/Paraguay 💧
97 J 8 **Represa Porto Primavera**, Brazil 💧
97 J 8 **Represa São Simão**, Brazil 💧
97 K 8 **Represa Três Marias**, Brazil 💧
97 J 5 **Represa Tucuruí**, Brazil 💧
74 H 5 **Repulse Bay**, NU, Canada
75 K 9 **Réservoir Cabonga**, QC, Canada 💧
75 J 8 **Réservoir la Grande Deux**, QC, Canada 💧
75 J 8 **Réservoir la Grande Trois**, QC, Canada 💧
75 K 8 **Réservoir Manicouagan**, QC, Canada 💧
98 H 8 **Resistencia**, Argentina
60 F 7 **Reşiţa**, Romania
32 C 6 **Resolute**, Canada
150 A 10 **Resolution Island**, New Zealand 🌴
75 K 5 **Resolution Island**, NU, Canada 🌴
61 H 15 **Rethymno**, Greece
30 F 6 **Réunion**, France 🌴
141 O 8 **Réunion**, France ▣
53 D 11 **Reutlingen**, Germany
22 C 5 **Revillagigedo Islands**, North America 🏝
119 F 9 **Rewa**, India
84 I 8 **Rexburg**, ID, United States
28 G 2 **Reykjanes Basin**, Atlantic Ocean ▬
28 F 3 **Reykjanes Ridge**, Atlantic Ocean ▬
68 B 6 **Reykjavík**, Iceland 🏛
89 K 5 **Reynosa**, Mexico
65 J 3 **Rēzekne**, Latvia
52 C 6 **Rheine**, Germany
22 H 3 **Rhine**, Europe ∿
79 N 7 **Rhode Island**, United States ▣
61 J 14 **Rhodes**, Greece 🌴
45 K 7 **Rhône**, France ∿
37 G 11 **Ribble**, United Kingdom ∿
40 E 2 **Ribeira**, Spain
40 C 9 **Ribeira Grande**, Portugal
97 J 8 **Ribeirão Preto**, Brazil
98 F 3 **Riberalta**, Bolivia
65 K 9 **Ribniţa**, Moldova
81 J 4 **Richard B. Russell Lake**, GA, United States 💧
150 E 7 **Richmond**, New Zealand
78 H 10 **Richmond**, KY, United States
79 K 10 **Richmond**, VI, United States ⌂
85 F 13 **Ridgecrest**, CA, United States
65 I 3 **Riga**, Latvia 🏛
33 N 1 **Riiser-Larsen Peninsula**, Antarctica ◗
29 J 12 **Riiser-Larsen Sea**, Atlantic Ocean 🌊
61 A 7 **Rijeka**, Croatia
48 J 7 **Rijssen**, Netherlands
56 F 7 **Rimini**, Italy
69 D 14 **Ringsted**, Denmark
68 G 4 **Ringvassoy**, Norway 🌴
96 G 6 **Rio Branco**, Brazil
99 G 9 **Rio Cuarto**, Argentina
97 K 9 **Rio de Janeiro**, Brazil
99 F 15 **Rio Gallegos**, Argentina
99 F 15 **Rio Grande**, Argentina
97 J 11 **Rio Grande**, Brazil
22 D 4 **Rio Grande**, North America ∿
89 J 6 **Rio Grande**, Mexico
89 I 7 **Rio Grande de Santiago**, Mexico ∿
29 G 9 **Rio Grande Fracture Zone**, Atlantic Ocean ▬
29 F 9 **Rio Grande Rise**, Atlantic Ocean ▬
99 F 13 **Rio Mayo**, Argentina
97 J 7 **Rio Verde**, Brazil
89 K 7 **Rio Verde**, Mexico
96 E 4 **Riobamba**, Ecuador
96 F 1 **Riohacha**, Colombia
41 N 3 **Ripoll**, Spain
130 G 2 **Rishiri-tō**, Japan 🌴
90 F 7 **Rivas**, Nicaragua
22 F 8 **River Plate**, South America ∿
99 I 9 **Rivera**, Uruguay
85 F 14 **Riverside**, CA, United States
75 J 7 **Rivière aux Feuilles**, Canada ∿
75 L 9 **Rivière-du-Loup**, QC, Canada
65 J 7 **Rivne**, Ukraine
56 A 6 **Rivoli**, Italy
115 K 6 **Riyadh**, Saudi Arabia 🏛
108 J 6 **Rize**, Turkey
91 M 4 **Road Town**, British Virgin Islands 🏛
45 K 7 **Roanne**, France
79 J 10 **Roanoke**, VI, United States
81 O 2 **Roanoke Island**, NC, United States 🌴
140 H 11 **Robben Island**, South Africa 🌴
98 H 5 **Robore**, Bolivia
99 J 10 **Rocha**, Uruguay
44 G 7 **Rochefort**, France
79 K 6 **Rochester**, NY, United States
82 I 7 **Rochester**, MN, United States
81 K 3 **Rock Hill**, SC, United States
91 I 2 **Rock Sound**, The Bahamas
82 C 8 **Rock Springs**, WY, United States
28 H 3 **Rockall Bank**, Atlantic Ocean ▬
28 H 3 **Rockall Trough**, Atlantic Ocean ▬
78 E 7 **Rockford**, IL, United States
147 L 6 **Rockhampton**, QLD, Australia
81 M 2 **Rocky Mount**, NC, United States
22 C 4 **Rocky Mountains**, North America ▲
45 I 9 **Rodez**, France
30 G 5 **Rodrigues Island**, Indian Ocean 🌴
49 I 10 **Roermond**, Netherlands
49 C 11 **Roeselare**, Belgium
83 I 10 **Rogers**, AR, United States
27 L 8 **Roggeveen Basin**, Pacific Ocean ▬
118 D 8 **Rohtak**, India
83 I 9 **Rolla**, MO, United States
147 K 7 **Roma**, QLD, Australia
60 I 6 **Romania**, Europe □
57 F 9 **Rome**, Italy 🏛
80 H 3 **Rome**, GA, United States
65 M 7 **Romny**, Ukraine
40 H 9 **Ronda**, Spain
97 I 7 **Rondonópolis**, Brazil
151 M 2 **Rongelap Atoll**, Marshall Islands 🌴
151 M 3 **Rongrik**, Marshall Islands 🌴
69 E 15 **Rønne**, Denmark
33 K 3 **Ronne Ice Shelf**, Antarctica ◇
49 E 9 **Roosendaal**, Netherlands
33 L 6 **Roosevelt Island**, Antarctica 🌴
69 D 9 **Røros**, Norway
65 K 8 **Ros'**, Ukraine ∿
99 H 9 **Rosario**, Argentina
88 E 4 **Rosarito**, Mexico
78 H 5 **Roscommon**, MI, United States
91 N 6 **Roseau**, Dominica 🏛
84 C 8 **Roseburg**, OR, United States
137 L 6 **Roseires Reservoir**, Sudan 💧
53 G 12 **Rosenheim**, Germany
150 C 8 **Ross**, New Zealand
80 E 4 **Ross Barnett Reservoir**, MS, United States 💧
33 L 6 **Ross Ice Shelf**, Antarctica ◇
33 M 6 **Ross Island**, Antarctica 🌴
26 H 11 **Ross Sea**, Southern Ocean 🌊
136 D 4 **Rosso**, Mauritania
52 G 4 **Rostock**, Germany
104 B 7 **Rostov-na-Donu**, Russia
83 D 11 **Roswell**, NM, United States
151 L 5 **Rota**, Northern Mariana Islands 🌴
123 K 11 **Rote**, Indonesia 🌴
33 I 3 **Rothera**, United Kingdom ≡
37 H 11 **Rotherham**, United Kingdom
150 F 4 **Rotorua**, New Zealand
48 F 8 **Rotterdam**, Netherlands
45 J 1 **Roubaix**, France
44 H 3 **Rouen**, France
68 I 7 **Rovaniemi**, Finland
56 E 6 **Rovigo**, Italy
123 K 5 **Roxas**, Philippines
44 G 7 **Royan**, France
150 B 11 **Ruapuke Island**, New Zealand 🌴
150 H 4 **Ruatoria**, New Zealand
115 J 8 **Rub' al Khālī**, Saudi Arabia ◓
104 G 9 **Rubtsovsk**, Russia
111 J 2 **Rudnyy**, Kazakhstan
99 G 10 **Rufino**, Argentina
37 H 12 **Rugby**, United Kingdom
36 D 7 **Rum**, United Kingdom 🌴
140 H 7 **Rundu**, Namibia
61 I 8 **Ruse**, Bulgaria
104 H 7 **Russia**, Asia/Europe □
33 K 6 **Russkaya**, Russia ≡
109 M 5 **Rust'avi**, Georgia
141 I 9 **Rustenburg**, South Africa
83 I 12 **Ruston**, LA, United States
141 L 5 **Ruvuma**, Mozambique/Tanzania ∿
141 J 3 **Rwanda**, Africa □
104 C 6 **Ryazan'**, Russia
33 J 4 **Ryberg Peninsula**, Antarctica ◗
104 D 5 **Rybinsk**, Russia
64 F 8 **Rybnik**, Poland
131 J 15 **Ryukyu Islands**, Japan 🏝
26 D 4 **Ryukyu Trench**, Pacific Ocean ▬
64 H 8 **Rzeszów**, Poland

S

52 F 8 **Saale**, Germany ∿
53 B 10 **Saarbrücken**, Germany
64 H 2 **Saaremaa**, Estonia 🌴
61 D 7 **Šabac**, Serbia and Montenegro
41 N 4 **Sabadell**, Spain
52 J 7 **Sabah**, Malaysia ⠿
137 I 3 **Sabhā**, Libya
89 J 4 **Sabinas**, Mexico
89 K 5 **Sabinas Hidalgo**, Mexico
115 M 2 **Sabzevār**, Iran
85 C 11 **Sacramento**, CA, United States ⌂
85 C 10 **Sacramento**, United States ∿
130 G 8 **Sadoga-shima**, Japan 🌴
69 D 12 **Säffle**, Sweden
85 K 15 **Safford**, AZ, United States
136 F 2 **Safi**, Morocco
131 B 13 **Saga**, Japan
122 E 3 **Sagaing**, Myanmar
131 H 10 **Sagami-nada**, Japan ≈
119 E 9 **Sagar**, India
78 H 6 **Saginaw**, MI, United States
41 L 6 **Sagunto**, Spain
22 H 5 **Sahara**, Africa ◓
118 D 7 **Saharanpur**, India
22 H 5 **Sahel**, Africa ◇
111 L 9 **Sahiwal**, Pakistan
31 L 5 **Sahul Shelf**, Southern Ocean ▬
114 H 3 **Saïda**, Lebanon
119 H 9 **Saidpur**, Bangladesh
69 J 10 **Saimaa**, Finland 💧
37 I 13 **St Albans**, United Kingdom
79 I 9 **St Albans**, WV, United States
81 K 7 **St Augustine**, FL, United States
75 K 11 **St Catharines**, ON, Canada
82 H 6 **St Cloud**, MN, United States
78 D 4 **St Croix**, United States ∿
37 E 13 **St David's Head**, United Kingdom ◗
53 D 12 **St Gallen**, Switzerland
147 K 7 **St George**, QLD, Australia
85 H 12 **St George**, UT, United States
91 N 7 **St George's**, Grenada 🏛
37 D 13 **St George's Channel**, Ireland/United Kingdom ⧗
37 E 13 **St Govan's Head**, United Kingdom ◗
28 I 8 **St Helena**, Atlantic Ocean 🌴
140 H 11 **Saint Helena Bay**, South Africa ≈
28 G 8 **Saint Helena Fracture Zone**, Atlantic Ocean ▬
37 G 11 **St Helens**, United Kingdom
37 H 16 **St Helier**, United Kingdom
78 G 4 **St Ignace**, MI, United States
75 L 9 **St John**, NB, Canada
75 N 7 **St John's**, NL, Canada ⌂
91 N 5 **St John's**, Antigua and Barbuda 🏛
83 H 9 **St Joseph**, MO, United States
91 N 5 **St Kitts and Nevis**, North America □
22 E 3 **St Lawrence**, North America ∿
32 D 3 **St Lawrence Island**, United States 🌴

≈ Bay ⧗ Channel □ Country ▣ Dependent Territory ◓ Desert ⠿ Geographic Area ◗ Headland 🌴 Island 🏝 Island Group 💧 Lake ▲ Mountain

91	O 6	St Lucia, North America ▣
147	L 1	St Matthias Group, Papua New Guinea ⁂
53	E 13	St Moritz, Switzerland
82	H 6	St Paul, MN, United States ⌂
28	F 7	Saint Paul Fracture Zone, Atlantic Ocean ▼
23	L 8	St Paul I Island, Antarctica ⌓
30	H 8	St Paul Island, France ⌓
37	G 16	St Peter Port, United Kingdom
81	J 9	St Petersburg, FL, United States
104	C 4	St Petersburg, Russia
75	M 8	St Pierre & Miquelon, France, France ▣
53	J 11	St Pölten, Austria
49	G 12	St Truiden, Belgium
91	O 6	St Vincent, St Vincent and the Grenadines ⌓
91	O 6	St Vincent and the Grenadines, North America ▣
44	E 4	St-Brieuc, France
141	O 8	St-Denis, Réunion ■
45	L 4	St-Dié, France
45	K 8	St-Étienne, France
45	J 8	St-Flour, France
44	H 10	St-Gaudens, France
75	K 10	St-Jean-sur-Richelieu, QC, Canada
44	G 3	St-Lô, France
136	D 5	St-Louis, Senegal
44	F 4	St-Malo, France
44	F 5	St-Nazaire, France
49	E 10	St-Niklaas, Belgium
45	I 1	St-Omer, France
45	J 2	St-Quentin, France
151	L 4	Saipan, Northern Mariana Islands ■
131	F 11	Sakai, Japan
115	I 4	Sakākah, Saudi Arabia
108	E 7	Sakarya, Turkey ∫
130	H 7	Sakata, Japan
105	N 9	Sakhalin, Russia ⌓
109	N 6	Şäki, Azerbaijan
28	B 7	Sal, Cape Verde ⌓
27	K 7	Sala y Gómez, Pacific Ocean ⌓
27	K 8	Sala y Gómez Ridge, Pacific Ocean ▼
99	F 11	Salado, Argentina ∫
99	H 9	Salado, Argentina ∫
115	M 9	Şalālah, Oman
40	H 4	Salamanca, Spain
98	F 7	Salar de Arizaro, Argentina ◒
98	F 7	Salar de Atacama, Chile ◒
98	F 6	Salar de Coipasa, Bolivia ◒
98	F 6	Salar de Uyuni, Bolivia ◒
122	H 10	Salatiga, Indonesia
123	M 8	Salawati, Indonesia ⌓
147	K 10	Sale, VIC, Australia
84	C 7	Salem, OR, United States ⌂
119	E 14	Salem, India
57	K 11	Salentina Peninsula, Italy ▶
57	H 11	Salerno, Italy
65	J 6	Salihorsk, Belarus
83	G 9	Salina, KS, United States
89	M 10	Salina Cruz, Mexico
85	D 13	Salinas, CA, United States
98	F 7	Salinas Grandes, Argentina ◒
37	H 14	Salisbury, United Kingdom
79	L 9	Salisbury, MD, United States
69	H 11	Salo, Finland
45	K 10	Salon-de-Provence, France
85	I 10	Salt Lake City, UT, United States ⌂
98	G 7	Salta, Argentina
89	J 5	Saltillo, Mexico
99	I 9	Salto, Uruguay
85	G 15	Salton Sea, CA, United States ◒
97	L 7	Salvador, Brazil
23	L 5	Salween, Asia ∫
109	O 7	Salyan, Azerbaijan
53	H 12	Salzburg, Austria
52	E 7	Salzgitter, Germany
123	K 5	Samar, Philippines ⌓
104	D 7	Samara, Russia
123	J 8	Samarinda, Indonesia
111	K 6	Samarkand, Uzbekistan
119	G 10	Sambalpur, India
49	E 13	Sambre, Belgium ∫
151	K 9	Samoa, Pacific Ocean ▣
61	I 13	Samos, Greece
61	I 12	Samos, Greece ⌓
61	I 10	Samotharaki, Greece ⌓
108	H 6	Samsun, Turkey
109	K 5	Samtredia, Georgia
122	F 5	Samut Prakan, Thailand
64	H 7	San, Poland ∫
89	M 9	San Andrés Tuxtla, Mexico
83	F 12	San Angelo, TX, United States
99	E 10	San Antonio, Chile
83	G 13	San Antonio, TX, United States
99	G 12	San Antonio Oeste, Argentina
85	F 14	San Bernardino, CA, United States
99	E 10	San Bernardo, Chile
88	G 5	San Blas, Mexico
98	F 4	San Borja, Bolivia
99	E 12	San Carlos de Bariloche, Argentina
96	F 2	San Cristóbal, Venezuela
40	B 10	San Cristóbal de la Laguna, Spain
89	N 10	San Cristóbal de las Casas, Mexico
85	F 15	San Diego, CA, United States
40	G 10	San Fernando, Spain
99	E 10	San Fernando, Chile
85	E 14	San Fernando, CA, United States
91	O 7	San Fernando, Trinidad and Tobago
123	K 4	San Fernando, Philippines
96	G 2	San Fernando de Apure, Venezuela
85	C 12	San Francisco, CA, United States
91	K 4	San Francisco de Macoris, Dominican Republic
98	H 5	San Ignacio, Bolivia
85	D 12	San Joaquin, United States ∫
85	D 12	San Joaquin Valley, CA, United States ◇
151	L 5	San Jose, Northern Mariana Islands
85	D 12	San Jose, CA, United States
90	G 8	San José, Costa Rica ■
96	F 3	San José del Guaviare, Colombia
99	F 9	San Juan, Argentina
91	M 4	San Juan, Puerto Rico ■
90	F 7	San Juan, Nicaragua ∫
98	I 8	San Juan Bautista, Paraguay
83	C 9	San Juan Mountains, CO/NM, United States ▲
98	I 7	San Lorenzo, Paraguay
99	F 10	San Luis, Argentina
85	D 14	San Luis Obispo, CA, United States
89	J 7	San Luis Potosí, Mexico
88	F 2	San Luis Rio Colorado, Mexico
83	H 13	San Marcos, TX, United States
56	F 7	San Marino, San Marino ■
56	F 7	San Marino, Europe ▣
33	J 3	San Martin, Argentina ▬
99	E 12	San Martín de Los Andes, Argentina
98	I 5	San Matias, Bolivia
98	G 4	San Miguel, Bolivia ∫
90	E 6	San Miguel, Netherlands Antilles
98	G 8	San Miguel de Tucumán, Argentina
90	H 8	San Miguelito, Panama
99	H 10	San Nicolás de los Arroyos, Argentina
123	K 5	San Pablo, Philippines
98	F 7	San Pedro de Atacama, Chile
89	J 5	San Pedro de las Colonias, Mexico
91	L 4	San Pedro de Macoris, Dominican Republic
90	E 5	San Pedro Sula, Honduras
99	F 10	San Rafael, Argentina
98	G 7	San Ramón, Argentina
56	B 7	San Remo, Italy
90	E 6	San Salvador, El Salvador ■
91	J 2	San Salvador, The Bahamas ⌓
98	G 7	San Salvador de Jujuy, Argentina
57	I 10	San Severo, Italy
115	J 9	Şan'ā', Yemen ■
33	M 1	Sanae, South Africa ▬
115	K 2	Sanandaj, Iran
90	H 3	Sancti Spiritus, Cuba
52	J 7	Sandakan, Malaysia
61	G 10	Sandanski, Bulgaria
36	G 4	Sanday, United Kingdom ⌓
85	K 14	Sanders, AZ, United States
69	A 12	Sandnes, Norway
122	E 4	Sandoway, Myanmar
84	G 5	Sandpoint, ID, United States
123	K 7	Sangir, Indonesia ⌓
119	C 12	Sangli, India
83	D 11	Sangre de Cristo Mountains, CO/NM, United States ▲
81	J 10	Sanibel Island, FL, United States ⌓
109	I 9	Şanliurfa, Turkey
40	G 9	Sanlúcar de Barrameda, Spain
127	L 7	Sanmenxia, China
127	M 9	Sanming, China
136	E 7	San-Pédro, Côte d'Ivoire
41	M 5	Sant Carles de la Ràpita, Spain
85	F 15	Santa Ana, CA, United States
90	E 6	Santa Ana, Netherlands Antilles
85	E 14	Santa Barbara, CA, United States
85	C 12	Santa Clara, CA, United States
90	H 3	Santa Clara, Cuba
98	G 5	Santa Cruz, Bolivia
99	F 14	Santa Cruz, Argentina ∫
85	C 12	Santa Cruz, CA, United States
40	A 10	Santa Cruz de la Palma, Spain
40	B 10	Santa Cruz de Tenerife, Spain
150	H 9	Santa Cruz Islands, Solomon Islands ⁂
99	H 9	Santa Fé, Argentina
83	D 11	Santa Fe, NM, United States ⌂
88	G 6	Santa Genoveva, Mexico, ▲
97	K 5	Santa Inês, Brazil
99	F 10	Santa Isabel, Argentina
40	C 10	Santa Maria, Portugal ⌓
97	I 10	Santa Maria, Brazil
28	B 7	Santa Maria, Cape Verde
85	D 14	Santa Maria, CA, United States
96	E 1	Santa Marta, Colombia
99	G 11	Santa Rosa, Argentina
85	C 11	Santa Rosa, CA, United States
90	E 6	Santa Rosa de Copán, Honduras
41	J 1	Santander, Spain
40	E 6	Santarém, Portugal
97	I 4	Santarém, Brazil
90	H 2	Santaren Channel, Cuba/The Bahamas ⧗
81	L 4	Santee, United States ∫
99	E 10	Santiago, Chile ■
91	K 4	Santiago, Dominican Republic
90	H 9	Santiago, Panama
91	J 4	Santiago de Cuba, Cuba
40	F 2	Santiago del Compostela, Spain
98	G 8	Santiago del Estero, Argentina
28	A 7	Santo Antão, Cape Verde ⌓
91	L 4	Santo Domingo, Dominican Republic ■
98	I 8	Santo Tomé, Argentina
61	H 14	Santorini, Greece ⌓
97	K 9	Santos, Brazil
29	F 9	Santos Plateau, Atlantic Ocean ▼
28	B 8	São Filipe, Cape Verde
97	K 7	São Francisco, Brazil ∫
97	K 9	São Gonçalo, Brazil
40	B 9	São Jorge, Portugal ⌓
97	J 8	São José do Rio Preto, Brazil
97	K 4	São Luís, Brazil
97	I 6	Sao Manuel, Brazil ∫
40	C 9	São Miguel, Portugal ⌓
28	B 7	São Nicolau, Cape Verde ⌓
97	K 9	São Paulo, Brazil
28	B 8	São Tiago, Cape Verde ⌓
140	E 3	São Tomé, São Tomé and Príncipe ⌓
140	D 3	São Tomé, São Tomé and Príncipe ■
140	D 3	São Tomé and Principe, Africa ▣
28	A 7	São Vicente, Cape Verde ⌓
45	K 6	Saône, France ∫
130	H 4	Sapporo, Japan
57	I 11	Sapri, Italy
61	D 8	Sarajevo, Bosnia-Herzegovina ■
61	E 11	Sarandë, Albania
104	D 7	Saransk, Russia
104	D 7	Sarapul, Russia
81	J 9	Sarasota, FL, United States
104	C 7	Saratov, Russia
122	I 7	Sarawak, Malaysia ⁙
57	B 11	Sardinia, Italy ⌓
80	F 3	Sardis Lake, MS, United States ◒
111	J 7	Sar-e Pol, Afghanistan
28	E 5	Sargasso Sea, Atlantic Ocean ≋
111	L 8	Sargodha, Pakistan
137	J 6	Sarh, Chad
115	L 2	Sārī, Iran
61	J 14	Saria, Greece ⌓
108	K 7	Sarikamiş, Turkey
127	N 5	Sariwon, North Korea
37	G 16	Sark, United Kingdom ⌓
108	H 8	Şarkişla, Turkey
75	J 11	Sarnia, ON, Canada
65	J 7	Sarny, Ukraine
61	G 13	Saronic Gulf, Greece ≃
108	B 6	Saros Körfezi, Turkey ≃
45	N 11	Sartène, Corsica
111	M 4	Saryozek, Kazakhstan
111	K 4	Sarysu, Kazakhstan ∫
131	A 13	Sasebo, Japan
74	F 8	Saskatchewan, Canada ▣
74	F 9	Saskatoon, SK, Canada
141	I 9	Sasolburg, South Africa
57	B 11	Sassari, Italy
48	F 7	Sassenheim, Netherlands
131	B 15	Sata-misaki, Japan ▶
119	E 9	Satna, India
111	K 3	Satpayev, Kazakhstan
119	C 10	Satpura Range, India ▲
60	G 5	Satu Mare, Romania
115	K 7	Saudi Arabia, Asia ▣
78	H 4	Sault Ste Marie, MI, United States
44	G 5	Saumur, France
140	H 5	Saurimo, Angola
61	C 7	Sava, Croatia ∫
151	J 9	Savai'i, Samoa ⌓
81	K 5	Savannah, GA, United States
81	J 4	Savannah, United States ∫
45	M 4	Saverne, France
56	B 7	Savona, Italy
123	K 11	Savu, Indonesia ⌓
123	K 10	Sawu Sea, Indonesia ≋
115	K 9	Say'ūn, Yemen
37	G 10	Scafell Pike, United Kingdom ▲
23	I 3	Scandinavian Shield, Europe ◇
37	H 10	Scarborough, United Kingdom
48	F 6	Schagen, Netherlands
49	D 11	Schelde, Belgium ∫
79	L 6	Schenectady, NY, United States
48	I 4	Schiermonnikoog, Netherlands ⌓
53	E 11	Schwäbisch Gmünd, Germany
52	H 5	Schwedt, Germany
53	E 9	Schweinfurt, Germany
52	F 5	Schwerin, Germany
52	F 5	Schweriner See, Germany ◒
53	D 13	Schwyz, Switzerland
29	E 12	Scotia Ridge, Atlantic Ocean ▼
29	F 11	Scotia Sea, Atlantic Ocean ≋
36	E 8	Scotland, United Kingdom ▣
33	M 6	Scott Base, New Zealand ▬
82	E 8	Scottsbluff, NE, United States
80	H 3	Scottsboro, AL, United States
85	I 15	Scottsdale, AZ, United States
79	L 7	Scranton, PA, United States
65	N 10	Sea of Azov, Russia/Ukraine ≋
61	H 14	Sea of Crete, Greece ≋
26	E 2	Sea of Japan, Pacific Ocean ≋
108	D 6	Sea of Marmara, Turkey ≋
26	F 1	Sea of Okhotsk, Pacific Ocean ≋
84	D 6	Seattle, WA, United States
60	G 6	Sebeş, Romania
136	E 4	Sebkhet Chemchâm, Mauritania ◒
136	F 3	Sebkhet Ti-n-Bessaïs, Mauritania ◒
119	E 12	Secunderabad, India
45	K 3	Sedan, France
136	E 5	Ségou, Mali
41	I 4	Segovia, Spain
69	H 9	Seinäjoki, Finland
44	H 3	Seine, France ∫
122	H 8	Selat Karimata, Indonesia ⧗
122	F 8	Selat Mentawai, Indonesia
82	F 6	Selby, SD, United States
127	J 2	Selenga, Mongolia ∫
45	M 4	Sélestat, France
136	E 5	Sélibabi, Mauritania
74	H 9	Selkirk, MB, Canada
80	G 5	Selma, AL, United States
122	H 10	Semarang, Indonesia
123	M 8	Semenanjung Bomberai, Indonesia ▶
111	M 2	Semipalatinsk, Kazakhstan
115	L 2	Semnān, Iran
49	F 14	Semois, Belgium ∫
130	H 8	Sendai, Japan
130	I 8	Sendai-wan, Japan ≃
136	E 5	Senegal, Africa ▣
136	D 4	Sénégal, Mauritania/Senegal ∫
61	B 7	Senj, Croatia
68	F 5	Senja, Norway ⌓
45	I 3	Senlis, France
45	J 4	Sens, France
127	O 5	Seoul, South Korea ■
147	J 1	Sepik, Papua New Guinea ∫
75	L 8	Sept-Îles, QC, Canada
49	H 12	Seraing, Belgium
123	L 9	Seram, Indonesia ⌓
123	L 8	Seram Sea, Indonesia ≋
122	G 9	Serang, Indonesia
61	E 8	Serbia and Montenegro, Europe ▣
52	G 7	Seremban, Malaysia
141	K 3	Serengeti Plain, Tanzania ◇
61	H 13	Serifos, Greece ⌓
104	E 7	Serov, Russia
141	I 8	Serowe, Botswana
97	L 8	Serra, Brazil
61	G 10	Serres, Greece
61	B 6	Sesvete, Croatia
45	J 10	Sète, France
131	K 14	Seteuchi, Japan
136	H 1	Sétif, Algeria
131	D 12	Seto-naikai, Japan ≋
40	E 7	Setúbal, Portugal
109	M 6	Sevana Lich, Armenia ◒
65	M 11	Sevastopol', Ukraine
105	N 4	Sevenyy Anyuyskiy Khrebet, Russia ▲
37	G 13	Severn, United Kingdom ∫
74	H 9	Severn, Canada ∫
105	I 3	Severnaya Zemlya, Russia ⁂
104	E 5	Severodvinsk, Russia
105	I 5	Severo-Sibirskaya Nizmennost', Russia ◇
85	I 11	Sevier, United States ∫
85	H 11	Sevier Lake, UT, United States ◒
40	H 9	Seville, Spain
30	F 4	Seychelles, Africa ▣
60	H 6	Sfântu Gheorghe, Romania
137	I 1	Sfax, Tunisia
126	E 5	Shache, China
33	P 5	Shackleton Ice Shelf, Antarctica ◇
150	D 10	Shag Point, New Zealand ▶
118	E 8	Shahjahanpur, India
111	J 8	Shahrak, Afghanistan
104	B 7	Shakhty, Russia
130	G 4	Shakotan-misaki, Japan ▶
122	F 3	Shan Plateau, Myanmar ◇
127	N 7	Shanghai, China
127	M 7	Shangqiu, China
127	N 8	Shangrao, China
37	C 12	Shannon, Ireland ∫
105	M 9	Shantarskiye Ostrova, Russia ⁂
127	M 10	Shantou, China
127	M 9	Shaoguan, China
127	N 8	Shaoxing, China
127	L 9	Shaoyang, China
130	J 2	Shari, Japan
115	M 6	Sharjah, United Arab Emirates
146	D 7	Shark Bay, WA, Australia ≃
85	D 10	Shasta Lake, CA, United States ◒
111	K 2	Shchuchinsk, Kazakhstan
137	N 7	Shebeli, Ethiopia/Somalia ∫
78	F 6	Sheboygan, WI, United States
37	H 11	Sheffield, United Kingdom
111	M 8	Shekhupura, Pakistan
82	B 5	Shelby, MT, United States
127	N 4	Shenyang, China
127	M 10	Shenzhen, China
75	L 9	Sherbrooke, QC, Canada
82	D 7	Sheridan, WY, United States
83	H 11	Sherman, TX, United States
49	G 9	's-Hertogenbosch, Netherlands
36	G 3	Shetland Islands, United Kingdom ⁂
127	M 6	Shijiazhuang, China
111	K 10	Shikarpur, Pakistan
131	H 11	Shikine-shima, Japan ⌓
131	D 12	Shikoku, Japan ⌓
26	E 3	Shikoku Basin, Pacific Ocean ▼
130	H 4	Shikotsu-ko, Japan ◒
119	I 9	Shillong, India
131	H 11	Shimizu, Japan
119	C 13	Shimoga, India
131	B 12	Shimonoseki, Japan
141	K 4	Shinyanga, Tanzania
131	F 12	Shiono-misaki, Japan ▶
83	C 10	Shiprock, NM, United States
115	L 4	Shīrāz, Iran
130	J 2	Shiretoko-misaki, Japan ▶
130	H 5	Shiriya-zaki, Japan ▶
119	D 9	Shivpuri, India
127	L 7	Shiyan, China
127	K 5	Shizuishan, China
131	H 11	Shizuoka, Japan
61	D 9	Shkodër, Albania
29	I 10	Shona Ridge, Atlantic Ocean ▼

▲ Mountain Range ■ National Capital ≈ Ocean ◇ Physical Feature ▬ Polar Base ∫ River ≋ Sea ★ Special Feature ⌂ State Capital ▼ Underwater Feature

85	J 14	**Show Low**, AZ, United States
83	I 12	**Shreveport**, LA, United States
37	G 12	**Shrewsbury**, United Kingdom
127	O 3	**Shuangyashan**, China
84	I 6	**Shumagin Islands**, AL, United States 🌴
61	I 8	**Shumen**, Bulgaria
111	K 5	**Shymkent**, Kazakhstan
65	I 3	**Šiauliai**, Lithuania
61	B 8	**Šibenik**, Croatia
104	F 7	**Siberia**, Russia ⁙
122	F 8	**Siberut**, Indonesia 🏝
60	G 6	**Sibiu**, Romania
52	I 7	**Sibu**, Malaysia
127	K 8	**Sichuan Basin**, China ◇
57	E 14	**Sicilian Channel**, Italy ⧗
57	G 14	**Sicily**, Italy 🏝
57	J 13	**Siderno**, Italy
136	G 1	**Sidi Bel Abbès**, Algeria
61	G 10	**Sidirokastro**, Greece
82	E 5	**Sidney**, MT, United States
64	H 6	**Siedlce**, Poland
52	C 8	**Siegen**, Germany
122	G 5	**Siem Reap**, Cambodia
56	E 8	**Siena**, Italy
99	G 12	**Sierra Grande**, Argentina
136	E 6	**Sierra Leone**, Africa □
28	H 6	**Sierra Leone Basin**, Atlantic Ocean ▬
89	J 9	**Sierra Madre del Sur**, Mexico ⛰
88	G 3	**Sierra Madre Occidental**, Mexico ⛰
89	J 4	**Sierra Madre Oriental**, Mexico ⛰
40	G 8	**Sierra Morena**, Spain ⛰
85	D 11	**Sierra Nevada**, CA, United States ⛰
88	E 2	**Sierra San Pedro Martir**, Mexico ⛰
85	J 16	**Sierra Vista**, AZ, United States
61	H 13	**Sifnos**, Greece 🏝
49	I 12	**Signal de Botrange**, Belgium ▲
33	I 1	**Signy**, United Kingdom ⊟
136	E 6	**Siguiri**, Guinea
109	K 9	**Siirt**, Turkey
118	C 8	**Sikar**, India
136	F 6	**Sikasso**, Mali
83	J 10	**Sikeston**, MO, United States
105	M 11	**Sikhote-Alin'**, Russia ⛰
119	J 9	**Silchar**, India
109	G 10	**Silifke**, Turkey
118	H 8	**Siliguri**, India
126	G 7	**Siling Co**, China ∽
69	E 11	**Siljan**, Sweden ∽
108	K 8	**Silvan Baraji**, Turkey ∽
122	E 7	**Simeulue**, Indonesia 🏝
65	M 11	**Simferopol'**, Ukraine
147	I 6	**Simpson Desert**, NT/SA, Australia ◓
74	H 5	**Simpson Peninsula**, NU, Canada ►
96	E 2	**Sincelejo**, Colombia
40	E 8	**Sines**, Portugal
122	G 8	**Singapore**, Singapore ♜
122	G 8	**Singapore**, Asia □
122	H 8	**Singkawang**, Indonesia
108	G 5	**Sinop**, Turkey
108	G 5	**Sinop Burnu**, Turkey ►
40	E 7	**Sintra**, Portugal
127	N 5	**Sinŭiju**, North Korea
53	C 13	**Sion**, Switzerland
82	G 8	**Sioux City**, IA, United States
82	G 7	**Sioux Falls**, SD, United States
127	N 4	**Siping**, China
33	K 6	**Siple Island**, Antarctica 🏝
122	F 8	**Sipura**, Indonesia 🏝
147	I 4	**Sir Edward Pellew Group**, NT, Australia 🌴
69	B 12	**Sira**, Norway
115	M 4	**Sīrjān**, Iran
109	L 9	**Şirnak**, Turkey
118	C 7	**Sirsa**, India
137	I 2	**Sirte**, Libya
61	B 7	**Sisak**, Croatia
40	H 5	**Sistema Central**, Spain ⛰
41	J 3	**Sistema Ibérico**, Spain ⛰
41	I 9	**Sistemas Béticos**, Spain ⛰
118	E 8	**Sitapur**, India
61	I 15	**Siteia**, Greece
41	N 4	**Sitges**, Spain
84	K 6	**Sitka**, AL, United States
122	F 4	**Sittang**, Myanmar ≀
122	E 3	**Sittwe**, Myanmar
108	H 7	**Sivas**, Turkey
109	J 9	**Siverek**, Turkey
137	K 3	**Siwa**, Egypt
69	C 14	**Sjaelland**, Denmark 🏝
69	B 13	**Skagerrak**, Denmark ⧗
68	G 8	**Skellefteå**, Sweden
69	D 11	**Ski**, Norway
61	G 11	**Skiathos**, Greece
69	C 12	**Skien**, Norway
136	H 1	**Skikda**, Algeria
61	G 12	**Skopelos**, Greece
61	F 9	**Skopje**, Macedonia ♜
36	D 7	**Skye**, United Kingdom 🏝
61	H 12	**Skyros**, Greece
61	H 12	**Skyros**, Greece 🏝
69	C 14	**Slagelse**, Denmark
60	H 7	**Slatina**, Romania
74	F 7	**Slave**, Canada ≀
61	C 7	**Slavonski Brod**, Croatia
37	B 10	**Sligo**, Ireland
61	I 9	**Sliven**, Bulgaria
60	I 7	**Slobozia**, Romania
65	I 5	**Slonim**, Belarus
37	I 13	**Slough**, United Kingdom
64	G 8	**Slovakia**, Europe □
60	B 6	**Slovenia**, Europe □
65	N 8	**Slov"yans'k**, Ukraine
65	J 7	**Sluch**, Ukraine ≀
65	J 6	**Slutsk**, Belarus
37	A 11	**Slyne Head**, Ireland ►
75	L 7	**Smallwood Reservoir**, NL, Canada ∽
61	E 7	**Smederevska Palanka**, Serbia and Montenegro
69	C 9	**Smøla**, Norway 🏝
104	C 5	**Smolensk**, Russia
61	H 10	**Smolyan**, Bulgaria
33	J 4	**Smyley Island**, Antarctica 🏝
85	G 9	**Snake**, United States ≀
85	H 9	**Snake River Plain**, ID, United States ◇
48	H 5	**Sneek**, Netherlands
64	E 7	**Sněžka**, Czech Republic/Poland ▲
37	F 12	**Snowdon**, United Kingdom ▲
137	L 6	**Sobat**, Sudan ≀
97	L 5	**Sobral**, Brazil
104	B 8	**Sochi**, Russia
151	M 10	**Society Archipelago**, French Polynesia 🌴
83	C 11	**Socorro**, NM, United States
115	M 10	**Socotra**, Yemen 🏝
68	I 6	**Sodankylä**, Finland
69	F 10	**Söderhamn**, Sweden
69	F 12	**Södertälje**, Sweden
61	G 9	**Sofia**, Bulgaria
69	A 10	**Sogna Fjord**, Norway ≈
137	L 3	**Sohâg**, Egypt
28	E 4	**Sohm Abyssal Plain**, Atlantic Ocean ▬
45	J 3	**Soissons**, France
108	C 8	**Söke**, Turkey
109	J 5	**Sokhumi**, Georgia
136	G 6	**Sokodé**, Togo
136	H 6	**Sokoto**, Nigeria
119	C 11	**Solapur**, India
104	E 6	**Solikamsk**, Russia
52	C 8	**Solingen**, Germany
150	H 8	**Solomon Islands**, Pacific Ocean □
147	M 3	**Solomon Sea**, Pacific Ocean 🌊
141	I 6	**Solwezi**, Zambia
30	E 4	**Somali Basin**, Indian Ocean ▬
137	O 7	**Somalia**, Africa □
78	G 10	**Somerset**, KY, United States
74	G 4	**Somerset Island**, NU, Canada 🏝
68	D 7	**Sømna**, Norway 🏝
119	F 9	**Son**, India ≀
122	G 3	**Son La**, Vietnam
90	H 9	**Soná**, Panama
141	K 5	**Songea**, Tanzania
122	F 6	**Songkhla**, Thailand
111	J 11	**Sonmiani Bay**, Pakistan ≈
88	F 4	**Sonora**, Mexico ≀
85	G 15	**Sonoran Desert**, AZ/CA, United States ◓
105	O 7	**Sopka Klyuchevskaya**, Russia ▲
75	K 9	**Sorel**, QC, Canada
108	G 7	**Sorgun**, Turkey
41	K 3	**Soria**, Spain
151	J 1	**Sorol**, Federated States of Micronesia 🏝
123	M 8	**Sorong**, Indonesia
68	H 4	**Sørøya**, Norway 🏝
141	I 9	**Soshanguve**, South Africa
64	G 7	**Sosnowiec**, Poland
61	I 10	**Soufli**, Greece
114	G 3	**Soûr**, Lebanon
141	I 10	**South Africa**, Africa □
119	J 14	**South Andaman**, India 🏝
146	H 8	**South Australia**, Australia ▣
31	K 7	**South Australian Basin**, Southern Ocean ▬
31	M 8	**South Australian Plain**, Southern Ocean ▬
78	G 7	**South Bend**, IN, United States
81	K 3	**South Carolina**, United States ▣
26	C 4	**South China Sea**, Pacific Ocean 🌊
82	E 7	**South Dakota**, United States ▣
147	K 11	**South East Cape**, TAS, Australia ►
26	G 7	**South Fiji Basin**, Pacific Ocean ▬
33	N 5	**South Geomagnetic Pole**, Antarctica ◇
29	F 11	**South Georgia**, United Kingdom 🏝
26	E 5	**South Honshu Ridge**, Pacific Ocean ▬
119	B 16	**South Huvadhu Atoll**, Maldives 🏝
31	L 10	**South Indian Basin**, Southern Ocean ▬
150	D 8	**South Island**, New Zealand 🏝
127	O 6	**South Korea**, Asia □
85	E 11	**South Lake Tahoe**, CA, United States
119	A 14	**South Maalhosmadulu Atoll**, Maldives 🏝
119	B 14	**South Male Atoll**, Maldives 🏝
119	B 14	**South Miladunmadulu Atoll**, Maldives 🏝
29	F 11	**South Orkney Islands**, Atlantic Ocean 🌴
82	E 8	**South Platte**, NE, United States ≀
33	M 4	**South Pole**, Antarctica ◇
29	G 11	**South Sandwich Islands**, Atlantic Ocean 🌴
29	G 11	**South Sandwich Trench**, Atlantic Ocean ▬
22	F 9	**South Shetland Islands**, Antarctica 🌴
29	D 12	**South Shetland Trough**, Atlantic Ocean ▬
37	H 9	**South Shields**, United Kingdom
150	E 5	**South Taranaki Bight**, New Zealand ≈
26	F 9	**South Tasman Rise**, Pacific Ocean ▬
36	D 7	**South Uist**, United Kingdom 🏝
150	B 11	**South West Cape**, New Zealand ►
37	H 14	**Southampton**, United Kingdom
75	I 6	**Southampton Island**, NU, Canada 🏝
30	H 7	**Southeast Indian Ridge**, Indian Ocean ▬
27	J 10	**Southeast Pacific Basin**, Pacific Ocean ▬
37	J 13	**Southend-on-Sea**, United Kingdom
150	B 9	**Southern Alps**, New Zealand ⛰
151	L 10	**Southern Cook Islands**, Cook Islands 🌴
151	M 9	**Southern Line Islands**, Kiribati 🌴
23	L 9	**Southern Ocean** ≋
37	F 9	**Southern Uplands**, United Kingdom ⛰
30	E 8	**Southwest Indian Ridge**, Indian Ocean ▬
26	H 8	**Southwest Pacific Basin**, Pacific Ocean ▬
64	H 4	**Sovetsk**, Russia
141	I 8	**Sowa Pan**, Botswana ∽
141	I 9	**Soweto**, South Africa
130	G 2	**Sōya-wan**, Japan ≈
65	L 5	**Sozh**, Belarus ≀
41	K 6	**Spain**, Europe □
91	I 4	**Spanish Town**, Jamaica
85	E 11	**Sparks**, NV, United States
81	J 3	**Spartanburg**, SC, United States
147	I 9	**Spencer Gulf**, SA, Australia ≈
36	F 7	**Spey**, United Kingdom ≀
53	D 10	**Speyer**, Germany
29	I 11	**Spiess Seamount**, Atlantic Ocean ▬
32	E 8	**Spitsbergen**, Svalbard 🏝
61	B 8	**Split**, Croatia
84	F 6	**Spokane**, WA, United States
61	G 12	**Sporades**, Greece 🌴
78	G 8	**Springfield**, OH, United States
79	M 7	**Springfield**, MA, United States
78	E 8	**Springfield**, IL, United States ⌂
83	I 10	**Springfield**, MO, United States
84	C 8	**Springfield**, OR, United States
150	D 7	**Springs Junction**, New Zealand
147	K 6	**Springsure**, QLD, Australia
79	J 9	**Spruce Knob**, WV, United States ▲
37	I 11	**Spurn Head**, United Kingdom ►
150	E 7	**Spy Glass Point**, New Zealand ►
119	E 15	**Sri Jayewardenepura Kotte**, Sri Lanka
119	E 15	**Sri Lanka**, Asia □
118	C 6	**Srinagar**, India
83	J 9	**St. Louis**, MO, United States
48	K 5	**Stadskanaal**, Netherlands
37	G 12	**Stafford**, United Kingdom
64	H 7	**Stalowa Wola**, Poland
79	M 7	**Stamford**, CT, United States
99	H 15	**Stanley**, Falkland Islands
105	K 8	**Stanovoy Khrebet**, Russia ⛰
105	J 9	**Stanovoye Nagor'ye**, Russia ◇
48	I 6	**Staphorst**, Netherlands
61	H 9	**Stara- Zagora**, Bulgaria
64	E 5	**Stargard- Szczeciński**, Poland
80	F 4	**Starkville**, MS, United States
104	C 6	**Staryy Oskol**, Russia
79	K 8	**State College**, PA, United States
81	K 5	**Statesboro**, GA, United States
32	D 8	**Station Nord**, Greenland
79	J 10	**Staunton**, VI, United States
69	A 12	**Stavanger**, Norway
104	B 8	**Stavropol'**, Russia
82	D 8	**Steamboat Springs**, CO, United States
48	I 6	**Steenwijk**, Netherlands
74	G 4	**Stefansson Island**, NU, Canada 🏝
52	F 6	**Stendal**, Germany
83	G 12	**Stephenville**, TX, United States
82	E 8	**Sterling**, CO, United States
78	H 6	**Sterling Heights**, MI, United States
104	D 7	**Sterlitamak**, Russia
78	E 5	**Stevens Point**, WI, United States
150	B 11	**Stewart Island**, New Zealand 🏝
53	I 11	**Steyr**, Austria
69	F 12	**Stockholm**, Sweden ♜
37	H 11	**Stockport**, United Kingdom
85	D 12	**Stockton**, CA, United States
37	G 12	**Stoke-on-Trent**, United Kingdom
37	G 14	**Stonehenge**, United Kingdom ✱
69	C 14	**Store Baelt**, Denmark ⧗
69	D 9	**Støren**, Norway
74	F 4	**Storkerson Peninsula**, NU, Canada ►
36	D 6	**Stornoway**, United Kingdom
69	E 9	**Storsjön**, Sweden ∽
68	F 8	**Storuman**, Sweden
37	J 13	**Stour**, United Kingdom ≀
37	C 10	**Strabane**, Ireland
57	B 10	**Strait of Bonifacio**, Italy/France ⧗
136	F 1	**Strait of Gibraltar**, Morocco/Spain ⧗
115	M 6	**Strait of Hormuz**, Asia ⧗
99	E 15	**Strait of Magellan**, Chile ⧗
122	F 6	**Strait of Malacca**, Indonesia/Malaysia ⧗
57	I 14	**Strait of Messina**, Italy ⧗
90	G 2	**Straits of Florida**, Caribbean Sea ⧗
52	G 4	**Stralsund**, Germany
37	E 10	**Stranraer**, United Kingdom
45	M 4	**Strasbourg**, France
150	E 5	**Stratford**, New Zealand
69	F 9	**Strömsund**, Sweden
61	G 9	**Struma**, Bulgaria ≀
61	F 10	**Strumica**, Macedonia
65	I 8	**Stryy**, Ukraine
53	D 11	**Stuttgart**, Germany
65	I 7	**Styr**, Ukraine ≀
61	E 6	**Subotica**, Serbia and Montenegro
60	I 5	**Suceava**, Romania
98	G 6	**Sucre**, Bolivia ♜
65	N 11	**Sudak**, Ukraine
137	K 5	**Sudan**, Africa □
75	J 10	**Sudbury**, ON, Canada
137	K 7	**Sudd**, Sudan ◇
41	L 6	**Sueca**, Spain
137	L 2	**Suez**, Egypt
137	L 2	**Suez Canal**, Egypt ⧗
115	M 6	**Şuḩār**, Oman
52	F 8	**Suhl**, Germany
127	L 7	**Suizhou**, China
122	H 10	**Sukabumi**, Indonesia
111	K 10	**Sukkur**, Pakistan
131	D 13	**Sukumo**, Japan
111	K 9	**Sulaiman Ranges**, Pakistan ⛰
123	J 9	**Sulawesi**, Indonesia 🏝
96	D 5	**Sullana**, Peru
123	J 7	**Sulu Archipelago**, Philippines 🌴
123	J 6	**Sulu Sea**, Philippines 🌊
33	L 6	**Sulzberger Bay**, Antarctica ≈
122	G 8	**Sumatra**, Indonesia 🏝
123	J 10	**Sumba**, Indonesia 🏝
123	J 10	**Sumbawa**, Indonesia 🏝
141	J 5	**Sumbawanga**, Tanzania
109	O 6	**Sumqayit**, Azerbaijan
81	K 3	**Sumter**, SC, United States
65	M 7	**Sumy**, Ukraine
147	J 10	**Sunbury**, VIC, Australia
127	O 6	**Sunch'ŏn**, South Korea
26	C 5	**Sunda Shelf**, Pacific Ocean ▬
122	G 9	**Sunda Strait**, Indonesia ⧗
37	H 10	**Sunderland**, United Kingdom
69	F 10	**Sundsvall**, Sweden
85	C 12	**Sunnyvale**, CA, United States
147	L 7	**Sunshine Coast**, QLD, Australia ⁙
68	J 8	**Suomussalmi**, Finland
131	C 13	**Suō-nada**, Japan ≈
78	D 4	**Superior**, WI, United States
108	L 8	**Süphan Dagları**, Turkey ▲
115	J 4	**Sūq ash Shuyūkh**, Iraq
127	M 7	**Suqian**, China
115	N 7	**Şūr**, Oman
123	I 10	**Surabaya**, Indonesia
123	I 10	**Surakarta**, Indonesia
119	B 10	**Surat**, India
122	F 6	**Surat Thani**, Thailand
49	H 14	**Sûre**, Luxembourg ≀
119	B 10	**Surendranagar**, India
147	L 8	**Surfers Paradise**, QLD, Australia
104	G 7	**Surgut**, Russia
123	K 6	**Surigao**, Philippines
97	I 3	**Suriname**, South America □
131	H 11	**Suruga-wan**, Japan ≈
56	A 6	**Susa**, Italy
85	D 10	**Susanville**, CA, United States
84	C 8	**Sutherlin**, OR, United States
111	L 9	**Sutlej**, India/Pakistan ≀
151	I 10	**Suva**, Fiji ♜
64	H 5	**Suwałki**, Poland
131	B 16	**Suwanose-jima**, Japan 🏝
127	O 5	**Suwon**, South Korea
127	N 7	**Suzhou**, China
127	M 7	**Suzhou**, China
131	F 11	**Suzuka**, Japan
32	E 8	**Svalbard**, Norway ▣
69	E 10	**Sveg**, Sweden
69	E 9	**Svenstavik**, Sweden
64	F 8	**Svitavy**, Czech Republic
65	K 6	**Svyetlahorsk**, Belarus
140	G 8	**Swakopmund**, Namibia
37	F 13	**Swansea**, United Kingdom
141	J 9	**Swaziland**, Africa □
69	E 13	**Sweden**, Europe □
83	F 12	**Sweetwater**, TX, United States
74	F 10	**Swift Current**, SK, Canada
37	H 13	**Swindon**, United Kingdom
53	D 13	**Switzerland**, Europe □
147	L 9	**Sydney**, NSW, Australia ⌂
75	M 8	**Sydney**, NS, Canada
65	O 8	**Syeverodonets'k**, Ukraine
104	E 6	**Syktyvkar**, Russia
119	J 9	**Sylhet**, Bangladesh
33	O 2	**Syowa**, Japan ⊟
57	I 15	**Syracuse**, Italy
79	K 6	**Syracuse**, NY, United States
111	K 5	**Syrdar'ya**, Kazakhstan ≀
114	H 3	**Syria**, Asia □
114	H 3	**Syrian Desert**, Asia ◓
61	H 13	**Syros**, Greece 🏝
104	D 7	**Syzran'**, Russia
64	E 5	**Szczecin**, Poland
64	G 10	**Szeged**, Hungary
64	F 9	**Székesfehérvár**, Hungary
64	F 10	**Szekszárd**, Hungary
64	G 10	**Szolnok**, Hungary
64	E 9	**Szombathely**, Hungary

≈ Bay ⧗ Channel □ Country ▣ Dependent Territory ◓ Desert ⁙ Geographic Area ► Headland 🏝 Island 🌴 Island Group ∽ Lake ▲ Mountain

T

141 J 4 Tabora, Tanzania
115 J 1 Tabrīz, Iran
114 H 5 Tabūk, Saudi Arabia
123 K 5 Tacloban, Philippines
96 F 8 Tacna, Peru
84 D 6 Tacoma, WA, United States
99 I 9 Tacuarembó, Uruguay
127 O 6 Taegu, South Korea
127 O 6 Taejŏn, South Korea
28 H 4 Tagus Abyssal Plain, Atlantic Ocean
127 N 1 Tahe, China
151 N 10 Tahiti, French Polynesia
136 G 5 Tahoua, Niger
127 N 9 T'aichung, Taiwan
150 C 10 Taieri, New Zealand
150 F 5 Taihape, New Zealand
147 I 9 Tailem Bend, SA, Australia
127 N 10 T'ainan, Taiwan
127 N 9 Taipei, Taiwan
52 F 7 Taiping, Malaysia
127 O 10 Taiwan, Asia
127 N 10 Taiwan Strait, China/Taiwan
127 L 6 Taiyuan, China
127 N 8 Taizhou, China
115 J 10 Ta'izz, Yemen
111 L 6 Tajikistan, Asia
40 H 6 Tajo, Spain
131 D 12 Takamatsu, Japan
131 F 9 Takaoka, Japan
150 F 3 Takapuna, New Zealand
131 H 9 Takasaki, Japan
131 F 11 Takatsuki, Japan
23 L 4 Taklimakan Desert, Asia
136 F 7 Takoradi, Ghana
111 L 5 Talas, Kyrgyzstan
41 I 5 Talavera de la Reina, Spain
99 E 10 Talca, Chile
99 E 11 Talcahuano, Chile
111 M 4 Taldykorgan, Kazakhstan
123 K 8 Taliabu, Indonesia
81 I 6 Tallahassee, FL, United States
65 I 1 Tallinn, Estonia
98 E 7 Taltal, Chile
136 F 6 Tamale, Ghana
136 H 4 Tamanrasset, Algeria
37 F 14 Tamar, United Kingdom
89 K 8 Tamazunchale, Mexico
136 D 5 Tambacounda, Senegal
104 C 7 Tambov, Russia
81 J 8 Tampa, FL, United States
81 J 9 Tampa Bay, FL, United States
69 I 10 Tampere, Finland
89 L 7 Tampico, Mexico
147 L 8 Tamworth, NSW, Australia
68 I 4 Tana Bru, Norway
146 H 5 Tanami Desert, NT, Australia
99 H 11 Tandil, Argentina
131 C 15 Tanega-shima, Japan
141 L 4 Tanga, Tanzania
136 F 1 Tangier, Morocco
126 G 7 Tangra Yumco, China
127 M 5 Tangshan, China
123 I 8 Tanjung, Indonesia
122 H 9 Tanjung Bugel, Indonesia
122 G 9 Tanjung Cina, Indonesia
123 N 8 Tanjung d'Urville, Indonesia
122 G 10 Tanjung Guhakolak, Indonesia
122 G 9 Tanjung Lumut, Indonesia
123 L 7 Tanjung Sopi, Indonesia
123 N 10 Tanjung Vals, Indonesia
123 J 7 Tanjungredeb, Indonesia
137 L 2 Tanta, Egypt
141 J 4 Tanzania, Africa
136 F 4 Taoudenni, Mali
127 N 9 T'aoyüan, Taiwan
89 N 11 Tapachula, Mexico
97 I 5 Tapajós, Brazil
61 D 8 Tara, Serbia and Montenegro
123 J 7 Tarakan, Indonesia
41 J 6 Tarancón, Spain
57 J 11 Taranto, Italy
96 E 5 Tarapoto, Peru
45 K 7 Tarare, France
151 I 7 Tarawa, Kiribati
111 L 5 Taraz, Kazakhstan
44 H 10 Tarbes, France
146 H 8 Tarcoola, SA, Australia
147 L 9 Taree, NSW, Australia
60 H 7 Târgovişte, Romania
60 G 7 Târgu Jiu, Romania
60 H 6 Târgu Mureş, Romania
98 G 6 Tarija, Bolivia
126 F 5 Tarim Basin, China
126 F 4 Tarim He, China
123 N 8 Taritatu, Indonesia
123 J 4 Tarlac, Philippines
64 G 8 Tarnów, Poland
41 N 4 Tarragona, Spain
109 G 9 Tarsus, Turkey
65 J 2 Tartu, Estonia
114 H 3 Ţarţūs, Syria
56 G 4 Tarvisio, Italy
111 K 5 Tashkent, Uzbekistan
111 L 5 Tash-Kömür, Kyrgyzstan
52 G 7 Tasik Kenyir, Malaysia
26 F 9 Tasman Basin, Pacific Ocean
150 E 6 Tasman Bay, New Zealand
26 F 8 Tasman Sea, Southern Ocean
147 J 11 Tasmania, Australia
136 H 3 Tassili n'Ajjer, Algeria
64 F 9 Tatabánya, Hungary
105 M 9 Tatarskiy Proliv, Russia
108 K 8 Tatvan, Turkey
37 G 14 Taunton, United Kingdom
150 G 4 Taupo, New Zealand
64 H 4 Tauragė, Lithuania
150 F 4 Tauranga, New Zealand
150 E 2 Tauroa Point, New Zealand
23 I 4 Taurus Mountains, Europe
109 D 9 Tavas, Turkey
122 F 5 Tavoy, Myanmar
122 F 5 Tavoy Point, Myanmar
119 D 10 Tawa Reservoir, India
89 K 9 Taxco, Mexico
36 F 8 Tay, United Kingdom
40 F 9 TaÙira, Portugal
104 H 6 Taz, Russia
109 M 6 T'bilisi, Georgia
64 G 5 Tczew, Poland
150 F 4 Te Kuiti, New Zealand
89 N 9 Teapa, Mexico
109 M 5 Tebulosmt'a, Georgia/Russia
89 I 9 Tecomán, Mexico
89 K 10 Técpan, Mexico
111 I 7 Tedzhen, Turkmenistan
37 G 10 Tees, United Kingdom
90 F 6 Tegucigalpa, Honduras
115 L 2 Tehran, Iran
89 L 9 Tehuacán, Mexico
89 M 10 Tehuantepec, Mexico
108 C 6 Tekirdağ, Turkey
114 G 3 Tel Aviv-Jaffa, Israel
37 G 12 Telford, United Kingdom
64 H 3 Telšai, Lithuania
123 K 9 Teluk Bone, Indonesia
122 H 7 Teluk Datu, Malaysia
123 M 9 Teluk Kamrau, Indonesia
123 K 8 Teluk Tomini, Indonesia
111 L 3 Temirtau, Kazakhstan
85 I 15 Tempe, AZ, United States
83 G 12 Temple, TX, United States
99 E 11 Temuco, Chile
119 J 14 Ten Degree Channel, India
81 J 10 Ten Thousand Islands, FL, United States
119 E 12 Tenali, India
136 H 4 Ténéré du Tafassâsset, Niger
40 B 11 Tenerife, Spain
146 H 5 Tennant Creek, NT, Australia
80 G 1 Tennessee, United States
80 G 2 Tennessee, United States
68 I 6 Tenniöjoki, Finland
68 I 5 Tenojoki, Finland
97 L 7 Teófilo Otôni, Brazil
89 K 8 Teotiuacan, Mexico
89 I 7 Tepic, Mexico
64 E 7 Teplice, Czech Republic
89 J 8 Tequila, Mexico
57 G 9 Teramo, Italy
40 B 9 Terceira, Portugal
97 K 5 Teresina, Brazil
111 K 7 Termez, Uzbekistan
49 D 10 Terneuzen, Netherlands
57 F 9 Terni, Italy
65 I 8 Ternopil', Ukraine
33 M 7 Terra Nova Bay, Italy
57 F 10 Terracina, Italy
78 F 9 Terre Haute, IN, United States
48 G 4 Terschelling, Netherlands
41 L 5 Teruel, Spain
130 G 2 Teshio, Japan
141 J 7 Tete, Mozambique
65 K 7 Teteriv, Ukraine
61 E 9 Tetovo, Macedonia
83 I 11 Texarkana, TX, United States
83 F 12 Texas, United States
48 F 5 Texel, Netherlands
122 H 3 Thai Nguyên, Vietnam
122 F 4 Thailand, Asia
115 M 9 Thamarīt, Oman
37 H 13 Thames, United Kingdom
150 F 3 Thames, New Zealand
119 B 11 Thane, India
122 H 3 Thanh Hoa, Vietnam
119 E 14 Thanjavur, India
23 K 5 Thar Desert, Asia
61 G 10 Thasos, Greece
122 F 4 Thaton, Myanmar
85 J 14 Theodore Roosevelt Lake, AZ, United States
61 G 10 Thessaloniki, Greece
82 G 5 Thief River Falls, MN, United States
45 J 7 Thiers, France
136 D 5 Thiès, Senegal
119 B 13 Thiladhunmathee Atoll, Maldives
118 I 8 Thimphu, Bhutan
45 L 3 Thionville, France
61 H 14 Thira, Greece
61 G 12 Thiva, Greece
81 I 6 Thomasville, GA, United States
74 H 8 Thompson, MB, Canada
45 L 6 Thonon-les-Bains, France
33 M 1 Thorshavnheiane Mountains, Antarctica
127 K 8 Three Gorges Dam, China
150 D 1 Three Kings Island, New Zealand
49 E 13 Thuin, Belgium
32 C 7 Thule, Greenland
53 C 13 Thun, Switzerland
75 I 10 Thunder Bay, ON, Canada
36 F 5 Thurso, United Kingdom
33 J 5 Thurston Island, Antarctica
126 F 4 Tian Shan, China
127 M 5 Tianjin, China
127 K 7 Tianshui, China
137 I 4 Tibesti, Chad
126 G 6 Tibet, China
89 O 8 Ticul, Mexico
136 E 4 Tidjikja, Mauritania
127 O 3 Tieli, China
127 N 4 Tieling, China
23 K 4 Tien Shan, Asia
49 F 11 Tienen, Belgium
69 F 11 Tierp, Sweden
99 F 16 Tierra del Fuego, Argentina
97 J 8 Tietê, Brazil
81 J 6 Tifton, GA, United States
65 K 10 Tighina, Moldova
96 E 4 Tigre, Peru
23 J 4 Tigris, Asia
88 D 2 Tijuana, Mexico
90 E 5 Tikal, Guatemala
27 J 6 Tiki Basin, Pacific Ocean
115 J 3 Tikrīt, Iraq
49 G 9 Tilburg, Netherlands
61 J 14 Tilos, Greece
150 D 9 Timaru, New Zealand
136 F 5 Timbuktu, Mali
60 F 6 Timişoara, Romania
75 J 9 Timmins, ON, Canada
123 K 10 Timor, Asia,
31 L 5 Timor Sea, Indian Ocean
69 F 10 Timrå, Sweden
136 F 3 Tindouf, Algeria
151 L 5 Tinian, Northern Mariana Islands
61 H 13 Tinos, Greece
61 H 13 Tinos, Greece
118 K 8 Tinsukia, India
61 E 10 Tirana, Albania
65 K 10 Tiraspol, Moldova
36 D 8 Tiree, United Kingdom
150 F 4 Tirua Point, New Zealand
119 E 14 Tiruchchirappalli, India
119 D 15 Tirunelveli, India
119 E 13 Tirupati, India
119 D 14 Tiruppur, India
119 E 13 Tiruvannamalai, India
136 H 1 Tizi Ouzou, Algeria
89 P 7 Tizimín, Mexico
89 I 8 Tlaquepaque, Mexico
136 G 1 Tlemcen, Algeria
141 N 7 Toamasina, Madagascar
91 O 7 Tobago, Trinidad and Tobago
111 J 2 Tobol, Kazakhstan
104 F 7 Tobol'sk, Russia
137 K 2 Tobruk, Libya
97 J 6 Tocantins, Brazil
98 E 7 Tocopilla, Chile
151 M 2 Tofol, Federated States of Micronesia
136 G 6 Togo, Africa
131 G 11 Tōkai, Japan
131 B 16 Tokara-rettō, Japan
131 J 16 Tokasiki-jima, Japan
108 H 7 Tokat, Turkey
151 K 8 Tokelau Islands, New Zealand
130 I 4 Tokkachi, Japan
150 G 4 Tokoroa, New Zealand
131 K 14 Toku-no-shima, Japan
131 K 14 Tokunoshima, Japan
131 E 12 Tokushima, Japan
131 C 12 Tokuyama, Japan
131 H 10 Tokyo, Japan
41 I 6 Toledo, Spain
78 H 7 Toledo, OH, United States
83 I 12 Toledo Bend Reservoir, LA/TX, United States
141 L 8 Toliara, Madagascar
60 A 6 Tolmin, Slovenia
41 K 2 Tolosa, Spain
89 K 9 Toluca, Mexico
104 D 7 Tol'yatti, Russia
78 E 5 Tomah, WI, United States
130 H 4 Tomakomai, Japan
80 G 5 Tombigbee, United States
104 G 8 Tomsk, Russia
123 K 8 Tondano, Indonesia
151 J 11 Tonga, Pacific Ocean
26 G 7 Tonga Trench, Pacific Ocean
151 K 10 Tongatapu, Tonga
127 K 6 Tongchuan, China
127 O 4 Tonghua, China
127 N 4 Tongliao, China
118 D 8 Tonk, India
122 G 5 Tônlé Sap, Cambodia
85 F 12 Tonopah, NV, United States
69 C 12 Tønsberg, Norway
85 I 10 Tooele, UT, United States
147 L 7 Toowoomba, QLD, Australia
146 H 4 Top Springs, NT, Australia
83 H 9 Topeka, KS, United States
115 N 2 Torbat-e Heydarīyeh, Iran
115 N 2 Torbat-e Jām, Iran
49 C 11 Torhout, Belgium
68 G 5 Torneälven, Sweden
68 H 7 Tornio, Sweden
40 H 4 Toro, Spain
75 K 10 Toronto, ON, Canada
37 F 15 Torquay, United Kingdom
85 E 14 Torrance, CA, United States
41 I 2 Torrelavega, Spain
89 I 6 Torreón, Mexico
40 F 6 Torres Novas, Portugal
147 J 3 Torres Strait, QLD, Australia
40 E 6 Torres Vedras, Portugal
82 E 8 Torrington, WY, United States
64 G 5 Toruń, Poland
131 D 13 Tosa-wan, Japan
131 H 11 To-shima, Japan
98 H 8 Tostado, Argentina
131 D 11 Tottori, Japan
45 L 4 Toul, France
45 L 10 Toulon, France
45 I 10 Toulouse, France
45 J 1 Tourcoing, France
49 C 12 Tournai, Belgium
44 H 5 Tours, France
130 H 6 Towada-ko, Japan
147 K 5 Townsville, QLD, Australia
130 H 4 Tōya-ko, Japan
131 F 10 Toyama, Japan
131 F 9 Toyama-wan, Japan
131 G 11 Toyohashi, Japan
131 G 11 Toyota, Japan
109 L 5 Tqibuli, Georgia
108 J 6 Trabzon, Turkey
37 B 12 Tralee, Ireland
33 L 4 Transantarctic, Antarctica
23 L 10 Transantarctic Mountains, Antarctica
30 D 7 Transkei Basin, Indian Ocean
60 F 6 Transylvania, Romania
60 F 7 Transylvanian Alps, Romania
57 F 14 Trapani, Italy
53 I 11 Traun, Austria
78 G 5 Travers City, MI, United States
99 J 10 Treinta y Tres, Uruguay
99 F 12 Trelew, Argentina
37 I 12 Trent, United Kingdom
56 E 5 Trento, Italy
79 L 8 Trenton, NJ, United States
56 F 5 Treviso, Italy
53 B 9 Trier, Germany
56 G 5 Trieste, Italy
61 F 11 Trikala, Greece
119 E 15 Trincomalee, Sri Lanka
99 I 10 Trinidad, Uruguay
98 G 4 Trinidad, Bolivia
83 E 10 Trinidad, CO, United States
91 O 7 Trinidad, Trinidad and Tobago
91 O 7 Trinidad and Tobago, North America
61 F 13 Tripoli, Greece
114 G 3 Tripoli, Lebanon
137 I 2 Tripoli, Libya
29 I 9 Tristan da Cunha, Atlantic Ocean
29 G 9 Tristan da Cunha Fracture Zone, Atlantic Ocean
119 D 15 Trivandrum, India
75 L 9 Trois-Rivières, QC, Canada
69 D 12 Trollhättan, Sweden
68 G 5 Tromsø, Norway
69 D 9 Trondheim, Norway
80 H 5 Troy, AL, United States
79 L 6 Troy, NY, United States
45 J 4 Troyes, France
40 H 6 Trujillo, Spain
96 E 6 Trujillo, Peru
90 F 5 Trujillo, Honduras
75 M 9 Truro, NS, Canada
61 J 9 Tsarevo, Bulgaria
140 H 4 Tshikapa, Democratic Republic of Congo
131 F 11 Tsu, Japan
131 I 10 Tsuchiura, Japan
130 G 5 Tsugaru-kaikyō, Japan
140 G 7 Tsumeb, Namibia
130 H 7 Tsuruoka, Japan
131 A 12 Tsushima, Japan
151 N 9 Tuamotu Archipelago, French Polynesia
27 J 7 Tuamotu Fracture Zone, Pacific Ocean
85 J 13 Tuba City, AZ, United States
53 D 11 Tübingen, Germany
85 J 15 Tucson, AZ, United States
83 E 11 Tucumcari, NM, United States
41 K 3 Tudela, Spain
27 I 2 Tufts Abyssal Plain, Pacific Ocean
123 K 4 Tuguegarao, Philippines
74 D 4 Tuktoyaktuk, NT, Canada
104 C 6 Tula, Russia
89 L 8 Tulancingo, Mexico
85 E 13 Tulare, CA, United States
60 J 7 Tulcea, Romania
83 H 10 Tulsa, OK, United States
119 D 13 Tumkur, India
61 I 9 Tundzha, Bulgaria
119 D 12 Tungabhadra Reservoir, India
137 I 1 Tunis, Tunisia
137 I 1 Tunisia, Africa
96 F 3 Tunja, Colombia
80 F 3 Tupelo, MS, United States
98 G 6 Tupiza, Bolivia
23 K 4 Turan Lowland, Asia
114 H 4 Turayf, Saudi Arabia
111 J 10 Turbat, Pakistan
60 G 6 Turda, Romania
61 I 8 Tŭrgovishte, Bulgaria
41 L 6 Turia, Spain
56 B 6 Turin, Italy
111 K 5 Turkestan, Kazakhstan

Mountain Range · National Capital · Ocean · Physical Feature · Polar Base · River · Sea · Special Feature · State Capital · Underwater Feature

108 H 8 **Turkey**, Asia/Europe
108 G 11 **Turkish Republic of Northern Cyprus**, Asia/Europe
110 H 6 **Turkmenbashi**, Turkmenistan
111 I 6 **Turkmenistan**, Asia
91 K 3 **Turks and Caicos Islands**, United Kingdom
91 K 3 **Turks Islands**, Turks and Caicos Islands
69 H 11 **Turku**, Finland
49 F 10 **Turnhout**, Belgium
126 H 4 **Turpan**, China
23 L 4 **Turpan Depression**, Asia
80 G 4 **Tuscaloosa**, AL, United States
56 D 7 **Tuscan Archipelago**, Italy
56 D 8 **Tuscany**, Italy
119 D 15 **Tuticorin**, India
151 K 9 **Tutuila**, American Samoa
151 I 8 **Tuvalu**, Pacific Ocean
89 I 8 **Tuxpan**, Mexico
89 L 8 **Tuxpan**, Mexico
89 L 9 **Tuxtepec**, Mexico
89 N 10 **Tuxtla Gutiérrez**, Mexico
108 F 8 **Tuz Gölü**, Turkey
61 D 7 **Tuzla**, Bosnia-Herzegovina
104 C 5 **Tver'**, Russia
37 G 9 **Tweed**, United Kingdom
85 H 9 **Twin Falls**, ID, United States
64 G 7 **Tychy**, Poland
83 H 12 **Tyler**, TX, United States
61 H 15 **Tympaki**, Greece
105 K 9 **Tynda**, Russia
37 G 9 **Tyne**, United Kingdom
61 G 11 **Tyrnavos**, Greece
45 O 11 **Tyrrhenian Sea**, France/Italy
104 F 8 **Tyumen'**, Russia

U

41 J 8 **Úbeda**, Spain
97 J 8 **Uberaba**, Brazil
97 J 8 **Uberlândia**, Brazil
122 G 4 **Ubon Ratchathani**, Thailand
96 E 5 **Ucayali**, Peru
130 G 4 **Uchiura-wan**, Japan
119 C 9 **Udaipur**, India
69 D 12 **Uddevalla**, Sweden
56 G 5 **Udine**, Italy
27 I 10 **Udintsev Fracture Zone**, Pacific Ocean
122 G 4 **Udon Thani**, Thailand
141 I 2 **Uele**, Democratic Republic of Congo
137 K 8 **Uele**, Somalia
52 E 6 **Uelzen**, Germany
104 D 7 **Ufa**, Russia
141 J 2 **Uganda**, Africa
140 G 5 **Uíge**, Angola
151 J 1 **Uithi**, Federated States of Micronesia
151 M 3 **Ujae**, Marshall Islands
119 D 10 **Ujjain**, India
123 J 9 **Ujung Pandang**, Indonesia
104 E 6 **Ukhta**, Russia
85 C 11 **Ukiah**, CA, United States
65 I 4 **Ukmergė**, Lithuania
65 I 8 **Ukraine**, Europe
127 K 3 **Ulaanbaatar**, Mongolia
127 I 2 **Ulaangom**, Mongolia
126 H 6 **Ulan Ul Hu**, China
105 J 10 **Ulan-Ude**, Russia
127 L 2 **Uldz**, Mongolia
119 C 11 **Ulhasnagar**, India
53 E 11 **Ulm**, Germany
127 P 6 **Ulsan**, South Korea
151 L 1 **Ulul**, Federated States of Micronesia
74 F 4 **Uluqsaqtuuq**, NT, Canada
146 H 7 **Uluru**, NT, Australia
104 D 7 **Ul'yanovsk**, Russia
65 K 8 **Uman'**, Ukraine
69 G 9 **Umeå**, Sweden
68 G 8 **Umeälven**, Sweden
32 C 7 **Ummannaq**, Greenland
84 I 5 **Umnak Island**, AL, United States
61 B 7 **Una**, Bosnia-Herzegovina
75 K 6 **Ungava Bay**, QC, Canada
80 F 1 **Union City**, TN, United States
79 J 8 **Uniontown**, PA, United States
115 L 7 **United Arab Emirates**, Asia
37 G 10 **United Kingdom**, Europe
36 H 3 **Unst**, United Kingdom
151 J 9 **Upolu**, Samoa
150 F 6 **Upper Hutt**, New Zealand
85 D 9 **Upper Klamath Lake**, OR, United States
82 H 5 **Upper Red Lake**, MN, United States
69 F 11 **Uppsala**, Sweden
110 H 2 **Ural**, Kazakhstan/Russia
23 J 2 **Ural Mountains**, Asia
110 H 2 **Ural'sk**, Kazakhstan
131 H 10 **Urawa**, Japan
111 J 5 **Urgench**, Uzbekistan
111 K 6 **Ŭroteppa**, Tajikistan
89 J 9 **Uruapan**, Mexico
97 I 10 **Uruguai**, Argentina/Uruguay
99 I 10 **Uruguay**, South America
22 F 8 **Uruguay**, South America
126 H 4 **Ürümqi**, China
60 I 7 **Urziceni**, Romania
108 D 8 **Uşak**, Turkey
99 F 16 **Ushuaia**, Argentina
105 I 9 **Usol'ye-Sibirskoye**, Russia
45 I 7 **Ussel**, France
105 M 11 **Ussuriysk**, Russia
105 I 9 **Ust'-Ilimsk**, Russia
111 M 2 **Ust'-Kamenogorsk**, Kazakhstan
111 I 5 **Ustyurt Plateau**, Uzbekistan
89 N 9 **Usumacinta**, Mexico
85 I 11 **Utah**, United States
85 I 10 **Utah Lake**, UT, United States
65 I 4 **Utena**, Lithuania
79 L 6 **Utica**, NY, United States
48 G 8 **Utrecht**, Netherlands
151 N 3 **Utrik**, Marshall Islands
131 H 9 **Utsunomiya**, Japan
83 F 13 **Uvalde**, TX, United States
127 I 2 **Uvs Nuur**, Mongolia
131 D 13 **Uwajima**, Japan
98 F 6 **Uyuni**, Bolivia
111 J 5 **Uzbekistan**, Asia
64 H 9 **Uzhhorod**, Ukraine
61 E 8 **Užice**, Serbia and Montenegro

V

23 I 8 **Vaal**, Africa
49 I 12 **Vaals**, Luxembourg
69 H 9 **Vaasa**, Finland
119 C 10 **Vadodara**, India
53 E 12 **Vaduz**, Liechtenstein
151 J 9 **Vaiaku**, Tuvalu
83 D 9 **Vail**, CO, United States
41 J 7 **Valdepeñas**, Spain
99 D 11 **Valdivia**, Chile
29 I 9 **Valdivia Seamount**, Atlantic Ocean
75 J 9 **Val-d'Or**, QC, Canada
81 J 6 **Valdosta**, GA, United States
45 K 8 **Valence**, France
41 L 6 **Valencia**, Spain
96 G 2 **Valencia**, Venezuela
45 J 2 **Valenciennes**, France
65 I 2 **Valga**, Estonia
61 E 8 **Valjevo**, Serbia and Montenegro
49 H 10 **Valkenswaard**, Netherlands
41 I 4 **Valladolid**, Spain
89 P 8 **Valladolid**, Mexico
96 F 2 **Valledupar**, Colombia
85 C 12 **Vallejo**, CA, United States
98 E 8 **Vallenar**, Chile
57 H 16 **Valletta**, Malta
91 N 4 **Valley, The**, Anguilla
41 M 4 **Valls**, Spain
65 I 2 **Valmiera**, Latvia
119 D 14 **Valparai**, India
99 E 10 **Valparaíso**, Chile
108 L 8 **Van**, Turkey
146 H 3 **Van Diemen Gulf**, NT, Australia
109 M 6 **Vanadzor**, Armenia
74 D 9 **Vancouver**, BC, Canada
74 D 9 **Vancouver Island**, BC, Canada
69 D 12 **Vänern**, Sweden
147 J 1 **Vanimo**, Papua New Guinea
44 F 5 **Vannes**, France
69 I 11 **Vantaa**, Finland
151 J 10 **Vanua Levu**, Fiji
150 H 10 **Vanuatu**, Pacific Ocean
119 F 9 **Varanasi**, India
68 I 4 **Varanger Fjord**, Norway
61 C 6 **Varaždin**, Croatia
69 D 13 **Varberg**, Sweden
61 F 10 **Vardar**, Macedonia
69 B 14 **Varde**, Denmark
56 C 5 **Varese**, Italy
69 J 9 **Varkaus**, Finland
61 J 8 **Varna**, Bulgaria
60 I 6 **Vaslui**, Romania
69 F 12 **Västerås**, Sweden
69 E 10 **Västerdalälven**, Sweden
69 F 13 **Västervik**, Sweden
57 H 9 **Vasto**, Italy
57 F 9 **Vatican City**, Vatican City
57 F 9 **Vatican City**, Europe
68 C 6 **Vatnajökull**, Iceland
69 E 12 **Vättern**, Sweden
83 D 11 **Vaughn**, NM, United States
69 E 13 **Växjö**, Sweden
48 H 8 **Veenendaal**, Netherlands
68 D 7 **Vega**, Norway
119 A 15 **Veimandu Channel**, Maldives
69 C 14 **Vejke**, Denmark
104 C 5 **Velikiye Luki**, Russia
104 C 5 **Velikiye Novgorod**, Russia
61 H 8 **Veliko Tŭrnovo**, Bulgaria
61 G 9 **Velingrad**, Bulgaria
119 E 13 **Vellore**, India
28 E 6 **Vema Fracture Zone**, Atlantic Ocean
99 H 10 **Venado Tuerto**, Argentina
44 H 5 **Vendôme**, France
96 F 2 **Venezuela**, South America
28 D 6 **Venezuelan Basin**, Atlantic Ocean
56 F 6 **Venice**, Italy
49 I 10 **Venlo**, Netherlands
64 H 3 **Venta**, Lithuania
56 A 7 **Ventimiglia**, Italy
64 H 2 **Ventspils**, Latvia
85 E 14 **Ventura**, CA, United States
99 H 9 **Vera**, Argentina
89 L 9 **Veracruz**, Mexico
119 B 10 **Veraval**, India
56 B 6 **Vercelli**, Italy
23 L 2 **Verkhoyanskiy Khrebet**, Asia
82 I 5 **Vermilion Lake**, MN, United States
79 M 6 **Vermont**, United States
33 I 2 **Vernadsky**, Ukraine
85 J 10 **Vernal**, UT, United States
83 F 11 **Vernon**, TX, United States
74 E 9 **Vernon**, BC, Canada
61 F 10 **Veroia**, Greece
56 E 5 **Verona**, Italy
45 I 4 **Versailles**, France
49 I 12 **Verviers**, Belgium
45 L 5 **Vesoul**, France
68 E 6 **Vest Fjord**, Norway
68 E 5 **Vesterålen**, Norway
57 H 10 **Vesuvius**, Italy
64 F 10 **Veszprém**, Hungary
49 B 11 **Veurne**, Belgium
40 E 3 **Viana do Castelo**, Portugal
56 D 7 **Viareggio**, Italy
57 I 13 **Vibo Valentia**, Italy
69 C 14 **Viborg**, Denmark
41 N 3 **Vic**, Spain
56 E 5 **Vicenza**, Italy
45 J 7 **Vichy**, France
80 E 5 **Vicksburg**, MS, United States
147 K 10 **Victoria**, Australia
146 G 5 **Victoria**, NT, Australia
83 H 13 **Victoria**, TX, United States
74 D 10 **Victoria**, BC, Canada
141 I 7 **Victoria Falls**, Zimbabwe
141 I 7 **Victoria Falls**, Zambia/Zimbabwe
74 F 5 **Victoria Island**, NT/NU, Canada
33 M 6 **Victoria Land**, Antarctica
75 L 9 **Victoriaville**, QC, Canada
99 G 12 **Viedma**, Argentina
53 J 11 **Vienna**, Austria
122 G 4 **Vientiane**, Laos
45 I 5 **Vierzon**, France
122 H 4 **Vietnam**, Asia
44 G 11 **Vignemale**, France
40 F 3 **Vigo**, Spain
119 F 12 **Vijayawada**, India
68 D 8 **Vikna**, Norway
69 B 10 **Vikøyri**, Norway
28 B 7 **Vila da Ribeira Brava**, Cape Verde
28 B 7 **Vila da Sal Rei**, Cape Verde
28 B 8 **Vila do Tarrafal**, Cape Verde
40 F 4 **Vila Nova de Gaia**, Portugal
28 A 8 **Vila Nova Sintra**, Cape Verde
40 F 4 **Vila Real**, Portugal
40 G 2 **Vilalba**, Spain
68 F 8 **Vilhelmina**, Sweden
65 I 2 **Viljandi**, Estonia
99 G 9 **Villa María**, Argentina
98 F 6 **Villa Martin**, Bolivia
98 G 6 **Villa Montes**, Bolivia
41 J 8 **Villacarrillo**, Spain
53 H 13 **Villach**, Austria
89 N 9 **Villahermosa**, Mexico
41 L 7 **Villajoyosa**, Spain
41 J 7 **Villanueva de los Infantes**, Spain
98 I 8 **Villarrica**, Paraguay
96 F 3 **Villavicencio**, Colombia
40 H 1 **Villaviciosa de Asturias**, Spain
98 G 6 **Villazon**, Bolivia
41 L 7 **Villena**, Spain
65 I 4 **Vilnius**, Lithuania
105 K 8 **Vilyuy**, Russia
105 J 7 **Vilyuyskoye Vodokhranilishche**, Russia
99 E 9 **Viña del Mar**, Chile
41 M 5 **Vinarós**, Spain
78 F 9 **Vincennes**, IN, United States
33 P 5 **Vincennes Bay**, Antarctica
119 C 10 **Vindhya Ranges**, India
122 H 4 **Vinh**, Vietnam
65 K 8 **Vinnytsya**, Ukraine
33 K 4 **Vinson Massif**, Antarctica
91 M 4 **Virgin Islands**, United States
79 J 10 **Virginia**, United States
82 I 5 **Virginia**, MN, United States
79 L 11 **Virginia Beach**, VI, United States
61 C 6 **Virovitica**, Croatia
49 H 15 **Virton**, Belgium
61 B 8 **Vis**, Croatia
85 E 13 **Visalia**, CA, United States
69 G 13 **Visby**, Sweden
74 F 4 **Viscount Melville Sound**, NU, Canada
40 F 5 **Viseu**, Portugal
119 F 12 **Vishakhapatnam**, India
64 G 6 **Vistula**, Poland
57 E 9 **Viterbo**, Italy
151 I 10 **Viti Levu**, Fiji
23 L 3 **Vitim**, Asia
97 L 8 **Vitória**, Brazil
97 L 7 **Vitória da Conquista**, Brazil
28 F 8 **Vitoria Seamount**, Atlantic Ocean
41 J 2 **Vitoria-Gasteiz**, Spain
65 K 4 **Vitsyebsk**, Belarus
119 F 11 **Vizianagaram**, India
61 F 9 **Vladičin Han**, Serbia and Montenegro
104 C 6 **Vladimir**, Russia
105 M 11 **Vladivostok**, Russia
48 K 5 **Vlagtwedde**, Netherlands
48 F 4 **Vlieland**, Netherlands
49 D 10 **Vlissingen**, Netherlands
45 L 8 **Voiron**, France
96 A 6 **Volcán Darwin**, Galapagos Islands
96 A 7 **Volcán La Cumbre**, Galapagos Islands
98 F 7 **Volcán Licancábur**, Bolivia/Chile
98 F 7 **Volcán Llullaillaco**, Argentina/Chile
96 A 6 **Volcán Wolf**, Galapagos Islands
23 J 3 **Volga**, Europe
104 C 7 **Volgograd**, Russia
104 D 5 **Vologda**, Russia
61 G 11 **Volos**, Greece
136 F 6 **Volta**, Ghana,
104 F 5 **Vorkuta**, Russia
104 C 6 **Voronezh**, Russia
65 I 2 **Võrtsjärv**, Estonia
65 J 2 **Võru**, Estonia
45 L 5 **Vosges**, France
33 N 5 **Vostok**, Russia
61 G 8 **Vratsa**, Bulgaria
61 F 7 **Vršac**, Serbia and Montenegro
96 F 3 **Vuaupés**, Brazil/Colombia
61 D 7 **Vukovar**, Croatia

W

49 G 9 **Waal**, Netherlands
49 G 9 **Waalwijk**, Netherlands
78 F 9 **Wabash**, United States
83 H 12 **Waco**, TX, United States
137 L 5 **Wad Medani**, Sudan
137 I 3 **Waddān**, Libya
48 G 5 **Waddenzee**, Netherlands
137 L 4 **Wadi Halfa**, Sudan
114 G 4 **Wadi Rum**, Jordan
131 J 15 **Wadomari**, Japan
147 K 9 **Wagga Wagga**, NSW, Australia
146 E 9 **Wagin**, WA, Australia
111 L 8 **Wah**, Pakistan
123 L 9 **Wahai**, Indonesia
85 B 15 **Wahiawa**, HI, United States
150 B 10 **Waiau**, New Zealand
123 M 8 **Waigeo**, Indonesia
150 F 3 **Waihi**, New Zealand
123 J 10 **Waikabubak**, Indonesia
150 F 4 **Waikato**, New Zealand
85 C 15 **Wailuku**, HI, United States
150 D 9 **Waimate**, New Zealand
85 C 15 **Waimea**, HI, United States
150 F 5 **Waiouru**, New Zealand
150 G 5 **Waipawa**, New Zealand
150 E 7 **Wairau**, New Zealand
150 G 5 **Wairoa**, New Zealand
150 E 3 **Waitakere**, New Zealand
150 C 9 **Waitaki**, New Zealand
150 E 3 **Waiuku**, New Zealand
131 E 10 **Wakasa-wan**, Japan
131 E 12 **Wakayama**, Japan
130 G 2 **Wakkanai**, Japan
64 F 7 **Wałbrzych**, Poland
37 F 13 **Wales**, United Kingdom
147 K 8 **Walgett**, NSW, Australia
85 E 11 **Walker Lake**, NV, United States
84 F 7 **Walla Walla**, WA, United States
31 J 5 **Wallaby Plateau**, Indian Ocean
151 J 9 **Wallis**, Wallis and Futuna Islands
151 J 9 **Wallis and Futuna Islands**, France
80 H 5 **Walter F. George Reservoir**, AL, United States
30 E 7 **Walters Shoal**, Indian Ocean
140 G 8 **Walvis Bay**, Namibia
29 I 9 **Walvis Ridge**, Atlantic Ocean
150 C 9 **Wanaka**, New Zealand
32 D 7 **Wandel Sea**, Arctic Ocean
150 F 5 **Wanganui**, New Zealand
150 F 5 **Wanganui**, New Zealand
147 J 9 **Wangaratta**, VIC, Australia
119 E 11 **Warangal**, India
119 E 10 **Wardha**, India
49 C 11 **Waregem**, Belgium
147 L 6 **Warginburra Peninsula**, QLD, Australia
150 F 2 **Warkworth**, New Zealand
79 J 7 **Warren**, PA, United States
78 H 7 **Warren**, MI, United States
136 H 7 **Warri**, Nigeria
37 G 11 **Warrington**, United Kingdom
147 J 10 **Warrnambool**, VIC, Australia
64 G 6 **Warsaw**, Poland
64 F 6 **Warta**, Poland
147 L 8 **Warwick**, QLD, Australia
79 N 7 **Warwick**, RI, United States
37 I 12 **Wash, The**, United Kingdom
0 K 9 **Washington**, DC, United States
84 D 6 **Washington**, United States
79 M 7 **Waterbury**, CT, United States
37 D 13 **Waterford**, Ireland
82 I 7 **Waterloo**, IA, United States
79 K 6 **Watertown**, NY, United States
82 G 6 **Watertown**, SD, United States
37 I 13 **Watford**, United Kingdom
85 D 12 **Watsonville**, CA, United States
81 I 2 **Watts Bar Lake**, TN, United States

Bay · Channel · Country · Dependent Territory · Desert · Geographic Area · Headland · Island · Island Group · Lake · Mountain

137 K 7 **Wau**, Sudan
78 F 7 **Waukegan**, WI, United States
78 F 6 **Waukesha**, WI, United States
78 E 5 **Wausau**, WI, United States
49 F 12 **Wavre**, Belgium
75 J 10 **Wawa**, ON, Canada
81 J 6 **Waycross**, GA, United States
29 F 12 **Weddell Abyssal Plain**, Atlantic Ocean
99 H 15 **Weddell Island**, Falkland Islands
29 F 13 **Weddell Sea**, Atlantic Ocean
49 H 10 **Weert**, Netherlands
127 M 6 **Weifang**, China
52 F 8 **Weimar**, Germany
84 F 8 **Weiser**, ID, United States
80 H 3 **Weiss Lake**, AL, United States
49 I 14 **Weiswampach**, Luxembourg
150 D 6 **Wekakura Point**, New Zealand
141 I 9 **Welkom**, South Africa
147 I 4 **Wellesley Islands**, QLD, Australia
150 F 7 **Wellington**, New Zealand
85 G 10 **Wells**, NV, United States
53 H 11 **Wels**, Austria
84 E 6 **Wenatchee**, WA, United States
151 L 1 **Weno**, Federated States of Micronesia
127 N 8 **Wenzhou**, China
49 H 13 **Werbomont**, Belgium
52 E 8 **Werra**, Germany
52 B 7 **Wesel**, Germany
52 D 6 **Weser**, Germany
147 I 3 **Wessel Islands**, NT, Australia
33 K 4 **West Antarctica**, Antarctica
150 A 10 **West Cape**, New Zealand
26 E 5 **West Caroline Basin**, Pacific Ocean
99 H 15 **West Falkland**, Falkland Islands
151 K 1 **West Fayu**, Federated States of Micronesia
48 F 4 **West Frisian Islands**, Netherlands
81 L 9 **West Palm Beach**, FL, United States
29 D 12 **West Scotia Ridge**, Atlantic Ocean
23 K 3 **West Siberian Plain**, Asia
79 I 9 **West Virginia**, United States
146 F 7 **Western Australia**, Australia
65 J 3 **Western Dvina**, Belarus/Latvia
119 C 11 **Western Ghats**, India
136 E 3 **Western Sahara**, Morocco
49 D 10 **Westerschelde**, Netherlands
37 B 11 **Westport**, Ireland
150 C 7 **Westport**, New Zealand
123 L 10 **Wetar**, Indonesia
147 J 1 **Wewak**, Papua New Guinea
37 D 13 **Wexford**, Ireland
74 G 10 **Weyburn**, SK, Canada
150 G 4 **Whakatane**, New Zealand
150 E 2 **Whangarei**, New Zealand
31 I 5 **Wharton Basin**, Indian Ocean
80 G 3 **Wheeler Lake**, AL, United States
79 I 8 **Wheeling**, WV, United States
78 F 9 **White**, United States
85 G 12 **White**, United States
150 G 3 **White Island**, New Zealand
83 I 13 **White Lake**, LA, United States
23 I 5 **White Nile**, Africa
104 D 4 **White Sea**, Russia
136 F 6 **White Volta**, Burkina Faso/Ghana
37 F 10 **Whitehaven**, United Kingdom
74 D 6 **Whitehorse**, YT, Canada
83 C 11 **Whitewater Baldy**, NM, United States
147 K 5 **Whitsunday Group**, QLD, Australia
147 I 9 **Whyalla**, SA, Australia
83 G 10 **Wichita**, KS, United States
83 G 11 **Wichita Falls**, TX, United States
36 G 5 **Wick**, United Kingdom
85 I 14 **Wickenburg**, AZ, United States
53 K 11 **Wiener Neustadt**, Austria
53 C 9 **Wiesbaden**, Germany
147 J 8 **Wilcannia**, NSW, Australia
52 C 5 **Wilhelmshaven**, Germany
79 K 7 **Wilkes Barre**, PA, United States
33 O 6 **Wilkes Land**, Antarctica
85 J 15 **Willcox**, AZ, United States
91 L 7 **Willemstad**, Netherlands Antilles
84 C 8 **Williamette**, United States

79 K 7 **Williamsport**, PA, United States
82 E 5 **Williston**, ND, United States
82 H 6 **Wilmar**, MN, United States
81 M 3 **Wilmington**, NC, United States
79 L 8 **Wilmington**, DE, United States
140 G 8 **Windhoek**, Namibia
75 J 11 **Windsor**, ON, Canada
91 O 6 **Windward Islands**, Caribbean Sea
91 J 4 **Windward Passage**, Caribbean Sea
75 I 8 **Winisk**, Canada
85 F 10 **Winnemucca**, NV, United States
85 E 10 **Winnemucca Lake**, NV, United States
74 H 10 **Winnipeg**, MB, Canada
85 J 14 **Winslow**, AZ, United States
81 K 1 **Winston Salem**, NC, United States
48 J 8 **Winterswijk**, Netherlands
53 D 12 **Winterthur**, Switzerland
150 B 10 **Winton**, New Zealand
147 J 6 **Winton**, NSW, Australia
78 E 5 **Wisconsin**, United States
52 F 5 **Wismar**, Germany
52 F 6 **Wittenberge**, Germany
64 G 6 **Włocławek**, Poland
64 F 7 **Wodzisław Śląski**, Poland
151 K 1 **Woleai**, Federated States of Micronesia
53 I 13 **Wolfsberg**, Austria
52 F 6 **Wolfsburg**, Germany
74 G 8 **Wollaston Lake**, SK, Canada
74 F 5 **Wollaston Peninsula**, NU, Canada
147 K 9 **Wollongong**, NSW, Australia
48 I 5 **Wolvega**, Netherlands
37 G 12 **Wolverhampton**, United Kingdom
127 O 5 **Wŏnsan**, North Korea
78 E 4 **Woodruff**, WI, United States
150 F 6 **Woodville**, New Zealand
79 N 7 **Worcester**, MA, United States
37 F 10 **Workington**, United Kingdom
82 C 7 **Worland**, WY, United States
53 D 10 **Worms**, Germany
37 I 14 **Worthing**, United Kingdom
82 H 7 **Worthington**, MN, United States
151 M 3 **Wotho**, Marshall Islands
151 N 3 **Wotje**, Marshall Islands
105 N 4 **Wrangel Island**, Russia
32 E 5 **Wrangel Sea**, Arctic Ocean
64 F 7 **Wrocław**, Poland
127 K 5 **Wuhai**, China
127 M 8 **Wuhan**, China
127 N 7 **Wuhu**, China
52 C 8 **Wuppertal**, Germany
53 E 9 **Würzburg**, Germany
127 N 7 **Wuxi**, China
127 K 6 **Wuzhong**, China
127 L 10 **Wuzhou**, China
37 G 13 **Wye**, United Kingdom
146 G 4 **Wyndham**, WA, Australia
82 C 7 **Wyoming**, United States

X

109 O 5 **Xaşmaz**, Azerbaijan
141 K 9 **Xai-Xai**, Mozambique
89 L 8 **Xalapa**, Mexico
122 G 3 **Xam Hua**, Laos
109 N 7 **Xankändi**, Azerbaijan
61 H 10 **Xanthi**, Greece
41 L 7 **Xátiva**, Spain
127 N 9 **Xiamen**, China
127 L 7 **Xi'an**, China
127 L 7 **Xiangfan**, China
127 L 8 **Xiangtan**, China
127 K 7 **Xianyang**, China
127 N 2 **Xiao Higgan Ling**, China
126 G 8 **Xigaz**, China
127 M 4 **Xilinhot**, China
127 M 6 **Xingtai**, China
97 J 5 **Xingu**, Brazil
127 J 6 **Xining**, China
127 M 6 **Xintai**, China
127 L 6 **Xinxiang**, China
127 M 7 **Xinyang**, China
127 M 7 **Xuchang**, China

127 L 11 **Xuwen**, China
127 M 7 **Xuzhou**, China

y

61 G 8 **Yablanitsa**, Bulgaria
98 G 6 **Yacuiba**, Bolivia
137 I 2 **Yafran**, Libya
29 D 11 **Yaghan Basin**, Atlantic Ocean
127 M 2 **Yakeshi**, China
84 E 6 **Yakima**, WA, United States
131 C 16 **Yaku-shima**, Japan
105 L 7 **Yakutsk**, Russia
65 M 11 **Yalta**, Ukraine
130 H 8 **Yamagata**, Japan
131 C 12 **Yamaguchi**, Japan
104 G 5 **Yamal Peninsula**, Russia
61 I 9 **Yambol**, Bulgaria
136 F 7 **Yamoussoukro**, Côte d'Ivoire
126 H 8 **Yamzho Yumco**, China
105 L 6 **Yana**, Russia
127 L 6 **Yan'an**, China
114 H 6 **Yanbu' al Bahr**, Saudi Arabia
111 K 6 **Yangiyul**, Uzbekistan
127 L 6 **Yangquan**, China
127 J 9 **Yangtze**, China
127 M 7 **Yangzhou**, China
127 O 4 **Yanji**, China
82 G 7 **Yankton**, SD, United States
127 N 6 **Yantai**, China
137 I 8 **Yaoundé**, Cameroon
151 J 1 **Yap**, Federated States of Micronesia
123 N 8 **Yapen**, Indonesia
88 G 4 **Yaqui**, Mexico
109 D 10 **Yardimci Burnu**, Turkey
37 J 12 **Yare**, United Kingdom
150 H 7 **Yaren**, Nauru
126 F 5 **Yarkant He**, China
75 L 9 **Yarmouth**, NS, Canada
104 D 6 **Yaroslavl'**, Russia
108 I 6 **Yasun Burnu**, Turkey
131 B 14 **Yatsushiro**, Japan
119 E 11 **Yavatmal**, India
115 L 4 **Yazd**, Iran
80 E 4 **Yazoo City**, MS, United States
104 E 7 **Yekaterinburg**, Russia
36 H 3 **Yell**, United Kingdom
127 K 5 **Yellow**, China
127 N 6 **Yellow Sea**, China
74 F 7 **Yellowknife**, NT, Canada
82 C 6 **Yellowstone**, MT, United States
82 C 7 **Yellowstone Lake**, WY, United States
111 I 7 **Yeloten**, Turkmenistan
115 J 10 **Yemen**, Asia
122 E 3 **Yenangyaung**, Myanmar
104 H 7 **Yenisey**, Russia
104 H 8 **Yeniseyskiy Kryazh**, Russia
37 G 14 **Yeovil**, United Kingdom
109 M 7 **Yerevan**, Armenia
109 N 6 **Yevlax**, Azerbaijan
65 M 11 **Yevpatoriya**, Ukraine
127 K 8 **Yibin**, China
127 L 8 **Yichang**, China
127 O 2 **Yichun**, China
127 K 6 **Yinchuan**, China
127 N 5 **Yingkou**, China
126 G 4 **Yining**, China
127 L 8 **Yiyang**, China
122 H 10 **Yogyakarta**, Indonesia
131 F 11 **Yokkaichi**, Japan
131 H 10 **Yokohama**, Japan
131 I 10 **Yokosuka**, Japan
131 D 11 **Yonago**, Japan
127 N 9 **Yong'an**, China
79 M 8 **Yonkers**, NY, United States
37 I 11 **York**, United Kingdom
79 K 8 **York**, PA, United States
147 I 9 **Yorke Peninsula**, SA, Australia
74 G 9 **Yorkton**, SK, Canada
131 K 15 **Yoron-tō**, Japan
104 D 6 **Yoshkar-Ola**, Russia
79 I 8 **Youngstown**, OH, United States
85 C 9 **Yreka**, CA, United States
111 M 5 **Ysyk-Köl**, Kyrgyzstan
127 J 9 **Yuan**, China

85 D 11 **Yuba City**, CA, United States
89 O 7 **Yucatan Channel**, Mexico
89 O 8 **Yucatan Peninsula**, Mexico
127 O 8 **Yueyang**, China
105 N 5 **Yukagirskoye Ploskogor'ye**, Russia
22 C 2 **Yukon**, North America
74 D 6 **Yukon Territory**, Canada
127 L 10 **Yulin**, China
127 L 6 **Yulin**, China
85 H 15 **Yuma**, AZ, United States
127 I 5 **Yumen**, China
27 L 7 **Yupanqui Basin**, Pacific Ocean
131 J 8 **Yuwan-dake**, Japan
105 N 10 **Yuzhno-Sakhalinsk**, Russia
65 L 9 **Yuzhnoukrayinsk**, Ukraine

Z

48 F 7 **Zaandam**, Netherlands
64 F 7 **Zabrze**, Poland
89 J 7 **Zacatecas**, Mexico
61 B 8 **Zadar**, Croatia
40 G 7 **Zafra**, Spain
61 B 6 **Zagreb**, Croatia
23 J 4 **Zagros Mountains**, Asia
115 N 4 **Zähedän**, Iran
61 E 13 **Zakynthos**, Greece
61 E 13 **Zakynthos**, Greece
64 E 10 **Zalaegerszeg**, Hungary
127 N 3 **Zalantun**, China
110 H 5 **Zaliv Kara-Bogaz-Gol**, Turkmenistan
105 N 7 **Zaliv Shelikhova**, Russia
60 G 5 **Zalžu**, Romania
23 I 7 **Zambezi**, Africa
141 I 6 **Zambia**, Africa
123 K 6 **Zamboanga**, Philippines
40 H 4 **Zamora**, Spain
89 J 7 **Zamora de Hidalgo**, Mexico
64 H 7 **Zamość**, Poland
79 I 9 **Zanesville**, OH, United States
115 K 2 **Zanjän**, Iran
141 L 4 **Zanzibar**, Tanzania
127 M 6 **Zaozhuang**, China
104 G 9 **Zapadnyy Sayan**, Russia
99 F 11 **Zapala**, Argentina
29 G 9 **Zapiola Seamount**, Atlantic Ocean
65 M 9 **Zaporizhzhya**, Ukraine
108 I 7 **Zara**, Turkey
111 K 8 **Zarafshon**, Tajikistan
41 L 4 **Zaragoza**, Spain
111 J 9 **Zaranj**, Afghanistan
111 K 8 **Zarghün Shahr**, Afghanistan
136 H 6 **Zaria**, Nigeria
48 G 8 **Zeist**, Netherlands
64 G 4 **Zelenogradsk**, Russia
61 D 8 **Zenica**, Bosnia-Herzegovina
105 L 9 **Zeyskoye Vodokhranilishche**, Russia
127 O 4 **Zhangguangcai Ling**, China
127 M 5 **Zhangjiakou**, China
127 N 9 **Zhangzhou**, China
127 L 10 **Zhanjiang**, China
126 G 7 **Zhari Namco**, China
127 L 7 **Zhengzhou**, China
127 N 7 **Zhenjiang**, China
111 K 3 **Zhezkazgan**, Kazakhstan
65 K 5 **Zhlobin**, Belarus
33 P 3 **Zhongshan**, China
127 M 8 **Zhuzhou**, China
110 H 2 **Zhympity**, Kazakhstan
65 K 7 **Zhytomyr**, Ukraine
127 M 6 **Zibo**, China
64 E 6 **Zielona Góra**, Poland
127 K 8 **Zigong**, China
136 D 5 **Ziguinchor**, Senegal
89 J 9 **Zihuatanejo**, Mexico
141 I 7 **Zimbabwe**, Africa
136 H 6 **Zinder**, Niger
115 J 9 **Zinjibär**, Yemen
104 E 7 **Zlatoust**, Russia
64 F 8 **Zlín**, Czech Republic
137 I 2 **Zlītan**, Libya
48 G 8 **Zoetermeer**, Netherlands
108 E 6 **Zonguldak**, Turkey

136 E 3 **Zouérat**, Mauritania
115 L 9 **Zufär**, Oman
53 D 12 **Zug**, Switzerland
53 F 12 **Zugspitze**, Germany
48 I 4 **Zuidhorn**, Netherlands
127 K 9 **Zunyi**, China
61 D 7 **Županja**, Croatia
53 D 12 **Zürich**, Switzerland
48 I 7 **Zutphen**, Netherlands
136 E 7 **Zwedru**, Liberia
52 G 8 **Zwickau**, Germany
48 I 7 **Zwolle**, Netherlands
111 N 2 **Zyryanovsk**, Kazakhstan

▲ Mountain Range ■ National Capital ⊚ Ocean ◆ Physical Feature ▬ Polar Base ⋟ River ⊋ Sea ★ Special Feature ⌂ State Capital ◼ Underwater Feature

Acknowledgments

Conceived and produced by Weldon Owen Pty Ltd
59 Victoria Street, McMahons Point
Sydney, NSW 2060, Australia

Chief Executive Officer John Owen
President Terry Newell
Publisher Sheena Coupe
Creative Director Sue Burk
Vice President International Sales Stuart Laurence
Administrator International Sales Kristine Ravn

Project Editors Angela Handley, Emma Hutchinson
Text Janine Flew, Lynn Humphries, Limelight Press, Margaret McPhee

Designers Melanie Calabretta, Avril Makula, Heather Menzies, Craig Peterson
Design Consultant John Bull

Maps Map Illustrations
Chief Cartographer Laurie Whiddon
Cartographers Encompass Graphics
Cartographic Consultant Colin Arrowsmith
Information Graphics Andrew Davies
Flags Flag Society of Australia

Editorial Coordinator Jennifer Losco
Production Manager Caroline Webber
Production Coordinator James Blackman

Color reproduction by Chroma Graphics (Overseas) Pte Ltd
Printed by Kyodo Printing Co. (S'pore) Pte Ltd
Printed in Singapore

A Weldon Owen Production

Key t=top; l=left; r=right; tl=top left; tc=top center; tr=top right; cl=center left; c=center; cr=center right; b=bottom; bl=bottom left; bc=bottom center; br=bottom right

AA = The Art Archive; AAA = The Ancient Art & Architecture Collection Ltd.; AAP = Australian Associated Press; AFP = Agence France-Presse; AMNH = American Museum of Natural History; APL/Corbis = Australian Picture Library/Corbis; AVA = The Advertising Archive Ltd.; BA = Bridgeman Art Library (www.bridgeman.co.uk); GC = The Granger Collection; GI = Getty Images; KC = Kobal Collection; MEPL = Mary Evans Picture Library; APL/MP = Australian Picture Library/Minden Pictures; N_G = NASA/Great Images in NASA; N_J = NASA/Jet Propulsion Laboratory; N_T = NASA/Total Ozone Mapping Spectrometer; NASA = National Aeronautics and Space Administration; PD = Photodisc; PE = PhotoEssentials; SML = The Science Museum, London; TPL = photolibrary.com; TPL/SPL = photolibrary.com/ Science Photo Library

8b Craig Mahew/Robert Simmon/NASA/GSFC tc NASA/GSFC/METI/ERSDAC/JAROS & US/Japan Aster Science Team **9**tl NASA/GSFC/METI/ERSDAC/JAROS & US/Japan Aster Science Team tr Restec Japan/TPL/SPL **10**b NASA Goddard Space Flight Center/Reto Stöckli/Robert Simmon/ MODIS/USGS/Defense Meteorological Satellite Program tc N_G **11**tl NASA/TPL/SPL tr N_T **12**bl N_J br Adastra/GI cl APL/Corbis cr The Image Bank/GI tc NASA/TPL/SPL **13**br SRTM Team/ NASA/JPL/NIMA c NASA/GSFC/MITI/ERSDAC/JAROS & US/Japan Aster Science Team tl NASA/ GSFC/METI/ERSDAC/JAROS & US/Japan Aster Science Team tr Jacques Descloitres/MODIS Rapid Response Team/NASA/GSFC **16**c Shin Yoshino/APL/MP c Jim Brandenburg/APL/MP **17**c, cr APL/ Corbis cr Mitsuaki Iwogo/APL/MP tr Norbert Wu/APL/MP **18**bc Tom Owen Edmunds/GI bc Connie Coleman/GI cl APL/Corbis **19**cr APL/Corbis **38**br, cl, cr, tr APL/Corbis **39**bc Belvoir Castle, Leicestershire, UK/BA bl, br, c, cl, cr APL/Corbis c Paul Maeyaert/BA cl Lambeth Palace Library, London, UK/BA cl Christie's Images/BA tr Ashmolean Museum, Oxford, UK/BA **42**bc AFP bl APL/Corbis **43**bc AA/Museo Picasso Barcelona/Dagli Orti c, cl, cr BA tl Rafael Macia/photolibrary.com **46**cl APL/Corbis tr PD tr TPL/David Barnes **47**bc TPL bl APL/Corbis br AA/Bibliotheque Nationale Paris c Lauros/Giraudon/BA cr GI/BA/Rossetti tr AVA **50**bc, bl APL/Corbis **51**bc, br, c, cl, cr, tr APL/Corbis c, tc AFP tl Graphische Sammlung Albertina, Vienna, Austria/BA **54**c APL/Corbis **55**bl AVA br, cl APL/Corbis cl Germanisches National Museum, Nuremberg, Germany/BA tl Lauros/Giraudon/BA tr Christie's Images/BA **58**bl, br APL/Corbis c Peter Johnson **59**bc, tr APL/Corbis bc Alessi cl Valerie Martin **62**cl APL/Corbis **63**bc, cl, cr APL/ Corbis bc AA/Nicolas Sapieha tl GC **66**bc, bl, cl APL/Corbis tr GI/Taxi/Dan Sams **67**bc, bl, br, cr, tr APL/Corbis c Tretyakov Gallery, Moscow, Russia/BA cl BA/Archives Charmet tc Museo Civico di Storia ed Arte, Modena, Italy/Alinari/BA **70**bl, br APL/Corbis **71**bc, cr, tc, tr APL/Corbis br Polar Music/Reg Grundy Prods/KC cl AA/Nasjonal Gallericht, Oslo/Album/Joseph Martin **75**tr AMNH **76**bl, c APL/Corbis tr AA/Tate Gallery, London **77**bc, bl, br, c, tr APL/Corbis cr AA/ National Trust Quebec House/Eileen Tweedy cr AVA **86**c APL/Corbis tr Angela Handley **87**bc, bl, c, tl, tr APL/Corbis br PE **92**br, cr, tr APL/Corbis **93**bc, c, cl, cr, tc, tr APL/Corbis c Andrew Furlong **100**bl, br Angela Handley cl PD **101**bc, c, cl, cr, t, tl APL/Corbis br AFP br Bibliotheque Nationale, Paris, France/BA cr American Museum of Natural History, New York, USA/BA **106**br, c, cl, tc APL/Corbis **107**bc, c, cl, cr, tr APL/Corbis tc Mark Gallery/London, UK/BA tl Museum of Tropinin & His Contemporaries, Moscow, Russia/BA **112**bc APL/Corbis View bl APL/Corbis cl Persian School/British Museum London, UK/BA **113**bc, bl, br, c, tc, tr APL/ Corbis cr Topkapi Palace Museum, Istanbul, Turkey/BA **116**bl David W. Hamilton/GI cr APL/ Corbis **117**bc MEPL bl, br, cl, cr, tc APL/Corbis **120**cr APL/Corbis **121**bc, br, c, cl, tl APL/Corbis cl AA/Bodleian Library Oxford/The Bodleian Library cr Victoria & Albert Museum, London/BA tr British Library, London, UK/BA **124**c Digital Vision/GI cr APL/Corbis tc MEPL **125**bc, bl, c, cr, tc APL/Corbis tr Bushnell/Soifer/GI **128**br AAP Image/Xinhua Photo/Du Huajau **129**bc, c, tc APL/ Corbis bl Bibliotheque Nationale, Paris, France/BA bl SML (Science & Society Picture Library) tr Paul Freeman/BA **132**br, cr Japan National Tourist Organisation c Chris Shorten cl, tr APL/ Corbis **133**bc, bl, br, tc, tr APL/Corbis **138**bc, bl, tc APL/Corbis **139**bc, c APL/Corbis br PE c AAA tl APL/Zefa **142**br APL/Corbis **143**bl, br, c, cr, tc, tr APL/Corbis c Pascal Goetgheluck/TPL/SPL **148**bl, c APL/Corbis **149**bc, br, c, tl APL/Corbis c AAP Image cl By permission of the National Library of Australia cr Allport Library and Museum of Fine Arts, State Library of Tasmania tr By permission of the South Australian Museum **152**bl, br, cl APL/Corbis **153**bc, bl, br, c, cr APL/Corbis bl AAP Image/AP c PE tl La Trobe Picture Collection, State Library of Victoria

Illustrators: Susanna Addario; Paul Bachem; Graham Back; Anne Bowman; Gregory Bridges; Danny Burke; Fiammetta Dogi; Simone End; Christer Eriksson; Chris Forsey; John Crawford Fraser; Mark A. Garlick/space-art.co.uk; Jon Gittoes; Mike Gorman; Lorraine Hannay; Robert Hynes; INKLINK; David Kirshner; Frank Knight; Mike Lamble; Iain McKellar; James McKinnon; Marlene McLoughlin; Rob Mancini; Peter Mennim; Moonrunner Design Ltd.; Nicola Oram; Peter Bull Art Studio; Evert Ploeg; Tony Pyrzakowski; Oliver Rennert; John Richards; Edwina Riddell; Barbara Rodanska; Trevor Ruth; Claudia Saraceni; Michael Saunders; Peter Schouten; Marco Sparaciari; Roger Swainston; Steve Trevaskis; Thomas Trojer; Guy Troughton; Glen Vause; Rod Westblade; Ann Winterbotham; Murray Zanoni.

Bernard Thornton Artists UK: Tony Gibbons, Adam Hook, Christa Hook, Richard Hook, Stephen Seymour.

Illustrationweb.com: Andrew Beckett, Steinar Lund, Sharif Tarabay.

Wildlife Art Ltd: Robin Carter, Tom Connell, Ray Grinaway, David Hardy, Philip Hood, Ian Jackson, Ken Oliver, Michael Langham Rowe, Myke Taylor.